THE MIDDLE LENGTH SAYINGS

MAJJHIMA-NIKĀYA

VOLUME I

Pali Text Society

TRANSLATION SERIES, NO. 29

THE COLLECTION OF THE MIDDLE LENGTH SAYINGS

(MAJJHIMA-NIKĀYA)

VOL. I

THE FIRST FIFTY DISCOURSES
(MŪLAPAṆṆĀSA)

TRANSLATED FROM THE PALI BY

I. B. HORNER, M.A.

Associate of Newnham College, Cambridge

Translator of "The Book of the Discipline," volumes I-V

Published by

THE PALI TEXT SOCIETY · LONDON

Distributed by

ROUTLEDGE & KEGAN PAUL

LONDON, HENLEY & BOSTON

1976

First published 1954
Second impression 1976

ISBN 0 7100 8392 0

PRINTED IN GREAT BRITAIN
BY UNWIN BROTHERS LIMITED
THE GRESHAM PRESS, OLD WOKING, SURREY
A MEMBER OF THE STAPLES PRINTING GROUP

CONTENTS

PAGE

Translator's Introduction - - - - - - - ix

THE FIRST FIFTY DISCOURSES (MŪLAPAṆṆĀSA)

I. THE DIVISION OF THE SYNOPSIS OF FUNDAMENTALS (MŪLAPARIYĀYAVAGGA)

1. Discourse on the Synopsis of Fundamentals - - - 3
   (Mūlapariyāyasutta)
2. Discourse on All the Cankers - - - - - - 8
   (Sabbâsavasutta)
3. Discourse on Heirs of Dhamma - - - - - 16
   (Dhammadāyādasutta)
4. Discourse on Fear and Dread - - - - - 21
   (Bhayabheravasutta)
5. Discourse on No Blemishes - - - - - - 31
   (Anaṅgaṇasutta)
6. Discourse on What one may Wish - - - - - 41
   (Ākaṅkheyyasutta)
7. Discourse on the Simile of the Cloth - - - - 45
   (Vatthûpamasutta)
8. Discourse on Expunging - - - - - - 51
   (Sallekhasutta)
9. Discourse on Perfect View - - - - - - 57
   (Sammādiṭṭhisutta)
10. Discourse on the Applications of Mindfulness - - - 70
   (Satipaṭṭhānasutta)

II. THE DIVISION OF THE LION'S ROAR (SĪHANĀDAVAGGA)

11. Lesser Discourse on the Lion's Roar - - - - 85
   (Cūḷasīhanādasutta)
12. Greater Discourse on the Lion's Roar - - - - 91
   (Mahāsīhanādasutta)

PAGE

13. Greater Discourse on the Stems of Anguish - - - 110
(Mahādukkhakkhandhasutta)

14. Lesser Discourse on the Stems of Anguish - - - 119
(Cūḷadukkhakkhandhasutta)

15. Discourse on Measuring in Accordance with - - - 124
(Anumānasutta)

16. Discourse on Mental Barrenness - - - - - 132
(Cetokhilasutta)

17. Discourse on the Forest Grove - - - - - 136
(Vanapatthasutta)

18. Discourse of the Honey-ball - - - - - - 141
(Madhupiṇḍikasutta)

19. Discourse on the Twofold Thought - - - - 148
(Dvedhāvitakkasutta)

20. Discourse on the Forms of Thought - - - - 152
(Vitakkasanthānasutta)

III. THE THIRD DIVISION (TATIYAVAGGA)

21. Discourse on the Parable of the Saw - - - - 159
(Kakacûpamasutta)

22. Discourse on the Parable of the Water-snake - - - 167
(Alagaddûpamasutta)

23. Discourse on the Anthill - - - - - - 183
(Vammīkasutta)

24. Discourse on the Relays of Chariots - - - - 187
(Rathavinītasutta)

25. Discourse on Crops - - - - - - - 194
(Nivāpasutta)

26. Discourse on the Ariyan Quest - - - - - 203
(Ariyapariyesanasutta)

27. Lesser Discourse on the Simile of the Elephant's Footprint 220
(Cūḷahatthipadopamasutta)

28. Greater Discourse on the Simile of the Elephant's Footprint 230
(Mahāhatthipadopamasutta)

PAGE

29. Greater Discourse on the Simile of the Pith - - - 238
(Mahāsāropamasutta)

30. Lesser Discourse on the Simile of the Pith - - - 245
(Cūḷasāropamasutta)

IV. THE GREATER DIVISION OF THE PAIRS
(MAHĀYAMAKAVAGGA)

31. Lesser Discourse in Gosiṅga - - - - - - 257
(Cūḷagosiṅgasutta)

32. Greater Discourse in Gosiṅga - - - - - - 263
(Mahāgosiṅgasutta)

33. Greater Discourse on the Cowherd - - - - - 271
(Mahāgopālakasutta)

34. Lesser Discourse on the Cowherd - - - - - 277
(Cūḷagopālakasutta)

35. Lesser Discourse to Saccaka - - - - - - 280
(Cūḷasaccakasutta)

36. Greater Discourse to Saccaka - - - - - - 291
(Mahāsaccakasutta)

37. Lesser Discourse on the Destruction of Craving - - 306
(Cūḷataṇhāsaṅkhayasutta)

38. Greater Discourse on the Destruction of Craving - - 311
(Mahātaṇhāsaṅkhayasutta)

39. Greater Discourse at Assapura - - - - - 325
(Mahāassapurasutta)

40. Lesser Discourse at Assapura - - - - - - 334
(Cūḷaassapurasutta)

V. THE LESSER DIVISION OF THE PAIRS
(CŪḶAYAMAKAVAGGA)

41. Discourse to the People of Sālā - - - - - 343
(Sāleyyakasutta)

42. Discourse to the People of Verañjā - - - - 349
(Verañjakasutta)

43. Greater Discourse of the Miscellany - - - - 350
(Mahāvedallasutta)

PAGE

44. Lesser Discourse of the Miscellany - - - - - - 360
(Cūḷavedallasutta)
45. Lesser Discourse on the (Ways of) undertaking Dhamma 368
(Cūḷadhammasamādānasutta)
46. Greater Discourse on the (Ways of) undertaking Dhamma 372
(Mahādhammasamādānasutta)
47. Discourse on Inquiring - - - - - - - - 379
(Vīmaṁsakasutta)
48. Discourse at Kosambī - - - - - - - - 383
(Kosambiyasutta)
49. Discourse on a Challenge to a Brahmā - - - - 388
(Brahmanimantaṇikasutta)
50. Discourse on a Rebuke to Māra - - - - - 395
(Māratajjaniyasutta)

INDEXES

I. Topics - - - - - - - - - - 404
II. Similes - - - - - - - - - - 412
III. Names - - - - - - - - - - 413
IV. Some Pali Words in the Notes - - - - - 416

TRANSLATOR'S INTRODUCTION

The *Majjhima-Nikāya* is the second "book" or Collection of Discourses in the Suttapiṭaka. It consists of 152 Discourses (*sutta*) and is divided into three Sections (*paṇṇāsa*) of fifty Discourses each, the last Section, however, containing fifty-two.[1] These Sections are further sub-divided into Divisions (*vagga*) of ten Discourses each, the penultimate Division containing the two extra Discourses. There are fifteen Divisions, five in each Section.

This present volume of translation covers the first Section and thus comprises the First Fifty Discourses. I hope to follow it with two more volumes for the Middle Fifty and the Last, or Further, Fifty (-two). My translation is based on the edition of the *Majjhima* published in three volumes for the Pali Text Society by V. Trenckner, vol. i, 1888, and Lord Chalmers, vols. ii and iii, 1898, 1899 (all reprinted in 1949, 1951).

Two complete translations have already appeared, the one by E. K. Neumann: *Die Reden Gotamo Buddho's aus der mittleren Sammlung Majjhima-nikāyo*, three vols., Leipzig, 1896-1902; and the other by Lord Chalmers: *Further Dialogues of the Buddha*, two vols., in the Sacred Books of the Buddhists Series, vols. v, vi, 1926, 1927. Both of these works are now unfortunately out of print. Translations of individual Discourses have also been made and still appear from time to time both in the East and the West. They are too numerous to catalogue; but Professor Rhys Davids' translations of Suttas Nos. 2, 6 and 16, together with his masterly Introductions (Sacred Books of the East, vol. xi), should not be overlooked.

With this considerable amount of material available, I have found it best on the whole to take an independent course, while duly consulting my predecessors. I do not claim that my translation makes any advance, simply that it differs in some respects. It must be left to anyone interested to compare the various transla-

---

[1] Perhaps the Bhaddekaratta (No. 131) should be counted as one Discourse, and the Ānanda-, Mahākaccāna- and the Lomasakangiya-bhaddekaratta Suttas as together accounting for one Discourse instead of three.

tions, for my footnotes would have become overburdened had I done so. As it is, they are chiefly concerned with noting parallel passages (a labour some day to be rendered superfluous by the publication of the *Pali Tipiṭakaṁ Concordance*, at present in the course of appearing), and, with the help of the *Majjhima* Commentary, the *Papañcasūdanī*, trying to elucidate perplexing or specially interesting and unusual points in the text itself.

Another difficulty, and one that I have not overcome with consistency, concerns the abbreviation of long and repetitious passages. Repetitions produce a rhythm in the *hearer* (as he was originally), and, as he sat listening after the heat of the day had passed, were calculated to drive home point after point. But the *reader*, especially perhaps the Western one, is apt to find repetitions so tedious and delaying that he may skip what he should have read. Mostly, however, considerations of space and of the size this volume would have attained had everything been put in full, led me to make the abbreviations I have. In addition, I naturally did not expand the abbreviations I found in the P.T.S. printed edition of the *Majjhima*.

This brings us to the question of why this Collection is called *Majjhima*, Middle—a name commonly assumed to derive from the length of the Discourses it contains. The commentators appear to suggest (*e.g.*, at *VA*. 26-27, *DA*. 23) that "length," *pamāṇa*, refers to the length as well as to the number of the Discourses assigned to each of the five Nikāyas. For they speak of the "Suttas of long length," *dīghappamāṇānaṁ suttānaṁ*, as numbering thirty-four, the "middle length Suttas," *majjhimappamāṇāni suttāni*, as numbering 152, while there are 7,762 Suttas in the *Saṁyutta* and 9,557 in the *Anguttara*. Thus the Suttas of "middle length," while being shorter than those of "long length," although more numerous, are longer than the Suttas in the two remaining chief Nikāyas, but not so numerous. Therefore on both counts, their position is a "middle" one. A certain amount of research, however, might be needed to establish whether or not one or two of the very brief *Majjhima* Discourses, such as the Vammīka or the Cūḷagopālaka, were in fact shorter than some of the longer Suttas in *S*. or *A*. On the other hand, it seems doubtful whether, even if some of the longer ones were printed in full, they would turn out to be longer than any of the *Dīgha* Suttantas if these were printed in full.

An interesting feature of the *Majjhima*, and one that is peculiar to it, is its possession of two Vaggas or Divisions called Yamaka, pair, twin, double, couple (Vaggas IV and V). These are distinguished one from the other by prefixing Mahā- (Great or Greater) in the first case and Cūḷa- (Small or Lesser) in the second to the otherwise identical title of Yamakavagga. In the *Dhammapada* there is a Yamakavagga where the verses are arranged by pairs; and Yamakavagga is also the title of one Chapter in the *Saṁyutta* (*S.* iv. 6-15) and of the two in the *Anguttara* (*A.* iv. 314-335, v. 113-131).

The *Majjhima* carries the idea of *yamaka*, but not the name, further than its Mahāyamakavagga and Cūḷayamakavagga. As these form a pair, so, out of the total of 152 Discourses, there are seventeen pairs. In each of these one Discourse is called Mahā- and the other Cūḷa- to distinguish an otherwise identical title shared in common.

Except for a concentration of five such pairs in the Mahāyamakavagga, the remaining pairs occur here and there throughout the *M.* This Vagga is well named since it is the only one of the fifteen Divisions to contain nothing but pairs of Discourses. The Cūḷayamakavagga had, one may suppose, to stand in some close relation to the Mahāyamakavagga and, with its two pairs, follows it. But these two pairs are not placed at the beginning of the Vagga as though they are continuing from the Mahāyamakavagga, but are its Discourses Nos. 3-6.

Immediately before the Mahāyamakavagga comes the Tatiya (Third) Vagga, unique among the M. Vaggas in apparently having no specific name. It contains two pairs, and as they are its last four Discourses, they lead straight on to the five sets of pairs in the Mahāyamakavagga. It might, therefore, have been appropriately named the Cūḷayamakavagga, had there not been another consideration, a cross-division as it were. For the two pairs that conclude this Vagga, as well as its first two Discourses, are further distinguished by the word *upama* in their titles. As this is so, and as there are only two other *upama*-Discourses in the *M.* (Nos. 7, 66), it seems strange that this Division was not called by a name that was to hand: Opammavagga.[1] This name has been suggested by Lord Chalmers, perhaps following Neumann.[2] But at least this

---

[1] *Cf.* Opamma Saṁyutta (*S.* ii. 262 *ff.*), so called because it is rich in parables and similes.

[2] See Tables of Contents in their translations.

assemblage of six *upama*-Discourses in the Third Division provides a good and acceptable reason for *not* calling it Cūḷayamakavagga. It is difficult to know why Suttas 7 and 66 were not included in this Third Division.

There is no such problem with the title of the second Division, with its two pairs placed at the beginning of the Division for, in naming it the Sīhanāda-vagga, the not uncommon practice was being followed of naming a Vagga after its first Sutta, chapter or section as the case might be—a plan also adopted in Vaggas I, XI, XII and XIII of the *M.* The name may also have been determined by the recognition that in the *M.* the technical term *sīhanāda*, the lion's roar, is found (or so I believe) only in the Cūḷa- and Mahā-sīhanāda Suttas. Therefore, once the idea of grouping Suttas by pairs had arisen, such a focusing of attention on a rare but important word, and all that it implied, would provide not only a suitable title for a pair, but also one from which a Division might well take its name. When we call to mind Rhys Davids' intimation that all Sīhanāda Suttas are Discourses on asceticism[1] together with Chalmers' emphasis on this subject,[2] we can see that the Buddhist teaching would not wish to ignore a subject that was uppermost in some of the contemporary and rival teachings, but would have wanted to put forward its own interpretation of false and true asceticism. Moreover in neither of the *M.* Sīhanāda Suttas could either the persons addressed or the places where the utterances were pronounced provide a sufficiently distinctive title: monks, Sāvatthī, Sāriputta and Vesālī all appear too frequently.

A few points concerning the pairs of Discourses may now be briefly noticed, a full discussion being impossible here.

(1) The method of beginning a pair with its Mahā- or Cūḷa-member is reversible. In fact the Cūḷa- member precedes its Mahā- nine times, the Mahā- thus preceding its Cūḷa- member eight times.

(2) With the exception of the Mahā- and Cūḷa-puṇṇamā Suttas (Nos. 109, 110) which are named after a *time*, all the other sixteen pairs are called either after the main topic treated; or after a proper name, that of a person or a place; or after some simile or parable that they contain.

(3) There are no pairs in Vaggas I, VI, IX, X or XII, and only one member of a pair in Vagga XV.

(4) Pairs occur with greater frequency in the Vaggas placed

---

[1] *Dial.* i. 208.

[2] *Fur. Dial.* i. Introduction.

earlier in the *M.* They culminate in the Mahāyamakavagga and, dwindling again through the Cūḷayamakavagga, appear more sporadically afterwards while displaying, to all seeming, a few interesting diversities not found among the pairs placed more at the beginning.

(5) Where a Discourse has no pair of the type under discussion, it is invariably the Cūḷa-member that is lacking. Thus, in the sequence of the three Vacchagotta Suttas, one is called Mahā- (No. 73), but neither of the other two (Nos. 71, 72) is called Cūḷa-Vacchagottasutta. There is a Mahācattārīsaka Sutta (No. 117) and a Mahāsaḷâyatanika (No. 149), but in neither case is there a corresponding Cūḷa-member, although there is a Saḷâyatanavibhaṅga-sutta (No. 137).

(6) Occasionally the members of a pair are divided by one or more intervening Discourses. The Mahā- and Cūḷa-Sakuludāyin Suttas (Nos. 77, 79) in Vagga VIII have one other Discourse between them; but of the three Rāhulovāda Suttas, although the Mahā- (No. 62 in Vagga VII) follows immediately after the Ambalaṭṭhikā-Rāhulovāda, the Cūḷa-Rāhulovāda is placed as far on as Discourse No. 147 in Vagga XV (referred to under (3) above). Vaggas VII and XV, therefore, each contain one member of the same pair.

One of the chief points of interest in connection with the *M.* pairs of Suttas is whether these prefixes of Mahā- and Cūḷa- are intended to qualify the title of the Discourses, or the Discourses themselves, or have they a double reference? For example, when both members of a pair are dealing with the same topic, does the Mahā- give the main gist, or approach the topic from some more significant angle, and does it therefore become of greater length than the Cūḷa-? Or is the length independent of these other features? There is probably little doubt for example that the Mahā-sīhanāda Sutta may be regarded as the "Discourse on the Lion's Roar that is Great," "great" because uttered by the Tathāgata and setting forth his ten Powers and four Confidences, and much else besides of his comprehensions and autobiographical reminiscences. The Cūḷa-sīhanāda, on the other hand, does no more than urge monks to roar a Lion's Roar and then quits the topic. In this sense it is therefore the Lion's Roar that is lesser than the Tathāgata's Roar. Again, the Mahā- is longer than the Cūḷa-sīhanāda, so on this count, too, it may be legitimately regarded as the "Greater."

Of those Discourses that are paired because their titles share the name of some simile, we may take the Gopālaka Suttas (although not strictly speaking *upama*-Suttas) in exemplification of the problem. Here the Cūḷa- makes use of only one simile deriving from the "cowherd," while the Mahā- puts forward eleven. It is also shorter than the Mahā-. Both of these reasons may have been operative in determining which Discourse was to be perpetuated as the Greater and which as the Lesser.

When we come to those Discourses whose titles are united by the same proper name, it is never the person or the place denoted by the proper name that is great or small. No Mahā-saccaka or Cūḷa-saccaka, for example, is known to have existed—only Saccaka; there was no place known either as Mahā-Assapura or as Cūḷa-Assapura—merely Assapura.[1] In such Discourses, therefore, the name is to be ignored as that to which Maha- or Cuḷa- refers. We are, however, still left with the same problems as are to be looked for in the pairs of Discourses deriving their titles from topics or similes.

In order to arrive at some solution, I think that each pair would have to be examined separately in the first place, but always in conjunction with other comparable Suttas, wherever these may be found in the *M.* or in other parts of the Pali Canon. Only then, if ever, could any general conclusion be established. I will now take one Sutta, whose case has already been discussed by the Rhys Davids and Lord Chalmers, and which serves well to indicate the possible lines such a wider investigation might follow.

As the *Dīgha* contains three Sīhanāda Suttantas (Nos. 8, 25, 26) while the *M.* has two; and as it has a Subha Suttanta (No. 10), which is also the title of *M.* Sutta 99 so it has a Mahāsatipaṭṭhāna-suttanta (No. 22), the *M.* likewise containing a Satipaṭṭhāna Sutta (No. 10). Yet while the Sīhanāda Suttas have a varying degree of identity, and sometines none at all, and while the Subha Suttas are quite different in both Nikāyas, the *Dīgha's* Mahāsatipaṭṭhāna Suttanta contains not only word for word the material of *M.* Sutta 10, but also that of *M.* Sutta 141. Lord Chalmers is of the opinion that it "accordingly is distinguished from ours here (*i.e.*, *M.* Sutta 10) "as 'the Long' or *Mahā*-sati-paṭṭhāna sutt*anta*."[2] And the translators of *Dīgha*, vol. ii, have a note to the same effect.[3] Should the conclusion, therefore, be drawn that the

[1] In the case of the Mahā-kaccāna-bhaddekaratta Sutta, Mahā- is of course part of this Kaccāna's name, serving to distinguish him from other Kaccānas.

[2] *Fur. Dial.* i. 41.

[3] *Dial.* ii. 337.

Satipaṭṭhāna Sutta of *M.* is really a Cūḷa-satipaṭṭhāna Sutta? I do not think that this can be assumed with any degree of certainty without some prior examination of the reasons why the Mahā-Suttantas of the *Dīgha* are so named. Meanwhile we do know that, within the *M.* itself, even if the pairs are dealing with the same topic (which is not necessarily the case if they are named after a place) each member handles it differently. So that, it seems a little difficult to believe that the *M.* Satipaṭṭhāna Sutta has a pair that not only occurs in a different Nikāya but a pair with which, as far as it goes, it is identical. For the *D.* Suttanta only gains its greater length by adding paragraphs on the Four Truths, which in the *M.*, form a separate Sutta (No. 141). Apart from this, the space devoted to the chief topic, namely the *sati-paṭṭhāna*, and the manner of presentation are exactly the same in *D.* 22 and *M.* 10, and inevitably the same since there is only one way, fixed and systematic, to study and practise the applications of mindfulness.

Yet, owing to the greater completeness of the *D.* Suttanta its translators argue that, because it is prefixed by the term *mahā-*, " that would show that when the title was first used the *M.* recension was already known. It would not follow that the *Dīgha* is younger than the *Majjhima*; they may have been edited at the same time from older material." It might also show that it was deliberately decided to have a Satipaṭṭhāna Sutta in both Nikāyas owing to the importance of the subject. But again, if we judge by the inner arrangement and the naming of the *M.* Suttas, a Mahā- can exist without a Cūḷa-. Therefore, if the naming of the *D.* Suttantas follows this same plan, and it contains no discourses called Cūḷa-, its Mahā-satipaṭṭhāna Suttanta need not necessarily have a corresponding Cūḷa- either within its own framework or in any other Nikāya.

The Buddha is sometimes shown as spontaneously naming the Discourse he is about to deliver. This leaves open the question of whether he had already given a Discourse in the same terms, with or without naming it, and which is to be repeated now; or whether the name and the Discourse were both being given for the first time. Thus, in *M.* Sutta No. 1, he is recorded as saying: " I will give you the (or, a) *sabbadhammamūlapariyāya*," of which compound the title as it has come down to us is but an abbreviation. And at the beginning of Sutta No. 2 he is recorded to say: " I will give you the (or, a) *sabbâsavasaṁvarapariyāya*," a compound that has apparently been contracted into the title of Sabbâsavasutta. In Sutta 17 he is shown as saying: " I will give you the (or, a) *vanapatthapariyāya.*" As in Sutta No. 2, the word *pariyāya* has been omitted from the title as handed down both in the *M.* itself and in Buddhaghosa's Commentary, although variant readings of the latter recognise it. Where, in the Discourses placed later in the Collection, Gotama is recorded to give a name to the Discourse he is about to utter, the word *vibhaṅga* may take the place of *pariyāya,* as in Suttas Nos. 137, 138, 139.

Sometimes alternative names for the Suttas, attributed to Gotama, are to be found in the Suttas themselves. Thus Nāgasamāla is to remember the Mahā-sīhanāda (No. 12) as the Lomahaṁsanapariyāya, a title also used for this Discourse at *Miln.* 398. At the end of Sutta No. 115 five alternative titles are given for it, as happens in *Dīgha* Suttanta No. 1. On the other hand Ānanda is told he may remember the Discourse just given as the Madhupiṇḍika (No. 18) which is the name by which the *M.* knows this Discourse, and which one may therefore presume had probably not been heard by Ānanda before.

In addition, Buddhaghosa supplies some of the Discourses with alternative or variant titles. These are too numerous to assemble here, and I can only draw attention to the interesting case of the Dīghanakha Sutta (No. 74). In the *Papañcasūdanī* he gives no hint of another title. But in his Commentary on the *Dīgha* (*DA.* 418) he refers to it as the Vedanāpariggahasuttanta, as do both the commentator of the *Dhammapada* (*DhA.* i. 96) and Dhammapāla in his Commentary on the *Theragāthā* for Sāriputta's verses (beginning with *Thag.* verse 981). Alternative titles known to Buddhaghosa for the Anumāna Sutta (No. 15) and the Ariyapariyesanā (No. 26) are noticed in the appropriate footnotes below.

In the Tipiṭaka are a number of constantly recurring leading terms each having such a wide range and richness in connotation that an adequate, sufficiently expressive or true translation becomes impossible. It is not unlikely that the early contemporary auditors appreciated the background, associations and the " religious " application and use of these words and were able to fill in more or less correctly and fully the significance they held in the Teaching that was in the course of being promulgated. In trying to recapture and reconstruct the meaning such terms had then, it is essential not to distort them as may be done by using a word from another and different tradition. For this may merely succeed in stressing one aspect only, or it may conjure up a false or inappropriate set of values. If the meaning and full significance of these Eastern terms cannot be expressed justly and truly by one or more English word or even by a circumlocution, rather than to mislead, fall short or call up wrong conceptions it seems better to leave them to speak for themselves. Words that for these reasons I think it justifiable not to translate include Tathāgata, Bodhisatta, Nibbāna, Dhamma and Brahma.

But lest a translation should become overloaded with words left in the original Pali, renderings have to be attempted of other technical terms, such as *dukkha*, *āsava* and *saṅkhārā*, even although the adequacy of the renderings remains a matter for debate. It is now necessary to make a few remarks about the Pali words I have mentioned in these two groups.

Tathāgata. Five reasons why a Tathāgata is so called are given at *D.* iii. 135 (*cf. A.* ii. 24; *It.* p. 121) and the Commentaries provide another eight reasons (*e.g.*, *MA.* i. 45 *f.*, *DA.* 59 *ff.*, *UdA.* 128 *ff.*, *ItA.* i. 115 *ff.*, *KhpA.* 196). Each is somewhat complex, so it would appear that the word Tathāgata had no simple, narrow or rigid meaning but was, on the contrary, one with a wide sweep. In sense probably "Accomplished One" or "Perfect One" comes nearest although having no etymological justification and being, moreover, equally applicable to any arahant, the perfect one who has done all there was to be done. Various contexts insist on the tracklessness of a Tathāgata (*e.g.*, *M.* i. 139; *Dhp.* 179, 180); on his having cut off and rooted out the five *khandhas* so that it is impossible he should be known or "reckoned" by these; and on being, even when actually present, incomprehensible (or, not to be got at, *anupalabbhamāna*). Although, therefore, he cannot be defined or described as the man so-and-so, he can for this very reason be called *uttamapurisa paramapurisa paramapattipatta*, Highest Person, Supernal Person, Attainer of the Supernal (*S.* iii. 118). This renders it as inept to speak of him as "is" or "is not" or "both is and is not" or "neither is nor is not" after dying as to speak of him as "arising," "not arising," "both arising and not arising" or "neither arising nor not arising" (*M.* i. 488). The Tathāgata has cut off the conduit for Becoming (or, the "cord" tying to Becoming, *bhavanetti*). He is deep, unfathomable as is the great ocean (*M.* i. 487), the body of Dhamma, the body of Brahma, Dhamma-become and Brahma-become (*D.* iii. 84). But yet, so long as his body remains *devas* and men shall see him; at the breaking up of his body at the end of his life-time *devas* and men shall see him not (*D*. i. 46).

Bodhisatta. In general terms this means the Being both set on and actively determined to win *bodhi*, Awakening, Enlightenment or Illumination for himself. The Bodhisatta in the Pali canon is always, unless otherwise stated as at *e.g.*, *D*. ii. 30 and *S*. ii. 5, the Being who became the Fully Self-enlightened or awakened One of our epoch, Gotama the Buddha and who, in his last " birth " in this or any world, finally accomplished the vow he took eons ago under Dīpaṅkara, the first Buddha of all, of himself becoming Buddha. When, as recorded in the Nikāyas, he wished to exemplify some point by recourse to " autobiography," he sometimes spoke of himself as bodhisatta (see Index, s.v.) without necessarily, however, referring to a previous " birth " as is the burden of his " identification " at the end of each Jātaka story, but rather meaning some time in this " birth " before the Night of Awakening when, on becoming Buddha, his career as the Bodhisatta came to an end.

Nibbāna. It is commonly said that nibbāna cannot be described, any more than can the other great negative word *amata*, the Deathless or Undying, which is more or less equivalent. That these words are negative points to the illimitability of their connotations as surely as the Upanishadic *neti neti*, It is not this, it is not this, points to the indefinability of Brahman. It is therefore probably true that the state of mind called nibbāna and the vision of nibbāna baffle all description. Yet a good deal may be said, externally as it were, as can be seen from the following few examples. In the first place there is Sāriputta's dictum that nibbāna is the destruction of attachment, aversion and confusion (*S*. iv. 251), and which, besides having the merit of brevity, also indicates that nibbāna is a state of mind devoid of these three roots of unskill, *akusala*. As a state of mind, as " the real, the excellent " (*A*. v. 322), as there " where there is no-thing, where naught is grasped—the utter destruction of ageing and dying " (*Sn*. 1093, 1094), and where ageing and dying refer as much, if not more, to the rise and fall of sensations and desires as to physical decrepitude and death, nibbāna can be attained here and now (*e.g.*, *S*. iii. 164). In this sense it is also the " stopping of becoming," *bhavanirodho nibbānaṁ* (*S*. ii. 117; *A*. v. 9) because there has been a getting rid of that craving (*S*. i. 39, *Sn*. 1109) that sews one to becoming after becoming (*A*. iii. 400 *ff*.). Nibbāna is (*tiṭṭhat' eva nibbānaṁ*, *M*. iii, 6; *atthi nibbānaṁ*, *Miln*. 271); and it is *lokuttara*, of another, a further world, not of this ordinary realm of sense, but beyond it. It is a world where, because of a new attitude to the senses brought about by disciplining them, the fuel for the lamp of sensory and saṁsāric becoming is exhausted. When this lamp goes out, one may penetrate, in meditation, the layers of ordinary sense-imposed consciousness and, seeing them as they really are, *yathābhūtaṁ*, enter into and have mastery in the transcendent and abounding plenitude of the extra-sensory Wisdom beyond, *paññāpāripūrī vepullatā* (*D.* iii. 57). As *asaṅkhata*, nibbāna is uncaused and uncausing. It is, and it is "unborn, unageing, undecaying, undying, unsorrowing and stainless —the uttermost security from the bonds" (*M.* i. 163), the ultimate "escape" from all that has been born, has become, been made or compounded (*Ud.* 80).

Dhamma. Dhamma, from the root *dhr*, meaning to hold, support, has been treated at some length in the *PED* and by W. Geiger in *Pali Dhamma*, Munich, 1920, and I have also written on *Early Buddhist Dhamma* in *Artibus Asiae*, XI. 1/2, 1948.

Primarily, Dhamma means the natural state or condition of beings and things, what supports them, the law of their being, what it is right for them to be, the very stuff of their being, *evaṁ-dhammo*. If they are what it is right for them to be, if they are right without being righteous, *sīlavā no ca sīlamayo* (*M.* ii. 27), then they are true to themselves. So Dhamma also means truth (*S.* i. 169), with the derived meaning of "religious" truth, hence the Buddhist doctrine, Dhamma or *saddhamma*, the Teaching itself, our Teaching or the true Teaching. If beings and things are true to themselves they will know how to act in body, speech and thought. If not, Dhamma will still have to be pointed out to them, their duty taught, as in the *Bhagavadgītā* Kṛṣṇa pointed out to Arjuna what was his *dharma*, and as in the Suttapiṭaka Gotama tells his disciples the Dhamma that they should strive to follow and practise. There are, moreover, general terms in which he keeps the pursuit of Dhamma before them: "Fare along having *attā* for island and refuge, having Dhamma for island and refuge"—an exhortation that has special reference to the four applications of mindfulness (for which see Sutta 10 below) which, if properly developed, are powers for passing from ignorance to knowledge. The exhortation, moreover, perfectly agrees with Gotama's saying at the end of his life: "After I am gone, the Dhamma taught and the Discipline laid down by me will be your Teacher." In some sense the Buddha and the Dhamma are one. He is *Dhamma-bhūta*, Dhamma-become (*M.* i. 111) so that " Who sees me sees Dhamma " (*S.* iii. 121); and while the Buddha is constantly referred to as the charioteer, Dhamma, too, is the charioteer (*S.* i. 33).

Again Dhamma is identified with Conditioned Genesis or Dependent Origination, *paṭicca-samuppāda*, among the most important doctrines enunciated by the Buddha. For, " Who sees Conditioned Genesis sees Dhamma, who sees Dhamma sees Conditioned Genesis " (*M.* i. 190-191).

Dhamma is, moreover, not infrequently paralleled by *sama*, even, as in the phrases *dhammacariya samacariya* and *dhammacārin samacārin,* which in the *M.* occur, for example, in Suttas Nos. 41, 42. The ultimate fruits of this Dhamma- and even-faring are freedom of mind and freedom through intuitive wisdom, arrived at when the cankers have been destroyed and the arahant is a " mover-at-will " in the high planes of meditation, free to engage upon them where, when and for as long as he wills. " Even " is an epithet of the Way and of those who tread it: " Even is the ariyans' Way; ariyans are even amid things uneven " (*S.* i. 48), for they have arrived at *upekkhā*, such steady even-mindedness and mental balance that they are unaffected by sensory impingement and craving for it.

As we find *dhammacariya* and *samacariya,* so we find, and much more frequently, *brahmacariya.* Similarly, either *dhamma* or *brahma* can be prefixed, as it seems indiscriminately, to various other terms such as *yāna*, *kāya*, *bhūta* and *cakka.* So we must now turn to this term Brahma, far from negligible in the Pali canon.

Brahma. The Commentaries always gloss this by *seṭṭha,* best, but this only puts the meaning the term had for Buddhism a step further back, for they never say what they think of as " Best." Perhaps, however, the vagueness was deliberate. One who has developed the four *Brahmavihāra*, meditative abidings in Brahma, is said as related in a story of the past (*M.* ii. 76) to attain the Brahma-world. But this is after dying and may refer to Brahmā's world. While still alive here, he may be called *brahmapatta*, attained to Brahma, also one of the many epithets by which Upāli, the Jain " convert," praised the Buddha (*M.* i. 368). The Buddha, not caught or stuck fast at any extreme (*cf. Sn.* 1042), either ethical or doctrinal, pointed out the Middle Way, the pursuit of which leads to Brahma-attainment (*S.* i. 169). Success results from concentration of mind and harmlessness to all that lives and breathes:

A mind well concentrated,
Stainless, undefiled,
Without harshness for all that has come to be——
This is the Way for Brahma-attainment.

This, therefore, depends upon perfect fulfilment of the ethical precepts and of mental cultivation. The aspect of harmlessness, necessary for attaining and thereby becoming and so being Brahma, is again evident in a context occurring not infrequently, and taken to be the criterion of Buddhist morality: " He who neither torments himself or another, who is here and now allayed, gone out, become cool, an experiencer of bliss, lives with a self become Brahma " (as at *M*. i. 342). Brahma is thus perhaps not a goal to be reached after physical death, but a goal to be won here and now by the death of the greed and craving from which all cruelty springs. The death of unskilled psychological states induces a new condition of mind, one that is supreme, highest and best, and a new generation of spiritual powers. The *Sn*. (verse 508) is therefore much to the point when it asks: " By which self does one go to the Brahma-world?" An answer may be found at *Sn*. 139: " having cast out sensual desire and attachment, he came to the Brahma-world."

I therefore take it that the *Brahmaloka* in the formula of the *iddhis*, the psychic powers of the spirit, as on pp. 43, 92 below, has reference to a world of mentality and mental activity, supernormal though this may be, but none the less attainable while one is " in the body," *kāyena*. And this I think is the point: for if there is no entity that survives from one " birth " to another, if then it is " the being that is bound to *saṁsāra* while his *kamma* passes on" (*S*. i. 38), the being must make the utmost efforts *now* to win what is not yet won. It follows that all speculations on what one was in the past, will be in the future or doubts about the present are worthless (*M*. i. 8, 265). So, " be free of the past, be free of things hereafter, be free of middle things " (*Dhp*. 348). The real things to put in the place of vain speculation are the *jhānas*, the meditations, which are of the purest mentality, *ābhicetasika* (*M*. i. 33, 354, etc.). They lead on to the " three knowledges " (*e.g.*, below, pp. 27 *ff*., 229, 302, 332) all of which, on p. 227 *ff*., are called, rather strangely since he was mostly thought of as " trackless," the Tathāgata's footprints; and they lead on to " the abidings that are peaceful " (below, p. 53); and they lead on to the stopping of perception and feeling (below, pp. 202, 218, 252, 261), the ultimate meditative state, higher than any known to either of Gotama's former teachers, Āḷāra the Kālāma or Uddaka Rāmaputta (see below, Sta. 26). The unshakable freedom of mind that results is called the goal, the pith and the culmination of the Brahma-faring (*M.* i. 197, 201), that faring in or towards the Highest and Sublime which, I have suggested, was not transcendent for Buddhism, but within, and realisable in the highest reaches of a mind capable of sustained and uninterrupted meditation. When the Brahma-faring has been brought to a close (*vusitaṁ brahmacariyaṁ*), when done is all that there was to be done, the Brahma-farer, who is the Dhamma-farer and the even-farer, has become Brahman, *brahmabhūta*, is of the stuff of his own being, *evaṁ-dhammo*, and fares evenly amid things uneven.

We come now to a short discussion of three technical terms for which I, in common with other English translators, have attempted a rendering.

Dukkha. I have translated this on the whole as " anguish," and have always done so in the various formulae such as the Four Truths and in one of the occurrences of the word in the formula of the fourth *jhāna*, but not in its other occurrence there. The reason for this is that " there is no word in English covering the same ground as Dukkha does in Pali. Our modern words are too specialised, too limited and usually too strong " (*P.E.D.* s.v. *dukkha*). " Anguish," I am aware, may be considered too strong. But where it has been used the stress appears to be wanted more on the mental than on the physical dis-ease; where physical dis-ease is more clearly intended, I have used other words. Short of keeping *dukkha* itself, untranslated, the only alternative seemed to use these various renderings.

The word *dukkha* appears to be derived from *duh* or *dus*+*kha*, the bad or evil hollow or cavern, zero, empty of that which should rightly fill, and which may perhaps be taken as nibbāna. For once nibbāna has been gained *dukkha* has been stopped, or to put it the other way, with the eradication of *dukkha* nibbāna supervenes. This is tantamount to the Third Truth. The five *khandhas* are groups of grasping; if uncontrolled by the ariyan disciple, they are the source of desire, sensual pleasure and so on, and hence, partly owing to their impermanence, of the uprising of *dukkha*. But the desire and attachment to which they give rise may be controlled and ejected (see below, p. 237), not by the atrophy of sense-perceptions, but by the refusal to be either entranced or repelled by them (*e.g.*, below, p. 323 *f.*). The attitude to them must therefore be new. It is that required in the fourth *jhāna*, which itself is a means for getting rid of the ignorance (p. 367 below), which, as the first and fundamental condition in the whole series of *paṭiccasamuppāda*, leads on to the arising of this whole mass of *dukkha*.

In the absence of success in the " watch over the senses " and in rectitude of *sīla*, in the absence of proper mind-control and cultivation,

> " Man's heart is anguished with the fever of unrest,
> With the poison of self-seeking,
> With a thirst that knows no end."[1]

Āsava. As Rhys Davids remarks (*S.B.E.* xi, p. 294) the term *āsava* is " simple "—but yet it has always been a problem to translators. I have used Lord Chalmers' " canker," as I have come on no other translation that seems preferable. The root *sru* suggests a flowing, discharge, leak, trickling, oozing, while the prefix *ā*-, especially with verbs of motion, means " towards." Therefore the " influx " used in the Anthology compiled by the late Dr. A. K. Coomaraswamy and myself,[2] although lacking useful connotation for the general reader, has some etymological advantage. Canker, on the other hand, is well known as " anything that frets, corrodes, corrupts or consumes slowly and secretly " (*O.E.D.*). If we therefore take the prefix *ā*- in its sense of " around " or " from all sides," which it has when prefixed to a verb or noun, the term " canker " is quite apt. *MA*. i. 61 indeed seems to regard the *āsavas* both as what flow in and what flow out. " They flow, *savanti*, they proceed, *pavattanti*, from the eye, . . . from the mind. Or, they flow (towards), they enter, *pavasanti*, the long *saṁsāradukkha*."[3]

The Sanskrit lexicons give " discharge " among other meanings, such as flowing, running, distress, pain, affliction, and they also give " fault, transgression." I would suggest that in general the implication is that the mind should be so compact of beneficial and skilled mental activities and thoughts as to have no " fault " in it, in the geological sense (see Rhys Davids, *S.B.E.*, xi, p. 295), no break in the continuity of its determination to develop skill, *kusala*, thus giving no possible entrance for or manufacture of the three, or four, corroding *āsavas*. In the *M*. the *āsava* of *diṭṭhi* is not mentioned. For it, the *āsavas* number three: *kāma*, *bhava* and

---

[1] From Rabindranath Tagore's *Hymn to the Buddha*.

[2] *Living Thoughts of Gotama the Buddha*. [3] *Cf*. *Asl*. 48.

avijjā. From Sta. 2 onwards a major theme is the extirpation of these *āsavas*.

Saṅkhārā. This is "one of the most difficult terms in Buddhist metaphysics,"[1] and for a fuller analysis than is possible here the reader is referred to the *P.E.D.* Here I can only draw attention to contexts where the word occurs in the First Fifty Discourses, and to the different meanings—or shades of meaning—attached to it in each of these, and which therefore each require a different English word to convey some import of the idea of the Pali word, but without being regarded as a definite translation.

When *saṅkhārā* occurs as the fourth of the five *khandhas*, I have translated it as "habitual tendencies," such as are inherent in, or effect and synthesise, *abhisankharoti*, these groups of grasping with the possible exception of the first, *rūpa* or *kāya*. It is thus "synthetic activity," one of the two senses ascribed to the word by Dasgupta.[2]

When *saṅkhārā* occurs in the *paṭiccasamuppāda*, I have translated it as "karma-formations"[3] or, more simply, formations, in the sense that *saṅkhārā* denote the act of forming, karmically and causally, as required in producing through condition, *paṭicca*.

When the word is used as a suffix to *kāya*, *vacī*, *citta* or *mano-* (as at *M.* i. 301), its sense appears to be that of function, impulse or activity. Dr. E. J. Thomas suggests that this simpler analysis may be earlier.[4] In such passages I have rendered the word by "activities," a word I have also used in translating the formulation of the bases of psychic power, where each of the four is called *padhānasaṅkhārasamannāgata*, "possessed of the activities of striving" (p. 135 below). I have also translated *saṅkhārā* by "activities" in the sequence *sabbasaṅkharasamathāya sabbûpadhipaṭinissaggāya taṇhakkhayāya* (on pp. 176, 211 below). This *sabbasaṅkhāra-*, however, may have more affinities with the *popular*[5] meaning of the word as found in the formula *sabbe saṅkhārā aniccā . . . dukkhā*,[6] as may also be the case on p. 400 below, but where I have rendered it as "all constructions" (*sabbasaṅkhāresu aniccâ-*

---

[1] *P.E.D.*, s.v. *saṅkhāra*.

[2] *Hist. Ind. Philosophy*, i. 96.

[3] Following Nyanatiloka, *Bud. Dictionary*, p. 142, although as *P.E.D.* notes (s.v. *saṅkhāra* 3) "if we render it by 'formations' (*cf.* Oldenberg's "Gestaltungen," Buddha, 1920, p. 254) we imply the mental 'constitutional' element as well as the physical."

[4] *Hist. Bud. Thought*, p. 61, n. 2.

[5] See *P.E.D.*, s.v. *saṅkhāra*.

[6] *Dhp.* 277, 278; and *aniccā vata saṅkhārā* at *D.* ii. 157, etc.

nupassino). This phrase is here ascribed to an earlier Buddha, Kakusandha, which may again point to this use being "earlier" and more "popular" than that of the more philosophical appearances of the word as a *handha* and in the *paṭiccasamuppāda*.

Still one other occurrence of *saṅkhārā* in these First Fifty Discourses is when it forms a compound with *āyu*, as *āyusaṅkhārā* (*M*. i. 295 *f*.). This I believe may be yet another meaning of the word and have accordingly rendered it by "properties."[1]

These different meanings attributed to the word may, of course, be essentially invalid, for in all its appearances in this context or that there may be some inner bond of reference that has so far escaped interpreters of Buddhist thought. A case in point may be found in Sutta 9, where the statement of the *paṭiccasamuppāda* is interrupted at each factor to ask what that factor is, what its uprising, its stopping and the course leading to its stopping. Here *saṅkhārā*, "formations," are commentarially taken as sixty-nine types of action of body, speech and thought. So when it is asked: "What are the formations?" the answer can be given in terms of "activity" of body, speech and mind.[2]

Dasgupta makes the interesting suggestion[3] that "The Buddha was one of the first few earliest thinkers to introduce proper philosophical terms and phraseology with a distinct philosophical method and he had often to use the same word in more or less different senses. Some of the philosophical terms at least are therefore somewhat elastic. . . ." This would indicate a certain insufficiency of them, rather than an unsettled state of philosophical and psychological terminology by the time the Nikāyas came into being. In the assumed absence of any inner point of reference, it would seem that not enough terms had been coined or taken over from other systems of thought—usually to be given a new meaning[4]—to fill the growing content of the Buddhist teaching. As Mrs. Rhys Davids sometimes said of other words, one has to do duty for several. In addition, the Commentaries recognise clearly that some words have different meanings, and not infrequently assemble

---

[1] The word occurs, also in the plural, in a different context at *S*. ii. 266; and in still another context, but in the singular, at *D*. ii. 106, *A*. iv. 311, *Ud*. 64.

[2] *Cf*. *Vism*. 527.

[3] *Hist*. *Ind*. *Phil*., i. 86, n. 1.

[4] At *e.g.*, *Manu*, ii. 26 *ff*., ix., x. the "sacraments" are called *samskāra*; see also *P.E.D.*, s.v. *saṅkhāra*, and Winternitz, *Ind. Lit.*, i. 272.

examples of these before stating which meaning is intended " here." Buddhaghosa gave a full analysis of *saṅkhārā* at *Vism.* 526 *ff.*

Thirty-six Discourses are addressed to monks, either in general or to particular ones, such as Mahācunda (Sta. 8), Sāriputta (No. 12) or Kumārakassapa (No. 23). Nine, or part of them, are addressed to others, such as brahmans (No. 4, part of No. 7, and Nos. 27, 30), brahman householders (Nos. 41, 42), Sakyans (No. 14 and first part of No. 18), a Jain (No. 36), and Māra (No. 50). The remaining Suttas are remarkable for the diversity of characters recorded to take part (Nos. 18, 31, 32, 35, 37).

The majority of the Discourses are said to have been delivered by Gotama. Others are ascribed to Sāriputta (second part of No. 3, and Nos. 5, 9, 28); Sutta 24 records a dialogue held between Sāriputta and Puṇṇa Mantāṇī's son, while in Sutta 43 questions put by Mahākoṭṭhita are answered by Sāriputta. Suttas 15 and 50 are ascribed to Moggallāna, who also figures in Sutta 37. The second part of No. 18 is ascribed to Mahākaccāna and the first part of No. 23 to a *deva*. The beginning of Sutta 27 records a short conversation between the wanderer Pilotika and the brahman Jāṇussoṇi, while in Sutta 44 questions are put by the monk Visākha and answered by the nun Dhammadinnā. Unlike the *Suttanipāta* which, as Chalmers has pointed out, contains no reference to nuns, the *Majjhima* is aware of their existence as is shown in Suttas 21, 44, and in other contexts.

The false way of asceticism, set out in detail in *e.g.*, the Mahāsīhanādasutta, is to give way to self-discipline and mind-control. Only so will be achieved the freedom of mind and the freedom through wisdom that are cankerless, the calm and tranquillity, the knowledge and vision, the evenness and the unshakability of mind that ensue when an end has been made of the unrest, the agitation and the anguish which is *dukkha*. This is not so much perhaps the inherent necessity or existence of pain in the world's constituents, but the wrong mental grasp of these very constituents, the unskilled mental attitude of craving for them thinking that they are " mine," I am they or they are my self (see *e.g.*, Sutta No. 1).

I. B. HORNER.

London, 1953.

ABBREVIATIONS

A.	= Anguttara-Nikāya.
AA.	= Commentary on A.
Asl.	= Atthasālinī.
B.D.	= *Book of the Discipline.*
Budv.	= Buddhavaṁsa.
Comy.	= Commentary.
Cpd.	= *Compendium of Philosophy.*
C.P.D.	= *Critical Pali Dictionary* (Dines Andersen and Helmer Smith).
D.	= Dīgha-Nikāya.
DA.	= Commentary on D.
Dh., or *Dhp.*	= Dhammapada.
DhA.	= Commentary on Dh.
Dhs.	= Dhammasangani.
Dial.	= *Dialogues of the Buddha.*
Divy.	= Divyâvadāna.
D.P.P.N.	= *Dictionary of Pali Proper Names* (G. P. Malalasekera).
Fur. Dial.	= *Further Dialogues of the Buddha.*
G.S.	= *Gradual Sayings.*
It.	= Itivuttaka.
Jā.	= Jātaka.
J.P.T.S.	= *Journal of the Pali Text Society.*
Khp.	= Khuddakapāṭha.
KhpA.	= Commentary on Khp.
K.S.	= *Kindred Sayings.*
Kvu.	= Kathāvatthu.
M.	= Majjhima-Nikāya.
MA.	= Commentary on M.
Mhvs.	= Mahāvaṁsa.
Mhvu.	= Mahāvastu.
Miln.	= Milindapañha.
Min. Anth.	= *Minor Anthologies of the Pali Canon.*
MT.	= Vaṁsatthappakāsinī.
Nd.	= Niddesa.

Nissag.	= Nissaggiya.
P. Purity	= *Path of Purity.*
Pāc.	= Pācittiya.
P.E.D.	= *Pali-English Dictionary* (T. W. Rhys Davids and W. Stede).
Pṭs.	= Paṭisambhidāmagga.
P.T.S.	= Pali Text Society.
Pug.	= Puggalapaññatti.
PugA.	= Commentary on Pug.
Pv.	= Petavatthu.
PvA.	= Commentary on Pv.
S.	= Saṁyutta-Nikāya.
SA.	= Commentary on S.
Sn.	= Suttanipāta.
SnA.	= Commentary on Sn.
Sta.	= Sutta.
Thag.	= Theragāthā.
Thīg.	= Therīgāthā.
Ud.	= Udāna.
UdA.	= Commentary on Ud.
VA.	= Commentary on Vin.
Vbh.	= Vibhaṅga.
VbhA.	= Commentary on Vbh.
Vin.	= Vinaya-piṭaka.
Vism.	= Visuddhimagga.
Vv.	= Vimānavatthu.

I. THE DIVISION OF THE SYNOPSIS OF FUNDAMENTALS

(Mūlapariyāyavagga)

Praise to the Lord, the Perfected One, the Completely Self-awakened One.

1. DISCOURSE ON THE SYNOPSIS OF FUNDAMENTALS

(Mūlapariyāyasutta).[1]

[**1**] THUS have I heard: At one time the Lord[2] was staying near Ukkaṭṭhā in the Subhaga Grove[3] close to[4] the great sāl-tree. While he was there the Lord addressed the monks,[5] saying: " Monks." " Revered One,"[6] these monks answered the Lord in assent. The Lord spoke thus:

" I will teach you, monks, the synopsis of the fundamentals of all things.[7] Listen, attend carefully, and I will speak."

" Yes, Lord," these monks answered the Lord in assent. The Lord spoke thus:

" This is a case, monks, where an uninstructed[8] average person, taking no count of the pure ones,[9] unskilled in the *dhamma* of the

---

[1] Both *mūla* and *pariyāya* are words of several meanings. *MA*. i. 16-17 expands the title into *sabbadhammamūlapariyāya*, a compound attributed to Gotama in his first speech in this *Sutta*. The Comy. further says that the meaning is the breaking of pride; for the reason for this see p. 20, *n*. 4. *Cf*. *Jātaka* No. 245, the *Mūlapariyāyajātaka*, which is quoted at *MA*. i. 56-8.

[2] *Bhagavā*. This means, according to *MA*. i. 10, esteemed, *garu*, esteemed in the world. Or *garu* may mean " teacher." *Cf*. *guru*.

[3] *vana*. *MA*. i. 11 says a grove is of two kinds: one that is planted (by men) and one that is self-sown, or, growing on its own,—i.e. groves are cultivated or wild. To the former class belong, according to *MA*. i. 11, the Bamboo Grove, the Jeta Grove, etc.; to the latter the Blind Men's Grove, the Great Grove, the Añjana Grove, etc. The Subhaga Grove is self-sown, or self-grown.

[4] *MA*. i. 12 = *VA*. i. 109 says *mūlam* here means *samīpaṃ*, near, close.

[5] Part of the definition of " monk " at *Vin*. iii. 24 is quoted at *MA*. i. 13, which also states that the word " monk " is used (by the Buddha) in addressing his ordained disciples.

[6] *bhadante*, a term of respect.

[7] *dhammā*, an important word with several meanings, such as conditions, mental objects, states of mind, and things.

[8] One who does not hear the teaching or tradition. *Cf*. *S*. iii, 3, 113; *M*. i. 7, 135, iii. 17; *Dhs*. 1003, 1217.

[9] *ariyānaṃ*, restricted at *MA*. i. 21 to Buddhas, Paccekabuddhas and

pure ones,[1] untrained[2] in the *dhamma* of the pure ones, taking no count of the true men,[3] unskilled in the *dhamma* of the true men, untrained in the *dhamma* of the true men, recognises extension[4] as extension;[5] having recognised extension as extension, he thinks of extension, he thinks (of self) in (regard to) extension, he thinks (of self as) extension, he thinks, 'Extension is mine'[6]—he rejoices in extension.[7] What is the reason for this? I say that it is not thoroughly understood by him.

He recognises liquid[8] as liquid . . . heat[9] as heat . . . motion[10] as

---

disciples of Buddhas, "or here, just Buddhas are pure ones." *Cf. S.* v. 435, *tathāgato ariyo, tasmā ariyasaccānî ti vuccanti,* "the Tathāgata is pure, therefore they (the four truths) are called the pure truths (or the truths of the pure one(s))."

[1] According to *MA.* i. 22, this consists of the categories of the applications of mindfulness, and so on.

[2] *avinīta,* untrained, not led, not disciplined. *MA.* i. 22 mentions two kinds of *vinaya* or discipline, that of restraint, and that of getting rid of. Each of these is further subdivided into a fivefold division.

[3] *sappurisa.* *MA.* i. 21 says that these are paccekabuddhas and disciples of tathāgatas. Identified with the "pure ones" at *MA.* i. 21, 24.

[4] *paṭhavī,* as a *mahābhūta* or *dhātu,* is an element, a fundamental or essential part of every existing thing, meaning "extension." Its symbol is "earth." See *Cpd.* 155. *MA.* i. 25 gives four aspects of the word *paṭhavī* and says they are all to be taken into account here: the *paṭhavī* that (1) is a characteristic feature, (2) has ingredients or constituent parts, (3) is a subject for meditation, (4) that is so called by convention. On *paṭhavī-dhātu* see *M.* i. 185, also *M.* i. 329, 421, and *Vism.* 352.

[5] All of these headings from "extension" down to "the Conqueror" occur also at *M.* i. 329.

[6] *paṭhavim me,* or "extension is in me" or "for me."

[7] *MA.* i. 29, "Who thinks in these ways is not able to get rid of his false view of or craving for extension. Who rejoices in extension rejoices in suffering. 'I say that he who rejoices in suffering is not freed from suffering'" (quoting *S.* ii. 174).

[8] Symbolised by *āpo,* water. In distinction to *paṭhavī tejo* and *vāyo,* what is liquid or cohesive is intangible, but is that which unifies atoms. See *M.* i. 187 for analysis of this element, also *M.* i. 423. *Cf. Vbh.* 83; *Vism.* 352.

[9] *tejo.* This includes cold as well as heat. Vitalising energy and decay are due to this element. See *M.* i. 188, 424; *Vism.* 352.

[10] *vāyo,* the wind, symbolising movement and motion. See *Vbh.* 84; *Vism.* 352; and *M.* i. 188-189, 424. *MA.* i. 31 says "these are four ways of regarding material shapes that are conceits and false views as to one's own body: (1) to see material shape as self; (2) to see self in material shape; (3) to think self is other than material shape; (4) to see self as having material shape or material shape as in self. One is a view of annihilism, three are views of eternalism."

motion . . . [2] beings[1] as beings . . . *devas*[2] . . . Pajāpati[3] . . . Brahmā[4] . . . the Radiant ones . . . the Lustrous ones . . . the Vehapphalā[5] (*devas*) . . . the Overlord[6] . . . the plane of infinite ether[7] . . . the plane of infinite consciousness . . . [3] . . . the plane of no-thing . . . the plane of neither-perception-nor-non-perception . . . the seen[8] as the seen . . . the heard[8] . . . the sensed[8] . . . the cognised[8] . . . unity as unity[9] . . . diversity as diversity . . . universality[10] as universality . . . [4] . . . he recognises nibbāna[11] as nibbāna; having recognised nibbāna as nibbāna, he thinks of nibbāna,[12] he thinks (of the self) in (regard to) nibbāna, he thinks (of self as) nibbāna, he thinks, 'Nibbāna is mine'—he rejoices in nibbāna

---

[1] *bhūtā*. See *Pṭs*. i. 159. *MA*. i. 31 gives various kinds: that which is among the *khandhas*, those which are non-human, those which are among the (four) elements (symbolised by earth, water, heat, air), that which exists as a fact, that which is in one whose cankers are destroyed, creatures, and that which inhabits trees and so on. *MA*. i. 33 says that these ways of thinking about "beings" (sons and daughters, sheep and goats, cocks and swine, elephants, cows, horses, mares) arouse selfishness, affection and pride.

[2] *MA*. i. 33 says *devas* shine with the five strands of sense-pleasures or with their own natural power; they amuse themselves or they illumine. They are threefold: *devas* by convention (kings, queens, princes), those reborn or uprisen as *devas* (the Four Great Regents, and the *devas* beyond them), and the *devas* of purity (arahants whose cankers are destroyed). The second class is meant here.

[3] Here to be called Māra, so *MA*. i. 33. Usually Pajāpati is the lord of creation, but the story given at *MA*. shows Māra pretending to be this. For the following classes of *devas* see *Dīgha Sta*. 31 and *M*. *Sta*. 49.

[4] *MA*. i. 34 gives Mahābrahmā, tathāgata, brahman, parents and best as synonyms.

[5] Explained at *MA*. i. 35 as *vipulā phalā*, of extensive fruits, at the stage of the fourth *jhāna*.

[6] *Abhibhu*. *MA*. i. 35 says that this is a synonym for being without perception—hence advanced in the contemplative process.

[7] This and the three following planes, *āyatana*, are the fifth to the eighth of the nine stages in the contemplative process.

[8] *diṭṭha-suta-muta-viññāta*. As at *Vin*. iv. 2. See *B.D*. ii. 166, n. 3. *Diṭṭha* and *suta* mean seen and heard by both the physical and the *deva*-like (*dibba*) eye and ear.

[9] *ekatta*.

[10] *MA*. i. 38 says, he thinks "great is my self . . . this self of mine is in everything."

[11] Here *nibbāna* signifies the enjoyment of the five kinds of sensory pleasures. The "average man" regards these as the highest *nibbāna* in this very life. *Nibbāna* is therefore not being used here in its Buddhist sense.

[12] The nibbāna clauses are quoted at *Kvu*. 404.

What is the reason for this? I say that it is not thoroughly understood by him.

Monks, whatever monk is a learner,[1] not attained to perfection,[2] but who lives striving for the incomparable security from bondage, he intuitively knows extension as extension;[3] from intuitively knowing extension as extension, let him not think of extension, let him not think (of self) in (regard to) extension, let him not think (of self) as extension, let him not think, 'Extension is mine'—let him not rejoice in extension. What is the reason for this? I say it is because it may be thoroughly understood by him.

(*The same repeated for* liquid *down to* nibbāna.)

Monks, whatever monk is one perfected,[4] canker-waned, who has lived the life,[5] done what was to be done, laid down the burden,[6] attained his own goal, whose fetters of becoming[7] are utterly worn away, who is freed[8] by perfect profound knowledge—he too intuitively knows extension as extension; from intuitively knowing extension as extension, he does not think of extension, he does not think (of self) in (regard to) extension, he does not think (of self) as extension, he does not think, 'Extension is mine'—he does not rejoice in extension. What is the reason for this? I say it is because it is thoroughly understood by him.

(*The same repeated for* liquid *down to* nibbāna.)

Monks, whatever monk is one perfected, canker-waned, who has

---

[1] The learner, "undergraduate," *sekha*, the one under training, here appears as the middle term between the average worldling, *puthujjana*, and the *asekha*, the adept, "graduate," who has no further need of training. Moreover the worldling does not understand, the learner may understand, the arahant does understand.

[2] *appattamānasa*. *MA*. i. 41 says that *mānasa* is of three kinds: *rāga*, *citta*, *arahatta* (attachment, mind or consciousness, and arahantship or perfection), but here *arahatta* is meant. *Cf*. *appattamānasa* at *M*. i. 477; *S*. i. 121, ii. 229, v. 327; *A*. ii. 90; and *pattamānasa* at *It*. p. 76.

[3] Not by wrong perception as does the ordinary man, but by most excellent knowledge he knows intuitively that it is impermanent, ill, not-self.

[4] *arahant*. See also *M*. i. 280.

[5] *MA*. i. 42, "who has lived according to the ten ariyan modes." These are given at *D*. iii. 269.

[6] *ohitabhāra*. *MA*. i. 43 gives three burdens: the *khandhas* (constituents, components of the psycho-physical compound), the *kilesas* (impurities, defilements), and *abhisankhāra* (material for rebirth). See also *M*. i. 139; *A*. iii. 85 on "the burden laid low," *pannabhāra*.

[7] *MA*. i. 43 gives ten fetters which bind one to "becoming."

[8] *MA*. i. 43 gives two kinds of freedom: freedom of mind, and nibbāna.

lived the life, done what was to be done, laid down the burden, attained his own goal, whose fetters of becoming are utterly worn away, who is freed by perfect profound knowledge—he too [5] intuitively knows extension as extension . . . he does not rejoice in extension. What is the reason for this? It is because he is without attachment owing to the waning of attachment.

(*The same repeated for* liquid *down to* nibbāna.) . . . It is because he is without aversion owing to the waning of aversion. . . . It is because he is without confusion owing to the waning of confusion.

(*The same repeated for* liquid *down to* nibbāna.)

The Tathāgata,[1] monks, perfected one, fully Self-awakened One,[2] also intuitively knows extension as extension; from intuitively knowing extension as extension, he does not think of extension, he does not think (of self) in (regard to) extension, he does not think (of self) as extension, he does not think 'Extension is mine'—he does not rejoice in extension. [6] What is the reason for this? I say it is because it is thoroughly understood[3] by the Tathāgata.

(*The same repeated for* liquid *down to* nibbāna.)

And, monks, the Tathāgata also, perfected one, fully Self-awakened One, intuitively knows extension as extension; from intuitively knowing extension as extension, he does not think of extension, he does not think (of self) in (regard to) extension, he does not think (of self) as extension, he does not think, 'Extension is mine'—he does not rejoice in extension. What is the reason for this? It is because he, having known that delight is the root of anguish,[4] knows that from becoming[5] there is birth, and that there

---

[1] *tathāgata*. According to *MA*. i. 45 the Lord is a Tathāgata for eight reasons. Other Comys. give much the same. It is therefore impossible to find one English word to convey all these meanings.

[2] Because he is thoroughly or perfectly, *sammā*, awakened to all things, and of himself, *sāmaṃ*, (*i.e.* not with another's help), he is thoroughly awakened, *sammāsambuddha*, *MA*. i. 52. For full discussion of this compound see *Vism*. i. 198.

[3] *MA*. i. 52 here reads *pariññātantaṃ*, thoroughly understood to the end (or, to the full), while the text reads *pariññātaṃ*, which the Comy. also recognises.

[4] *MA*. i. 52 calls *dukkha* the five *khandhas*. *Dukkha* is therefore deep, almost cosmic, anguish of the many, the "individuals," owing to their separation from the One.

[5] Becoming, *bhava*, is here explained as "karmical becoming," *kammabhava*, becoming through deeds, see *MA*. i. 52.

is old age and dying for the being.[1] Consequently I say, monks, that the Tathāgata, by the waning of all cravings, by dispassion,[2] by stopping, by abandoning, by completely renouncing, is wholly self-awakened to the incomparable full self-awakening."[3]

(*The same repeated for* liquid *down to* nibbāna.)

Thus spoke the Lord. Delighted, these monks rejoiced in what the Lord had said.[4]

Discourse on the Synopsis of Fundamentals:
The First.

2. DISCOURSE ON ALL THE CANKERS

(Sabbâsavasutta).

THUS have I heard: At one time the Lord was staying near Sāvatthī in the Jeta Grove in Anāthapiṇḍika's monastery. While he was there the Lord addressed the monks, saying: " Monks." " Revered One," these monks answered the Lord in assent. The Lord spoke thus:

" I will discourse to you, monks, on the means[5] of controlling all

---

[1] *MA*. i. 52 explains *bhūta*, what has become, by *satta*, creature. At *MA*. i. 53 it is said that " delight " is of the past, " birth, old age and dying " of the future, " suffering and becoming " of the present.

[2] *MA*. i. 54 ascribes this and the following three achievements to the first, the second, and the third and fourth Ways respectively.

[3] *MA*. i. 54, *bodhi* is a tree, the Way, omniscience, nibbāna.

[4] According to *MA*. i. 56 the five hundred monks to whom this Discourse was addressed were *not* delighted and did *not* rejoice. They were ignorant and did not understand its meaning. Moreover they had thought that they were as learned as the Buddha, and said so. He then preached the *Mūlapariyāya-jātaka* to them, and their pride was humbled—and to humble pride is in a way the purpose of this Discourse, see p. 3, *n*. 1. Later, as the Buddha was on tour, he preached the *Gotamakasutta* (*A*. i. 276) to them and they became arahants. It is unusual for monks not to feel satisfied and pleased at the end of a discourse, but such is the tradition in this case.

[5] Here *MA*. i. 61 says *pariyāya* is *kāraṇa*, means or method.

the cankers.[1] [7] Listen and attend carefully, and I will speak."

"Yes, Lord," these monks answered the Lord in assent. The Lord spoke thus:

"I, monks, am speaking of the destruction of the cankers in one who knows, in one who sees, not in one who does not know, does not see. And what, monks, is the destruction of the cankers in one who knows, in one who sees? There is wise attention[2] and unwise attention. Monks, from unwise attention cankers arise that had not arisen, and also cankers that have arisen increase. But, monks, from wise attention cankers that had not arisen do not arise, and also cankers that have arisen decline. There are, monks, cankers that should be got rid of by vision,[3] there are cankers that should be got rid of by control, there are cankers that should be got rid of by use, there are cankers that should be got rid of by endurance, there are cankers that should be got rid of by avoidance, there are cankers that should be got rid of by elimination, there are cankers that should be got rid of by development.[4]

And what, monks, are the cankers to be got rid of by vision? Herein, monks, an uninstructed ordinary person,[5] taking no count

---

[1] *āsava*. There are four cankers, "influxes" or corruptions: *kāmâsava*, or attachment to the fivefold sensual realm; *bhavâsava*, attachment to *bhava*, literally "becoming," meaning attachment to the planes of form and formlessness; *diṭṭhâsava*, the attachment to (false) views; and the *āsava* of *avijjā*, ignoring, nescience (here of the four Truths); see *MA*. i. 67 and *cf*. Nārada Mahāthera, *Dhp*., p. 16, *n*. 5.

[2] *yoniso manasikāraṃ*, attention to the means, the Way; *ayoniso mana-*, is not attending to the means, or attending to (or, in) the wrong way, turning the mind against the truth so that you think permanence is in the impermanent, happiness in suffering, self in what is not-self, and the fair in the foul; and if there is ignorance, then "conditioned by ignorance are the *saṅkhāras*," and so on to the end of the "causal" chain: "the arising of this whole mass of anguish." See *MA*. i. 64-65.

[3] *Cf*. *A*. iii. 387-390, where, however, "vision," the first of the seven ways of riddance, is omitted; and see *G.S*. iii. 276, *n*. 1. Above "vision" refers to the vision pertaining to the first stage of arahantship or perfection, the *sotāpattimagga*, from its giving the first vision of nibbāna, *MA*. i. 74. Hence *saṃsāra*, or *vaṭṭa*, the endless round of births, is grounded on unwise attention. But a man of rational attention will develop the eightfold Way, beginning with perfect view. This is knowledge (*yā ca sammādiṭṭhi sā vijjā*): from the arising of knowledge, from the stopping of ignorance is the stopping of the *saṅkhāras*, and so on to the stopping of this whole mass of anguish. Thus nibbāna (here called *vivaṭṭa*, being devoid of the round of births) is said to be grounded on wise attention; *MA*. i. 64 *f*.

[4] *bhāvanā*, meaning mind-development. [5] As above, p. 3.

of the pure ones, unskilled in the *dhamma* of the pure ones, untrained in the *dhamma* of the pure ones; taking no count of the true men, unskilled in the *dhamma* of the true men, untrained in the *dhamma* of the true men, does not comprehend the things which should be wisely attended to, does not comprehend the things which should not be wisely attended to. He, not comprehending the things that should be wisely attended to, not comprehending the things that should not be wisely attended to, wisely attends to those things which should not be wisely attended to, does not wisely attend to those things which should be wisely attended to.

And what, monks, are the things that should not be wisely attended to, but to which he wisely attends? From his wisely attending to these things, monks, the canker of sense-pleasure arises which had not arisen before or the canker of sense-pleasure, arisen, increases; or the canker of becoming arises which had not arisen before or the canker of becoming, arisen, increases; or the canker of ignorance[1] arises which had not arisen before or the canker of ignorance, arisen, increases. These are the things to which he wisely attends but which should not be wisely attended to.

And what, monks, are the things that should be wisely attended to, but to which he does not wisely attend? From his wisely attending to these things, monks, either the canker of sense-pleasure which had not arisen does not arise, or if the canker of sense-pleasure has arisen it declines; or if the canker of becoming . . . or if the canker of ignorance has arisen it declines. These are things that should be wisely attended to, but to which he does not wisely attend. If he [8] wisely attends to things which should not be wisely attended to, if he does not wisely attend to things which should be wisely attended to, cankers arise which had not arisen before and also the cankers, arisen, increase.

In these ways he is not wisely attending: if he thinks, ‘ Now, was I in a past period ?[2] Now, was I not in a past period ? Now,

---

[1] *MA*. i. 67 explains the absence of the canker of false views, which often appears as the third of the four cankers, by saying: “ the canker of sense-pleasure is the attraction connected with the five strands of sense-pleasure; the canker of becoming is the attachment to desire for the planes of form and formlessness; it is craving for the jhānas accompanied by the false views of eternalism and annihilationism. In this way the canker of false views is included in the canker of becoming itself. The canker of ignorance is not knowing in regard to the four Truths.”

[2] *Cf. M*. i. 265 for these questions.

what was I in a past period? Now, how was I[1] in a past period? Now, having been what, what did I become in a past period? Now, will I come to be in a future period? Now, will I not come to be in a future period? Now, what will I come to be in a future period? Now, how will I come to be in a future period? Having become what, what will I come to be in a future period?' Or, if he is now subjectively[2] doubtful about the present period, and thinks: 'Now, am I? Now, am I not? Now, what am I? Now, how am I? Now, whence has this being come? Where-going will it come to be?' To one who does not pay wise attention in these ways, one of six (wrong) views arises: 'There is for me a self'[3]—the view arises to him as though it were true, as though it were real.[4] Or, 'There is not for me a self.'[5] . . . Or, 'Simply by self am I aware of self.' . . . Or, 'Simply by self am I aware of not-self.' . . . Or, 'Simply by not-self am I aware of self'—the view arises to him as though it were true, as though it were real. Or a wrong view occurs to him thus: 'Whatever is this self for me that speaks, that experiences and knows,[6] that experiences now here, now there, the fruition of deeds that are lovely and that are depraved,[7] it is this self for me that is permanent, stable, eternal, not subject to change, that will stand firm like unto the eternal.'[8] This, monks, is called going to

---

[1] *MA*. i. 69: what was I like, tall or short, fair or dark?

[2] *ajjhatta*. He doubts his own components, *khandhā*, his own existence, *atthibhāva*, *MA*. i. 69.

[3] This is the view of the Eternalists. It holds that the self exists permanently through all time.

[4] *saccato thetato*, as at e.g. *S*. iii. 112.

[5] This is the view of the Annihilationists, from their holding to the de-becoming (destruction, *vibhava*) here and there of the essential being, *sato sattassa*, *MA*. i. 70.

[6] As at *M*. i. 258. *Vado vedeyyo*, that speaks, that knows and feels, is explained at *MA*. i. 71 as "This is a conviction of those who hold eternalist views. Here 'that speaks' is *vado*. It is a mode of vocal act. 'That experiences (or, feels), *vediyati*, is *vedeyyo*. And it means 'that knows, that experiences' (*anubhavati*, partakes of, undergoes). What does it know-and-feel (*vedeti*)? It experiences (*paṭisamvedeti*) now here, now there, the fruits of deeds that are lovely and that are depraved. 'Now here, now there' means in this or that class of womb, bourn, station, abode." *Cf*. *MA*. ii. 305 on *vado vedeyyo*: "that which speaks, that knows-and-feels, and that which experiences now here, now there, the fruits of deeds that are lovely and depraved, this is that consciousness that I am speaking about."

[7] As at *M*. i. 258.

[8] As at *D*. i. 18 *ff*. "Like unto the Eternal" means what is usually taken to be eternal by the world: moon, sun, sea, great earth, mountains; *MA*. i. 71.

wrong views,[1] holding wrong views, the wilds of wrong views, the wriggling of wrong views, the scuffling of wrong views, the fetter of wrong views.

Fettered with the fetter of wrong views, monks, the uninstructed ordinary person is not set free from birth, from old age and dying, from griefs, from sorrows, from ills, from tribulations, from miseries, he is not set free from anguish, I say.

But the instructed disciple of the pure ones who takes count of the pure ones, who is skilled in the *dhamma* of the pure ones, well trained in the *dhamma* of the pure ones, who takes count of the true men, who is skilled in the *dhamma* of the true men, well trained in the *dhamma* of the true men—he comprehends the things that should be wisely attended to, he comprehends the things that should not be wisely attended to; he, comprehending the things that should be wisely attended to, comprehending the things that should not be wisely attended to, [9] does not wisely attend to those things which should not be wisely attended to, he wisely attends to those things which should be wisely attended to. And which, monks, are those things which he does not wisely attend to because they should not be wisely attended to? Those things, monks, by wisely attending to which there arises the canker of sense-pleasure which had not arisen before, or the canker of sense-pleasure which, arisen before, increases. Or there arises the canker of becoming. . . . Or there arises the canker of ignorance which had not arisen before, or the canker of ignorance which, arisen before, increases. These are the things to which he does not wisely attend because they should not be wisely attended to.

And which, monks, are the things to which he wisely attends because they should be wisely attended to? Those things, monks, by wisely attending to which there does not arise the canker of sense-pleasure which had not arisen before or the canker of sense-pleasure which, arisen before, declines . . . canker of becoming . . . canker of ignorance . . . arisen before, declines. These are the things to which he wisely attends because they should be wisely attended to.

If he is one who does not wisely attend to things that should not be wisely attended to, if he is one who wisely attends to things that should be wisely attended to, both the cankers which have not arisen do not arise, and the cankers which have arisen decline. He,

---

[1] As at *M*. i. 486; *Dhs*. 381.

thinking: 'This is anguish,' wisely attends. . . . 'This is the origin of anguish.' . . . 'This is the stopping of anguish.' . . . 'This is the course leading to the stopping of anguish,' wisely attends. Because he wisely attends thus, the three fetters decline: wrong view as to one's own body,[1] doubt, adherence to (wrongful) rites and ceremonies. These, monks, are called the cankers to be got rid of by vision.

And what, monks, are the cankers to be got rid of by control?[2] In this teaching,[3] monks, a monk, wisely reflective, lives controlled with control over the sense-organ of the eye . . . of the ear . . . of the nose . . . of the tongue . . . of the body . . . of the mind. Whereas, monks, if he lived uncontrolled in regard to control over these sense-organs, cankers which are destructive and consuming might arise. **[10]** But if he lives controlled with control over these organs, then the cankers which are destructive and consuming are not. These, monks, are called the cankers to be got rid of by control.

And what, monks, are the cankers to be got rid of by use? In this teaching, monks, a monk,[4] wisely reflective, uses a robe simply for warding off the cold, for warding off the heat, for warding off the touch of gadfly, mosquito, wind and sun, creeping things, simply for the sake of covering his nakedness. Wisely reflective, he uses almsfood not for sport,[5] not for indulgence, not for personal charm, not for beautification, but just enough for the support and sustenance of the body, for keeping it unharmed,[6] for furthering the Brahma-faring,[7] thinking: 'Thus do I crush out former feeling and do not set going new feeling; and there will be for me faultlessness and living in comfort.' Wisely reflective, he uses lodgings only for warding off the cold, for warding off the heat, for warding off the touch of gadfly, mosquito, wind, sun and creeping things, only for dispelling the dangers of the seasons, for the purpose of enjoying seclusion. Wisely reflective, he uses the requisite of medicines for

---

[1] *MA.* i. 73 says this and adherence to rites and ceremonies are reckoned as *āsavas*—that of wrong views as well as fetters. But doubt is a fetter only.

[2] *Cf. A.* iii. 387 *ff.*

[3] *idha*, so explained at *MA.* i. 75.

[4] *MA.* i. 77 does not comment on the following terms, but refers to *Vism.* (pp. 30-36=*P. Purity*, i. 35 *ff.*).

[5] Stock, as at *M.* i. 355; *A.* ii. 40, 145; *Dhs.* 1346; *Pug.* 21; *Vbh.* 249.

[6] *vihiṁsūparatīyā*, or "for allaying the pangs of hunger" as at *G.S.* iii. 277, *P. Purity*, i. 38.

[7] Two kinds discriminated at *Vism.* 32, that of complete instruction, and that of the Way(s).

the sick for warding off injurious feelings that have arisen, for the maximum of well-being. Whereas, monks, if he does not use (the requisites), the cankers which are destructive and consuming might arise, but because he does use (them), therefore these cankers which are destructive and consuming are not. These, monks, are called the cankers to be got rid of by use.

And what, monks, are the cankers to be got rid of by endurance ? In this teaching, monks, a monk, wisely reflective, is one who bears cold, heat, hunger, thirst, the touch of gadfly, mosquito, wind and sun, creeping things, ways of speech that are irksome, unwelcome; he is of a character to bear bodily feelings which, arising, are painful, acute, sharp, shooting, disagreeable, miserable, deadly.[1] Whereas, monks, if he lacked endurance, the cankers which are destructive and consuming might arise. But because he endures, therefore these cankers which are destructive and consuming are not. These, monks, are called the cankers to be got rid of by endurance.

And what, monks, are the cankers to be got rid of by avoidance ? In this teaching, monks, a monk, wisely reflective, avoids a fierce elephant, avoids a fierce horse, avoids a fierce bull, avoids a fierce dog, a snake, the stump of a tree, a thorny brake, [**11**] a deep hole, a mountain slope, a refuse pool,[2] a rubbish pit.[2] Wisely reflecting, he avoids that which is not an (allowable) seat,[3] and that which is not a (lawful) resort (for alms),[4] and those who are depraved friends. For if he were sitting on what is not an (allowable) seat like that, if he were walking in what is not a (lawful) resort (for alms) like that, if he were associating with depraved friends like that, his intelligent fellow Brahma-farers would suspect him of depraved qualities. Whereas, monks, if he does not avoid (these occasions), the cankers which are destructive and consuming might arise, but if he avoids (them), therefore these cankers which are destructive and consuming are not. These, monks, are called the cankers to be got rid of by avoidance.

---

[1] A person under twenty years of age is not considered able to endure these hardships, and is therefore not to be ordained at such an early age; see *Vin.* iv. 130. See *B.D.* iii. 12 for further references to this stock description.

[2] Both words occur at *M.* i. 448; *A.* i. 161.

[3] *anāsana*. *MA.* i. 80 says what is not a proper seat is *anāsana*, and refers to the Aniyatas where monks are forbidden to sit down with a woman in a private place or on a secluded seat (*Vin.* iii. 188, where these terms are defined. See *B.D.* i. 332).

[4] *agocara*. Five kinds, referred to at *MA.* i. 80, are given at *Vbh.* 247.

And what, monks, are the cankers to be got rid of by elimination? In this teaching, monks, a monk, wisely reflective, does not give in to thought about sense-pleasures[1] that has arisen, he gets rid of it, he eliminates it, makes an end of it, sends it to its ceasing; he does not give in to malevolent thought that has arisen . . . he does not give in to thought of harming that has arisen, he gets rid of it, he eliminates it, he makes an end of it, sends it to its ceasing; he does not give in to evil unskilled mental objects that have constantly arisen, he gets rid of them, eliminates them, makes an end of them, sends them to their ceasing. Whereas, monks, if he does not eliminate (these thoughts), the cankers which are destructive and consuming might arise, but if he eliminates (them), therefore these cankers which are destructive and consuming are not. These, monks, are called the cankers to be got rid of by elimination.

And what, monks, are the cankers to be got rid of by (mental) development? In this teaching, monks, a monk, wisely reflective, develops mindfulness as a link in awakening and which is dependent on aloofness,[2] dependent on lack of attraction, dependent on ceasing, ending in renunciation.[3] Wisely reflective, he develops investigation of *dhamma*[4] as a link in awakening . . . energy . . . rapture . . . serenity . . . concentration . . . even-mindedness as a link in awakening and which is dependent on aloofness, dependent on lack of attraction, dependent on ceasing, ending in renunciation.[5] Whereas, monks, if he does not develop (these links in awakening), the cankers which are destructive and consuming might arise. But if he develops (them), therefore these cankers which are destructive and consuming are not. These, monks, are called the cankers to be got rid of by development.

---

[1] This, and the two following "thoughts" are three evil modes of thought. Mentioned also at *M*. i. 114 (with their opposites); *D*. iii. 215, 226; *A*. i. 276, ii. 252, iii. 429, 446; *Vbh*. 362 (cited at *MA*. i. 81), etc.

[2] *MA*. i. 85 enumerates the five aspects of aloofness as at *VbhA*. 316; *Pṭs*. ii. 220.

[3] *vossaggapariṇāmī*. *MA*. i. 85 f.=*VbhA*. 316=*SA*. i. 159 explain this as the abandonment of the depravities, *kilesa*, and the resulting leaping or springing forward to nibbāna, and say that the Way itself is an ending in renunciation, *maggo eva ca vossaggapariṇāmī*. This and the three preceding terms are used at *S*. i. 88 in connection with developing each of the factors of the eightfold Way. *Cf*. *Pṭs*. i. 194, *pariccāga*- and *pakkhandana-nissagga*.

[4] *MA*. 1. 83, that is, into the four true things. *Dhammavicaya* might be "investigation of things," or "mental objects." *Cf*. below, p. 80.

[5] With the above passage *cf*. *M*. iii. 88.

Monks, in whatever monk those cankers to be got rid of by vision are got rid of by vision . . . by control . . . by use . . . by endurance . . . by avoidance [12] . . . by elimination . . . by mental development are got rid of by mental development, this monk is called, monks, one who is controlled with control over all the cankers. He has cut off craving,[1] done away with fetter,[2] and by fully mastering[3] pride[4] will make an end of anguish."

Thus spoke the Lord. Delighted, these monks rejoiced in what the Lord had said.

Discourse on All the Cankers:
the Second.

3. DISCOURSE ON HEIRS OF DHAMMA

(Dhammadāyādasutta)[5]

THUS have I heard: At one time the Lord was staying near Sāvatthī in the Jeta Grove in Anāthapiṇḍika's monastery. While he was there the Lord addressed the monks, saying: "Monks." "Revered One," these monks answered the Lord in assent. The Lord spoke thus:

"Monks, become my heirs of *dhamma*, not heirs of material things.[6] I have sympathy with you and think: How may disciples become my heirs of *dhamma*, not heirs of material things? If you, monks, should become heirs of material things, not heirs of *dhamma*, not only may you become in consequence those of whom it is said: 'The Teacher's disciples are heirs of material things, not heirs of

---

[1] *Cf. M.* i. 122; *A.* i. 134, ii. 249, iii. 246, 445, iv. 8; *S.* i. 12, iv. 205; *It.* 47; *Expositor*, i. 77.

[2] *MA.* i. 87 says that this means a tenfold fetter.

[3] By vision and by getting rid of, *MA.* i. 87.

[4] As at *Sn.* 342. A tenfold aspect given at *Nd.* i. 80=*Nd.* ii. 505.

[5] Referred to at *MA.* ii. 246.

[6] *Cf. It.*, p. 101. *Āmisa* is material goods or gains, such as the four types of requisites, which, however, *MA.* i. 89-90 says are only figuratively *āmisa*.

dhamma,' but I too may become in consequence one of whom it is said: 'The Teacher's disciples are . . . not heirs of *dhamma.*' But if you, monks, should become my heirs of *dhamma,* not heirs of material things, then you may become in consequence those of whom it is said: 'The Teacher's disciples are heirs of *dhamma,* not heirs of material things,' and I too may become in consequence one of whom it is said: 'The Teacher's disciples are heirs of *dhamma,* not heirs of material things.' Therefore, monks, become my heirs of *dhamma,* not heirs of material things. I have sympathy with you and think: How may disciples become my heirs of *dhamma,* not heirs of material things?

Take a case where I, monks, may have eaten[1] and be satisfied,[2] (the meal) ended, finished, I having had enough, as much as I pleased. But it may be that some of my almsfood is over and is to be thrown away, when two monks may arrive [**13**] worn out with exhaustion and hunger.[3] If I should speak to them thus: 'I, monks, have eaten and am satisfied . . . some of my almsfood is over and is to be thrown away. Do eat it if you (so) desire;[4] if you do not eat it I will now throw it away where there is no grass or I will drop it into water that has no living creatures in it.'[5] Then it may occur to one monk: 'Now, the Lord having eaten and being satisfied . . . this almsfood of the Lord's is to be thrown away; if we do not eat it, the Lord will now throw it away where there is no grass or he will drop it into water that has no living creatures in it. But this was said by the Lord: Monks, become my heirs of *dhamma,* not heirs of material things. But this is a material thing, that is to say, almsfood. Suppose that I, not having eaten this almsfood, in spite of this hunger and exhaustion, should pass this night and day thus?' He, not having eaten that almsfood, in spite of that hunger and exhaustion, may pass this night and day thus. Then it occurs to the second monk, thus: 'Now, the Lord, having eaten and being satisfied . . . this almsfood of the Lord's is to be thrown away; if we do not eat it, the Lord will now throw it

---

[1] *bhuttāvin.*

[2] *pavārita,* see *B.D.* ii. 326, n. 2; *MA.* i. 93 distinguishes four kinds of *pavāraṇā,* "invitation" to take and therefore "satisfying."

[3] *Cf. M.* i. 114, 364.

[4] At Pāc. 35 (*Vin.* iv. 81 *ff.*) monks may eat food that is left over.

[5] For this sentence *cf. Vin.* i. 157, 225, ii. 216; *S.* i. 169; *M.* i. 207, iii. 157; *Sn.* p. 15. At Pāc. 20 and 62 it is made an offence for monks knowingly to make use of water that contains life (*Vin.* iv. 48 *f.,* 125).

away where there is no grass or he will drop it into water that has no living creatures in it. Suppose that I, having eaten this almsfood, having driven away this hunger and exhaustion, should pass this night and day thus ?' He, having eaten that almsfood, having driven away that hunger and exhaustion, may spend that night and day thus. Although, monks, that monk, having eaten that almsfood . . . may spend that night and day thus, yet that first monk is for me the more to be honoured and the more to be praised.[1] What is the reason for this ? It is, monks, that it will conduce for a long time to that monk's desirelessness, to his contentment, expunging (of evil), to his being easily supported, to his putting forth energy.[2] Therefore, monks, become my heirs of *dhamma*, not heirs of material things. I have sympathy with you and think: How may disciples become my heirs of *dhamma*, and not heirs of material things ?"

Thus spoke the Lord; when the Well-farer had spoken thus, rising from his seat, he entered the dwelling-place.

Thereupon the venerable Sāriputta, not long after the Lord had gone away, addressed the monks, saying: " Reverend monks." " Your reverence," **[14]** these monks answered the venerable Sāriputta in assent. Then the venerable Sāriputta spoke thus:

" In what respects, your reverences, while the Teacher is staying in seclusion, do disciples not follow his example of aloofness ? And in what respects, while the Teacher is staying in seclusion, do disciples follow his example of aloofness ?"

" We would come even from afar to learn from the venerable Sāriputta the meaning of this that is said. It were good indeed if the meaning of this that is said should be spoken out by the venerable Sāriputta, so that monks, having heard the venerable Sāriputta, might master it."

" Very well, your reverences, listen, attend carefully, and I will speak."

" Yes, your reverence," these monks answered the venerable Sāriputta in assent. Then the venerable Sāriputta spoke thus:

" This is a case, your reverences, where, while the Teacher is staying in seclusion, disciples do not follow his cxample as to aloofness, they do not get rid of those things of which the Teacher

---

[1] Quoted at *Miln.* 242.

[2] *Cf. Vin.* iii. 21, and see *B.D.* i. 37, *n.* 6.

has spoken of getting rid, they are ones for abundance[1] and are lax, taking the lead in backsliding,[2] throwing off the yoke[3] of seclusion.[4] Among them,[5] your reverences, monks who are elders become contemptible in three ways: if, while the Teacher is staying in seclusion, disciples do not follow his example as to aloofness—this is the first way in which monks who are elders become contemptible. If they do not get rid of those things of which the Teacher has spoken of getting rid—this is the second way in which monks who are elders become contemptible. If they are ones for abundance and are lax, taking the lead in backsliding, throwing off the yoke of seclusion—this is the third way in which monks who are elders become contemptible. So, your reverences, monks who are elders become contemptible in these three ways. Among them, your reverences, monks who are of middle standing[6] . . . newly ordained monks[7] become contemptible in three ways. . . . So, your reverences, monks of middle standing . . . newly ordained monks become contemptible in these three ways. In these respects, your reverences, while the Teacher is staying in seclusion, do disciples not follow his example as to aloofness.

But in what respects, while the Teacher is staying in seclusion, do disciples [**15**] follow his example as to aloofness? This is a case, your reverences, where, while the Teacher is staying in seclusion, disciples follow his example as to aloofness and get rid of those things of which the Teacher has spoken of getting rid, they are not ones for abundance, they are not lax, they throw off the yoke of backsliding and take the lead in seclusion. Among them, your reverences, monks who are elders become praiseworthy in three ways: if, while the Teacher is staying in seclusion, disciples follow his example as to aloofness—this is the first way in which monks who are elders become praiseworthy. If they get rid of those things of which the Teacher has spoken of getting rid—this is the second way in which monks who are elders become praiseworthy.

---

[1] *I.e.* of robes, etc., *MA.* i. 101. *Cf. A.* i. 71 (where monks such as these are put among the unariyan company), *A.* ii. 148, iii. 108, 179 f.; *M.* i. 32.

[2] *okkamana*, in regard to the five hindrances, *MA.* i. 101.

[3] *nikkhittadhura*, throwing off responsibility. *Cf. dhuraṃ nikkhipati* at *Vin.* iii. 50, and *dhuraṃ nikkhittamatte* at *Vin.* iv. 128, 280, 291, 297, 302.

[4] Aloofness from attachment, nibbāna, *MA.* i. 101.

[5] *tatra*, explained at *MA.* i. 102 to mean among these disciples.

[6] Those, as *MA.* i. 102 remarks, who have been ordained from five to nine years.

[7] Those who have been ordained for less than five years.

If they are not ones for abundance, if they are not lax, if they throw off the yoke of backsliding and take the lead in seclusion—this is the third way in which monks who are elders become praiseworthy. So, your reverences, monks who are elders become praiseworthy in these three ways. Among them, your reverences, monks who are of middle standing . . . newly ordained monks become praiseworthy in three ways. So, your reverences, monks of middle standing . . . newly ordained monks become praiseworthy in these three ways. In these respects, your reverences, while the Teacher is staying in seclusion, do disciples follow his example as to aloofness.

Herein,[1] your reverences, greed is evil and ill-will[2] is evil; for getting rid of greed and for getting rid of ill-will there is the Middle Course[3] which, making for vision,[4] making for knowledge,[4] conduces to tranquillity,[5] to super-knowledge, to awakening,[6] to nibbāna.[7] And what, your reverences, is this Middle Course which, making for vision, making for knowledge, conduces . . . to nibbāna ? It is this ariyan Eightfold Way itself,[8] that is to say, perfect view, perfect thought, perfect speech, perfect action, perfect mode of livelihood, perfect exertion, perfect mindfulness, perfect concentration. It is this, your reverences, that is the Middle Course which, making for vision, making for knowledge, conduces . . . to nibbāna.

Herein, your reverences, anger[9] is evil and malevolence is evil . . . hypocrisy is evil and spite is evil . . . envy is evil and stinginess is evil . . . deceit is evil and treachery is evil . . . obstinacy is evil

---

[1] *I.e.* in the foregoing teaching, *MA*. i. 103.

[2] *I.e.* ill-will or anger or resentment at not getting the foods you were greedy to get. Following terms occur at *A*. i. 299; *cf*. also *A*. i. 95, 100.

[3] *MA*. i. 104 says that it is the Way, called " Middle," because the two ends (or, dead-ends) of greed and ill-will do not touch it, it is free from them.

[4] Of the Truths, *MA*. i. 104.

[5] By the allaying of attachment, *rāga*, and so on.

[6] *sambodho ti maggo*, awakening is called the Way; because it conduces to this it conduces to awakening, *MA*. i. 104.

[7] Because it conduces to the realisation of the deathlessness of nibbāna, by making it clear (or, present), it is said that it conduces to nibbāna, *MA*. i. 104.

[8] *MA*. i. 105 quotes *Dhp*. 274: " This itself is the Way—there is not another —for the purification of vision (*dassanā*)." The (Way) goes slaying the corruptions, or it tracks out nibbāna, or it is followed by one seeking nibbāna. Each factor of the Way—and each is the Way—gets rid of its opposite, and nibbāna is made a mental object, *MA*. i. 105-106. Taken together the eight factors constitute a process (see *M*. iii. 76) with right or perfect view (understanding or knowledge, *vijjā*) as the forerunner (*M*. iii. 71; *A*. v. 214).

[9] The following terms down to *sātheyya*, treachery, are defined at *Vbh*. 357.

and [16] impetuosity is evil . . . arrogance is evil and pride is evil . . . conceit is evil and indolence is evil. For getting rid of conceit and for getting rid of indolence there is the Middle Course which, making for vision, making for knowledge, conduces . . . to nibbāna. And what, your reverences, is the Middle Course which, making for vision, making for knowledge, conduces . . . to nibbāna? It is this ariyan Eightfold Way itself, that is to say, perfect view, perfect thought, perfect speech, perfect action, perfect way of living, perfect exertion, perfect mindfulness, perfect concentration. It is this, your reverences, that is the Middle Course which, making for vision, making for knowledge, conduces to tranquillity, to super-knowledge, to awakening, to nibbāna."

Thus spoke the venerable Sāriputta. Delighted, these monks rejoiced in what the venerable Sāriputta had said.

Discourse on Heirs of Dhamma:
the Third.

4. DISCOURSE ON FEAR AND DREAD

(Bhayabheravasutta)

THUS have I heard: At one time the Lord was staying near Sāvatthī in the Jeta Grove in Anāthapiṇḍika's monastery. Then Jāṇussoṇi the brahman[1] approached the Lord; having approached, he exchanged greetings with the Lord; having exchanged greetings of friendliness and courtesy, he sat down at a respectful distance.[2] As he was sitting down at a respectful distance, Jāṇussoṇi the brahman spoke thus to the Lord:

"Good[3] Gotama, these who are sons of respectable families,[4] who

---

[1] A brahman by birth. But the pure ones (ariyans) are called brahmans because they exclude evil, *MA*. i. 109. Jāṇussoṇi was not a name given him by his parents, but was that which he received in virtue of his office as chaplain to the king.

[2] See *B.D.* ii. 42, n. 5.

[3] *bho.*

[4] *MA*. i. 111 divides these into two kinds: those who are such by birth, and those who are such by right conduct.

have gone forth from home into homelessness out of faith in the honoured Gotama, of these the honoured Gotama is the leader, to these the honoured Gotama is of great service, of these the honoured Gotama is the adviser,[1] and these people emulate the views of the honoured Gotama."

"That is so, brahman, that is so, brahman. These who are sons of respectable families, who have gone forth from home into homelessness out of faith in me, of these I am the leader, to these I am of great service, of these I am the adviser. And these people emulate my views."

"But, good Gotama, remote lodgings in forest[2] and in woodland wildernesses[2] are hard to put up with, arduous is aloofness, it is difficult to delight in solitude; methinks forests distract the mind of a monk who does not secure concentration."

[17] "That is so, brahman, that is so, brahman. Remote lodgings in forest and in woodland wildernesses are hard to put up with . . . methinks forests distract the mind of a monk who does not secure concentration. Brahman, before my Awakening, and while I was yet merely the Bodhisatta, not a fully self-awakened one, it occurred to me also; 'Remote lodgings in forest . . . distract the mind of a monk who does not secure concentration.' In connection with this it occurred to me, brahman: Whatever recluses or brahmans, not wholly pure in bodily actions, frequent remote lodgings in forest and woodland wildernesses, these worthy recluses and brahmans, because they are not wholly pure in bodily actions, indeed evoke (in themselves) unskilled[3] fear and dread. But I, not of impure bodily actions, frequent remote lodgings in forest and woodland wildernesses. I am wholly pure in bodily actions, I am one of those ariyans who, wholly pure in bodily actions, frequent remote lodgings in forest and woodland wildernesses. I, brahman, beholding in myself this complete purity of bodily actions, gained greater assurance[4] for living in the forest.

---

[1] *samādapetā*, as at *M.* iii. 4, 6, of Gotama as the adviser or instructor in the Way to nibbāna. *MA.* i. 111 however says "training them in moral habit and the rest."

[2] Defined at *Vbh.* 251, and quoted at *MA.* i. 112.

[3] *akusala*, explained at *MA.* i. 113 as *sāvajja akkhema*, blameable, faulty; and unsafe, insecure . . . fear is unskilled through being based on *sāvajja*, dread through being based on *akkhema*.

[4] *palloma*. Word occurs at *D.* i. 96. See *JPTS.* 1889, p. 206 for notes, *MA.* i. 114 gives *pannalomata*; and also *khema*, *sotthibhāva*, security.

In connection with this, it occurred to me, brahman: Whatever recluses or brahmans, not wholly pure in speech . . . not wholly pure in thought . . . not wholly pure in their mode of living . . . gained greater assurance for living in the forest.

In connection with this, it occurred to me, brahman: Whatever recluses or brahmans, covetous, strongly passionate in their desires,[1] frequent remote lodgings in the forest and woodland wildernesses, these worthy recluses and brahmans, because they are covetous and strongly passionate in their desires, indeed evoke (in themselves) unskilled fear and dread. But I, not covetous or strongly passionate in my desires, frequent remote lodgings in forest and woodland wildernesses. Without covetousness am I, I am one of those ariyans who, being without covetousness, frequent remote lodgings in forest and woodland wildernesses. [**18**] I, brahman, beholding in myself this lack of covetousness, gained greater assurance for living in the forest.

In connection with this, brahman, it occurred to me: Whatever recluses or brahmans, corrupt in heart, wicked in thought and purpose, frequent remote lodgings in forest and woodland wildernesses, these worthy recluses and brahmans because they are corrupt in heart, wicked in thought and purpose, indeed evoke (in themselves) unskilled fear and dread. Not corrupt in heart, nor wicked in thought and purpose do I frequent remote lodgings in forest and woodland wildernesses. Of a mind of friendliness am I, I am one of those ariyans who, with a mind of friendliness, frequent remote lodgings in forest and woodland wildernesses. I, brahman, beholding in myself this mind of friendliness, gained greater assurance for living in the forest.

In connection with this, brahman, it occurred to me: Whatever recluses or brahmans, obsessed by sloth or torpor,[2] frequent remote lodgings in forest and woodland wildernesses, these worthy recluses, and brahmans, because they are obsessed by sloth and torpor, indeed evoke (in themselves) unskilled fear and dread. Not obsessed by sloth and torpor do I frequent remote lodgings in forest and woodland wildernesses. I have got rid of sloth and torpor, I am one of those ariyans who, rid of sloth and torpor, frequent remote lodgings in forest and woodland wildernesses. I, brahman, beholding in myself that sloth and torpor were got rid of, gained greater assurance for living in the forest.

---

[1] *Cf. A.* ii. 30.

[2] See *A.* i. 3; ii. 211. iii. 92, v. 163; *D.* i. 71.

In connection with this, brahman, it occurred to me: Whatever recluses or brahmans, unbalanced, of unquiet minds, frequent . . . because they are unbalanced, of unquiet minds, they indeed evoke (in themselves) unskilled fear and dread. Not unbalanced, not of unquiet mind do I frequent remote lodgings in forest and woodland wildernesses. Of quiet mind am I, I am one of those ariyans who, with quiet minds, frequent remote lodgings in forest and woodland wildernesses. I, brahman, beholding in myself this quiet mind, gained greater assurance for living in the forest.

In connection with this, brahman, it occurred to me: Whatever recluses or brahmans, doubting, perplexed, frequent . . . because they are doubting, perplexed, they indeed evoke (in themselves) unskilled fear and dread. Not doubting, not perplexed do I frequent remote lodgings in forest and woodland wildernesses. Crossed over doubt[1] am I, I am one of those ariyans who, crossed over doubt, frequent remote lodgings in forest and woodland wildernesses. I, brahman, beholding in myself this doubt crossed over, [**19**] gained greater assurance for living in the forest.

In connection with this, brahman. . . . Whatever recluses or brahmans, extolling themselves, disparaging others,[2] frequent. . . . Not extolling myself, not disparaging others do I frequent remote lodgings in forest and woodland wildernesses. Not an extoller of self am I, not a disparager of others, I am one of those ariyans who, not extolling self, not disparaging others, frequent remote lodgings in forest and woodland wildernesses. I, brahman, beholding in myself this lack of extolling self, this lack of disparaging others, gained greater assurance for living in the forest.

In connection with this, brahman. . . . Whatever recluses or brahmans, terrified, affrighted, frequent. . . . Not terrified, not affrighted do I frequent remote lodgings in forest and woodland wildernesses. Not horrified[3] am I, I am one of those ariyans who, not horrified . . . gained greater assurance for living in the forest.

In connection with this, brahman. . . . Whatever recluses or brahmans, striving after gains, honours, fame, frequent remote lodgings . . . because they are striving after gains, honours, fame they indeed evoke (in themselves) unskilled fear and dread. Not striving after gains, honours, fame do I frequent remote lodgings in forest and woodland wildernesses. Of few desires am I, I am one

---

[1] *tiṇṇavicikiccha*, as at *D.* i. 71, 110; *A.* iii. 297, iv. 186. [2] *Cf. M.* i. 95.
[3] *vigatalomahaṃsa*, "gone is horripilation, hair standing on end."

of those ariyans of few desires who frequent remote lodgings . . . greater assurance for living in the forest.

In connection with this, brahman. . . . Whatever recluses or brahmans, lethargic, lacking in energy,[1] frequent remote lodgings . . . because they are lethargic and lacking in energy, they indeed evoke (in themselves) unskilled fear and dread. Not lethargic, not lacking in energy do I frequent remote lodgings in forest and woodland wildernesses. Of stirred up energy am I, I am one of those ariyans of stirred up energy who frequent remote lodgings . . . greater assurance for living in the forest.

In connection with this, brahman [**20**]. . . . Whatever recluses, of muddled mindfulness, not clearly conscious, frequent remote lodgings . . . because they are of muddled mindfulness, not clearly conscious, they indeed evoke (in themselves) unskilled fear and dread. Not of muddled mindfulness, not not clearly conscious, do I frequent remote lodgings in forest and woodland wildernesses. Of raised up mindfulness am I, I am one of those ariyans of raised up mindfulness who frequent remote lodgings . . . greater assurance for living in the forest.

In connection with this, brahman, it occurred to me: Whatever recluses or brahmans, not composed, their minds wavering, frequent remote lodgings in forest and woodland wildernesses, these worthy recluses and brahmans, because they are not composed, because their minds are wavering, indeed evoke (in themselves) unskilled fear and dread. Not not composed, my mind not wavering do I frequent remote lodgings in forest and woodland wildernesses. Possessed of concentration am I, I am one of those ariyans who, possessed of concentration, frequent remote lodgings in forest and woodland wildernesses. I, brahman, beholding in myself this possession of concentration, gained greater assurance for living in the forest.

In connection with this, brahman, it occurred to me: Whatever recluses or brahmans, weak in intuitive wisdom,[2] drivellers,[3]

---

[1] *Cf. Dhp.* 7, 112; *It.* p. 27, 71, 116.

[2] *paññā*, extra-sensory wisdom or knowledge.

[3] *eḷamugā*, as at *M*. i. 32. Translated at *G.S.* iii. 305 as "dullard." See also *G.S.* ii. 257, n. 1. *Cf. mūgasūkara* at *Vin*. i. 102. The idea is a "driveller." *MA*. i. 118 says "*eḷamugā* means *eḷamukhā*: the *ga* comes from the *kha*. It comes to be called *lālāmukhā* (saliva-mouths). While those of poor wisdom are talking, saliva drips from their mouths. It is called *lālā* and *eḷa*. Accordingly it is said: 'See the saliva-mouthed two-tongued snake'

frequent remote lodgings in forest and woodland wildernesses, these worthy recluses and brahmans, because they are weak in intuitive wisdom, drivellers, indeed evoke (in themselves) unskilled fear and dread. Not weak in intuitive wisdom, not a driveller do I frequent remote lodgings in forest and woodland wildernesses. Possessed of intuitive wisdom am I, I am one of those ariyans who, possessed of intuitive wisdom, frequent remote lodgings in forest and woodland wildernesses. I, brahman, beholding in myself this possession of intuitive wisdom, gained greater assurance for living in the forest.

In connection with this, brahman, it occurred to me: Suppose that I, on those recognised and fixed nights: the fourteenth, fifteenth and eighth of the half-months,[1] should stay in such frightening and horrifying lodgings as park-shrines,[2] forest-shrines,[3] tree-shrines,[4] so that I should see that fear and dread. So I, brahman, after a time, on those recognised and fixed nights, the fourteenth, the fifteenth and the eighth of the half-months, stayed in such frightening and horrifying places as park-shrines, forest-shrines, tree-shrines. As I was staying there, brahman, either an animal came along, or a peacock[5] [**21**] broke off a twig, or the wind rustled the fallen leaves. It occurred to me: Surely this is that fear and dread coming. Then it occurred to me, brahman: Why am I staying longing for nothing but fear? Suppose now that I, in whatever posture I may be as that fear and dread come upon me should, while in that same posture, drive out that fear and dread? If, brahman, that fear and dread came upon me while I was pacing up and down, I, brahman, neither stood still nor sat down nor lay down, but drove out

---

(reference to *Jā*. iii. 347, which should be inserted at *MA*. i. 118). Therefore they are called *eḷamugā*. *Eḷamūgā* is also a reading. Some also read *eḷamūkā*. Further, there is also *eḷamukhā*. Everywhere the meaning is *eḷamukhā*." It seems that *lālā*, saliva, is the real synonym. *Jā*. iii. 347 explains that *eḷamūgaṃ* is so called because *eḷa* trickles, or oozes, from the mouth. "To drivel" is given in the *OED* as "to let saliva or mucus flow from the mouth or nose, as infants and idiots do; to slaver. To flow ineptly from the lips."

[1] The three days originally designated for teaching *dhamma*, *Vin*. i. 102.

[2] Park, *ārāma*, is defined at *MA*. i. 119 as flower parks and orchards, as at *Vin*. iii. 49.

[3] Forests where oblations should be taken.

[4] According to *MA*. i. 119 these are trees to be worshipped at the entrance gates to villages, little towns and so on. On going to all three when afraid, *cf*. *Dhp*. 188.

[5] *MA*. i. 120 says that here a peacock signifies all birds.

that fear and dread as I was pacing up and down. While I was standing, brahman, that fear and dread came upon me. So I, brahman, neither paced up and down nor sat down nor lay down until I had, while I was standing, driven out that fear and dread. While I was sitting down, brahman, that fear and dread came upon me. So I, brahman, neither lay down nor stood up nor paced up and down until, while I was sitting down, I drove out that fear and dread. While I was lying down, brahman, that fear and dread came upon me. So I, brahman, neither sat down nor stood up nor paced up and down until I had, while I was lying down, driven out that fear and dread.

Now there are, brahman, some recluses and brahmans who suppose that night is similar to day and who suppose that day is similar to night. Of these recluses and brahmans I say that they are living in bewilderment. For I, brahman, suppose that night is similar to night, I suppose that day is similar to day. Whoever, brahman, in speaking aright should say: 'A being not liable to bewilderment has arisen in the world for the welfare of the manyfolk, for the happiness of the manyfolk, out of compassion for the world, for the good, the welfare, the happiness of devas and men, then, in speaking aright of me he would say: 'A being not liable to bewilderment . . . the happiness of devas and men.'[1] Unsluggish energy is stirred up by me, brahman, unmuddled mindfulness is raised up, my body is tranquil, impassible, my mind composed, one-pointed. So I, brahman, aloof from pleasures of the senses, aloof from unskilled states of mind, entered into the first meditation[2] which is accompanied by initial thought and discursive thought, is born of aloofness, and is rapturous and joyful. By allaying initial and discursive thought, with the mind subjectively tranquillised and fixed on one point, [22] I entered into and abided in the second meditation which is devoid of initial and discursive thought, is born of concentration, and is rapturous and joyful. By the fading out of rapture, I dwelt with equanimity, attentive, and clearly conscious; and I experienced in my person that joy of which the ariyans say: 'Joyful lives he who has equanimity and is mindful,' and I entered into and abided in the third meditation.

---

[1] As at *M.* i. 83.

[2] *jhāna*, meditation, mental absorption. As being of the fine-material sphere, *rūpajjhāna*, they are conditioned by concentration, *samādhi*, and by the absence of the five hindrances, *nīvaraṇāni*. This statement of the meditation processes is of frequent occurrence in the *Majjhima*.

By getting rid of joy, by getting rid of anguish, by the going down of my former pleasures and sorrows, I entered into and abided in the fourth meditation which has neither anguish nor joy, and which is entirely purified by equanimity and mindfulness.

Thus with the mind composed, quite purified, quite clarified, without blemish, without defilement, grown soft and workable, fixed, immovable, I directed my mind to the knowledge and recollection of former habitations[1]: I remembered a variety of former habitations, thus: one birth, two births, three . . . four . . . five . . . ten . . . twenty . . . thirty . . . forty . . . fifty . . . a hundred . . . a thousand . . . a hundred thousand births, and many an eon of integration and many an eon of disintegration and many an eon of integration-disintegration; such a one was I by name, having such and such a clan, such and such a colour, so was I nourished, such and such pleasant and painful experiences were mine, so did the span of life end. Passing from this, I came to be in another state[2] where such a one was I by name, having such and such a clan, such and such a colour, so was I nourished, such and such pleasant and painful experiences were mine, so did the span of life end. Passing from this, I arose here.[3] Thus I remember divers former habitations in all their modes and detail. This, brahman, was the first knowledge attained by me in the first watch of the night; ignorance was dispelled, knowledge arose, darkness was dispelled, light arose, even as I abided diligent, ardent, self-resolute.

Then with the mind composed, quite purified, quite clarified, without blemish, without defilement, grown soft and workable, fixed, immovable, I directed my mind to the knowledge of the passing hence and the arising of beings. With the purified *deva*-vision surpassing that of men I see beings as they pass hence or come to be; I comprehend that beings are mean, excellent, comely, ugly, well-going, ill-going, according to the consequences of their deeds, and I think: Indeed these worthy beings who were possessed of wrong conduct in body, who were possessed of wrong conduct of

---

[1] On these three " knowledges " see e.g. *Vin.* iii. 3-4, and notes at *B.D.* i. 7-10.

[2] *MA.* i. 125 says this was the Tusita abode (where the Bodhisatta passes his last " birth " before being born for the final time as a man). Here he was a *devaputta* called Setaketu, in the same class as those devas, the colour of gold, nourished on beautiful deva-food. He experienced deva-like happiness, but his painful experiences were those connected only with the *saṅkhāras.*

[3] *MA.* i. 126, " here in the womb of the lady Mahāmāyā."

speech, who were possessed of wrong conduct of thought, scoffers at the ariyans, holding a wrong view, incurring deeds consequent on a wrong view—these, at the breaking up of the body after dying, have arisen in a sorrowful state, a bad bourn, the abyss, Niraya Hell. But these worthy beings who were possessed of good conduct in body, [**23**] who were possessed of good conduct in speech, who were possessed of good conduct in thought, who did not scoff at the ariyans, holding a right view, incurring deeds consequent on a right view—these, at the breaking up of the body after dying, have arisen in a good bourn, a heaven world. Thus with the purified *deva*-vision surpassing that of men do I see beings as they pass hence, as they arise; I comprehend that beings are mean, excellent, comely, ugly, well-going, ill-going according to the consequences of their deeds. This, brahman, was the second knowledge attained by me in the middle watch of the night; ignorance was dispelled, knowledge arose, darkness was dispelled, light arose, even as I abided diligent, ardent, self-resolute.

Then with the mind composed . . . fixed, immovable, I directed my mind to the knowledge of the destruction of the cankers. I understood as it really is: This is anguish, this is the arising of anguish, this is the stopping of anguish, this is the course leading to the stopping of anguish. I understood as it really is: These are the cankers, this is the arising of the cankers, this is the stopping of the cankers, this is the course leading to the stopping of the cankers. Knowing this thus, seeing thus, my mind was freed from the canker of sense-pleasures, and my mind was freed from the canker of becoming, and my mind was freed from the canker of ignorance.[1] In freedom the knowledge came to be: I am freed; and I comprehended: Destroyed is birth, brought to a close is the Brahma-faring, done is what was to be done, there is no more of being such or such.[2] This, brahman, was the third knowledge attained by me in the last watch of the night; ignorance was dispelled, knowledge arose, darkness was dispelled, light arose even as I abided diligent, ardent, self-resolute.

---

[1] At the parallel passage at *Vin.* iii. 5. the four cankers are mentioned. But only three at *A.* ii. 211, iv. 179.

[2] *nâparaṃ itthattāya*. *MA.* i. 128 (*cf. DA.* 112, *SA.* i. 205) say there is not now again *itthambhāvā* (being thus) owing to development in the Way or to the destruction of the depravities. Or it means that for me there is no further continuity of the *khandhas*, for, being thoroughly understood, they are like trees cut down at the roots.

But it may be, brahman, that this occurs to you: 'Is the recluse Gotama even today not devoid of attachment, not devoid of aversion, not devoid of confusion, and that therefore he frequents remote lodgings in forest and woodland wildernesses?' But this is not to be taken in this way, brahman. I frequent[1] remote lodgings in forest and woodland wildernesses, brahman, beholding two special reasons: beholding for the self[2] an abiding in ease here and now,[3] and being compassionate for the folk that come after.[4]"

"The folk that come after have the compassion of the revered Gotama **[24]** because of his perfection, because of his complete self-awakening. Excellent, good Gotama, excellent, good Gotama. It is as if one might set upright what had been upset, or might disclose what was covered, or show the way to one who had gone astray, or bring an oil-lamp into the darkness so that those with vision might see material shapes—even so in many a figure has *dhamma* been made clear by the revered Gotama. Thus I am going to the revered Gotama for refuge, to *dhamma* and to the Order of monks. May the revered Gotama accept me as a layfollower going for refuge from today forth for as long as life lasts."

Discourse on Fear and Dread:
the Fourth

---

[1] Also at *A*. i. 60.

[2] *MA*. i. 128, for the individuality that is present here and now.

[3] In regard to the four postures, *MA*. i. 128.

[4] *pacchimaṃ janataṃ*. See *B.D.* i. 66, n. *MA*. i. 129 says: "the young men of family, gone forth from faith, seeing that the Lord dwells in the forest, think that the Lord would not undertake forest lodgings if there were not something to be known, something to be got rid of, something to be developed, something to be realised—so why should not they? And they think that they should dwell there. Thus do they quickly become end-makers of anguish. Thus there comes to be compassion for those who come after (or, the lowest of folk)."

5. DISCOURSE ON NO BLEMISHES

(Anaṅgaṇasutta)[1]

THUS have I heard: At one time the Lord was staying near Sāvatthī in the Jeta Grove in Anāthapiṇḍika's monastery. While he was there the venerable Sāriputta addressed the monks, saying: "Reverend monks." "Your reverence," these monks answered the venerable Sāriputta in assent. Then the venerable Sāriputta spoke thus:

"Your reverences, these four kinds of persons[2] are found existing in the world[3]. What are the four? Your reverences, there is here some person with a blemish[4] who thinks: 'I have a subjective blemish,' but who does not comprehend it as it really is. And there is the person with a blemish who, thinking: 'I have a subjective blemish,' comprehends it as it really is.

There is here the person without a blemish who thinks: 'I have no subjective blemish,' but who does not comprehend it as it really is. And there is the person without a blemish who, thinking: 'I have no subjective blemish,' comprehends it as it really is.

Where, your reverences, there is this person with a subjective blemish who thinks, 'I have a subjective blemish,' but does not comprehend it as it really is, this one, of these two persons with a blemish, is shown to be the inferior man.[5] Where, your reverences, there is a person with a subjective blemish who thinks, 'I have a subjective blemish,' and comprehends it as it really is,

---

[1] Referred to at *MA.* ii. 246: *Vism.* 377. The *Anaṅgaṇavatthusutta*, mentioned at *VA.* i. 158, probably refers to this *Majjhima Sutta*.

[2] *MA.* i. 137 notes that there is both a conventional teaching and a teaching according to ultimate truth (*paramatthadesanā*). Herein "individual person, being, woman, man, khattiya, brahman, deva, Māra" come under conventional meaning; and "impermanence, anguish, insubstantiality, the khandhas, the elements, the planes, the applications of mindfulness" under ultimate truth. "The four persons are to be understood in the conventional way" (*MA.* i. 139).

[3] *MA.* i. 139 calls this *sattaloka*, the world of beings.

[4] *Vbh.* 368: "attachment, hatred and folly are called the three blemishes." *MA.* i. 139ff. equates them with the defilements, the *kilesa*.

[5] *hīnapurisa*.

this one, of these two persons with a blemish, is shown to be the best man.

Where, your reverences, there is a person without a subjective blemish [**25**] who thinks, 'I have no subjective blemish,' but does not comprehend it as it really is, this one, of these two persons without a blemish, is shown to be the inferior man. Where, your reverences, there is a person without a subjective blemish who thinks, 'I have no subjective blemish,' and comprehends it as it really is, this one, of these two persons without a blemish, is shown to be the best man."

When this had been said, the venerable Moggallāna the Great spoke thus to the venerable Sāriputta: "Now, reverend Sāriputta, what is the cause, what the reason why, of these two persons with a blemish, one is shown as being the inferior man, while the other is shown as being the best man?"

"Where, your reverence, there is this person with a blemish who thinks: 'I have a subjective blemish,' but who does not comprehend it as it really is, this may be expected for him: that he will not generate desire, or strive, or stir up energy for getting rid of that blemish; he will pass away while he has attachment, aversion, and confusion, while he has the blemish, while his mind is tarnished. Your reverence, it is like a bronze bowl, brought back from a shop or smithy covered with dust and dirt and that the owners would not make use of or clean, but would throw away in the dust. In consequence, your reverence, would that bronze bowl become more tarnished with dirt after a time?"

"Yes, your reverence."

"Even so, your reverence, for that person with a blemish who thinks: 'I have a subjective blemish,' but does not comprehend it as it really is, this is to be expected: that he will not generate desire, or strive, or stir up energy for getting rid of that blemish; he will pass away while he has attachment, aversion, confusion, while he has the blemish, while his mind is tarnished.

Where, your reverence, there is this person with a blemish who thinks: 'I have a subjective blemish,' and comprehends it as it really is, this may be expected for him: that he will generate desire, and strive, and stir up energy for getting rid of that blemish; he will pass away without attachment, without aversion, without confusion, without the blemish, his mind untarnished. Your reverence, it is like a bronze bowl, brought back from a shop or smithy covered with dust and dirt, but which the owners would use and would clean, and would not throw away in the dust. **[26]** In consequence, your reverence, would that bronze bowl become more clean after a time with the cleaning?"

"Yes, your reverence."

"Even so, your reverence, for that person with a blemish who thinks: 'I have a subjective blemish,' and who comprehends it as it really is, this is to be expected: that he will generate desire and strive, and stir up energy for getting rid of that blemish; he will pass away without attachment, without aversion, without confusion, without the blemish, his mind untarnished.

Where, your reverence, there is this person without a blemish who thinks, 'I have no subjective blemish,' but who does not comprehend it as it really is, this may be expected for him: that he will attend to the fair aspect (of things); because of attention to the fair aspect, attachment will deprave his mind; he will pass away while he has attachment, aversion and confusion, while he has a blemish, while his mind is tarnished. Your reverence, it is like a bronze bowl, brought back from a shop or smithy quite pure, quite clean, but which its owners would neither use nor clean, but would throw away in the dust. In consequence, your reverence, would that bronze bowl become more tarnished with dirt after a time?"

"Yes, your reverence."

"Even so, your reverence, for that person without a blemish who thinks: 'I have no subjective blemish,' but who does not comprehend it as it really is, this may be expected for him; that he will attend to the fair aspect (of things); because of attention to the fair aspect, attachment will deprave his mind; he will pass away while he has attachment, aversion and confusion, while he has a blemish, while his mind is tarnished.

Where, your reverence, there is this person without a blemish who thinks, 'I have no subjective blemish,' and comprehends it as it really is, this may be expected for him: that he will not attend to the fair aspect (of things); because there is no attention to the fair aspect, attachment will not deprave his mind; he will pass away without attachment, without aversion, without confusion, without a blemish, his mind untarnished. Your reverence, it is like a bronze bowl, brought back from a shop or smithy quite pure, quite clean, but which the owners would use and would clean, and would not throw away in the dust. In consequence, your reverence, would that bronze bowl become more clean after a time with the cleaning?"

"Yes, your reverence."

"Even so, your reverence, for this person without a blemish who thinks, 'I have no subjective blemish' and who comprehends it as it really is, this may be expected for him: that he will not attend to the fair aspect (of things); because there is no attention to the fair aspect, attachment will not deprave his mind; he will pass away without attachment, without aversion, without confusion, without blemish, his mind untarnished. This, reverend [27] Moggallāna, is the cause, this the reason why, of these two persons with a blemish, the one is shown to be the inferior man, while the other is shown to be the best man. This, reverend Moggallāna, is the cause, this the reason why, of these two persons without a blemish, the one is shown to be the inferior man, while the other is shown to be the best man."

"'Blemish, blemish,' is it called, your reverence? Now, of what is this a synonym, your reverence, that is to say 'blemish'?"

"Your reverence, this—that is to say 'blemish'—is a synonym for being occupied with evil unskilled wishes. This situation occurs, your reverence, when a wish such as this may arise in some monk here: 'Indeed, should I fall into an offence, the monks might not find out about me[1]—that I have fallen into an offence.' This situation occurs, your reverence, when monks may find out about that monk, that he has fallen into an offence. He, thinking that the monks have found out that he has fallen into an offence, becomes angry and discontented. Whatever is anger, your reverence, whatever is discontent, both are a blemish.

This situation occurs, your reverence, when a wish such as this may arise in some monk here: 'But if I have fallen into an offence, the monks might reprove me in private, not in the midst of an Order.' This situation occurs, your reverence, when monks might reprove him in the midst of an Order, not in private. He, thinking: 'The monks are reproving me in the midst of an Order, not in private, becomes angry and discontented. Whatever is anger, your reverence, whatever is discontent, both are a blemish.

This situation occurs, your reverence, when a wish such as this may arise in some monk here: 'Should I have fallen into an offence, an equal[2] should reprove me, not one who is not an equal.' This

---

[1] See *Vin.* ii. 32.

[2] *sappaṭipuggala.* *MA.* i. 144 says this means "an equal person. 'Equal' means one who has an offence. '*Paṭipuggala*' means the reprover. He thinks it possible to say, wishing for reproof from one who has an offence, 'You have fallen into this and that offence. You can reprove me after you

situation occurs, your reverence, when one who is not an equal might reprove that monk. He, thinking: 'One who is not an equal is reproving me, not one who is an equal,' becomes angry and discontented. Whatever is anger, your reverence, whatever is discontent, both are a blemish.

This situation occurs, your reverence, when a wish such as this may arise in some monk here: 'O may the Teacher teach *dhamma* to the monks, having interrogated me only time and again.' This situation occurs, your reverence, when the Teacher may teach *dhamma* to the monks having interrogated some other monk time and again, [**28**] and when the Teacher may teach *dhamma* to the monks not having interrogated *that* monk time and again. He, thinking: 'The Teacher teaches *dhamma* to the monks having interrogated another monk time and again; the Teacher teaches *dhamma* to the monks not having interrogated me time and again,' becomes angry and discontented. Whatever is anger, your reverence, whatever is discontent, both are a blemish.

This situation occurs, your reverence, when a wish such as this may arise in some monk here: 'O may the monks enter the village for rice having put me in front;[1] may the monks not enter the village for rice having put another monk in front.' This situation occurs, your reverence, when the monks may enter the village for rice having put another monk in front, they may enter a village for rice not having put *that* monk in front. He, thinking: 'The monks are entering the village for rice having put another monk in front, they are entering the village for rice not having put me in front,' becomes angry and discontented. Whatever is anger, your reverence, whatever is discontent, both are a blemish.

This situation occurs, your reverence, when a wish such as this may arise in some monk here: 'O may I receive the best seat, the best water, the best almsfood in a refectory,[2] may no other monk receive the best seat, the best water, the best almsfood in the refectory.' This situation occurs; your reverence, when another monk may receive the best seat, the best water, the best almsfood in a refectory, when *that* monk does not receive the best seat . . . in the refectory. He, thinking: 'Another monk is receiving the best seat . . . in the refectory; I am not receiving the best seat . . . in the

---

have confessed it.' Or, he may wish for reproof from one of his own birth, family, learning, experience, or ascetic practice."

[1] I.e. of the procession walking for almsfood to be put into their bowls.

[2] See *Vin.* ii. 161, where a list of those monks fit for such an honour is given.

refectory,' becomes angry and discontented. Whatever is anger, your reverence, whatever is discontent, both are a blemish.

This situation occurs, your reverence, when a wish such as this may arise in some monk here: 'O may I, when I have eaten in a refectory, give the thanks, may no other monk, when he has eaten in a refectory, give the thanks.' This situation occurs, your reverence, when another monk, when he has eaten in the refectory, may give the thanks, when *that* monk, when he has eaten in the refectory, may not give the thanks. He, thinking: 'Another monk, when he has eaten in the refectory, is giving the thanks; I, when I have eaten in the refectory, am not giving the thanks,' becomes angry and discontented. Whatever is anger, your reverence, whatever is discontent, both are a blemish.

This situation occurs, your reverence, when a wish such as this may arise in some monk here: 'O may I teach *dhamma* to the monks who are in a monastery, may no other monk teach *dhamma* to the monks who are in the monastery.' This situation occurs, your reverence, when another monk may teach *dhamma* . . . when *that* monk [**29**] may not teach *dhamma* to the monks who are in a monastery. He, thinking, 'Another monk is teaching *dhamma* to the monks who are in a monastery, I am not teaching *dhamma* to the monks who are in the monastery,' becomes angry and discontented. Whatever is anger, your reverence, whatever is discontent, both are a blemish.

This situation occurs, your reverence, when a wish such as this may arise in some monk here: 'O may I teach *dhamma* to the nuns who are in a monastery . . . to layfollowers who are in a monastery . . . to women layfollowers who are in a monastery, may no other monk teach *dhamma* to the women layfollowers who are in a monastery.' This situation occurs, your reverence, when some other monk may teach *dhamma* to the women layfollowers who are in a monastery, when *that* monk does not teach *dhamma* . . . in a monastery. He, thinking: 'Another monk is teaching . . . I am not teaching . . . in a monastery,' becomes angry and discontented. Whatever is anger, your reverence, whatever is discontent, both are a blemish.

This situation occurs, your reverence, when a wish such as this may arise in some monk here: 'O may the monks revere, esteem, venerate, honour me, may they revere, esteem, venerate, honour no other monk. . . . O may the nuns . . . the layfollowers, the women layfollowers revere, esteem, venerate, honour me, may they revere

. . . honour no other monk.' This situation occurs, your reverence, when the monks . . . the nuns . . . the layfollowers . . . the women layfollowers may revere, esteem, venerate, honour some other monk, when they do not revere . . . honour *that* monk. He, thinking: 'The monks . . . the nuns . . . the layfollowers . . . the women layfollowers are revering, esteeming, venerating, honouring some other monk, they are not revering . . . honouring me,' becomes angry and discontented. Whatever is anger, your reverence, whatever is discontent, both are a blemish.

This situation occurs, your reverence, when a wish such as this may arise in some monk here: 'O may I receive fine robe-material, may no other monk receive fine robe-material . . . **[30]** . . . fine almsfood . . . fine lodgings . . . fine requisites of medicines for the sick, may no other monk receive fine requisites of medicines for the sick.' This situation occurs, your reverence, when another monk may receive fine requisites of medicines for the sick, when *that* monk does not receive fine requisites of medicines for the sick. He, thinking: 'Another monk is receiving fine requisites of medicines for the sick, I am not receiving fine requisites of medicines for the sick,' becomes angry and discontented. Whatever is anger, your reverence, whatever is discontent, both are a blemish. This, your reverence—that is to say 'blemish'—is a synonym for being occupied with evil unskilled wishes.

In whatever monk, your reverence, it is seen and also heard that these occupations with evil unskilled wishes are not destroyed—even though he be a forest-dweller whose lodgings are remote, one who walks for almsfood on continuous almsround,[1] a rag-robe wearer who wears robes that are worn thin[2]—then his fellow Brahma-farers do not revere, esteem, venerate, honour him. What is the cause of this? It is that these see and also hear of this reverend one that his occupations with evil unskilled wishes are not destroyed. Your reverence, it is like a bronze bowl brought back from a shop or smithy quite pure, quite clean; its owners, having filled it with a dead snake or a dead dog or a dead human being, and having enclosed it in another bronze bowl, might take it back inside the shop. People, on seeing it, would say: 'Just

---

[1] I.e. not picking and choosing between the houses he would visit, but taking them in the order in which they come, according to Sekhiya 33.

[2] *MA*. i. 149 says that this may be due to three causes: because they are cut with a knife, sewn with a coarse long thread, or stained by dust.

look, what is this that has been brought back like a very lovely thing?' Having lifted it up and opened it, they would look at it; at the sight of it, repugnance would set in and loathing would set in and disgust would set in; those who had been hungry would have no desire for food, far less those who had eaten already—even so, your reverence, of whatever monk it is seen and heard that these occupations with evil unskilled wishes are not destroyed—even though he be a forest-dweller . . . who wears robes that are worn thin—then his fellow Brahma-farers do not revere, [**31**] esteem, venerate, honour him. What is the cause of this? This reverend one's occupations with evil unskilled wishes are seen as well as heard to be not destroyed.

In whatever monk, your reverence, these occupations with evil unskilled wishes are seen and are heard to be destroyed—even though he were staying near a village, were one who is invited,[1] were one who wears householder's robe-material[2]—then his fellow Brahma-farers would revere, esteem, venerate, honour him. What is the cause of this? It is that these see and also hear of that reverend one that his occupations with evil unskilled wishes are destroyed. Your reverence, it is like a bronze bowl, brought back from a shop or smithy quite pure, quite clean. Its owners, having filled it with fine rice; rice-water, the black grains removed, with various curries, various vegetables, and having enclosed it in another bronze bowl, might take it back inside the shop. People, seeing it, would say: 'Just look, what is this that has been brought back like a very lovely thing?' Having lifted it up, having opened it, they would look at it. On seeing it, liking would set in, and no loathing would set in and no disgust would set in; even those who had eaten would have a desire for food, how much more those who were hungry?—even so, your reverence, of whatever monk it is seen and heard that these occupations with evil unskilled wishes are destroyed—even though he were staying near a village . . . then his fellow Brahma-farers would revere . . . honour him. What is the cause of this? It is that these see and also hear of this reverend one that his occupations with evil unskilled wishes are destroyed."

When this had been said, the venerable Moggallāna the Great

---

[1] I.e. to go and take his meals at houses (either as a regular diner, or as one specially invited) instead of walking for his almsfood. *Cf. A.* iii. 391.

[2] I.e. robe-material given by householders—superior to robes made of rags taken from the dust-heap. *Cf. M.* iii. 126.

spoke thus to the venerable Sāriputta: " A simile occurs[1] to me, reverend Sāriputta."

" Let it be evident,[2] reverend Moggallāna."

" Once I, your reverence, was staying near Rājagaha in the mountain Cowpen.[3] Then I, your reverence, having dressed in the morning, taking my bowl and robe, entered Rājagaha for alms-food. Now at that time Samīti, the son of a vehicle maker, was shaping a felloe, and the Naked Ascetic, Paṇḍu's son, who had formerly been the son of a vehicle maker, was standing near him. Then, your reverence, this reasoning arose in the mind of the Naked Ascetic,[4] Paṇḍu's son, who had formerly been the son of a vehicle maker: ' O that this Samīti, the son of a vehicle maker, might shape away this felloe's crookedness, its twist and notch, so that the felloe, without crookedness, without twist, without notch, might be clear and placed on the pith.' [**32**] Even while there was this reasoning in the mind of the Naked Ascetic, Paṇḍu's son, who had formerly been a vehicle maker, so did Samīti, the son of a vehicle maker, shape away that crookedness and that twist and that notch from the felloe. Then, your reverence, the Naked Ascetic, Paṇḍu's son, who had formerly been the son of a vehicle maker, was delighted; he let forth a cry of delight: ' It seems as if he is shaping it away because with his heart[5] he knows my heart.' Even so, your reverence, those persons who are without faith, but who, in want of a way of living, have gone forth from home into homelessness, not from faith, who are crafty, fraudulent, deceitful, who are unbalanced[6] and puffed up, who are shifty, scurrilous and of loose talk, the doors of whose sense-faculties are not guarded, who do not know moderation in eating, who are not intent on vigilance, indifferent to recluseship, not of keen respect for the training, ones for abundance, lax, taking the lead in backsliding, shirking the burden of seclu-

---

[1] *paṭibhāti* explained by *upaṭṭhāti* at *MA*. i. 151.

[2] *paṭibhātu*. *MA*. i. 151 says, " let it occur, let it rise up. The meaning is: you speak."

[3] Giribbaje. *MA*. i. 151 says, " it (Rājagaha) was called Giribbaja because it stood like a cattle pen (*vaja*) with a circle of mountains all round." So Giribbaja, which is usually taken as a name for Rājagaha, is the Cowpen in the mountains which surround Rājagaha.

[4] *MA*. i. 151 explains *ājīvika* as *naggasamaṇa*. See A. L. Basham, *History and Doctrines of the Ājīvikas*, London, 1951.

[5] *hadaya*.

[6] This word and the next four also occur at *M*. i. 470, *S*. i. 61, 203; all at *A*. iii. 198-199.

sion,[1] who are indolent, of feeble energy, of confused mindfulness, not clearly conscious, not concentrated but of wandering minds, who are weak in wisdom, drivellers[2]—it seems that the venerable Sāriputta, because he knows their hearts with his heart, is shaping them by means of this disquisition on *dhamma*.

But those young men of respectable families who, from faith, have gone forth from home into homelessness, who are not crafty, fraudulent or deceitful, who are not unbalanced, not puffed up, not shifty, not scurrilous or of loose talk, the doors of whose sense-faculties are guarded, who know moderation in eating, who are intent on vigilance, who long for recluseship, who are of keen respect for the training, not ones for abundance, not lax, shirking back-sliding, taking the lead in seclusion, who are of stirred up energy, self-resolute, with mindfulness aroused, clearly conscious, who are concentrated, their minds one-pointed, who have wisdom, are not drivellers—these, having heard this disquisition on *dhamma* from the venerable Sāriputta, seem to drink it, seem to savour it with speech as well as with mind. Indeed it is good that a fellow Brahma-farer, having caused one to rise up from[3] what is unskilled, establishes him in what is skilled. Your reverence, it is like[4] a woman or a man, young and of tender years, fond of adornment, who, having washed the head, having acquired a garland of lotuses or a garland of jasmine or a garland of acacia creeper, and having taken it in both hands should place it on the top of the head—even so, your reverence, those young men of respectable families who have gone forth from home into homelessness from faith, who are not crafty . . . having heard this disquisition on *dhamma* from the venerable Sāriputta, seem to drink it, seem to savour it with speech as well as with mind. Indeed it is good that a fellow Brahma-farer, having caused one to rise up from what is unskilled, establishes him in what is skilled."

In this wise did each of these great beings[5] rejoice together in what was well spoken by the other.

Discourse on No Blemishes:
the Fifth

---

[1] As at *M*. i. 14. [2] As at *M*. i. 20.

[3] *vuṭṭhāpetvā*. Or having caused one to remove himself from.

[4] As at *Vin*. ii. 255, *A*. iv. 278, etc.

[5] *mahānāga*. *MA*. i. 153 says that this is what the two chief disciples and called; it gives three derivations for *nāga*, and quotes *Sn*. 522.

6. DISCOURSE ON WHAT ONE MAY WISH

(Ākaṅkheyyasutta[1])

[**33**] THUS have I heard[2]: At one time the Lord was staying near Sāvatthī in the Jeta Grove in Anāthapiṇḍika's monastery. While he was there the Lord addressed the monks, saying: "Monks." "Revered one," these monks answered the Lord in assent. The Lord spoke thus:

"Fare along, monks, possessed of moral habit, possessed of the Obligations, fare along controlled by the control of the Obligations, possessed of right conduct and resort, seeing danger in the slightest faults; undertaking them rightly, train yourselves in the rules of training.[3]

Monks, if a monk should wish: 'May I be agreeable to my fellow Brahma-farers, liked by them, revered and respected,' he should be one who fulfils the moral habits, who is intent on mental tranquillity within,[4] whose meditation is uninterrupted, who is endowed with vision,[5] a cultivator of empty places.[6]

Monks, if a monk should wish: 'May I be one who receives the requisites of robes, almsfood, lodgings, and medicines for the sick,' he should be one who fulfils the moral habits . . . a cultivator of empty places.

Monks, if a monk should wish: 'May these services of those[7] from whom I enjoy the requisites of robes, almsfood, lodgings, requisites for the sick, be of great merit, of great advantage,' he should be one who fulfils the moral habits . . . a cultivator of empty places.

Monks, if a monk should wish: 'May this be a great fruit, a great

---

[1] At *MA*. i. 15, *DA*. i. 50 this Sutta is mentioned as an example of a discourse preached by the Buddha of his own accord, *attano ajjhāsayen' eva*.

[2] *Cf*. *A*. v. 131.

[3] *MA*. i. 155 says all is given in detail in *Vism*. (p. 16f.). *Cf*. *D*.i. 63; *Miln*. 375.

[4] *Cf*. *M*. i. 213; *It*. p. 39.

[5] *vipassanā*. A sevenfold viewing, *anupassanā*, is mentioned at *MA*. i. 157, *Pṭs*. i. 10.

[6] *Cf*. *Khp*. VII.

[7] *MA*. i. 159 says devas or men.

advantage to those of my kith and kin who, their minds pleased, recollect the departed who have passed away,[1] he should be one who fulfils the moral habits . . . a cultivator of empty places.

Monks, if a monk should wish: 'May I be one who overcomes aversion[2] and liking[3], and may aversion not overcome me, may I fare along constantly conquering any aversion that has arisen,' he should be one who fulfils the moral habits . . . a cultivator of empty places.

Monks, if a monk should wish: 'May I be one who overcomes fear and dread, and may fear and dread not overcome me, may I fare along constantly conquering any fear and dread that has arisen,' he should be one who fulfils the moral habits . . . a cultivator of empty places.

Monks, if a monk should wish: 'May I be one who, at will,[4] without trouble, without difficulty, acquires the four meditations which are of the purest mentality, abidings in ease here-now,[5] he should be one who fulfils the moral habits . . . a cultivator of empty places.

Monks, if a monk should wish: 'Those incorporeal deliverances[6] which are calmed, transcending forms, may I fare along having realised[7] them while in the body,'[8] he should be one who fulfils the moral habits . . . a cultivator of empty places.

[**34**] Monks, if a monk should wish: 'By the total destruction of the three fetters may I be a stream-attainer,[9] not liable to the Downfall, assured, bound for awakening,' he should be one who fulfils the moral habits . . . a cultivator of empty places.

Monks, if a monk should wish: 'By the total destruction of the three fetters, by the reduction of attachment, aversion, confusion, may I be a once-returner; having come back once only to this

---

1 *Cf. Sn.* 590.

2 *MA.* i. 160, for remote lodgings. *Cf. M.* iii. 97, *A.* iv. 291, v, 132 for this whole passage.

3 *MA.* i. 160, to the five strands of sense-pleasures.

4 *Cf. M.* i. 354; *A.* ii 23, iii. 114, 133, v. 132, etc.

5 *diṭṭhadhamma* is called the present individuality. Here the meaning is "of beings abiding in ease," for which a synonym is the four meditations on the fine-material plane.

6 *Cf. D.* ii. 70.

7 *phassitvā. MA.* i. 162 says *nāmakāyena phusitvā; pāpuṇitvā adhigantvā.*

8 *kāyena.*

9 *MA.* i. 162 says "stream" is a synonym for the Way and quotes *S.* v. 347, adding that here (i.e. above) the name is given for a fruit of the Way.

world, may I make an end of anguish,'[1] he should be one who fulfils the moral habits . . . a cultivator of empty places.

Monks, if a monk should wish: 'By the total destruction of the five fetters that bind one to the lower world,[2] may I be of spontaneous uprising, one who has utterly attained to nibbāna there,[3] not liable to return from that world,[4] he should be one who fulfils the moral habits . . . a cultivator of empty places.

Monks, if a monk should wish: 'May I experience the various forms of psychic power[5]; having been one may I be manifold, having been manifold may I be one; manifest or invisible may I go unhindered through a wall, through a rampart, through a mountain as if through air; may I plunge into the ground and shoot up again as if in water; may I walk upon the water without parting it as if on the ground; sitting cross-legged may I travel through the air like a bird on the wing; with my hand may I rub and stroke this moon and sun although they are of such mighty power and majesty; and even as far as the Brahma-world may I have power in respect of my body,'[6] he should be one who fulfils the moral habits . . . a cultivator of empty places.

Monks, if a monk should wish: 'By the purified *deva*-like hearing which surpasses that of men, may I hear both (kinds of) sounds—*deva*-like ones and human ones, whether they be far or near,' he should be one who fulfils the moral habits . . . a cultivator of empty places.[7]

Monks, if a monk should wish: 'May I know intuitively by mind the minds of other beings,[8] of other individuals, so that I may know intuitively of a mind that is full of attachment[9] . . . aversion . . . confusion, that it is full of attachment . . . aversion . . . confusion; or of a mind that is without attachment . . . without aversion . . . without confusion, that it is without attachment . . . without

---

[1] *MA.* i. 163 explains *dukkha* here as *vaṭṭadukkha,* the anguish of whirling (on in recurrent birth).

[2] *See M.* Sutta 64.

[3] This formula therefore is not "peculiar to Samy. and Ang.", as stated at *G.S.* ii. 243, n. 1.

[4] The Brahma-world, *MA.* i. 164.

[5] *M.* i. 494; *D.* i. 78; *A.* i. 170, 255, etc.

[6] This is called the marvel of psychic power at *A.* i. 170. *Cf.* also *S.* v. 282, etc.

[7] *Cf. A.* i. 255.

[8] As at e.g. *M.* i. 59, 69. See notes at p. 76, below.

[9] *Cf. M.* i. 59, 69, 495; *A.* i. 255; *D.* i. 80, etc.

aversion . . . without confusion; or so that I may know intuitively of a mind that is contracted that it is contracted, or of a mind that is distracted that it is distracted, or of a mind that has become great that it has become great, or of a mind that has not become great that it has not become great, or of a mind with (some other mental state) superior to it that it has (some other mental state) superior to it, or of a mind that has no (other mental state) superior to it that it has no (other mental state) superior to it, or of a mind that is composed that it is composed, [**35**] or of a mind that is not composed that it is not composed, or of a mind that is freed that it is freed, or of a mind that is not freed that it is not freed,' he should be one who fulfils the moral habits . . . empty places.

Monks, if a monk should wish: ' May I recollect (my) manifold former habitations,[1] that is to say, one birth, two births, three . . . four . . . five . . . ten . . . twenty . . . forty . . . fifty . . . a hundred . . . a thousand . . . a hundred thousand births, many an eon of integration, many an eon of disintegration, many an eon of integration-disintegration; such a one was I by name, having such and such a clan, such and such a colour, so was I nourished, such and such pleasant and painful experiences were mine, so did the span of life end. Passing from this, I came to be in another state where such a one was I by name, having such and such a clan, such and such a colour, so was I nourished, such and such pleasant and painful experiences were mine, so did the span of life end. Passing from this I arose here. Thus may I remember (my) divers former habitations in all their modes and detail,' he should be one who fulfils the moral habits . . . empty places.

Monks, if a monk should wish: ' With the purified *deva*-vision surpassing that of men,[2] may I behold beings as they pass hence or come to be—mean, excellent, fair, foul, in a good bourn, in a bad bourn, according to the consequences of their deeds; may I comprehend: Indeed these worthy beings were possessed of wrong conduct in body, speech and thought, they were scoffers at the ariyans, holding a wrong view, incurring deeds consequent on a wrong view—these, at the breaking up of the body after dying, have arisen in a sorrowful state, a bad bourn, the abyss, Niraya Hell. But these worthy beings who were possessed of good conduct in body, speech and thought, who were not scoffers at the ariyans, holding a right view, incurring deeds consequent on a right view—

[1] *Cf. M.* i. 22; *A.* i. 255, etc.

[2] *Cf. M.* i. 22-23; *A.* i. 256, etc.

these at the breaking up of the body after dying have arisen in a good bourn, a heaven world. Thus, with the purified *deva*-vision surpassing that of men may I behold beings as they pass hence, as they arise—mean, excellent, fair, foul, in a good bourn, in a bad bourn, according to the consequences of their deeds,' he should be one who fulfils the moral habits . . . empty places.

Monks, if a monk should wish: 'By the destruction of the cankers,[1] having realised by my own super-knowledge here and now the freedom of mind,[2] and freedom through wisdom[3] that are cankerless, **[36]** entering thereon, may I abide therein,' he should be one who fulfils the moral habits, who is intent on mental tranquillity within, who does not interrupt (his) meditation, who is endowed with vision, a cultivator of empty places. That of which I have spoken thus was spoken in relation to this: Fare along, monks, possessed of moral habit, possessed of the Obligations, fare along controlled by the control of the Obligations, possessed of right conduct and resort, seeing danger in the slightest faults; undertaking them rightly, train yourselves in the rules of training."

Thus spoke the Lord. Delighted, these monks rejoiced in what the Lord had said.

Discourse on What one may Wish:
the Sixth

7. DISCOURSE ON THE SIMILE OF THE CLOTH

(Vatthûpamasutta)[4]

THUS have I heard: At one time the Lord was staying near Sāvatthī in the Jeta Grove in Anāthapiṇḍika's monastery. While he was there the Lord addressed the monks, saying: "Monks." "Revered

[1] *Cf. M.* i. 22-23, *A.* i. 256.

[2] *MA.* i. 164 says this is contemplation that is freed from attachment.

[3] *MA.* i. 164 says this should be so called because it is freed from ignorance.

[4] Called at *MA.* i. 165 Vatthasutta. It states that there are four ways of presenting a similitude or parable in relation to its meaning; here the simile is given first, then the meaning.

one," these monks answered the Lord in assent. The Lord spoke thus:

"Monks, as a cloth that is stained and dirty and which a dyer might dip into this and that dye—be it dark green or yellow or red or crimson—would be dyed a bad colour; it would not be clear in colour. What is the reason for this? Monks, it is because the cloth was not clean. Even so, monks, a bad bourn[1] is to be expected when the mind is stained. Monks, as a cloth that is quite clean, quite pure, and which a dyer might dip into this or that dye—be it dark green or yellow or red or crimson—would be dyed a good colour; it would be clear in colour. What is the reason for this? Monks, it is because the cloth was clean. Even so, monks, a good bourn[2] is to be expected when the mind is not stained.

And what, monks, are the defilements of the mind? Greed and covetousness[3] is a defilement of the mind, malevolence . . . anger . . . malice . . . hypocrisy . . . spite . . . envy . . . stinginess . . . deceit . . . treachery . . . obstinacy . . . impetuosity . . . arrogance . . . pride . . . conceit . . . **[37]** indolence is a defilement of the mind. Monks, a monk thinks that greed and covetousness is a defilement of the mind, and having known it thus, he gets rid of the defilement of the mind that is greed and covetousness; a monk thinks that malevolence . . . anger . . . indolence is a defilement of the mind, and having known it thus, he gets rid of the defilement of the mind that is indolence. When, monks, the monk thinks that greed and covetousness is a defilement of the mind . . . that indolence is a defilement of the mind, and having known it thus, the defilement of the mind that is indolence is got rid of, he becomes possessed of unwavering confidence in the Awakened One and thinks: 'Thus indeed is he the Lord, perfected, wholly self-awakened, endowed with knowledge and right conduct, well-farer, knower of the world(s), incomparable charioteer of men to be tamed, teacher of *devas* and mankind, the Awakened One, the Lord.' He becomes

---

[1] Niraya Hell, animal birth or the realm of the departed (*petavisaya*). These bad bourns are alike for householders and the homeless (recluses) if their conduct is bad in the ways specified at *MA*. i. 167-168.

[2] A householder arises to greatness as a man and greatness as a deva (*manussamahattam pi devamahattam pi*). A homeless one, if he has certain qualifications, arises in the three great families in the human world or among the six Kāmâvacara devas, or among the ten Brahma-abodes, or in the five Pure Abodes, or in the four formless (realms), *MA*. i. 168.

[3] Greed is the passion of delight for one's own possessions, covetousness that for another's possessions, *MA*. i. 169.

possessed of unwavering confidence in *dhamma* and thinks: '*Dhamma* is well taught by the Lord, it is self-realised, it is timeless,[1] it is a come-and-see thing, leading onwards,[2] to be understood individually by the wise.' He becomes possessed of unwavering confidence in the Order and thinks: 'The Lord's Order of disciples is of good conduct, the Lord's Order of disciples is upright, the Lord's Order of disciples is of wise conduct, the Lord's Order of disciples is of dutiful conduct, that is to say the four pairs of men, the eight individuals.[3] This Order of the Lord's disciples is worthy of alms, worthy of hospitality, worthy of offerings, worthy of reverence, it is a matchless field of merit for the world.'[4] At this stage[5] there is for him giving up, renouncing, rejecting, getting rid of, forsaking. He, thinking: 'Possessed of unwavering confidence in the Awakened One am I,' acquires knowledge of the goal,[6] acquires knowledge of *dhamma*,[7] acquires the delight that is connected with *dhamma*; rapture is born from that delight, being rapturous, his body is impassible, with the body impassible, joy[8] is felt, because of joy the mind is (well) concentrated.[9] Thinking: 'Possessed of unwavering confidence in *dhamma* am I,' he acquires knowledge of the goal . . . **[38]** . . . the mind is (well) concentrated. Thinking: 'Possessed of unwavering confidence in the Order am I,' he acquires knowledge of the goal . . . because of joy the mind is (well) concentrated. Thinking: 'At this stage there comes to be for me giving up, renouncing, rejecting, getting rid of, forsaking,' he acquires knowledge of the goal, acquires knowledge of *dhamma* . . . the mind is (well) concentrated.

---

[1] *akālika*, not belonging to time. The meaning is: of immediate fruit. The fruit is immediately followed by the Way (without any interval of time). On these terms see *Vism.* 198-221.

[2] I.e. to nibbāna.

[3] Those on the four stages of the Way, and those who have attained the fruits of the four stages of the Way.

[4] For this formula of "confidence" see also *D.* iii. 227; *S.* ii. 69, iv. 271; *A.* i. 222, etc.

[5] *yathodi*, i.e. he is now a non-returner, *MA.* i. 172.

[6] *atthaveda*. *MA.* i. 173 gives three kinds of *veda*: (1) (literary) composition, *gantha*; (2) knowledge, *ñāṇa*; (3) mental ease or happiness, *somanassa*; and says here mental ease and the knowledge attached to it is meant. *Cf. M.* i. 221, 325; *A.* iii. 285, v. 349.

[7] *dhammaveda*.

[8] Mental joy is meant, *MA.* i. 174

[9] *cittaṁ samādhiyati*, the mind is rightly synthesised, it remains unmoving as though fastened. With this passage, *cf. Vin.* i. 294; *D.* i. 73; *Miln.* 84, etc.

A monk, monks, of such moral habit,[1] of such *dhamma*,[2] of such wisdom—even if he eat fine almsfood, the black grains removed, with various curries, various vegetables,[3] that will not be a stumbling-block for him. Monks, even as a stained and dirty cloth, if put in clear water becomes pure and clean, or as gold put into a smelting-pot becomes pure and clean, in like manner, monks, a monk of such moral habit, of such *dhamma*, of such wisdom, even if he eat fine almsfood, the black grains removed, with various curries, various vegetables, that will not be a stumbling-block for him.

He dwells, having suffused the first quarter with a mind of friendliness, likewise the second, likewise the third, likewise the fourth; just so above, below, across; he dwells having suffused the whole world everywhere, in every way, with a mind of friendliness that is far-reaching, wide-spread, immeasurable, without enmity, without malevolence. He dwells having suffused the first quarter with a mind of compassion . . . sympathetic joy . . . equanimity . . . that is far-reaching, wide-spread, immeasurable, without enmity, without malevolence.

He comprehends: ‘There is this,[4] there is a low,[5] there is the excellent,[6] there is a further escape from perceptions.’[7] For one thus knowing, thus seeing, the mind is freed from the canker of sense-pleasures and the mind is freed from the canker of becoming and the mind is freed from the canker of ignorance. In freedom the knowledge comes to be that he is freed, and he comprehends: ‘Destroyed is birth, brought to a close is the Brahma-faring, done is what was to be done, there is no more of being such or such.’ [**39**] Monks, this is called a monk who is washed with an inner washing.”[8]

---

[1] *MA*. i. 174, the body (or mass) of moral habit connected with the way of no-return.

[2] *Ibid.*, the body of concentration also connected, as is the body of wisdom, with the way of non-returners. *Sīla samādhi paññā* form the three main branches of the Teaching. Here, *dhamma* takes the place, but only in name, of *samādhi*, which also is sometimes called *citta* in this connection.

[3] As at *M*. i. 31.

[4] *MA*. i. 176, the attainment of arahantship.

[5] *Ibid.*, anguish and its uprising. [6] *Ibid.*, the means of ejecting anguish.

[7] *saññāgata*. According to *MA*. i. 176 nibbāna is this further escape for one who has perception of the four *brahmavihāras* (referred to just above). It is the truth of “stopping,” *i.e.* the third truth. Traditionally the development of the *brahmavihāras* leads to companionship with Brahmā. Here, *MA*. takes the result of such development to be nibbāna.

[8] *sināta*. *Cf*. *Sn*. 521, *nhātaka*. See also *S*. i. 169; *M*. i. 280.

Now at that time the brahman Sundarika-Bhāradvāja[1] was sitting not far from the Lord. Then the brahman Sundarika-Bhāradvāja spoke thus to the Lord: "Does the revered Gotama go down to wash in the river Bāhukā ?"[2]

"Brahman, what is there to the river Bāhukā ? Of what use is the river Bāhukā ?"

"But, good Gotama, the river Bāhukā is considered by the manyfolk as a means of purification,[3] the river Bāhukā is considered by the manyfolk to be for merit. For in the river Bāhukā the manyfolk wash away the evil deeds that have been done."

Then the Lord addressed the brahman Sundarika-Bhāradvāja in verses:

"In the Bāhukā, and at Adhikakkā,[4]
At Gayā,[4] and in the Sundarikā,
In the Sarassatī, and at Payāga,[5]
Then in the river Bāhumatī,[6]
The fool, though entering constantly,
Does not cleanse his dark deed.[7]

What can the Sundarikā do ?
What Payāga, what the Bāhukā river ?
They do not cleanse that hostile guilty man
Intent on evil deeds.
For the pure every day is auspicious, for the pure every day is holy,[8]

---

[1] Mentioned at *S.* i. 167; *Sn.* p. 79 as performing fire-worship on the banks of the river Sundarikā.

[2] At *Jā.* v. 387, 388 *bahuka* does not seem to be the name of a river. *Cf.* also *Mhvu.* ii. 51.

[3] *M.* text reads *mokkhasammatā. MA.* i. 177 *lokhyasammatâ ti lūkhabhāvasammatā. Cokkhabhāvaṃ visuddhibhāvaṃ detî ti.* See also *M.* i. 530 (Trenckner's notes) and *MA.* i. 177, *n.* 3, 4.

[4] Both are fords, *MA.* i. 178. [5] A ford across the Ganges, *MA.* i. 178.

[6] *MA.* i. 178 says that these four are rivers: Bāhukā, Sundarikā, Sarassatī, Bāhumatī.

[7] On *kaṇhakamma* (and light, or bright, *i.e.* good deeds) see *M.* i. 389.

[8] Quoted at *DA.* i. 139. Phaggu is an auspicious constellation, and so the word has here been translated "auspicious." *MA.* i. 179 explains by saying that the brahman view is that whoever bathes in the month of Phagguna on the day after the full moon is cleansed of evil done during the year. *Uposatha,* here translated "holy," has no good English equivalent. Ordinarily there are four uposatha days a month when people observe the higher *sīla* or fast. But for the pure every day, not necessarily only the four

For the pure of bright deeds[1] there is ever the practice of
(good) custom.
Bathe in this only,[2] brahman,
Make all creatures secure,[3]

If you do not speak a lie,[4] if you harm no living thing,[5]
If you take not the ungiven,[5] are believing, not stingy——
What can you do by going to Gayā, when Gayā is only a well[6]
for you ?"

When this had been said, the brahman Sundarika-Bhāradvāja spoke thus to the Lord:

"It is excellent, good Gotama; it is excellent, good Gotama. It is as if, good Gotama, one might set upright what had been upset, or disclose what had been covered, or show the way to one who had gone astray, or bring an oil lamp into the darkness so that those with vision might see material shapes; even so in many a figure has *dhamma* been made clear by the good Gotama, I, even I, am going to the revered Gotama for refuge, and to *dhamma*, and to the Order of monks. May I receive the going forth[7] in the presence of the good Gotama, may I receive ordination."[8]

Then the brahman Sundarika-Bhāradvāja received the going forth in the Lord's presence, he received ordination. [**40**] Soon after he had been ordained the venerable Bhāradvāja, abiding alone,[9] aloof,[10] diligent, ardent,[11] self-resolute,[12] not long afterwards, by his own super-knowledge, having precisely here-now[13] realised

---

prescribed days, is *uposatha*, an " observance " day when all the observances and rules of discipline are observed.

[1] *sucikamma*, pure deeds, *cf. Dhp.* 24.

[2] In this teaching of mine, *MA.* i. 179.

[3] security, *khemata*; *MA.* i. 179 says *abhaya hitabhāva mettā*, lack of fear, welfare, friendliness. This is purity by way of mind.

[4] Purity by way of speech. [5] Purity by way of gesture or body.

[6] *udapāna.*

[7] *pabbajjā*, the initial entry or lesser ordination into the Order.

[8] *upasampadā*, the subsequent or higher ordination, not necessarily " final," as it was possible to return to " the low life of the layman." On the ordination ceremony and the regulations for carrying it out in the prescribed way, see *Vin. Mahāvagga* I.

[9] *MA.* i. 179, as to the body. [10] *MA.* i. 180, as to mind.

[11] *MA.* i. 180, with ardour in physical and mental energy.

[12] *MA.* i. 180 says " by absence of longing as to the body and the life-principle."

[13] In this very individuality, *attabhāva*, *MA.* i. 180 and at *MA.* i. 165.

that matchless culmination of the Brahma-faring[1] for the sake of which young men of family[2] rightly go forth from home into homelessness, abided in it. He comprehended: Destroyed is birth, brought to a close is the Brahma-faring, done is what was to be done, there is no more of being such or such. So the venerable Bhāradvāja became one of the perfected ones.

Discourse on the Simile of the Cloth:
the Seventh

8. DISCOURSE ON EXPUNGING
(Sallekhasutta)

THUS have I heard: At one time the Lord was staying near Sāvatthī in the Jeta Grove in Anāthapiṇḍika's monastery. Then the venerable Cunda the Great,[3] emerging towards evening from solitary meditation, approached the Lord; having approached, having greeted the Lord, he sat down at a respectful distance. As he was sitting down at a respectful distance the venerable Cunda the Great spoke thus to the Lord:

"Those various types of views,[4] Lord, that arise in the world and are connected with theories of the self or with theories of the world, does there come to be ejection of these views, does there come to be renunciation of these views for a monk who wisely reflects from the beginning?"

---

[1] *MA*. i. 180 calls this culmination of the Brahma-faring or the Way the "fruit of arahantship." At *M*. i. 197, 205 freedom of mind is said to be the goal and culmination.

[2] Those by birth and those by habits: both meant here, *MA*. i. 180 as at *MA*. i. 111.

[3] Mentioned with other great theras at *M*. iii. 78; *A*. iii. 299; *Ud*. 3; *Vin*. iv. 66. Verses ascribed to him at *Thag*. 141-142.

[4] Wrong views are meant, *MA*. i. 182. Wrong views about self (in connection with the *khandhas*) number twenty (*four* for each of the five *khandhas*). See *A*. ii. 214, *S*. iii. 16. Wrong views about the world number eight: that the world and the self are eternal, not eternal, both eternal and not, neither eternal nor not eternal; see *D*. i. 14 *ff*.

"Those various types of views, Cunda, that arise in the world and are connected with theories of the self or with theories of the world—wherever these views arise and wherever they obsess (the mind) and wherever they are current, it is by seeing them with perfect wisdom as they really are, thus: 'This is not mine,[1] this am I not,[2] this is not my self,'[3] that there is ejection of these views, that there is renunciation of these views.

The situation occurs, Cunda, when a monk here, aloof from pleasures of the senses, aloof from unskilled states of mind, may enter on and abide in the first meditation which is accompanied by initial thought and discursive thought, is born of aloofness, and is rapturous and joyful. It may occur to him: 'I fare along[4] by expunging.' But these,[5] Cunda, are not called expungings in the discipline for an ariyan; these are called 'abidings in ease here-now' **[41]** in the discipline for an ariyan.

This situation occurs, Cunda, when some monk here, by allaying initial thought and discursive thought, with the mind subjectively tranquillised and fixed on one point, may enter on and abide in the second meditation which is devoid of initial and discursive thought, is born of concentration, and is rapturous and joyful. It may occur to him: 'I fare along by expunging' . . . in the discipline for an ariyan.

This situation occurs, Cunda, when some monk here, by the fading out of rapture, may abide with equanimity, attentive, and clearly conscious, and may experience in his person that joy of which the ariyans say: 'Joyful lives he who has equanimity and is mindful,' and may enter on and abide in the third meditation. It may occur to him: 'I fare along by expunging' . . . in the discipline for an ariyan.

This situation occurs, Cunda, when some monk here, by getting rid of joy, by getting rid of anguish, by the going down of his former pleasures and sorrows, may enter on and abide in the fourth meditation which has neither anguish nor joy, and that is entirely purified by equanimity and mindfulness. It may occur to him:

---

[1] To think *etaṁ mama*, this is mine, is to be in the grip of craving.

[2] To think *eso aham asmi*, I am this, is to be in the grip of pride.

[3] To think *eso me attā*, this is my self, is to be in the grip of wrong view, *MA*. i. 183.

[4] At *MA*. i. 244-5, *Vbh*. 252 (quoted *Asl*. 167), *Nd*. ii. 237, *viharati* is explained by verbs of motion. The idea is that the expunger moves from higher things to higher.

[5] The plural number is used in reference to the properties of the jhānas.

'I fare along by expunging.' But these, Cunda, are not called 'expungings' in the discipline for an ariyan; these are called 'abidings in ease here-now' in the discipline for an ariyan.

This situation occurs, Cunda, when some monk here, by wholly transcending perceptions of material shapes, by the going down of perceptions due to sensory impressions, by not reflecting on the perceptions of multiformity, thinking: 'Ether is unending,' may enter on and abide in the plane of infinite ether.[1] It may occur to him: 'I fare along by expunging.' But these, Cunda, are not called 'expungings' in the discipline for an ariyan; these are called 'abidings that are peaceful'[2] in the discipline for an ariyan.

This situation occurs, Cunda, when some monk here, by wholly transcending the plane of infinite ether, thinking: 'Consciousness is unending,' may enter on and abide in the plane of infinite consciousness. It may occur to him: 'I fare along by expunging.' But these, Cunda, are not called 'expungings' in the discipline for an ariyan; these are called 'abidings that are peaceful' in the discipline for an ariyan.

This situation occurs, Cunda, when some monk here, by wholly transcending the plane of infinite consciousness, thinking: 'There is no-thing,' may enter on and abide in the plane of no-thing. It may occur to him . . . in the discipline for an ariyan.

This situation occurs, Cunda, when some monk here, by wholly transcending the plane of no-thing, may enter on and abide in the plane of neither-perception-nor-non-perception. It may occur to him: 'I fare along by expunging.' **[42]** But these, Cunda, are not called 'expungings' in the discipline for an ariyan; these are called 'abidings that are peaceful' in the discipline for an ariyan.

Herein, Cunda, is expunging to be done by you, thinking: 'Others may be harmful; we, as to this, will not be harmful'—so is expunging to be done. 'Others may be those to make onslaught on creatures; we, as to this, will be those who are restrained from making onslaught on creatures'—so is expunging to be done. 'Others may be takers of what is not given; we, as to this, will be restrained from taking what is not given'—so is expunging to be done. 'Others may be non-Brahma-farers; we, as to this will be Brahma-farers'[3]—so is expunging to be done. 'Others may be

---

[1] See *Vism.* Ch. X.

[2] *santā ete vihārā . . . vuccanti.* *MA.* i. 186 explains *santa* by *nibbuta* and *sukha*, quenched and easeful.

[3] *abrahmacārī* follow a non-brahma, a low inferior *dhamma* . . . the *brahma-*

speakers of lies; we, as to this, will be restrained from lying speech '—so is expunging to be done. ' Others may be of harsh speech . . . of rough speech . . . of frivolous speech; we, as to this, will be restrained from harsh speech . . . from rough speech . . . from frivolous speech '—so is expunging to be done. ' Others may be covetous; we, as to this, will be non-covetous '—so is expunging to be done. ' Others may be corrupt in mind; we, as to this, will be incorrupt in mind.' . . . ' Others may be of wrong view; we, as to this, will be of perfect view '—so is expunging to be done. ' Others may be of wrong thoughts; we, as to this, will be of perfect thoughts.' . . . ' Others may be of wrong speech . . . of wrong activity . . . of a wrong way of living . . . of wrong endeavour . . . of wrong mindfulness . . . of wrong concentration . . . of wrong knowledge . . . of wrong freedom; we as to this, will be of perfect speech . . . of perfect freedom '—so is expunging to be done. ' Others may be encompassed by sloth and torpor; we, as to this, will be without sloth and torpor.' . . . ' Others may be puffed up; we, as to this, will not be puffed up.' . . . ' Others may be doubtful; we, as to this, will be crossed over doubt.' . . . ' Others may be wrathful; we, as to this, will be without wrath.' . . . ' Others may be rancorous; we, as to this, will not be rancorous.' . . . [**43**] ' Others may be harsh; we, as to this, will not be harsh.' . . . ' Others may be spiteful . . . without spite.' . . . ' Others may be envious . . . without envy.' . . . ' Others may be grudging . . . not grudging.' . . . ' Others may be treacherous . . . not treacherous.' . . . ' Others may be deceitful . . . not deceitful.' . . . ' Others may be stubborn . . . not stubborn.' . . . ' Others may be proud . . . not proud.' . . . ' Others may be difficult to speak to;[1] we, as to this, will be easy to speak to.' . . . ' Others may be friends of those who are evil[2]; we, as to this, will be friends of those who are lovely.'[3] . . . ' Others may be indolent; we, as to this, will be diligent.' . . . ' Others may be lacking in faith;[4] we, as to this, will be of faith.' . . . ' Others may be shameless;[4] we, as to this, will feel shame.' . . . ' Others may be reckless;[4]

---

cāri follow along the course to Brahman, the best (or, as this could be translated, they follow along the highest, *brahman*, the best course). It also means chastity; see *MA*. i. 188. The *Sallekhasutta* is, at *DA*. 178, given as an example of a Discourse where *brahmacariya* is defined as *methuna-virati*.

[1] See *Vin*. iii. 178, and *B.D*. i. 310, *n*. 1; also *M*. i. 95.

[2] *MA*. i. 189 adduces Devadatta as an example.

[3] *MA*. i. 189 cites Buddhas and those like Sāriputta.

[4] These five terms form a series at *Vin*. i. 63. See *B.D*. iv. 82.

we, as to this, will be cautious.' . . . 'Others may be those who have heard little . . . heard much.' . . . 'Others may be lazy;[1] we, as to this, will be of stirred up energy.' . . . 'Others may be of muddled mindfulness;[1] we, as to this, will be those with mindfulness set up before us.' . . . 'Others may be weak in wisdom; we, as to this, will be endowed with wisdom'—so is expunging to be done. 'Others may seize the temporal, grasping it tightly, not letting go of it easily;[2] we, as to this, will not seize the temporal, not grasping it tightly, letting go of it easily'—so is expunging to be done.

Now I, Cunda, say that the arising of thought is very helpful in regard to skilled states (of mind), not to speak of gesture and speech that are in conformity (with thought). Therefore, Cunda, the thought should arise: 'Others may be harmful; we, as to this, will not be harmful.' The thought should arise; 'Others may be those who make onslaught on creatures; we, as to this, will be those who are restrained from making onslaught on creatures. . . . Others may seize the temporal . . . we, as to this, will not seize the temporal, not grasping it tightly, letting go of it easily.'

Cunda, like an uneven road although there may be another even road for going by; and, Cunda, like an uneven ford although there may be another even ford for going by; [**44**] even so, Cunda, there is non-harming for a harmful individual to go by; there is restraint from onslaught on creatures for an individual to go by who makes onslaught on creatures; there is restraint from taking what is not given for an individual to go by who is a taker of what is not given; there is the Brahma-faring to go by for a non-Brahma-farer; there is restraint from lying speech . . . from harsh speech . . . from rough speech . . . from frivolous speech . . . there is non-coveting . . . incorruption of mind . . . perfect view . . . perfect thought . . . perfect speech . . . perfect activity . . . perfect way of living . . . perfect endeavour . . . perfect mindfulness . . . perfect concentration . . . perfect knowledge . . . perfect freedom . . . being without sloth and torpor . . . not being puffed up . . . being crossed over doubt . . . being without wrath . . . non-rancour . . . non-disparagement . . . non-spite . . . non-jealousy . . . non-miserliness . . . non-treachery . . . non-deceit . . . non-stubbornness . . . non-pride . . . ease of being spoken to . . . friendship with those who are lovely . . . diligence . . . faith . . . shame . . . caution . . . having heard much . . . stirred up

---

[1] These five terms form a series at *Vin.* i. 63. See *B.D.* iv. 82.

[2] As at *M.* i. 96, ii. 246; *A.* iii. 335, v. 150; *Vin.* ii. 89; *D.* iii. 48, 247.

energy . . . mindfulness before one . . . endowment with wisdom . . . there is not seizing the temporal, not grasping it tightly, letting it go easily for the individual to go by who seizes the temporal, grasps it tightly, letting go of it with difficulty.

Cunda, as every unskilled state (of mind) leads downwards, as every skilled state (of mind) leads upwards, even so, Cunda, does non-harming come to be a higher state for an individual who is harmful, does restraint from onslaught on creatures come to be a higher state for the individual who makes onslaught on creatures . . . does not [**45**], seizing the temporal, not grasping it tightly, letting go of it easily come to be a higher state for the individual who seizes the temporal, grasps it tightly, letting go of it with difficulty.

This situation does not occur, Cunda, when one sunk into mud will by himself pull out another who is sunk into mud. But this situation occurs, Cunda, when one not sunk into mud will by himself pull out another who is sunk into mud.

This situation does not occur, Cunda, when one who is not tamed, not trained, not utterly quenched,[1] will by himself tame, train, make another utterly quenched. But this situation occurs, Cunda, when one who is tamed, trained, utterly quenched, will by himself tame, train, make another utterly quenched. Even so, Cunda, there is non-harming by means of utter quenching for the individual who is harmful, there is restraint from onslaught on creatures by means of utter quenching for the individual who makes onslaught on creatures . . . there is [**46**] endowment with wisdom by means of utter quenching for an individual of weak wisdom, there is not seizing the temporal, not grasping it tightly, ease in letting go of it through utter burning up for the individual who seizes the temporal, grasping it tightly, letting go of it with difficulty.

In this manner, Cunda, is taught by me the disquisition on expunging, is taught the disquisition on the uprising of thought, is taught the disquisition on going by, is taught the disquisition on upwards, is taught the disquisition on utter quenching. Whatever, Cunda, is to be done from compassion by a teacher seeking the welfare of his disciples, that has been done by me out of compassion for you. These, Cunda, are the roots of trees,[2] these are empty

---

[1] *aparinibbuto*, not utterly quenched, or burnt out, as to the *kilesas*, *A*. i. 194.

[2] *MA*. i. 195, lodgings at the roots of trees.

places.[1] Meditate, Cunda; do not be slothful; be not remorseful later. This is our instruction to you."[2]

Thus spoke the Lord. Delighted, the venerable Cunda rejoiced in what the Lord had said.

Discourse on Expunging:
the Eighth

9. DISCOURSE ON PERFECT VIEW

(Sammādiṭṭhisutta)[3]

THUS have I heard: At one time the Lord was staying near Sāvatthī in the Jeta Grove in Anāthapiṇḍika's monastery. There the venerable Sāriputta addressed the monks, saying: "Monks." "Your reverence," these monks answered the venerable Sāriputta in assent. Then the venerable Sāriputta spoke thus:

"Your reverences, it is said, 'Perfect view,[4] perfect view.' To what extent indeed, your reverences, does a disciple of the ariyans come to be of perfect view, one whose view is upright, one who is possessed of unwavering confidence in *dhamma*, who is come into this true *dhamma*?"

"From afar, your reverence, would we come into the venerable Sāriputta's presence to learn the meaning of this utterance. It were good if the meaning of this utterance were to be made clear by[5] the venerable Sāriputta himself; the monks, having heard it from the venerable Sāriputta, will bear it in mind."

---

[1] *Ibid.*, removed from people.

[2] That is, to meditate and not to be slothful, *MA*. i. 196. This exhortation is fairly frequent throughout the Piṭakas, *e.g.* at *M*. i. 118. *Cf:* the "cultivator of empty places" at *M*. i. 33.

[3] Translated with the Comy. into English by the Bhikkhu Soma: *Right Understanding: Discourse and Commentary*, Buddha Sāhitya Sabhā, Colombo, 1946.

[4] Right, or perfect, understanding, or view, is twofold: worldly and ultra-worldly. Three kinds of people may have it: the worldling, the learner and the adept. The worldling may be either outside the Buddha's dispensation or within it.

[5] *paṭibhātu*, let it occur to.

"Very well, your reverences, listen and attend carefully and I will speak."

"Yes, your reverence," these monks answered the venerable Sāriputta in assent. The venerable Sāriputta spoke thus:

"When a disciple of the ariyans comprehends unskill and unskill's root, and comprehends skill and skill's root, [**47**] to this extent, your reverences, does a disciple of the ariyans come to be of perfect view, one whose view is upright, who is possessed of unwavering confidence in *dhamma*, one who has come into this true *dhamma*.

And what, your reverences, is unskill? what is unskill's root? what is skill? what is skill's root?

Onslaught on creatures, your reverences, is unskill, taking what is not given is unskill, sexual misconduct is unskill, lying speech is unskill, slanderous speech is unskill, harsh speech is unskill, gossip is unskill, covetise is unskill, wrath is unskill, wrong view is unskill. This, your reverences, is called unskill.

And what, your reverences, is unskill's root? Greed is unskill's root, hatred is unskill's root, confusion is unskill's root. This, your reverences, is called unskill's root.

And what, your reverences, is skill? Restraint from onslaught on creatures is skill, restraint from taking what is not given is skill, restraint from sexual misconduct is skill, restraint from lying speech is skill, restraint from slanderous speech is skill, restraint from harsh speech is skill, restraint from gossip is skill, non-covetise is skill, non-wrath is skill, perfect view is skill. This, your reverences, is called skill.

And what, your reverences, is skill's root? Non-greed is skill's root, non-hatred is skill's root, non-confusion is skill's root. This, your reverences, is called skill's root.

When, your reverences, a disciple of the ariyans comprehends unskill thus, comprehends unskill's root thus, comprehends skill thus, comprehends skill's root thus, he, having got rid of all addiction to attachment,[1] having dispelled addiction to shunning,[1] having abolished addiction to the latent view 'I am,' having got rid of ignorance, having made knowledge arise, is here-now an end-maker of anguish. To this extent also, your reverences, does a disciple of the ariyans come to be of perfect view, one whose view is upright, one who is possessed of unwavering confidence in *dhamma*, one who has come into this true *dhamma*."

---

[1] *Cf. S.* iv. 205.

Saying, "Good, your reverence," these monks, having rejoiced in what the venerable Sāriputta had said, having approved of it, asked the venerable Sāriputta a further question: "Might there be, your reverence, also another method by which a disciple of the ariyans comes to be of perfect view, one whose view is upright, one who has unwavering confidence in *dhamma*, one who has come into this true *dhamma* ?"

"There might be, your reverences. When, your reverences, a disciple of the ariyans comprehends sustenance[1] and comprehends the uprising of sustenance and comprehends the stopping of sustenance and comprehends the course leading to the stopping of sustenance, to this extent also, your reverences, does a disciple of the ariyans come to be of perfect view . . . who has come into [**48**] this true *dhamma*.

And what, your reverences, is sustenance, what the uprising of sustenance, what the stopping of sustenance, what the course leading to the stopping of sustenance ? Your reverences, there are these four[2] (kinds of) sustenance for the stability of creatures who have come to be or for the assistance of those who are seeking to be. What are the four ? Material food, coarse or fine; (sense-) impingement is the second; volition is the third; consciousness[3] is the fourth.

From the uprising of craving is the uprising of sustenance, from the stopping of craving is the stopping of sustenance; the course leading to the stopping of sustenance is this ariyan eightfold Way itself, that is to say: perfect view, perfect thought, perfect speech, perfect action, perfect way of living, perfect endeavour, perfect mindfulness, perfect concentration. When a disciple of the ariyans comprehends sustenance thus, comprehends the uprising of sustenance thus, comprehends the stopping of sustenance thus, comprehends the course leading to the stopping of sustenance thus, he, having got rid of all addiction to attachment, having dispelled addiction to shunning, having abolished addiction to the latent view 'I am,' having got rid of ignorance, having made knowledge arise, is here-now an end-maker of anguish. To this extent, also, your reverences, does a disciple of the ariyans come

---

[1] *āhāra*, sustenance or nutriment, is a condition, *paccaya*, that brings, *āharati*, its own fruit.

[2] *Cf. M.* i. 261; *S.* ii. 11; *D.* iii. 228, 276; *Dhs.* 71-73 and see notes at *K.S.* ii. 8.

[3] *viññāṇa; MA.* i. 209 says "whatever is mind (*citta*)."

to be of perfect view, one whose view is upright, one who is possessed of unwavering confidence in *dhamma*, one who has come into this true *dhamma*."

Saying, "Good, your reverence," these monks, having rejoiced in what the venerable Sāriputta had said, having approved of it, asked the venerable Sāriputta a further question: "Might there be, your reverence, also another method by which a disciple of the ariyans comes to be of perfect view . . . one who has come into this true *dhamma* ?"

"There might be, your reverences. When, your reverences, a disciple of the ariyans comprehends anguish, its uprising, its stopping, and the course leading to its stopping, to this extent also, your reverences, does a disciple of the ariyans come to be of perfect view . . . one who has come into this true *dhamma*.

And what, your reverences, is anguish,[1] what its uprising, what its stopping, what the course leading to its stopping ? Birth is anguish, and old age is anguish, and disease is anguish, and dying is anguish, and grief, lamentation, suffering, tribulation and despair are anguish; and if one does not get what one wants, that too is anguish; in short, the five groups of grasping are anguish. This, your reverences, is called anguish.

And what, your reverences, is the uprising of anguish ? That craving which is connected with again-becoming, accompanied by delight and attachment, finding delight in this and that, namely the craving for sense-pleasures, [**49**] the craving for becoming,[2] the craving for annihilation[3]—this, your reverences, is called the origin of anguish.

And what, your reverences, is the stopping of anguish ? Whatever is the stopping, with no attachment remaining, of that selfsame craving, the giving up of it, the renunciation of it, the release from it, the doing away with it—this, your reverences, is called the stopping of anguish.

And what, your reverences, is the course leading to the stopping of anguish ? The course leading to the stopping of anguish is this ariyan eightfold Way itself, that is to say: perfect view . . . perfect concentration. When, your reverences, the disciple of the ariyans comprehends anguish thus, comprehends its origin thus, compre-

---

[1] *Cf. Vin.* i. 10; *D.* ii. 305; *M.* iii. 249.

[2] Connected with the view of Eternalism.

[3] *vibhava*, de-becoming. *DA.* iii. 800 says it is a synonym for the attachment connected with the view of Annihilationism.

hends its stopping thus, comprehends the course leading to its stopping thus, he, having got rid of all addiction to attachment, having dispelled addiction to shunning . . . is here-now an end-maker of anguish. To this extent also, your reverences, does a disciple of the ariyans come to be . . . one who has come into this true *dhamma*."

Saying, "Good, your reverence," these monks . . . asked the venerable Sāriputta a further question: "Might there be, your reverence, also another method by which a disciple of the ariyans comes to be perfect view . . . one who has come into this true *dhamma* ?"

"There might be, your reverences. When, your reverences, a disciple of the ariyans comprehends old age and dying . . . the course leading to the stopping of old age and dying, to this extent also, your reverences, does a disciple of the ariyans come to be of perfect view . . . one who has come into this true *dhamma*.

And what, your reverences, is old age and dying,[1] what the origin of old age and dying, what the stopping of old age and dying, what the course leading to the stopping of old age and dying ? Whatever of various beings in various groups of beings is old age, decrepitude, broken teeth, greying hair, wrinkly skin, the dwindling of the life-span, the collapse of the (sense-)organs, this, your reverences, is called old age. Whatever is the falling away, the passing away, the breaking up, the disappearance, the death and dying,[2] the action of time,[3] the breaking up of the groups (of grasping), the laying down of the body—this, your reverences, is called dying. Thus, your reverences, this ageing and this dying are called ageing-and-dying.

From the uprising of birth is the uprising of ageing-and-dying, from the stopping of birth is the stopping of ageing-and-dying; the course leading to the stopping of ageing-and-dying is this ariyan eightfold Way itself, that is to say perfect view . . . perfect concentration. When, your reverences, a disciple of the ariyans comprehends ageing-and-dying thus, its uprising and stopping, and the

---

[1] *Cf. S.* ii. 2; *D.* ii. 305; *M.* iii. 249.

[2] *maccumaraṇa.* *MA.* i. 216, "the dying called death."

[3] *kālakiriya.* *MA.* i. 216 *kālo nāma antiko,* time is an ender, whose action, *kiriya,* is the action of time. As far as here "dying" is explained in conventional terms, *MA.* i. 216-7, *DA.* iii. 798-9. But now it is to be explained in the real sense, *paramattha.* According to this it is the *khandhas* which are broken, not any being named So-and-so who dies.

course leading to its stopping thus, he, having got rid of all addiction to attachment, having dispelled addiction to shunning . . . is here-now an end-maker of anguish. To this extent also, your reverences, does a disciple of the ariyans come to be . . . one who has come into this true *dhamma.*"

Saying, "Good, your reverence," these monks . . . asked the venerable Sāriputta a further question: "Might there be, your reverence . . . ?"

[50] "There might be, your reverences. When, your reverences, a disciple of the ariyans comprehends birth and its uprising and stopping and the course leading to its stopping, to this extent also, your reverences, does a disciple of the ariyans come to be of perfect view . . . one who has come into this true *dhamma.*

And what, your reverences, is birth, what its uprising, what its stopping, what the course leading to its stopping? Whatever is the conception,[1] the production,[2] the descent,[3] the coming forth[4] of various beings in various groups of beings, the appearance of the groups (of grasping), the acquiring of the sense-bases,[5] this, your reverences, is called birth.[6]

From the uprising of becoming[7] is the uprising of birth, from the stopping of becoming is the stopping of birth; the course leading to the stopping of birth is this ariyan eightfold Way itself—that is to say, perfect view . . . perfect concentration. When, your reverences, a disciple of the ariyans comprehends birth thus, comprehends the uprising of birth thus, comprehends the stopping of birth thus, comprehends the course leading to the stopping of birth thus, he,

---

[1] *jāti* may be birth or conception. *MA.* i. 217 says it is called *jāti* on account of the sense-organs not being complete.

[2] *sañjāti*, so called when the sense-organs are complete, *MA.* i. 217.

[3] *okkanti* refers to "birth" from eggs or from a womb. *MA.* i. 217 says "they take on reinstatement as if entering an egg-shell or a membranous sheath."

[4] *abhinibbatti*, so called referring to spontaneous generation and birth from moisture, *MA.* i. 217. Up to here the explanation has referred to what is *vohāra*, the common or conventional usage of the terms. But there is an explanation according to the higher sense (or philosophical truth, *paramattha*); and "of the groups" (*khandha*) means the taking up of one, four or five of the constituents of being, *vokārabhava* (see *Kvu.* 261; *Vbh.* 137; *SnA.* 19, 158; *KhpA.* 245). *Cf. DA.* iii. 797.

[5] *āyatana.*

[6] *Cf. S.* ii. 3; *M.* iii. 249; *D.* ii. 305; *Vbh.* 137.

[7] *MA.* i. 217 says "here the condition for birth should be known as *kammabhava*, karmical becoming." This is explained at *Vbh.* 137.

having got rid of all addiction to attachment . . . comes to be of perfect view . . . one who has come into this true *dhamma*."

Saying, "Good, your reverence," these monks . . . asked the venerable Sāriputta a further question: "Might there be, your reverence . . . ?"

"There might be, your reverences. When, your reverences, a disciple of the ariyans comprehends becoming and comprehends its uprising and its stopping and comprehends the course leading to its stopping, to this extent also, your reverences, does a disciple of the ariyans come to be of perfect view . . . one who has come into this true *dhamma*.

And what, your reverences, is becoming, what its uprising, what its stopping, what the course leading to its stopping? Your reverences, there are these three (kinds of) becoming: becoming as to sense-pleasures, becoming as to fine-materiality, becoming as to non-materiality.

From the uprising of grasping is the uprising of becoming, from the stopping of grasping is the stopping of becoming; the course leading to the stopping of becoming is this ariyan eightfold Way itself, that is to say: perfect view . . . perfect concentration. When, your reverences, a disciple of the ariyans comprehends becoming thus and its uprising and stopping and the course leading to its stopping thus, he, having got rid of all addiction to attachment . . . comes to be of perfect view . . . one who has come into this true *dhamma*."

Saying, "Good, your reverence," these monks . . . asked the venerable Sāriputta a further question: "Might there be, your reverence . . . ?"

"There might be, your reverences. When, your reverences, a disciple of the ariyans comprehends grasping and its uprising and its stopping and the course leading to its stopping, to this extent also, your reverences, does the disciple of the ariyans . . . come into this true *dhamma*.

And what, your reverences, is grasping, what its uprising, what its stopping, what the course leading to its stopping? There are, your reverences, these four [**51**] (kinds of) grasping: grasping after sense-pleasures,[1] grasping after view,[1] grasping after rites and customs,[1] grasping after the theory of 'self.'[2]

---

[1] *Cf. Dhs.* p. 212.

[2] *Cf. M.* i. 66; *D.* ii. 58, iii. 230; *S.* ii. 3; *Dhs.* p. 212. In explanation of *attavādupādāna*, grasping after the view of "self," *MA.* i. 219 says they talk about, they grasp (the) self. See also *attavāda* at *M.* i. 40 (Sutta 8).

From the uprising of craving is the uprising of grasping, from the stopping of craving is the stopping of grasping; the course leading to the stopping of grasping is this ariyan eightfold Way itself, that is to say, perfect view . . . perfect concentration. When, your reverences, a disciple of the ariyans comprehends grasping thus, its uprising, its stopping, the course leading to its stopping thus, he, having got rid of all addiction to attachment . . . comes to be of perfect view . . . one who has come into this true *dhamma*."

Saying, "Good, your reverence," these monks . . . asked the venerable Sāriputta a further question: "Might there be, your reverence . . . ?"

"There might be, your reverences. When an ariyan disciple comprehends craving and comprehends the uprising of craving and comprehends the stopping of craving and comprehends the course leading to the stopping of craving, to this extent also, your reverences, does the disciple of the ariyans . . . come into this true *dhamma*.

And what, your reverences, is craving, what its uprising, what the stopping of craving, what the course leading to its stopping? Your reverences, there are these six (kinds of) craving: craving for material shapes, craving for sounds, craving for smells, craving for flavours, craving for touches, craving for mental objects.[1]

From the uprising of feeling is the uprising of craving, from the stopping of feeling is the stopping of craving; the course leading to the stopping of craving is this ariyan eightfold Way itself, that is to say, perfect view . . . perfect concentration. When, your reverences, a disciple of the ariyans comprehends craving thus, comprehends its uprising, its stopping, the course leading to its stopping thus, he, getting rid of all addiction to attachment . . . comes to be of perfect view . . . one who has come into this true *dhamma*."

Saying, "Good, your reverence," these monks . . . asked the venerable Sāriputta a further question: "Might there be, your reverence . . . ?"

"There might be, your reverences. When, your reverences, a disciple of the ariyans comprehends feeling and its uprising and

---

[1] *Cf. S.* ii. 3. There are 108 modes of craving; craving is for sense-pleasures, becoming, annihilation (*vibhava*). These three, multiplied by the six kinds of sensory data, give eighteen. These eighteen may be of a subjective or an objective nature, so we get to thirty-six. These again may apply to past, future, present, thus we arrive at the 108; see *MA*. i. 219.

stopping and the course leading to its stopping, to this extent also, your reverences, does the disciple of the ariyans . . . come into this true *dhamma*.

And what, your reverences, is feeling, what the uprising of feeling, what the stopping of feeling, what the course leading to the stopping of feeling? There are, your reverences, these six classes of feeling: feeling arising from sensory impingement on the eye . . . on the ear . . . on the nose . . . on the tongue . . . on the body . . . on the mind.[1]

From the uprising of sensory impingement is the uprising of feeling, from the stopping of sensory impingement is the stopping of feeling; the course leading to the stopping of feeling is this ariyan eightfold Way itself, that is to say, perfect view . . . perfect concentration. [**52**] When, your reverences, the disciple of the ariyans comprehends feeling thus, its uprising, its stopping and the course leading to its stopping thus, he, having got rid of all addiction to attachment . . . comes to be of perfect view . . . one who has come into this true *dhamma*."

Saying, "Good, your reverence" . . . these monks . . . asked the venerable Sāriputta a further question: "Might there be, your reverence . . . ?"

"There might be, your reverences. When a disciple of the ariyans comprehends sensory impingement and its uprising and its stopping and the course leading to its stopping, to this extent also, your reverences, does the disciple of the ariyans . . . come into this true *dhamma*.

And what, your reverences, is sensory impingement, what its uprising, what its stopping, what the course leading to its stopping? Your reverences, there are these six classes of sensory impingement: sensory impingement on the eye . . . on the ear . . . on the nose . . . on the tongue . . . on the body . . . on the mind.[2]

From the uprising of the six bases of sense-impressions is the uprising of sensory impingement, from the stopping of the six bases of sense-impressions is the stopping of sensory impingement; this ariyan eightfold Way itself is the course leading to the stopping of sensory impingement, that is to say, perfect view . . . perfect concentration. When, your reverences, the disciple of the ariyans comprehends sensory impingement thus, comprehends its uprising, its stopping, and the course leading to its stopping thus, he, having

---

[1] *Cf. S.* ii. 3.

[2] *Cf. S.* ii. 3; *Vism.* 444-6.

got rid of all addiction to attachment . . . comes to be of perfect view . . . one who has come into this true *dhamma*."

Saying, "Good, your reverence," these monks . . . asked the venerable Sāriputta a further question: "Might there be, your reverence . . . ?"

"There might be, your reverences. When a disciple of the ariyans comprehends the six bases of sense-impressions and their uprising and stopping and comprehends the course leading to their stopping, to this extent also, your reverences, does the disciple of the ariyans . . . come into this true *dhamma*.

And what, your reverences, are the six bases of sense-impression, what their uprising, what their stopping, what the course leading to their stopping? Your reverences, there are these six bases: the basis for eye . . . for ear . . . for nose . . . for tongue . . . for body . . . for mind.

From the uprising of mind-and-matter[1] is the uprising of the six bases of sense-impression, from the stopping of mind-and-matter is the stopping of the six bases of sense-impression; the course leading to the stopping of the six bases of sense-impression is this ariyan eightfold Way itself, that is to say, perfect view . . . perfect concentration. When, your reverences, the disciple of the ariyans comprehends the six bases of sense-impressions thus, their uprising, their stopping, [**53**] the course leading to their stopping thus, he, getting rid of all addiction to attachment . . . comes to be of perfect view . . . one who has come into this true *dhamma*."

Saying, "Good, your reverence," these monks . . . asked the venerable Sāriputta a further question: "Might there be, your reverence . . . ?"

"There might be, your reverences. When a disciple of the ariyans comprehends mind-and-matter and comprehends the uprising of mind-and-matter and comprehends the stopping of mind-and-matter and comprehends the course leading to the stopping of mind-and-matter, to this extent also, your reverences, does the disciple of the ariyans . . . come into this true *dhamma*.

And what, your reverences, is mind-and-matter, what its uprising, its stopping, what the course leading to its stopping? Feeling, perception, volition, sensory impingement, reflectiveness,[2] this,

---

[1] *nāma-rūpa*, psycho-physicality. See *Vism.* 562-566.

[2] *MA.* i. 221 says that among the *khandhas* these last three form the *sankhāras*.

your reverences, is called mind. The four great elements[1] and the material shape derived from the four great elements, this, your reverences, is called matter. So, your reverences, this that is mind and this that is matter is called mind-and-matter.[2]

From the uprising of consciousness is the uprising of mind-and-matter, from the stopping of consciousness is the stopping of mind-and-matter; the course leading to the stopping of mind-and-matter is this ariyan eightfold Way itself, that is to say, perfect view . . . perfect concentration. When, your reverences, a disciple of the ariyans comprehends mind-and-matter thus, its uprising, its stopping, the course leading to its stopping thus, he, getting rid of all addiction to attachment . . . comes to be of perfect view . . . one who has come into this true *dhamma*."

Saying, "Good, your reverence," these monks . . . asked the venerable Sāriputta a further question: "Might there be, your reverence . . . ?"

"There might be, your reverences. When, your reverences, a disciple of the ariyans comprehends consciousness and comprehends the uprising of consciousness and comprehends the stopping of consciousness and comprehends the course leading to the stopping of consciousness, to this extent also, your reverences, does the disciple of the ariyans . . . come into this true *dhamma*.

And what, your reverences, is consciousness, what its uprising, what its stopping, what the course leading to its stopping? Your reverences, there are these six classes of consciousness: visual consciousness, auditory consciousness, olfactory consciousness, gustatory consciousness, bodily consciousness, mental consciousness.[3]

From the uprising of the formations[4] is the uprising of consciousness, from the stopping of the formations is the stopping of consciousness; the course leading to the stopping of consciousness is this ariyan eightfold Way itself, that is to say, perfect view . . . perfect concentration. When, your reverences, the disciple of the ariyans comprehends consciousness thus, its uprising, its stopping, the course leading to its stopping thus [**54**], he, having got rid of

---

[1] Extension, cohesion, heat and mobility. See *M. Sutta* 1, and *Vism.* 443.

[2] *Cf. S.* ii. 3-4.

[3] *Cf. S.* ii. 4; *Vism.* 545-58.

[4] *sankhāra*, potential energy, habitual, karmical, innate or reflex tendencies; and here seeming to mean unskilled and skilled (types of) deeds: eight skilled in regard to the body, twelve unskilled=twenty; and twenty in regard to speech, twenty-nine in regard to thought.

all addiction to attachment . . . comes to be of perfect view . . . one who has come into this true *dhamma*."

Saying, "Good, your reverence," these monks . . . asked the venerable Sāriputta a further question: "Might there be, your reverence . . . ?"

"There might be, your reverences. When, your reverences, a disciple of the ariyans comprehends the formations and comprehends the uprising of the formations and comprehends the stopping of the formations and comprehends the course leading to the stopping of the formations, to this extent also, your reverences, does the disciple of the ariyans . . . come into this true *dhamma*.

And what, your reverences, are the formations, what their uprising, their stopping, the course leading to their stopping? Your reverences, there are these three (kinds of) formations: activity of the body, activity of speech, activity of mind.

From the uprising of ignorance is the uprising of the formations, from the stopping of ignorance is the stopping of the formations; the course leading to the stopping of the formations is this ariyan eightfold Way itself, that is to say, perfect view . . . perfect concentration. When, your reverences, the disciple of the ariyans comprehends the formations thus, their uprising, their stopping, the course leading to their stopping thus, he, having got rid of all addiction to attachment . . . comes to be of perfect view . . . one who has come into this true *dhamma*."

Saying, "Good, your reverence," these monks . . . asked the venerable Sāriputta a further question: "Might there be, your reverence . . . ?"

"There might be, your reverences. When, your reverences, a disciple of the ariyans comprehends ignorance and comprehends the uprising of ignorance and comprehends the stopping of ignorance and comprehends the course leading to the stopping of ignorance, to this extent also, your reverences, does the disciple of the ariyans . . . come into this true *dhamma*.

And what, your reverences, is ignorance, what its uprising, what its stopping, what the course leading to its stopping? Whatever, your reverences, is not-knowing[1] in regard to anguish, not-knowing in regard to the uprising of anguish, not-knowing in regard to the stopping of anguish, not-knowing in regard to the course

[1] *aññāṇa*, nescience; it is folly or confusion, *moha*. *MA*. i. 223.

leading to the stopping of anguish, this, your reverences, is called ignorance.[1]

From the uprising of the cankers[2] is the uprising of ignorance, from the stopping of the cankers is the stopping of ignorance; the course leading to the stopping of the cankers is this ariyan eightfold Way itself, that is to say, perfect view . . . perfect concentration. When, your reverences, the disciple of the ariyans comprehends ignorance thus, its uprising, its stopping, the course leading to its stopping thus, he, getting rid of all addiction to attachment . . . comes to be of perfect view . . . one who has come into this true *dhamma*."

Saying, "Good, your reverence," these monks, having rejoiced in what the venerable Sāriputta had said, having approved of it, asked the venerable Sāriputta a further question: "Might there be, your reverence, another [**55**] method also by which a disciple of the ariyans comes to be of perfect view, one whose view is upright, who is possessed of unwavering confidence in *dhamma*, one who has come into this true *dhamma* ?"

"There might be, your reverences. When, your reverences, a disciple of the ariyans comprehends the cankers and comprehends the uprising of the cankers and comprehends the stopping of the cankers and comprehends the course leading to the stopping of the cankers, to this extent, your reverences, does the disciple of the ariyans come to be of perfect view, one whose view is upright, one who is possessed of unwavering confidence in *dhamma*, one who has come into this true *dhamma*.

And what, your reverences, is a canker, what the uprising of a canker, what the stopping of a canker, what the course leading to the stopping of a canker ? Your reverences, there are these

---

[1] *Cf. S.* ii. 4.

[2] *MA*. i. 223 *f*. says: "Here the cankers of sense-pleasures and becoming are, through co-nascence, the causes (or conditions) of ignorance." And again, "Ignorance is the cause, through co-nascence, of the cankers of sense-pleasures and becoming . . . This exposition of the cankers is spoken of as an explanation of the conditions of that chief ignorance which is among the clauses of 'dependent origination.' Through the exposition made known thus, the fact that the end of samsāric existence is inconceivable is proved. How? From the arising of ignorance is the arising of the cankers; from the arising of the cankers is the arising of ignorance. Having made the cankers the cause of ignorance and ignorance the cause of the cankers, the earliest point of ignorance is not perceptible, therefore the fact that the end of samsāric existence is inconceivable is proved."

three cankers: the canker of sense-pleasures, the canker of becoming, the canker of ignorance.

From the uprising of ignorance is the uprising of the cankers, from the stopping of ignorance is the stopping of the cankers; the course leading to the stopping of the cankers is this ariyan eightfold Way itself, that is to say, perfect view, perfect thought, perfect speech, perfect action, perfect way of living, perfect endeavour, perfect mindfulness, perfect concentration. When the disciple of the ariyans comprehends the cankers thus, comprehends the uprising of the cankers thus, comprehends the stopping of the cankers thus, comprehends the course leading to the stopping of the cankers thus, he, having got rid of all addiction to attachment, having dispelled addiction to shunning, having abolished addiction to the latent view 'I am,' having got rid of ignorance, having made knowledge arise, is here-now an end-maker of anguish. To this extent also, your reverences, does a disciple of the ariyans come to be of perfect view, one whose view is upright, one who is possessed of unwavering confidence in *dhamma*, one who has come into this true *dhamma*."[1]

Thus spoke the venerable Sāriputta. Delighted, these monks rejoiced in what the venerable Sāriputta had said.

Discourse on Perfect View:
the Ninth

10. DISCOURSE ON THE APPLICATIONS OF MINDFULNESS

(Satipaṭṭhānasutta)[2]

THUS have I heard: At one time the Lord was staying among the Kuru people in a township of the Kurus called Kammāssadhamma. While he was there, the Lord addressed the monks, saying: "Monks."

---

[1] *MA*. i. 224 says that only in this Discourse, even in the whole great fivefold classified collection of the Buddha's words, are the four truths proclaimed thirty-two times and arahantship thirty-two times.

[2] Translated by the Bhikkhu Soma, *The Way of Mindfulness*, 2nd edn., Colombo, 1949. *Cf. D.* Sta. XXII; and *Ānāpāna-saṃyutta* (*S.* v. 311 *ff.*); also *M*. iii. 82 *f.*

"Revered one," these monks answered the Lord in assent. The Lord spoke thus:

"There is this one way,[1] monks, for the purification of beings, [**56**] for the overcoming of sorrows and griefs, for the going down of sufferings and miseries, for winning the right path,[2] for realising nibbāna,[3] that is to say, the four applications[4] of mindfulness. What are the four?

Herein, monks, a monk fares along[5] contemplating the body in the body, ardent, clearly conscious (of it), mindful (of it) so as to control the covetousness and dejection in the world;[6] he fares along contemplating the feelings[7] in the feelings, ardent, clearly conscious (of them), mindful (of them) so as to control the covetousness and dejection in the world; he fares along contemplating the mind[8] in the mind, ardent, clearly conscious (of it), mindful (of it) so as to control the covetousness and dejection in the world; he fares along contemplating the mental objects in the mental objects, ardent, clearly conscious (of them), mindful (of them) so as to control the covetousness and dejection in the world.

And how, monks, does a monk fare along contemplating the body in the body? Herein,[9] monks, a monk who is forest-gone or gone to the root of a tree or gone to an empty place, sits down cross-legged, holding his back erect, arousing mindfulness in front of him. Mindful he breathes in, mindful he breathes out. Whether he is breathing in a long (breath) he comprehends, 'I am breathing in

---

[1] Quoted at *Kvu.* 158.

[2] *ñāya* is explained at *MA.* i. 236 as *ariyo atthaṅgiko maggo*; and it says that when the mundane way of the applications of mindfulness is developed it leads on to reaching the ultramundane way, and gradually effects the realisation of nibbāna.

[3] *MA.* i. 236 says that this is deathlessness which has got the name of nibbāna by reason of the absence in it of the lust (*vāna*, sewing or weaving) called craving. It further says that it is seen by each for himself (individually).

[4] *paṭṭhāna* is application or arousing.

[5] *MA.* i. 243 explains *viharati* by *iriyati*. I retain the verb of motion rather than the verb of rest so as to stress the symbolism of the Way and the endeavour needed to travel along it. *Cf. Vbh.* 252; *Nd.* II. 237.

[6] *MA.* i. 243-4 explains *loke* by *kāye*, and quotes *Vbh.* 195 in support. See also *S.* iv. 95, 157, where the "world" and the "sea" are taken to stand for the sense-organs.

[7] The three feelings; of pleasure, pain and those that are neutral.

[8] *citta* is mind or thought or consciousness. Here called *lokiya*, worldly. of the world, at *MA.* i. 245, as are also *dhammā*, mental objects.

[9] Following as at *M.* i. 425; *A.* v. 111.

a long (breath)'; or whether he is breathing out a long (breath) he comprehends, 'I am breathing out a long (breath)'; or whether he is breathing in a short (breath) he comprehends, 'I am breathing in a short (breath)'; or whether he is breathing out a short (breath) he comprehends, 'I am breathing out a short (breath).' He trains himself, thinking: 'I shall breathe in experiencing the whole body.' He trains himself, thinking: 'I shall breathe out experiencing the whole body.' He trains himself, thinking: 'I shall breathe in tranquillising the activity of the body.' He trains himself, thinking: 'I shall breathe out tranquillising the activity of the body.'[1]

Monks, it is like a clever turner or turner's apprentice who, making a long (turn), comprehends, 'I am making a long (turn)'; or when making a short (turn) comprehends, 'I am making a short (turn).' Even so, monks, does a monk who is breathing in a long (breath) comprehend, 'I am breathing in a long (breath);' . . . or when breathing out a short (breath) comprehends, 'I am breathing out a short (breath)'. He trains himself with the thought, 'I shall breathe in experiencing the whole body . . . I shall breathe out tranquillising the activity of the body.'

In this way, monks, he fares along contemplating the body in the body internally,[2] or he fares along contemplating the body in the body externally,[3] or he fares along contemplating the body in the body internally and externally.[4] Or he fares along contemplating origination-things in the body, or he fares along contemplating dissolution-things in the body, or he fares along contemplating origination-and-dissolution things in the body.[5] Or, thinking, 'There is the body,' his mindfulness is established precisely to the extent necessary just for knowledge, just for remembrance, and he fares along independently of[6] and not grasping anything in the world.[7] It is thus too, monks, that a monk fares along contemplating the body in the body.

And again, monks, a monk, when he is walking, comprehends, 'I am walking'; or when he is standing still, comprehends, 'I am

[1] And so the four *jhānas* arise. Or, he takes up in-breathing and out-breathing after he has developed the *jhānas*, or factors in the *jhānas*, *MA*. i. 249.

[2] His own body. [3] Someone else's body.

[4] Now internally, now externally, but not both together.

[5] Separately, not together.

[6] *anissito*—that is, not leaning on, but being independent of craving and view, *MA*. i. 250.

[7] *I.e.* not grasping any of the five *khandhas*, and not holding that "This is my self or belonging to self."

standing still'; or when he is sitting down, [**57**] comprehends, 'I am sitting down'; or when he is lying down, comprehends, 'I am lying down.' So that however his body is disposed he comprehends that it is like that. Thus he fares along contemplating the body in the body internally, or he fares along contemplating the body in the body externally, or he fares along contemplating the body in the body internally and externally. Or he fares along contemplating origination-things in the body, or he fares along contemplating dissolution-things in the body, or he fares along contemplating origination-and-dissolution things in the body. Or, thinking, 'There is the body,' his mindfulness is established precisely to the extent necessary just for knowledge, just for remembrance, and he fares along independently of and not grasping anything in the world. It is thus too, monks, that a monk fares along contemplating the body in the body.

And again, monks, a monk, when he is setting out or returning[1] is one acting in a clearly conscious way; when he is looking in front or looking around . . . when he has bent in or stretched out (his arm) . . . when he is carrying his outer cloak, bowl and robe . . . when he is eating, drinking, chewing, tasting . . . when he is obeying the calls of nature . . . when he is walking, standing, sitting, asleep, awake, talking, silent, he is one acting in a clearly conscious way. Thus he fares along contemplating the body in the body internally, or he fares along contemplating the body in the body externally, or he fares along contemplating the body in the body internally and externally. Or he fares along contemplating origination-things in the body, or he fares along contemplating dissolution-things in the body, or he fares along contemplating origination-and-dissolution things in the body. Or, thinking, 'There is the body,' his mindfulness is established precisely to the extent necessary just for knowledge, just for remembrance, and he fares along independently of and not grasping anything in the world. It is thus too, monks, that a monk fares along contemplating the body in the body.

And again, monks, a monk reflects on precisely this body itself, encased in skin and full of various impurities, from the soles of the feet up and from the crown of the head down, that: 'There is connected with this body hair of the head, hair of the body, nails, teeth, skin, flesh, sinews, bones, marrow, kidneys, heart, liver,

---

[1] *Cf. M.*i. 274.

membranes, spleen, lungs, intestines, mesentary, stomach, excrement, bile, phlegm, pus, blood, sweat, fat, tears, serum, saliva, mucus, synovic fluid, urine.'[1]

Monks, it is like a double-mouthed provision bag[2] that is full of various kinds of grain such as hill-paddy, paddy, kidney beans, peas, sesamum, rice; and a keen-eyed man, pouring them out, were to reflect: 'That's hill-paddy, that's paddy, that's kidney beans, that's peas, that's sesamum, that's rice.' Even so, monks, does a monk reflect on precisely this body itself, encased in skin and full of various impurities, from the soles of the feet up and from the crown of the head down, that: 'There is connected with this body hair of the head . . . urine.' Thus he fares along contemplating the body in the body internally . . . and he fares along independently of and not grasping anything in the world. It is thus too, monks, that a monk fares along contemplating the body in the body.

And again, monks, a monk reflects on this body according to how it is placed or disposed[3] in respect of the elements,[4] thinking: 'In this body there is the element of extension, the element of cohesion, the element of heat, the element of motion.' **[58]** Monks, even as a skilled cattle-butcher, or his apprentice, having slaughtered a cow, might sit displaying its carcase at a cross-roads, even so, monks, does a monk reflect on this body itself according to how it is placed or disposed in respect of the elements, thinking: 'In this body there is the element of extension, the element of cohesion, the element of heat, the element of motion.' Thus he fares along contemplating the body in the body internally . . . and he fares along independently of and not grasping anything in the world. It is thus too, monks, that a monk fares along contemplating the body in the body.

And again, monks, as a monk might see a body thrown aside in a cemetery, dead for one day or for two days or for three days, swollen, discoloured, decomposing; he focuses on this body itself,[5] thinking: 'This body, too, is of a similar nature, a similar constitution, it has not got past that (state of things).' It is in this way that a monk fares along . . . not grasping anything in the

---

1 As at *A.* iii. 323, v. 109; *D.* ii. 293.

2 *mutoḷī*, as at *M.* iii. 90; *D.* ii 293. See *Dial.* ii. 330, "sample-bag." This simile is not found at *A.* iii. 323.

3 *yathāpaṇihita*, controlled or directed.

4 *dhātu*, called by the Bhikkhu Soma "modes of materiality."

5 *I.e.* on his own body.

world. It is thus too, monks, that a monk fares along contemplating the body in the body.

And again, monks, a monk might see a body thrown aside in a cemetery, and being devoured by crows or ravens or vultures or wild dogs or jackals or by various small creatures; he focuses on this body itself, thinking: 'This body too is of a similar nature, a similar constitution, it has not got past that (state of things).' It is in this way that a monk fares along . . . not grasping anything in the world. It is thus too, monks, that a monk fares along contemplating the body in the body.

And again, monks, as a monk might see a body thrown aside in a cemetery, a skeleton[1] with (some) flesh and blood, sinew-bound; . . . or fleshless but blood-bespattered, sinew-bound; . . . or without flesh and blood, sinew-bound; . . . or the bones scattered here and there, no longer held together: here a bone of the hand, there a foot-bone, here a leg-bone, there a rib, here a hip-bone, there a back-bone, here the skull; he focuses on this body itself. . . . It is in this way that a monk fares along . . . not grasping anything in the world. It is thus too, monks, that a monk fares along contemplating the body in the body.

And again, monks, a monk might see a body thrown aside in a cemetery: the bones white and something like sea-shells . . . a heap of dried up bones more than a year old . . . the bones gone rotten and reduced to powder; [**59**] he focuses on this body itself, thinking: 'This body, too, is of a similar nature, a similar constitution, it has not got past that (state of things).' Thus he fares along contemplating the body in the body internally, or he fares along contemplating the body in the body externally, or he fares along contemplating the body in the body internally and externally. Or he fares along contemplating origination-things in the body, or he fares along contemplating dissolution-things in the body, or he fares along contemplating origination-dissolution-things in the body. Or, thinking, 'There is the body,' his mindfulness is established precisely to the extent necessary just for knowledge, just for remembrance, and he fares along independently of and not grasping anything in the world. It is thus too, monks, that a monk fares along contemplating the body in the body.

And how, monks, does a monk fare along contemplating the feelings in the feelings? Herein, monks, while he is experiencing

---

[1] As at *M*. i. 89, *A*. iii. 324.

a pleasant feeling he comprehends: 'I am experiencing a pleasant feeling;'[1] while he is experiencing a painful feeling he comprehends, 'I am experiencing a painful feeling'; while he is experiencing a feeling that is neither painful nor pleasant he comprehends: 'I am experiencing a feeling that is neither painful nor pleasant.' While he is experiencing a pleasant feeling in regard to material things[2] . . . in regard to non-material things he comprehends, 'I am experiencing a pleasant feeling in regard to non-material things'; while he is experiencing a painful feeling in regard to material things . . . in regard to non-material things he comprehends, 'I am experiencing a painful feeling in regard to non-material things'; while he is experiencing a feeling that is neither painful nor pleasant in regard to material things . . . in regard to non-material things he comprehends, 'I am experiencing a feeling that is neither painful nor pleasant in regard to non-material things.' Thus he fares along contemplating the feelings in the feelings internally, or he fares along contemplating the feelings in the feelings externally, or he fares along contemplating the feelings in the feelings internally and externally. Or he fares along contemplating origination-things in the feelings, or he fares along contemplating dissolution-things in the feelings, or he fares along contemplating origination-dissolution-things in the feelings. Or, thinking, 'There is feeling,' his mindfulness is established precisely to the extent necessary just for knowledge, just for remembrance, and he fares along independently of and not grasping anything in the world. It is thus, monks, that a monk fares along contemplating feelings in the feelings.

And how, monks, does a monk fare along contemplating mind in the mind? Herein, monks, a monk knows intuitively[3] the mind with attachment as a mind with attachment; he knows intuitively the mind without attachment as a mind without attachment . . . the mind with hatred as a mind with hatred . . . the mind without hatred as a mind without hatred . . . the mind with confusion as a mind with confusion . . . the mind without confusion as a mind

---

[1] *MA.* i. 278 quotes *M.* i. 500 to show that neither all the three feelings nor any two of them can be experienced simultaneously.

[2] *āmisa*, sometimes put into opposition to *dhamma*, as at *M.* i. 12. But here in opposition to *nirāmisa*. According to *MA.* i. 279 *sāmisa sukha* means the worldling's feelings of pleasure connected with the five senses, whereas *nirāmisa sukha* are the feelings of pleasure connected with renunciation. All is set out at *M.* iii. 217-19.

[3] As at, *e.g.*, *M.* i. 34, 68.

without confusion . . . the mind that is contracted[1] as a mind that is contracted . . . the mind that is distracted[2] as a mind that is distracted . . . the mind that has become great[3] as a mind that has become great . . . a mind that has not become great[4] as a mind that has not become great . . . the mind with (some other mental state) superior to it[5] as a mind with (some other mental state) superior to it . . . the mind with no (other mental state) superior to it[6] as a mind with no (other mental state) superior to it . . . the mind that is composed[7] as a mind that is composed . . . the mind that is not composed[8] as a mind that is not composed . . . the mind that is freed[9] as a mind that is freed . . . the mind that is not freed[10] as a mind that is not freed. Thus he fares along contemplating the mind in the mind internally, or he fares along contemplating the mind in the mind externally, or he fares along contemplating the mind in the mind internally and externally. [**60**] Or he fares along contemplating origination-things in the mind, or he fares along contemplating dissolution-things in the mind, or he fares along contemplating origination-dissolution-things in the mind. Or, thinking, 'There is mind,' his mindfulness is established precisely to the extent necessary just for knowledge, just for remembrance, and he fares along independently of and not grasping anything in the world. It is thus, monks, that a monk fares along contemplating mind in the mind.

And how, monks, does a monk fare along contemplating mental objects in mental objects ? Herein, monks, a monk fares along contemplating mental objects in mental objects from the point of view of the five hindrances. And how, monks, does a monk fare along contemplating mental objects in mental objects from the point of view of the five hindrances ? Herein, monks, when a subjective desire for sense-pleasures is present, a monk comprehends that he has a subjective desire for sense-pleasures; or when a subjective desire for sense-pleasures is not present he comprehends

---

[1] The mind fallen into sloth and torpor. [2] Accompanied by restlessness.
[3] Connected with the fine-material and the non-material planes.
[4] Connected with the sensuous plane of existence.
[5] This state of consciousness is also connected with the sensuous plane.
[6] This refers to the fine-material or the non-material plane.
[7] This refers to the person who has full or partial concentration.
[8] Where neither of these forms of concentration is present.
[9] See *Vism.* 410.
[10] Here (for the beginner) there is no place for the freedoms through extirpation, calming and escape, *MA.* i. 280.

that he has no subjective desire for sense-pleasures. And in so far as there comes to be an uprising of desire for sense-pleasures that had not arisen before, he comprehends that; and in so far as there comes to be a getting rid of desire for sense-pleasures that has arisen, he comprehends that. And in so far as there comes to be no future uprising of desire for the sense-pleasures that has been got rid of, he comprehends that. Or when ill-will is subjectively present he comprehends that he has subjective ill-will. . . . Or when sloth and torpor are subjectively present he comprehends that he has subjective sloth and torpor. . . . Or when restlessness and worry are subjectively present he comprehends that he has subjective restlessness and worry. . . . Or when doubt is present subjectively he comprehends that he has subjective doubt; when doubt is not present subjectively he comprehends that he has no subjective doubt. And in so far as there is an uprising of doubt that had not arisen before, he comprehends that; and in so far as there is a getting rid of doubt that has arisen, he comprehends that; and in so far as there is in the future no uprising of the doubt that has been got rid of, he comprehends that. It is thus that he fares along contemplating mental objects in mental objects internally, or he fares along contemplating mental objects in mental objects externally, or he fares along contemplating mental objects in mental objects internally and externally. Or he fares along contemplating origination-things in mental objects, or he fares along contemplating dissolution-things in mental objects, or he fares along contemplating origination-things and dissolution-things in mental objects. Or, thinking, 'There are mental objects,' his mindfulness is established precisely to the extent necessary just for knowledge, just for remembrance, and he fares along independently of and not grasping anything in the world. It is thus, monks, that a monk fares along contemplating mental objects in mental objects from the point of view of the five hindrances.

And again, monks, a monk fares along contemplating mental objects in mental objects **[61]** from the point of view of the five groups[1] of grasping. And how, monks, does a monk fare along contemplating mental objects in mental objects from the point of view of the five groups of grasping? Herein, monks, a monk thinks, 'Such is material shape, such is the arising of material shape,

---

[1] *upādānakkhandha*, or the five aggregates, *khandha*, of clinging or grasping, and which arise as a result of grasping. See *Vism.* Ch. XX.

such is the setting of material shape; such is feeling, such the arising of feeling, such the setting of feeling; such is perception, such the arising . . . such the setting of perception; such are the tendencies, such the arising . . . such the setting of the tendencies; such is consciousness, such the arising of consciousness, such the setting of consciousness.' It is in this way that he fares along contemplating mental objects in mental objects internally, or he fares along . . . contemplating origination-things and dissolution-things in mental objects. Or, thinking, 'There are mental objects,' his mindfulness is established precisely to the extent necessary just for knowledge, just for remembrance, and he fares along independently of and not grasping anything in the world. It is thus, monks, that a monk fares along contemplating mental objects in mental objects from the point of view of the five groups of grasping.

And again, monks, a monk fares along contemplating mental objects in mental objects from the point of view of the six internal-external sense-bases. And how, monks, does a monk fare along contemplating mental objects in mental objects from the point of view of the six internal-external sense-bases? Herein, monks, a monk comprehends the eye and he comprehends material shapes, and he comprehends the fetter[1] that arises dependent on both, and he comprehends the uprising of the fetter not arisen before, and he comprehends the getting rid of the fetter that has arisen, and he comprehends the non-uprising in the future of the fetter that has been got rid of. And he comprehends the ear . . . and he comprehends sounds . . . and he comprehends the nose and he comprehends smells . . . and he comprehends the tongue and he comprehends flavours . . . and he comprehends the body and he comprehends tactile objects . . . and he comprehends the mind and he comprehends mental objects, and he comprehends the fetter that arises dependent on both, and he comprehends the uprising of the fetter that had not arisen before, and he comprehends the getting rid of the fetter that has arisen, and he comprehends the non-arising in the future of the fetter that has been got rid of. It is in this way that he fares along contemplating mental objects in mental objects internally, or he fares along contemplating mental objects in mental objects externally, or he fares along contemplating mental objects

---

[1] Tenfold; the fetter of sense-pleasure being based on two conditions, and that of ignorance on eight.

in mental objects internally and externally. Or he fares along contemplating origination-things in mental objects. . . . Or, thinking, 'There are mental objects,' . . . he fares along independently of and not grasping anything in the world. It is thus, monks, that a monk fares along contemplating mental objects in mental objects from the point of view of the six internal-external sense-bases.

And again, monks, a monk fares along contemplating mental objects in mental objects from the point of view of the seven links in awakening. And how, monks, does a monk fare along contemplating mental objects in mental objects from the point of view of the seven links in awakening? Herein, monks, when the link in awakening that is mindfulness is present internally he comprehends that he has internally the link in awakening that is mindfulness; when the link in awakening that is mindfulness is not internally present [**62**] he comprehends that he has not internally the link in awakening that is mindfulness. And in so far as there is an uprising of the link in awakening that is mindfulness that had not uprisen before, he comprehends that; and in so far as there is completion by the mental development of the uprisen link in awakening that is mindfulness, he comprehends that. When the link in awakening that is investigation of mental objects is present internally . . . and in so far as there is completion by mental development of the uprisen link in awakening that is investigation of mental objects, he comprehends that. When the link in awakening that is energy is present internally . . . in so far as there is completion by mental development of the uprisen link in awakening that is energy, he comprehends that. When the link in awakening that is rapture is present internally. . . . When the link in awakening that is serenity is present internally. . . . When the link in awakening that is concentration is present internally. . . . When the link in awakening that is equanimity is present internally he comprehends that he has the link in awakening that is equanimity; when the link in awakening that is equanimity is not present internally, he comprehends that he has not the link in awakening that is equanimity. And in so far as there is an uprising of the link in awakening that is equanimity that had not uprisen before, he comprehends that; and in so far as there is completion by mental development of the uprisen link in awakening that is equanimity, he comprehends that. It is in this way that he fares along contemplating mental objects in mental objects . . . both internally and externally. Or he fares along contemplating origination-things in mental objects. . . . Or, thinking, 'There are mental objects,' his mindfulness is established . . . he fares along independently of and not grasping anything in the world. It is thus, monks, that a monk fares along contemplating mental objects in mental objects from the point of view of the seven links in awakening.[1]

And again, monks, a monk fares along contemplating mental objects in mental objects from the point of view of the four ariyan truths. And how, monks, does a monk fare along contemplating mental objects in mental objects from the point of view of the four ariyan truths? Herein, monks, a monk comprehends as it really is, 'This is anguish'; he comprehends as it really is, 'This is the arising of anguish'; he comprehends as it really is, 'This is the stopping of anguish'; he comprehends as it really is, 'This is the course leading to the stopping of anguish.' It is thus that he fares along contemplating mental objects in mental objects internally, or he fares along contemplating mental objects in mental objects externally, or he fares along contemplating mental objects in mental objects internally and externally. Or he fares along contemplating origination-things in mental objects, or he fares along contemplating dissolution-things in mental objects, or he fares along contemplating origination-things and dissolution-things in mental objects. Or, thinking, 'There are mental objects,' his mindfulness is established precisely to the extent necessary just for knowledge, just for remembrance, and he fares along independently of and not grasping anything in the world. It is thus, monks, that a monk fares along contemplating mental objects in mental objects from the point of view of the four ariyan truths.

Whoever,[2] monks, should thus develop these four applications of mindfulness for seven years, one of two fruits is to be expected for him: either profound knowledge[3] here-now, or, if there is any residuum remaining,[4] the state of non-returning.[5] Monks, let be the seven years. Whoever, [**63**] monks, should thus develop these four applications of mindfulness for six years, five years, four years, three years, two years, for one year, one of two fruits is to

---

[1] For the above paragraph *MA*. i. 289 *ff*. refers to *S*. v. 65, 66.

[2] *MA*. i. 301: whatever monk, nun, man or woman lay follower.

[3] *aññā*, equivalent to arahantship.

[4] The grasping that leads to again-becoming or recurrent birth, but not necessarily in this world.

[5] The third stage in supramundane fulfilment.

be expected for him: either profound knowledge here-now, or, if there is any residuum remaining, the state of non-returning. Monks, let be the one year. Whoever, monks, should thus develop these four applications of mindfulness for seven months, one of two fruits is to be expected for him: either profound knowledge here-now, or, if there is any residuum remaining, the state of non-returning. Monks, let be the seven months. Whoever, monks, should thus develop these four applications of mindfulness for six months, five months, four months, three months, two months, for one month, for half a month. . . . Monks, let be the half month. Whoever, monks, should thus develop these four applications of mindfulness for seven days, one of two fruits is to be expected for him: either profound knowledge here-now, or, if there is any residuum remaining, the state of non-returning.

What has been spoken in this way has been spoken in reference to this: 'There is this one way, monks, for the purification of beings, for the overcoming of sorrows and griefs, for the going down of sufferings and miseries, for winning the right path, for realising nibbāna, that is to say, the four applications of mindfulness.' "

Thus spoke the Lord. Delighted, these monks rejoiced in what the Lord had said.

Discourse on the Applications of Mindfulness:
the Tenth

Division of the Synopsis of Fundamentals:
the First

II. THE DIVISION OF THE LION'S ROAR
(Sīhanādavagga)

11. LESSER DISCOURSE ON THE LION'S ROAR

(Cūḷasīhanādasutta)

THUS have I heard: At one time the Lord was staying near Sāvatthī in the Jeta Grove in Anāthapiṇḍika's monastery. While he was there, the Lord addressed the monks, saying: " Monks." " Revered one," these monks answered the Lord in assent. The Lord spoke thus:

" Monks, thinking: ' Just here[1] is a recluse, here a second recluse, here a third recluse, here a fourth recluse;[2] void of recluses [**64**] are other (systems teaching) alien views,'[3] it is thus, monks, that you may rightly[4] roar a lion's roar.[5] But this situation occurs, monks, when wanderers belonging to other sects might herein speak thus: ' What confidence have the venerable ones, what authority, by reason of which the venerable ones speak thus: " Just here is a recluse, here a second recluse, here a third recluse, here a fourth recluse; void of recluses are other (systems teaching) alien views ?' " Monks, if there are wanderers belonging to other sects who speak thus, they should be spoken to thus: ' It is because we see for ourselves four things made known to us by the Lord who knows, who sees, perfected one, fully self-awakened one, that we speak thus: " Just here is a recluse, here a second recluse, here a third recluse, here a fourth recluse; void of recluses are other (systems teaching) alien views." What are the four ? Your reverences, we have confidence in the Teacher,[6] we have confidence in *dhamma*,[6] there is fulfilment of the moral habits, and our fellow *dhamma*-men,[7]

---

[1] *idh'eva*; *MA*. ii. 4, " in this very teaching."

[2] *Cf*. *D*. ii. 151. *MA*. ii. 4, citing *A*. ii. 238, states that the first *samaṇa* is a stream-winner, the second a once-returner, the third a non-returner, the fourth an arahant. *Cf*. the four kinds of recluses at *A*. ii. 86-90, and see *G.S*. ii. 96, *n*. 1.

[3] As at *D*. ii. 151, 152; *A*. ii. 238. *MA*. ii. 5 mentions the ten groups into which the sixty-two " heretical views " fall, and says that they are all recorded in the *Brahmajāla Sta*.

[4] *MA*. ii. 7 says here *sammā* means with cause, with reason.

[5] *Sīhanāda* is the roar of the best, of a fearless one, an unequalled one, *MA*. ii. 7=*AA*. ii. 303.

[6] As stated at *e.g*. *M*. i. 37.

[7] *sahadhammikā*. *MA*. ii. 8 calls them monks, nuns, probationers, male

as well as householders and those who have gone forth, are dear to us and liked (by us). It is, your reverences, because of these four matters, made known to us by the Lord who knows, who sees, perfected one, fully self-awakened one, that we speak thus: "Just here is a recluse . . . alien views." '

But this situation occurs, monks, when wanderers belonging to other sects might speak thus: 'Your reverences, we too have confidence in that teacher of ours[1] who is our teacher, and we have confidence in that *dhamma* of ours which is our *dhamma*, and we fulfil those which are our moral habits,[2] and our fellow *dhamma*-men, as well as householders and those who have gone forth, are dear to us and liked (by us). So, your reverences, what is the distinction, what the divergence, what the difference between you and us?' Monks, if there are wanderers belonging to other sects who speak thus, they should be spoken to thus: 'But, your reverences, is the goal[3] one or is the goal manifold?' Monks, if answering rightly wanderers belonging to other sects would answer thus: 'The goal is one, your reverences, the goal is not manifold.' 'But, your reverences, is this goal for one with attachment or for one without attachment?' Monks, if answering rightly wanderers belonging to other sects would answer: 'This goal is for one without attachment, this goal is not for one with attachment.' 'But, your reverences, is this goal for someone with aversion or for someone without aversion . . . for someone with confusion or for someone without confusion . . . for someone with craving or for someone without craving [**65**] . . . for someone with grasping or for someone without grasping . . . for someone who is intelligent or for someone who is unintelligent . . . for someone who is yielding[4] and hindered[5] or for someone who is unyielding and unhindered . . . for someone

---

and female novices, men and women lay followers. All these are *sahadhammikā*, for which a synonym is *ariyasāvakā*. They are all under one and the same *dhamma*.

[1] *MA*. ii. 9 mentions Pūraṇa Kassapa and the other six (heretical) teachers.

[2] *MA*. ii. 9 instances the moral habits of those following the goat, cow, ram and dog practices. For the bovine and canine practices see *M.-Sta*. 57.

[3] *niṭṭhā*, glossed at *MA*. ii. 9 as *pariyosānabhūta*, what has become the consummation or culmination. *MA*. here gives as examples of "many": the Brahma-world is the fulfilment or goal of brahmans, Ābhassarā of ascetics, Subhakiṇha of wanderers, unending mind of Ājīvakas. But in this teaching arahantship is the goal.

[4] *anuruddha*, *MA*. ii. 10 to attachment.

[5] *paṭiviruddha*, *MA*. ii. 10 by anger.

with delight in impediments[1] or for someone without delight in impediments ?' Monks, if answering rightly wanderers belonging to other sects would answer thus: 'This goal is for someone without aversion, not for someone with aversion . . . for someone without confusion, not for someone with confusion . . . for someone without craving, not for someone with craving . . . for someone without grasping, not for someone with grasping . . . for someone who is intelligent, not for someone who is not intelligent . . . for someone who is unyielding and unhindered, not for someone who is yielding and hindered . . . for someone who is without delight in impediments, not for someone with delight in impediments.'

Monks, there are these two views: view of becoming, and view of annihilation.[2] Monks, whatever recluses and brahmans adhere to the view of becoming, have come under the view of becoming, cleave to the view of becoming, these are obstructed from the view of annihilation. Monks, whatever recluses and brahmans adhere to the view of annihilation, have come under the view of annihilation, cleave to the view of annihilation, these are obstructed from the view of becoming. Monks, whatever recluses or brahmans do not comprehend as they really are the rise and fall of, and satisfaction in, and peril of these two views and the escape[3] from them, these have attachment, these have aversion, these have confusion, these have craving, these have grasping, these are unintelligent, these are yielding and hindered, these delight in impediments. these are not utterly freed from birth, ageing, dying, grief, sorrow, suffering, lamentation, despair—these are not utterly freed from anguish,[4] I say. But whatever recluses or brahmans comprehend as they really are the rise and fall of, and the satisfaction in, and the peril of these two views and the escape from them, these are without attachment, these are without aversion, these are without confusion, these are without craving, these are without grasping, these are intelligent, these are unyielding and unhindered, these do not delight in impediments, these are utterly freed from birth, ageing,

---

[1] *papañcārāmassa papañcaratino.* See *G.S.* ii. 168, *n.* 3. *MA.* ii. 10 says that here synonyms are craving, views, and pride.

[2] *bhavadiṭṭhi ca vibhavadiṭṭhi ca.* *MA.* ii. 10 calls the former the Eternalist view, and the latter the Annihilationist view.

[3] *nissaraṇa.* *MA.* ii. 11 here calls it *nibbāna.*

[4] Anguish is here the whole rolling or whirling on, *vaṭṭa* (in recurrent birth), *MA.* ii. 12.

dying, grief, sorrow, suffering, lamentation, despair—these are utterly freed from anguish, I say.

[**66**] Monks, there are these four (kinds of) grasping. What are the four? The grasping of sense-pleasures, the grasping of view, the grasping of rule and custom, the grasping of the theory of self. There are some recluses and brahmans who, although pretending to a comprehension of all the graspings, do not lay down rightly a comprehension of all the graspings; they lay down a comprehension of the grasping of sense-pleasures, but do not lay down a comprehension of the grasping of view, of the grasping of rule and custom, of the grasping of the theory of self. What is the cause of this? It is that these worthy recluses and brahmans do not understand three situations as they really are. Therefore these worthy recluses and brahmans, although pretending to a comprehension of all the graspings, do not lay down rightly a comprehension of all the graspings; they lay down a comprehension of the grasping of sense-pleasures, but do not lay down a comprehension of the grasping of view, do not lay down a comprehension of the grasping of rule and custom, do not lay down a comprehension of the grasping of the theory of self.

Monks, there are some recluses and brahmans who, although pretending to a comprehension of all the graspings, do not lay down rightly a comprehension of all the graspings; they lay down a comprehension of the grasping of sense-pleasures, they lay down a comprehension of the grasping of view, but they do not lay down a comprehension of the grasping of rule and custom, they do not lay down a comprehension of the grasping of the theory of self. What is the cause of this? It is that these worthy recluses and brahmans do not comprehend two situations as they really are. Therefore these worthy recluses and brahmans, although pretending to a comprehension of all the graspings, do not rightly lay down a comprehension of all the graspings; they lay down a comprehension of the grasping of sense-pleasure, they lay down a comprehension of the grasping of view, they do not lay down the comprehension of the grasping of rule and custom, they do not lay down a comprehension of the grasping of the theory of self.

Monks, there are some recluses and brahmans who, although pretending to a comprehension of all the graspings, do not lay down rightly a comprehension of all the graspings; they lay down a comprehension of the grasping of sense-pleasures, they lay down a comprehension of the grasping of view, they lay down a comprehension of the grasping of rule and custom, but they do not lay down a comprehension of the grasping of the theory of self. What is the cause of this? It is that these worthy recluses and brahmans do not understand one situation as it really is. Therefore these worthy recluses and brahmans, although pretending to a comprehension of all the graspings, do not rightly lay down a comprehension of all the graspings; they lay down a comprehension of the grasping of sense-pleasure, they lay down a comprehension of the grasping of view, they lay down a comprehension of the grasping of rule and custom, but they do not lay down a comprehension of the grasping of the theory of self.

In such a *dhamma* and discipline as this, monks, that which is confidence in the Teacher is shown to be not perfect, that which is confidence in *dhamma* is shown to be not perfect, that which is fulfilment of the moral habits is shown to be not perfect, that which is regard and affection for one's fellow *dhamma*-men is shown to be not perfect. What is the cause of this? It comes to be thus, monks, [**67**] in a *dhamma* and discipline that are wrongly shown, wrongly taught, not leading onwards,[1] not conducive to allayment,[2] taught by one who is not fully self-awakened.

But the Tathāgata, monks, perfected one, fully self-awakened one, claiming a comprehension of all the graspings, rightly lays down a comprehension of all the graspings; he lays down a comprehension of the grasping of sense-pleasures, he lays down a comprehension of the grasping of view, he lays down a comprehension of the grasping of rule and custom, he lays down a comprehension of the grasping of the theory of self. In such a *dhamma* and discipline as this, monks, that which is confidence in the Teacher is shown to be perfect, that which is confidence in *dhamma* is shown to be perfect, that which is fulfilment of the moral habits is shown to be perfect, that which is regard and affection for one's fellow *dhamma*-men is shown to be perfect. What is the cause of this? It comes to be thus, monks, in a *dhamma* and discipline that are rightly shown, rightly taught, leading onwards, conducive to allayment, taught by one who is fully self-awakened.

Monks, what is the provenance, what the origin, what the birth, what the source of these four (kinds of) grasping? Craving, monks, is the provenance, craving is the origin, craving is the birth, craving

---

[1] Only round and round in animal births, of which *MA*. ii. 13-14 gives examples.

[2] Of attachment and so on, *MA*. ii. 15.

is the source of these four (kinds of) grasping. And what, monks, is the provenance, what the origin, what the birth, what the source of craving ? Feeling, monks, is the provenance, the origin, the birth, the source of craving. And what, monks, is the provenance, the origin, the birth, the source of feeling ? Sensory impingement is the provenance, the origin, the birth, the source of feeling. And what, monks, is the provenance, the origin, the birth, the source of sensory impingement ? The six bases of sensory impression, monks, is the provenance . . . the source of sensory impingement. And what, monks, is the provenance . . . the source of the six bases of sensory impression ? Name-and-form, monks, is the provenance . . . the source of the six bases of sensory impression. And what, monks, is the provenance . . . the source of name-and-form ? Consciousness, monks, is the provenance . . . the source of name-and-form. And what, monks, is the provenance . . . the source of consciousness ? The karma-formations, monks, are the provenance . . . the source of consciousness. And what, monks, is the provenance . . . the source of the karma-formations ? Ignorance, monks, is the provenance, ignorance is the origin, ignorance is the birth, ignorance is the source of the karma-formations

When, monks, ignorance is got rid of by a monk and knowledge[1] has arisen, he, by the going down of ignorance, by the uprising of knowledge,[2] neither grasps after the grasping of sense-pleasures, nor grasps after the grasping of view, nor grasps after the grasping of rule and custom, nor grasps after the theory of self. Not grasping, he is not troubled; being untroubled he himself is individually attained to nibbāna,[3] and he comprehends: 'Destroyed is birth, brought to a close is the Brahma-faring, done is what was to be done, there is no more of being such or such.' "

[68] Thus spoke the Lord. Delighted, these monks rejoiced in what the Lord had said.

Lesser Discourse on the Lion's Roar:
the First

---

[1] *vijjā*; here knowledge of the Way to arahantship, *MA*. ii. 18.

[2] As at *M*. i. 294; *S*. ii. 82, iii. 47; *A*. ii. 196.

[3] *paccattam yeva parinibbāyati*. *Cf*. *M*. i. 251-52; *S*. iii. 54. *MA*. ii. 18, 299 say *sayam eva kilesaparinibbānena parinibbāyati*, himself he is brought to nibbāna through the nibbāna (quenching or burning up) of the defilements.

12. GREATER DISCOURSE ON THE LION'S ROAR

(Mahāsīhanādasutta)

THUS have I heard: At one time the Lord was staying near Vesālī outside the town in a woodland thicket to the west.[1] Now at that time Sunakkhatta, the son of a Licchavi,[2] having recently left this *dhamma* and discipline, spoke these words to a group (of people) at Vesālī: " There are no states of further-men,[3] (no) excellent knowledge and insight[4] befitting the ariyans in the recluse Gotama; the recluse Gotama teaches *dhamma* on (a system) of his own devising beaten out by reasoning and based on investigation;[5] and says that *dhamma*, taught for the sake of something specific,[6] leads onwards[7] the doer of it to the complete destruction of anguish."

Then the venerable Sāriputta, having dressed early in the morning, taking his bowl and robe, entered Vesālī for almsfood. Then the venerable Sāriputta heard that speech of Sunakkhatta, the son of a Licchavi, as it was being spoken to the group (of people) in Vesālī: " There are no states of further-men . . . and says that *dhamma*, taught for the sake of something specific, leads onwards

---

[1] Not like Ambapālī's Grove, which was inside the town, but like Jīvaka's Mango Grove, which was outside it, *MA*. ii. 21. This Sutta should be compared with *Jā*. No. 94 (*Lomahaṁsajātaka*) in which the Lord was said to be staying in the Pāṭikârāma, depending for alms on Vesālī.

[2] Licchaviputta, *MA*. ii. 21 saying that he was so called because he was the son of a Licchavi rajah. On the use of °*putta*, see *B.D*. ii. p. xliv *ff*.

[3] See Pārājika IV, *Vin*. iii. 87-109, and especially p. 92, where *uttarimanussadhamma* is defined; also *B.D*. i. xxiv *f*.; and *M*. i. 246, etc.

[4] *ñāṇadassana*, or, insight into knowledge. *MA*. ii. 21 defines it as the deva-like sight and vision (*vipassanā*) and the Way and the fruit and knowledge due to reflecting on, and omniscience.

[5] *Cf*. *M*. i. 520; *D*. i. 16. Sunakkhatta is saying that *dhamma* is based by Gotama on empirical knowledge instead of being known and realised intuitively.

[6] *yassa ca khvāssa atthāya*. *MA*. ii. 22 says " meditation on the foul for repugnance to attachment, mental development of friendliness for repugnance to hatred, the five things for repugnance to confusion, breathing for cutting off discursive thought."

[7] *niyyāti*, to lead out or onwards, has the sense (as recognised at *MA*. ii. 23) of helping the escape from the anguish of *vaṭṭa*, the whirl of *saṁsāra*. Its object is therefore nibbāna.

the doer of it to the complete destruction of anguish." Then the venerable Sāriputta, having walked in Vesālī for almsfood, after the meal returning from (his quest for[1]) alms, approached the Lord; having approached, having greeted the Lord, he sat down at a respectful distance. As he was sitting down at a respectful distance, the venerable Sāriputta spoke thus to the Lord:

"Lord, Sunakkhatta, the son of a Licchavi, spoke these words to a group (of people) at Vesālī: 'There are no states of further-men, (no) excellent knowledge and insight befitting the ariyans in the recluse Gotama; the recluse Gotama teaches *dhamma* on (a system) of his own devising beaten out by reasoning and based on investigation; and says that *dhamma*, taught for the sake of something specific, leads onwards the doer of it to the complete destruction of anguish.' "

"Sāriputta, Sunakkhatta is a man of wrath and folly, and these words were spoken by him in wrath. Thinking, 'I will speak dispraise,' he, Sāriputta, the foolish man Sunakkhatta, really spoke praise of the Tathāgata. **[69]** For this, Sāriputta, is praise of a Tathāgata: when someone should speak thus: '*Dhamma*, taught for the sake of something specific, leads onwards the doer of it to the complete destruction of anguish.' But, Sāriputta, there will not be for Sunakkhatta, the foolish man, this inference from *dhamma* about me: 'This is the Lord, perfected one, fully Self-awakened One, endowed with knowledge and right conduct, well-farer, knower of the world(s), incomparable trainer of men to be tamed, teacher of devas and men, the Awakened one, the Lord.' Nor, Sāriputta, will there be for Sunakkhatta, the foolish man, this inference from *dhamma* about me: 'This is the Lord who enjoys the manifold forms of psychic power: from having been one he becomes manifold; from having been manifold he becomes one; manifest or invisible, he goes unhindered through a wall, through a rampart, through a mountain as if through air; he plunges into the ground and shoots up again as if in water; he walks upon the water without parting it as if on the ground; sitting cross-legged he travels through the air like a bird on the wing. Even this moon and sun, although of such mighty power and majesty, he rubs and strokes them with his hand. Even as far as the Brahma-world he has power in respect of his body.'

Nor, Sāriputta, will there be for Sunakkhatta, the foolish man,

---

[1] Supplied by *MA*. ii. 23.

this inference from *dhamma* about me: 'This is the Lord who, through the purified *deva*-condition of hearing, surpassing that of men, hears both (kinds of) sounds: *deva*-like ones and human ones, and those which are distant and those which are near.'

Nor, Sāriputta, will there be for Sunakkhatta, the foolish man, this inference from *dhamma* about me: 'This is the Lord who knows intuitively by mind the minds of other beings, of other individuals; he knows intuitively of a mind that is full of attachment that it is full of attachment; he knows intuitively of a mind that is without attachment that it is without attachment; he knows intuitively of a mind that is full of aversion . . . full of confusion that it is full of aversion . . . full of confusion; he knows intuitively of a mind that is without aversion . . . without confusion . . . that it is without aversion . . . without confusion; he knows intuitively of a mind that is contracted that it is contracted, or of a mind that is distracted that it is distracted, or of a mind that has become great that it has become great, or of a mind that has not become great that it has not become great, or of a mind with (some other mental state) superior to it that it is a mind with (some other mental state) superior to it; of a mind with no (other mental state) superior to it that it is a mind with no (other mental state) superior to it; he knows intuitively of a mind that is composed that it is composed . . . that is not composed that it is not composed; he knows intuitively of a mind that is freed that it is freed; he knows intuitively of a mind that is not freed that it is not freed.'

Now, Sāriputta, a Tathāgata has these ten powers of a Tathāgata,[1] endowed with which powers a Tathāgata claims the leader's place,[2] roars his lion's roar in assemblies, and sets rolling the Brahma-wheel.[3] What are the ten?

Herein, Sāriputta, a Tathāgata comprehends as it really is causal occasion as such and what is not causal occasion as such.[4] Inasmuch, Sāriputta, as a Tathāgata comprehends as it really is causal occasion as such and what is not causal occasion as such, this, Sāriputta, [**70**] is a Tathāgata's power of a Tathāgata, having which power a Tathāgata claims the leader's place, roars his lion's roar in assemblies, and sets rolling the Brahma-wheel.

And again, Sāriputta, a Tathāgata comprehends as it really is the

---

[1] As at *e.g. A.* v. 32 *ff.*, *Cf. A.* iii. 417 (six powers).

[2] *āsabhaṭṭhāna*, bull's place. *MA.* ii. 26 says "the best, the highest place. Or, bulls are the previous Buddhas—their place."

[3] *Brahmacakka*, also at *S.* ii. 27.

[4] See *VbhA.* 400; *Dhs.* 1337.

acquiring of deeds for oneself, past, future and present, both in their causal occasion and their result. Inasmuch, Sāriputta, as a Tathāgata comprehends . . . as it really is the acquiring of deeds . . . and sets rolling the Brahma-wheel.

And again, Sāriputta, a Tathāgata comprehends as it really is the course[1] leading to all bourns.[2] Inasmuch, Sāriputta, as a Tathāgata also comprehends . . . and sets rolling the Brahma-wheel.

And again, Sāriputta, a Tathāgata comprehends as it really is the world[3] with its various and diverse features. Inasmuch, Sāriputta, as a Tathāgata also comprehends . . . and sets rolling the Brahma-wheel.

And again, Sāriputta, a Tathāgata comprehends as they really are the divers characters of beings.[4] Inasmuch, Sāriputta, as a Tathāgata also comprehends . . . and sets rolling the Brahma-wheel.

And again, Sāriputta, a Tathāgata comprehends as it really is the higher or lower state of the faculties[5] of other beings, of other persons. Inasmuch, Sāriputta, as a Tathāgata also comprehends . . . and sets rolling the Brahma-wheel.

And again, Sāriputta, a Tathāgata comprehends as they really are the defilement of, the purification of, the emergence from attainments in meditation, the deliverances and concentration. Inasmuch, Sāriputta, as a Tathāgata also comprehends . . . and sets rolling the Brahma-wheel.

And again, Sāriputta, a Tathāgata remembers his manifold former habitations, that is to say one birth and two births . . . three . . . four . . . five . . . ten . . . twenty . . . thirty . . . forty . . . fifty . . . a hundred . . . a thousand births, and a hundred thousand births, and many an eon of integration and many an eon of disintegration and many an eon of integration-disintegration, thinking: 'Such and such was I by name, having such a clan, such a colour, so was I nourished, I experienced this and that pleasure and pain, so did the span of life end. As that one I, passing from this, rose up again elsewhere. There, too, such a one was I by name, having such a clan, such a colour, so was I nourished, experienced this or that pleasure and pain, so did the span of life end. I, deceasing thence, rose up here.' Thus with all their modes and detail does

---

[1] *paṭipadā*, called *magga* at *MA*. ii. 29. [2] Both good and bad ones.

[3] The world of the *khandhas*, *āyatanas*, and *dhātus*, *MA*. ii. 29.

[4] *adhimutti*, will, intention. *Cf*. *Vbh*. 339.

[5] The faculties, *indriya*, are here the five of faith, *saddhā*, and so on. It means also their growth or decline. *Cf*. *Vbh*. 340.

he remember his manifold former habitations. Inasmuch, Sāriputta, as a Tathāgata also comprehends . . . and sets rolling the Brahma-wheel.

And again, Sāriputta, a Tathāgata, with his purified *deva* vision, surpassing that of men, sees beings as they are deceasing and uprising—he comprehends that beings are mean, excellent, comely, ugly, well-going, ill-going according to the consequences of their deeds, and thinks: 'Indeed, these worthy beings who were possessed of wrong conduct in body, in speech, in thought, scoffers at the ariyans, of wrong view, incurring deeds consequent on a wrong view—these, at the breaking up of the body **[71]** after dying, arise in the sorrowful state, a bad bourn, the abyss, Niraya Hell. But, on the other hand, these worthy beings, endowed with good conduct in body, speech, and thought, not scoffers at the ariyans, of right view, incurring deeds consequent on right view—these, at the breaking up of the body after dying arise in a good bourn, the heaven world.' In this way, with his purified *deva* vision, surpassing that of men, he sees beings as they are deceasing and uprising; he comprehends that beings are mean, excellent, comely, ugly, well-going, ill-going according to their deeds. Inasmuch, Sāriputta, as a Tathāgata comprehends . . . and sets rolling the Brahma-wheel.

And again, Sāriputta, a Tathāgata, by the destruction of the cankers, enters on and abides in freedom of mind, freedom through wisdom that are cankerless, having realised them here and now through his own super-knowledge. Inasmuch, Sāriputta, as a Tathāgata, by the destruction of the cankers, enters on and abides in freedom of mind, freedom through wisdom that are cankerless, having realised them here and now through his own super-knowledge, this too, Sāriputta, is a Tathāgata's power of a Tathāgata, having which power a Tathāgata claims the leader's place, roars his lion's roar in assemblies, and sets rolling the Brahma-wheel.

These, Sāriputta, are the Tathāgata's ten powers of a Tathāgata, endowed with which powers the Tathāgata claims the leader's place, roars his lion's roar in assemblies, and sets rolling the Brahma-wheel. Whoever, Sāriputta, knowing me thus, seeing me thus, should speak thus: 'There are no states of further-men, (no) excellent knowledge and insight befitting the ariyans in the recluse Gotama; the recluse Gotama teaches *dhamma* on (a system of) his own devising beaten out by reasoning and based on investigation' if he does not retract that speech, Sāriputta, if he does not retract that thought, if he does not give up that view, he is consigned to Niraya Hell just as a burden is set aside.[1] Sāriputta, as a monk, endowed with moral habit, endowed with concentration, endowed with intuitive wisdom, might attain profound knowledge here-now, so I say that this, Sāriputta, results thus:[2] not retracting that speech, not retracting that thought, not giving up that view, he is consigned to Niraya Hell just as a burden is set aside.

Sāriputta, there are these four convictions[3] of a Tathāgata endowed with which convictions a Tathāgata claims the leader's place, roars his lion's roar in assemblies, and sets rolling the Brahma-wheel. What are the four ? If anyone says: 'These matters are not fully awakened to although you claim to be fully self-awakened' —as to this, I do not behold the ground, Sāriputta, on which a recluse or a brahman or a *deva* or Māra or Brahmā or anyone in the world [**72**] can legitimately reprove me. Because I, Sāriputta, do not behold this ground, I fare along attained to security, attained to fearlessness, attained to conviction.

If anyone says: 'These cankers are not utterly destroyed, although you claim to be one whose cankers are destroyed,' as to this, I do not behold the ground . . . I fare along attained to . . . conviction.

If anyone says: 'In following those things called stumbling-blocks there is no stumbling-block at all,'[4] as to this, I do not behold the ground . . . I fare along attained to . . . conviction.

If anyone says: '*Dhamma*, taught by you for the sake of something specific, does not lead onward the doer of it to the complete destruction of anguish,'—as to this, I do not behold the ground, Sāriputta, on which a recluse or brahman or a *deva* or Māra or Brahmā or anyone in the world can legitimately reprove me. Because I, Sāriputta, do not behold this ground, I fare along attained to security, attained to fearlessness, attained to conviction.

These, Sāriputta, are the four convictions of a Tathāgata, en

---

[1] *yathābhataṃ nikkhitto evaṃ niraye*, as at *e.g. A.* i. 8, 96, 105, 292, *It.* p. 12. See note on this obscure phrase at *G.S.* i. 6, *n.* 2, and *Min. Anth.* II. 124, *n.* 2.

[2] *evaṁsampadam-idaṃ vadāmi.*

[3] *vesārajjāni*; as at *A.* ii. 8; *cf. A.* iv 83 *f.* Perhaps self-confidences, self-satisfactions.

[4] *Cf.* Pācittiya 68, *Vin.* iv. 133 *ff.*, and see *B.D.* iii. 21, *n.* 5. *MA.* ii. 33 says that there *methunadhamma* (unchastity) is meant. It is a stumbling-block to the fruits of the ways.

dowed with which convictions the Tathāgata claims the leader's place, roars his lion's roar in assemblies, and sets rolling the Brahma-wheel. Whoever, Sāriputta, knowing me thus . . . is consigned to Niraya Hell just as a burden is set aside.

These, Sāriputta, are the eight (kinds of) assemblies.[1] What are the eight? Assemblies of nobles, assemblies of brahmans, assemblies of householders, assemblies of recluses, assemblies of the retinue of the Four Great Regents, assemblies of the Thirty-Three, Māra's assemblies,[2] assemblies of Brahmās. These eight, Sāriputta, are the assemblies. A Tathāgata who is endowed with those four convictions, Sāriputta, approaches these eight assemblies, enters them. Now I, Sāriputta, call to mind approaching many hundred assemblies of nobles[3] . . . many hundred assemblies of brahmans . . . of householders . . . of recluses . . . of the retinue of the Four Great Regents . . . of the Thirty-Three . . . many hundreds of Māra's assemblies . . . many hundred assemblies of Brahmās. Yet before I sat down there and before I held converse there and before I fell into conversation there, I did not behold, Sāriputta, any ground for thinking that fear or nervousness would come upon me there. So I, Sāriputta, not beholding this ground, fare along attained to security, attained to fearlessness, attained to conviction. [**73**] Whoever, Sāriputta, knowing me thus . . . is consigned to Niraya Hell just as a burden is set aside.

These, Sāriputta, are the four modes of life.[4] What are the four? The mode of life born from an egg, the mode of life born from a womb, the mode of life born from moisture, the mode of life of spontaneous uprising.[5] And what, Sāriputta, is the mode of life born from an egg? Whatever beings are produced, Sāriputta, breaking through an egg-shell, this, Sāriputta, is called the mode of life born from an egg. And what, Sāriputta, is the mode of life born from a womb? Whatever beings are produced, Sāriputta, breaking through a membranous sheath, this, Sāriputta, is called the mode of life born from a womb. And what, Sāriputta, is the

---

[1] As at *A*. iv. 307; *D*. ii. 109.

[2] *MA*. ii. 34 expressly says "not (assemblies) of Māras, but an occasion when those in Māra's retinue gather together."

[3] *MA*. ii. 34 says this means a concourse round Bimbisāra, a concourse of relations, a concourse of Licchavis and so forth. See note at *Dial*. ii. 117.

[4] *D*. iii. 230.

[5] *MA*. ii. 36 says that *opapātika* means that, having arisen, not through these (other) circumstances, they are as though existing (*nibbattā*, being reborn).

mode of life born of moisture? Whatever beings are produced, Sāriputta, in rotting fish or in rotting corpses or rotting rice or in a dirty pool near a village, this, Sāriputta, is called the mode of life born of moisture. And what, Sāriputta, is the mode of life of spontaneous uprising? *Devas*,[1] those in Niraya Hell, and some men and some in the sorrowful state—this is called, Sāriputta, the mode of life of spontaneous uprising. These, Sāriputta, are the four modes of life. Whoever, Sāriputta, knowing me thus . . . is verily consigned to Niraya Hell, just as a burden is set aside.

These, Sāriputta, are the five bourns.[2] What are the five? Niraya Hell, animal birth, the realm of the departed,[3] men, *devas*. I, Sāriputta, comprehend Niraya Hell and the way[4] leading to Niraya Hell and the course[4] leading to Niraya Hell, and that according to how one is faring along one uprises, at the breaking up of the body after dying, in a sorrowful state, a bad bourn, the abyss, Niraya Hell—that too I comprehend. And I, Sāriputta, comprehend animal birth and the way leading to animal birth and the course leading to animal birth, and that according to how one is faring along one uprises, at the breaking up of the body after dying, in animal birth—that too I comprehend. And I, Sāriputta, comprehend the realm of the departed and the way leading to the realm of the departed and the course leading to the realm of the departed, and that according to how one is faring along one uprises, at the breaking up of the body after dying, in the realm of the departed—that too I comprehend. And I, Sāriputta, comprehend men, and the way leading to the world of men and the course leading to the world of men, and that according to how one is faring along one uprises, at the breaking up of the body after dying, among men—that too I comprehend. And I, Sāriputta, comprehend *devas* and the way leading to *deva*-worlds and the course leading to *deva*-worlds, and that according to how one is faring along one uprises, at the breaking up of the body after dying, in a good

---

[1] *MA*. ii. 36 says "beginning with the Four Great Regents, *devas* who are higher are of spontaneous uprising. But the earth-*devas* belong to the four modes of life. Some men are of spontaneous uprising, but for the most part they are womb-born."

[2] *gati*, going, destiny, where one must go according to one's deeds, whether well or ill done. *MA*. ii. 36 gives five other kinds of *gati* and says here *gatigati* is meant; as exemplified at *Dh*. 420.

[3] *MA*. ii. 37, *peccabhāvaṃpattānaṃ visayo ti*.

[4] Way and course here identified, *MA*. ii. 37.

bourn, a heaven-world—that too I comprehend. And I, Sāriputta, comprehend nibbāna[1] and the way leading to nibbāna [**74**] and the course leading to nibbāna, and that according to how one is faring along, by the destruction of the cankers one enters on and abides in the freedom of mind, the freedom through intuitive wisdom which are cankerless, having realised them here-now by one's own super-knowledge—that too I comprehend.

Now I, Sāriputta, with my mind comprehend the mind of some person thus: As that person fares along and as he is going along and has entered that way, so will he arise at the breaking up of the body after dying in a sorrowful state, a bad bourn, the abyss, Niraya Hell. After a time I see by purified *deva* vision, surpassing that of men that, at the breaking up of the body after dying, he has arisen in a sorrowful state, a bad bourn, the abyss, Niraya Hell, and is experiencing feelings that are exclusively[2] painful, sharp, severe. Sāriputta, it is as if there were a pit of charcoal, deeper than man's height, full of embers that are neither flaming nor smoking;[3] then a man might come along overcome and overpowered by the hot-weather heat, exhausted, parched and thirsty,[4] heading direct for that pit of charcoal itself by the one sole way. A man with vision, having seen him, might say: 'As that good man is faring along and as he is going along and has entered on that way, so will he come to that pit of charcoal itself.' After a time he may see him, fallen into that charcoal pit, experiencing feelings that are exclusively painful, sharp, severe. Even so do I, Sāriputta, with my mind comprehend the mind of some person thus: As that person fares along and as he is going along and has entered on that way, so will he arise at the breaking up of the body after dying in a sorrowful state, a bad bourn, the abyss, Niraya Hell. After a time I see by purified *deva* vision, surpassing that of men, that, at the breaking up of the body after dying, he has arisen in a sorrowful state, a bad bourn, the abyss, Niraya Hell, and is experiencing feelings that are exclusively painful, sharp, severe.

Then I, Sāriputta, with my mind comprehend the mind of some person thus: As that person fares along and as he is going along and has entered on that way, so will he arise, at the breaking up of the body after dying, in an animal birth. After a time I see with

---

[1] *MA*. ii. 37, "I know that nibbāna is the escape from the bourns." *Cf. SnA*. 368: *gativippamokkhaṃ parinibbānaṃ*.

[2] *ekanta*. *MA*. ii. 37 gives *nicca, nirantara*, constantly, incessantly.

[3] *Cf. M*. i. 365; *S*. ii. 99.

[4] As at *M*. i. 284.

purified *deva* vision, surpassing that of men, that, at the breaking up of the body after dying, he has arisen in an animal birth and is experiencing feelings which are painful,[1] sharp, severe. Sāriputta, it is as if there were a cesspool, deeper than a man's height, full of filth; then a man might come along overcome and overpowered by the hot-weather heat, [**75**] exhausted, parched and thirsty, heading direct for that cesspool itself by the one sole way. A man with vision, having seen him, might say: 'As that good man is faring along, and as he is going along and has entered on that way, so will he come to that cesspool itself.' After a time he may see him, fallen into that cesspool and experiencing feelings that are painful, sharp, severe. Even so do I, Sāriputta, with my mind comprehend the mind of some person thus . . . feelings that are painful, sharp, severe.

Then I, Sāriputta, with my mind comprehend the mind of some person thus: As that person fares along . . . so will he arise, at the breaking up of the body after dying, in the realm of the departed. After a time I see . . . that he has arisen in the realm of the departed and is experiencing feelings that are abundantly painful.[2] Sāriputta, it is like a tree growing on uneven ground, with sparse leaves and foliage (giving) patchy shade.[3] Then a man might come along overcome and overpowered by the hot-weather heat, exhausted, parched and thirsty, heading direct for that tree itself by the one sole way. A man with vision, having seen him, might say: 'As that good man is faring along and as he is going along and has entered on that way, so will he come to that tree itself.' After a time he may see him sitting down or lying down in the shade of that tree, experiencing feelings that are abundantly painful. Even so do I, Sāriputta, with my mind comprehend the mind of some person thus . . . feelings that are abundantly painful.

Then I, Sāriputta, with my mind comprehend the mind of some person thus: As that person fares along . . . so will he arise, at the breaking up of the body after dying, among men. After a time I see . . . that he has arisen among men and is experiencing feelings that are abundantly pleasant.[4] Sāriputta, it is like a tree growing

---

[1] Not "exclusively painful" here, because there is no burning, as in the ember-pit.

[2] In this realm, pain is abundant, pleasure slight, *MA*. ii. 39.

[3] *kabaracchāya*. *MA*. ii. 38 says "not like a thin layer of clouds."

[4] Such feelings can be experienced among *khattiya* (royal or noble) families, and so on, *MA*. ii. 39.

on even ground, with dense leaves and foliage (giving) thick shade. Then a man might come along overcome and overpowered by the hot-weather heat, exhausted, parched, thirsty, heading direct for that tree itself by the one sole way. A man with vision, having seen him, might speak thus: 'As that good man is faring along, and as he is going along and has entered on that way, so he will come to that tree itself.' After a time he may see him sitting down or lying down in the shade of that tree, experiencing feelings that are abundantly pleasant. Even so do I, Sāriputta, with my mind comprehend the mind of some person thus . . . feelings that are abundantly pleasant.

[76] Then I, Sāriputta, with my mind comprehend the mind of some person thus: As that person fares along . . . so will he arise, at the breaking up of the body after dying, in a good bourn, a heaven world. After a time I see . . . that he has arisen in a good bourn, a heaven world and is experiencing feelings that are exclusively pleasant. Sāriputta, it is as if there were a long house[1] where there might be a building with a gabled roof, smeared inside and out,[2] protected from the wind, with bolts that are fastened,[3] windows[4] that are closed.[5] Therein might be a divan[6] spread with a long-haired coverlet,[7] spread with a white coverlet, spread with a wool coverlet besprent with flowers, a splendid sheeting of the hide of the *kadali*-deer, with an awning overhead and a scarlet cushion at either end.[8] Then a man might come along overcome and overpowered by the hot-weather heat, exhausted, parched, thirsty, heading direct for that long house itself by the one sole way. A man with vision, having seen him, might say: 'As that good

---

[1] *pāsādo ti dīghapāsādo, MA.* ii. 39=*VA.* 654. See *B.D.* ii. 16, *n.* 5. This simile occurs at *A.* i. 137. *Cf.* also the burning gabled house at *A.* i. 101=*M.* iii. 61.

[2] This word, *ullittâvalitta,* is used in defining *vihāra* at *Vin.* iii. 156, iv, 47, and " hut," *kuṭī,* at *Vin.* iii. 149.

[3] *phassitaggaḷaṃ, M.* iii. 61; *A.* i. 101, 137; *MA.* ii, 39 read *phussita,* which is to be preferred. *MA.* ii. 39 explains that the door, *kavāṭa,* (*i.e.* that by which the aperture is closed) is closed tight against the door-posts.

[4] *vātapāna* are really shutters, I think. Various ways of ornamenting them are given at *Vin.* iv. 47; see also *Vin.* ii. 148.

[5] *Cf. M.* iii. 61, *A.* i. 101 for this description.

[6] *pallaṅka,* see *B.D.* iii. 271, *n.* 3.

[7] These words are found in longer lists at *Vin.* i. 192, ii. 163; *D.* i. 7; *A.* i. 181.

[8] *MA.* ii. 39 says one for the head and one for the feet.

man is faring along and as he is going along and has entered on that way, so will he come to that long house itself.' After a time he may see him sitting down or lying down in that long house, in that building with the gabled roof, on that divan, experiencing feelings that are exclusively pleasant. Even so do I, Sāriputta, with my mind comprehend of some person thus . . . feelings that are exclusively pleasant.

Then I, Sāriputta, with my mind comprehend the mind of some person thus: As that person fares along and as he is going along and has entered on that way, so will he, by the destruction of the cankers, enter and abide in the freedom of mind, the freedom through intuitive wisdom that are cankerless, having realised them here-now by his own super-knowledge. After a time I see that he, by the destruction of the cankers, having entered on freedom of mind, freedom through intuitive wisdom that are cankerless, and having realised them here-now by his own super-knowledge, is abiding in them, experiencing feelings that are exclusively pleasant.[1] Sāriputta, it is as if there were a lovely lotus-pool[2] with clear water, sweet water, cool water, limpid, with beautiful banks,[3] and close to it a dim forest thicket. Then a man might come along overcome and overpowered by the hot-weather heat, exhausted, parched and thirsty, heading direct for that pond itself by the one sole way. A man with vision, having seen him, might say: 'As that good man is faring along and as he is going along and has entered on that way, so will he come to that lotus-pool itself.' After a time he may see that he has plunged into that lotus-pool, has bathed in it and drunk of it, and having allayed all distress, exhaustion and fever, has got out again[4] and is sitting down or lying down in that forest thicket[5] [77] experiencing feelings that are exclusively pleasant. Even so do I, Sāriputta, with my mind comprehend the mind of some person thus: As that person is faring along and as he is going along and has entered on that way, so will he, by the destruction of the cankers, having entered on freedom of mind, freedom through

---

[1] *MA.* ii. 40 says "exclusively pleasant here and in the *deva*-worlds are the same in denotation but not in connotation. That of the *deva*-worlds is not really exclusively pleasant because there is still the fever of passion. But the bliss of nibbāna is exclusively pleasant because in every way all fevers have been allayed."

[2] As at *M.* i. 283; *A.* iii. 190; *S.* i. 91.

[3] *M.* reads *sūpatitthā*.

[4] *paccuttaritvā*, possibly meaning: having crossed the pool.

[5] *MA.* ii 40 says this is like nibbāna.

intuitive wisdom that are cankerless, having realised them here-now by his own super-knowledge, abide therein. After a time I see that he, by the destruction of the cankers, having entered on freedom of mind, freedom through intuitive wisdom that are cankerless, having realised them here-now by his own super-knowledge, is abiding therein, experiencing feelings that are exclusively pleasant.

These, Sāriputta, are the five bourns. Whoever, Sariputta, knowing me thus, seeing me thus, should say: 'The recluse Gotama has no conditions of further-men, (no) excellent knowledge and insight befitting the ariyans; the recluse Gotama teaches *dhamma* on (a system of) his own devising beaten out by reasoning and based on investigation;' if he, Sāriputta, does not retract that speech, if he does not retract that thought, if he does not give up that view, he is verily consigned to Niraya Hell just as a burden is set aside. Sāriputta, as a monk, endowed with moral habit, endowed with concentration, endowed with intuitive wisdom, might here and now attain profound knowledge, so I say that this, Sāriputta, results thus: 'Not retracting that speech, not retracting that thought, not giving up that view, he is verily consigned to Niraya Hell just as a burden is set aside.'

Now I, Sāriputta, as one who fares, fully know a Brahma-faring[1] that is endowed with four constituent parts[2]: I became an ascetic, the foremost ascetic; I became loathly, the foremost loathly one; I became a detester,[3] the foremost detester; I became aloof, the foremost aloof one.

In that,[4] Sāriputta, there was this for me through asceticism: I was unclothed,[5] flouting life's decencies,[6] licking my hands (after

---

[1] *MA.* i. 41 says that the Brahma-faring is generosity, doing services, the rules of training, the *brahmavihāras*, the teaching of *dhamma*, abstention from unchastity, satisfaction in one's own wife, the Observance, the ariyan Way, the whole teaching, being intent on, energy . . . (*MA.* ii. 43). But here energy is a synonym for the Brahmacariya, and this Sutta is itself about the Brahma-faring that is energy.

[2] *Cf. Jā* i. 390-91, where it is said that the Bodhisatta, when dying, realised that this practice was no good, so he took a right view and passed to a *deva*-world.

[3] *MA.* ii. 43, of evil.

[4] *MA.* ii. 43, in that fourfold Brahma-faring.

[5] The following occurs at *M.* i. 342; *A.* i. 295, ii. 206; *D.* i. 166; *Pug.* 55; *cf. M.* i. 238.

[6] I borrow this expression from Chalmers. *MA.* ii. 44 from here=*AA.* ii. 383 *ff.*= *PugA.* 231.

meals), not one to come when asked to do so, not one to stand still when asked to do so.[1] I did not consent (to accept food) offered to (me) or specially prepared for (me) nor to (accept) an invitation (to a meal). I did not accept (food) straight from a cooking pot or pan, nor within the threshold, nor among the faggots, nor among the rice-pounders,[2] nor when two people were eating,[3] nor from a pregnant woman, nor from one giving suck,[4] nor from one co-habiting with a man,[5] nor from gleanings,[6] nor near where a dog is standing, nor where flies are swarming, nor fish, nor meat. I drank neither fermented liquor nor spirits nor rice-gruel. I was a one-house-man, a one-piece-man,[7] or [**78**] a two-house-man, a two-piece-man . . . or a seven-house-man, a seven-piece-man. I subsisted on one little offering,[8] and I subsisted on two little offerings . . . and I subsisted on seven little offerings. I took food only once a day, and once in two days . . . and once in seven days. Then I lived intent on the practice of eating rice at regular fortnightly intervals. I came to be one feeding on[9] potherbs or feeding on millet or on wild rice or on snippets of skin or on water-plants or on the red powder of rice husks or on the discarded scum of rice on the boil or on the flour of oil-seeds or grass or cowdung. I was one who subsisted on forest roots and fruits, eating the fruits that had fallen. I wore coarse hempen cloths,[10] and I wore mixed cloths,[11] and I wore cerements, and I wore rags taken from the dust heap, and I wore tree-bark fibre, and I wore antelope skins, and I wore strips of antelope skin, and I wore cloths of *kusa*-grass, and I wore cloths of bark, and I wore cloths of wood shavings, and I wore

---

[1] *I.e.* when receiving food on the begging round.

[2] See *G.S.* i. 273, *n.* 6.

[3] *MA.* ii. 44, *AA.* ii. 384 not helpful. They say "When it is given by one only of them. Why? There is a stumbling-block (danger) in (only) a mouthful."

[4] *Vin.* iv. 318, a mother or a foster-mother. *MA.* ii. 44, and the other Comys., say that this comes to endanger the milk for the child.

[5] *purisantaragatā*. At *Vin.* iv. 322 this word is used to define *gihigatā*; at *MA.* ii. 209, *DA.* 78 to define *itthi*. The Comys. say that this is a danger to (their) pleasure.

[6] According to the Comys., done in times of scarcity by unclothed ascetics.

[7] Visiting only one house or asking for only one piece of food.

[8] *MA.* ii. 45 says that *datti* is one small bowlful from which they leave out the main food.

[9] As at *M.* i. 156; *D.* i. 166.

[10] On *sāṇāni*, see *B.D.* ii. 143, *n.* 3, 4. Following garments as at *A.* i. 240.

[11] *masāṇāṇi*, perhaps meaning a mixture of coarse hemp and other fibres.

a blanket of human hair, and I wore a blanket of animal hair, and I wore owls' feathers. I was one who plucked out the hair of his head and beard, intent on the practice of plucking out the hair of head and beard. I became one who stood upright, refusing a seat; I became one who squats on his haunches, intent on the practice of squatting. I became one for covered thorns,[1] I made my bed on covered thorns; and I was intent on the practice of going down to the water to bathe up to three times in an evening.[2] Thus in many a way did I live intent on the practice of mortifying and tormenting my body. This then was for me, Sāriputta, through asceticism.

In that, Sāriputta, there was this for me through loathliness: on my body there accumulated the dust and dirt of years, so that it fell off in shreds. Just as the stump of the *tindukā*-tree comes to accumulate the dust and dirt of years, so that it falls off in shreds, even so, Sāriputta, on my body there accumulated the dust and dirt of years, so that it fell off in shreds. But it did not occur to me, Sāriputta, to think: 'Indeed now, I could rub off this dust and dirt with my hand, or others could rub off this dust and dirt for me with their hands.' It did not occur to me thus, Sāriputta. This then was for me, Sāriputta, through loathliness.

In that, Sāriputta, there was this for me through detesting: Sāriputta, whether I was going out, whether I was returning, there was set up in me kindliness even towards a drop of water, and I thought: 'Do not let me bring small creatures in their various places[3] to destruction.' This then was for me, Sāriputta, through detesting.

In that, Sāriputta, there was this for me through aloofness: [**79**] if I had plunged into a certain stretch of forest,[4] and if I saw a cow-herd or a cattle-herd or a gatherer of grass or sticks or anyone roaming about for bulbs and roots and so on,[5] I fled from grove to grove, from thicket to thicket, from low ground to low ground, from high ground to high ground. What was the reason for this?

---

[1] Iron spikes or thorns were placed in the ground, covered with a hide, and then an ascetic stood there, paced up and down and so forth.

[2] To get rid of the day's evil. *Cf. M.* i. 39.

[3] *visamagate.* The idea at *MA.* ii. 46 seems to be lest a drop of water splash the place where any small creature was at that time.

[4] *Cf. M.* i. 152.

[5] This is how *MA.* ii. 46 explains *vanakammika.* It therefore appears not to be " one who works in the forests."

I thought: 'Do not let them see me, do not let me see them.'[1] Even as a deer in the forest, Sāriputta, having seen a man, flees from grove to grove, from thicket to thicket, from low ground to low ground, from high ground to high ground, even so did I, Sāriputta, when I saw a cow-herd or a cattle-herd or a gatherer of grass or sticks or anyone roaming about for bulbs and roots and so on, flee from grove to grove, from thicket to thicket, from low ground to low ground, from high ground to high ground. What was the reason for this? I thought: 'Do not let them see me, do not let me see them.' This then was for me, Sāriputta, through aloofness.

Then I, Sāriputta, having approached on all fours those cow-pens that the cows had quitted, the cow-herds having departed,[2] I subsisted there on the droppings of the young suckling calves. So long as my own dung and urine held out, I subsisted on that. This then was for me, Sāriputta, through partaking of the great filthy things.[3]

Then I, Sāriputta, having plunged into a terrifying forest thicket, stayed there. It comes to be said of a terrifying forest thicket, because it is so terrifying: 'Whoever, not rid of attachment, enters that forest thicket, his hair stands on end.' Then I, Sāriputta, during the cold winter nights, between the 'eights' in a time of snowfall,[4] spent such nights as these in the open air, the days in the forest thicket. I spent the days of the last month of the hot weather in the open air, the nights in the forest thicket.[5] Then, Sāriputta, this verse, never heard before, occurred spontaneously to me:

> Now scorched, now cold, alone in terrifying forest,
> Naked and sitting fireless, the sage is intent on his quest.[6]

Then I, Sāriputta, lay down to sleep in a cemetery, leaning on a skeleton.[7] Cowherds' boys,[8] having come up to me, spat and staled on me, and showered me with dust and stuck twigs into my

---

[1] *Miln.* 396.

[2] *paṭṭhitagāvo apagatagopālakā.*

[3] As at *D.* i. 167. Usually four in number, as at *Vin.* i. 206, applied against snake-bite; and at *Vin.* iv. 90 where they do not count as "nutriment," so a monk may himself take them even if there is no one to make them "allowable."

[4] As at *Vin.* i. 31, 288; *A.* i. 136; *Ud.* I. 9; *Miln.* 396. See *B.D.* iv. 41, *n.* 3.

[5] *Miln.* 396 quotes this passage. *Cf.* also *Jā.* i. 390.

[6] *Verse* at *Jā.* i. 390, whose Comy. is more detailed than that at *MA.* ii. 48.

[7] *Jā* i. 47 ; *Cp.* III. 15. 1 (p. 102).

[8] *gomaṇḍala.* At *Cp.* III. 15. 1 *gāmaṇḍala.* *MA.* ii. 48-9 explains by *gopāladārakā.*

ears. But I, Sāriputta, well know that I was not the creator of a malign heart against them.[1] This then came to be for me, Sāriputta, through abiding in even-mindedness.[2]

[**80**] There are, Sāriputta, some recluses and brahmans who speak thus and are of this view: 'Purity is through food.' These speak thus: 'We subsist on jujube fruits,' and they eat jujube fruits and they eat crushed jujube fruits and they drink jujube fruit water, and they make use of jujube fruits in a variety of ways.[3] Now I, Sāriputta, claim to have subsisted on one single jujube fruit. It may be, Sāriputta, that this occurs to you: 'But at that time the jujube fruit was large.' But this must not be regarded in this way, Sāriputta, for the jujube fruit was then as it is now. While I, Sāriputta, was subsisting on one single jujube fruit, my body became exceedingly emaciated.[4]

Because I ate so little, all my limbs became like the knotted joints of withered creepers; because I ate so little, my buttocks became like a bullock's hoof; because I ate so little, my protruding backbone became like a string of balls; because I ate so little, my gaunt ribs became like the crazy rafters of a tumble-down shed; because I ate so little, the pupils of my eyes appeared lying low and deep in their sockets as sparkles of water in a deep well appear lying low and deep; because I ate so little, my scalp became shrivelled and shrunk as a bitter white gourd cut before it is ripe becomes shrivelled and shrunk by a hot wind. If I, Sāriputta, thought: 'I will touch the skin of my belly,' it was my backbone that I took hold of. If I thought, 'I will touch my backbone,' it was the skin of my belly that I took hold of. For because I ate so little, the skin on my belly, Sāriputta, came to be cleaving to my backbone. If I, Sāriputta, thought: 'I will obey the calls of nature,' I fell down on my face then and there, because I ate so little. If I, Sāriputta, soothing my body, stroked my limbs with my hand, the hairs, rotted at the roots, fell away from my body as I stroked my limbs with my hand, because I ate so little.

There are, Sāriputta, some recluses and brahmans who speak thus and are of this view: 'Purity is through food.' These speak thus: 'We subsist on beans . . . we subsist on sesamum . . . we subsist on rice-grains,' and they eat rice-grains and they eat crushed

---

[1] *MA*. ii. 49 explains as "not by me was an evil heart created against them."

[2] *upekhā* is a *pāramī*; also a *bojjhanga*, and a *brahmavihāra*.

[3] *MA*. ii. 49, salads, cakes, balls.

[4] *Cf*. what follows with *M*. i. 247.

rice-grains [**81**] and they drink rice-grain water, and they make use of rice-grains in a variety of ways. Now I, Sāriputta, claim to have subsisted on one single rice-grain. It may be, Sāriputta, that this occurs to you: 'But at that time a rice-grain was large.' But this is not to be regarded in this way, Sāriputta, for the rice-grain was then as it is now. While I, Sāriputta, was subsisting on one single rice-grain, my body became exceedingly emaciated.

Because I ate so little, all my limbs became like the knotted joints . . . (*as before*) . . . the hairs, rotted at the roots, fell away from my body as I stroked my limbs with my hand, because I ate so little. But I, Sāriputta, even by this procedure, by this course, by this mortification, did not reach states of further-men or the excellent knowledge and insight befitting the ariyans. What was the cause of this? It was that by these there is no reaching the ariyan intuitive wisdom which, when reached, is ariyan, leading onwards, and which leads onwards the doer of it to the complete destruction of anguish.

Now, Sāriputta, there are some recluses and brahmans who speak thus and are of this view: 'Purity is through faring on.'[1] But, Sāriputta, it is not easy to find that faring-on [**82**] that I have not formerly fared-on in during this long past except among the *devas* of the Pure Abodes. For if I, Sāriputta, were to have fared on among the *devas* of the Pure Abodes, I could not have come back again to this world.

Now, Sāriputta, there are some recluses and brahmans who speak thus and are of this view: 'Purity is through uprising.' But, Sāriputta, it is not easy to find that uprising that has not formerly been uprisen in by me during this long past, except among the *devas* of the Pure Abodes. For if I, Sāriputta, were to have uprisen among the *devas* of the Pure Abodes, I could not have come back again to this world.

Now, Sāriputta, there are some recluses and brahmans who speak thus and are of this view: 'Purity is through abode.' But, Sāriputta, it is not easy to find that abode that I have not abided in during this long past, except among the *devas* of the Pure Abodes.[2] For if I, Sāriputta, were to have abided among the *devas* of the Pure Abodes, I could not have come back again to this world.

Now, Sāriputta, there are some recluses and brahmans who speak thus and are of this view: 'Purity is through oblation.' But,

---

[1] *saṁsāra*.

[2] Quoted at *DA*. ii. 511.

Sāriputta, it is not easy to find that oblation that has not formerly been offered by me during this long past when I was a noble, anointed king, or a wealthy brahman.

Now, Sāriputta, there are some recluses and brahmans who speak thus and are of this view: 'Purity is through tending the (sacrificial) fire.' But, Sāriputta, it is not easy to find that fire that has not formerly been tended by me during this long past when I was a noble, anointed king, or a wealthy brahman.

Now, Sāriputta, there are some recluses and brahmans who speak thus and are of this view: 'So long as this good man is young, endowed with the coal-black hair of youth, in his early prime, so long is he possessed of the utmost lucidity of wisdom. But when this good man is worn, old, stricken in years, has lived his span, and is at the close of his life[1]—eighty or ninety or a hundred years of age—then he falls from that lucidity of wisdom.' But this is not to be regarded in this way, Sāriputta. I, Sāriputta, am now worn, old, stricken in years, I have lived my span, and am at the close of my life, being round about eighty.[2] Sāriputta, I might have four disciples here, each of a hundred years' life-span, living a hundred years, and possessed of the utmost mindfulness, and attentiveness, and resolute energy,[3] and with the utmost lucidity of wisdom. As, Sāriputta, a skilled archer, trained, deft, a marksman, may with ease wing a slender shaft across a palm-tree's shadow,[4] so are these of extreme mindfulness, of extreme attentiveness, **[83]** of extreme resolute energy, so are they possessed of the utmost lucidity of wisdom. If these were to ask me again and again a question about the four applications of mindfulness,[5] and if I, questioned again and again, were to explain to them, and if they, on being explained to by me, should understand as explained, and if they were not to question me about any secondary and further matter (nor pause), except for feeding, drinking, eating, tasting, except for answering the calls of nature, except for dispelling fatigue by sleep, still unfinished, Sāriputta, would be the Tathāgata's teaching of *dhamma*, still unfinished would be the Tathāgata's expositions on the phrases of *dhamma*, still unfinished would be the Tathāgata's ways of

---

[1] Stock, as at *Vin.* ii. 88, iii. 2.

[2] *MA.* ii 51, "they say the Lord spoke this discourse in the year of the *parinibbāna.*"

[3] *dhiti.* [4] As at *A.* ii. 48, iv. 429; *S.* i. 62, ii. 266. See *G.S.* iv. 288, *n.* 3.

[5] *MA.* ii. 52-3, about these and then about the rest of the thirty-seven links in awakening.

putting questions[1] when these four disciples of mine, of life-spans of a hundred years, living for a hundred years, would pass away at the end of a hundred years. Yet, if you should have to carry me about on a litter, Sāriputta, verily there is no change in the Tathāgata's lucidity of wisdom. Whoever, Sāriputta, speaking rightly, should say: 'A being not liable to delusion has arisen in the world for the welfare of the manyfolk, for the happiness of the manyfolk, out of compassion for the world, for the good, the welfare, the happiness of *devas* and men,' so, when he is speaking rightly of me, he would say: 'A being not liable to delusion has arisen in the world for the welfare of the manyfolk, for the happiness of the manyfolk, out of compassion for the world, for the good, the welfare, the happiness of *devas* and men.'"

Now at that time the venerable Nāgasamāla[2] spoke thus to the Lord: "It is wonderful, Lord, it is marvellous, Lord, that when, Lord, this disquisition on *dhamma* had been heard by me, my hair stood on end. What is the name, Lord, of this disquisition on *dhamma* ?"

"Wherefore do you, Nāgasamāla, remember this disquisition on *dhamma* as the Hair-raising Disquisition."[3]

Thus spoke the Lord. Delighted the venerable Nāgasamāla rejoiced in what the Lord had said.

The Greater Discourse on the Lion's Roar:
The Second

13. GREATER DISCOURSE ON THE STEMS OF ANGUISH

(Mahādukkhakkhandhasutta)

THUS have I heard: At one time the Lord was staying near Sāvatthī in the Jeta Grove in Anāthapiṇḍika's monastery. Then several[4] monks, having dressed in the morning, taking their bowls and

---

[1] *pañhapaṭibhāna*. Word occurs at *M*. i. 378.

[2] Verses at *Thag*. 267-70. And see *Ud*. 90, *Jā*. iv. 95.

[3] Called by this name, *Lomahaṃsanapariyāya*, at *Miln*. 398, and in *DA*. i; and in Jātaka No. 94 it is called *Lomahaṃsajātaka*.

[4] *sambahulā*; not a technical term here, as in *Vin*. where it means a

robes, [**84**] entered Sāvatthī for almsfood. Then it occurred to these monks: "It is too early to walk for almsfood in Sāvatthī. Suppose we were to approach the park[1] of the wanderers belonging to other sects?" Then these monks approached the park of the wanderers belonging to other sects; having approached, they exchanged greetings with the wanderers belonging to other sects, and having exchanged greetings of courtesy and friendliness, they sat down at a respectful distance. As these monks were sitting down at a respectful distance, these wanderers belonging to other sects spoke thus to them:

"Your reverences, the recluse Gotama lays down the full understanding[2] of sense-pleasures; we too lay down the full understanding of sense-pleasures. Your reverences, the recluse Gotama lays down the full understanding of material shapes;[3] we too lay down the full understanding of material shapes. Your reverences, the recluse Gotama lays down the full understanding of feelings; we too lay down the full understanding of feelings. So, your reverences, herein what is the divergence, what the discrepancy, what the difference between the recluse Gotama and us, that is to say in *dhamma*-teaching as against *dhamma*-teaching, in instruction as against instruction?" Then those monks neither rejoiced in nor scoffed at what the wanderers belonging to other sects had said. Rising from their seats they departed, not rejoicing, not scoffing, but thinking: "We shall learn the meaning of what has been said in the Lord's presence."

Then these monks having walked for almsfood in Sāvatthī, returning from the alms-gathering after the meal, approached the Lord; having approached, having greeted the Lord, they sat down at a respectful distance. As they were sitting down at a respectful distance, these monks spoke thus to the Lord:

"Now we, Lord, having dressed in the morning, taking our bowls and robes, entered Sāvatthī for almsfood. It occurred to us, Lord: 'It is too early to walk for almsfood in Sāvatthī. Suppose

"group." *i.e.* less than a *saṁgha*. It is noticed at *MA.* ii. 54 that in *Vin. sambahulā* is three people, but in the Suttas three is called just three, and (a number) higher than that is *sambahulā*.

[1] *ārāma*. Not here a "monastery" as wanderers were not monastically constituted. *MA.* ii. 54 says it was not far from the Jeta Grove.

[2] *MA.* ii. 54, the ejection and transcending of sense-pleasures and of material shapes and feelings.

[3] *Cf. S.* iv. 16.

we were to approach the park of the wanderers belonging to other sects ?' So we, Lord, approached the park . . . As we were sitting down at a respectful distance, Lord, these wanderers belonging to other sects spoke thus to us: 'Your reverences, the recluse Gotama lays down the full understanding of sense-pleasures; we too lay down the full understanding of sense-pleasures. **[85]** . . .' Rising from our seats, we departed, thinking: 'We shall learn the meaning of what has been said in the Lord's presence.'"

"Monks, wanderers belonging to other sects who speak thus should be spoken to thus: 'But what, your reverences, is the satisfaction in pleasures of the senses, what the peril, what the escape (from them) ?' Monks, when wanderers belonging to other sects are questioned in this way, they will not be able to explain, and moreover they will get into further difficulties.[1] What is the reason for this ? It is that it is not within their scope. I, monks, do not see anyone in the world with its *devas*, Māras and Brahmās, in creation with its recluses and brahmans, its *devas* and men, who could win approbation with his answers to these questions except a Tathāgata or a Tathāgata's disciple or one who has heard (the teaching) from them.

And what, monks, is the satisfaction in pleasures of the senses ?[2] These five, monks, are the strands of sense-pleasures.[3] What five ? Material shapes cognisable by the eye, agreeable, pleasant, liked, enticing, connected with sensual pleasures, alluring. Sounds cognisable by the ear . . . Smells cognisable by the nose . . . tastes cognisable by the tongue . . . touches cognisable by the body, agreeable, pleasant, liked, enticing, connected with sensual pleasures, alluring. These, monks, are the five strands of sense-pleasures. Whatever pleasure, whatever happiness arises in consequence of these five strands of sense-pleasures, this is the satisfaction in sense-pleasures.

And what, monks, is the peril in sense-pleasures ? In this case, monks, a young man of family earns his living by some craft, such as reckoning on the fingers,[4] such as calculation,[5] such as

---

[1] *Cf. D.* i. 26, *S.* iv. 15.

[2] From here to *M.* i. 87=*M.* i. 92=398=454.

[3] *M.* i. 92, 398, 454; *A.* iii. 411, etc. quoted *Kvu.* 369.

[4] *muddā.* See *B.D.* ii. 176, *n.* 4 for further references, etc. *MA.* ii. 56 says, "having established awareness through the joints of the fingers, it is called *hatthamuddā* (hand-reckoning)."

[5] *gaṇanā* See *B.D.* ii. 176, *n.* 5.

computing,[1] such as agriculture,[2] such as being in a rajah's service,[3] such as by another craft.[4] He is afflicted by the cold,[5] he is afflicted by the heat, suffering from the touch of gadflies, mosquitoes, wind, sun, creeping things, dying of hunger and thirst. This, monks, is a peril in pleasures of the senses that is present, a stem of ill,[6] having pleasures of the senses as the cause, having pleasures of the senses as the provenance, [**86**] being a consequence of pleasures of the senses, the very cause of pleasures of the senses.

If, monks, this young man of family rouses himself, exerts himself, strives thus, but if these possessions do not come to his hand, he grieves, mourns, laments, beating his breast and wailing, he falls into disillusionment,[7] and thinks: 'Indeed my exertion is vain, indeed my striving is fruitless.' This too, monks, is a peril in the pleasures of the senses that is present . . . the very cause of pleasures of the senses.

If, monks, this young man of family rouses himself, exerts himself, strives thus, and these possessions come to his hand, he experiences suffering and sorrow in consequence of looking after them, and thinks: 'Now by what means may neither kings nor thieves take away my possessions, nor fire burn them, nor water carry them away, nor heirs whom I do not like take them away?'[8] Although he looks after these possessions and guards them, kings do take them away or thieves take them away, or fire burns them or water carries them away, or heirs whom he does not like take them away. He grieves, mourns, laments, beating his breast and wailing, he falls into disillusionment, and thinks: 'I do not even have that which was mine.' This too, monks, is a peril in the pleasures of the senses that is present . . . the very cause of pleasures of the senses.

And again, monks, when sense-pleasures are the cause, sense-pleasures the provenance, sense-pleasures the consequence, the very

---

[1] *sankhānaṃ.* According to the Comy., computing how much rice there will be, how much fruit, how many birds in the sky, by looking at a field, at a tree, or at the sky respectively.

[2] See *B.D.* ii. 175.

[3] Perhaps a government official, *rājaporisa.* As at *D.* i. 135, *A.* iv. 281, 286.

[4] *MA.* ii. 56 instances elephant-craft and horse-craft.

[5] *MA.* ii. 56, "like an arrow's target, he stands before (*purato*) the cold." It (*i.e. purakkhata*) also means 'being oppressed.'"

[6] *MA.* ii. 57 says, a heap, *rāsi.*

[7] *sammoha,* or confusion, delusion.

[8] *Cf. A.* iv. 282.

cause of sense-pleasures, kings dispute with kings, nobles dispute with nobles, brahmans dispute with brahmans, householders dispute with householders, a mother disputes with her son, a son disputes with his mother, a father disputes with his son, a son disputes with his father, a brother disputes with a brother, a brother disputes with a sister, a sister disputes with a brother, a friend disputes with a friend. Those who enter into quarrel, contention, dispute and attack one another with their hands and with stones[1] and with sticks and with weapons,[2] these suffer dying then and pain like unto dying. This too, monks, is a peril in the pleasures of the senses that is present . . . the very cause of pleasures of the senses.

And again, monks, when sense-pleasures are the cause, sense-pleasures the provenance, sense-pleasures the consequence, the very cause of sense-pleasures, having taken sword and shield, having girded on bow and quiver, both sides mass for battle and arrows are hurled and knives are hurled and swords are flashing. These who wound with arrows and wound with knives and decapitate with their swords, these suffer dying then and pain like unto dying. This too, monks, is a peril in the pleasures of the senses that is present . . . the very cause of pleasures of the senses.

And again, monks, when sense-pleasures are the cause, sense-pleasures the provenance, sense-pleasures the consequence, the very cause of sense-pleasures, having taken sword and shield, having girded on bow and quiver, they leap on to the newly daubed[3] ramparts, and arrows are hurled and knives **[87]** are hurled and swords are flashing. Those who wound with arrows and wound with knives and pour boiling cow-dung[4] over them and crush them with the (falling) portcullis and decapitate them with their swords, these suffer dying then and pain like unto dying. This too, monks, is a peril in the pleasures of the senses . . . the very cause of pleasures of the senses.

And again, monks, when sense-pleasures are the cause, sense-pleasures the provenance, sense-pleasures the consequence, the very cause of sense-pleasures, they break into a house and carry off the booty and behave as a thief and wait in ambush and go to other

---

[1] *leḍḍu*. See *Vin*. iii. 46, iv. 40.

[2] This sequence also found at *M*. i. 123, *Ud*. 71.

[3] *addāvalepana*. The word also occurs at *S*. iv. 187. *MA*. ii 58 renders by "hot mud."

[4] *pakkaṭṭhī*, explained by *MA*. ii. 58 as *kuthita* (=*kaṭh*-) *gomaya*, while *Nd*. ii. 199 reads *chakaṇatī*.

men's wives.[1] Kings, having arrested such a one, deal out various punishments:[2] they lash him with whips and they lash him with canes and they lash him with (birch) rods, and they cut off his hand ... his foot ... his hand and foot ... his ear ... his nose and they cut off his ear and nose, and they give him the 'gruel-pot'[3] punishment ... the 'shell-tonsure' punishment ... 'Rāhu's mouth,' ... the 'fire-garland' ... the 'flaming hand' ... the 'hay-twist' ... the 'bark-dress' ... the 'antelope' ... 'flesh-hooking' ... the 'disc-slice' ... the 'pickling process' ... 'circling the pin,' and they give him the 'straw mattress,' and they spray him with boiling oil, give him as food to the dogs, impale him alive on stakes and decapitate him with a sword. This too, monks, is a peril in the pleasures of the senses ... the very cause of pleasures of the senses.

And again, monks, when sense-pleasures are the cause, sense-pleasures the provenance, sense-pleasures the consequence, the very cause of sense-pleasures, they behave wrongly in body, they behave wrongly in speech, they behave wrongly in thought. These, having behaved wrongly in body, in speech, in thought, at the breaking up of the body after dying, arise in a sorrowful state, a bad bourn, the abyss, Niraya Hell. This, monks, is a peril in pleasures of the senses that is of the future, a stem of ill, having pleasures of the senses as the cause, having pleasures of the senses as the provenance, being a consequence of pleasures of the senses, the very cause of pleasures of the senses.

And what, monks, is the escape from pleasures of the senses? Whatever, monks, is the control of desire for and attachment to pleasures of the senses, the getting rid of the desire and attachment, this is the escape from pleasures of the senses.[4]

Monks, whatever recluses or brahmans[5] do not thus comprehend the satisfaction in pleasures of the senses as satisfaction, the peril as peril, the escape as escape as it really is, these indeed will neither know their own sense-pleasures accurately, nor will they arouse another to a similar condition[6] so that, as he fares along, he will know sense-pleasures accurately—this situation does not exist.

---

[1] As at *M*. ii. 88, and *cf*. *M*. i. 404.

[2] As at *M*. iii. 163 *f*., *A*. i. 47, ii. 122, *Miln*. 197.

[3] These punishments are described in greater detail at *G.S.* i. 42, 43 in the notes.

[4] At other passages, *e.g.* *A*. iii. 245, *It*. p. 61, *D*. iii. 239, 275, renunciation of sense-pleasures is called the escape from them. *MA*. ii. 60 says it is nibbāna.

[5] *Cf*. *S*. iii. 191-92.

[6] *tathattāya samādapessanti*.

But, monks, whatever recluses or brahmans [**88**] comprehend thus the satisfaction in pleasures of the senses as satisfaction, the peril as peril, the escape as escape as it really is, these indeed either know their own sense-pleasures accurately, or they will arouse another to a similar condition, so that, as he fares along, he will know sense-pleasures accurately—this situation exists.

And what, monks, is the satisfaction in material shapes ? Monks, it is like a girl in a noble's family or a brahman's family or a householder's family who at the age of fifteen or sixteen is not too tall, not too short, not too thin, not too fat, not too dark, not too fair—is she, monks, at the height of her beauty and loveliness at that time ?"

"Yes, Lord."

"Monks, whatever happiness and pleasure arise because of beauty and loveliness, this is satisfaction in material shapes.[1]

And what, monks, is peril in material shapes ? As to this, monks, one might see that same lady[2] after a time, eighty or ninety or a hundred years old, aged, crooked as a rafter, bent, leaning on a stick, going along palsied, miserable, youth gone, teeth broken, hair thinned, skin wrinkled, stumbling along, the limbs discoloured. What would you think, monks ? That that which was former beauty and loveliness has vanished, a peril has appeared ?"

"Yes, Lord."

"This too, monks, is a peril in material shapes. And again, monks, one might see that same lady diseased, suffering, sorely ill, lying in her own excrement, having to be lifted up by others, having to be laid down by others.[3] What would you think, monks ? That that which was former beauty and loveliness has vanished, a peril has appeared ?"

"Yes, Lord."

"This too, monks, is a peril in material shapes. And again, monks, one might see that same lady, her body thrown aside in a cemetery, dead for one, two or three days, swollen, discoloured, decomposing. What would you think, monks ? That that which was former beauty and loveliness has vanished, a peril has appeared ?"

"Yes, Lord."

"This too, monks, is a peril in material shapes. And again, monks, one might see this same lady, her body thrown aside in

---

[1] *Cf. S.* iv. 8.

[2] *tam eva bhaginī* (literally, sister).

[3] As at *A.* i. 139.

a cemetery, being devoured by crows or ravens or vultures or wild dogs or jackals or by a variety of animals.[1] What would you think, monks? [**89**] That that which was former beauty and loveliness has vanished, a peril has appeared?"

"Yes, Lord."

"This too, monks, is a peril in material shapes. And again, monks, one might see that same lady, her body thrown aside in a cemetery, a skeleton with (some) flesh and blood, sinew-bound . . . a fleshless skeleton with a smear of blood, sinew-bound . . . a skeleton without flesh or blood, sinew-bound . . . the bones no longer held together, scattered in this direction and that: here a hand-bone, there a foot-bone, here a leg-bone, there a rib, here a hip-bone, there a back-bone, here the skull.[2] What would you think, monks? That that which was former beauty and loveliness has vanished, a peril has appeared?"

"Yes, Lord."

"This too, monks, is a peril in material shapes. And again, monks, one might see that same lady, her body thrown aside in a cemetery, the bones white and something like sea-shells . . . a heap of dried-up bones more than a year old . . . the bones gone rotten and reduced to powder. What would you think, monks? That that which was former beauty and loveliness has vanished, a peril has appeared?"

"Yes, Lord."

"This too, monks, is a peril in material shapes.

And what, monks, is the escape from material shapes? Whatever, monks, is the control of desire and attachment, the getting rid of desire and attachment to material shapes, this is the escape from material shapes.[3]

Monks, whatever recluses or brahmans do not thus comprehend the satisfaction in material shapes as satisfaction, the peril as peril, the escape as escape as it really is, these indeed will neither know material shapes accurately themselves nor will they arouse another to a similar condition, so that, as he fares along, he will know material shapes accurately—this situation does not exist. But, monks, whatever recluses or brahmans comprehend thus the satisfaction in material shapes as satisfaction, the peril as peril, the escape as escape as it really is, these indeed either know material shapes

---

[1] As at *M.* i. 58.

[2] As at *A.* iii. 324.

[3] As at *S.* iii. 62.

accurately themselves or they will arouse another to a similar condition, so that, as he fares along, he will know material shapes accurately—this situation exists.

And what, monks, is the satisfaction of feelings ? As to this, monks, a monk aloof from pleasures of the senses, aloof from unskilled states of mind, enters into and abides in the first meditation which is accompanied by initial thought and discursive thought, is born of aloofness, and is rapturous and joyful. Monks, at the time in which the monk, aloof from pleasures of the senses, aloof from unskilled states of mind, enters into and abides in the first meditation . . . and is rapturous and joyful, if at that time he does not strive for his own hurt, if he does not strive for the hurt of others, if he does not strive for the hurt of both, **[90]** at that very time he experiences a feeling that is not hurtful. I, monks, say that not-hurtfulness is the highest satisfaction among feelings.

And again, monks, a monk, by allaying initial thought and discursive thought, with the mind subjectively tranquillised and fixed on one point, enters into and abides in the second meditation which is devoid of initial and discursive thought, is born of concentration, and is rapturous and joyful . . . the third meditation . . . enters into and abides in the fourth meditation. Monks, at the time in which the monk by getting rid of joy and by getting rid of anguish, and by the going down of his former pleasures and sorrows, enters into and abides in the fourth meditation, which has neither anguish nor joy and which is entirely purified by equanimity and mindfulness, if at that time he does not strive for his own hurt, if he does not strive for the hurt of others, if he does not strive for the hurt of both, at that very time he experiences a feeling that is not hurtful. I, monks, say that not-hurtfulness is the highest satisfaction among feelings.

And what, monks, is the peril of feelings ? Inasmuch, monks, as feelings are impermanent, ill, liable to change, this is the peril of feelings.[1]

And what, monks, is the escape from feelings ? Whatever, monks, is the control of desire and attachment, the getting rid of desire and attachment to feelings, this is the escape from feelings.

Monks, whatever recluses or brahmans do not thus comprehend the satisfaction in feelings as satisfaction, the peril as peril, the escape as escape as it really is, these indeed will neither know

---

[1] As at *S*. iii. 63.

feelings accurately themselves nor will they arouse another to a similar condition, so that, as he fares along, he will know feelings accurately—this situation does not exist. But, monks, whatever recluses or brahmans comprehend thus the satisfaction in feelings as satisfaction, the peril as peril, the escape as escape as it really is, these indeed know feelings accurately themselves or they will arouse another to a similar condition, so that, as he fares along, he will know feelings accurately—this situation exists."

Thus spoke the Lord. Delighted, these monks rejoiced in what the Lord had said.

The Greater Discourse on the Stems of Anguish:
The Third

14. LESSER DISCOURSE ON THE STEMS OF ANGUISH

(Cūḷadukkhakkhandhasutta)

[**91**] Thus have I heard: At one time the Lord was staying among the Sakyans at Kapilavatthu in Nigrodha's park.[1] Then Mahānāma the Sakyan[2] approached the Lord; having approached, having greeted the Lord, he sat down at a respectful distance. As Mahānāma the Sakyan was sitting down at a respectful distance, he spoke thus to the Lord:

"For a long time, Lord, I have thus understood *dhamma* taught by the Lord: Greed is a depravity of the mind,[3] aversion is a depravity of the mind, confusion is a depravity of the mind. It is thus that I, Lord, understand *dhamma* taught by the Lord: Greed is a depravity of the mind, aversion is a depravity of the mind, confusion is a depravity of the mind. But at times things belonging to greed, taking hold of my mind, persist, and things belonging to aversion, taking hold of my mind, persist, and things belonging

---

[1] *MA*. ii. 61 says Nigrodha was a Sakyan. He came to Kapilavatthu and made a dwelling-place for the Lord in his own park, *ārāma*, and gave it to the Lord.

[2] Suddhodana's nephew, son of Sukkodana, and brother of Anuruddha, Gotama's cousin.

[3] *Cf. M*. i. 36.

to confusion, taking hold of my mind, persist. It occurred to me thus, Lord: Now what can be the quality in me, not got rid of subjectively, on account of which at times things belonging to greed . . . and things belonging to aversion . . . and things belonging to confusion, taking hold of my mind, persist ?"

" Indeed there is a quality in you, Mahānāma, not got rid of subjectively, on account of which at times things belonging to greed, taking hold of your mind, persist, and things belonging to aversion . . . and things belonging to confusion, taking hold of your mind, persist. But this quality could be got rid of subjectively by you, Mahānāma, if you would not dwell in a house, if you would not enjoy pleasures of the senses. But inasmuch as this quality, Mahānāma, is not got rid of by you subjectively, therefore you dwell in a house and enjoy pleasures of the senses.

Pleasures of the senses are of little satisfaction, of much ill, of much tribulation wherein is more peril.[1] Yet if this, Mahānāma, comes to be well seen as it really is, through perfect intuitive wisdom by an ariyan disciple, but if he does not come to rapture and joy apart from pleasures of the senses, apart from unskilled states of mind, or to something better than that,[2] then he is not yet one unseduced by pleasures of the senses. But when, Mahānāma, an ariyan disciple thinks: ' Pleasures of the senses are of little satisfaction, of much ill, of much tribulation wherein is more peril,' and if this comes to be well seen, as it really is, through perfect intuitive wisdom by the ariyan disciple, and if he comes to rapture and joy apart from pleasures of the senses, apart from unskilled states of mind, and to something better than that, then he is one who is not seduced by pleasures of the senses.

And I too, [**92**] Mahānāma, before my awakening while I was still the *bodhisatta*, not fully awakened, thought: ' Pleasures of the senses are of little satisfaction, of much ill, of much tribulation, wherein is more peril; ' and although this came to be well seen thus, as it really is, through perfect intuitive wisdom, I came to no rapture and joy apart from pleasures of the senses, apart from unskilled states of mind, nor to anything better than that. So I was conscious that I was not yet one unseduced by pleasures of the senses. But when, Mahānāma, I thought: ' Pleasures of the senses are of little

---

[1] *Vin.* iv. 134.

[2] *MA.* ii. 63 points out that rapture and joy pertain to the first two meditations. Something higher than that will be connected with the third and fourth meditations.

satisfaction . . . wherein is more peril,' and when this was well seen thus, as it really is, through perfect intuitive wisdom, and I came to rapture and joy apart from the pleasures of the senses, apart from unskilled states of mind, and to something better than that, then was I conscious that I was one not seduced by pleasures of the senses.

And what, Mahānāma, is the satisfaction in pleasures of the senses ? These five, Mahānāma, are the strands of sense-pleasures.[1] What five ? Material shapes cognisable by the eye, agreeable, pleasant, loved, enticing, connected with sensual pleasures, alluring. Sounds cognisable by the ear . . . Smells cognisable by the nose . . . Tastes cognisable by the tongue . . . Touches cognisable by the body . . . agreeable, pleasant, loved, enticing, connected with sensual pleasure, alluring. These, Mahānāma, are the five strands of sense-pleasures. Whatever pleasure, whatever happiness arises in consequence of these five strands of sense-pleasures, this is the satisfaction in sense-pleasures.

And what, Mahānāma, is the peril in sense-pleasures ? . . . (*repeat from p.* **85**, *l.* **30** to *p.* **87**, *l.* **26**, text, *with* Mahānāma *substituted for* monks). . . . This, Mahānāma, is a peril in sense-pleasures[2] that is of the future, a stem of ill, having pleasures of senses as the cause, having pleasures of senses as the provenance, being a consequence of pleasures of the senses, the very cause of pleasures of the senses.

At one time I, Mahānāma, was staying near Rājagaha on Mount Vulture Peak. Now at that time several Jains[3] on the Black Rock on the slopes of (Mount) Isigili came to be standing erect and refusing a seat;[4] they were experiencing feelings that were acute, painful, sharp, severe. Then I, Mahānāma, having emerged from solitary meditation towards evening, approached the slopes of (Mount) Isigili, the Black Rock and those Jains; having approached I spoke thus to those Jains: 'Why do you, reverend Jains, standing erect and refusing a seat, experience feelings that are acute, painful sharp, severe ?' When I had thus spoken, Mahānāma, those Jains spoke thus to me:

---

[1] As at *M.* i. 85; *A.* iii. 411; *D.* i. 245.

[2] *MA.* ii. 63 points out that " escape " is not spoken of here. " This teaching is resolved to speak of it. One dead-end is devotion to pleasures of the senses, the other is devotion to self-mortification. My teaching is freed from these dead-ends." *Cf. Vin.* i. 10.

[3] *nigaṇṭha.*

[4] As at *M.* i. 78, 308, *A.* i. 296, ii. 206.

'Your reverence, Nāthaputta the Jain is all-knowing,[1] all-seeing; he claims all-embracing knowledge-and-vision,[2] saying: "Whether I am walking or standing still or asleep or [**93**] awake, knowledge-and-vision is permanently and continuously before me." He speaks thus: "If there is, Jains, an evil deed that was formerly done by you, wear it away by this severe austerity. That which is the non-doing of an evil deed in the future is from control of body, from control of speech, from control of thought here, now.[3] Thus by burning up,[4] by making an end of former deeds, by the non-doing of new deeds, there is no flowing[5] in the future. From there being no flowing in the future is the destruction of deeds;[6] from the destruction of deeds is the destruction of ill; from the destruction of ill is the destruction of feeling; from the destruction of feeling all ill will become worn away." And because that is approved of by us as well as being pleasing to us, therefore we are delighted.'

When they had spoken thus, I, Mahānāma, spoke thus to those Jains: 'But do you, reverend Jains, know[7] that you yourselves were in the past, that you were not not?'

'Not this, your reverence.'

'But do you, reverend Jains, know that you yourselves did this evil deed in the past, that you did not not do it?'

'Not this, your reverence.'

'But do you, reverend Jains, know that you did not do an evil deed like this or like that?'

'Not this, your reverence.'

'But do you, reverend Jains, know that so much ill is worn away, or that so much ill is to be worn away, or that when so much ill is worn away, all ill will become worn away?'

'Not this, your reverence.'

'But do you, reverend Jains, know the getting rid of unskilled states of mind here and now, the uprising of skilled states?'

'Not this, your reverence.'

'From what you say, reverend Jains, you do not know then whether you yourselves were in the past, whether you were not not; you do not know whether in the past you yourselves did this evil deed, whether you did not not do it; you do not know whether

---

[1] *Cf. A.* i. 220, 221; iv. 428. [2] *M.* i. 482, 519, ii. 31.

[3] Not *diṭṭh'eva dhamma*, but *ettha etarahi*. [4] *tapasā*, incandescence.

[5] *anavassavo. MA.* does not explain. *Cf. Vin.* ii. 89, *M.* ii. 246. At *A.* i. 220-21 the reading is *setughātam*, bridge-breaking.

[6] *Cf. M.* ii. 217 as well as *A.* i. 221. [7] *Cf. M.* ii. 214-15.

you did an evil deed like this or like that; you do not know so much ill is worn away, or that so much ill is to be worn away, or that when so much ill is worn away all ill will become worn away; you do not know the getting rid of unskilled states of mind, the uprising of skilled states.

'This being so, reverend Jains, do those who are born again among men in the world and are hunters, bloody-handed, dealing in cruelty[1]—do these go forth among the Jains?'

'Now, reverend Gotama, happiness is not to be achieved through happiness, happiness is to be achieved through pain. If, reverend Gotama, [**94**] happiness were to be achieved through happiness, King Seniya Bimbisāra of Magadha could achieve happiness, King Seniya Bimbisāra of Magadha would be more of a dweller in happiness than the venerable Gotama.'

'Undoubtedly this speech was made hastily by the reverend Jains, without deliberation: "Now, reverend Gotama, happiness is not to be achieved through happiness. . . . King Seniya Bimbisāra of Magadha would be more of a dweller in happiness than the venerable Gotama." For it is I who should be questioned thus on this subject: Which of these venerable ones is more of a dweller in happiness: King Seniya Bimbisāra of Magadha or the venerable Gotama?'

'Undoubtedly, reverend Gotama, this speech was made by us hastily, without deliberation: "Now, reverend Gotama, happiness is not to be achieved through happiness, happiness is to be achieved through pain. If, reverend Gotama, happiness were to be achieved through happiness, King Seniya Bimbisāra of Magadha could achieve happiness, King Seniya Bimbisāra of Magadha would be more of a dweller in happiness than the venerable Gotama." But let that be, for now we will question the venerable Gotama: Which of the venerable ones is more of a dweller in happiness: King Seniya Bimbisāra of Magadha or the venerable Gotama?'

'Well then, reverend Jains, I will ask you a question in return on that very subject. As it pleases you, so reply to it. What do you think about this, reverend Jains: Is King Seniya Bimbisāra of Magadha, without moving his body, without uttering a word, able to stay experiencing nothing but happiness for seven nights and days?'

'No, your reverence.'

'What do you think about this, reverend Jains: Is King Seniya

---

[1] *kurūrakammantā*, as at *A*. iii. 383.

Bimbisāra of Magadha, without moving his body, without uttering a word, able to stay experiencing nothing but happiness for six nights and days, for five, for four, for three, for two nights and days, for one night and day?'

'No, your reverence.'

'But I, reverend Jains, am able, without moving my body, without uttering a word, to stay experiencing nothing but happiness for one night and day. I, reverend Jains, am able, without moving my body, without uttering a word, to stay experiencing nothing but happiness[1] for two nights and days, for three, four, five, six, for seven[2] nights and days. What do you think about this, reverend Jains: This being so, who is more of a dweller in happiness, King Seniya Bimbisāra of Magadha or I?'

'This being so, the venerable [**95**] Gotama himself is more of a dweller in happiness than King Seniya Bimbisāra of Magadha.'"

Thus spoke the Lord. Delighted, Mahānāma the Sakyan rejoiced in what the Lord had said.

The Lesser Discourse on the Stems of Anguish:
The Fourth

15. DISCOURSE ON MEASURING IN ACCORDANCE WITH

(Anumānasutta)[3]

THUS have I heard: At one time the venerable Moggallāna the Great was staying among the Bhaggas in Sumsumāragira[4] in Bhesakaḷā Grove in the deer-park. Then the venerable Moggallāna the Great addressed the monks, saying: "Reverend monks". "Your

---

[1] The happiness of attaining the fruits (of the Way).

[2] Quoted *Kvu.* 459.

[3] Referred to at *MA.* ii. 246. *MA.* ii. 67 says that this Sutta was known to the Ancients as the Bhikkhupātimokkha, and should be reflected upon three times daily. It should be compared with Sangh. XII (*Vin.* iii. 177-79) and see *B.D.* i. Intr. xxviii *f.* and pp. 309-13 for notes. Note that the Buddha is not mentioned in this discourse. *Anumāna* may mean "inference," or "argument."

[4] This is not *giri*, hill, but *gira*, a sound, utterance. *MA.* ii. 65 says

reverence," these monks answered the venerable Moggallāna the Great in assent. Then the venerable Moggallāna the Great spoke thus:

"Now, if, your reverences, a monk invites, saying: 'Let the venerable ones speak[1] to me, I should be spoken to by the venerable ones,' but if he is one whom it is difficult to speak to,[2] endowed with qualities which make him difficult to speak to, intractable, incapable of being instructed,[3] then his fellow Brahmafarers judge that he should not be spoken to and that he should not be instructed[4] and that trust should not be placed in that individual.

Now what, your reverences, are the qualities which make him difficult to speak to? Herein, your reverences, a monk comes to be of evil desires and in the thrall of evil desires. Whatever monk, your reverences, comes to be of evil desires and in the thrall of evil desires, this is a quality that makes him difficult to speak to. And again, your reverences, a monk exalts himself and disparages others.[5] Whatever monk exalts himself and disparages others, this too is a quality that makes him difficult to speak to. And again, your reverences, a monk comes to be wrathful, overpowered by wrath. Whatever monk is wrathful, overpowered by wrath, this too is a quality.... And again, your reverences, a monk comes to be wrathful and because of his wrath is a fault-finder.[6] Whatever monk is wrathful and because of his wrath is a fault-finder, this too is a quality.... And again, your reverences, a monk comes to be wrathful and because of his wrath is one who takes offence. Whatever monk is wrathful and because of his wrath is one who takes offence, this too is a quality.... And again, your reverences, a monk comes to be wrathful and because of his wrath utters words bordering on wrath. Whatever monk is wrathful and because of his wrath utters

---

Sumsumāragira is the name of a town. When the foundations were being laid, a crocodile, *sumsumāra*, in a pool nearby made a sound, let forth an utterance, *giraṃ nicchāresi*, and so they gave the town this name when it had been built. See *B.D.* ii. 398.

[1] *MA.* ii. 66, let them exhort and instruct.

[2] *dubbaca,* see *B.D.* i. 310, *n.* 1.

[3] *MA.* ii. 66: he says, Why do you speak to me? I know for myself what is allowable and what is not, what has error and what has not, what is the goal and what is not.

[4] *Cf. A.* ii. 113: This is destruction in the discipline for an ariyan: when both a Tathāgata and fellow Brahma-farers deem that a man to be tamed is not to be spoken to, not to be instructed.

[5] *Cf. M.* i. 19.

[6] Or, grudge-bearer.

words bordering on wrath, this too is a quality that makes him difficult to speak to. And again, your reverences, a monk, reproved,[1] blurts out reproof against the reprover. Whatever monk, reproved, blurts out reproof against the reprover, this too is a quality that makes him difficult to speak to. And again, your reverences, a monk, reproved, disparages the reprover for the reproof. Whatever monk, reproved, disparages the reprover for the reproof, this too is a quality. . . . And again, [**96**] your reverences, a monk, reproved, rounds on[2] the reprover for the reproof. Whatever monk, reproved, rounds on the reprover for the reproof, this too is a quality . . . And again, your reverences, a monk, reproved, shelves the question by (asking) the reprover another,[3] answers off the point,[4] and evinces temper and ill-will and sulkiness. Whatever monk, reproved, shelves the question by asking the reprover another, answers off the point, and evinces temper and ill-will and sulkiness, this too is a quality. . . . And again, your reverences, a monk, reproved, does not succeed in explaining his movements[5] to the reprover. Whatever monk, reproved, does not succeed in explaining his movements to the reprover, this too is a quality that makes him difficult to speak to. And again, your reverences, a monk comes to be harsh, spiteful.[6] Whatever monk comes to be harsh, spiteful, this too is a quality. . . . And again, your reverences, a monk comes to be envious, grudging. Whatever monk comes to be envious, grudging, this too is a quality. . . . And again, your reverences, a monk comes to be treacherous, deceitful. Whatever monk comes to be treacherous, deceitful, this too is a quality. . . . And again, you reverences, a monk comes to be stubborn, proud. Whatever monk comes to be stubborn, proud, this too is a quality. . . . And again, your reverences, a monk comes to seize the temporal, grasping it tightly, not letting go of it easily. Whatever monk comes to seize the temporal,

---

[1] *cudito*, reproved for a fault. *Cf. A.* iv. 193, and *Vin.* i. 173, ii. 248 *ff.*

[2] *paccāropeti.* He says, But it is *you* who have fallen into such and such an offence—*you* confess first. *Cf. A.* iv. 193.

[3] *aññen' aññaṃ paṭicarati*; see *B.D.* ii. 164, *n.* 4.

[4] *bahiddhā kathaṃ apanāmeti*, takes the talk outside. *M.A.* ii. 66 gives as an example, if he is asked whether he has fallen into such and such an offence, he answers that he is going to Pāṭaliputta.

[5] *apadāne. MA.* ii. 66 *attano cariyāya.* He is not able to explain where he was staying, on whom or what depending, what he was doing at that time or where he was or what another was doing or where *he* was. Colloquially " goings on."

[6] As at *M.* i. 42-3, ii. 245; *Vin.* ii. 89; *A.* iii. 335; *D.* iii. 45, 246-47.

grasping it tightly, not letting go of it easily,[1] this too is a quality that makes him difficult to speak to. These, your reverences, are called the qualities which make it difficult to speak to (a monk).

But if, your reverences, a monk invites, saying: 'Let the venerable ones speak to me, I should be spoken to by the venerable ones' and if he is one whom it is easy to speak to, endowed with qualities which make him easy to speak to, tractable, capable of being instructed, then his fellow Brahma-farers judge that he should be spoken to and that he should be instructed and that trust should be placed in that individual.

And what, your reverences, are the qualities which make him easy to speak to? Herein, your reverences, a monk does not come to be of evil desires nor in the thrall of evil desires. Whatever monk comes to be not of evil desires nor in the thrall of evil desires, this is a quality that makes him easy to speak to. And again, your reverences, a monk does not come to exalt himself nor to disparage others . . . easy to speak to. And again, your reverences, a monk does not come to be wrathful, overpowered by wrath . . . easy to speak to. And again, your reverences, a monk does not come to be wrathful and a fault-finder because of his wrath . . . easy to speak to. And again, your reverences, a monk does not come to be wrathful and because of his wrath takes offence . . . easy to speak to. And again, your reverences, a monk does not come to be wrathful and because of his wrath utters words bordering on wrath. Whatever monk does not come to be wrathful and because of his wrath utters words bordering on wrath, this too is a quality that makes him easy to speak to. And again, your reverences, a monk, reproved, does not blurt out reproof against the reprover . . . easy to speak to. And again, your reverences, a monk, reproved, does not disparage the reprover for the reproof . . . [**97**] easy to speak to. And again, your reverences, a monk, reproved, does not round on the reprover for the reproof . . . easy to speak to. And again, your reverences, a monk, reproved, does not shelve the question by asking the reprover another, he does not answer off the point, he does not evince temper and ill-will and sulkiness. Whatever monk, reproved, does not shelve the question by asking the reprover another, does not answer off the point, does not evince temper, ill-will and sulkiness, this too is a quality that makes him easy to speak to. And again, your reverences, a monk, reproved, succeeds in

---

[1] As at *M.* i. 43.

explaining his movements to the reprover . . . easy to speak to. And again, your reverences, a monk comes to be not harsh, not spiteful . . . easy to speak to. And again, your reverences, a monk comes to be not envious, not grudging . . . easy to speak to. And again, your reverences, a monk comes to be not treacherous, not deceitful . . . easy to speak to. And again, your reverences, a monk comes to be not stubborn, not proud . . . easy to speak to. And again, your reverences, a monk comes not to seize the temporal, not grasping it tightly, letting go of it easily. Whatever monk comes not to seize the temporal, not grasping it tightly, letting go of it easily, this too is a quality that makes him easy to speak to. These, your reverences, are called the qualities that make it easy to speak to (a monk).

Therein[1], your reverences, self ought to be measured against self[2] thus by a monk: 'That person who is of evil desires and who is in the thrall of evil desires, that person is displeasing and disagreeable to me; and, similarly, if I were of evil desire and in the thrall of evil desires, I would be displeasing and disagreeable to others.' When a monk, your reverences, knows this, he should make up his mind that: 'I will not be of evil desires nor in the thrall of evil desires.' 'That person who exalts himself and disparages others is displeasing and disagreeable to me; and, similarly, if I were one to exalt myself and disparage others, I would be displeasing and disagreeable to others.' When a monk knows this, your reverences, he should make up his mind and think: 'I will not be one who exalts himself and disparages others.' 'Whatever person is wrathful, overcome by wrath . . . I will not be one who is wrathful nor overcome by wrath.' 'Whatever person is wrathful and because of his wrath is a fault-finder . . . I will not be one who is wrathful nor one who is a fault-finder because of wrath.' 'Whatever person is wrathful and because of his wrath is one who takes offence . . . I will not be one who is wrathful nor one who takes offence because of his wrath.' 'Whatever person is wrathful and because of his wrath utters words bordering on wrath . . . I will not be one who is wrathful nor one who utters words bordering on wrath because of wrath.' 'Whatever person, reproved, blurts out

[1] *I.e.* in these sixteen qualities, *MA*. ii. 67.

[2] *attanā va attānaṃ anuminitabbam.* The last word no doubt helps to give this Sutta its title, *anumāna*. It means inferring, drawing a deduction, and is explained at *MA*. ii. 67 by *anumetabbo, tuletabbo, tīretabbo,* to be measured, weighed, decided upon.

reproof against the reprover . . . **[98]** I, reproved, will not blurt out reproof against the reprover.' 'Whatever person, reproved, disparages the reprover for the reproof . . . I, reproved, will not disparage the reprover for the reproof.' 'Whatever person, reproved, rounds on the reprover for the reproof . . . I, reproved, will not round on the reprover for the reproof.' 'Whatever person, reproved, shelves the question by asking the reprover another, answers off the point, and evinces temper, ill-will and sulkiness . . . I, reproved, will not shelve the question by asking the reprover another, I will not answer off the point, I will not evince temper, ill-will and sulkiness.' 'Whatever person, reproved, does not succeed in explaining his movements to the reprover . . . I will explain my movements to the reprover.' 'Whatever person is harsh, spiteful . . . I will be not harsh, not spiteful.' 'Whatever person is envious, grudging . . . I will not be envious, grudging.' 'Whatever person is treacherous, deceitful . . . I will not be treacherous, deceitful.' 'Whatever person is stubborn, proud . . . I will not be stubborn, proud.' 'Whatever person comes to seize the temporal, grasping it tightly, not letting go of it easily, that person is displeasing and disagreeable to me; and, similarly, if I were to seize the temporal, grasping it tightly, not letting go of it easily, I would be displeasing and disagreeable to others.' When a monk, your reverences, knows this, he should make up his mind and think: 'I will not be one to seize the temporal, not grasping it tightly, letting go of it easily.'

Therein, your reverences, self ought to be reflected upon by self thus by a monk: 'Now, am I of evil desires, in the thrall of evil desires?' If, your reverences, while the monk is reflecting, he knows thus: 'I am of evil desires, in the thrall of evil desires,' then, your reverences, that monk should strive to get rid of those evil unskilled states. But if, your reverences, that monk, while reflecting, knows thus: 'I am not of evil desires, not in the thrall of evil desires,' then, with rapture and delight, they should be forsaken by that monk, training day and night in skilled states. And again, your reverences, self ought to be reflected on by self thus by a monk: 'Now, am I one who exalts himself, disparages others?' If, your reverences, the monk, while reflecting, knows thus . . . that monk should strive to get rid of those evil unskilled states. But if, your reverences, . . . **[99]** that monk, while reflecting, knows thus: 'I am not one who exalts himself, disparages others' . . . in skilled states. And again . . . 'Now, am I one who is wrathful, overpowered by wrath ?' . . . 'I am not one who is wrathful, overpowered by wrath' . . . in skilled states. And again . . . 'Now, am I one who is wrathful and a fault-finder because of wrath ?' . . . 'I am not one who is wrathful and a fault-finder because of wrath' . . . in skilled states. And again . . . 'Now, am I one who is wrathful and takes offence because of wrath ?' . . . 'I am not one who is wrathful and takes offence because of wrath' . . . in skilled states. And again . . . 'Now, am I one who is wrathful and who because of wrath utters words bordering on wrath ?' . . . 'I am not one who is wrathful and who because of wrath utters words bordering on wrath' . . . in skilled states. And again . . . 'Now, am I one who, reproved, blurts out reproof against the reprover ?' . . . 'I, reproved, do not blurt out reproof against the reprover' . . . in skilled states. And again . . . 'Now, do I, reproved, disparage the reprover for the reproof ?' . . . 'I, reproved, do not disparage the reprover for the reproof' . . . in skilled states. And again . . . 'Now, do I, reproved, round on the reprover for the reproof ?' .. 'I, reproved, do not round on the reprover for the reproof' . . . in skilled states. And again . . . 'Now do I, reproved, shelve the question by (asking) the reprover another, do I speak off the point, do I evince temper, ill-will and sulkiness ?' . . . 'I, reproved, do not shelve the question by (asking) the reprover another, I do not speak off the point, I do not evince temper, ill-will and sulkiness' . . . in skilled states. And again . . . 'Now, do I, reproved, succeed in explaining my movements to the reprover ?' . . . 'I, reproved, succeed in explaining my movements to the reprover' . . . in skilled states. And again . . . 'Now, am I harsh, spiteful ?' . . . 'I am not harsh, spiteful' . . . in skilled states. And again . . . 'Now, am I envious, grudging ?' . . . 'I am not envious, grudging' . . . in skilled states. And again . . . 'Now, am I treacherous, deceitful ?' . . . 'I am not treacherous, deceitful' . . . in skilled states. And again . . . 'Now, am I stubborn, proud ?' . . . 'I am not stubborn, proud' . . . in skilled states. And again, your reverences, self ought to be reflected upon by self thus by a monk: 'Now, am I one to seize the temporal, grasping it tightly, not letting go of it easily ?' If, your reverences, the monk, while reflecting, knows thus: 'I am one to seize the temporal, grasping it tightly, not letting go of it easily,' then, your reverences, **[100]** that monk should strive to get rid of those evil unskilled states. But if, your reverences, that monk, while reflecting, knows thus: 'I am not one to seize the temporal, not grasping it tightly, letting go of it easily,' then, your reverences, with rapture and delight they should be forsaken by that monk, training day and night in skilled states.

If, your reverences, while reflecting, a monk beholds that all these evil unskilled states are not got rid of in himself, then, your reverences, that monk must strive to get rid of all these evil unskilled states. But if, your reverences, while reflecting, a monk beholds that all these evil unskilled states are got rid of in himself, then, your reverences, with rapture and delight that monk should forsake them, training day and night in skilled states.[1]

Your reverences, it is like a woman or a man, young, in the prime of life, and fond of ornaments who is pondering on his own reflection in a mirror that is quite clear, quite pure, or in a bowl of limpid water.[2] If he sees dust or blemish there, he strives to get rid of that dust or blemish. But if he does not see dust or blemish there, he is pleased in consequence and thinks: 'Indeed, this is good for me, indeed I am quite clean.' Even so, your reverences, if a monk, while reflecting, beholds that all these evil unskilled states in the self are not got rid of, then, your reverences, he strives to get rid of all these evil, unskilled states. But if, your reverences, the monk, while reflecting, beholds that all these evil unskilled states in the self are got rid of, then, your reverences, with rapture and delight that monk should forsake them, training day and night in skilled states."

Thus spoke the venerable Moggallāna the Great. Delighted, these monks rejoiced in what the venerable Moggallāna the Great had said.

Discourse on Measuring in Accordance with: the Fifth

---

[1] *MA.* ii. 67 notices the fivefold *pahāna*, getting rid of. The last one is the getting rid of by "escape," *nissaraṇa*, when one has come to *nibbāna*. *Cf. SnA.* 8; *Asl.* 351 (*Expos.* ii. 454).

[2] *Cf. Vin.* ii. 107; *D.* i. 80; *S.* iii. 105.

16. DISCOURSE ON MENTAL BARRENNESS[1]

(Cetokhilasutta)

[**101**] Thus have I heard: At one time the Lord was staying near Sāvatthī in the Jeta Grove in Anāthapiṇḍika's monastery. There the Lord addressed the monks, saying: "Monks." "Revered One," these monks answered the Lord in assent. The Lord spoke thus:

"Monks, by whatever monk five mental barrennesses[2] are not got rid of, five mental bondages[3] are not rooted out, that he should come to growth, expansion, maturity[4] in this *dhamma* and discipline —such a situation does not occur. Which are the five mental barrennesses that are not got rid of by him? Herein, monks, the monk has doubts about the Teacher, is perplexed, is not convinced, is not sure. Monks, whatever monk has doubts about the Teacher, is perplexed, is not convinced, is not sure, his mind does not incline to ardour, to continual application, to perseverance, to striving. This is the first mental barrenness that thus comes not to be got rid of by him whose mind does not incline to ardour, to continual application, to perseverance, to striving.

And again, monks, the monk has doubts about *dhamma* . . . has doubts about the Order . . . has doubts about the training, is perplexed, is not convinced, is not sure. Monks, whatever monk has doubts about the training, is perplexed, is not convinced, is not sure, his mind does not incline to ardour, to continual application, to perseverance, to striving. This is the fourth mental barrenness that thus comes to be not got rid of by him whose mind does not incline to ardour . . . to striving.

And again, monks, a monk comes to be angry, displeased with his fellow Brahma-farers, the mind worsened, barren.[5] Monks, whatever monk comes to be angry, displeased with his fellow Brahma-farers, his mind worsened, barren, his mind does not incline to

---

[1] Or "spikes," *khila* being a post.

[2] *Cf. D.* iii. 237; *A.* iii. 248, iv. 460, v. 17.

[3] The same references apply here; and see below, *M.* i. 103.

[4] *MA.* ii. 68, in the moral habits, the Way, nibbāna, respectively; or, in moral habit and concentration, insight and the way, the fruits and nibbāna.

[5] *Cf. Vin.* iii. 163, 255, iv. 236, 238; *D.* iii. 238.

ardour, to continual application, to perseverance, to striving. This is the fifth mental barrenness that thus comes not to be got rid of by him whose mind does not incline to ardour, to continual application, to perseverance, to striving. These are the five mental barrennesses that are not got rid of.

And what are the five mental bondages that are not rooted out in him? In this case, monks, a monk is not without attachment to sense-pleasures, not without desire, not without affection, not without thirst, not without fever, not without craving. Monks, whatever monk is not without attachment to sense-pleasures . . . not without craving, his mind does not incline to ardour, to continual application, to perseverance, to striving. This is the first mental bondage that thus comes not to be rooted out by him whose mind does not incline to ardour, to continual application, to perseverance, to striving.

And again, monks, a monk is not without attachment to body[1] . . . the second mental bondage that thus comes to be not rooted out . . .

[102] And again, monks, a monk is not without attachment to material shapes[2] . . . the third mental bondage that thus comes to be not rooted out. . . .

And again, monks, a monk having eaten as much as his belly will hold, lives intent on the ease of bed, on the ease of lying down, on the ease of slumber. Whatever monk, having eaten as much as his belly will hold, lives intent on the ease of bed, on the ease of lying down, on the ease of slumber, his mind does not incline to ardour, to continual application, to perseverance, to striving. This is the fourth mental bondage that comes to be not rooted out by him whose mind does not incline to ardour, to striving.

And again, monks, a monk fares the Brahma-faring aspiring after some class of *devas*, thinking: 'By this moral habit or custom or austerity or Brahma-faring I will become a *deva*[3] or one among the *devas*.[3] Whatever monk fares the Brahma-faring aspiring after some class of *devas*, thinking: 'By this moral habit or custom or austerity or Brahma-faring I will become a *deva* or one among the *devas*', his mind does not incline to ardour, to continual application, to perseverance, to striving. This is the fifth mental bondage that comes not to be rooted out by him whose mind does not incline

---

[1] *MA.* ii. 69, his own body. [2] *Ibid.*, external ones.
[3] *Ibid.*, a *deva* of great or little esteem.

to ardour . . . to striving. These are his five mental bondages that are not rooted out. Monks, by whatever monk these five mental barrennesses are not got rid of, these five mental bondages are not rooted out, that he should come to growth, expansion, maturity in this *dhamma* and discipline—such a situation does not occur.

Monks, by whatever monk five mental barrennesses are got rid of, five mental bondages are properly rooted out, that he should come to growth, expansion, maturity in this *dhamma* and discipline—this situation occurs. Which are the five mental barrennesses that are got rid of by him? Herein, monks, a monk has no doubts about the Teacher, is not perplexed, is convinced, is sure. Monks, whatever monk has no doubts about the Teacher . . . is sure, his mind inclines to ardour, to continual application, to perseverance, to striving. This is the first mental barrenness that comes to be got rid of by him whose mind inclines to ardour . . . to striving.

And again, monks, a monk has no doubts about *dhamma* . . . about the Order . . . about the training . . . is sure. Monks, whatever monk has no doubts about the training . . . is sure, his mind inclines to ardour, to continual application, to perseverance, to striving. This is the fourth mental barrenness that comes to be got rid of by him whose mind inclines to ardour . . . to striving.

And again, monks, a monk does not come to be angry, displeased, with his fellow Brahma-farers, the mind worsened, barren. Monks, whatever monk does not come to be angry, displeased, with his fellow Brahma-farers, his mind worsened, barren, his mind inclines to ardour, [**103**] to continual application, to perseverance, to striving. This is the fifth mental barrenness that thus comes to be got rid of by him whose mind inclines to ardour, to continual application, to perseverance, to striving. These are the five mental barrennesses that are got rid of by him.

And what are the five mental bondages that are properly rooted out by him? In this case, monks, a monk comes to be without attachment to sense-pleasures, without desire, without affection, without thirst, without fever, without craving. Whatever monk is without attachment to sense-pleasures . . . without craving, his mind inclines to ardour, to continual application, to perseverance, to striving. This is the first mental bondage that comes to be properly rooted out by him whose mind inclines to ardour . . . to striving.

And again, monks, a monk comes to be without attachment to body . . without attachment to material shapes . . . not having eaten as much as his belly will hold, does not live intent on the ease of bed, on the ease of lying down, on the ease of slumber. Whatever monk, not having eaten as much as his belly will hold, does not live intent on the ease of bed . . . on the ease of slumber, his mind inclines to ardour, to continual application, to perseverance, to striving. This is the fourth mental bondage that comes to be properly rooted out by him whose mind inclines to ardour . . . to striving.

And again, monks, a monk does not fare the Brahma-faring aspiring after some class of *devas* and thinking: 'By this moral habit or custom or austerity or Brahma-faring I will become a *deva* or one among the *devas*.' Whatever monk does not fare the Brahma-faring aspiring after some class of *devas* and thinking: 'By this moral habit or custom or austerity or Brahma-faring I will become a *deva* or one among the *devas*' his mind inclines to ardour, to continual application, to perseverance, to striving. This is the fifth mental bondage that comes to be properly rooted out by him whose mind inclines to ardour . . . to striving. These are the five forms of mental bondage that are properly rooted out in him. Monks, by whatever monk these five forms of mental barrenness are got rid of, these five forms of mental bondage are properly rooted out, that he should come to growth, expansion, maturity in this *dhamma* and discipline—such a situation occurs.

He cultivates the basis of psychic power[1] that is possessed of concentration of intention with activities of striving; he cultivates the basis of psychic power that is possessed of concentration of energy with activities of striving; he cultivates the basis of psychic power that is possessed of concentration of consciousness with activities of striving; he cultivates the basis of psychic power that is possessed of concentration of investigation with activities of striving, with exertion as the fifth. Monks, if a monk is thus possessed of fifteen factors including exertion[2] **[104]** he becomes one[3] for successful breaking through,[4] he becomes one for awakening, he becomes one for winning the incomparable security from the bonds.[5] Monks,

---

[1] *Cf. D.* iii. 77, 221; *A.* i. 39; *S.* v. 263 *ff.*; *Vbh.* 216 *ff.*; *Vism.* 385.

[2] *MA.* ii. 69, the five mental barrennesses, the five mental bondages, the four bases of psychic power, with exertion. "Exertion," *ussoḷhi*, is rendered at *MA.* ii. 69 as energy (*viriya*) in regard to all that should be done. *Viriya* is virility, manliness, heroism.

[3] *bhabbo. MA.* ii. 69, *anurūpo anucchaviko,* fit, suitable for.

[4] *MA.* ii. 69, of the *kilesa* by knowledge. *Cf. M.* i. 357.

[5] *MA.* ii. 69, from the four bonds, *yoga* (which is equivalent to arahantship).

it is as if[1] there were eight or ten or a dozen hen's eggs properly sat on, properly incubated, properly hatched by that hen; such a wish as this would not arise in that hen: 'O may my chicks, having pierced through the egg-shells with the point of the claw on their feet or with their beaks, break forth safely,' for these chicks were ones who were able to break forth safely having pierced through the egg-shells with the point of the claw on their feet or with their beaks. Even so, monks, is it that a monk who is thus possessed of the fifteen factors including exertion becomes one . . . for winning the incomparable security from the bonds."

Thus spoke the Lord. Delighted, these monks rejoiced in what the Lord had said.

Discourse on Mental Barrenness:
The Sixth

17. DISCOURSE ON THE FOREST GROVE

(Vanapatthasutta)

THUS have I heard. At one time the Lord was staying near Sāvatthī in the Jeta Grove in Anāthapiṇḍika's monastery. There the Lord addressed the monks, saying: "Monks." "Revered One," these monks answered the Lord in assent. The Lord spoke thus: "Monks, I will teach you the disquisition on the forest grove.[2] Listen to it, pay careful attention to it, and I will speak."

"Yes, Lord," the monks answered the Lord in assent.

"In this connection, monks, a monk is staying in a certain forest grove. While he is staying in that forest grove mindfulness which had not been aroused is not aroused, and thought which was not composed is not composed, and the cankers which were not totally destroyed do not come to total destruction, and the incomparable security from the bonds which had not been attained is not attained, and those necessities of life which should be procured by one who

---

[1] =*M.* i. 357=*A.* iv. 126=*S.* iii. 154; *cf. A.* iv. 176, *Vin.* iii. 3.

[2] *vanapattha*, as at *D.* i. 71. *MA.* ii. 72 says: depending on lodgings in a *vanasaṇḍa*, woodland or forest thicket, beyond human habitations, he dwells performing the *dhamma* of recluses. *Cf. DA.* i. 210.

has gone forth—robe-material, almsfood, lodgings, medicines for the sick—these are to be got (only) with difficulty. Monks, this monk [**105**] should reflect thus: 'I am staying in this forest grove. While I am staying in this forest grove mindfulness which had not been aroused is not aroused, and thought which was not composed is not composed, and the cankers which were not totally destroyed do not come to total destruction, and the incomparable security from the bonds which had not been attained is not attained, and those necessities of life which should be procured by one who has gone forth—robe-material, almsfood, lodgings, medicines for the sick—these are to be got (only) with difficulty.' Monks, that monk —whether it be by night or day[1]—should depart from that forest grove, he should not remain.

But in this connection, monks, a monk is staying in a certain forest grove. While he is staying in that forest grove, mindfulness that had not been aroused is not aroused, and thought which was not composed is not composed, and the cankers which were not totally destroyed do not come to total destruction, and the incomparable security from the bonds which had not been attained is not attained, but those necessities of life which should be procured by one who has gone forth—robe-material, almsfood, lodgings, medicines for the sick—these are to be got with (only) a little difficulty. Monks, this monk should reflect thus: 'I am staying in this forest grove. While I am staying in this forest grove mindfulness which had not been aroused is not aroused . . . and the incomparable security from the bonds which had not been attained is not attained, but those necessities of life which should be procured by one who has gone forth—robe-material, almsfood, lodgings, medicines for the sick—these are to be got with (only) a little difficulty.[2] But I did not go forth from home into homelessness for the sake of robe-material. I did not go forth . . . for the sake of almsfood. I did not go forth . . . for the sake of lodgings. I did not go forth from home into homelessness for the sake of medicines for the sick.[3] But while I am staying in this forest grove mindfulness which

---

[1] *MA*. ii. 72: if he knows all this by pondering over it during the night, he should leave that same night, although if there are fierce wild animals on the road he can wait until sunrise. Similarly, if he finds all this out during the day, he should leave by day, but he can wait until sunset if there is some danger by day.

[2] *appakasirena*, also meaning "without difficulty."

[3] *Cf*. *Vin*. i. 57-8 where a certain brahman acknowledges that he went forth for the sake of his stomach.

had not been aroused is not aroused . . . the incomparable security from the bonds which had not been attained is not attained.' Monks, just on this count,[1] that monk should depart from that forest grove, he should not remain.

In this connection, monks, a monk is staying in a certain forest grove. While he is staying in that forest grove mindfulness which had not been aroused is aroused, and thought which was not composed is composed, and the cankers which had not been totally destroyed come to total destruction, and the incomparable security from the bonds which had not been attained is attained, but those necessities of life which should be procured by one who has gone forth—robe-material, almsfood, lodgings, medicines for the sick—these are to be got (only) with difficulty. Monks, this monk should reflect thus: [**106**] 'I am staying in this forest grove. While I am staying in this forest grove, mindfulness which had not been aroused is aroused . . . and the incomparable security from the bonds which had not been attained is attained, but those necessities of life . . . these are to be got (only) with difficulty. But I did not go forth from home into homelessness for the sake of robe-material . . . for the sake of almsfood . . . for the sake of lodgings. I did not go forth from home into homelessness for the sake of medicines for the sick. But while I am staying in this forest grove, mindfulness which had not been aroused is aroused . . . the incomparable security from the bonds which had not been attained is attained.' Monks, just on this count, that monk should remain in that forest grove, he should not depart.

But in this connection, monks, a monk is staying in a certain forest grove. While he is staying in that forest grove mindfulness that had not been aroused is aroused . . . and the incomparable security from the bonds which had not been attained is attained, and those necessities of life which should be procured by one who has gone forth—robe-material, almsfood, lodgings, medicines for the sick—these are to be got with (only) a little difficulty. Monks, that monk should reflect thus: 'I am staying in this forest grove. While I am staying in this forest grove, mindfulness which had not been aroused is aroused . . . and the incomparable security from the bonds which had not been attained is attained, and those necessities of life . . . these are to be got with (only) a little difficulty.' Monks,

---

[1] *sankhā pi*. *MA*. ii. 72: knowing there was not—also that there was—this result (or procedure) in the recluse-*dhamma*.

that monk should remain in that forest grove even as long as life lasts, he should not depart.

In this connection, monks, a monk is staying near[1] a village . . . near a little town . . . near a town . . . in a country district . . . a monk is staying near a certain man. While he is staying near that man, mindfulness which had not been aroused is not aroused . . . and the incomparable security from the bonds which had not been attained is not attained . . . these are to be got (only) with difficulty. Monks, that monk should reflect thus: 'I am staying near this man. While I am staying near this man, mindfulness which had not been aroused is not aroused . . . is not attained . . . these are to be got (only) with difficulty.' Monks, that monk, whether it be night or day, should depart without having asked that man (for permission),[2] he should not be waited on by him.[3]

But in this connection, monks, a monk is staying near a certain man. While he is staying near that man, [**107**] mindfulness which had not been aroused is not aroused . . . is not attained, but those necessities of life . . . these are to be got with (only) a little difficulty. Monks, that monk should reflect thus: 'I am staying near this man. While I am staying near this man, mindfulness which had not been aroused is not aroused . . . is not attained, but those necessities of life . . . are to be got with (only) a little difficulty. But I did not go forth from home into homelessness for the sake of robe-material . . . for the sake of almsfood . . . for the sake of lodgings . . . for the sake of medicines for the sick. But while I am staying near this man, mindfulness which had not been aroused is not aroused . . . the incomparable security from the bonds which had not been attained is not attained.' Monks, just on this count that monk should depart without having asked that man (for permission), he should not be waited on (by him).

In this connection, monks, a monk is staying near a certain man. While he is staying near that man, mindfulness that had not been aroused is aroused . . . and that incomparable security from the bonds which had not been attained is attained, but those necessities of life . . . these are (only) to be got with difficulty. Monks, that monk should reflect thus: 'I am staying near this man. While I am staying near this man, mindfulness which had not been aroused is

---

[1] *upanissāya*, near, in, dependent on.

[2] *anāpucchā*, a common *Vinaya* idiom. It is an exception to the usual practice for a monk to go away without asking his supporter for his permission.

[3] *nânubandhitabbo*. *Cf. nânubandheyya* at *Vin.* iv. 326, and see *VA.* 941.

aroused . . . is attained, but those necessities of life . . . these are to be got (only) with difficulty. But I did not go forth from home into homelessness for the sake of robe-material . . . for the sake of almsfood . . . for the sake of lodgings . . . for the sake of medicines for the sick, and while I am staying near this man, mindfulness which had not been aroused is aroused . . . and the incomparable security from the bonds which had not been attained is attained.' Monks, just on this count, that monk may be waited on by that man, he should not depart.

But in this connection, monks, a monk is staying near a certain man. While he is staying near that man, mindfulness which had not been aroused is aroused, and thought which had not been composed is composed, and the cankers which had not been totally destroyed came to total destruction, and the incomparable security from the bonds which had not been attained is attained, and those necessities of life which should be procured by one who has gone forth—robe-material, almsfood, lodgings, medicines for the sick—these are to be got with (only) a little difficulty. Monks, that monk should reflect thus: 'I am staying near this man. [**108**] While I am staying near this man, mindfulness which had not been aroused is aroused, thought which had not been composed is composed, the cankers which had not been totally destroyed come to total destruction, and the incomparable security from the bonds which had not been attained is attained, and those necessities of life which should be procured by one who has gone forth—robe-material, almsfood, lodgings, medicines for the sick—these are to be got with (only) a little difficulty.' Monks, that monk may be waited on by that man even for as long as life lasts, he should not depart even if he is being driven away."[1]

Thus spoke the Lord. Delighted, these monks rejoiced in what the Lord had said.

Discourse on the Forest Grove:
The Seventh

---

[1] As at *A*. iv. 32. *MA*. ii. 72 says even if the man has a stick (*daṇḍa*, punishment) brought, and saying, "Do not stay here," has him thrown out; (the monk) having apologised to him, should simply remain as long as life lasts.

18. DISCOURSE OF THE HONEY-BALL

(Madhupiṇḍikasutta)

THUS have I heard. At one time the Lord was staying among the Sakyans in Nigrodha's monastery in Kapilavatthu. Then the Lord, having dressed in the morning, taking his bowl and robe, entered Kapilavatthu for almsfood. Having walked in Kapilavatthu for almsfood, returning from (the quest for) alms after the meal, he approached the Great Wood[1] for the day-sojourn. Having plunged into the Great Wood, he sat down for the day-sojourn at the root of a young vilva tree. Then the Sakyan, Stick-in-hand,[2] who was always pacing up and down, always roaming about on foot,[3] approached the Great Wood; having plunged into the Great Wood, he approached the young vilva tree and the Lord; having approached, he exchanged greetings with the Lord; having exchanged greetings of friendliness and courtesy, he stood at one side leaning on his stick. As he was standing at one side leaning on his stick, the Sakyan, Stick-in-hand, spoke thus to the Lord:

"What is the teaching[4] of the recluse, of what views[5] is he ?"

"According to my teaching, sir, in the world with its *devas*, Māras and Brahmās, with its creation with recluses and brahmans, with *devas* and men, there is no contending with anyone in the world;[6] for which reason perceptions do not obsess that brahman[7] as he

---

[1] This Mahāvana near Kapilavatthu was virgin forest, uncultivated, stretching up to the Himalayas. It was not like the Mahāvana at Vesālī which was partly natural, partly cultivated, *MA*. ii. 73.

[2] Daṇḍapāṇi; so called because he used a golden walking stick although he was not old. He sided with Devadatta; so *MA*. ii. 73.

[3] Stock phrase, as *e.g.* at *M*. i. 227, ii. 118, iii. 128; *D*. i. 235; *Sn*. p. 105; *A*. i. 136, iii. 76. "For the sake of seeing parks, woods, mountains," *MA*. ii. 73.

[4] *kimvādī*. *MA*. ii. 73 *kimdiṭṭhiko*, of what views? *Cf*. *Vin*. i. 40.

[5] *kimakkhāyī*, what does he point out or show? *MA*. ii. 73, what does he talk about? *Cf*. *Vin*. i. 40.

[6] *Cf*. *S*. iii. 138 (quoted *MA*. ii. 74), "I do not dispute with the world, but the world disputes with me"; and an untraced quotation, "A *dhamma*-speaker disputes with no one, but a speaker of non-*dhamma* disputes" on such problems as impermanence, not-self, ill, the unlovely and their opposites.

[7] Who has destroyed the cankers, *MA*. ii. 74.

fares along not fettered to sense-pleasures, without questionings, remorse[1] cut off, and who is devoid of craving for becoming and non-becoming.[2] This, sir, is my teaching, this my view."

When this had been said, the Sakyan, Stick-in-hand, shaking his head[3] and [**109**] wagging his tongue, departed leaning on his stick, his brow furrowed into three wrinkles.[4]

Then the Lord, emerging from solitude towards evening, approached Nigrodha's monastery; having approached, he sat down on the appointed seat. As he was sitting down the Lord addressed the monks, saying: "Now I, monks, having dressed in the morning, taking my bowl and robe, entered Kapilavatthu for almsfood. Having walked in Kapilavatthu for almsfood, returning from the (quest for) alms after the meal, I approached the Great Wood for the day-sojourn. Having plunged into the Great Wood, I sat down for the day-sojourn at the root of a young vilva tree. Then the Sakyan, Stick-in-hand . . . [*as above*] . . . spoke thus to me: 'What is the teaching of the recluse, of what views is he?' When he had said this, I, monks, spoke thus to the Sakyan, Stick-in-hand:

'According to (my) teaching, sir, in the world with its *devas*, Māras, Brahmās, with its creation with recluses and brahmans, with *devas* and men, there is no contending with anyone in the world; for which reason perceptions do not obsess that brahman as he fares along not fettered to sense-pleasures, without questionings, remorse cut off, and who is devoid of craving for becoming and non-becoming. This, sir, is my teaching, this my view.' When I had said this, monks, the Sakyan, Stick-in-hand, shaking his head and wagging his tongue, departed leaning on his stick, his brow furrowed into three wrinkles."

When he had spoken thus, a certain monk spoke thus to the Lord: "But what is this teaching, Lord, whereby the Lord, in the world with its *devas*, Māras and Brahmās, with its creation with recluses and brahmans, would not contend with anyone in the world? And how is it, Lord, that perceptions do not obsess the Lord, that brahman,[5] as he is faring along, not fettered to sense-pleasures, without

---

[1] *chinnakukkucca*, *MA*. ii. 74, gives two meanings for *chinnakukkucca*: *vippaṭisāri*, remorse, and *hatthapāda*, hands and feet.

[2] *bhavâbhave*. *MA*. ii. 74, again and again becoming, or becoming that is low, or excellent; for an excellent becoming is called *abhava*, non-becoming, come to growth.

[3] As at *M*. i. 171.

[4] As at *S*. i. 118.

[5] Here the Lord is being referred to as "brahman."

questionings, remorse cut off, and who is devoid of craving for becoming and non-becoming?"

"Whatever is the origin, monk, of the number of obsessions and perceptions[1] which assail a man, if there is nothing to rejoice at, to welcome, to catch hold of, this is itself an end of a propensity to attachment, this is itself an end of a propensity to repugnance, this is itself an end [**110**] of a propensity to views, this is itself an end of a propensity to perplexity, this is itself an end of a propensity to pride, this is itself an end of a propensity to attachment to becoming, this is itself an end of a propensity to ignorance, this is itself an end of taking the stick, of taking a weapon, of quarrelling, contending, disputing, accusation, slander, lying speech.[2] In these ways, these evil unskilled states are stopped without remainder."

Thus spoke the Lord. Having said this, the Well-farer, rising from his seat, entered a dwelling-place. Soon after the Lord had gone away it occurred to these monks: "Your reverences, the Lord, having recited this recital to us in brief, but not having explained the meaning in full, rising from his seat, entered a dwelling-place: 'Whatever is the origin, monk . . . are stopped without remainder.' Now, who can explain the meaning in full of this recital recited in brief by the Lord but whose meaning was not explained in full?" Then it occurred to these monks: "Now the venerable Kaccāna the Great is both praised by the Lord and revered by intelligent fellow Brahma-farers. The venerable Kaccāna the Great is able to explain in full the meaning of this recital recited in brief by the Lord, but whose meaning was not explained in full. Suppose we were to approach the venerable Kaccāna the Great and, having approached, were to question him on this meaning?"

Then these monks approached the venerable Kaccāna the Great; having approached, they exchanged greetings with the venerable Kaccāna the Great; having exchanged greetings of friendliness and courtesy, they sat down at a respectful distance. As they were sitting down at a respectful distance, these monks spoke thus to the venerable Kaccāna the Great:

"Reverend Kaccāna, the Lord having recited this recital to us in brief, but not having explained the meaning in full, rising from his seat, entered a dwelling-place: 'Whatever is the origin, monk . . . are stopped without remainder.' Soon after the Lord had gone

---

[1] *papañcasaññāsankhā*. *MA*. ii. 75 explains *sankhā* by *koṭṭhāsa*, and *papañcasaññā* as perceptions connected with obsessions, views, craving.

[2] *Cf*. *M*. i. 410, from "taking a stick."

away, it occurred to us: 'This venerable Kaccāna the Great is both praised by the Lord and revered by intelligent fellow Brahma-farers; [**111**] the venerable Kaccāna the Great is able to explain in full the meaning of this recital recited in brief by the Lord but whose meaning was not explained in full. Suppose we were to approach the venerable Kaccāna the Great and, having approached, were to question him on this meaning.' May the venerable Kaccāna the Great explain it."

"Your reverences, as a man walking about aiming at the pith,[1] searching for the pith, looking about for the pith of a great, stable and pithy tree, passing by the root, passing by the trunk, might think that the pith is to be looked for in the branches and foliage—even so is this performance of the venerable ones, for (although) you had the Teacher face to face, yet having ignored that Lord, you judge that it is I who should be questioned on this meaning. But, your reverences, the Lord knows what should be known, sees what should be seen,[2] he has become vision, become knowledge, become *dhamma*, become Brahma, he is the propounder, the expounder, the bringer to the goal,[3] the giver of the Deathless, *dhamma*-lord, Tathāgata. That was the time when you should have questioned the Lord on this meaning so that you might have understood what the Lord explained to you."

"Undoubtedly, Kaccāna, the Lord knows what should be known, sees what should be seen, he has become vision, become knowledge, become *dhamma*, become Brahma, he is the propounder, the expounder, the bringer to the goal, the giver of the Deathless, *dhamma*-lord, Tathāgata. But the venerable Kaccāna the Great is both praised by the Lord, and revered by intelligent fellow Brahma-farers, and the venerable Kaccāna the Great is able to explain in full the meaning of that recital recited in brief by the Lord but whose meaning was not explained in full. Let the venerable Kaccāna explain, without finding it troublesome."

"Well then, your reverences, listen, pay careful attention and I will speak."

"Yes, your reverence," these monks answered the venerable Kaccāna the Great in assent. The venerable Kaccāna the Great spoke thus:

---

[1] As at *M*. i. 195, iii. 194; *A*. v. 226 *ff*., 256 *ff*., etc.

[2] He knows and sees what is to be known and seen; he knows by knowing, sees by seeing, *MA*. ii. 76.

[3] *attha*, or matter, meaning.

"In regard to that recital, your reverences, which the Lord recited in brief . . . 'Whatever is the origin, monk, of the number of obsessions and perceptions which assail a man . . . are stopped without remainder,' of that recital recited by the Lord in brief but whose meaning was not explained in full, I understand the meaning in full thus: Visual consciousness,[1] your reverences, arises because of eye and material shapes; the meeting of the three is sensory impingement;[2] feelings are because of sensory impingement; what one feels one [**112**] perceives; what one perceives one reasons about;[3] what one reasons about obsesses one; what obsesses one is the origin of the number of perceptions and obsessions which assail a man in regard to material shapes cognisable by the eye, past, future, present. And, your reverences, auditory consciousness arises because of ear and sounds. . . . And, your reverences, olfactory consciousness arises because of nose and smells. . . . And, your reverences, gustatory consciousness arises because of tongue and tastes. . . . And, your reverences, bodily consciousness arises because of body and touches. . . . And, your reverences, mental consciousness[4] arises because of mind[5] and mental objects. The meeting of the three is sensory impingement; feelings are because of sensory impingement; what one feels one perceives; what one perceives one reasons about; what one reasons about obsesses one; what obsesses one is the origin of the number of perceptions and obsessions which assail a man in regard to mental objects cognisable by mind, past, future, present. This situation occurs: that when there is eye, your reverences, when there is material shape, when there is visual consciousness, one will recognise the manifestation of sensory impingement. This situation occurs: that when there is the manifestation of sensory impingement, one will recognise the manifestation of feeling. This situation occurs: that when there is the manifestation of feeling, one will recognise the manifestation of perception. This situation occurs: that when there is the manifestation of perception, one will recognise the manifestation of reasoning. This situation occurs: that when there is the manifestation of reasoning, one will recognise

---

[1] As at *S.* iv. 32.

[2] *phassa*, contact.

[3] *vitakketi*. On *vitakka* see *D.* ii. 277.

[4] Explained at *MA.* ii. 77 as "advertence" (*āvajjana*) and impulsion (*javana*).

[5] Explained at *MA.* ii. 77 as *bhavangacitta*, the unconscious or "subconsciousness."

the manifestation of the assault of a number of obsessions and perceptions.

This situation occurs: that when there is ear, your reverences, when there is sound . . . when there is nose, when there is smell . . . when there is tongue, when there is taste . . . when there is body, when there is touch . . . when there is mind, when there is a mental object, when there is mental consciousness, one will recognise a manifestation of sensory impingement.

This situation does not occur: that when there is not eye, your reverences, when there is not material shape, when there is not visual consciousness, one will recognise a manifestation of sensory impingement. This situation does not occur: that when there is not a manifestation of sensory impingement, one will recognise a manifestation of feeling. This situation does not occur: that when there is not a manifestation of feeling one will recognise a manifestation of perception. This situation does not occur: that when there is not a manifestation of perception one will recognise a manifestation of reasoning. This situation does not occur: that when there is not a manifestation of reasoning one will recognise a manifestation of the assault of a number of obsessions and perceptions.

This situation does not occur: that when there is not ear, your reverences, when there is not sound . . . when there is not nose, when there is not smell . . . when there is not tongue, when there is not taste. . . when there is not body, when there is not touch . . . when there is not mind, when there is not a mental object, when there is not mental consciousness, one will recognise a manifestation of sensory impingement. . . .

In regard to that recital, your reverences, which the Lord, [**113**] having recited in brief. . . . 'Whatever is the origin, monks, of the number of obsessions and perceptions which assail a man . . . are stopped without remainder,' of that recital which was recited in brief by the Lord but whose meaning was not explained in full, I understand the meaning in full thus. But if you, venerable ones, so desire, having approached the Lord, you can question him as to this meaning so that as the Lord explains it to you so may you understand it."

Then these monks, delighting and rejoicing in what the venerable Kaccāna the Great had said, rising from their seats, approached the Lord; having approached, having greeted the Lord, they sat down at a respectful distance. As they were sitting down at a respectful distance, these monks spoke thus to the Lord:

"Lord, the Lord having recited this recital to us in brief, rising from his seat, entered a dwelling-place: 'Whatever is the origin, monk, of the number of obsessions and perceptions which assail a man . . . are stopped without remainder.' Now, Lord, soon after the Lord had gone away, it occurred to us: 'The Lord, having recited this recital to us in brief, but without explaining its meaning in full, rising from his seat, entered a dwelling-place: "Whatever is the origin, monk, of the number of obsessions and perceptions which assail a man, if there is nothing here to rejoice at, to welcome, to catch hold of, this is itself an end of a propensity to attachment, this is itself an end of a propensity to repugnance, this is itself an end of a propensity to views, this is itself an end of a propensity to perplexity, this is itself an end of a propensity to pride, this is itself an end of a propensity to attachment for becoming, this is itself an end of a propensity to ignorance, this is itself an end of taking the stick, of taking a weapon, of quarrelling, contending, disputing, accusation, slander, lying speech. Herein, these evil unskilled states are stopped without remainder." Now, who can explain in full the meaning of this recital recited in brief by the Lord but whose meaning was not explained in full?' Then, Lord, it occurred to us: 'Now the venerable Kaccāna the Great is both praised by the Lord and revered by intelligent fellow Brahma-farers. The venerable Kaccāna the Great is able to explain in full the meaning of this recital recited in brief by the Lord, but whose meaning was not explained in full. Suppose we were to approach the venerable Kaccāna the Great; and having approached were to question the venerable Kaccāna the Great on this meaning?' Then we, Lord, approached the venerable Kaccāna the Great; having approached, [**114**] we questioned the venerable Kaccāna the Great on this meaning. The meaning of those (words) was explained to us, Lord, by the venerable Kaccāna the Great by these methods, by these sentences,[1] by these words."[2]

"Learned, monks, is Kaccāna the Great, of great wisdom is Kaccāna the Great. For if you, monks, had questioned me as to this meaning, I too would have explained it precisely as it was explained by Kaccāna the Great. Indeed, this is the exact meaning of that, and thus should you understand it."

When this had been said, the venerable Ānanda spoke thus to the

---

[1] *MA*. ii. 78, by a group of syllables (*akkhara*).

[2] *Ibid.*, by individual syllables. Also *M*. i. 320.

Lord: " Lord, even as a man overcome by hunger and exhaustion might come upon a honey-ball;[1] from each bit that he would taste he would get a sweet delicious[2] flavour—even so, Lord, is a monk who is naturally able in mind; from each bit that he would examine with intuitive wisdom as to the meaning of this disquisition on *dhamma*, he would get delight, he would get satisfaction for the mind. What is this disquisition on *dhamma* called, Lord ? "

" Wherefore you, Ānanda, may understand this disquisition on *dhamma* as the Disquisition of the Honey-ball."

Thus spoke the Lord. Delighted, the venerable Ānanda rejoiced in what the Lord had said.

Discourse of the Honey-Ball:
the Eighth

19. DISCOURSE ON THE TWOFOLD THOUGHT

(Dvedhāvitakkasutta)

THUS have I heard: At one time the Lord was staying near Sāvatthī in the Jeta Grove in Anāthapiṇḍika's monastery. While he was there the Lord addressed the monks, saying: " Monks." " Revered One," these monks answered the Lord in assent. The Lord spoke thus:

" Monks, before my awakening, while I was the *bodhisatta*, not fully awakened, this occurred to me: ' Suppose that I should fare along with a twofold thought ? '[3] So, monks, whatever is thought of sense-pleasures and whatever is thought of malevolence and whatever is thought of harming—that I made into one part; and whatever is thought of renunciation and whatever is thought of non-malevolence and whatever is thought of non-harming, that I made into the other part. While I, monks, was faring on thus, diligent, ardent, self-resolute, [**115**] thought of sense-pleasures arose, and I comprehended thus: ' This thought of sense-pleasures has

---

[1] *Ibid.*, a large sweet cake; or, sugared meal made into cakes.

[2] *asecanaka*, to which nothing need be added, *e.g.* condiments; complete in itself.

[3] *Cf. It.* p. 82.

arisen in me, but it conduces to self-hurt and it conduces to the hurt of others and it conduces to the hurt of both, it is destructive of intuitive wisdom, associated with distress, not conducive to nibbāna.' But while I was reflecting, 'It conduces to self-hurt,' it subsided; and while I was reflecting, 'It conduces to the hurt of others,' it subsided; and while I was reflecting, 'It is destructive of intuitive wisdom, it is associated with distress, it is not conducive to nibbāna,' it subsided. So I, monks, kept on getting rid of the thought of sense-pleasures as it constantly arose, I kept on driving it out, I kept on making an end of it.

While I, monks, was faring on thus, diligent, ardent, self-resolute, thought of malevolence arose . . . thought of harming arose, and I comprehended thus: 'This thought of malevolence . . . of harming has arisen in me, but it conduces to self-hurt . . . not conducive to nibbāna.' But while I was reflecting, 'It conduces to self-hurt' . . . while I was reflecting, 'It is . . . not conducive to nibbāna,' it subsided. So I, monks, kept on getting rid of the thought of harming as it constantly arose, I kept on driving it out, I kept on making an end of it.

Monks, according to whatever a monk ponders and reflects on much his mind in consequence gets a bias that way. Monks, if a monk ponder and reflect much on thought of sense-pleasures he ejects thought of renunciation; if he makes much of the thought of sense-pleasures, his mind inclines to the thought of sense-pleasures. Monks, if a monk ponder and reflect much on the thought of malevolence . . . on the thought of harming, he ejects the thought of non-harming; if he makes much of the thought of harming, his mind inclines to the thought of harming.

Monks, it is as if in the last month of the rains, in the autumn when the corn is thick, a cowherd might be looking after the cows, and might hit them above and below[1] with a stick, and might restrain and check them. What is the reason for this? Monks, that cowherd sees death or imprisonment or degradation[2] from that source. Even so did I, monks, see the peril in unskilled states of mind, the vanity, the defilement, and the advantage, allied to cleansing, in renouncing them for skilled states of mind.[3]

[**116**] While I, monks, was faring on, diligent, ardent, self-

---

[1] *ākoṭeyya patikoṭeyya*. *MA*. ii. 82, he would strike them straight, on their backs, he would strike them across, on the ribs.

[2] *Cf*. *D*. i. 135, *A*. i. 201.

[3] *M*. i. 403. *Cf*. *M*. i. 379, *Vin*. i. 15.

resolute, thought of renunciation arose and I comprehended thus: 'This thought of renunciation has arisen in me, and it conduces neither to self-hurt nor does it conduce to the hurt of others nor does it conduce to the hurt of both, it is for growth in intuitive wisdom, it is not associated with distress, it is conducive to nibbāna.' If during the night, monks, I should ponder and reflect upon this, not from that source do I behold fear; and if during the day, monks, I should ponder and reflect upon this, not from that source do I behold fear; and if during the night and day, monks, I should ponder and reflect upon this, not from that source do I behold fear. But I thought that after pondering and reflecting too long my body would be weary; if the body was weary the mind would be disturbed:[1] if the mind is disturbed it is a mind far from concentration. So I, monks, subjectively steadied the mind, I calmed it, I made it one-pointed, I concentrated.[2] What was the reason for this? I thought, 'Do not let my mind be disturbed.'

While I, monks, was faring on diligent, ardent, self-resolute, thought of non-malevolence . . . thought of non-harming arose, and I comprehended thus: 'This thought of non-malevolence . . . of non-harming has arisen in me, and it conduces neither to self-hurt nor does it conduce to the hurt of others nor does it conduce to the hurt of both, it is for growth in intuitive wisdom, it is not associated with distress, it is conducive to nibbāna.' If, during the night, monks, . . . not from that source do I behold fear. But I thought that after pondering and reflecting too long my body would be weary; if the body was weary the mind would be disturbed; if the mind is disturbed, it is a mind far from concentration. So I, monks, subjectively steadied the mind, I calmed it, I made it one-pointed, I concentrated. What was the reason for this? I thought, 'Do not let my mind be disturbed.'

Monks, according to whatever a monk ponders and reflects on much his mind in consequence gets a bias that way. Monks, if a monk ponder and reflect much on thought of renunciation he ejects thought of sense-pleasures; if he makes much of the thought of renunciation, his mind inclines to the thought of renunciation. Monks, if a monk ponder and reflect much on the thought of non-malevolence . . . of non-harming, he ejects thought of harming; if he makes much of the thought of non-harming his mind inclines to the thought of non-harming.

---

[1] *ūhanati*, to shake, to be restless. [2] *Cf. M.* iii. 111; *A.* ii. 94.

Monks, it is as if in the last month of the hot weather when all the corn is stored at the confines of a village a cowherd might be looking after the cows; [**117**] while he is at the root of a tree or in the open he remembers there is something to be done, and thinks: Those are the cows.[1] Even so, monks, remembering there is something to be done, did I think: Those are mental states.[2]

Monks, unsluggish energy[3] was stirred up in me, unmuddled mindfulness was set up, the body was tranquil, impassible, the mind composed, one-pointed. Then I, monks, aloof from pleasures of the senses, aloof from unskilled states of mind, entered on and abided in the first meditation . . . [*As at p.* 27 *above*] . . . This, monks, was the third knowledge attained by me in the last watch of the night; ignorance was dispelled, knowledge arose, darkness was dispelled, light arose, even as I abided diligent, ardent, self-resolute.

Monks, as there might be a large piece of low-lying marshy ground in a forest grove,[4] near which might live a large herd of deer, towards which some man might come along, not desiring their good, not desiring their weal, not desiring their security from bonds; if there were a road that was secure, safe, leading to rapture, he might block that road, might open up a treacherous road, might place a decoy and might tether a female decoy as a lure, even so, monks, after a time that great herd of deer might come to calamity and dwindle away.

But, monks, if some man came along towards that great herd of deer, desiring their good, desiring their weal, desiring their security from bonds, and if there were a road that was secure, safe, leading to rapture, he might open up that road, he might block the treacherous road, he would disturb the male decoy, he would let loose[5] the female lure; thus, monks, after a time that great herd of deer would come to growth, expansion, maturity.

Monks, this parable has been made by me for [**118**] illustrating the meaning. And this is the meaning here:

'The large piece of low-lying marshy ground,' monks, this is a synonym for sense-pleasures.

---

[1] *MA*. ii. 84 says he need not herd them but must be mindful of them.

[2] Namely *samatha* (calm) and *vipassanā* (insight), *MA*. ii. 84.

[3] =*M*. i. 21-3 to beginning of next simile.

[4] *araññe pavane*. *MA*. ii. 85 says that these two words mean the same; and *pavana* is *vanasaṇḍa*, forest grove, or woodland thicket.

[5] *nāseti*, to expel, with the added sense of spoiling or ruining, here the purpose for which she was tethered.

'The great herd of deer,' monks, this is a synonym for beings.

'The man not desiring their good, not desiring their weal, not desiring their security from bonds,' monks, this is a synonym for Māra, the Evil One.

'The treacherous way,' monks, this is a synonym for the eightfold wrong way, that is to say, wrong view, wrong thought, wrong speech, wrong action, wrong way of living, wrong endeavour, wrong mindfulness, wrong concentration.

'The male decoy,' monks, this is a synonym for the passion of delight.

'The female lure,' monks, this is a synonym for ignorance.

'The man desiring good, desiring weal, desiring security from the bonds,' monks, this is a synonym for the Tathāgata, perfected one, fully self-awakened one.

'The way that is secure, safe, leading to rapture,' monks, this is a synonym for the ariyan eightfold Way, that is to say, right view, right thought, right speech, right action, right way of living, right endeavour, right mindfulness, right concentration.

Thus is the secure, safe way leading to rapture opened by me, monks, the treacherous way blocked, the decoy disturbed, the lure let loose. Whatever, monks, is to be done from compassion by a Teacher seeking the welfare of his disciples, that has been done by me out of compassion for you. These, monks, are the roots of trees, these are empty places. Meditate, monks; do not be slothful, be not remorseful later. This is our instruction to you."[1]

Thus spoke the Lord. Delighted, these monks rejoiced in what the Lord had said.

The Discourse on the Twofold Thought:
the Ninth

20. DISCOURSE ON THE FORMS OF THOUGHT

(Vitakkasanthānasutta)

THUS have I heard: At one time the Lord was staying near Sāvatthī in the Jeta Grove in Anāthapiṇḍika's monastery. There the Lord addressed the monks, saying: "Monks." "Revered One," **[119]**

---

[1] As at *M*. i. 46.

these monks answered the Lord in assent. The Lord spoke thus:

" Monks, if a monk is intent on the higher thought,[1] from time to time he should attend to five characteristics. What five ?

Herein, monks, whatever may be the characteristic which a monk attends to, if there arise evil unskilled thoughts associated with desire and associated with aversion and associated with confusion, that monk should attend, instead of to that characteristic, to another characteristic which is associated with what is skilled. By attending to this other characteristic which is associated with what is skilled instead of to that characteristic, those evil unskilled thoughts associated with desire and associated with aversion and associated with confusion are got rid of, they come to an end. From getting rid of these, his mind subjectively steadies, calms, is one-pointed, concentrated. As, monks, a skilled carpenter[2] or a carpenter's apprentice might knock out, drive out, draw out a large peg with a small peg—even so, monks, whatever may be the characteristic which a monk attends to, if there arise evil unskilled thoughts associated with desire and associated with aversion and associated with confusion, that monk should attend, instead of to that characteristic, to another characteristic which is associated with what is skilled. By attending to this other characteristic which is associated with what is skilled instead of to that characteristic, those evil unskilled thoughts associated with desire and associated with aversion and associated with confusion—these are got rid of, these come to an end. From getting rid of these, his mind subjectively steadies, calms, is one-pointed, concentrated.

Monks, if while the monk is attending, instead of to that characteristic, to this other characteristic which is associated with what is skilled, there still arise evil unskilled thoughts associated with desire and associated with aversion and associated with confusion, then the peril of these thoughts should be scrutinised by that monk, thinking: ' Indeed these are unskilled thoughts, indeed these are

---

[1] *adhicitta*. *MA*. ii. 87 explains: " the thought that arises in relation to the ten skilled ways of acting is just thought; the thought that is higher than that thought—the higher thought—is based on vision, it is thought in respect of the eight attainments." The ways of acting are ten: 3 of body, 4 of speech, 3 of thought. The eight attainments are the four *jhānas* and the four succeeding planes of the meditative process.

[2] *palagaṇḍa*, occurring in another simile at *S*. iii. 154 (*phalag-*) and *A*. iv. 127. *MA*. ii. 90, *vaḍḍhakī*.

thoughts that have errors, indeed these are thoughts that are of painful results.' While he is scrutinising the peril of these thoughts, those evil unskilled thoughts that are associated with desire, associated with aversion, associated with confusion, these are got rid of, these come to an end. By getting rid of these, his mind subjectively steadies, calms, is one-pointed, concentrated. Monks, it is like[1] a woman or a man, young, in the prime of life, fond of adornment, who, if the carcase of a snake or the carcase of a dog or the carcase of a human being [**120**] were hanging round the neck, would be revolted, ashamed, disgusted—even so, monks, while the monk is attending, instead of to this characteristic, to that other characteristic . . . concentrated.

Monks, if while the monk is scrutinising the peril of those thoughts, there still arise evil unskilled thoughts associated with desire and associated with aversion and associated with confusion, that monk should bring about forgetfulness of and lack of attention to those thoughts; having come to forgetfulness[2] of and lack of attention to these thoughts, those evil unskilled thoughts associated with desire and associated with aversion and associated with confusion—these are got rid of, these come to an end. By getting rid of these, the mind subjectively steadies, calms, is one-pointed, concentrated. Monks, it is like a man with vision who might not want to see the material shapes that come within his range of vision; he would close his eyes or look another way—even so, monks, if while the monk is scrutinising the peril of those thoughts . . . concentrated.

Monks, if when the monk has brought about forgetfulness of and lack of attention to those thoughts, there still arise evil unskilled thoughts associated with desire and associated with aversion and associated with confusion, monks, that monk should attend to the thought function and form of those thoughts. While he is attending to the thought function and form of those thoughts, those that are evil unskilled thoughts associated with desire and associated with aversion and associated with confusion, these are got rid of, these come to an end. By getting rid of these the mind subjectively steadies, calms, is one-pointed, concentrated. Monks, even as it might occur to a man who is walking quickly: 'Now, why do I walk quickly? Suppose I were to walk slowly?' It might occur to him as he was walking slowly: 'Now, why do I walk

---

[1] *Cf. A.* iv. 376; *Vin.* iii. 68.

[2] *asati-amanasikāra. MA.* ii. 90 says that they should neither be remembered nor attended to. *Cf. A.* iii. 186.

slowly ? Suppose I were to stand ? ' It might occur to him as he was standing: 'Now, why do I stand ? Suppose I were to sit down ? ' It might occur to him as he was sitting down: 'Now, why do I sit down ? Suppose I were to lie down ? '—even so, monks, the man, having abandoned the very hardest posture, might take to the easiest posture itself. Even so, monks, if while the monk has brought about forgetfulness of and lack of attention to those thoughts . . . concentrated.

Monks, if while the monk is attending to the thought function and form of those thoughts, there still arise evil unskilled thoughts associated with desire and associated with aversion and associated with confusion, monks, that monk, his teeth clenched,[1] his tongue pressed against his palate, should by his mind subdue, restrain and dominate the mind. [**121**] While, with his teeth clenched, his tongue pressed against his palate, he is with the mind subduing, restraining and dominating the mind, those evil unskilled thoughts associated with desire and associated with aversion and associated with confusion, these are got rid of, these come to an end. By getting rid of these, the mind subjectively steadies, calms, is one-pointed, concentrated. Monks, even as a strong man, having taken hold of a weaker man by the head or shoulders, might subdue, restrain and dominate him, even so, monks, if while that monk is attending to the thought function and form of those thoughts, there still arise evil unskilled thoughts associated with desire and associated with aversion and associated with confusion, then, monks, that monk, his teeth clenched, his tongue pressed against his palate, should by his mind subdue, restrain and dominate his mind. While, with his teeth clenched, his tongue pressed against his palate, he is by the mind subduing, restraining and dominating the mind, those evil unskilled thoughts associated with desire and associated with aversion and associated with confusion, are got rid of, they come to an end. By getting rid of these, the mind subjectively steadies, calms, is one-pointed, concentrated.

Monks, if while a monk, in regard to some characteristic, is attending to that characteristic, there arise evil unskilled thoughts associated with desire and associated with aversion and associated with confusion, then if he attends, instead of to that characteristic, to some other characteristic which is associated with what is skilled, those evil unskilled thoughts associated with desire and associated

---

[1] As at *M.* i. 242.

with aversion and associated with confusion, these are got rid of, these come to an end. By getting rid of these, the mind subjectively steadies, calms, is one-pointed, concentrated.

And by scrutinising the peril of these thoughts, those evil unskilled thoughts associated with desire and associated with aversion and associated with confusion, these are got rid of, these come to an end. By getting rid of these, the mind subjectively steadies, calms, is one-pointed, concentrated.

If he comes to forgetfulness of and lack of attention to those evil unskilled thoughts that are associated with desire and associated with aversion and associated with confusion, these are got rid of, these come to an end. By getting rid of these, the mind subjectively steadies, calms, is one-pointed, concentrated.

And by attending to the thought function and form of these thoughts, those evil unskilled thoughts associated with desire and associated with aversion and associated with confusion, these are got rid of, these come to an end. By getting rid of these, the mind subjectively steadies, calms, is one-pointed, concentrated.

With the teeth clenched, with the tongue pressed against the palate, if he subdues, restrains, dominates the mind by the mind, those evil unskilled thoughts associated with desire and associated with aversion and associated with confusion, these are got rid of, these come to an end. By getting rid of these, the mind subjectively steadies, calms, [**122**] is one-pointed, concentrated.

Monks, this monk is called one who is master in the method and paths of thought; he can think whatever thought he wishes; he will not think any thought that he does not wish; he has cut off craving,[1] done away with fetter, and, by fully mastering pride, has made an end of anguish."

Thus spoke the Lord. Delighted, these monks rejoiced in what the Lord had said.

Discourse on the Forms of Thought:
the Tenth

Division of the Lion's Roar:
the Second

---

[1] As at *M*. i. 12; see above, p. 16, for further references.

III. THE THIRD DIVISION

(Tatiyavagga)

21. DISCOURSE ON THE PARABLE OF THE SAW

(Kakacûpamasutta)[1]

THUS have I heard: At one time the Lord was staying near Sāvatthī in the Jeta Grove in Anāthapiṇḍika's monastery. Now at that time the venerable Moliyaphagguna lived too closely[2] associated with the nuns. While the venerable Moliyaphagguna was living associated thus with the nuns, if any monk face to face with the venerable Moliyaphagguna spoke dispraise of those nuns, then the venerable Moliyaphagguna was angry, displeased, and made a legal question.[3] And if some monk face to face with those nuns spoke dispraise of the venerable Moliyaphagguna, then those nuns were angry, displeased, and made a legal question. It was in this way that the venerable Moliyaphagguna was living associated with nuns.

Then a certain monk approached the Lord; having approached, having greeted the Lord, he sat down at a respectful distance. As he was sitting down at a respectful distance, this monk spoke thus to the Lord: " Lord, the venerable Moliyaphagguna lives too closely associated with nuns. It is thus, Lord, that the venerable Moliyaphagguna lives associated with the nuns: if any monk . . . and make a legal question. It is thus, Lord, that the venerable Moliyaphagguna lives associated with nuns." Then the Lord addressed this monk, saying: " Come [**123**] you, monk, summon the monk Moliyaphagguna on my behalf, saying: ' The Lord is summoning you, Phagguna.' "

" Very well, Lord," and this monk, having answered the Lord in assent, approached the venerable Moliyaphagguna and having approached, spoke thus to the venerable Moliyaphagguna: " The Lord is summoning you, Phagguna."

" Very well, your reverence," and the venerable Moliyaphagguna,

---

[1] Mentioned at *DA*. 123 as a sutta preached on account of someone's lack of patience.

[2] *atївelā*. *MA*. ii. 95 names three *velās*: *kālav°*, *sīmav°*, *sīla°*. Phagguna infringed all these limits: he exhorted nuns until late in the evening, for too long at a time; and in more than five or six sentences (see *Vin*. iv. 55, 21); and he spoke in fun of serious offences, *duṭṭhullâpattipahonaka*. *Cf. Vin*. iv. 31, 127.

[3] *adhikaraṇa*, see *Vin*. ii. 88 *ff*., 99 *ff*.

having answered this monk in assent, approached the Lord; having approached, having greeted the Lord, he sat down at a respectful distance. The Lord spoke thus to the venerable Moliyaphagguna as he was sitting down at a respectful distance:

"Is it true, as is said, that you, Phagguna, are living too closely associated with nuns? So that if some monk, face to face with you, speaks in dispraise of the nuns you are angry, displeased and make a legal question; or if some monk, face to face with the nuns, speaks dispraise of you, these nuns are angry, displeased and make a legal question? Is it true, as is said, that you, Phagguna, are living associated with the nuns thus?"

"Yes, Lord."

"But did not you, Phagguna, the son of a respectable family, go forth from home into homelessness out of faith?"

"Yes, Lord."

"But this is not suitable in you, Phagguna, a son of a respectable family who has gone forth from home into homelessness out of faith, that you should live too closely associated with nuns. Wherefore, Phagguna, even if anyone face to face with you should speak dispraise of those nuns, even so should you, Phagguna, get rid of those which are worldly desires, those which are worldly thoughts; and you, Phagguna, should train yourself thus: 'Neither will my mind become perverted, nor will I utter an evil speech, but kindly and compassionate will I dwell with a mind of friendliness and void of hatred.' It is thus that you must train youself, Phagguna. Wherefore, Phagguna, even if anyone face to face with you should give a blow with the hand to these nuns, should give a blow with a clod of earth, should give a blow with a stick, should give a blow with a weapon, even then, Phagguna, should you train yourself thus: . . . It is thus that you must train yourself, Phagguna. Wherefore, Phagguna, even if anyone face to face with you should speak dispraise, even then should you . . . train yourself thus. Wherefore, Phagguna, even if anyone should give a blow with his hand, should give a blow with a clod of earth, should give a blow with a stick, should give a blow with a weapon, [**124**] even so should you, Phagguna, get rid of those desires that are worldly, those thoughts that are worldly; and you, Phagguna, should train yourself thus: 'Neither will my mind become perverted, nor will I utter an evil speech, but kindly and compassionate will I dwell with a mind of friendliness and void of hatred.' It is thus that you must train yourself, Phagguna."

Then the Lord addressed the monks, saying: "Monks, my monks at one time were indeed accomplished in mind. Then I, monks, addressed the monks, saying: 'Now I, monks, partake of a meal at one session.[1] Partaking of a meal at one session, I, monks, am aware of good health and of being without illness and of buoyancy and strength and living in comfort.[2] Come you too, monks, partake of a meal at one session; partaking of a meal at one session you too, monks, will be aware of good health and of being without illness and of buoyancy and strength and living in comfort.' There was nothing to be done by me, monks, by way of instruction to those monks; all that was to be done by me, monks, was the production of mindfulness among those monks. Monks, even as[3] on level ground at crossroads a chariot is standing harnessed with thoroughbreds, the goad hanging handy; and a skilled groom, a charioteer of horses to be tamed, having mounted it, having taken the reins in his left hand, having taken the goad in his right, might drive up and down where and how he likes; even so, monks, there was nothing to be done by me by way of instruction to those monks; all that was to be done by me, monks, was the production of mindfulness among those monks. Wherefore, monks, do you get rid of what is unskilled, make exertion[4] among things that are skilled—so will you too come to growth, development, maturity in this *dhamma* and discipline.

Monks, close to some village or little town, a great sāl-wood may be overgrown with creepers, but some man might approach it desiring its good, desiring its welfare, desiring its security from bonds;[5] he, having cut off those sāl-tree sprouts which are bent and crushed by the strength (of the creepers), would carry them out (of the wood) and would thoroughly clear the inside of the wood. But he would tend properly those sāl-tree sprouts which are straight and well grown. Thus, monks, after a time this sāl-tree wood would come to growth, development, maturity. Even so, do you, monks, get rid of what is unskilled, make exertion among things that are skilled, [**125**]—so will you too come to growth, development, maturity in this *dhamma* and discipline.

Once upon a time, monks, in this very Sāvatthī, there was a lady

---

[1] *ekâsanabhojanaṃ bhuñjāmi*. *Cf*. *Vism*. 60. *MA*. ii. 97 says this is a meal in the morning, one of the seven (*v. ll.* ten, a hundred) times for eating meals between sunrise and noon.

[2] *Cf*. *M*. i. 437, 473, ii. 91, 125, 141; *D*. i. 204, ii. 72.

[3] *M*. iii. 97; *A*. iii. 28; *S*. iv. 176.

[4] *āyogaṃ karotha*. Comy. does not explain.

[5] As at *M*. i. 117.

householder named Vedehikā.[1] Monks, a lovely reputation had gone forth thus about the lady Vedehikā: The lady householder Vedehikā is gentle, she is meek, she is tranquil. Now, monks, the lady householder Vedehikā had a slave woman, named Kāḷī, who was clever,[2] diligent, a careful worker.[3] Then, monks, it occurred to the slave woman Kāḷī: 'A lovely reputation has gone forth about my mistress thus: The lady householder Vedehikā is gentle, she is meek, she is tranquil. Now does my mistress have an inward ill-temper that she does not show, or does she not have one? Or is it that my mistress, because I do my work so carefully, whether she has an inward ill-temper or not, does not show it? Suppose now that I should test the mistress?'

Then, monks, the slave woman Kāḷī got up late next day. Then, monks, the lady householder Vedehikā spoke thus to the slave woman Kāḷī: 'Well now,[4] Kāḷī.' 'What is it, mistress?' 'Now why did you get up late today?[5]' 'That's nothing, mistress.' 'That's nothing indeed, bad slave—you got up late today,'[6] and angry, displeased, she frowned. Then, monks, it occurred to the woman slave Kāḷī: 'Whether my mistress has an inward ill-temper or not, she does not show it. Is it because my work is so careful that my mistress, whether she has an inward ill-temper or not, does not show it? Suppose that I were to test the mistress even further?' Then, monks, the woman slave Kāḷī got up later the next day. Then, monks, the lady householder Vedehikā spoke thus to the slave woman Kāḷī: 'Well now, Kāḷī.' 'What is it, mistress?' 'Now why did you get up late today?' 'That's nothing, mistress.' 'That's nothing indeed, bad slave—you got up late today,' and angry, displeased, she spoke a word of displeasure. Then it occurred to the slave woman Kāḷī: 'Whether my mistress has an inward ill-temper or not, she does not show it. Is it because my work is so careful that my mistress, whether she has an inward ill-temper or not, does not show it? Suppose I were to test the mistress even further?' Then, monks, the slave woman Kāḷī got

---

[1] *MA*. ii. 98, "a daughter of a family resident in the kingdom of Videha. Or, *veda* means wisdom, so Vedehikā is a farer by wisdom. It means she is clever."

[2] *MA*. ii. 99 among other work in cooking the food, making (lit. spreading) the beds, making the lamps burn.

[3] She did not break or chip things in spite of being diligent, *MA*. ii. 99.

[4] *he je*, explained at *MA*. ii. 99 by *are*, an exclamation of astonishment.

[5] *MA*. ii. 99, have you some discomfort?

[6] If you have no discomfort, why did you get up late?

up even later the next day. Then, monks, the lady householder Vedehikā spoke thus to the slave-woman Kāḷī: **[126]** 'Well now, Kāḷī.' 'What is it, mistress?' 'Now why did you get up late today?' 'That's nothing, mistress.' 'That's nothing indeed, bad slave—you got up late today,' and angry, displeased, having seized the pin for securing the bolt (of a door), she gave her a blow on the head, which cracked her head.[1] Then, monks, the slave woman Kāḷī, her head broken and streaming with blood, spread it about among the neighbours, saying: 'See, sirs, the deed of the gentle one; see, sirs, the deed of the meek one; see, sirs, the deed of the tranquil one. How can she, saying to her only slave woman, 'You got up late today,' angry, displeased, having seized the pin for securing the bolt (of a door), give a blow on the head and crack the head?' And then, monks, after a time an evil reputation went forth about this lady householder Vedehikā: The lady householder Vedehikā is violent, she is not meek, she is not tranquil.

Even so, monks, some monk here is very gentle, very meek, very tranquil so long as disagreeable ways of speech do not assail him. But when disagreeable ways of speech assail the monk it is then that he is to be called gentle, is to be called meek, is to be called tranquil. I, monks, do not call that monk easy to speak to who is easy to speak to about robe-material, almsfood, lodgings, medicines for the sick, who falls into suavity. What is the reason for this? It is, monks, that this monk, not getting robe-material, almsfood, lodgings, medicines for the sick, is not easy to speak to, does not fall into suavity. Monks, whatever monk, respecting only *dhamma*, revering *dhamma*, honouring *dhamma*, comes to be easy to speak to, falls into suavity—him do I call easy to speak to. Wherefore, monks, thinking: Respecting only *dhamma*, revering *dhamma*, honouring *dhamma*, we will become easy to speak to, we will fall into suavity, thus must you train yourselves, monks.

There are, monks, these five ways of speaking in which others when speaking to you might speak: at a right time or at a wrong time; according to fact or not according to fact; gently or harshly; on what is connected with the goal or on what is not connected with the goal; with a mind of friendliness or full of hatred. Monks, when speaking to others you might speak at a right time or at a wrong time; monks, when speaking to others you might speak according to fact or not according to fact; monks, when speaking to

---

[1] As at *M*. i. 336.

others you might speak gently or harshly; monks, when speaking to others you might speak about what is connected with the goal [**127**] or about what is not connected with the goal; monks, when speaking to others you might speak with minds of friendliness or full of hatred. Herein, monks, you should train yourselves thus: ' Neither will our minds become perverted nor will we utter an evil speech, but kindly and compassionate will we dwell, with a mind of friendliness, void of hatred; and we will dwell having suffused that person with a mind of friendliness; and, beginning with him, we will dwell having suffused the whole world with a mind of friendliness that is far-reaching, widespread, immeasurable, without enmity, without malevolence.' This is how you must train yourselves, monks.

Monks, as a man might come along bringing a shovel and basket, and might speak thus: ' I will make this great earth not earth '; so he digs here and there, tosses it here and there, spits here and there, stales here and there, thinking: ' You are becoming not-earth, you are becoming not-earth.' What do you think about this, monks ? Could that man make this great earth not earth ?'

" No, Lord. What is the reason for this ? It is that this great earth, Lord, is deep, it is immeasurable, it is not easy to make it not-earth before that man would be worn out and defeated."[1]

" Even so, monks, are these five ways of speaking in which others when speaking to you might speak: at a right time . . . or full of hatred. Herein, monks, you should train yourselves thus: ' Neither will our minds become perverted nor will we utter an evil speech, but kindly and compassionate will we dwell, with a mind of friendliness, void of hatred; and we will dwell having suffused that person with a mind of friendliness; and, beginning with him, we will dwell having suffused the whole world with a mind like the earth—far-reaching, widespread, immeasurable, without enmity, without malevolence.' This is how you must train yourselves, monks.

Monks, as a man might come along bringing lac or yellow or dark green[2] or crimson, and might speak thus: ' I will delineate[3] material shapes in this space[4], I will make material shapes appear.'[5] What do

---

[1] *kilimathassa vighātassa bhāgī assa*, he would be a partaker in exhaustion and slaying.

[2] *MA*. ii.100=*Vin*. iv. 120, the *nīla* (green) of bronze, the *nīla* of foliage. See *VA*. 863.

[3] *likhissāmi*, smear, scrape.

[4] *ākāsa* is not air. It is ether or empty space, what is void.

[5] *Cf. Thag.* 1155 *f.*

you think about this, monks ? Could that man delineate a material shape in this space, could he make material shapes appear ? "

" No, Lord. What is the reason for this ? It is, Lord, that this space is without shape,[1] it is viewless. It is not easy to delineate a material shape there, to make material shapes appear before [**128**] that man would be worn out and defeated."

" Even so, monks, are these five ways of speaking in which others when speaking to you might speak: at a right time or at a wrong time . . . ' . . . . and beginning with him, we will live having suffused the whole world with a mind like space—far-reaching, widespread, immeasurable, without enmity, without malevolence.' This is how you must train yourselves, monks.

Monks, as a man might come along bringing a burning grass-torch[2] and might speak thus: ' I, with this burning grass-torch will set fire to the river Ganges, I will make it scorch up.' What do you think about this, monks ? Could that man, with the burning grass-torch set fire to the river Ganges and make it scorch up ? "

" No, Lord. What is the reason for this ? It is, Lord, that the river Ganges is deep, it is immeasurable. It is not easy to set fire to it with a burning grass-torch and make it scorch up before that man would be worn out and defeated."

" Even so, monks, are these five ways of speaking in which others when speaking to you might speak: at a right time or at a wrong time . . . ' . . . . and, beginning with him, we will live having suffused the whole world with a mind like the river Ganges—far-reaching, widespread, immeasurable, without enmity, without malevolence.' This is how you must train yourselves, monks.

Monks, it is like a catskin bag[3] that is cured, well cured, cured all over, and is supple, silky, with no hisses, no purrs.[4] Then a man might come along bringing a piece of wood or a potsherd and might speak thus: ' I, with a piece of wood or a potsherd will get a hiss, will get a purr out of this catskin bag that is cured, well cured, cured all over, and is supple, silky, with no hisses, no purrs.' What do you think about this, monks ? Could that man with a piece of wood or a potsherd get a hiss, get a purr out of that catskin bag that is cured, well cured, cured all over, and is supple, silky, with no hisses, no purrs ? "

---

[1] *Cf. Dh.* 254, 255.

[2] *Cf. M.* i. 365.

[3] *Cf. Thag.* 1138, *biḷārabhastā*.

[4] *chinnasassarā chinnababbharā*, and below *sarasara bharabhara*. See *JPTS*. 1889, p. 209. *Cf. surusuru* (*kāraka*) at *Vin.* iv. 197.

"No, Lord. What is the reason for this? It is, Lord, that that catskin bag is cured, well cured, cured all over, and is supple, silky, with no hisses, no purrs. It is not easy, with a piece of wood or with a potsherd, to get a hiss out of it or to get a purr, before that man would be worn out and defeated."

"Even so, monks, are these five ways of speaking in which others when speaking to you might speak: at a right time [**129**] or at a wrong time; according to fact or not according to fact; gently or harshly; on what is connected with the goal or on what is not connected with the goal; with a mind of friendliness or full of hatred. Monks, when speaking to others you might speak at a right time or at a wrong time . . . according to fact or not according to fact . . . gently or harshly . . . on what is connected with the goal or on what is not connected with the goal . . . with a mind of friendliness or full of hatred. Herein, monks, you should train yourselves thus: 'Neither will our minds become perverted nor will we utter an evil speech, but kindly and compassionate will we dwell, with a mind of friendliness, void of hatred; and we will dwell having suffused that man with a mind of friendliness; and, beginning with him, we will dwell having suffused the whole world with a mind like a catskin bag—far-reaching, widespread, immeasurable, without enmity, without malevolence.' This is how you must train yourselves, monks.

Monks, as low-down thieves might carve one limb from limb with a double-handled saw[1], yet even then whoever[2] sets his mind at enmity, he, for this reason, is not a doer of my teaching. Herein, monks, you should train yourselves thus: 'Neither will our minds become perverted, nor will we utter an evil speech, but kindly and compassionate will we dwell, with a mind of friendliness, void of hatred; and, beginning with him, we will dwell having suffused the whole world with a mind of friendliness that is far-reaching, widespread, immeasurable, without enmity, without malevolence.' This is how you must train yourselves, monks.

If you, monks, were to attend repeatedly to this exhortation on the Parable of the Saw, would you, monks, see any way of speech, subtle or gross, that you could not endure?"

"No, Lord."

"Wherefore, monks, consider repeatedly this exhortation on the

---

[1] Referred to and quoted at *M.* i. 186, 189.

[2] *MA.* ii. 102, either a monk or a nun.

Parable of the Saw; for a long time it will be for your welfare and happiness."

Thus spoke the Lord. Delighted, these monks rejoiced in what the Lord had said.

Discourse on the Parable of the Saw:
the First

22. DISCOURSE ON THE PARABLE OF THE WATER-SNAKE

(Alagaddûpamasutta)

[**130**] THUS have I heard: At one time the Lord was staying near Sāvatthī in the Jeta Grove in Anāthapiṇḍika's monastery. Now at that time a pernicious view had arisen like this in a monk named Ariṭṭha who had formerly been a vulture-trainer[1]:

" In so far as I understand *dhamma* taught by the Lord, it is that in following those things called stumbling-blocks by the Lord, there is no stumbling-block at all." Several monks heard: " A pernicious view has arisen to the monk named Ariṭṭha, who was formerly a vulture-trainer, like this: ' In so far as I understand *dhamma* taught by the Lord, it is that in following those things called stumbling-blocks by the Lord, there is no stumbling-block at all.' "

Then these monks approached the monk Ariṭṭha, who had formerly been a vulture-trainer; having approached, they spoke thus to the monk Ariṭṭha, who had formerly been a vulture-trainer: " Is it true, as is said, reverend Ariṭṭha, that a pernicious view has arisen in you, like this: ' In so far as I understand *dhamma* . . . there is no stumbling-block at all ? ' "

" Undoubtedly, your reverences, as I understand *dhamma* taught by the Lord, it is that in following those things called stumbling-blocks by the Lord, there is no stumbling-block at all."

Then these monks, anxious to dissuade the monk Ariṭṭha who had formerly been a vulture-trainer from that pernicious view, questioned him, cross-questioned him, and pressed for the reasons,[2]

---

[1] This episode also at *Vin.* ii. 25, iv. 133 *ff.* For notes, etc. see *B.D.* iii. 21 *ff.*

[2] As at *M.* i. 233.

and said: "Do not speak thus, reverend Ariṭṭha, do not misrepresent the Lord; misrepresentation of the Lord is not at all seemly, and the Lord certainly would not speak thus. For, in many a figure, reverend Ariṭṭha, are things called stumbling-blocks by the Lord,[1] and in following these there is a veritable stumbling-block. Sense-pleasures are said by the Lord to be of little satisfaction, of much pain, of much tribulation, wherein is more peril. Sense-pleasures are likened by the lord to a skeleton,[2] of much pain. . . . Sense-pleasures are likened by the Lord to a lump of meat . . . to a torch of dry grass . . . to a pit of glowing embers . .. to a dream . . . to something borrowed . . . to the fruits of a tree . . . to a slaughter-house . . . to an impaling stake. . . . Sense-pleasures are likened by the Lord to a snake's head, of much pain, of much tribulation, wherein is more peril."

Yet the monk Ariṭṭha who had formerly been a vulture-trainer even while being questioned, cross-questioned and pressed for his reasons by these monks, expressed that pernicious view as before, obstinately holding and adhering to it: "Undoubtedly, your reverences, in so far as I understand *dhamma* taught by the Lord . . . there is no stumbling-block at all."

Since these monks were unable to dissuade the monk Ariṭṭha **[131]** who had formerly been a vulture-trainer from that pernicious view, then these monks approached the Lord; having approached, having greeted the Lord, they sat down at a respectful distance. While they were sitting down at a respectful distance, these monks spoke thus to the Lord:

"Lord, a pernicious view like this arose in the monk called Ariṭṭha who had formerly been a vulture-trainer: 'In so far as I understand *dhamma* taught by the Lord . . . there is no stumbling-block at all.' And we heard, Lord, that a pernicious view like this had arisen in the monk called Ariṭṭha who had formerly been a vulture-trainer: 'In so far as I understand *dhamma* taught by the Lord . . . there is no stumbling-block at all.' Then we, Lord, approached the monk Ariṭṭha who had formerly been a vulture-trainer; having approached, we spoke thus to the monk Ariṭṭha who had formerly been a vulture-trainer: 'Is it true, as is said, reverend Ariṭṭha, that a pernicious view has arisen in you like this: "In so far as I under-

---

[1] *Vin.* iv. 134 reads "are things that are stumbling-blocks called stumbling-blocks by the Lord."

[2] *Cf.* following with *M.* i. 364 *f.*

stand *dhamma* taught by the Lord . . . no stumbling-block at all ? " ' When this had been said, Lord, the monk Ariṭṭha, who had formerly been a vulture-trainer, spoke thus to us: ' Undoubtedly as I, your reverences, understand *dhamma* taught by the Lord . . . there is no stumbling-block at all.' Then we, Lord, anxious to dissuade the monk Ariṭṭha, who had formerly been a vulture-trainer, from that pernicious view, questioned him, cross-questioned him, pressed him for reasons, and said: ' Do not speak thus, reverend Ariṭṭha, do not misrepresent the Lord; misrepresentation of the Lord is not at all seemly, and the Lord certainly would not speak thus. For in many a figure, reverend Ariṭṭha, are things called stumbling-blocks by the Lord, and in following these there is a veritable stumbling-block. Sense-pleasures are said by the Lord to be of little satisfaction, of much pain, of much tribulation, wherein is more peril. Sense-pleasures are likened by the Lord to a skeleton. . . . Sense-pleasures are likened by the Lord to a snake's head, of much pain, of much tribulation, wherein is more peril.' Yet, Lord, the monk Ariṭṭha who had formerly been a vulture-trainer, even while being questioned, cross-questioned and pressed for his reasons by us, expressed that pernicious view as before, obstinately holding and adhering to it: ' Undoubtedly, as I, your reverences, understand *dhamma* taught by the Lord . . . there is no stumbling-block at all.' Since we, Lord, were unable to dissuade the monk Ariṭṭha who had formerly been a vulture-trainer from that pernicious view, we are therefore telling this matter to the Lord."

Then the Lord addressed a certain monk, saying: " Come you, monk, summon the monk Ariṭṭha who had formerly been a vulture-trainer in my name, saying: ' The Lord is summoning you, Ariṭṭha.' "

[132] " Very well, Lord," and this monk, having answered the Lord in assent, approached the monk Ariṭṭha who had formerly been a vulture-trainer, and having approached, spoke thus to the monk Ariṭṭha who had formerly been a vulture-trainer: " The Lord is summoning you, reverend Ariṭṭha."

" Very well, your reverence," and the monk Ariṭṭha who had formerly been a vulture-trainer, having answered this monk in assent, approached the Lord; having approached, having greeted the Lord, he sat down at a respectful distance. As the monk Ariṭṭha who had formerly been a vulture-trainer was sitting down at a respectful distance, the Lord spoke thus to him:

" Is it true, as is said, that in you, Ariṭṭha, a pernicious view arose like this: 'In so far as I understand *dhamma* taught by the Lord . . . no stumbling-block at all.' ? "

" Undoubtedly, Lord, as I understand *dhamma* . . . no stumbling-block at all."

" To whom then do you, foolish man, understand that *dhamma* was taught thus by me ? Have not things that are stumbling-blocks been spoken of by me in many a figure, and in following these is there not a veritable stumbling-block ? Sense-pleasures are said by me to be of little satisfaction, of much pain, of much tribulation, wherein is more peril. Sense-pleasures are likened by me to a skeleton . . . to a lump of meat . . . to a torch of dry grass . . . to a pit of glowing embers . . . to a dream . . . to something borrowed . . . to the fruits of a tree . . . to a slaughter-house . . . to an impaling stake. . . . Sense-pleasures are likened by me to a snake's head, of much pain, of much tribulation, wherein is more peril. And yet you, foolish man, not only misrepresent me because of your own wrong grasp, but also injure yourself and give rise to much demerit which will be for a long time, foolish man, for your woe and sorrow."[1]

Then the Lord addressed the monks, saying: " What do you think about this, monks ? Has the monk Ariṭṭha who was formerly a vulture-trainer even a glimmering[2] of this *dhamma* and discipline ?"

" How could this be, Lord ? It is not so, Lord." When this had been said, the monk Ariṭṭha who had formerly been a vulture-trainer sat down silent, ashamed, his shoulders drooped, his head lowered, brooding, speechless. Then the Lord, understanding why the monk Ariṭṭha who had formerly been a vulture-trainer was silent, ashamed, his shoulders drooped, his head lowered, brooding, speechless, spoke thus to the monk Ariṭṭha who had formerly been a vulture-trainer:

" You, foolish man, will be known through this pernicious view of your own, for I will now interrogate the monks." Then the Lord addressed the monks, saying:

" Do you too, [**133**] monks, understand that *dhamma* was taught by me thus, so that the monk Ariṭṭha who had formerly been a vulture-trainer not only misrepresents me because of his own wrong grasp, but is also injuring himself and giving rise to much demerit ?"

---

[1] To here = *Vin.* iv. 133-35, with the difference that in *Vin.* Gotama does not summon Ariṭṭha to speak to him, but convenes an Order and questions him there.

[2] *usmīkata*, as at *M.* i. 258. *MA.* ii. 104 " has he the least glimmering of knowledge, *ñaṇusmā?*"

"No, Lord. For, Lord, in many a figure are things that are stumbling-blocks spoken of to us by the Lord, and in following these there is a veritable stumbling-block. Sense-pleasures are said by the Lord to be of little satisfaction, of much pain, of much tribulation, wherein is more peril. Sense-pleasures are likened by the Lord to a skeleton. . . . Sense-pleasures are likened by the Lord to a snake's head, of much pain, of much tribulation, wherein is more peril."

"It is good, monks, it is good that you, monks, have thus understood *dhamma* taught by me. For in many a figure have things that are stumbling-blocks been spoken of by me to you, monks, and in following these there is a veritable stumbling-block. Sense-pleasures are said by me to be of little satisfaction, of much pain, of much tribulation, wherein is more peril. Sense-pleasures are likened by me to a skeleton. . . . Sense-pleasures are likened by me to a snake's head, of much pain, of much tribulation, wherein is more peril. But when this monk Ariṭṭha who had formerly been a vulture-trainer not only misrepresents me, but also injures himself and gives rise to much demerit, this will be for a long time for the woe and sorrow of this foolish man. Indeed, monks, this situation does not occur when one could follow sense-pleasures apart from sense-pleasures themselves, apart from perceptions of sense-pleasures, apart from thoughts of sense-pleasures.

Herein, monks, some foolish men master *dhamma*: the Discourses in prose, in prose and verse,[1] the Expositions,[2] the Verses,[3] the Uplifting Verses, the 'As it was Saids,' the Birth Stories, the Wonders, the Miscellanies.[4] These, having mastered that *dhamma*, do not test the meaning of these things by intuitive wisdom; and these things whose meaning is untested by intuitive wisdom do not become clear; they master this *dhamma* simply for the advantage of reproaching others and for the advantage of gossiping,[5] and they do not arrive at that goal for the sake of which they mastered *dhamma*. These things, badly grasped by them conduce for a long time to their woe and sorrow. What is the reason for this?

---

[1] Stock passage. *MA*. ii. 106 says "in prose and verse" refers to *Viuaya* and various Suttas in the *Suttanipāta*.

[2] *veyyākaraṇa* is explained as *Abhidhamma*.

[3] *MA*. ii. 106: *Thag-thīg*, and *Dhp*. and part of the *Sn*.

[4] Cūḷa-and Mahā-vedalla Suttas, Sammādiṭṭhi, Sakkapañha, Sankhārabhājanīya and Mahāpuṇṇamā Suttas.

[5] *Cf*. *A*. ii. 26.

Monks, it is because of a wrong grasp of things. Monks, it is like[1] a man walking about aiming after a water-snake,[2] searching for a water-snake, looking about for a water-snake. He might see a large water-snake, and he might take hold of it by a coil or by its tail; the water-snake, having rounded on him, might bite him on his hand or arm or on another part of his body; [**134**] from this cause he might come to dying or to pain like unto dying. What is the reason for this ? Monks, it is because of his wrong grasp of the water-snake. Even so, monks, do some foolish men here master *dhamma*: the Discourses in prose. . . . Monks, it is because of a wrong grasp of things.

In this case, monks, some young men of family master *dhamma*: the Discourses in prose, in prose and verse, the Expositions, the Verses, the Uplifting Verses, the 'As it was Saids,' the Birth Stories, the Wonders, the Miscellanies. These, having mastered that *dhamma*, test the meaning of these things by intuitive wisdom; and these things whose meaning is tested by intuitive wisdom become clear to them. They master *dhamma* neither for the advantage of reproaching others nor for the advantage of gossiping, and they arrive at the goal for the sake of which they mastered *dhamma*. These things, being well grasped by them, conduce for a long time to their welfare and happiness. What is the reason for this? It is, monks, because of a right grasp of things. Monks, it is like a man walking about aiming after a water-snake, searching for a water-snake, looking about for a water-snake. He might see a large water-snake, and he might hold it back skilfully[3] with a forked[4] stick; having held it back skilfully with a forked stick, he might grasp it properly by the neck. However that water-snake, monks, might wind its coils round that man's hand or arm or round another part of his body, he would not come to dying or to pain like unto dying. What is the reason for this ? Monks, it is because of his right grasp of the water-snake. Even so, monks, some young men of family master *dhamma*. . . . It is, monks, because of a right grasp of things. Wherefore, monks, understand the meaning of what I have said, then learn it. But in case you do not understand the meaning of what I have said, I should be questioned about it by you, or else those who are experienced monks.

---

[1] Quoted *DA*. i. 21. *Asl*. 23. [2] *alagadda*=*āsivisa, MA*. ii. 107.

[3] Lit.; he might hold it back well held back.

[4] *ajapada*, cleft like a goat's hoof.

Monks, I will teach you *dhamma*—the Parable of the Raft—for crossing over, not for retaining.[1] Listen to it, pay careful attention, and I will speak."

"Yes, Lord," these monks answered the Lord in assent.

"Monks, as a man going along a highway might see a great stretch of water, the hither bank dangerous[2] and frightening,[2] the further bank secure, not frightening, but if there were not a boat for crossing by or a bridge across for going from the not-beyond to the beyond, this might occur to him: [**135**] 'This is a great stretch of water, the hither bank dangerous and frightening, the further bank secure and not frightening, but there is not a boat for crossing by or a bridge across for going from the not-beyond to the beyond. Suppose that I, having collected grass, sticks, branches and foliage, and having tied a raft, depending on that raft, and striving with hands and feet,[3] should cross over safely to the beyond?' Then, monks, that man, having collected grass, sticks, branches and foliage, having tied a raft, depending on that raft and striving with his hands and feet, might cross over safely to the beyond. To him, crossed over, gone beyond, this might occur: 'Now, this raft has been very useful to me. I, depending on this raft, and striving with my hands and feet, crossed over safely to the beyond. Suppose now that I, having put this raft on my head, or having lifted it on to my shoulder, should proceed as I desire?' What do you think about this, monks? If that man does this, is he doing what should be done with that raft?"

"No, Lord."

"What should that man do, monks, in order to do what should be done with that raft? In this case, monks, it might occur to that man who has crossed over, gone beyond: 'Now, this raft has been very useful to me. Depending on this raft and striving with my hands and feet, I have crossed over safely to the beyond. Suppose now that I, having beached this raft on dry ground or having submerged it under the water, should proceed as I desire? In doing this, monks, that man would be doing what should be done with that raft. Even so, monks, is the Parable of the Raft *dhamma* taught by me for crossing over, not for retaining. You, monks,

---

[1] Referred to at *MA*. i. 260.

[2] *MA*. ii. 109 defines these words in accordance with definitions given at *Vin*. iii. 263, iv. 63.

[3] *Cf*. *S*. iv. 174 for this symbolism.

by understanding the Parable of the Raft, should get rid even of (right) mental objects,[1] all the more of wrong ones.[2]

Monks, there are these six views with causal relations.[3] What are the six ? In this connection, monks, an uninstructed average person,[4] taking no count of the pure ones, unskilled in the *dhamma* of the pure ones, untrained in the *dhamma* of the pure ones, taking no count of the true men, unskilled in the *dhamma* of the true men, untrained in the *dhamma* of the true men, regards material shape as: 'This is mine, this am I, this is my self;'[5] he regards feeling as: 'This is mine . . . ;' he regards perception as: 'This is mine . . . ;' he regards the habitual tendencies as: 'These are mine . . . ;' he regards consciousness as: 'This is mine, this am I, this is my self.' And also he regards whatever is seen, heard, sensed,[6] cognised, reached, looked for, pondered by the mind as: 'This is mine, this am I, this is my self.' Also whatever view with causal relation says: 'This the world this the self;[7] after dying[8] I [9] will become permanent, lasting, eternal, not liable to change, [**136**] I will stand fast like unto the eternal,' he regards this as: 'This is mine, this am I, this is my self.'

But, monks, an instructed disciple of the pure ones, taking count of the pure ones, skilled in the *dhamma* of the pure ones, well trained in the *dhamma* of the pure ones, taking count of the true men, skilled in the *dhamma* of the true men, well trained in the *dhamma* of the

---

1 *MA*. ii. 109 says that the Lord makes us get rid of the desire and passion for calm and for insight; and in regard to the former the Comy. quotes *M*. i. 456, "I speak of getting rid of the plane of neither-perception-nor-non-perception"; and in regard to the latter it quotes *M*. i. 260, "Even if this view of yours is purified thus, do not cling to it."

2 Such as Ariṭṭha's; *MA*. ii 109.

3 *diṭṭhiṭṭhānāni*. *Cf*. *A*. v. 198. *MA*. ii. 110 says, "There is view and the *ṭhāna* of view; both the cause of view and the result of view."

4 As at *M*. i. 1, 7, etc.

5 Through desire, pride, false view respectively.

6 *muta*. The fields of sight and hearing are separately mentioned; *muta* refers to the fields of smell, taste and touch, so *MA*. ii. 110, with which *cf*. definition of *muta* at *Vin*. iv. 2.

7 *so loko so attā*, meaning, I think, that what is the world, that is the self, thus identifying them. The "world" at *S*. iv. 97 is the world of the senses and as such is impermanent, ill, not the self. See *MA*. ii. 110 which quotes *M*. iii. 17: *rūpam attato samanupassati*, he regards material shapes from the point of view of self. Or *so* may stand for "I," as below; thus we would get: "I the world, I the self."

8 Having gone to a world beyond, *MA*. ii. 110. 9 *so*=*so aham*.

true men, regards material shape as: 'This is not mine, this am I not, this is not my self;' he regards feeling as: 'This is not mine . . . ;' he regards perception as: 'This is not mine . . . ;' he regards the habitual tendencies as: 'These are not mine . . . ;' he regards consciousness as: 'This is not mine, this am I not, this is not my self.' And also he regards whatever is seen, heard, sensed, cognised, reached, looked for, pondered by the mind as: 'This is not mine, this am I not, this is not my self.' Also whatever view with causal relation says: 'This the world this the self, after dying I will become permanent, lasting, eternal, not liable to change, I will stand fast like unto the eternal,' he regards this as: 'This is not mine, this am not I, this is not my self.' He, regarding thus that which does not exist,[1] will not be anxious."[2]

When this had been said, a certain monk spoke thus to the Lord: "But Lord, might there not be anxiety about something objective that does not exist?"[3]

"There might be, monk," the Lord said. "In this case, monk, it occurs to somebody: 'What was certainly mine[4] is certainly not mine (now);[5] what might certainly be mine, there is certainly no chance of my getting.' He grieves, mourns, laments, beats his breast, and falls into disillusionment. Even so, monks, does there come to be anxiety about something objective that does not exist."

"But might there be, Lord, no anxiety about something objective that does not exist?"

"There might be, monk," the Lord said. "In this case, monk, it does not occur to anybody: 'What was certainly mine is certainly not mine (now); what might certainly be mine, there is certainly no chance of my getting.' He does not grieve, mourn, lament, he does not beat his breast, he does not fall into disillusionment. Even so, monk, does there come to be no anxiety about something objective that does not exist."

"But, Lord, might there be anxiety about something subjective that does not exist?"

"There might be, monk," the Lord said. "In this case, monk, the view occurs to someone: 'This the world this the self; after

---

[1] *asati*=*avijjamāne*, being inexistent, untrue, *MA*. ii. 111.

[2] *MA*. ii. 111, will not be disturbed by fear and craving.

[3] Externally, in the loss of requisites, *MA*. ii. 111.

[4] Valuables, vehicles, mounts, gold, *MA*. ii. 111.

[5] *MA*. ii. 111, it is taken by rajahs or thieves or it is burnt or carried away by water; *cf*. *M*. i. 86.

dying I will become permanent, lasting, eternal, not liable to change, I will stand fast like unto the eternal.' He hears *dhamma* as it is being taught by the Tathāgata or by a disciple of the Tathāgata for rooting out all resolve for, bias, tendency and addiction to view and causal relation, for tranquillising all the activities, for casting away all attachment, for the destruction of craving, for dispassion, stopping, nibbāna. It occurs to him thus: [**137**] 'I will surely be annihilated, I will surely be destroyed, I will surely not be.'[1] He grieves, mourns, laments, beats his breast, and falls into disillusionment. Thus, monk, there comes to be anxiety about something subjective that does not exist."

"But, Lord, might there be no anxiety about something subjective that does not exist?"

"There might be, monk," the Lord said. "In this case, monk, the view does not occur to anyone: 'This the world this the self, after dying I will become permanent, lasting, eternal, not liable to change, I will stand fast like unto the eternal.' He hears *dhamma* as it is being taught by the Tathāgata or by a disciple of the Tathāgata for rooting out all resolve for, bias, tendency and addiction to view and causal relation, for tranquillising all the activities, for casting away all attachment, for the destruction of craving, for dispassion, stopping, nibbāna. But it does not occur to him thus: 'I will surely be annihilated, I will surely be destroyed, I will surely not be.' So he does not grieve, mourn, lament, he does not beat his breast, he does not fall into disillusionment. Thus, monk, does there come to be no anxiety about something subjective that does not exist.

Monks, could you take hold of some possession, the possession of which would be permanent, lasting, eternal, not liable to change, that would stand fast like unto the eternal? But do you, monks, see that possession the possession of which would be permanent, lasting, eternal, not liable to change, that would stand fast like unto the eternal?"

"No, Lord."

"Good, monks. Neither do I, monks, see that possession the possession of which is permanent, lasting, eternal, not liable to change, that would stand fast like unto the eternal. Could you, monks, grasp that grasping of the theory of self, so that by grasping that theory of self there would not arise grief, suffering, anguish,

---

[1] *MA*. ii. 112 cites *S*. iii. 55 *ff*. *no c'assaṃ no ca me siyā*, "had it not been it were not mine." *Cf*. *Ud*. 66.

lamentation, despair ? But do you, monks, see that grasping of the theory of self, from the grasping of which theory of self there would not arise grief, suffering, anguish, lamentation, despair ? "

"No, Lord."

"Good, monks. Neither do I, monks, see that grasping of the theory of self from the grasping of which there would not arise grief, suffering, anguish, lamentation, despair. Could you, monks, depend on that dependence on view, depending on which dependence on view there would not arise grief, suffering, anguish, lamentation, despair ? But do you, monks, see that dependence on view . . . despair ? "

"No, Lord."

"Good, monks. Neither do I, monks, see that dependence on view by depending on which dependence on view [**138**] there would not arise grief, suffering, anguish, lamentation, despair. If, monks, there were Self, could it be said: 'It belongs to my self' ? "[1]

"Yes, Lord."

"Or, monks, if there were what belongs to Self, could it be said: 'It is my self' ? "[2]

"Yes, Lord."

"But if Self, monks, and what belongs to Self, although actually existing, are incomprehensible,[3] is not the view and the causal relation that: 'This the world this the self, after dying I will become permanent, lasting, eternal, not liable to change, I will stand fast like unto the eternal'—is not this, monks, absolute complete folly ? "

"Lord, how could it not be absolute complete folly ? "

"What do you think about this, monks:[4] Is material shape permanent or impermanent ? "[5]

"Impermanent, Lord."

"But is what is impermanent painful or pleasant ? "

"Painful, Lord."

"But is it fitting to regard that which is impermanent, painful, liable to change, as 'This is mine, this am I, this is my self' ? "

---

[1] *Cf. S.* iii. 127; also *S.* iii. 67; *Vin.* i. 13.

[2] *MA.* ii. 113, "If there is an I, there is a mine; if there is a mine, there is an I. So (the two) would become joined."

[3] *anupalabbhamāne*, either: not to be known, or, not-existing. *Cf. Sn.* 858: in him there exists (or is to be found) neither *attaṃ* nor *nirattaṃ*.

[4] As at *Vin.* i. 14. *Cf. S.* iv. 34, iii. 66, 82-3; also *M.* iii. 282.

[5] *MA.* ii. 113, "inasmuch as having been, it is not (now), therefore it is impermanent, and for these four reasons: because of uprising and decaying, temporariness, and being the opposite of permanence."

"No, Lord."[1]

"What do you think about this, monks: Is feeling . . . perception . . . are the habitual tendencies permanent or impermanent? What do you think about this, monks: Is consciousness permanent or impermanent?"

"Impermanent, Lord."

"Is that which is impermanent painful or pleasant?"

"Painful, Lord."

"But is it fitting to regard that which is impermanent, painful, liable to change as, 'This is mine, this am I, this is my self'?"

"No, Lord."

"Wherefore, monks, whatever is material shape, past, future, present, subjective or objective, [**139**] gross or subtle, mean or excellent, whether it is far or near—all material shape should be seen thus by perfect intuitive wisdom as it really is: This is not mine, this am I not, this is not my self. Whatever is feeling . . . whatever is perception . . . whatever are the habitual tendencies . . . whatever is consciousness, past, future, present, subjective or objective, gross or subtle, mean or excellent, whether it is far or near—all consciousness should be seen thus by perfect intuitive wisdom as it really is: This is not mine, this am I not, this is not myself.

Monks, the instructed disciple of the pure ones, seeing thus, disregards material shape, disregards feeling, disregards perception, disregards the habitual tendencies, disregards consciousness; disregarding, he is dispassionate; through dispassion he is freed; in freedom the knowledge comes to be that he is freed,[2] and he comprehends: Destroyed is birth, brought to a close is the Brahma-faring, done is what was to be done, there is no more of being such or such.

Monks, such a monk[3] is said to have lifted the barrier,[4] and he is said to have filled the moat, and he is said to have pulled up the pillar, and he is said to have withdrawn the bolts, and he is said to be a pure one, the flag laid low, the burden[5] dropped, without fetters.

And how, monks, has a monk lifted the barrier? In this connection, monks, ignorance is got rid of by the monk, cut down to the roots, made like a palm-tree stump, made so that it can come to no

---

[1] *MA* ii. 113, "Not-self for four reasons: because it is empty, has no owner, has no master, and because it is the opposite of Self."

[2] *MA.* ii. 115, "Here dispassion is the Way . . he is freed by the dispassionate Way."

[3] This passage also at *A.* iii. 84. [4] *Dhp.* 398.

[5] See *S.* iii. 25 on the burden and its bearer.

future existence, not liable to rise again. In this way, monks, a monk comes to be one who has lifted the barrier.

And how, monks, does a monk come to be one who has filled the moat? In this connection, monks, again-becoming, faring on in births come to be got rid of by a monk, cut down to the roots, made like a palm-tree stump, made so that they can come to no future existence, not liable to rise again. In this way, monks, a monk comes to be one who has filled the moat.

And how, monks, does a monk come to be one who has pulled up the pillar? In this connection, monks, craving comes to be got rid of by a monk . . . made so that it can come to no future existence, not liable to rise again. In this way, monks, is a monk one who has pulled up the pillar.

And how, monks, does a monk come to be one who has withdrawn the bolts? In this connection, monks, the five fetters binding to the lower (shore) come to be got rid of by a monk . . . made so that they can come to no future existence, not liable to rise again. In this way, monks, does a monk come to be one who has withdrawn the bolts.

And how, monks, does a monk come to be a pure one, the flag laid low, the burden dropped, without fetters? In this connection, monks, the conceit 'I am' comes to be got rid of by the monk, cut down to the roots, made like a palm-tree stump, made so that it can come to no future existence, [**140**] not liable to rise again. In this way, monks, a monk comes to be a pure one, the flag laid low, the burden dropped, without fetters.

Monks, when a monk's mind is freed thus, the *devas*—those with Inda,[1] those with Brahmā,[1] those with Pajāpati,[1] do not succeed in their search if they think: 'This is the discriminative consciousness attached[2] to a Tathāgata.'[3] What is the reason for this? I, monks, say here and now that a Tathāgata is untraceable.[4]

---

[1] Mentioned in different context at *D.* i. 244. *Sa-Indadeve sa-Brahmake* at *D.* ii. 261; *sa-Inda-devā sa-Pajāpatikā* at *D.* ii. 274. *Inda* at *D.* iii. 204, *Sn.* 310, 316, 679. *Brahmā vā Indo vā pi Sujumpati* at *Sn.* 1024.

[2] *nissata*, supporting, attached to, dependent on.

[3] *MA.* ii. 117 says here "tathāgata means both a being, *satta*, and the highest person, one who has destroyed the cankers." It then seems to take this back, saying there is nothing called a being in the highest meaning, and the Lord does not speak of *tathāgata, satta, puggala*. For the Tathāgata is untraceable. *Cf. UdA.* 340, which explains *tathāgata* by *attā*. *Cf. S.* i. 123, where Māra cannot find Godhika's discriminative consciousness, *viññāṇa*.

[4] *ananuvejja*. *Cf. Dhp.* 179; *Miln.* 73.

Although I, monks, am one who speaks thus, who points out thus, there are some recluses and brahmans who misrepresent me untruly, vainly, falsely, not in accordance with fact, saying: 'The recluse Gotama is a nihilist,[1] he lays down the cutting off, the destruction, the disappearance[2] of the existent entity. But as this, monks, is just what I am not, as this is just what I do not say, therefore these worthy recluses and brahmans misrepresent me untruly, vainly, falsely, and not in accordance with fact when they say: 'The recluse Gotama is a nihilist, he lays down the cutting off, the destruction, the disappearance of the existent entity.' Formerly[3] I, monks, as well as now, lay down simply anguish and the stopping of anguish. If, in regard to this, monks, others revile,[4] abuse, annoy[5] the Tathāgata, there is in the Tathāgata no resentment, no distress, no dissatisfaction of mind[6] concerning them.

If, in regard to this,[7] monks, others revere, esteem, respect and honour the Tathāgata, there is in the Tathāgata no joy, no gladness, no elation of mind[8] concerning them. If, in regard to this, monks, others revere, esteem, respect and honour the Tathāgata, it occurs to the Tathāgata, monks, concerning them: 'This that was formerly thoroughly known,[9] such kind of duties are to be done by me to it.'[10] Wherefore, monks, even if others should revile, abuse, annoy you, there should be in you no resentment, distress, dissatisfaction of mind concerning them. And wherefore, monks, even if others should revere, esteem, respect, honour you, there should not be in you joy, gladness, elation of mind concerning them. And wherefore, monks, even if others should revere, esteem, respect, honour you, it should occur to you: 'This that was formerly thoroughly known, such kind of duties are to be done by us to it.'

---

[1] *venayika*, a leader away, averter, diverter. *MA*. ii. 117 says he removes, he causes destruction.

[2] *vibhava*, or extirpation, annihilation.

[3] As early as the First Utterance, called the Rolling of the Dhamma-wheel.

[4] *MA*. ii. 118, with the ten ways of reviling or cursing. These are given at *Jā*. i. 191, *DhA*. i. 212, *SnA*. 342. See *B.D*. ii. 171, *n*. 3 and p. 173 for the ten kinds of *omasavāda*, insulting speech.

[5] *MA*. ii. 118 reads *rosenti vihesanti*, annoy, vex.

[6] As at *D*. i. 3; *A*. i. 79.

[7] *I.e.* the teaching on anguish.

[8] As at *D*. i. 3.

[9] *MA*. ii. 118 refers this to the five *khandhas*; see *Vin*. i. 13 *f*., etc.

[10] *tattha me evarūpā kārā karīyanti*. *MA*. ii. 118 says *tattha'me ti tasmiṃ khandhapañcake ime*. But "'*me*" must be wrong, for just below when the monks are being told how to comport themselves, we get *tattha no evarūpā*.

Wherefore, monks, what is not yours, put it away.[1] Putting it away will be for a long time for your welfare and happiness. And what, monks, is not yours? Material shape, monks, is not yours; put it away, putting it away will be for a long time for your welfare and happiness. Feeling, monks, is not yours; [**141**] put it away, putting it away will be for a long time for your welfare and happiness. Perception, monks, is not yours; put it away, putting it away will be for a long time for your welfare and happiness. The habitual tendencies, monks, are not yours; put them away, putting them away will be for a long time for your welfare and happiness. Consciousness is not yours; put it away, putting it away will be for a long time for your welfare and happiness. What do you think about this,[2] monks? If a person were to gather or burn or do as he pleases with the grass, twigs, branches and foliage in this Jeta Grove, would it occur to you: The person is gathering *us*, he is burning *us*, he is doing as he pleases with *us*?"

"No, Lord. What is the reason for this? It is that this, Lord, is not our self nor what belongs to self."

"Even so, monks, what is not yours, put it away; putting it away will be for a long time for your welfare and happiness. And what, monks, is not yours? Material shape, monks, is not yours; put it away, putting it away will be for a long time for your welfare and happiness. Feeling . . . Perception. . . . The habitual tendencies. . . . Consciousness, monks, is not yours; put it away, putting it away will be for a long time for your welfare and happiness.

Thus, monks, is *dhamma* well taught by me, made manifest, opened up, made known, stripped of its swathings. Because *dhamma* has been well taught by me thus, made manifest, opened up, made known, stripped of its swathings, those monks who are perfected ones, the cankers destroyed, who have lived the life, done what was to be done, laid down the burden, attained their own goal, the fetter of becoming utterly destroyed, and who are freed by perfect profound knowledge—the track of these cannot be discerned.

Thus, monks, is *dhamma* well taught by me . . . stripped of its swathings. Because *dhamma* has been well taught by me thus . . . stripped of its swathings, those monks in whom the five fetters binding the lower (shore) are got rid of—all these[3] are of spontaneous

---

[1] This passage also at *S.* iii. 33 *f.* [2] *S.* iii. 34 reads *seyyathā pi.*

[3] *anāgāmino*, non-returners, should, I think, be inserted after *sabbe te.*

uprising, they are attainers of utter nibbāna there, not liable to return from that world.[1]

Thus, monks, is *dhamma* well taught by me . . . stripped of its swathings. Because *dhamma* has been well taught by me thus . . . stripped of its swathings, those monks in whom the three fetters are got rid of, in whom attachment, aversion and confusion are reduced, all these are once-returners who, having come back to this world once, will make an end of anguish.

Thus, monks, is *dhamma* well taught by me . . . stripped of its swathings. Because *dhamma* has been well taught by me thus . . . stripped of its swathings, those monks in whom the three fetters are got rid of, all these are stream-attainers [**142**] who, not liable to the Downfall, are assured, bound for awakening.

Thus, monks, is *dhamma* well taught by me . . . stripped of its swathings. Because *dhamma* has been well taught by me thus . . . stripped of its swathings, all those monks who are striving for *dhamma*, striving for faith[2] are bound for awakening.

Thus, monks, is *dhamma* well taught by me, made manifest, opened up, made known, stripped of its swathings. Because *dhamma* has been well taught by me thus, made manifest, opened up, made known, stripped of its swathings, all those who have enough faith in me, enough affection, are bound for heaven."[3]

Thus spoke the Lord. Delighted, these monks rejoiced in what the Lord had said.

Discourse on the Parable of the Water-snake:
The Second

---

[1] See above, p. 43.

[2] Defined at *Pug.* 15; quoted at *MA.* ii. 120. *Cf. M.* i. 226.

[3] Not literally, but " ' as though,' *viya*, in heaven. Some say ' assured.' " *MA.* ii. 120 adds that the Porāṇakatheras call such a monk a lesser stream-attainer, *cūḷasotâpanno.* " Monk," however, is not mentioned in this clause of the text.

23. DISCOURSE ON THE ANTHILL

(Vammīkasutta)

Thus have I heard: At one time the Lord was staying near Sāvatthī in the Jeta Grove in Anāthapiṇḍika's monastery. Now at that time the venerable Kassapa the Boy[1] was staying in the Blind Men's Grove. Then, when the night was far spent[2] a certain *deva*[3] with a glorious skin,[4] having illuminated the whole of the Blind Men's Grove, approached the venerable Kassapa the Boy; and having approached stood at one side. While standing at one side this *deva* spoke thus to the venerable Kassapa the Boy: "Monk, monk,[5] this ant-hill smokes by night, blazes up by day. A brahman speaks thus: 'Bringing a tool, clever one, dig it up.' The clever one, digging when he had brought a tool saw a bolt and said: 'A bolt, revered one.' The brahman spoke thus: 'Take out the bolt, dig on, clever one, bringing a tool.' The clever one, digging on when he had brought a tool, saw a frog,[6] and said: 'A frog, revered one.' The brahman spoke thus: 'Take out the frog, dig on, clever one, bringing a tool.' The clever one, digging on when he had brought a tool, saw a forked path, and said: 'A forked path, revered one.' The brahman spoke thus: 'Take out the forked path, dig on, clever one, bringing a tool.' The clever one, digging on when he had brought

---

[1] This is Kumārakassapa, so called even when he was grown up, *MA*. ii. 120. He lived in the Blind Men's Grove fulfilling the course for learners, *MA*. ii. 124. He took this *sutta* as the subject of his meditations and so developed insight and won arahantship, *MA*. ii. 134. He was therefore not an arahant at the time when it was delivered.

[2] This is the meaning attributed to *abhikkantāya* by *MA*. ii. 124—the meaning of "waning" as against its other meaning of "lovely," "beautiful" and "wonderful" (in the sense of assenting).

[3] *MA*. ii. 124: "*devatā* is the common (general or joint) appellation of *devas* and daughters of *devas*. Here it means a *deva*." *Cf*. *SA*. ii. 14, which says here it means a *devaputta*.

[4] *abhikkantavaṇṇā*. *MA*. ii. 125 says *abhikkanta* is here in its sense of "beautiful," *abhirūpa*; and among seven meanings attributed to *vaṇṇa*, the first, that of "skin," *chavi*, is meant.

[5] The *deva* and Kassapa had been two of five friends in the time of the Buddha Kassapa. Therefore the *deva* did not greet him, *MA*. ii. 126.

[6] *uddhumāyikā*=*maṇḍūka*, *MA*. ii. 128.

a tool, saw a strainer,[1] and said: 'A strainer, revered one.' The brahman spoke thus: [**143**] 'Take out the strainer, dig on, clever one, bringing a tool.' The clever one, digging on when he had brought a tool, saw a tortoise, and said: 'A tortoise, revered one.' The brahman spoke thus: 'Take out the tortoise, dig on, clever one, bringing a tool.' The clever one, digging on when he had brought a tool, saw a slaughter-house,[2] and said: 'A slaughter-house, revered one.' The brahman spoke thus: 'Take out the slaughter-house, dig on, clever one, bringing a tool.' The clever one, digging on when he had brought a tool, saw a piece of flesh, and said: 'A piece of flesh, revered one.' The brahman spoke thus: 'Take out the piece of flesh, dig on, clever one, bringing a tool.' The clever one, digging on when he had brought a tool, saw a cobra,[3] and said: 'A cobra, revered one.' The brahman spoke thus: 'Let the cobra be, do not touch the cobra, do reverence to the cobra.' If you, monk, having approached the Lord, were to ask him about these questions, then you could remember as the Lord explains to you. I, monk, do not see anyone in the world with its *devas*, with its Māras, with its Brahmās, in creation, with its recluses and brahmans, its *devas* and men, who could turn his mind to expounding these questions except a Tathāgata or a Tathāgata's disciple or one who has heard (the teaching) from them."

Thus spoke that *deva*; and vanished then and there, having said this.

Then the venerable Kassapa the Boy approached the Lord towards the end of that night; having approached, having greeted the Lord, he sat down at a respectful distance. As he was sitting down at a respectful distance, the venerable Kassapa the Boy spoke thus to the Lord: " During this night, Lord, when the night was far spent, a certain *deva* with a glorious skin, having illumined the whole of the Blind Men's Grove, approached me; and having approached, stood at one side. While standing to one side, Lord, that *deva* spoke thus to me: 'Monk, monk, this ant-hill smokes by night, it blazes up by day. A brahman speaks thus: " Bringing a tool, clever one, dig it

---

[1] *caṅgavāra*, explained at *MA*. ii. 128 as *khāraparissāvana*, a strainer for potash? *Cf. cangavāraka* at *Miln*. 365, translated as " dyers' straining cloth "; and *Jā*. v. 186, translated as " sieve." *Jā*. *Comy*. says " as water placed in a dyers' *khāracaṅgavāra* quickly runs out." Neumann's translation, *Majjh*., I 239, gives *Geflecht*, basket-work. Chalmers has " strainer."

[2] *MA*. ii. 128 says a large knife for cutting up meat as well as a block.

[3] *nāga*.

up . . ." or one who has heard (the teaching) from them.' This is what the *deva* said, Lord, and vanished then and there, having said this.

Now what, Lord is the anthill, what is smoking by night, what is blazing up by day, who is the brahman, who the clever one, what is the tool, what the digging up, what the bolt, what the frog, what the forked path, what the strainer, what the tortoise, what the slaughter-house, what the piece of flesh, what the cobra ?"

[144] "The anthill, monk, this is a synonym for the body made of the four great elements, originated from mother and father, nourished on gruel and sour milk, of a nature to be constantly rubbed away, pounded away, broken up and scattered.[1]

Whatever, monk, one thinks upon and ponders upon during the night concerning the day's affairs, this is smoking by night.

Whatever affairs, monk, one sets going by day, whether by body, speech or thought, having pondered and reflected upon them during the night, this is blazing up by day.

Brahman,[2] monk, this is a synonym for the Tathāgata, perfected one, fully self-awakened one.

Clever one, monk, this is a synonym for a monk who is a learner.[3]

The tool, monk, this is a synonym for the ariyan intuitive wisdom.

Digging, monk, this is a synonym for the output of energy.[4]

The bolt, monk, this is a synonym for ignorance. Take out the bolt, get rid of ignorance, dig, clever one, bringing a tool. This is the meaning of that.

The frog, monk, this is a synonym for the turbulence of wrath. Take out the frog, get rid of the turbulence of wrath, dig, clever one, bringing a tool. This is the meaning of that.

The forked path, monk, this is a synonym for perplexity. Take out the forked path, get rid of perplexity, dig, clever one, bringing a tool. This is the meaning of that.

The strainer, monk, this is a synonym for the five hindrances: for the hindrance of desire for sense-pleasures, for the hindrance of malevolence . . . sloth and torpor. . . restlessness and worry, for the hindrance of perplexity. Take out the strainer, get rid of the five hindrances, dig, clever one, bringing a tool. This is the meaning of that.

---

[1] This description of the body occurs also at *M.* i. 500, ii. 17; *S.* iv. 83; *D.* i. 76.

[2] *Cf.* definition of brahman at *A.* iv. 144, quoted at *MA.* ii. 130.

[3] *Cf.* definition of *sikkhati . . . sekho* at *A.* i. 231, quoted at *MA.* ii. 131.

[4] *MA.* ii. 131, of bodily and mental energy.

The tortoise, monk, this is a synonym for the five grasping groups,[1] that is to say, for the group of grasping after material shape, for the group of grasping after feeling, for the group of grasping after perception, for the group of grasping after the habitual tendencies, for the group of grasping after consciousness. Take out the tortoise, get rid of the five grasping groups, dig, clever one, bringing a tool. This is the meaning of that.

The slaughter-house, monk, this is a synonym for the five strands of sense-pleasures: for material shapes cognisable by the eye, agreeable, pleasant, liked, enticing, connected with sensual pleasures, alluring; for sounds cognisable by the ear . . . for smells cognisable by the nose . . . for savours cognisable by the tongue . . . for touches cognisable by the body, agreeable, pleasant, liked, enticing, connected with sensual pleasures, [**145**] alluring. Take out the slaughter-house, get rid of the five strands of sense-pleasures, dig, clever one, bringing a tool. This is the meaning of that.

The piece of flesh, monk, this is a synonym for the passion of delight. Take out the piece of flesh, get rid of the passion of delight, dig, clever one, bringing a tool. This is the meaning of that.

The cobra, monk, this is a synonym for a monk whose cankers are destroyed.[2] Let the cobra be, do not touch the cobra, do reverence to the cobra. This is the meaning of that."

Thus spoke the Lord. Delighted the venerable Kassapa the Boy rejoiced in what the Lord had said.

The Discourse on the Ant-hill:
the Third

---

[1] *MA*. ii. 133 says that these are comparable to the four legs and the head of a tortoise.

[2] See end of Sta. 5, where the two chief disciples are referred to as *mahānāga*.

24. DISCOURSE ON THE RELAYS OF CHARIOTS

(Rathavinītasutta)[1]

THUS have I heard: At one time the Lord was staying near Rājagaha in the Bamboo Grove at the squirrels' feeding place. Then a number of monks, living in their native district,[2] having kept the rains locally,[2] approached the Lord; having approached, having greeted the Lord, they sat down at a respectful distance. The Lord spoke thus to these monks as they were sitting down at a respectful distance:

"Who, monks, among the monks living in their native district, is esteemed by his local fellow Brahma-farers in this way: both as one desiring little for himself and as being one who talks to the monks on desiring little; both as one who is content for himself and as one who talks to the monks on contentment; both as one who is aloof himself and as one who talks to the monks on aloofness; both as one who is not sociable[3] himself and as one who talks to the monks about not being sociable; both as one of stirred up energy himself and as one who talks to the monks on stirring up energy; both as one who is himself endowed with moral habit and as one who talks to the monks on the attainment of moral habit; both as one who is himself endowed with concentration and as one who talks to monks on the attainment of concentration; both as one who is himself endowed with intuitive wisdom[4] and as one who talks to monks on the attainment of intuitive wisdom; both as one who is himself endowed with freedom and as one who talks to monks on the attainment of freedom; both as one who is himself endowed with the knowledge and vision of freedom and as one who talks to

---

[1] Referred to at *MA*. i. 92, ii. 246, iii. 6; *Vism*. 93, 671; *SnA*. 446; *MT*. 553.

[2] *jātibhūmaka* and *jātibhūmiyaṃ*. Both words occur at *A*. iii. 366. *MA*. ii. 135 says *jātaṭṭhāna*, and instances Kapilavatthu as the *jātaṭṭhāna* of the Buddha, and hence his *jātibhūmi*.

[3] *asaṁsaṭṭha*. See on *saṁsaṭṭha viharati B.D.* iii. 207, *n*. 1. *MA*. ii. 143 gives five kinds of *saṁsagga*: association through hearing, seeing, conversation, eating with, body.

[4] *paññā*; *MA*. ii. 147 says this is worldly and other-worldly knowledge, *ñāṇa*.

the monks on the attainment of the knowledge and vision of freedom;[1] an exhorter,[2] instructor, one who can gladden, arouse, [**146**] incite, delight his fellow Brahma-farers ? "

" Lord, the venerable Puṇṇa, Mantāṇī's son[3], is among the monks living in his native district and who is esteemed by his fellow Brahma-farers in this way: both as one desiring little for himself . . . delight his fellow Brahma-farers."

Now at that time the venerable Sāriputta was sitting close to the Lord. Then it occurred to the venerable Sāriputta: " It is profitable for the venerable Puṇṇa, Mantāṇī's son, it is well gotten for the venerable Puṇṇa, Mantāṇī's son, that his well informed fellow Brahma-farers praise him point by point when they are face to face with the Teacher, and that the Teacher approves of him. Perhaps I might meet the venerable Puṇṇa, Mantāṇī's son, somewhere sometime. Perhaps there might be some conversation (with him)."

Then the Lord, having stayed near Rājagaha for as long as he found suitable, set out on tour for Sāvatthī; in due course, walking on tour, he arrived at Sāvatthī. The Lord stayed there near Sāvatthī in the Jeta Grove in Anāthapiṇḍika's monastery. Then the venerable Puṇṇa, Mantāṇī's son, heard: " They say the Lord has reached Sāvatthī and is staying near Sāvatthī in the Jeta Grove in Anāthapiṇḍika's monastery." Then the venerable Puṇṇa, Mantāṇī's son, having packed away his bedding,[4] taking his bowl and robe, set out on tour for Sāvatthī; in due course, walking on tour, he approached Sāvatthī, the Jeta Grove, Anāthapiṇḍika's monastery, and the Lord; having approached, having greeted the Lord, he sat down at a respectful distance. The Lord gladdened, roused, incited, delighted the venerable Puṇṇa, Mantāṇī's son, with talk on *dhamma* as he was sitting down at a respectful distance. Then the venerable Puṇṇa, Mantāṇī's son, gladdened, roused, incited, delighted by the Lord's talk on *dhamma*, having rejoiced and being satisfied, rising from his seat, having greeted the Lord, and keeping

---

[1] These five " attainments," *sampadā*, also at *Pug.* 54; *cf. S.* i. 139, *A.* iii. 12*ff*; and as *khandha* at *S.* v. 162.

[2] This and the following epithets are at *S.* v. 162 applied to Sāriputta (who had just died); see also *Miln.* 373.

[3] At *A.* i. 23, *S.* ii. 156 called chief of speakers on *dhamma*. Mentioned at *S.* iii. 105. His verse is at *Thag.* 4.

[4] See *B.D.* i. 153, *n.* 4; and *cf.* Pāc. 14, 15 (*Vin.* iv. 39 *ff*). Also *Vin.* ii. 211, quoted *MA.* ii. 152.

his right side towards him, set out for the day-sojourn in the Blind Men's Grove.[1]

Then a certain monk approached the venerable Sāriputta; having approached, he spoke thus to the venerable Sāriputta: "Inasmuch as you, reverend Sāriputta, are continually extolling the monk called Puṇṇa, Mantāṇī's son, he, [**147**] gladdened, roused, incited, delighted by the Lord's talk on *dhamma*, having rejoiced in what the Lord had said, and being satisfied, rising from his seat, having greeted the Lord and keeping his right side towards him, is setting out for the Blind Men's Grove for the day-sojourn."

Then the venerable Sāriputta, hurriedly taking his piece of cloth to sit upon,[2] followed close after the venerable Puṇṇa, Mantāṇī's son, keeping him in sight. Then the venerable Puṇṇa, Mantāṇī's son, having plunged into the Blind Men's Grove, sat down at the root of a tree for the day-sojourn. Then the venerable Sāriputta, having also plunged into the Blind Men's Grove, sat down at the root of a tree for the day-sojourn. Then the venerable Sāriputta, having emerged from solitary meditation towards evening, approached the venerable Puṇṇa, Mantāṇī's son; having approached, he exchanged greetings with the venerable Puṇṇa, Mantāṇī's son; having exchanged greetings of friendliness and courtesy, he sat down at one side. As he was sitting down at one side, the venerable Sāriputta spoke thus to the venerable Puṇṇa, Mantāṇī's son:

"Your reverence, is the Brahma-faring lived under our Lord?"

"Yes, your reverence."

"Your reverence, is the Brahma-faring lived under the Lord for purity of moral habit?"[3]

"Not for this, your reverence."

"Then, your reverence, is not the Brahma-faring lived under the Lord for purity of mind?"

"Not for this, your reverence."

"Then, your reverence, is the Brahma-faring lived under the Lord for purity of view?"[4]

"Not for this, your reverence."

---

[1] *MA.* ii. 154, "the Jeta grove was crowded after the meal with nobles, brahmans and so on, and it was impossible to find solitude. But the Blind Men's grove was secluded, like a place for striving."

[2] *nisīdana*, see *Vin.* iii. 207, 232, and *B.D.* ii. p. 34, *n.* 1; p. 87, *n.* 2.

[3] *MA.* ii. 155 refers to the fourfold purity in moral habit spoken of at length at *Vism.* (p. 15 *f.*).

[4] *sīla-* and *diṭṭhi-visuddhi* at *D.* iii. 214; *A.* i. 95.

"Then, your reverence, is not the Brahma-faring lived under the Lord for purity through crossing over doubt?"[1]

"Not for this, your reverence."

"Then, your reverence, is the Brahma-faring lived under the Lord for purity of knowledge and insight into the Way and what is not the Way?"

"Not for this, your reverence."

"Then, your reverence, is not the Brahma-faring lived under the Lord for purity of knowledge and insight into the course?"[2]

"Not for this, your reverence."

"Then, your reverence, is the Brahma-faring lived under the Lord for purity arising from knowledge and insight?"[3]

"Not for this, your reverence."

"But when you, your reverence, are being asked: 'Your reverence, is the Brahma-faring lived under the Lord for purity of moral habit?' you say: 'Not for this, your reverence.' And when you, your reverence, are being asked: 'Your reverence, is the Brahma-faring lived under the Lord for purity of mind . . . of view . . . through crossing over doubt . . . of knowledge and insight into the Way and what is not the Way . . . for purity of knowledge and insight into the course . . . for purity arising from knowledge and insight?' you say: 'Not for this, your reverence.' What is the reason, then, your reverence, [**148**] that the Brahma-faring is lived under the Lord?"

"The Brahma-faring under the Lord, your reverence, is lived for utter nibbāna without attachment."[4]

"Your reverence, is purity of moral habit utter nibbāna without attachment?"

"It is not this, your reverence."

"Then, your reverence, is not purity of mind utter nibbāna without attachment?"

"It is not this, your reverence."

---

[1] *Cf. Ud.* 60.

[2] *paṭipadā*. Quoted *MA*. ii. 115.

[3] All these seven acts of purity are found also at *D*. iii. 288 with two added: purification through wisdom and through freedom. See *Dial*. iii. 262, *n*. 3.

[4] *Cf. S*. iv. 48, v. 29; *A*. i. 44, iv. 74, v. 65. *MA*. ii. 156 says that in the view of those who assert that attachment is due to a condition, utter nibbāna with no attachment means utter nibbāna due to no condition; if the incomposite realm of deathlessness has not arisen on account of a condition, they speak of it as utter nibbāna without attachment. This is the end, the peak, the goal (*niṭṭhā*).

"Then, your reverence, is purity of view utter nibbāna without attachment?"

"It is not this, your reverence."

"Then, your reverence, is not purity through crossing over doubt utter nibbāna without attachment?"

"It is not this, your reverence."

"Then, your reverence, is purity of knowledge and insight into the Way and what is not the Way utter nibbāna without attachment?"

"It is not this, your reverence."

"Then, your reverence, is not purity of knowledge and insight into the course utter nibbāna without attachment?"

"It is not this, your reverence."

"Then, your reverence, is purity arising from knowledge and insight utter nibbāna without attachment?"

"It is not this, your reverence."

"But, your reverence, what is utter nibbāna without attachment except these states?"

"It is not this, your reverence."

"But when you, your reverence, are being asked: 'Is purity of moral habit utter nibbāna without attachment?' you say: 'It is not this, your reverence.' And when you, your reverence, are being asked: 'Then, your reverence, is not purity of mind utter nibbāna without attachment . . . of view . . . through crossing over doubt . . . of knowledge and insight into the Way and what is not the Way . . . of knowledge and insight into the course . . . arising from knowledge and insight?' you say: 'It is not this, your reverence.' And when you, your reverence, are being asked: 'What is utter nibbāna without attachment except these states?' you say: 'It is not this, your reverence.' But, your reverence, the meaning of what has been said should have been shown as it was spoken."

"If, your reverence, the Lord had laid down that purity of moral habit was utter nibbāna without attachment, he would have laid down that utter nibbāna without attachment is the same as that with attachment. If, your reverence, the Lord had laid down that purity of mind . . . of view . . . through crossing over doubt . . . of knowledge and insight into the Way and what is not the Way . . . of knowledge and insight into the course . . . that purity arising from knowledge and insight was utter nibbāna without attachment, he would have laid down that utter nibbāna without attachment is the same as that with attachment. And, your reverence, if there were utter nibbāna without attachment apart from these states, the average person would be (attained to) utter nibbāna, for the average person, your reverence, is apart from these states. Well then, your reverence, I will make you a parable, for by a parable well-informed men here understand the meaning of what is said. Your reverence, it is as though while King Pasenadi of Kosala was staying in Sāvatthī, [**149**] something to be done urgently should arise in Sāketa, and seven relays of chariots would be arranged for him between Sāvatthī and Sāketa. Then, your reverence, King Pasenadi of Kosala, having left Sāvatthī by the palace-gate, might mount the first chariot in the relay, and by means of the first chariot in the relay he would reach the second chariot in the relay. He would dismiss the first chariot in the relay and would mount the second chariot in the relay, and by means of the second chariot in the relay he would reach the third chariot in the relay . . . the fourth . . . the fifth . . . the sixth . . . and would mount the seventh chariot in the relay, and by means of the seventh chariot in the relay he would reach the palace-gate in Sāketa. While he was at the palace-gate, the chief ministers and his kith and kin would question him thus:

'Have you, sire, reached the palace-gate at Sāketa by means of this relay of chariots from Sāvatthī?' Answering in what way, your reverence, would King Pasenadi of Kosala when answering answer rightly?"

"Answering thus, your reverence, would King Pasenadi of Kosala when answering answer rightly: 'Now, as I was staying in Sāvatthī something to be done urgently arose in Sāketa. For this they had seven relays of chariots arranged for me between Sāvatthī and Sāketa. Then I, having left Sāvatthī by the palace-gate, mounted the first chariot in the relay, and by means of the first chariot in the relay reached the second chariot in the relay. I dismissed the first chariot in the relay and mounted the second chariot in the relay. By means of the second chariot in the relay I reached the third chariot in the relay . . . the fourth . . . the fifth . . . the sixth. . . . By means of the sixth chariot in the relay I reached the seventh chariot in the relay. I dismissed the sixth chariot in the relay and mounted the seventh chariot in the relay. By means of the seventh chariot in the relay I reached the palace-gate at Sāketa.' Answering, thus, your reverence, King Pasenadi of Kosala when answering would answer rightly."

"Even so, your reverence, purity of moral habit is of purpose as far as purity of mind;[1] purity of mind is of purpose as far as purity of view; purity of view is of purpose as far as purity through crossing over doubt; purity through crossing over doubt [**150**] is of purpose as far as purity of knowledge and insight into the Way and what is not the Way; purity of knowledge and insight into the Way and what is not the Way is of purpose as far as purity of knowledge and insight into the course; purity of knowledge and insight into the course is of purpose as far as purity arising from knowledge and insight; purity arising from knowledge and insight is of purpose as far as utter nibbāna without attachment. Your reverence, the Brahma-faring under the Lord is lived for the purpose of utter nibbāna without attachment."

When this had been said, the venerable Sāriputta spoke thus to the venerable Puṇṇa, Mantāṇī's son: "What is the venerable one's name? And how do the fellow Brahma-farers know the venerable one?"

"Puṇṇa is my name, your reverence, and the fellow Brahma-farers know me as Mantāṇī's son."

"It is wonderful, your reverence, it is marvellous, your reverence, that the very deep questions were explained step by step by an instructed disciple who knows the Teacher's instruction properly, namely by the venerable Puṇṇa, Mantāṇī's son. It is profitable for the fellow Brahma-farers, it is well gotten for the fellow Brahma-farers that they have a chance to see, that they have a chance to visit the venerable Puṇṇa, Mantāṇī's son. Also, if the fellow Brahma-farers, carrying the venerable Puṇṇa, Mantāṇī's son, on a roll of cloth on their heads,[2] should get a chance to see him, should get a chance to visit him, this would be profitable for them and this would be well gotten for them. It is profitable for us and it is well gotten for us that we have a chance to see, that we have a chance to visit the venerable Puṇṇa, Mantāṇī's son."

When this had been said, the venerable Puṇṇa, Mantāṇī's son, spoke thus to the venerable Sāriputta:

"What is the venerable one's name? And how do the fellow-Brahma-farers know the venerable one?"

"Upatissa is my name, your reverence, and the fellow-Brahma-farers know me as Sāriputta."

---

[1] Whatever is purity of mind, this is the goal (*attha*), this the peak, this the culmination of purity of moral habit, *MA*. ii. 157.

[2] *MA*. ii. 158, so that the crowd should see him and be able to question him and hear *dhamma*, instead of running about here and there asking where he was.

"I have been counselling the worthy disciple whom they liken to the Teacher without knowing that it was the venerable Sāriputta. If I had known that it was the venerable Sāriputta, I would not have spoken at such length. It is wonderful, your reverence, it is marvellous, your reverence, that the very deep questions were asked step by step by an instructed disciple who knows the Teacher's instruction properly, namely by the venerable Sāriputta. It is profitable for the fellow Brahma-farers, it is well gotten for the fellow Brahma-farers that they have a chance to see, that they have a chance to visit the venerable Sāriputta. Also if the fellow Brahma-farers, carrying the venerable Sāriputta on a roll of cloth on their heads, should get a chance to see him, should get a chance to visit him, [**151**] this would be profitable for them and this would be well gotten for them. It is profitable for us and it is well gotten for us that we have a chance to see, that we have a chance to visit the venerable Sāriputta."

In this way these two great beings applauded what the other had so well said.[1]

Discourse on Relays of Chariots:
the Fourth

25. DISCOURSE ON CROPS

(Nivāpasutta)

THUS have I heard: At one time the Lord was staying near Sāvatthī in the Jeta Grove, in Anāthapiṇḍika's monastery. There the Lord addressed the monks, saying: "Monks." "Revered one," these monks answered the Lord in assent. The Lord spoke thus:

"Monks, a sower does not sow a crop for herds of deer, thinking: 'Let the herds of deer, enjoying this crop sown by me, flourish in good condition for many a long day.' Monks, the sower sows the crop for herds of deer thinking: 'The herds of deer will eat fodder encroaching entranced on this crop sown by me; encroaching entranced and eating the fodder, they will get elated;

---

[1] As at Sutta 5.

being elated they will get careless; being careless they will become those to be done to as one wills amid this crop.'

Then, monks, the first herd of deer ate fodder encroaching entranced on this crop sown by the sower; encroaching entranced and eating the fodder these got elated; being elated they got careless; being careless they became those to be done to as the sower willed amid that crop. Thus, monks, this first herd of deer did not escape from the sower's mastery.[1]

Then, monks, the second herd of deer realised: 'The first herd of deer has eaten fodder encroaching entranced on that crop sown by the sower; these, eating fodder encroaching entranced there got elated; being elated they got careless; being careless [**152**] they became those to be done to as the sower willed amid that crop. Thus this first herd of deer did not escape from the sower's mastery. Suppose that we should all refrain from eating the crops; and refraining from enjoyment where there is fear, having plunged into a stretch of forest, should stay there?' So all these refrained from eating the crops; and refraining from enjoyment where there was fear, having plunged into a stretch of forest, they stayed there. In the last month of the hot weather the grass and water gave out, and their bodies became extremely emaciated so that their strength and energy diminished, and with diminished strength and energy they came back again to those crops sown by the sower; encroaching entranced they ate the fodder there; encroaching entranced and eating the fodder there, they got elated; being elated they got careless; being careless, they became those to be done to as the sower willed amid that crop. Thus, monks, neither did the second herd of deer escape from the sower's mastery.

Then, monks, the third herd of deer realised: 'The first herd of deer has eaten fodder encroaching entranced. . . . Thus this first herd of deer did not escape from the sower's mastery. Then that second herd of deer realised thus: "The first herd of deer has eaten fodder encroaching entranced. . . . Thus this first herd of deer did not escape from the sower's mastery. Suppose that we should all refrain from eating the crops; and refraining from enjoyment where there is fear, having plunged into a stretch of forest, should stay there?" So all these refrained from eating the crops; and refraining from enjoyment where there was fear, having plunged into a stretch of

---

[1] *iddhânubhāva*. *MA*. ii. 160 says here *iddhi* and *ānubhāva* are just *vasībhāva*.

forest, they stayed there. In the last month of the hot weather the grass and water gave out, and their bodies became extremely emaciated so that their strength and energy diminished, and with diminished strength and energy they came back again to those crops sown by the sower; encroaching entranced they ate the fodder there; encroaching entranced and eating the fodder there, they got elated; being elated they got careless; being careless, they became those to be done to as the sower willed amid that crop. Suppose that we should make a lair[1] near those crops sown by the sower, [**153**] so that we can eat fodder not encroaching entranced on those crops sown by the sower; and then, having made the lair and not encroaching entranced on the crops sown by the sower, we will not get elated; not being elated we will not get careless; not being careless, we will not become those to be done to as the sower wills amid that crop.' These made a lair near that crop sown by the sower; having made the lair, they ate fodder not encroaching entranced on the crops sown by the sower; these, eating fodder not encroaching entranced there, did not get elated; not being elated, they did not get careless; not being careless, they did not become those to be done to as the sower willed amid that crop.

Thereupon, monks, it occurred to the sower and his companions: 'This third herd of deer must be crafty and wily; this third herd of deer must have potency[2] and be demons;[3] they eat this crop that was sown, but we do not know of their comings or goings. Suppose that we were to enclose this crop that was sown with large stakes and snares on all sides? Then we might see the lair of the third herd of deer, where they might go to take it.[4] So these enclosed that crop that was sown with large stakes and snares on all sides. Then, monks, the sower and his companions saw the lair of the third herd of deer, where they went to take it. Thus, monks, neither did this third herd of deer escape from the sower's mastery.

Thereupon, monks, the fourth herd of deer realised thus: 'The

---

[1] Or, should lie down in an abode, *āsayaṃ kappeyyāma*. *MA*. ii. 161 says that the deer think the hunter will not be on the watch the whole time, and when he is away they can go and eat among the crops.

[2] *iddhimantā*.

[3] *parajanā*; "they are *yakkhas*, not a herd of deer," *MA*. ii. 161. *Cf*. *Dīgha parajana yakkha* at *M*. i. 210.

[4] The sower (or hunter=Death) had an idea, according to *MA*. ii. 161, that the deer did not go far away but lay down near the crops. In *yattha te gāhaṃ gaccheyyuṃ* the *gāha* probably refers to the place among the stakes that they go to; they shake it, and the watchers see.

first herd of deer has eaten fodder encroaching entranced. . . . Thus this first herd of deer did not escape from the sower's mastery. Then that second herd of deer realised thus: " The first herd of deer has eaten fodder encroaching entranced. . . . Thus this first herd of deer did not escape from the sower's mastery. Suppose that we should all refrain from eating the crops. . . ." Thus this second herd of deer did not escape from the sower's mastery. Then that third herd of deer realised thus: " That [**154**] first herd of deer. . . . Thus this first herd of deer did not escape from the sower's mastery. Then that second herd of deer realised thus: ' The first herd of deer has eaten fodder encroaching entranced. . . . Thus this first herd of deer has not escaped from the sower's mastery. Suppose that we should all refrain from eating the crops. . . .' Thus this second herd of deer did not escape from the sower's mastery. Suppose that we should make a lair near those crops sown by the sower, so that we can eat fodder not encroaching entranced on the crops sown by the sower; and then, having made the lair and not encroaching entranced on the crops sown by the sower, we will not get elated; not being elated, we will not get careless; not being careless, we will not become those to be done to as the sower wills amid that crop." These made a lair near that crop sown by the sower; having made the lair they ate fodder not encroaching entranced on the crop sown by the sower; these eating fodder not encroaching entranced there, did not get elated; not being elated, they did not get careless; not being careless, they did not become those to be done to as the sower wills amid that crop. Thereupon it occurred to the sower and his companions: " This third herd of deer must be crafty and wily; this third herd of deer must have potency and be demons; they eat this crop that was sown but we do not know of their comings or goings. Suppose that we were to enclose this crop that was sown with large stakes and snares on all sides ? Then we might see the lair of the third herd of deer, where they might go to take it." So these enclosed that crop that was sown with large stakes and snares on all sides. Then the sower and his companions saw the lair of the third herd of deer, where they went to take it. Thus neither did this third herd of deer escape from the sower's mastery. Suppose that we were to make a lair somewhere where the sower and his companions do not come ? Having made our lair there, we might eat fodder not encroaching entranced on that crop sown by the sower; eating fodder not encroaching entranced, we will not get elated; not being elated, we will not get careless; not being careless, we [**155**] will not become those to be done to as the sower wills amid that crop.' These made a lair somewhere where the sower and his companions did not come; having made a lair there, they ate fodder not encroaching entranced on that crop sown by the sower; these eating fodder not encroaching entranced there, did not get elated; not being elated, they did not get careless; not being careless, they did not become those to be done to as the sower willed amid that crop.

Thereupon, monks, it occurred to the sower and his companions: 'This fourth herd of deer must be crafty and wily; this fourth herd of deer must have potency and be demons; they eat this crop that was sown, but we do not know of their comings or goings. Suppose that we were to enclose this crop that was sown with large stakes and snares on all sides? Then we might see the lair of the fourth herd of deer, where they might go to take it.' So these enclosed that crop that was sown with large stakes and snares on all sides. But, monks, neither the sower nor his companions saw the lair of this fourth herd of deer, where they might go to take it. Thereupon, monks, it occurred to the sower and his companions: "If we beat up this fourth herd of deer, these, beaten up, will beat up others; these, beaten up, will beat up others, and so all the deer will neglect this crop that was sown. Suppose that we were not to interfere with the fourth herd of deer?" So, monks, neither the sower nor his companions interfered with the fourth herd of deer. Thus, monks, this fourth herd of deer escaped the sower's mastery.

Monks, this parable was made by me to illustrate the meaning. And just this is the meaning here:

'The crop,' monks, this is a synonym for the five strands of sense-pleasures.

'The sower,' monks, this is a name for Māra, the Evil One.

'The sower's companions,' monks, this is a synonym for Māra's companions.

'The herds of deer,' monks, this is a synonym for recluses and brahmans.

Where, monks, the first kind of recluse and brahman ate fodder encroaching entranced on that crop sown by Māra—material things of the world—[**156**] these, eating the fodder and encroaching entranced there, got elated; being elated, they got careless; being careless, they became those to be done to by Māra as he willed amid that crop—material things of the world. Thus, monks, the first kind of recluses and brahmans did not escape from Māra's mastery.

I, monks, say that this first kind of recluse and brahman is like that first herd of deer in the parable.

Then, monks, the second kind of recluse and brahman realised: 'That first kind of recluses and brahmans ate fodder encroaching entranced on a crop sown by Māra—material things of the world; these, eating the fodder and encroaching entranced there, got elated; being elated, they got careless; being careless, they became those to be done to by Māra as he willed amid that crop—material things of the world. Suppose that we should all refrain from eating the crop—material things of the world; and refraining from enjoyment where there is fear, having plunged into a stretch of forest, should stay there?' All these refrained from eating the crop—material things of the world; refraining from enjoyment where there was fear, having plunged into a stretch of forest, they stayed there. There these became those feeding[1] on potsherbs . . . on millet . . . on wild rice . . . on snippets of leather . . . on water plants . . . on the red powder of rice-husks . . . on the discarded scum of rice on the boil . . . on the flour of oil-seeds . . . on grass and they became those feeding on cow dung, and they subsisted on jungle roots and fruits, eating the fruits that had fallen. In the last month of the hot weather, when the grass and water dried up, their bodies became extremely emaciated; because their bodies were extremely emaciated their strength and energy diminished; because their strength and energy diminished, freedom of mind diminished; because freedom of mind diminished, they went back again to that very crop sown by Māra—material things of the world. They ate fodder encroaching entranced there; eating fodder encroaching entranced there, they got elated; being elated they got careless; being careless, they became those to be done to by Māra as he willed amid that crop—those material things of the world. Thus, monks, neither did this second kind of recluse and brahman escape from Māra's **[157]** mastery. I, monks, say that this second kind of recluse and brahman is like that second herd of deer in that parable.

Then, monks, the third kind of recluse and brahman realised: 'That first kind of recluse and brahman ate fodder encroaching entranced on that crop sown by Māra—material things of the world. Thus this first kind of recluse and brahman did not escape from Māra's mastery. And that second kind of recluse and brahman realised: "That first kind of recluse and brahman ate fodder en-

---

[1] As at *M*. i. 78, *D*. i. 166.

croaching entranced. . . . Thus this first kind of recluse and brahman did not escape from Māra's mastery. Suppose that we should all refrain from eating the crop . . . should stay there ? " All these refrained from eating the crop . . . they stayed there. There these became eaters of potsherbs. . . eating the fruits that had fallen. In the last month of the hot weather . . . they went back again to that very crop sown by Māra—material things of the world. Thus this second kind of recluse and brahman did not escape from Māra's mastery. Suppose that we should make a lair near that crop sown by Māra—material things of the world; having made a lair there, we will eat fodder not encroaching entranced on that crop sown by Māra—material things of the world; eating fodder not encroaching entranced, we will not get elated; not being elated, we will not get careless; not being careless, we will not become those to be done to by Māra as he wills amid that crop—material things of the world.' These made a lair near that crop sown by Māra—material things of the world; having made a lair there, they ate fodder not encroaching entranced on that crop sown by Māra—material things of the world; these, eating fodder not encroaching entranced there, did not get elated; not being elated, they did not get careless; not being careless, they did not become those to be done to by Māra as he willed amid that crop—material things of the world. Nevertheless they came to be of views like this: that the world is eternal, also that the world is not eternal; and that the world is an ending thing, also that the world is not an ending thing; and that the life principle and the body are the same, also that the life principle and the body are different; and that the Tathāgata becomes after dying, also that the Tathāgata does not become after dying, also that the Tathāgata both becomes and does not become after dying, also that the Tathāgata neither becomes nor does not become after dying. [**158**] Thus, monks, neither did this third kind of recluse and brahman escape from Māra's mastery. I, monks, say that this third kind of recluse and brahman is like that third herd of deer in the parable.

Then, monks, the fourth kind of recluse and brahman realised thus: ' That first kind of recluse and brahman ate fodder encroaching entranced on that crop sown by Māra—material things of the world. . . . Thus this first kind of recluse and brahman did not escape from Māra's mastery. And that second kind of recluse and brahman realised: " That first kind of recluse and brahman ate fodder. . . . Thus this first kind of recluse and brahman did not escape from

Māra's mastery. Suppose that we should all refrain from eating the crop . . . should stay there. . . . " Thus this second kind of recluse and brahman did not escape from Māra's mastery. Then it occurred to that third kind of recluse and brahman: "That first kind of recluse and brahman . . . did not escape from Māra's mastery. And that second kind of recluse and brahman realised: That first kind of recluse and brahman . . . did not escape from Māra's mastery. Suppose that we should all refrain from eating the crop. . . . Thus this second kind of recluse and brahman did not escape from Māra's mastery. Suppose that we should make a lair near that crop sown by Māra—material things of the world. . . ." These made a lair . . . they did not become those to be done to by Māra as he willed amid that crop—material things of the world. Nevertheless, they came to be of views like this: that the world is eternal . . . also that the Tathāgata neither becomes nor does not become after dying. Thus this third kind of recluse and brahman did not escape from Māra's mastery. Suppose that we should make a lair where Māra and Māra's companions do not come; having made that lair, we can eat fodder not encroaching entranced on that crop sown by Māra—material things of the world; eating fodder not encroaching entranced, we will not get elated; not being elated we will not get careless, not being careless we will not become those to be done to by Māra as he wills amid that crop—material things of the world.' These made a lair where Māra and Māra's companions did not come; having made a lair there, [**159**] they ate fodder not encroaching entranced on that crop sown by Māra—material things of the world. These, eating fodder not encroaching entranced there, did not get elated; not being elated, they did not get careless; not being careless, they did not become those to be done to by Māra as he willed amid that crop—material things of the world. Thus, monks, the fourth kind of recluses and brahmans escaped from Māra's mastery. I, monks, say that the fourth kind of recluse and brahman is like that fourth herd of deer in the parable.

And how, monks, is there non-entry[1] of Māra and Māra's companions? Herein, monks, a monk, aloof from the pleasures of the senses, aloof from unskilled states of mind, enters on and abides in the first meditation which is accompanied by initial thought and discursive thought, is born of aloofness, and is rapturous and joyful.

---

[1] *agati*, translated above "(where, *yattha*) Māra does not come." It is non-admission, where he does not come in.

Monks, this kind of monk is called one[1] who has put a darkness round Māra,[2] and who, having blotted out Māra's vision so that it has no range, goes unseen by the Evil One.

And again, monks, a monk, by allaying initial and discursive thought, his mind subjectively tranquillised and fixed on one point, enters on and abides in the second meditation which is devoid of initial and discursive thought, is born of concentration and is rapturous and joyful. Monks, this monk is called one who has put a darkness round Māra, and who, having blotted out Māra's vision so that it has no range, goes unseen by the Evil One.

And again, monks, a monk, by the fading out of rapture, dwells with equanimity, attentive and clearly conscious, and experiences in his person that joy of which the ariyans say: 'Joyful lives he who has equanimity and is mindful,' and he enters on and abides in the third meditation. Monks, this monk is called . . . by the Evil One.

And again, monks, a monk by getting rid of joy, by getting rid of anguish, by the going down of his former pleasures and sorrows, enters on and abides in the fourth meditation which has neither anguish nor joy, and which is entirely purified by equanimity and mindfulness. Monks, this monk is called . . . by the Evil One.

And again, monks, a monk by passing quite beyond perception of material shapes, by the going down of perception of sensory reactions, by not attending to perception of variety, thinking: 'Ether is unending,' enters on and abides in the plane of infinite ether. Monks, this monk is called . . . by the Evil One.

And again, monks, a monk by passing quite beyond the plane of infinite ether, thinking: Consciousness is unending,' enters on and abides in the plane of infinite consciousness. Monks, this monk is called . . . by the Evil One.

And again, monks, a monk, by passing quite beyond the plane of infinite consciousness, [**160**] thinking: 'There is not anything,' enters on and abides in the plane of no-thing. Monks, this monk is called . . . by the Evil One.

And again, monks, a monk, by passing quite beyond the plane of no-thing, enters on and abides in the plane of neither-perception-nor-non-perception. Monks, this monk is called one who has put a darkness round Māra, and who, having blotted out Māra's vision so that it has no range, goes unseen by the Evil One.

---

[1] *Cf. M.* i. 174; also at *A.* iv. 434 but in another connection.

[2] *andhaṃ akāsi Māraṃ* or, "makes Māra blind." Comy, explains *na Mārassa akkhīni bhindi . . . Māro passituṃ na sakkoti. Cf. G.S.* iv. 291, *n.* 1.

And again, monks, a monk, by passing quite beyond the plane of neither-perception-nor-non-perception, enters on and abides in the stopping of perception and feeling; and having seen by intuitive wisdom, his cankers are utterly destroyed. Monks, this monk is called one who has put a darkness round Māra, and who, having blotted out Māra's vision so that it has no range, goes unseen by the Evil One; he has crossed over the entanglement in the world."

Thus spoke the Lord. Delighted, these monks rejoiced in what the Lord had said.

Discourse on Crops:
the Fifth

26. DISCOURSE ON THE ARIYAN QUEST

(Ariyapariyesanasutta)[1]

THUS have I heard: At one time[2] the Lord was staying near Sāvatthī in the Jeta Grove in Anāthapiṇḍika's monastery. Then the Lord, having dressed early, taking his bowl and robe, entered Sāvatthī for almsfood. Then a number of monks approached the venerable Ānanda; having approached, they spoke thus to the venerable Ānanda: "It is long since we, reverend Ānanda, heard a talk on *dhamma* face to face with the Lord. It is good if we, reverend Ānanda, got a chance of hearing a talk on *dhamma* face to face with the Lord."

"Well then, the venerable ones should go to the hermitage of the brahman Rammaka, and probably you would get a chance of hearing a talk on *dhamma* face to face with the Lord."

"Yes, your reverence," these monks answered the venerable Ānanda in assent. Then the Lord, having walked for alms in Sāvatthī, returning from (the quest for) alms, after the meal, said to the venerable Ānanda: "We will go along, Ānanda, and approach the Eastern Park, the palace of Migāra's mother, for the day-sojourn."

"Very well, Lord," the venerable Ānanda answered the Lord in

[1] Called Pāsarāsi Sutta in the *Comy*. [2] *Cf. A.* iii. 344.

assent. [**161**] Then the Lord together with the venerable Ānanda approached the Eastern Park, the palace of Migāra's mother for the day-sojourn. Then the Lord, emerging from seclusion towards evening, said to the venerable Ānanda:

"We will go along, Ānanda, and approach the Eastern Porch[1] to bathe our limbs."

"Very well, Lord," the venerable Ānanda answered the Lord in assent. Then the Lord, together with the venerable Ānanda, approached the Eastern Porch to bathe their limbs. When he had bathed his limbs at the Eastern Porch and had come out (of the water), he stood in a single robe drying his limbs.[2] Then the venerable Ānanda spoke thus to the Lord:

"Lord, this hermitage of the brahman Rammaka is not far; the hermitage of the brahman Rammaka is lovely, Lord; the hermitage of the brahman Rammaka is beautiful, Lord. It were good, Lord, if out of compassion[3] the Lord were to approach the hermitage of the brahman Rammaka." The Lord consented by becoming silent. Then the Lord approached the hermitage of the brahman Rammaka. At that time a number of monks came to be sitting down and talking *dhamma* in the hermitage of the brahman Rammaka. Then the Lord stood outside the porch waiting for the talk to finish. Then the Lord, knowing that the talk had finished, coughed and knocked on the bar of the door;[4] those monks opened the door to the Lord.[5] Then the Lord, having entered the hermitage

---

[1] *MA.* ii. 166: When Kassapa was the Buddha there was a gate to the East, now known as the Eastern Porch, the river Aciravatī surrounded the town and made a great tank at the Eastern Porch. There were different fords (or bathing places): one for the king, one for the townspeople, one for the Order of monks, one for the Buddhas. Pubbakoṭṭhaka mentioned also at *S.* v. 220; *A.* iii. 345. See notes at *K.S.* v. 195, *G.S.* iii. 243.

[2] Besides *A.* iii. 345, *cf. A.* iii. 402, *S.* i. 8. *MA.* ii. 167 says the Lord went into the water in a bathing cloth, and when he came out the Elder handed him a dyed double cloth, which he put on, fastening it with his waistband; and having folded his large robe (*mahācīvara*; perhaps a reference to the *sugatacīvara* of *Vin.* iv. 173) end to end, making it like the heart of a lotus, he stood holding it at the corners. For if one puts on a robe while the limbs are still wet, the corners of the robe turn up, and the requisite is spoiled.

[3] *MA.* ii. 168, for the five hundred monks who wished to hear the Lord, and who had gone to the hermitage.

[4] As at *Vin.* i. 248; *A.* iv. 358 *f.* *MA.* ii. 168 says that *aggaḷam ākoṭesi* means: with the tip of his nail he gave a sign on the door.

[5] The moment they heard the sound, *MA.* ii. 168.

of the brahman Rammaka, sat down on the appointed seat.[1] As he was sitting down, the Lord said to the monks:

" As you were sitting down just now, what was your talk about, monks ? What was your talk that was interrupted ? "

" Lord, our talk that was interrupted was about the Lord himself; then he arrived."

" It were good, monks, that when young men of family such as you who have gone forth from home into homelessness out of faith are gathered together that you talk about *dhamma*. When you are gathered together, monks, there are two things to be done: either talk about *dhamma* or the ariyan silence.[2]

These, monks, are the two quests: the ariyan quest and the unariyan quest. And what, monks, is the unariyan quest ?[3] As to this, monks, someone, liable to birth because of self, seeks what is likewise liable to birth; being liable to ageing because of self, **[162]** seeks what is likewise liable to ageing; being liable to decay because of self . . . being liable to dying because of self . . . being liable to sorrow because of self . . . being liable to stain because of self, seeks what is likewise liable to stain. And what, monks, would you say is liable to birth ? Sons and wife, monks, are liable to birth, women-slaves and men-slaves are liable to birth, goats and sheep are liable to birth, cocks and swine are liable to birth, elephants, cows, horses and mares are liable to birth, gold and silver are liable to birth. These attachments, monks, are liable to birth; yet this (man), enslaved, infatuated, addicted,[4] being liable to birth because of self, seeks what is likewise liable to birth.

And what, monks, would you say is liable to ageing ? Sons and wife, monks, are liable to ageing, women-slaves and men-slaves . . .

---

[1] *MA*. ii. 168 says that in the time of a Buddha, everywhere where even one monk is staying a Buddha-seat comes to be appointed. For the Buddha may know that the monk is not thinking in the right way; and the monks think he will come and stand near them, showing himself. It is difficult to look about for a seat that moment, so the monks keep one ready. If there is a chair they appoint that. If not, they use a couch or a board of some wood or a stone or a heap of sand. Failing all this, having collected some dry leaves, they arrange a seat having spread rags from a dust-heap over them.

[2] *Cf*. *Ud*. 31; also *Sn*. 722. Here the ariyan silence is the second *jhāna*, *MA*. ii. 169.

[3] *MA*. ii. 169 says the Lord spoke about this first path as a man skilled in the way, when showing the way to go, would first exclude one path and say: Leaving the left-hand one alone, take the right-hand one (as at *S*. iii. 108).

[4] Stock, as at *D*. i. 245, iii. 43; *S*. ii. 270; *A*. v. 178, *etc*.

goats and sheep . . . cocks and swine . . . elephants, cows, horses and mares . . . gold and silver are liable to ageing. These attachments, monks, are liable to ageing; yet this (man), enslaved, infatuated, addicted, being liable to ageing because of self, seeks what is likewise liable to ageing.

And what, monks, would you say is liable to disease ? Sons and wife, monks, are liable to disease, women-slaves and men-slaves . . . goats and sheep . . . cocks and swine . . . elephants, cows, horses and mares are liable to disease.[1] These attachments, monks, are liable to disease . . . seeks what is likewise liable to disease.

And, what, monks, would you say is liable to dying ? Sons and wife, monks, are liable to dying, women-slaves and men-slaves . . . goats and sheep . . . cocks and swine . . . elephants, cows, horses and mares are liable to dying. These attachments, monks, are liable to dying . . . seeks what is likewise liable to dying.

And what, monks, would you say is liable to sorrow ? Sons and wife, monks, are liable to sorrow, women-slaves and men-slaves . . . goats and sheep . . . cocks and swine . . . elephants, cows, horses and mares are liable to sorrow. These attachments, monks, are liable to sorrow . . . seeks what is likewise liable to sorrow.

And what, monks, do you say is liable to stain ? Sons and wife, monks, are liable to stain, women-slaves and men-slaves . . . goats and sheep . . . cocks and swine . . . elephants, cows, horses and mares . . . gold and silver are liable to stain. These attachments, monks, are liable to stain; yet this (man), enslaved, infatuated, addicted, being liable to stain because of self, seeks what is likewise liable to stain. This, monks, is the unariyan quest.

And what, monks, is the ariyan quest ? As to this, monks, someone, being liable to birth because of self, having known the peril in what is likewise liable to birth, [**163**] seeks the unborn, the uttermost security from the bonds—nibbāna; being liable to ageing because of self, having known the peril in what is likewise liable to ageing, seeks the unageing, the uttermost security from the bonds—nibbāna; being liable to decay because of self, having known the peril in what is likewise liable to decay, seeks the undecaying, the uttermost security from the bonds—nibbāna; being liable to dying because of self, having known the peril in what is likewise liable to dying, seeks the undying, the uttermost security from the bonds—

[1] *MA*. ii. 170 points out that gold and silver are not liable to dying or sorrow; but iron, *etc.* becomes stained with stains, and ages because it takes up dust and dirt.

nibbāna; being liable to sorrow because of self, having known the peril in what is likewise liable to sorrow, seeks the unsorrowing, the uttermost security from the bonds—nibbāna; being liable to stain because of self, having known the peril in what is likewise liable to stain, seeks the stainless, the uttermost security from the bonds—nibbāna. This, monks, is the ariyan quest.

And I too, monks, before awakening, while I was still the *bodhisatta*, not fully awakened, being liable to birth because of self, sought what was likewise liable to birth; being liable to ageing because of self, sought what was likewise liable to ageing; being liable to disease because of self . . . being liable to dying because of self . . . being liable to sorrow because of self . . . being liable to stain because of self, sought what was likewise liable to stain. Then it occurred to me, monks: 'Why do I, liable to birth because of self, seek what is likewise liable to birth; being liable to ageing . . . being liable to stain because of self, seek what is likewise liable to stain? Suppose that I, (although) being liable to birth because of self, having known the peril in what is likewise liable to birth, should seek the unborn, the uttermost security from the bonds—nibbāna? Being liable to ageing because of self . . . should seek the unageing. . . . Being liable to decay because of self . . . should seek the undecaying. . . . Being liable to dying because of self . . . should seek the undying. . . . Being liable to sorrow because of self . . . should seek the unsorrowing. . . . Being liable to stain because of self, having known the peril in what is likewise liable to stain, should seek the stainless, the uttermost security from the bonds—nibbāna?

Then I, monks, after a time,[1] being young, my hair coal-black, possessed of radiant[2] youth, in the prime of my life—although my unwilling parents wept and wailed—having cut off my hair and beard, having put on yellow robes, went forth from home into homelessness. I, being gone forth thus, a quester for whatever is good, searching for the incomparable, matchless path to peace, approached Āḷāra the Kālāma; having approached, I spoke thus to Āḷāra the Kālāma: 'I, reverend Kālāma, want to fare the Brahma-faring in this *dhamma* and discipline.' This said, monks, Āḷāra the Kālāma spoke thus to me: 'Let the venerable one proceed;[3] this *dhamma* is such that an intelligent man, **[164]** having soon realised super-

---

[1] The following passage occurs at *M*. i. 240, ii. 93, 212.

[2] *bhadra*. *Bhaddaka* at *A*. iv. 255 is one of the ingredients of the moon and sun.

[3] *viharatu*.

knowledge for himself (as learnt from) his own teacher, may enter on and abide in it.' So I, monks, very soon, very quickly, mastered that *dhamma*. I, monks, as far as mere lip service, mere repetition were concerned, spoke the doctrine of knowledge,[1] and the doctrine of the elders,[2] and I claimed—I as well as others—that 'I know, I see.' Then it occurred to me, monks: 'But Āḷāra the Kālāma does not merely proclaim this *dhamma* simply out of faith: Having realised super-knowledge for myself, entering on it, I am abiding therein. For surely Āḷāra the Kālāma proceeds knowing, seeing this *dhamma*.' Then did I, monks, approach Āḷāra the Kālāma; having approached, I spoke thus to Āḷāra the Kālāma: 'To what extent do you, reverend Kālāma, having realised super-knowledge for yourself, entering thereon, proclaim this *dhamma* ?' When this had been said, monks, Āḷāra the Kālāma proclaimed the plane of no-thing. Then it occurred to me, monks: 'It is not only Āḷāra the Kālāma who has faith; I too have faith. It is not only Āḷāra the Kālāma who has energy; I too have energy. It is not only Āḷāra the Kālāma who has mindfulness; I too have mindfulness. It is not only Āḷāra the Kālāma who has concentration; I too have concentration. It is not only Āḷāra the Kālāma who has intuitive wisdom; I too have intuitive wisdom. Suppose now that I should strive for the realisation of that *dhamma* which Āḷāra the Kālāma proclaims: 'Having realised super-knowledge for myself, entering on it I am abiding therein ?' So I, monks, very soon, very quickly, having realised super-knowledge for myself, entering on that *dhamma*, abided therein. Then I, monks, approached Āḷāra the Kālāma; having approached, I spoke thus to Āḷāra the Kālāma: 'Is it to this extent that you, reverend Kālāma, proclaim this *dhamma*, entering on it, having realised it by your own super-knowledge ?'

'It is to this extent that I, your reverence, proclaim this *dhamma*, entering on it, having realised it by my own super-knowledge.'

'I too, your reverence, having realised this *dhamma* by my own super-knowledge, entering on it am abiding in it.'

'It is profitable for us, it is well gotten for us, your reverence, that we see a fellow Brahma-farer such as the venerable one. This *dhamma* that I, entering on, proclaim, having realised it by my own super-knowledge, is the *dhamma* that you, entering on, are abiding in,

---

[1] *ñāṇavāda*; *cf.* *A.* v. 42 *ff.*; *D.* iii. 13. *MA.* ii. 171, *jānāmî ti vādaṃ*, the doctrine (or theory) that "I know."

[2] *theravāda.* *MA.* ii. 171 says, *thirabhāvavādaṃ; thero aham atthâ ti etaṃ vacanaṃ*, a profession of strength.

having realised it by your own super-knowledge; the [**165**] *dhamma* that you, entering on, are abiding in, having realised it by your own super-knowledge, is the *dhamma* that I, entering on, proclaim, having realised it by my own super-knowledge. The *dhamma* that I know, this is the *dhamma* that you know. The *dhamma* that you know, this is the *dhamma* that I know. As I am, so are you; as you are, so am I. Come now, your reverence, being just the two of us, let us look after this group.' In this way, monks, did Āḷāra the Kālāma, being my teacher, set me—the pupil—on the same level as himself and honoured me with the highest honour. Then it occurred to me, monks: 'This *dhamma* does not conduce to disregard nor to dispassion nor to stopping nor to tranquillity nor to super-knowledge nor to awakening nor to nibbāna, but only as far as reaching the plane of no-thing.' So I, monks, not getting enough from this *dhamma*, disregarded and turned away from this *dhamma*.

Then I, monks, a quester for whatever is good, searching for the incomparable, matchless path to peace, approached Uddaka, Rāma's son; having approached, I spoke thus to Uddaka, Rāma's son: 'I, your reverence, want to fare the Brahma-faring in this *dhamma* and discipline.' This said, monks, Uddaka, Rāma's son, spoke thus to me: 'Let the venerable one proceed; this *dhamma* is such that an intelligent man, having soon realised super-knowledge for himself, (as learnt from) his own teacher, may enter on and abide in it.' So I, monks, very soon, very quickly, mastered that *dhamma*. I, monks, as far as mere lip service, mere repetition were concerned, spoke the doctrine of knowledge and the doctrine of the elders, and I claimed—I as well as others—that 'I know, I see.' Then it occurred to me, monks: 'But Uddaka, Rāma's son, does not merely proclaim this *dhamma* simply out of faith: Having realised super-knowledge for myself, entering on it, I am abiding in it. For surely Uddaka, Rāma's son, proceeds knowing and seeing this *dhamma*.' Then did I, monks, approach Uddaka, Rāma's son; having approached, I spoke thus to Uddaka, Rāma's son: 'To what extent do you, reverend Rāma, having realised super-knowledge for yourself, entering thereon proclaim this *dhamma*?' When this had been said, monks, Uddaka, Rāma's son, proclaimed the plane of neither-perception-nor-non-perception. Then it occurred to me, monks: 'It is not only Rāma who has faith; I too have faith. It is not only Rāma who has [**166**] energy; I too have energy. It is not only Rāma who has mindfulness; I too have mindfulness. It is not only Rāma who has concentration; I too have concentration. It is not only Rāma who has intuitive wisdom; I too have intuitive wisdom. Suppose now that I should strive for the realisation of that *dhamma* which Rāma proclaims: 'Having realised super-knowledge for myself, entering on it I am abiding in it?' So I, monks, very soon, very quickly, having realised super-knowledge for myself, entering on that *dhamma*, abided therein. Then I, monks, approached Uddaka, Rāma's son; having approached, I spoke thus to Uddaka, Rāma's son: 'Is it to this extent that you, reverend Rāma, proclaim this *dhamma*, entering on it, having realised it by your own super-knowledge?'

'It is to this extent that I, your reverence, proclaim this *dhamma*, entering on it, having realised it by my own super-knowledge.'

'I too, your reverence, having realised this *dhamma* by my own super-knowledge, entering on it am abiding in it.'

'It is profitable for us, it is well gotten by us, your reverence, that we see a fellow-Brahma-farer such as the venerable one. This *dhamma* that I, entering on, proclaim, having realised it by my own super-knowledge, is the *dhamma* that you, entering on, are abiding in, having realised it by your own super-knowledge; the *dhamma* that you, entering on, are abiding in, having realised it by your own super-knowledge, is the *dhamma* that I, entering on, proclaim, having realised it by my own super-knowledge. The *dhamma* that I know, this is the *dhamma* that you know. That *dhamma* that you know, this is the *dhamma* that I know. As I am, so are you; as you are, so am I. Come now, your reverence, being just the two of us, let us look after this group.' In this way, monks, did Uddaka, Rāma's son, being my teacher, set me—the pupil—on the same level as himself and honoured me with the highest honour. Then it occurred to me, monks: 'This *dhamma* does not conduce to disregard nor to dispassion nor to stopping nor to tranquillity nor to super-knowledge nor to awakening nor to nibbāna, but only as far as reaching the plane of neither-perception-nor-non-perception.' So I, monks, not getting enough from this *dhamma*, disregarded and turned away from this *dhamma*.

Then I, monks, a quester for whatever is good, searching for the incomparable, matchless path to peace, walking on tour through Magadha in due course arrived at Uruvelā, the camp township. **[167]** There I saw a delightful stretch of land and a lovely woodland grove, and a clear flowing river[1] with a delightful ford, and a

---

[1] The Nerañjarā.

village for support nearby. It occurred to me, monks: 'Indeed it is a delightful stretch of land, and the woodland grove is lovely, and the river flows clear with a delightful ford, and there is a village for support nearby. Indeed this does well for the striving of a young man set on striving.' So I, monks, sat down just there, thinking: 'Indeed this does well for striving.'

So I, monks, being liable to birth because of self, having known the peril in what is liable to birth, seeking the unborn, the uttermost security from the bonds—nibbāna—won the unborn, the uttermost security from the bonds—nibbāna; being liable to ageing because of self, having known the peril in what is liable to ageing, seeking the unageing, the uttermost security from the bonds—nibbāna—won the unageing, the uttermost security from the bonds—nibbāna; being liable to decay because of self, having known the peril in what is liable to decay, seeking the undecaying, the uttermost security from the bonds—nibbāna—won the undecaying, the uttermost security from the bonds—nibbāna; being liable to dying because of self, having known the peril in what is liable to dying, seeking the undying, the uttermost security from the bonds—nibbāna—won the undying, the uttermost security from the bonds—nibbāna; being liable to sorrow because of self, having known the peril in what is liable to sorrow, seeking the unsorrowing, the uttermost security from the bonds—nibbāna—won the unsorrowing, the uttermost security from the bonds—nibbāna; being liable to stain because of self, having known the peril in what is liable to stain, seeking the stainless, the uttermost security from the bonds—nibbāna—won the stainless, the uttermost security from the bonds—nibbāna. Knowledge and vision arose in me: unshakable is freedom for me, this is the last birth, there is not now again-becoming.

It occurred to me, monks: 'This *dhamma*,[1] won to by me is deep, difficult to see, difficult to understand, tranquil, excellent, beyond dialectic, subtle, intelligible to the learned. But this is a creation delighting in sensual pleasure, delighted by sensual pleasure, rejoicing in sensual pleasure. So that for a creation delighting in sensual pleasure, delighted by sensual pleasure, rejoicing in sensual pleasure, this were a matter difficult to see, that is to say causal uprising by way of condition. This too were a matter difficult to see, that is to say the tranquillising of all the activities, the renunciation of all attachment, the destruction of

---

[1] As at *Vin.* i. 4 *ff.* See *B.D.* iv. 6 *ff.* for notes, etc.

craving, dispassion, stopping, nibbāna. [**168**] But if I were to teach *dhamma* and others were not to understand me, that would be a weariness to me, that would be a vexation to me.

Moreover, monks, these verses not heard before in the past spontaneously occurred to me:

> This that through many toils I've won—
> Enough! why should I make it known?
> By folk with lust and hate consumed
> This *dhamma* is not understood.
> Leading on against the stream,
> Deep, subtle, difficult to see, delicate,
> Unseen 'twill be by passion's slaves
> Cloaked in the murk of ignorance.

In such wise, as I was pondering, monks, my mind inclined to little effort and not to teaching *dhamma*. Then, monks, it occurred to Brahmā Sahampati who knew with his mind the reasoning in my mind: 'Alas, the world is lost, alas, the world is destroyed, inasmuch as the mind of the Tathāgata, the perfected one, the fully awakened one, inclines to little effort and not to teaching *dhamma*.' Then, monks, as a strong man might stretch out his bent arm, or might bend back his outstretched arm, even so did Brahmā Sahampati, vanishing from the Brahma-world, become manifest before me. Then, monks, Brahmā Sahampati, having arranged his upper robe over one shoulder, having saluted me with joined palms, spoke thus to me: 'Lord, let the Lord teach *dhamma*, let the well-farer teach *dhamma*; there are beings with little dust in their eyes who, not hearing *dhamma*, are decaying, (but if) they are learners of *dhamma* they will grow.' Thus spoke Brahmā Sahampati to me, monks; having said this, he further spoke thus:

> 'There has appeared in Magadha before thee
> An unclean *dhamma* by (minds) with stains devised.
> Open this door of deathlessness; let them hear
> *Dhamma* awakened to by the stainless one.
>
> As on a crag on crest of mountain standing
> A man might watch the people all around,
> E'en so do thou, O Wisdom fair, ascending,
> O Seer of all, the terraced heights of truth,
> Look down, from grief released, upon the peoples
> Sunken in grief, oppressed with birth and age.

[169] Arise, thou hero! Conqueror in the battle!
Thou leader of the caravan, without a debt!
Walk in the world. Let the Blessed One
Teach *dhamma*; they who learn will grow.'

And then I, monks, having understood Brahmā's entreaty, out of compassion surveyed the world with the eye of an Awakened One. As I, monks, was surveying the world with the eye of an Awakened One, I saw beings with little dust in their eyes, with much dust in their eyes, with acute faculties, with dull faculties, of good dispositions, of bad dispositions, docile, indocile, few seeing from fear sins and the world beyond. Even as in a pond of blue lotuses or in a pond of red lotuses or in a pond of white lotuses, a few red and blue and white lotuses are born in the water, grow in the water, do not rise above the water but thrive while altogether immersed; a few blue or red or white lotuses are born in the water, grow in the water and reach the surface of the water; a few blue or red or white lotuses are born in the water, grow in the water, and stand rising out of the water, undefiled by the water; even so did I, monks, surveying the world with the eye of an Awakened One, see beings with little dust in their eyes, with much dust in their eyes, with acute faculties, with dull faculties, of good dispositions, of bad dispositions, docile, indocile, few seeing from fear sins and the world beyond. Then I, monks, addressed Brahmā Sahampati in verses:

Opened for those who hear are the doors of the Deathless, Brahmā,
Let them give forth their faith;
Thinking of useless fatigue, Brahmā, I have not preached *dhamma*
Sublime and excellent for men.

Then, monks, Brahmā Sahampati, thinking: 'The opportunity was made by me for the Lord to teach *dhamma*,' having greeted me, keeping his right side towards me, vanished then and there.

Then it occurred to me, monks: 'Now, to whom should I first teach this *dhamma*? Who will understand this *dhamma* quickly?' Then it occurred to me, monks: 'Indeed this Āḷāra the Kālāma is learned, experienced, wise, and for a long time has had little dust in his eyes. Suppose that I [170] were to teach *dhamma* first to Āḷāra the Kālāma; he will understand this *dhamma* quickly.'

Then *devatās* having approached me, spoke thus: 'Lord, Āḷāra the Kālāma passed away seven days ago.' So knowledge and vision arose in me that Āḷāra the Kālāma had passed away seven days ago.

Then it occurred to me, monks: 'Āḷāra the Kālāma has suffered a great loss.[1] For if he had heard this *dhamma*, he would have understood it quickly.' Then it occurred to me, monks: 'Now, to whom could I first teach this *dhamma*? Who will understand this *dhamma* quickly?' Then it occurred to me, monks: 'This Uddaka, Rāma's son, is learned, experienced, wise, and for a long time has had little dust in his eyes. Suppose that I were to teach *dhamma* first to Uddaka, Rāma's son? He will understand this *dhamma* quickly,' Then, monks, *devatās*, having approached me, spoke thus: 'Lord, Uddaka, Rāma's son, passed away last night,' So knowledge and vision arose in me that Uddaka, Rāma's son, had passed away last night. Then it occurred to me, monks: 'Uddaka, Rāma's son, has suffered a great loss. For if he had heard this *dhamma*, he would have understood it quickly.' Then it occured to me, monks: 'Now to whom could I first teach this *dhamma*? Who will understand this *dhamma* quickly?' Then it occurred to me, monks: 'This group of five monks who waited on me when I was self-resolute in striving, were very helpful. Suppose that I were to teach *dhamma* first to this group of five monks?' Then it occurred to me, monks: 'But where is the group of five monks staying at present?' Then, monks, I saw with *deva*-vision, purified and surpassing that of men, the group of five monks staying near Benares at Isipatana in the deer-park. Then I, monks, having stayed at Uruvelā for as long as I found suiting, set out on tour for Benares.

Then, monks, Upaka, a Naked Ascetic,[2] saw me as I was going along the high road between Gayā and the (Tree of) Awakening; having seen me, he spoke thus: 'Your reverence, your faculties are quite pure, your complexion is very bright, very clear. On account of whom have you, your reverence, gone forth, or who is your teacher, or whose *dhamma* do you [**171**] profess?' When this had been said, I, monks, addressed Upaka, the Naked Ascetic, in verses:

'Victorious over all, omniscient am I,
Among all things undefiled,
Leaving all, through death of craving freed,
By knowing for myself, whom should I point to?[3]

---

[1] *mahājāniyo.* I am indebted to the Ven. A. P. Buddhadatta for this interpretation of *jāni*=*hāri*, loss.

[2] *ājīvika*

[3] *I.e.* as my teacher.

For me there is no teacher,
One like me does not exist,
In the world with its *devas*
No one equals me.

For I am perfected in the world,
A teacher supreme am I,
I alone am all-awakened,
Become cool am I, nibbāna-attained.

To turn the *dhamma*-wheel
I go to Kasi's city,
Beating the drum of deathlessness
In a world that's blind become.'

'According to what you claim, your reverence, you ought to be victor of the unending.'

'Like me, they are victors indeed
Who have won destruction of the cankers;
Vanquished by me are evil things,
Therefore am I, Upaka, a victor.'

When this had been said, monks, Upaka the Naked Ascetic, having said: 'May it be (so), your reverence,' having shaken his head, went off having taken a different road. Then I, monks, walking on tour, in due course arrived at Benares, Isipatana, the deer-park and the group of five monks. Monks, the group of five monks saw me coming in the distance, and seeing me they agreed among themselves, saying: 'Your reverences, this recluse Gotama is coming, he lives in abundance, he is wavering in his striving, he has reverted to a life of abundance. He should be neither greeted, nor stood up for, nor should his bowl and robe be received; all the same a seat may be put out, he can sit down if he wants to.' But as I, monks, gradually approached this group of five monks, so this group of five monks were not able to adhere to their own agreement; having approached me, some received my bowl and robe, some made a seat ready, some brought water for washing the feet, and they addressed me by name and with the epithet 'your reverence.' When this had been said, I, monks, spoke thus to the group of five monks: 'Do not, monks, address a Tathāgata by his name or by the epithet 'your reverence.' Monks, the Tathāgata is one perfected, [**172**] a fully Self-awakened One. Give ear, monks, the deathless is found, I instruct, I teach *dhamma*. Going along in accordance with what is enjoined, having soon realised here and now by your own super-knowledge that supreme goal of the Brahma-faring for the sake of which young men of family rightly go forth from home into homelessness, you will abide in it.'

When this had been said, monks, the group of five monks addressed me thus: 'But you, reverend Gotama, did not come to a state of further-men, to knowledge and vision befitting the ariyans by this conduct, by this course, by this practice of austerities. So how can you now come to a state of further-men, to knowledge and vision befitting the ariyans when you live in abundance and, wavering in your striving, revert to a life of abundance ?'

When this had been said, monks, I spoke to the group of five monks thus: 'A Tathāgata, monks, does not live in abundance nor, wavering in striving, does he revert to a life of abundance. The Tathāgata, monks, is one perfected, a fully Self-awakened One. Give ear, monks, the deathless is found, I instruct, I teach *dhamma*. Going along in accordance with what is enjoined, having soon realised here and now by your own super-knowledge that supreme goal of the Brahma-faring for the sake of which young men of family rightly go forth from home into homelessness, you will abide in it.' And a second time, monks, the group of five monks spoke to me thus: 'But you, reverend Gotama . . .' . . . '. . . you will abide in it.' And a third time, monks, the group of five monks spoke to me thus: 'But you, reverend Gotama . . . revert to a life of abundance ?'

When this had been said, I, monks, spoke thus to the group of five monks: 'Do you allow, monks, that I have ever spoken[1] to you like this before ?'

'You have not, Lord.'

'A Tathāgata, monks, is a perfected one, a fully Self-awakened One. Give ear, monks, the deathless is found, I instruct, I teach *dhamma*. Going along in accordance with what is enjoined, having soon realised here and now by your own super-knowledge that supreme goal of the Brahma-faring for the sake of which young men of family rightly go forth from home into homelessness, **[173]** you will abide in it.' And I, monks, was able to convince the group of five monks.

Monks, I now exhorted two monks; three monks walked for almsfood.[2] Whatever the three monks who had walked for alms-

---

[1] *vabbhācitaṃ*. [2] As at *Vin.* i. 13.

food brought back, that the group of six[1] lived on. And then, monks, I exhorted three monks; two monks walked for almsfood. Whatever the two monks who had walked for almsfood brought back, that the group of six lived on. Then, monks, the group of five monks, being thus exhorted, thus instructed by me, being liable to birth because of self, having known the peril in what is liable to birth, seeking the unborn, the uttermost security from the bonds—nibbāna—won the unborn, the uttermost security from the bonds—nibbāna; being liable to ageing because of self . . . won the unageing . . . being liable to decay because of self . . . won the undecaying . . . being liable to dying because of self . . . won the undying . . . being liable to sorrow because of self . . . won the unsorrowing . . . being liable to stain because of self, having known the peril in what is liable to stain, seeking the stainless, the uttermost security from the bonds—nibbāna—won the stainless, the uttermost security from the bonds—nibbāna. Knowledge and vision arose in them: Unshakable is freedom for us, this is the last birth, there is not now again-becoming.

Monks, there are these five strands of sense-pleasures.[2] What are the five? Material shapes cognisable by the eye, alluring, agreeable, pleasant, liked, connected with sense-pleasures, enticing; sounds cognisable by the ear . . . smells cognisable by the nose . . . tastes cognisable by the tongue . . . touches cognisable by the body, alluring, agreeable, pleasant, liked, connected with sense-pleasures, enticing. These, monks, are the five strands of sense-pleasures. Monks, those recluses or brahmans who enjoy these five strands of sense-pleasures enslaved and infatuated by them, addicted to them, not seeing the peril in them, not aware of the escape from them—these should be told: 'You have come to calamity, you have come to misfortune and are ones to be done to by the Evil One as he wills. Monks, it is like a deer living in a forest who might be lying caught on a heap of snares—this may be said of it: It has come to calamity, it has come to misfortune, it is one to be done to by the trapper as he wills, for when the trapper comes it will not be able to go away as it wishes. Even so, monks, those recluses or brahmans . . . are ones to be done to by the Evil One as he wills.

Monks, those recluses or brahmans who enjoy these five strands of sense-pleasures, not enslaved, not infatuated by them, not

[1] *I.e.* Gotama and the group of five monks.

[2] According to *MA.* ii. 193 this is part of the unariyan quest.

addicted to them, seeing the peril in them, aware of the escape from them—**[174]** these should be told: You have not come to calamity, you have not come to misfortune, you are not ones to be done to by the Evil One as he wills. Monks, it is like a deer living in a forest who might lie down on a heap of snares but is not caught by it—this may be said of it: It has not come to calamity, it has not come to misfortune, it is not one to be done to by the trapper as he wills, for when the trapper comes it will be able to go away as it wishes. Even so, monks, those recluses or brahmans . . . are not ones to be done to by the Evil One as he wills.

Monks, it is like a deer living in a forest, roaming the forest slopes, who walks confidently, stands confidently, sits down confidently, goes to sleep confidently. What is the reason for this? Monks, it is out of the trapper's reach. Even so, monks, a monk, aloof from pleasures of the senses, aloof from unskilled states of mind, enters on and abides in the first meditation which is accompanied by initial thought and discursive thought, is born of aloofness, and is rapturous and joyful. Monks, this monk is called one[1] who has put a darkness round Māra, and having blotted out Māra's vision so that it has no range, goes unseen by the Evil One.

And again, monks, a monk, by allaying initial and discursive thought, his mind subjectively tranquillised and fixed on one point, enters on and abides in the second meditation which is devoid of initial and discursive thought, is born of concentration and is rapturous and joyful. Monks, this monk is called one . . . by the Evil One.

And again, monks, a monk, by the fading out of rapture, dwells with equanimity, attentive and clearly conscious, and experiences in his person that joy of which the ariyans say: 'Joyful lives he who has equanimity and is mindful'; and he enters on and abides in the third meditation. Monks, this monk is called one . . . by the Evil One.

And again, monks, a monk, by getting rid of joy, by getting rid of anguish, by the going down of his former pleasures and sorrows, enters on and abides in the fourth meditation which has neither anguish nor joy, and which is entirely purified by equanimity and mindfulness. Monks, this monk is called one . . . by the Evil One.

And again, monks, a monk, by passing quite beyond perception

---

[1] As at *M.* i. 159, where, in the *Nivāpasutta*, the four herds of deer may be compared with the four deer above.

of material shapes, by the going down of perception of sensory reactions, by not attending to perceptions of variety, thinking: 'Ether is unending,' enters on and abides in the plane of infinite ether. Monks, this monk is called one . . . by the Evil One.

And again, monks, a monk, by passing quite beyond the plane of infinite ether, thinking: 'Consciousness is unending,' enters on and abides in the plane of infinite consciousness. Monks, this monk is called one . . . by the Evil One.

And again, monks, a monk, by passing quite beyond the plane of infinite consciousness, thinking: 'There is not anything,' enters on and abides in the plane of no-thing. Monks, this monk is called . . . by the Evil One.

And again, monks, a monk, by passing quite beyond the plane of no-thing, [**175**] enters on and abides in the plane of neither-perception-nor-non-perception. Monks, this monk is called one who has put a darkness round Māra, and who, having blotted out Māra's vision so that it has no range, goes unseen by the Evil One.

And again, monks, a monk, by passing quite beyond the plane of neither-perception-nor-non-perception, enters on and abides in the stopping of perception and feeling; and having seen by intuitive wisdom, his cankers are utterly destroyed. Monks, this monk is called one who has put a darkness round Māra, and who, having blotted out Māra's vision so that it has no range, goes unseen by the Evil One; he has crossed over the entanglement in the world. He walks confidently, stands confidently, sits down confidently, goes to sleep confidently. What is the reason for this? Monks, he is out of reach of the Evil One."

Thus spoke the Lord. Delighted, these monks rejoiced in what the Lord had said.

Discourse on the Ariyan Quest:
The Sixth

27. LESSER DISCOURSE ON THE SIMILE OF THE ELEPHANT'S FOOTPRINT

(Cūḷahatthipadopamasutta)[1]

THUS have I heard: At one time the Lord was staying near Sāvatthī in the Jeta Grove in Anāthapiṇḍika's monastery. Now at that time the brahman Jāṇussoṇi was leaving Sāvatthī early in the day in an all-white chariot (drawn by) mares.[2] The brahman Jāṇussoṇi saw the wanderer Pilotika coming in the distance; seeing him, he spoke thus to the wanderer Pilotika: " Now, where is the revered Vacchāyana[3] coming from so early in the day ?"

" I, sir, am coming from the presence of the recluse Gotama."

" What do you think about this, Vacchāyana ? Has the recluse Gotama lucidity of wisdom[4] ? Do you think him clever ?"

" But who am I, sir, that I would know whether the recluse Gotama has lucidity of wisdom ? Surely only one like him could know whether the recluse Gotama has lucidity of wisdom."

" Undoubtedly it is with lofty praise that the revered Vacchāyana praises the recluse Gotama."

" But who am I, sir, that I should praise the recluse Gotama ? Praised by the praised[5] is the revered Gotama, chief among *devas* and men."

" But what good thing does the revered Vacchāyana see that he has this high confidence in the recluse Gotama ?"

" Sir, as a skilled elephant-tracker might enter an elephant-forest, and might see in the elephant-forest **[176]** a great footprint, long and broad; he might come to the conclusion: Indeed it is a

---

[1] At *Mhvs.* XIV. 22 this was the Sutta that Mahinda preached first of all to Devānampiyatissa on his arrival in Ceylon.

[2] *MA.* ii. 194 quotes *S.* v. 4 to indicate all the respects in which the chariot was white. It adds that it was harnessed to four white mares. Although the number of mares is not given in the text, Chalmers gives it as four in his translation.

[3] The name of his clan, *MA.* ii. 195. *Cf. M.* ii. 208, *A.* iii. 236 *f.*, as far as the simile.

[4] *paññāveyyattiyaṃ*, as at *M.* i. 82.

[5] *MA.* ii. 196 instances, among others, Pasenadi, Bimbisāra, Visākhā, Uppalavaṇṇā, Sāriputta, Sakka, Mahābrahmā. All are praised by their retinues, and all praise the Dasabala.

great elephant. Even so did I, sir,when I had seen the four footprints of the recluse Gotama, come to this conclusion: The fully Self-awakened One is the Lord; well taught is *dhamma* by the Lord; the Order is faring along well. What are the four ?

Here, sir, I see some clever nobles, subtle,[1] practised in disputing with others, skilled in hair-splitting, who go about, methinks, breaking to pieces in their wisdom the views (of others). These hear: 'Undoubtedly the recluse Gotama will visit a certain village or little town. They construct a question, thinking: Having approached the recluse Gotama, we will ask him this question of ours. If, on being asked by us thus, he answers thus, we will refute him thus; and if, on being asked by us thus, he answers thus, we will refute him thus.' These heard: 'It is certain that the recluse Gotama is visiting such and such a village or little town.' So they approached the recluse Gotama. The recluse Gotama gladdened, roused, incited, delighted them with talk on *dhamma*. These, gladdened, roused, incited, delighted by the recluse Gotama with talk on *dhamma*, did not ask the recluse Gotama the question at all—whence could they refute him ? On the contrary they became disciples of the recluse Gotama. When I, sir, saw this first footprint of the recluse Gotama, then I came to the conclusion: The fully Self-awakened One is the Lord; well taught is *dhamma* by the Lord; the Order fares along well.

And again I, sir, see here some clever brahmans, subtle, practised in disputing with others, skilled in hair-splitting, who go about, methinks, breaking to pieces in their wisdom the views (of others). These hear . . . On the contrary they became disciples of the recluse Gotama. When I, sir, saw this second footprint of the recluse Gotama, then I came to the conclusion: The fully Self-awakened One is the Lord; well taught is *dhamma* by the Lord; the Order fares along well.

And again I, sir, see here some clever householders . . . some clever recluses, subtle, practised in disputing with others, skilled in hair-splitting, who go about, methinks, breaking to pieces in their wisdom the views (of others). These hear: 'Undoubtedly the recluse Gotama [**177**] will visit a certain village or little town. They construct a question, thinking: 'Having approached the recluse Gotama, we will ask him this question of ours. If, on being asked thus by us, he answers thus, we will refute him thus; and if,

---

[1] **This sequence also at *D*. i. 26, 162; and *cf*. whole passage with *M*. ii. 122.**

on being asked thus by us, he answers thus, we will refute him thus.' These heard: 'It is certain that the recluse Gotama is visiting such and such a village or little town.' So they approached the recluse Gotama. The recluse Gotama gladdened, roused, incited, delighted them with talk on *dhamma*. These, gladdened, roused, incited, delighted by the recluse Gotama with talk on *dhamma*, did not ask the recluse Gotama the question at all—whence could they refute him? On the contrary, they asked leave of the recluse Gotama himself for the going forth from home into homelessness. The recluse Gotama let them go forth. These, gone forth like this, living alone, aloof, diligent, ardent, self-resolute, having by their own super-knowledge soon realised here and now that goal of the Brahma-faring for the sake of which young men of family rightly go forth from home into homelessness, entering on it, abided in it. These speak thus: 'Indeed we were nearly lost, indeed we nearly perished, for while formerly we were not (true) recluses, we claimed that we were, saying: We are recluses; not being (true) brahmans, we claimed that we were, saying: We are brahmans; not being (true) perfected ones, we claimed that we were, saying: We are perfected ones. But now we really are recluses, now we really are brahmans, now we really are perfected ones.' When I, sir, saw this fourth footprint of the recluse Gotama, then I came to the conclusion: The fully Self-awakened One is the Lord; well taught is *dhamma* by the Lord; the Order fares along well."

When this had been said, Jāṇussoṇi the brahman got down from his all-white chariot (drawn by) mares, and having arranged his outer cloak over one shoulder, having saluted the Lord three times with joined palms, he uttered this utterance: 'Reverence to this Lord, perfected one, fully Self-awakened One; Reverence to this Lord, perfected one, fully Self-awakened One; Reverence to this Lord, perfected one, fully Self-awakened One. Perhaps we, somewhere, [**178**] sometime will meet the honoured Gotama; perhaps there may be some conversation.'

Then Jāṇussoṇi the brahman approached the Lord; having approached, he exchanged greetings with the Lord; having exchanged greetings of friendliness and courtesy, he sat down at a respectful distance. As he was sitting down at a respectful distance, Jāṇussoṇi the brahman related to the Lord all the conversation he had had up till now with the wanderer Pilotika. When he had spoken thus, the Lord spoke thus to Jāṇussoṇi the brahman:

"Brahman, to a (certain) extent the simile of the elephant's footprints is not complete in all its detail. But, brahman, to the extent to which the simile of the elephant's footprints is complete in all its detail, listen, pay careful attention and I will speak."

"Yes, revered one," Jāṇussoṇi the brahman answered the Lord in assent. The Lord spoke thus:

"Brahman, an elephant tracker might enter an elephant forest, and might see in the elephant forest a large footprint, long and broad. But a skilled elephant tracker does not at once come to the conclusion: Indeed it is a great bull-elephant. What is the reason for this? There are, brahman, in an elephant forest stunted she-elephants who have large footprints, and he thinks this might be a footprint of theirs. He follows them and following them he sees in the elephant forest a great footprint, long and broad, and a grazing off of the high things.[1] A skilled elephant tracker does not at once come to the conclusion: Indeed it is a great bull-elephant. What is the reason for this? There are, brahman, in an elephant forest she-elephants who have tushes and who have large footprints, and he thinks this might be a footprint of theirs. He follows them and following them he sees in the elephant forest a great footprint, long and broad, and a grazing off of the high things and the high things slashed by tusks. A skilled elephant tracker does not at once come to the conclusion: Indeed it is a great bull-elephant. What is the reason for this? There are, brahman, in an elephant forest she-elephants with stumpy tusks who have large footprints, and he thinks this might be a footprint of theirs. He follows them and following them he sees in the elephant forest a great footprint, long and broad, and a grazing off of the high things and the high things slashed by tusks and the high things broken off at the boughs. And he sees that bull-elephant at the root of a tree or in the open, walking or standing or sitting or lying down. He comes to the conclusion: This is that bull-elephant himself.

In the same way, [**179**] brahman, a Tathāgata arises in the world, a perfected one, a fully Self-awakened One, endowed with right knowledge and conduct, well-farer, knower of the worlds,[2] the matchless charioteer of men to be tamed, the Awakened One, the Lord. He makes known this world with the *devas*, with Māra, with Brahmā,

---

[1] *uccā ca nisevitaṃ*. He sees where her shoulders have knocked against the trees, *MA*. ii. 198.

[2] *MA*. ii. 200 mentions the three worlds—that of space, that of beings, that of the habitual tendencies or activities—and says here the world of beings, and, more precisely, the world of men, is meant. *Cf. DA*. i. **173** *f*.

creation with its recluses and brahmans, its *devas* and men, having realised them by his own super-knowledge. He teaches *dhamma* which is lovely at the beginning, lovely in the middle, lovely at the ending, with the spirit and the letter; he proclaims the Brahma-faring wholly fulfilled, quite purified. A householder or a householder's son or one born in another family hears that *dhamma*. Having heard that *dhamma*, he gains faith in the Tathāgata. Endowed with this faith that he has acquired, he reflects in this way: 'The household life is confined and dusty,[1] going forth is in the open; it is not easy for one who lives in a house to fare the Brahma-faring wholly fulfilled, wholly pure, polished like a conch-shell. Suppose now that I, having cut off hair and beard, having put on saffron robes, should go forth from home into homelessness?' After a time, getting rid of his wealth,[2] be it small or great, getting rid of his circle of relations, be it small or great, having cut off his hair and beard, having put on saffron robes, he goes forth from home into homelessness.

He, being thus one who has gone forth and who is endowed with the training and the way of living of monks, abandoning onslaught on creatures,[3] is one who abstains from onslaught on creatures; the stick laid aside, the knife laid aside, he lives kindly, scrupulous, friendly and compassionate towards all breathing things and creatures. Abandoning the taking of what is not given, he is one who abstains from taking what is not given; being one who takes (only) what is given, who waits for what is given, not by stealing he lives with a self become pure. Abandoning unchastity, he is one who is chaste, keeping remote (from unchastity), abstaining from dealings with women.[4] Abandoning lying speech, he is one who abstains from lying speech, a truth-speaker, a bondsman to truth,[5] trustworthy, dependable, no deceiver of the world.[6]

---

[1] *rajāpatha*. *MA*. ii. 204=*DA*. i. 180 take this to mean, in accordance with the Mahā-aṭṭhakathā, the dust of passion, but say it is also *āgamanapatha*, full of comings and goings (?).

[2] *Cf*. *D*. ii. 85, 86.

[3] *Cf*. the following passage with *D*. i. 4-5; *M*. i. 287, iii. 33; *A*. ii. 208; *Pug*. 56; also *A*. iv. 249; *Kvu*. II.

[4] *gāmadhammā*. Explained at *MA*. ii. 206=*DA*. i. 72 as things (or states of mind, *dhammā*) of village dwellers. But this does not fit the context very well. *Cf*. *mātugāma*, women.

[5] *saccasandha*. *MA*. i. 206=*DA*. i. 73, *saccena saccaṃ sandahati*, he joins truth to truth.

[6] *Cf*. *D*. iii. 170.

Abandoning slanderous speech,[1] he is one who abstains from slanderous speech; having heard something here he is not one for repeating it elsewhere for (causing) variance among these (people), or having heard something elsewhere he is not one to repeat it there for (causing) variance among these (people). In this way he is a reconciler of those who are at variance, and one who combines those who are friends. Concord is his pleasure, concord his delight, concord his joy, concord is the motive of his speech. Abandoning harsh speech, he is one who abstains from harsh speech. Whatever speech is gentle, pleasing to the ear, affectionate, going to the heart, urbane, pleasant to the manyfolk, [**180**] agreeable to the manyfolk—he comes to be one who utters speech like this. Abandoning frivolous chatter, he is one who abstains from frivolous chatter. He is a speaker at a right time, a speaker of fact, a speaker on the goal,[2] a speaker on *dhamma*,[3] a speaker on discipline,[4] he speaks words that are worth treasuring, with similes at a right time that are discriminating, connected with the goal. He comes to be one who abstains from what involves destruction to seed-growth, to vegetable growth.[5] He comes to be one who eats one meal a day, refraining at night, abstaining from eating at a wrong time.[6] He comes to be one who abstains from watching shows of dancing, singing, music.[7] He comes to be one who abstains from using garlands, scents, unguents, adornments, finery.[8] He comes to be one who abstains from using high beds, large beds.[9] He comes to be one who abstains from accepting gold and silver.[10] He comes

---

[1] *Cf. M.* i. 286, iii. 49 for following passage.

[2] *MA.* ii. 208, *DA.* i. 76, he speaks about what is connected with the goal *attha*, of the here and now and of the beyond.

[3] *MA.* ii. 208=*DA.* i. 76, he speaks about what is connected with the nine other-worldly things; see *Dhs.* 1094.

[4] *MA.* ii. 208=*DA.* i. 76, the discipline of giving up and that of restraint.

[5] *bījagāmabhūtagāma.* *Cf.* Pāc. XI. (*Vin.* iv. 34), and see *D.* i. 5; also *MA.* ii. 208.

[6] Defined at *Vin.* iv. 86 as "after noon has passed until sunrise." *Cf. S.* v. 470; *A.* i. 212; *Kvu.* II. 6.

[7] Made into a *dukkata* offence for monks at *Vin.* ii. 108, and into a *pācittiya* for nuns at *Vin.* iv. 267. *Cf. D.* i. 6; *Kvu.* II. 7.

[8] *Cf. Kvu.* II. 8.

[9] *Cf. Pāc.* 87; *D.* i. 7; *A.* i. 181; *Vin.* i. 192, ii. 163. *MA.* ii. 209 says that "high beds" are those that exceed the (prescribed) measure, while "large beds" are those that are not allowable.

[10] *Cf. Vin.* iii. 236 *ff.* (Nissag. 18); *Kvu.* II. 10.

to be one who abstains from accepting raw grain . . . raw meat[1] . . . women and girls . . . women slaves and men slaves . . . goats and sheep . . . fowl and swine . . . elephants, cows, horses, mares . . . fields and sites . . . messages or going on such.[2] He comes to be one who abstains from buying and selling . . . from cheating with weights, from cheating with bronzes,[3] from cheating with measures.[4] He comes to be one who abstains from the crooked ways of bribery, fraud and deceit. He comes to be one who abstains from maiming, murdering, manacling, highway robbery.[5] He comes to be contented with the robes for protecting his body,[6] with the almsfood for sustaining his stomach. Wherever he goes he takes these things[7] with him as he goes. As a bird on the wing wherever it flies takes its wings with it as it flies, so a monk, contented with the robes for protecting his body, with the almsfood for sustaining his stomach, wherever he goes takes these things with him as he goes.

He, possessed of the ariyan body of moral habit, subjectively experiences unsullied well-being.[8] Having seen a material shape with the eye, he is not entranced by the general appearance, he is not entranced by the detail. If he dwells with this organ of sight uncontrolled,[9] covetousness and dejection, evil unskilled states of mind, might predominate. So he fares along controlling it; he guards the organ of sight, he comes to control over the organ of sight. Having heard a sound with the ear . . . Having smelt a smell with the nose . . . Having savoured a taste with the tongue . . . Having felt a touch with the body . . . Having cognised a mental object with the mind, he is not entranced by the general appearance, he is not entranced by the detail. If he lives with this organ of mind uncontrolled, covetousness and dejection, evil unskilled

---

[1] *Cf. Vin.* iii. 208, where the nun Uppalavaṇṇā prepared (or roasted) meat before offering it to the Lord.

[2] *Cf. D.* i. 8; *S.* iii. 239.

[3] *kaṃsa,* see Nuns' Nissag. XI, XII and note at *B.D.* iii. 239. But *MA.* ii. 210=*DA.* i 79 says a *kaṃsa* is called a golden bowl with reference to a method of cheating with copper bowls that have been made of a golden colour.

[4] *MA.* ii. 210=*DA.* i. 79 mention three methods: "heart-break," *hadayabheda,* used in measuring ghee, oil, etc.; "pyramid-break," *sikhābheda,* used in measuring sesamum, husked rice, etc.; "cord-break," *rajjubheda,* used in measuring fields and sites.

[5] *DA.* i. 80, this is twofold: hidden in the snow, hidden in a thicket, they kidnap people.

[6] As at *D.* i. 71.

[7] The eight requisites, *MA.* ii. 213=*DA.* i. 207.

[8] *Cf. D.* i. 70.

[9] *Cf. M.* i. 221.

states of mind might predominate. So he fares along controlling it; **[181]** he guards the organ of mind, he comes to control over the organ of mind. If he is possessed of this ariyan control of the (sense-) organs, he subjectively experiences unsullied well-being.

Whether he is setting out or returning,[1] he is one who comports himself properly; whether he is looking down or looking round, he is one who comports himself properly; whether he is bending back or stretching out (his arm), he is one who comports himself properly; whether he is carrying his outer cloak, his bowl, his robe, he is one who comports himself properly; whether he is munching, drinking, eating, savouring, he is one who comports himself properly; whether he is obeying the calls of nature, he is one who comports himself properly; whether he is walking, standing, asleep, awake, talking, silent, he is one who comports himself properly.

Possessed of[2] this ariyan body of moral habit and possessed of this ariyan control of the (sense-) organs and possessed of this ariyan mindfulness and clear consciousness, he chooses[3] a remote lodging in a forest, at the root of a tree, on a mountain slope, in a wilderness, in a hill-cave, in a cemetery, in a forest haunt, in the open or on a heap of straw. He, returning from alms-gathering after his meal, sits down cross-legged holding the back erect, having made mindfulness rise up in front of him. He, having got rid of covetousness for the world, lives with a mind devoid of coveting, he purifies the mind of coveting. By getting rid of the taint of ill-will, he lives benevolent in mind; and compassionate for the welfare of all creatures and beings, he purifies the mind of the taint of ill-will. By getting rid of sloth and torpor, he lives devoid of sloth and torpor; perceiving the light, mindful and clearly conscious, he purifies the mind of sloth and torpor. By getting rid of restlessness and worry, he lives calmly, the mind subjectively tranquillised, he purifies the mind of restlessness and worry. By getting rid of doubt, he lives doubt-crossed; unperplexed as to the states that are skilled, he purifies his mind of doubt.

He, by getting rid of these five hindrances[4]—defilements of a mind and weakening to intuitive wisdom—aloof from pleasures of the senses, aloof from unskilled states of mind, enters on and abides in the first meditation, which is accompanied by initial thought and discursive thought, is born of aloofness and is rapturous and joyful. This, brahman, is called the Tathāgata's footprint, and

---

[1] As at *D*. i. 70, etc.

[2] As at *D*. i. 71.

[3] *Cf*. *M*. i. 273, iii. 3, etc.

[4] Given also at *M*. i. 60, 274-75.

what is grazed against by the Tathāgata and what is slashed by the Tathāgata. But not yet does the ariyan disciple come to fulfilment[1] thinking: 'The fully Self-awakened One is the Lord; well taught is *dhamma* by the Lord; the Order fares along well.'

And again, brahman, a monk by allaying initial and discursive thought, his mind subjectively tranquillised and fixed on one point, enters on and abides in the second meditation, which is devoid of initial and discursive thought, is born of concentration and is rapturous and joyful. This too, brahman, is called the Tathāgata's footprint, and what is grazed against by the Tathāgata and what is slashed by the Tathāgata. But not yet does the ariyan [**182**] disciple come to fulfilment thinking: 'The fully Self-awakened One is the Lord; well taught is *dhamma* by the Lord; the Order fares along well.'

And again, brahman, a monk, by the fading out of rapture, dwells with equanimity, attentive and clearly conscious, and experiences in his person that joy of which the ariyans say: 'Joyful lives he who has equanimity and is mindful,' and he enters on and abides in the third meditation. This too, brahman, is called the Tathāgata's footprint, and what is grazed against by the Tathāgata and what is slashed by the Tathāgata. But not yet does the ariyan disciple come to fulfilment, thinking: 'The fully Self-awakened One is the Lord; well taught is *dhamma* by the Lord; the Order fares along well.'

And again, brahman, a monk, by getting rid of joy, by getting rid of anguish, by the going down of his former pleasures and sorrows, enters on and abides in the fourth meditation, which has neither anguish nor joy, and which is entirely purified by equanimity and mindfulness. This too, brahman, is called the Tathāgata's footprint, and what is grazed against by the Tathāgata, and what is slashed by the Tathāgata. But not yet does the ariyan disciple come to fulfilment, thinking: 'The fully Self-awakened One is the Lord; well taught is *dhamma* by the Lord; the Order fares along well.

Thus with the mind composed,[2] quite purified, quite clarified, without blemish, without defilement, grown soft and workable,

---

[1] *niṭṭhaṃ gacchati* can also mean "come to the conclusion" (in thought), as above. But *MA*. ii. 217 appears here to take it in the sense of fulfilment, saying *tīsu ratanesu niṭṭhaṃ gacchati*, he goes to fulfilment, or the goal, in the Three Jewels. *Cf. A*. ii. 175, iii. 450, v. 119 *ff*.

[2] Stock, as at *M*. i. 22, etc.

fixed, immovable, he directs his mind to the knowledge and recollection of former habitations: . . . (*As at p.* 28, *above*) . . . Thus he remembers divers former habitations in all their modes and detail. This too, brahman, is called the Tathāgata's footprint, and what is grazed against by the Tathāgata and what is slashed by the Tathāgata. But not yet does the ariyan disciple come to fulfilment, thinking: 'The fully Self-awakened One is the Lord; well taught is *dhamma* by the Lord; the Order fares along well.'

[**183**] Thus with the mind composed, quite purified, quite clarified, without blemish, without defilement, grown soft and workable, fixed, immovable, he directs his mind to the knowledge of the passing hence and arising of beings. With the purified *deva*-vision surpassing that of men, he sees beings . . . (*As at p.* 28, *above*) . . . Thus with the purified *deva*-vision surpassing that of men does he see beings as they pass hence or come to be, he comprehends that beings are mean, excellent, foul, fair, in a good bourn, in a bad bourn, according to the consequences of their deeds. This too, brahman, is called the Tathāgata's footprint, and what is grazed against by the Tathāgata and what is slashed by the Tathāgata. But not yet does the ariyan disciple come to fulfilment, thinking: 'The fully Self-awakened One is the Lord; well taught is *dhamma* by the Lord; the Order fares along well.'

Thus with the mind composed, quite purified, quite clarified, without blemish, without defilement, grown soft and workable, fixed, immovable, he directs his mind to the knowledge of the destruction of the cankers . . . (*As at p.* 29, *above*) . . . he comprehends as it really is: 'This is the course leading to the stopping of the cankers.' This too, brahman, is called the Tathāgata's footprint, and what is grazed against by the Tathāgata and what is slashed by the Tathāgata. But not yet does the ariyan disciple come to fulfilment, thinking: 'The fully Self-awakened One is the Lord; well taught is *dhamma* by the Lord: the Order fares along well.'

When he has known thus, when he has seen thus, the mind is freed from the canker of sense-pleasures [**184**] and the mind is freed from the canker of becoming and the mind is freed from the canker of ignorance. In freedom the knowledge comes to be that he is freed, and he comprehends: 'Destroyed is birth, brought to a close is the Brahma-faring, done is what was to be done, there is no more of being such or such.' This too, brahman, is called the Tathāgata's footprint, and what is grazed against by the Tathāgata and what is slashed by the Tathāgata. It is at this point, brahman, that the ariyan disciple comes to fulfilment, thinking: 'The fully·Self-awakened One is the Lord; well taught is *dhamma* by the Lord; the Order fares along well.' At this point, brahman, the simile of the elephant's footprint is complete in detail."

When this had been said, Jāṇussoṇi the brahman spoke thus to the Lord: "It is wonderful, good Gotama; good Gotama, it is wonderful. It is as if, good Gotama, one might set upright what had been upset, or might disclose what was covered, or might point out the way to one who had gone astray, or might bring an oil lamp into the darkness so that those with vision might see material shapes—even so is *dhamma* made clear in many a figure by the good Gotama. I am going to the revered Gotama for refuge, and to *dhamma* and to the Order of monks. May the good Gotama accept me as a lay-follower, one gone for refuge from today forth for as long as life lasts."

Lesser Discourse on the Simile of the Elephant's Footprint: the Seventh

28. GREATER DISCOURSE ON THE SIMILE OF THE ELEPHANT'S FOOTPRINT

(Mahāhatthipadopamasutta)

THUS have I heard: At one time the Lord was staying near Sāvatthī in the Jeta Grove in Anāthapiṇḍika's monastery. There the venerable Sāriputta addressed the monks, saying: "Reverend monks." "Your reverence," these monks answered the venerable Sāriputta in assent. The venerable Sāriputta spoke thus:

"As, your reverences, among all creatures that can walk[1] all pedal qualities are combined in an elephant's foot,[2] and as the elephant's foot is chief among these in point of size, so, your reverences, all skilled states of mind are included among the four ariyan truths. Among what four? Among the ariyan truth of anguish, [**185**] among the ariyan truth of the uprising of anguish, among the ariyan truth of the stopping of anguish, among the ariyan truth of the course leading to the stopping of anguish.

---

[1] Simile as at *S*. i. 86. [2] *Cf*. *A*. iii. 364.

And what, your reverences, is the ariyan truth of anguish ?[1] Birth is anguish and ageing is anguish and dying is anguish; and grief, lamentation, sorrow, tribulation and despair are anguish, and not getting what one wants, that too is anguish. In brief the five groups of grasping are anguish. And what, your reverences, are the five groups of grasping ? Just these: the group of grasping after material shape, the group of grasping after feeling, the group of grasping after perception, the group of grasping after the habitual tendencies, the group of grasping after consciousness.[2]

And what, your reverences, is the group of grasping after material shapes ? The four great elements, and the material shape that is derived from the four great elements. And what, your reverences, are the four great elements ? The element of extension, the liquid element, the element of heat, the element of motion.[3]

And what, your reverences, is the element of extension ? The element of extension may be internal, it may be external. And what,[4] your reverences, is the internal element of extension ? Whatever is[5] hard, solid, is internal,[6] referable to an individual[6] and derived therefrom, that is to say: the hair of the head, the hair of the body, nails, teeth, skin, flesh, sinews, bones, marrow of the bones, kidney, heart, liver, pleura, spleen, lungs, intestines, mesentary, stomach, excrement, or whatever other thing is hard, solid, is internal, referable to an individual or derived therefrom—this, your reverences, is called the internal element of extension. Whatever[7] is an internal element of extension and whatever is an external element of extension,[8] just these are the element of extension. By means of perfect intuitive wisdom it should be seen of this as it really is, thus: This is not mine, this am I not, this is not my self. Having seen this thus as it really is by means of perfect intuitive wisdom, he disregards the element of extension, he cleanses his mind of the element of extension.

---

[1] *MA*. ii. 218 says the teaching on the whole of anguish is meant here, but it has been set out in the *Vism*. (p. 494 *ff*.).

[2] As at *S*. iii. 58-59.

[3] See *M*. Sta. 1 for these elements.

[4] Quoted at *MA*. i. 25.

[5] As at *M*. i. 421, iii. 240 (six elements given). *Vism*. 348 says the four elements are treated briefly in the *Mahāsatipaṭṭhāna*, and at length in the *Mahāhatthipadopama*, the *Rāhulovāda* (*M*. i. 421) and the *Dhātuvibhaṅga* (*M*. iii. 237).

[6] *MA*. ii. 222 says both these are synonyms for " one's own," *niyaka*.

[7] As at *A*. ii. 164.

[8] *MA*. ii. 223 refers to *Vbh*., *ayo lohaṃ tipu sīsaṃ* (*Vbh*. 82), with which passage compare above.

There comes to be a time, your reverences, when the element of extension[1] that is external is agitated; at that time the external element of extension disappears. The impermanence of this ancient external element of extension can be shown, your reverences, its liability to destruction can be shown, its liability to decay can be shown, its liability to change can be shown. So what of this short-lived body derived from craving ? There is not anything here for saying, 'I' or 'mine' or 'I am.' Your reverences, if others abuse, revile, annoy,[2] vex this monk, he comprehends: 'This painful feeling that has arisen in me is born of sensory impingement on the ear, it has a cause, not no cause. What is the cause ? [**186**] Sensory impingement is the cause.' He sees that sensory impingement[3] is impermanent, he sees that feeling . . . perception . . . the habitual tendencies are impermanent, he sees that consciousness is impermanent. His mind rejoices, is pleased, composed and is set on[4] the objects of the element. If, your reverences, others comport themselves in undesirable, disagreeable, unpleasant ways towards that monk, and he receives blows from their hands and from clods of earth and from sticks and weapons, he comprehends thus: 'This body is such that blows from hands affect it and blows from clods of earth affect it and blows from sticks affect it and blows from weapons affect it. But this was said by the Lord in the Parable of the Saw:[5] "If, monks, low-down thieves should carve you limb from limb with a two-handled saw, whoever sets his heart at enmity, he, for this reason, is not a doer of my teaching." Unsluggish energy shall come to be stirred up by me, unmuddled mindfulness set up, the body tranquillised, impassible, the mind composed and one-pointed. Now, willingly, let blows from hands affect this body, let blows from clods of earth . . . from sticks . . . from weapons affect it, for this teaching of the Awakened Ones is being done.'

If, your reverences, this monk recollects the Awakened One thus, if he recollects *dhamma* thus, if he recollects the Order thus,[6] but there is not established (in him) the equanimity that depends on

---

[1] Text wrongly reads *āpodhātu* here instead of *paṭhavīdhātu*.

[2] As at *M*. i. 140.

[3] Here *phassa*, instead of, as is more usual in this sequence, *rūpa*. Just below, the word translated as "blows" is also *phassa*. It means a contact, something that impinges.

[4] *Cf*. *M*. i. 435, where instead of *adhimuccati*, is set on, the reading is *vimuccati*, is freed.

[5] *M*. i. 129.

[6] As in the formulæ, see *e.g.* *D*. ii. 93; *S*. i. 219 *f*.

skill;[1] he is strongly moved[2] because of this, he comes to a strongly moved condition, and thinks: 'It is unprofitable for me, it is not profitable for me, it is ill gotten by me, it is not well gotten by me that, although I recollect the Awakened One thus, although I recollect *dhamma* thus, although I recollect the Order thus, the equanimity that depends on skill is not established (in me).' Your reverences, as a daughter-in-law, having seen her father-in-law, is strongly moved and comes to a strongly moved condition, so, your reverences, if while this monk is recollecting the Awakened One . . . *dhamma* . . . the Order, the equanimity that depends on skill is not established (in him); he is strongly moved because of this, he comes to a strongly moved condition, and thinks: 'It is unprofitable for me . . . it is not well gotten by me that, although I recollect the Awakened One thus . . . *dhamma* . . . the Order thus, the equanimity that depends on skill is not established (in me).' But if, your reverences, while this monk is recollecting the Awakened One thus . . . *dhamma* thus . . . the Order thus, the equanimity that depends on skill is established (in him), he, because of this [**187**] is pleased. Up to this point, your reverences, much has been done by the monk.

And what, your reverences, is the liquid element? The liquid element[3] may be internal, it may be external. And what, your reverences, is the internal liquid element? Whatever is liquid, fluid, is internal, referable to an individual or derived therefrom, that is to say: bile, phlegm, pus, blood, sweat, fat, tears, serum, saliva, mucus, synovial fluid, urine or whatever other thing is liquid, fluid, is internal, referable to an individual or derived therefrom—this, your reverences, is called the internal liquid element. Whatever is an internal liquid element and whatever is an external liquid element, just these are the liquid element. By means of perfect intuitive wisdom it should be seen of this as it really is, thus: This is not mine, this am I not, this is not my self. Having seen this thus as it really is by means of perfect intuitive wisdom, he disregards the liquid element, he cleanses his mind of the liquid element.

There comes to be a time, your reverences, when the liquid element that is external is agitated; it carries away villages and it carries away little towns and it carries away towns and it carries away districts and it carries away districts and regions. There

---

[1] *upekhā kusalanissitā* here means the equanimity or indifference due to *vipassanā*, insight or vision.

[2] *saṃvijjati*.

[3] As at *M.* i. 422. *Cf. Vism.* 350.

comes to be a time, your reverences, when the waters in the great ocean[1] go down[2] a hundred *yojanas,* and when they go down two hundred . . . three hundred . . . four hundred . . . five hundred . . . six hundred *yojanas* and when they go down seven hundred *yojanas.* There comes to be a time, your reverences, when the water in the great ocean stands at (the height of) seven palm trees (in depth), when the water stands at (the height of) six . . . five . . . four . . . three . . . two palm trees (in depth) and when the water stands at (the height of) one palm tree (in depth). There comes to be a time, your reverences, when the water in the great ocean stands at (the depth of) seven men's stature . . . six men's stature . . . five . . . four . . . three . . . two men's stature and when the water stands at (the depth of) merely one man's stature. There comes to be a time, your reverences, when the water in the great ocean stands at (the depth of) half a man's stature, and when the water stands merely up to his hip . . . merely up to his knee . . . merely up to his ankle. There comes to be a time, your reverences, when the water in the great ocean does not wet even a toe-joint. The impermanence of this ancient liquid element that is external [**188**] can be shown, your reverences, its liability to destruction can be shown . . . But if, your reverences, while this monk is recollecting the Awakened One thus, is recollecting *dhamma* thus, is recollecting the Order thus, the equanimity that depends on skill is established (in him), he, because of this is pleased. Up to this point, your reverences, much has been done by the monk.

And what, your reverences, is the element of heat ?[3] The heat element may be internal, it may be external. And what, your reverences, is the internal heat element ? Whatever is heat, warmth, is internal, referable to an individual and derived therefrom, such as by whatever one is vitalised, by whatever one is consumed, by whatever one is burnt up, and by whatever one has munched, drunk, eaten and tasted that is properly transmuted (in digestion), or whatever other thing is heat, warmth, is internal, referable to an individual or derived therefrom—this, your reverences, is called the internal heat element. Whatever is an internal element of heat and whatever is an external element of heat, just these are the element of heat. By means of perfect intuitive

---

[1] *Cf. A.* iv. 101-2 as far as " ankle," and where all this is said to happen to the waters when a fifth sun appears.

[2] *ogacchanti. G.S.* iv. 66 " recede "; *MA.* ii. 227 gives *heṭṭhā gacchanti.*

[3] As at *M.* i. 422.

wisdom it should be seen of this as it really is, thus: This is not mine, this am I not, this is not myself. Having seen this thus as it really is by means of perfect intuitive wisdom, he disregards the heat element, he cleanses his mind of the heat element.

There comes a time, your reverences, when the element of heat that is external is agitated, and it burns up villages and it burns up little towns and it burns up towns and it burns up districts and it burns up districts and regions. When it has come to the end of the crops or to the end of a highway or to the end of a mountain or to the end of water or to a lovely stretch of level ground, it is extinguished[1] through lack of fuel. There comes to be a time, your reverences, when people seek to light a fire with a cock's feather or with snippets of gristle.[2] The impermanence of this ancient external element of heat can be shown, your reverences . . . the equanimity that depends on skill is established (in him), he, because of this is pleased. Up to this point, your reverences, much has been done by the monk.

And what, your reverences, is the element of motion ?[3] The element of motion may be internal, it may be external. And what, your reverences, is the internal element of motion ? Whatever is motion, wind, is internal, referable to an individual and derived therefrom, such as winds going upwards, winds going downwards, winds in the abdomen, winds in the belly, winds that shoot across the several limbs, in-breathing, out-breathing, or whatever other thing is motion, wind, is internal, referable to an individual and derived therefrom—this, your reverences, is called the internal element of motion. Whatever is an internal element of motion and whatever is an external element of motion, just these are the element of motion. By means of perfect intuitive wisdom it should be seen of this as it really is, thus: This is not mine, this am I not, this is not myself. Having seen this thus as it really is by means of perfect intuitive wisdom, he disregards the element of motion, he cleanses his mind of the element of motion.

[**189**] There comes a time, your reverences, when the element of motion that is external is agitated, and it carries away villages and it carries away little towns and it carries away towns and it carries away districts and it carries away districts and regions. There comes to be a time, your reverences, when in the last month of the hot weather people are looking about for wind by means of

---

[1] *nibbāyati*. [2] As at *A*. iv. 47. [3] As at *M*. i. 422.

a palm (leaf) fan[1] and a fan for fanning the fire,[1] and they do not expect grasses in the top of the thatch.[2] The impermanence of this ancient external element of motion can be shown, your reverences . . . [**190**] . . . But if, your reverences, while this monk is recollecting the Awakened one . . . *dhamma* . . . the Order thus, the equanimity that depends on skill is established (in him), he, because of this is pleased. Up to this point, your reverences, much has been done by the monk.

Your reverences, just as a space that is enclosed by stakes and creepers and grass and clay is known as a dwelling, so a space that is enclosed by bones and sinews and flesh and skin is known as a material shape. If, your reverences, the eye that is internal is intact[3] but external material shapes do not come within its range and there is no appropriate impact, then there is no appearance of the appropriate section[4] of consciousness. If, your reverences, the eye that is internal is intact and external material shapes come within its range but without an appropriate impact, then there is no appearance of the appropriate section of consciousness. But when, your reverences, the eye that is internal is intact and external material shapes come within its range and there is the appropriate impact, then there is thus an appearance of the appropriate section of consciousness. Whatever is material shape in what has thus come to be, it is included in the group of grasping after material shape. Whatever is feeling in what has thus come to be, it is included in the group of grasping after feeling. Whatever is perception in what has thus come to be, it is included in the group of grasping after perception. Whatever are the habitual tendencies in what has thus come to be, they are included in the group of grasping after the habitual tendencies. Whatever is consciousness in what has thus come to be, it is included in the group of grasping after consciousness. He comprehends thus: 'Thus there is, so it is said, the including, the collecting together, the coming together of these five groups of grasping,' This was said by the Lord: 'Whoever sees conditioned genesis [**191**] sees

---

[1] *tālavaṇṭena pi vidhūpanena pi.* On *vidhūpana* see *B.D.* iii. 253, *n.* 3. *MA.* ii. 229 calls this *aggivījanakena.*

[2] *ossavane. MA.* ii. 229, reading *ossāvane,* explains by *chadanagge,* and says " because the water flows out therefrom it is called *ossāvana.*" This means an outflow, running water, making the growth of grass possible.

[3] This passage is quoted at *Kvu.* 620.

[4] *bhāga,* but *Kvu.* reads *bhāva. Cf. Miln.* 56 *ff.*

dhamma, whoever sees *dhamma* sees conditioned genesis.'[1] These are generated by conditions: that is to say the five groups of grasping. Whatever among these five groups of grasping is desire, sensual pleasure, affection, catching at, that is the uprising of anguish. Whatever among these five groups of grasping is the control of desire and attachment,[2] the ejection of desire and attachment,[2] that is the stopping of anguish. Up to this point, your reverences, much has been done by the monk.

If, your reverences, the ear that is internal is intact . . . the nose that is internal is intact . . . the tongue that is internal is intact . . . the body that is internal is intact . . . the mind that is internal is intact, but external mental objects do not come within its range and there is no appropriate impact, then there is no appearance of the appropriate section of consciousness. If, your reverences, the mind that is internal is intact and external mental objects come within its range but there is no appropriate impact, then there is no appearance of the appropriate section of consciousness. But when, your reverences, the mind that is internal is intact and external mental objects come within its range and there is the appropriate impact, then there is thus an appearance of the appropriate section of consciousness. Whatever is material shape in what has thus come to be, it is included in the group of grasping after material shape. Whatever is feeling in what has thus come to be, it is included in the group of grasping after feeling. Whatever is perception in what has thus come to be, it is included in the group of grasping after perception. Whatever are the habitual tendencies in what has thus come to be, they are included in the group of grasping after the habitual tendencies. Whatever is consciousness in what has thus come to be, it is included in the group of grasping after consciousness. He comprehends thus: 'Thus there is, so it is said, the including, the collecting together, the coming together of these five groups of grasping.' This was said by the Lord: 'Whoever sees conditioned genesis sees *dhamma*, whoever sees *dhamma* sees conditioned genesis.' These are generated by conditions, that is to say the five groups of grasping. Whatever among these five groups of grasping is desire, sensual pleasure, affection, catching at, that is the uprising of anguish. Whatever among these five groups of grasping is the control of

---

[1] Untraced. "Conditioned genesis" is *paṭiccasamuppāda*.

[2] Synonyms for nibbāna, *MA*. ii. 230.

desire and attachment, the ejection of desire and attachment, that is the stopping of anguish. Up to this point, your reverences, much has been done by the monk."

Thus spoke the venerable Sāriputta. Delighted, these monks rejoiced in what the venerable Sāriputta had said.

The Greater Discourse on the Simile of the Elephant's Footprint: the Eighth

29. GREATER DISCOURSE ON THE SIMILE OF THE PITH

(Mahāsāropamasutta)

[**192**] THUS have I heard: At one time the Lord was staying near Rājagaha on Mount Vulture Peak not long after Devadatta had left (the Order).[1] There the Lord addressed the monks concerning Devadatta:

"Here, monks,[2] some young man of family has gone forth from home into homelessness through faith and thinks: 'I am beset by birth, ageing and dying, by grief, sorrow, suffering, lamentation and despair. I am beset by anguish, overwhelmed by anguish. Maybe the annihilation of this whole mass of anguish can be shown.' He, gone forth thus, receives gains, honours, fame.[3] Because of the gains, honours, fame, he becomes satisfied, his purpose is fulfilled. Because of the gains, honours, fame, he exalts himself and disparages others, saying: 'It is I who am a recipient, being famous, but those other monks[4] are little known, of little esteem.'[5] He, because of the gains, honours, fame, is exultant, indolent, and falls into sloth; being indolent, he dwells ill. Monks, it is like a man walking about aiming at the pith, seeking for the pith, looking

---

[1] As at *S.* i. 153; and *cf.* *Vin.* ii. 199, where it is said that Devadatta, having created a schism in the Order, went to Gayāsīsa with five hundred monks. See also *Miln.* 160.

[2] As at *M.* i. 200, 460=*A.* ii. 123. [3] *Cf.* *S.* ii. 226 *ff.*; *A.* ii. 73, ii. 343.

[4] *Cf.* *M.* iii. 38.

[5] See under *appesakkha* in *CPD.* *MA.* ii. 231 not only says *appaparivārā* (seldom "invited"), but "going before or after (the meal) they do not receive (anything)."

about for the pith of a great, stable and pithy tree,[1] who passes by the pith itself, passes by the softwood, passes by the bark, passes by the young shoots, and who, having cut down the branches and foliage, might go away taking them with him thinking they were the pith. A man with vision, having seen him, might say: 'Indeed this good man does not know the pith, he does not know the softwood, he does not know the bark, he does not know the young shoots, he does not know the branches and foliage, inasmuch as this good man, walking about aiming at the pith, seeking for the pith, looking about for the pith of a great, stable and pithy tree, passes by the pith itself, passes by the softwood, passes by the bark, passes by the young shoots, and having cut down the branches and foliage, is going away taking them with him thinking they are the pith. So will he not get the good that could be done by the pith because it is the pith.' Even so, monks, some young man of family here, having gone forth from home into homelessness through faith, thinks: 'I am beset by birth, ageing and dying, by grief, sorrow, suffering, lamentation and despair, I am beset by anguish, overwhelmed by anguish. Maybe the annihilation of this whole mass of anguish can be shown.' He, gone forth thus, receives gains, honours, fame. Because of the gains, honours, fame, he becomes satisfied, his purpose is fulfilled. Because of the gains, honours, fame, he exalts himself, [**193**] disparages others, thinking: 'It is I who am a recipient, but these other monks are little known, of little esteem.' He, because of the gains, honours, fame, is exultant, indolent and falls into sloth; being indolent, he dwells ill. Monks, this is called a monk who takes hold of the branches and foliage of the Brahma-faring, and because of this he fails of (full) accomplishment.[2]

But, monks, some young man of family here comes to have gone forth from home into homelessness through faith, and thinks: 'I am beset by birth, ageing and dying, by grief, sorrow, suffering, lamentation and despair. I am beset by anguish, overwhelmed by anguish. But perhaps the annihilation of this whole mass of anguish can be shown.' He, gone forth thus, receives gains, honours, fame. But because of the gains, honours, fame, he does not become satisfied, his purpose is not fulfilled. Because of the gains, honours, fame, he does not exalt himself, he does not

---

[1] See *S.* v. 163 *f.*

[2] *MA.* ii. 231, he thinks that it is enough that he has attained the essence up to this point.

disparage others. Because of the gains, honours, fame, he is not exultant, he is not indolent, he does not fall into sloth. Being diligent, he attains success in moral habit. He, because of this success in moral habit, becomes satisfied, his purpose is fulfilled. Because of this success in moral habit, he exalts himself, disparages others, thinking: 'It is I who am of (good) moral habit, lovely in character, but these other monks are of wrong moral habit, evil in character.' Because of this success in moral habit, he is exultant, he is indolent, he falls into sloth. Being indolent, he dwells ill. Monks, it is like a man walking about aiming at the pith, seeking for the pith, looking about for the pith of a great, stable and pithy tree, who passes by the pith itself . . . the softwood . . . the bark, and who, having cut off the young shoots, might go away taking them with him thinking they were the pith. A man with vision, having seen him, might say: 'Indeed this good man does not know the pith . . . the softwood . . . the bark . . . the young shoots, he does not know the branches and foliage, inasmuch as this good man, walking about aiming at, seeking and looking about for the pith of a great, stable and pithy tree, passes by the pith itself, passes by the softwood, passes by the bark, and having cut down the young shoots, is going away taking them thinking they are the pith. So will he not get the good that could be done by the pith because it is the pith.' Even so, monks, some young man of family, having gone forth from home into homelessness, thinks: . . . Because of this success in moral habit, he is exultant, indolent, he falls into sloth. Being indolent, he dwells ill. [**194**] Monks, this is called a monk who takes hold of the young shoots of the Brahma-faring, and because of this he fails of (full) accomplishment.

But, monks, some young man of family here comes to have gone forth from home into homelessness through faith, and thinks: 'I am beset by birth, by ageing and dying, by grief, sorrow, suffering, lamentation and despair, I am beset by anguish, overwhelmed by anguish. But perhaps the annihilation of this whole mass of anguish can be shown.' He, gone forth thus, receives gains, honours, fame. But because of the gains, honours, fame, he does not become satisfied, his purpose is not fulfilled. Because of the gains, honours, fame, he does not exalt himself, does not disparage others. Because of the gains, honours, fame, he is not exultant, not indolent, he does not fall into sloth. Being diligent, he attains success in moral habit. He, because of this success in moral habit, becomes satisfied, but not yet is his purpose fulfilled. He, because of this success in moral habit, does not exalt himself, does not disparage others. He, because of this success in moral habit, is not exultant, he is not indolent, he does not fall into sloth. Being diligent, he gains success in concentration. He, because of this success in concentration, becomes satisfied, his purpose is fulfilled. He, because of this success in concentration, exalts himself, disparages others, saying: 'It is I who am concentrated, their minds are wandering.' He, because of this success in concentration, is exultant, indolent, he falls into sloth. Being indolent, he dwells ill. Monks, it is like a man walking about aiming at the pith, seeking and looking about for the pith of a great, stable and pithy tree, who passes by the pith itself, passes by the softwood, and who, having cut off the bark, might go away taking it with him thinking it was the pith. A man with vision, having seen him, might say: 'Indeed this good man does not know the pith . . . the softwood . . . the bark . . . the young shoots, he does not know the branches and foliage, inasmuch as this good man walking about aiming at the pith, seeking for the pith, looking about for the pith of a great, stable and pithy tree, passes by the pith itself, passes by the softwood, and having cut off the bark, is going away taking it with him thinking it is the pith. So will he not get the good that could be done by the pith because it is the pith.' Even so,monks, some young man of family here, having gone forth from home into homelessness through faith, thinks. . . . He, because of this success in concentration, is exultant, indolent, he falls into sloth. Being indolent, he dwells ill. Monks, this [**195**] is called a monk who takes hold of the bark of the Brahma-faring, and because of this he fails of (full) accomplishment.

But, monks, some young man of family here comes to have gone forth from home into homelessness through faith, and thinks: 'I am beset by birth, by ageing and dying, by grief, sorrow, suffering, lamentation and despair, I am beset by anguish, overwhelmed by anguish. But perhaps the annihilation of this whole mass of anguish can be shown.' He, gone forth thus, receives gains, honours, fame. But because of the gains, honours, fame, he does not become satisfied, his purpose is not fulfilled. Because of the gains, honours, fame, he does not exalt himself, does not disparage others. Because of the gains, honours, fame, he is not exultant, not indolent, he does not fall into sloth. Being diligent, he attains success in moral habit. Because of this success in moral habit, he becomes satisfied, but not yet is his purpose fulfilled. He, because of this success in moral habit, does not exalt himself, does not disparage others. He, because of this success in moral habit, is not exultant, not indolent, he does not fall into sloth. Being diligent, he gains success in concentration. He, because of this success in concentration, is satisfied, but not yet is his purpose fulfilled. He, because of this success in concentration, does not exalt himself, does not disparage others. He, because of this success in concentration, is not exultant, not indolent, he does not fall into sloth. Being diligent, he gains knowledge and insight. He,because of this knowledge and insight, becomes satisfied, his purpose is fulfilled. Because of this knowledge and insight, he exalts himself, disparages others, saying: 'It is I who dwell knowing, seeing, but these other monks dwell not knowing, not seeing.' Because of this knowledge and insight he is exultant, indolent, he falls into sloth. Being indolent, he lives ill. Monks, it is like a man walking about aiming at the pith, seeking for the pith, looking about for the pith of a great, stable and pithy tree, and who, passing by the pith itself, having cut out the softwood might go away taking it with him thinking it was the pith. A man with vision, having seen him, might say: 'Indeed this good man does not know the pith . . . the softwood . . . the bark . . . the young shoots, he does not know the branches and foliage, inasmuch as this good man walking about aiming at the pith, seeking for the pith, looking about for the pith of a great, stable and pithy tree, passes by the pith itself, and having cut out of the softwood, goes away taking it with him thinking it is the pith. So will he not get the good that could be done by the pith because it is the pith.' [**196**] Even so, monks, some young man of family here has gone forth from home into homelessness through faith, and thinks: . . . He, because of this knowledge and vision is exultant, indolent, he falls into sloth. Being indolent he lives ill. Monks, this is called a monk who takes hold of the softwood of the Brahma-faring, and because of this he fails of (full) accomplishment.

But, monks, some young man of family here comes to have gone forth from home into homelessness through faith, and thinks: 'I am beset by birth, by ageing and dying, by grief, sorrow, suffering, lamentation and despair, I am beset by anguish, overwhelmed by anguish. But perhaps the annihilation of this whole mass of anguish can be shown.' He, gone forth thus, receives gains, honours, fame. But because of the gains, honours, fame, he is not satisfied, his purpose is not fulfilled. Because of the gains, honours, fame, he does not exalt himself, does not disparage others. Because of the gains, honours, fame, he is not exultant, he is not indolent, he does not fall into sloth. Being diligent, he attains success in moral habit. Because of this success in moral habit, he becomes satisfied, but not yet is his purpose fulfilled. He, because of this success in moral habit, does not exalt himself, does not disparage others. Because of this success in moral habit he is not exultant, he is not indolent, he does not fall into sloth. Being diligent, he attains success in concentration. Because of this success in concentration, he becomes satisfied, but not yet is his purpose fulfilled. Because of this success in concentration, he does not exalt himself, does not disparage others. Because of this success in concentration, he is not exultant, he is not indolent, he does not fall into sloth. Being diligent, he attains knowledge and vision. Because of this knowledge and vision, he becomes satisfied, but not yet is his purpose fulfilled. Because of this knowledge and vision he does not exalt himself, does not disparage others. Because of this knowledge and vision, he is not exultant, he is not indolent, he does not fall into sloth. Being diligent, he obtains release as to things of time.[1] The situation occurs, monks, when that monk falls away from freedom as to things of time.[2] Monks, it is like a man walking about aiming at the pith, seeking for the pith, looking about for the pith of a great, stable and pithy tree, and who, having cut out the pith itself, might go away taking it with him, knowing it to be the pith. A man with vision, having seen him, might say: 'Indeed this good man knows the pith, he knows the softwood, he knows the bark, he knows the young

---

[1] *samayavimokkha*. This is probably a release both as to things that are worldly, mundane and temporal, and as to what is passing or temporary in its nature. As such it is of a less high order than *asamayavimokkha*, below, from which there is no falling away, for it is "unshakable." *MA*. ii. 232, quoting *Pṭs*. ii. 40 says this is the four ways, the four fruits and nibbāna; while *samayavimokkha* is the four meditations and the four attainments in immateriality. *Vimokkha* may have an objective reference to the things one is freed from; while *vimutti* may be the subjective experience of (mental) freedom. It is curious that the preliminaries to attaining *samayavimokkha* and *asamayavimokkha* appear to be identical. This may be due either to some error on the part of a scribe or transcriber, or to some lacuna in the text. For this passage, speaking of ever greater and greater powers won by a monk, may have intended to show that *asamayavimokkha* was a higher achievement than *samayavimokkha*.

[2] *samayavimutti*. Word occurrs also at *Sn*. 54; *A*. iii. 349. And for *samayavimutta* see *A*. iii. 173; *Kvu*. 91; *Pug*. 4, 11.

shoots, he knows the branches and foliage, inasmuch as this good man walking about aiming at the pith, seeking for the pith, looking about for the pith [**197**] of a great, stable and pithy tree, having cut out the pith itself, is going away taking it with him, knowing it to be the pith. So will he get the good that could be done by the pith because it is the pith.' Even so, monks, some young man of family here comes to have gone forth from home into homelessness through faith, and thinks: 'I am beset by birth, by ageing and dying, by grief, sorrow, suffering, lamentation, despair. I am beset by anguish, overwhelmed by anguish. But perhaps the annihilation of the whole mass of anguish can be shown.' He, gone forth thus, receives gains, honours, fame. But because of these gains, honours, fame, he is not satisfied, his purpose is not fulfilled. Because of these gains, honours, fame, he does not exalt himself, does not disparage others. Because of these gains, honours, fame, he is not exultant, he is not indolent, he does not fall into sloth. Being diligent, he attains success in moral habit. Because of this success in moral habit, he becomes satisfied, but not yet is his purpose fulfilled. Because of the success in moral habit, he does not exalt himself, does not disparage others. Because of this success in moral habit, he is not exultant, he is not indolent, he does not fall into sloth. Being diligent, he attains success in concentration. Because of this success in concentration, he becomes satisfied, but not yet is his purpose fulfilled. Because of this success in concentration, he does not exalt himself, does not disparage others. Because of this success in concentration, he is not exultant, he is not indolent, he does not fall into sloth. Being diligent, he attains knowledge and vision. Because of this knowledge and vision, he becomes satisfied, but not yet is his purpose fulfilled. Because of this knowledge and vision, he does not exalt himself, does not disparage others. Because of this knowledge and vision, he is not exultant, he is not indolent, he does not fall into sloth. Being diligent, he obtains release as to things that are timeless. This is impossible, monks, it cannot come to pass, that a monk should fall away from freedom as to things that are timeless.

So it is, monks, that this Brahma-faring[1] is not for advantage in gains, honours, fame; it is not for advantage in moral habit, it is not for advantage in concentration, it is not for advantage in knowledge and vision. That, monks, which is unshakable freedom of

---

[1] As at *M.* i. 204-5.

mind,[1] this is the goal,[1] monks, of this Brahma-faring, this the pith,[1] this the culmination."[1]

Thus spoke the Lord. Delighted, these monks rejoiced in what the Lord had said.

Greater Discourse on the Simile of the Pith:
The Ninth

30. LESSER DISCOURSE ON THE SIMILE OF THE PITH

(Cūḷasāropamasutta)

[**198**] Thus have I heard: At one time the Lord was staying near Sāvatthī in the Jeta Grove in Anāthapiṇḍika's monastery. Then the brahman Piṅgalakoccha[2] approached the Lord; having approached, he exchanged greetings with the Lord; having exchanged greetings of friendliness and courtesy, he sat down at a respectful distance. As he was sitting down at a respectful distance, the brahman Piṅgalakoccha spoke thus to the Lord: "Good Gotama, those who are leaders in religious life,[3] heads of companies, heads of groups, teachers of groups, well known, famous, founders of sects,[4] much honoured[5] by the many folk, that is to say, Pūraṇa Kassapa,[6] Makkhali of the Cowpen, Ajita of the Hair-blanket, Pakudha Kaccāyana, Sañjaya Belaṭṭha's son,[7] the Jain

---

[1] *MA*. ii. 232 explains all these terms by the fruit of arahantship.

[2] *MA*. ii. 232 says Koccha was his name, and he was called *piṅgala* because he was tawny. A similar meeting with the following conversation with the Lord is ascribed to the wanderer Subhadda at *D*. ii. 150-51.

[3] *samaṇabrāhmaṇā*, but see reasons given at *Dial*. ii. 165 *n*. for translating here as above; also see *M*. i. 227.

[4] *titthakarā*, see *Fur. Dial*. i. 143, *n*.

[5] *sādhu*, *MA*. ii. 233 *sādhu, sundarā, sappurisā*.

[6] The doctrines of these six "heretical" teachers are set forth at *D*. i. 58-64. Their names occur also at *M*. i. 250. *MA*. ii. 233-34, in explaining them, resembles *DA*. 142-44. On Pūraṇa Kassapa and Makkhali Gosāla, see A. L. Basham, *History and Doctrines of the Ājīvikas*, 1950.

[7] *MA*. ii. 234=*DA*. i. 144 says *Belaṭṭhassa putto*. So "the son of the Belaṭṭhi slave-girl" of *Dial*. ii. 166 is not corroborated by these two commentarial passages. But there is also the reading Belaṭṭhiputto as at *M*. i. 547.

(Nigaṇṭha) Nātha's son—did all these, according to their own assertion, understand[1] or did they not all understand, or did some understand, and did some not understand ?"

"Enough, brahman, let this be: 'Did all these, according to their own assertion, understand or did they not all understand, or did some understand, and did some not understand ?' I will teach you *dhamma*, brahman, listen to it, attend carefully, and I will speak."

"Yes, Lord," the brahman Piṅgalakoccha answered the Lord in assent.

"Brahman, it is like a man walking about aiming at the pith, seeking for the pith, looking about for the pith of a great, stable and pithy tree, who passes by the pith itself, passes by the softwood, passes by the bark, passes by the young shoots, and who, having cut down the branches and foliage, might go away taking them with him thinking they were the pith. A man with vision, having seen him, might say: 'Indeed this good man does not know the pith . . . the softwood . . . the bark . . . the young shoots, he does not know the branches and foliage, inasmuch as this good man, walking about aiming at the pith, seeking for the pith, looking about for the pith of a great, stable and pithy tree, passes by the pith itself . . . the softwood . . . the bark . . . the young shoots, and having cut down the branches and foliage is going away taking them with him thinking they are the pith. So will he not get the good that could be done by the pith because it is the pith.'

Or, brahman, it is like a man walking about aiming at the pith, seeking for the pith, looking about for the pith of a great, stable and pithy tree, who passes by the pith itself . . . the softwood [**199**] . . . the bark, and who, having cut off the young shoots, might go away taking them with him thinking they were the pith. A man with vision, having seen him, might say: 'Indeed this good man does not know the pith . . . the softwood . . . the bark . . . the young shoots, he does not know the branches and foliage, inasmuch as this good man, walking about aiming at the pith . . . of a great, stable and pithy tree, passes by the pith itself . . . the softwood . . . the bark, and having cut down the young shoots, is going away taking them with him thinking they are the pith. So will he not get the good that could be done by the pith because it is the pith.'

---

[1]According to *MA*. ii. 234, if their assertion was one that led onwards, then they understood.

Or, brahman, it is like a man walking about aiming at the pith, seeking for the pith, looking about for the pith of a great, stable and pithy tree, who passes by the pith itself . . . the softwood, and who, having cut off the bark, might go away taking it with him thinking it was the pith. A man with vision, having seen him, might say: 'Indeed this good man does not know the pith . . . the softwood . . . the bark . . . the young shoots, he does not know the branches and foliage, inasmuch as this good man, walking about aiming at the pith . . . of a great, stable and pithy tree, passes by the pith itself, passes by the softwood, and having cut off the bark, is going away taking it with him thinking it is the pith. So will he not get the good that could be done by the pith because it is the pith.'

Or, brahman, it is like a man walking about aiming at the pith, seeking for the pith, looking about for the pith of a great, stable and pithy tree, who passes by the pith itself and who, having cut out the softwood, might go away taking it with him thinking it was the pith. A man with vision, having seen him, might say: 'Indeed this good man does not know the pith . . . the softwood . . . the bark . . . the young shoots, he does not know the branches and foliage, inasmuch as this good man, walking about aiming at the pith . . . of a great, stable and pithy tree, passes by the pith itself, and having cut out the softwood, is going away taking it with him thinking it is the pith. So will he not get the good that could be done by the pith because it is the pith.'

Or, brahman, it is like a man walking about aiming at the pith, seeking for the pith, looking about for the pith of a great, stable and pithy tree, and who, having cut out the pith itself knowing it to be the pith, might go away taking it with him. A man with vision, having seen him, might say: 'Indeed this good man knows the pith, he knows the softwood, he knows the bark, he knows the young shoots, he knows the branches and foliage, inasmuch as this good man, walking about aiming at the pith, seeking for the pith, looking about for the pith of a great, stable and pithy tree, having cut out the pith itself, [**200**] is going away taking it with him knowing it to be the pith. So will he get the good that could be done by the pith because it is the pith.'

Even so, brahman, some person here comes to have gone forth from home into homelessness out of faith, and thinks: 'I am beset by birth, by ageing and dying, by grief, sorrow, suffering, lamentation and despair, I am beset by anguish, overwhelmed by anguish.

But perhaps the annihilation of this whole mass of anguish can be shown.' He, gone forth thus, receives gains, honours, fame. Because of these gains, honours, fame, he is satisfied, his purpose is fulfilled. Because of the gains, honours, fame, he exalts himself, disparages others, saying: ' It is I who am a recipient, being famous, but these other monks are little known, of little esteem.' And he does not develop the desire for nor does he strive for realising those other things which are higher and more excellent than gains, honours, fame. He becomes remiss and lax. Brahman, it is like a man walking about aiming at the pith, seeking for the pith, looking about for the pith of a great, stable and pithy tree, who passing by the pith, passing by the softwood, passing by the bark, passing by the young shoots, having cut down the branches and foliage, is going away taking them with him thinking they are the pith. So will he not get the good that could be done by the pith because it is the pith. In accordance with this simile, brahman, do I call this person.

But, brahman, some person here comes to have gone forth from home into homelessness through faith, and thinks: ' I am beset by birth, by ageing and dying, by grief, sorrow, suffering, lamentation and despair. I am beset by anguish, overwhelmed by anguish. But perhaps the annihilation of this whole mass of anguish can be shown.' He, gone forth thus, receives gains, honours, fame. He, because of these gains, honours, fame, does not become satisfied, his purpose is not fulfilled. He, because of these gains, honours, fame, does not exalt himself, does not disparage others. And he develops a desire for and strives for realising those other things which are higher and more excellent than gains, honours, fame. He does not become remiss or lax. He attains success in moral habit. He, because of this success in moral habit, becomes satisfied, his purpose is fulfilled. He, because of this success in moral habit, exalts himself, disparages others, thinking: ' It is I who am of (good) moral habit, lovely in character, but these other monks are of wrong moral habit, evil in character.' And he does not develop a desire for nor does he strive for realising those other things which are higher and more excellent than success in moral habit. [**201**] He becomes remiss and lax. Brahman, it is like a man walking about aiming at the pith, seeking for the pith, looking about for the pith of a great, stable and pithy tree, who passing by the pith itself . . . the softwood . . . the bark, having cut off the young shoots, is going away taking them with him thinking they are the pith. So will he not get the good that could be done by the pith because it is the pith. In accordance with this simile, brahman, do I call this person.

But, brahman, some person here comes to have gone forth from home into homelessness through faith, and thinks: 'I am beset by birth, by ageing and dying, by grief, sorrow, suffering, lamentation and despair. I am beset by anguish, overwhelmed by anguish. But perhaps the annihilation of this whole mass of anguish can be shown.' He, gone forth thus, receives gains, honours, fame. He, because of these gains, honours, fame, does not become satisfied, his purpose is not fulfilled. He, because of these gains, honours, fame, does not exalt himself, does not disparage others. And he develops a desire for and strives for realising those other things which are higher and more excellent than gains, honours, fame. He does not become remiss or lax. He attains success in moral habit. He, because of this success in moral habit becomes satisfied, but not yet is his purpose fulfilled. He, because of this success in moral habit, does not exalt himself, does not disparage others, and he develops a desire for and strives for realising those other things which are higher and more excellent than success in moral habit. He does not become remiss or lax. He attains success in concentration. He, because of this success in concentration becomes satisfied, his purpose is fulfilled. He, because of this success in concentration, exalts himself, disparages others, thinking: 'It is I who am composed, my mind one-pointed, but these other monks are not composed, their minds are wandering.' And he does not develop a desire for nor does he strive for realising those other things which are higher and more excellent than success in concentration. He becomes remiss and lax. Brahman, it is like a man walking about aiming at the pith, seeking for the pith, looking about for the pith of a great, stable and pithy tree, and who, passing by the pith itself, passing by the softwood, having cut off the bark, is going away taking it with him thinking it is the pith. So will he not get the good that could be done by the pith because it is the pith. In accordance with this simile, brahman, do I call this person.

But, brahman, some person here comes to have gone forth from home into homelessness through faith, and thinks: 'I am beset by birth, by ageing and dying, [**202**] by grief, sorrow, suffering, lamentation and despair. I am beset by anguish, overwhelmed by anguish. But perhaps the annihilation of this whole mass of anguish can be shown.' He, gone forth thus, receives gains, honours, fame. He, because of these gains, honours, fame is not satisfied, his purpose is not fulfilled. He, because of these gains, honours, fame, does not exalt himself, does not disparage others. And he develops a desire for and strives for realising those other things which are higher and more excellent than gains, honours, fame. He does not become remiss or lax. He attains success in moral habit. He, because of this success in moral habit, becomes satisfied, but not yet is his purpose fulfilled. He, because of this success in moral habit, does not exalt himself, does not disparage others, And he develops a desire for and strives for realising those other things which are higher and more excellent than success in moral habit, He does not become remiss or lax. He attains success in concentration. He, because of this success in concentration, becomes satisfied, but not yet is his purpose fulfilled. He, because of this success in concentration, does not exalt himself, does not disparage others. And he develops a desire for and strives for realising those other things which are higher and more excellent than success in concentration. He does not become remiss or lax. He attains knowledge and vision. Because of that knowledge and vision he becomes satisfied, his purpose is fulfilled. He, because of that knowledge and vision, exalts himself, disparages others, thinking: 'It is I who dwell knowing and seeing, but these other monks dwell not knowing, not seeing.' And he does not develop a desire for, does not strive for realising those other things which are higher and more excellent than knowledge and vision. He becomes remiss and lax. Brahman, it is like a man walking about aiming at the pith, seeking for the pith, looking about for the pith of a great, stable and pithy tree, who, passing by the pith itself, having cut out the softwood, is going away taking it with him thinking it is the pith. So will he not get the good that could be done by the pith because it is the pith. In accordance with this simile, brahman, do I call this person.

But, brahman, some person here comes to have gone forth from home into homelessness through faith, and thinks: 'I am beset by birth, by ageing and dying, by grief, sorrow, suffering, lamentation and despair, I am beset by anguish, overwhelmed by anguish. But perhaps the annihilation of this whole mass of anguish can be shown.' He, gone forth thus, [**203**] receives gains, honours, fame. He, because of these gains, honours, fame, is not satisfied, his purpose is not fulfilled. He, because of these gains, honours, fame, does not exalt himself, does not disparage others. And he develops a desire for and strives for realising those other things which are higher and more excellent than gains, honours, fame. He does not become remiss or lax. He attains success in moral habit. He, because of this success in moral habit becomes satisfied, but not yet is his purpose fulfilled. He, because of this success in moral habit, does not exalt himself, does not disparage others. And he develops a desire for and strives for realising those other things which are higher and more excellent than success in moral habit. He does not become remiss and lax. He attains success in concentration. He, because of this success in concentration, becomes satisfied, but not yet is his purpose fulfilled. He, because of this success in concentration, does not exalt himself, does not disparage others. And he develops a desire for and strives for realising those things which are higher and more excellent than success in concentration. He does not become remiss or lax. He attains knowledge and vision. He, because of this knowledge and vision, becomes satisfied, but not yet is his purpose fulfilled. He, because of this knowledge and vision, does not exalt himself, does not disparage others. And he develops a desire for and strives for realising those other things which are higher and more excellent than knowledge and vision. He does not become remiss or lax.

And what, brahman, are the things that are higher and more excellent than knowledge and vision? Brahman, some monk here, aloof from pleasures of the senses, aloof from unskilled states of mind, entering into the first meditation which is accompanied by initial thought and discursive thought, is born of aloofness, and is rapturous and joyful, abides in it. This, brahman, is a state that is higher and more excellent than knowledge and vision. And again, brahman, the monk, by allaying initial and discursive thought, with the mind subjectively tranquillised and fixed on one point, enters into and abides in the second meditation, which is devoid of initial and discursive thought, is born of concentration, and is rapturous and joyful. This too, brahman, is a state that is higher and more excellent than knowledge and vision. And again, brahman, the monk, by the fading out of rapture, dwells with equanimity, attentive and clearly conscious; and he experiences in his person that joy of which the ariyans say: 'Joyful lives he who has equanimity and is mindful'; and entering into the third meditation, he abides in it. This too, **[204]** brahman, is a state that is higher and more excellent than knowledge and vision. And again, brahman, the monk by getting rid of joy, by getting rid of anguish, and by the going down of his former pleasures and sorrows, entering into the fourth meditation, which has neither anguish nor joy, and which is entirely purified by equanimity and mindfulness, abides in it. This too, brahman, is a state that is higher and more excellent than knowledge and vision. And again, brahman, a monk, by passing quite beyond all perception of material shapes, by the going down of perception of sensory reactions, by not attending to perceptions of variety, thinking: ' Ether is unending,' entering on the plane of infinite ether, abides in it. This too, brahman, is a state that is higher and more excellent than knowledge and vision. And again, brahman, a monk, by passing quite beyond the plane of infinite ether, thinking: ' Consciousness is unending,' entering on the plane of infinite consciousness, abides in it. This too, brahman, is a state that is higher and more excellent than knowledge and vision. And again, brahman, a monk, by passing quite beyond the plane of infinite consciousness, thinking, ' There is not anything,' entering on the plane of no-thing, abides in it. This too, brahman, is a state that is higher and more excellent than knowledge and vision. And again, brahman, a monk, by passing quite beyond the plane of no-thing, entering on the plane of neither-perception-nor-non-perception, abides in it. This too, brahman, is a state that is higher and more excellent than knowledge and vision. And again, brahman, a monk, by passing quite beyond the plane of neither-perception-nor-non-perception, entering on the stopping of perception and feeling, abides in it. And having seen by intuitive wisdom his cankers are utterly destroyed. This too, brahman, is a state that is higher and more excellent than knowledge and vision. These, brahman, are the states that are higher and more excellent than knowledge and vision.

Brahman, it is like a man walking about aiming at the pith, seeking for the pith, looking about for the pith of a great, stable and pithy tree, and who having cut out the pith itself, goes away taking it with him knowing it to be the pith. He will get the good that could be done by the pith because it is the pith. In accordance with this simile, brahman, do I call this person.

So it is, brahman, that this Brahma-faring is not for advantage in gains, honours, fame, it is not for advantage in moral habit, it is not for advantage in concentration, it is not for advantage in knowledge and vision. That, [**205**] brahman, which is unshakable freedom of mind, this is the goal, brahman, of this Brahma-faring, this the pith, this the culmination."

When this had been said, Piṅgalakoccha the brahman spoke thus to the Lord: "It is wonderful, good Gotama; good Gotama, it is wonderful. It is as if, good Gotama, one might set upright what had been upset, or might disclose what was covered, or might point out the way to one who had gone astray, or might bring an oil lamp into the darkness so that those with vision might see material shapes—even so is *dhamma* made clear in many a figure by the good Gotama. I am going to the revered Gotama for refuge, and to *dhamma* and to the Order of monks. May the good Gotama accept me as a lay-follower, one gone for refuge from this day forth for as long as life lasts."

Lesser Discourse on the Simile of the Pith:
the Tenth

The Third Division[1]

---

[1] This Division does not appear to have a name.

IV. THE GREATER DIVISION OF THE PAIRS

(Mahāyamakavagga)

31. LESSER DISCOURSE IN GOSIṄGA

(Cūḷagosiṅgasutta)

Thus have I heard: At one time the Lord was staying near Nādikā in the brick hall. Now at that time[1] the venerable Anuruddha and the venerable Nandiya and the venerable Kimbila were staying in a grove[2] in the Gosiṅga sāl-wood. Then the Lord, emerging from solitary meditation towards evening, approached that grove in the Gosiṅga sāl-wood. The keeper of the grove saw the Lord coming from a distance; and seeing him, he spoke thus to the Lord: "Do not, recluse, enter this grove; there are three young men of family staying here desiring Self;[3] do not cause them discomfort." The venerable Anuruddha heard the keeper of the grove conferring with the Lord; having heard, he spoke thus to the keeper of the grove: "Do not, good grove-keeper, impede the Lord. It is our teacher, the Lord, who is arriving." Then the venerable Anuruddha approached the venerable Nandiya and the venerable Kimbila; having approached, he spoke thus to the venerable Nandiya and the venerable Kimbila: "Go forward, venerable ones, go forward, venerable ones; our teacher, [**206**] the Lord is arriving."

Then the venerable Anuruddha and the venerable Nandiya and the venerable Kimbila, having gone out to meet the Lord, one received his bowl and robe, one made ready a seat, one set out water for (washing) the feet. Then the Lord sat down on the seat made ready; as he was sitting down the Lord bathed his feet. Then these venerable ones, having greeted the Lord, sat down at a respectful distance. As the venerable Anuruddha was sitting down at a respectful distance, the Lord spoke thus to him:

"I hope that things are going well with you, Anuruddhas,[4] I hope you are keeping going, I hope you are not short of almsfood?"

---

[1] This Sutta, as far as p. 259, is the same as *M.* iii. 155-57, except for a few variations, which include the locations given for the events. *Cf.* also *Vin.* i. 350-52 (and see *B.D.* iv. 501 *ff.* for notes); and also *M.* i. 462 and *Vin.* ii. 182.

[2] *MA.* ii. 235-36 speaks of *dāya* as *arañña*, jungle or forest.

[3] *attakāmarūpā*.

[4] The plural Anuruddhā is here used for the three names of the three separate monks.

" Things are going well, Lord, we are keeping going, Lord, and, Lord, we are not short of almsfood."

" I hope that you, Anuruddhas, are living all together on friendly terms and harmonious, as milk and water blend, regarding one another with the eye of affection ?"[1]

" Yes, certainly, Lord, we are living all together on friendly terms and harmonious, as milk and water blend, regarding one another with the eye of affection."

" And how is it that you, Anuruddhas, are living all together on friendly terms and harmonious, as milk and water blend, regarding one another with the eye of affection ?"

" As to this, Lord, it occurred to me:[2] Indeed it is a gain for me, indeed it is well gotten by me, that I am living with such fellow Brahma-farers. On account of this, Lord, for these venerable ones friendliness[3] as to acts of body, whether openly or in private, has risen up in me, friendliness as to acts of speech, whether openly or in private, has risen up in me, friendliness as to acts of thought, whether openly or in private, has risen up in me. Because of this, Lord, it occurred to me: Now, suppose that I, having surrendered my own mind, should live only according to the mind of these venerable ones ? So I, Lord, having surrendered my own mind, am living only according to the mind of these venerable ones. Lord, we have divers bodies,[4] but assuredly only one mind."

And the venerable Nandiya too. . . . And the venerable Kimbila too spoke thus to the Lord: " As to this, it occurred to me, Lord: Indeed it is a gain for me, indeed it is well gotten by me, that I am living with such fellow Brahma-farers. On account of this, Lord, for these venerable ones, friendliness as to acts of body, whether openly or in private, has risen up in me, friendliness as to acts of speech, whether openly or in private, has risen up in me, friendliness as to acts of thought, whether openly or in private, has risen up in me. Because of this, Lord, it occurred to me: Now, suppose that I, [**207**] having surrendered my own mind, should live only according to the mind of these venerable ones ? So I, Lord, having surrendered my own mind, am living only according to the mind of these venerable ones. Lord, we have divers bodies, but assuredly only one mind."

" Thus it is that we, Lord, are living all together on friendly

---

[1] Stock, as at *M*. i. 206, 398, iii. 156: *A*. i. 70, iii. 67, 104; *S*. iv. 225.

[2] Anuruddha himself is here supposed to be speaking.

[3] As at *M*. i. 222.

[4] *kāyā*.

terms and harmonious, as milk and water blend, regarding one another with the eye of affection."

"It is good, Anuruddhas, it is good. And I hope that you, Anuruddhas, are living diligent, ardent, self-resolute ?"

"Yes, certainly, Lord, we are living diligent, ardent, self-resolute."

"And how is it that you, Anuruddhas, are living diligent, ardent, self-resolute ?"

"As to this, Lord, whichever of us returns first[1] from (going to) a village for almsfood, he makes ready a seat, he sets out water for drinking and water for washing (the feet), he sets out a refuse-bowl. Whoever returns last from (going to) a village for almsfood, if there are the remains of a meal and if he so desires, he eats them; if he does not desire to do so, he throws them out where there are no crops or drops them into water where there are no living creatures; he puts up the seat, he puts away the water for drinking and the water for washing, he puts away the refuse-bowl, he sweeps the refectory. Whoever sees a vessel for drinking water or a vessel for washing water or a vessel (for water) for rinsing after evacuation, void and empty, he sets out (water). If it is impossible for him (to do this) by a movement of his hand, having invited a companion to help us by signalling (to him) with the hand, we set out (the water); but we do not, Lord, for such a reason, break into speech. And then we, Lord, once in every five nights sit down together for talk on *dhamma*. It is thus, Lord, that we are dwelling diligent, ardent, self-resolute."[2]

"It is good, Anuruddhas, it is good. But have you, Anuruddhas, thus living diligent, ardent, self-resolute, attained states of further-men, the excellent knowledge and insight befitting the ariyans, an abiding in comfort ?"[3]

"How could that not be, Lord ? For here we, Lord, for as long as we like, aloof from pleasures of the senses, aloof from unskilled states of mind, entering on the first meditation[4] which is accompanied by initial thought and discursive thought, is born of aloofness, and is rapturous and joyful, abide therein. This, Lord, is for us a state of further-men, an excellent knowledge and insight befitting the ariyans, an abiding in comfort reached while we are dwelling diligent, ardent, self-resolute."

---

[1] *Cf.* also *Vin.* i. 157. [2] *Vin.* i. 352 goes on differently from here.

[3] *M.* iii. 157 goes on differently from here.

[4] At *Vin.* iii. 92, iv. 24 the jhānas form part of the definition of *uttarimanussadhamma*.

"It is good, Anuruddhas, it is good. But did you, Anuruddhas, by passing quite beyond this abiding, [**208**] by allaying this abiding, reach another state of further-men, an excellent knowledge and vision befitting the ariyans, an abiding in comfort ?"

"How could that not be, Lord ? Here we, Lord, for as long as we like, by allaying initial thought and discursive thought, with the mind subjectively tranquillised and fixed on one point, enter into and abide in the second meditation which is devoid of initial and discursive thought, is born of concentration, and is rapturous and joyful. By passing quite beyond that abiding, Lord, by allaying that abiding, another state of further-men, an excellent knowledge and vision befitting the ariyans, an abiding in comfort, is reached."

"It is good, Anuruddhas, it is good. But did you, Anuruddhas, by passing quite beyond this abiding, by allaying this abiding, reach another state of further-men, an excellent knowledge and vision befitting the ariyans, an abiding in comfort ?"

"How could that not be, Lord ? Here we, Lord, for as long as we like, by the fading out of rapture, dwell with equanimity, attentive and clearly conscious; and experience in our persons that joy of which the ariyans say: 'Joyful lives he who has equanimity and is mindful,' and we enter into and abide in the third meditation. By passing quite beyond that abiding, Lord, by allaying that abiding, another state of further-men, an excellent knowledge and vision befitting the ariyans, an abiding in comfort, is reached."

"It is good, Anuruddhas, it is good. But did you, Anuruddhas, by passing quite beyond this abiding, by allaying this abiding, reach another state of further-men, an excellent knowledge and vision befitting the ariyans, an abiding in comfort ?"

"How could this not be, Lord ? Here we, Lord, for as long as we like, by getting rid of joy, by getting rid of anguish, by the going down of our former pleasures and sorrows, enter into and abide in the fourth meditation which has neither anguish nor joy, and which is entirely purified by equanimity and mindfulness. By passing quite beyond that abiding, Lord, by allaying that abiding, another state of further-men, an excellent knowledge and vision befitting the ariyans, an abiding in comfort, is reached."

"It is good, Anuruddhas, it is good. But did you, Anuruddhas, by passing quite beyond this abiding, by allaying this abiding, reach another state of further-men, an excellent knowledge and vision befitting the ariyans, an abiding in comfort ?"

"How could this not be, Lord? Here we, Lord, for as long as we like, by passing quite beyond all perception of material shapes, by the going down of perception of sensory reactions, by not attending to perception of variety, thinking, 'Ether is unending,' [**209**] entering on the plane of infinite ether, abide in it. By passing quite beyond that abiding, Lord, by allaying that abiding, another state of further-men, an excellent knowledge and vision befitting the ariyans, an abiding in comfort, is reached."

"It is good, Anuruddhas, it is good. But did you, Anuruddhas, by passing quite beyond this abiding, by allaying this abiding, reach another state of further-men, an excellent knowledge and vision befitting the ariyans, an abiding in comfort?"

"How could this not be, Lord? Here we, Lord, for as long as we like, by passing quite beyond the plane of infinite ether, thinking, 'Consciousness is unending,' entering on the plane of infinite consciousness, abide in it . . . by passing quite beyond the plane of infinite consciousness, thinking, 'There is not anything,' entering on the plane of no-thing, abide in it . . . by passing quite beyond the plane of no-thing, entering on the plane of neither-perception-nor-non-perception, we abide in it. By passing quite beyond this abiding, Lord, by allaying this abiding, another state of further-men, an excellent knowledge and vision befitting the ariyans, an abiding in comfort, is reached."

"It is good, Anuruddhas, it is good. But did you, Anuruddhas, by passing quite beyond this abiding, by allaying this abiding, reach another state of further-men, an excellent knowledge and vision befitting the ariyans, an abiding in comfort?"

"How could this not be, Lord? Here we, Lord, for as long as we like, by passing quite beyond the plane of neither-perception-nor-non-perception, entering on the stopping of perception and feeling, abide in it, and having seen through intuitive wisdom, our cankers come to be utterly destroyed. By passing quite beyond that abiding, Lord, by allaying that abiding, another state of further-men, an excellent knowledge and vision befitting the ariyans, an abiding in comfort, is reached. But we, Lord, do not behold another abiding in comfort that is higher or more excellent than this abiding in comfort."

"It is good, Anuruddhas, it is good. There is no other abiding in comfort that is higher or more excellent than this abiding in comfort."

Then the Lord, having gladdened, roused, incited, delighted the venerable Anuruddha and the venerable Nandiya and the venerable Kimbila with talk on *dhamma*, rising from his seat, departed. Then when the venerable Anuruddha and the venerable Nandiya and the venerable Kimbila, having escorted the Lord, had turned back again from there, the venerable [**210**] Nandiya and the venerable Kimbila spoke thus to the venerable Anuruddha:

"Now, did we ever speak thus to the venerable Anuruddha: 'We are acquirers of this or that attainment in abiding,'[1] in virtue of which the venerable Anuruddha when face to face with the Lord, made this known of us up to the destruction of the cankers?"

"The venerable ones have not said to me: 'We are acquirers of this and that attainment in abiding.' But by my mind the minds of the venerable ones are known to me, to the effect that the venerable ones are acquirers of this and that attainment in abiding. And *devatās* also told me this matter: 'These venerable ones are acquirers of this and that attainment in abiding.' It is in this way that the questions put by the Lord were answered."

Then Dīgha Parajana,[2] a *yakkha*,[3] approached the Lord; having approached, having greeted the Lord, he sat down at a respectful distance. As he was sitting down at a respectful distance, Dīgha Parajana, the *yakkha*, spoke thus to the Lord: "Indeed, it is profitable, Lord, for the Vajjis, it is well-gotten and profitable for the Vajji people[4] that the Tathāgata is staying (here), the perfected one, the fully Self-awakened One, and these three young men of family: the venerable Anuruddha and the venerable Nandiya and the venerable Kimbila." The four great Regent *devas*[5] having heard the sound of the earth-*devas*, made this sound heard . . . the *devas* of the Thirty-three . . . the Yama *devas* . . . the Happy *devas* . . . the *devas* who delight in creation . . . the *devas* who have power over the creation of others . . . the *devas* in the retinue of Brahmā made this sound heard: "Indeed it is profitable for the Vajjis, it is well-gotten and profitable for the Vajji people that the Tathāgata is staying (here), the perfected one,

---

[1] Worldly and transcendental, beginning with the first *jhāna*, *MA*. ii. 244.

[2] Mentioned at *D*. iii. 205 among the *yakkhas* to whom Gotama's followers may appeal for protection. *MA*. ii. 244 says Dīgha was a *devarājā*, and Parajana was his name.

[3] There being no exact English equivalent for words denoting non-human beings, they are best left untranslated.

[4] *MA*. ii. 244 says it is profitable for them to see the Lord and the three disciples, to honour them, to give them gifts of faith, and to hear *dhamma*.

[5] As at *Vin*. i. 12, iii. 18-19.

the fully Self-awakened One, and these three young men of family: the venerable Anuruddha, and the venerable Nandiya and the venerable Kimbila." Thus in this moment, in this second, these venerable ones became known as far as the Brahma-world.

"That is so, Dīgha, that is so, Dīgha. If, Dīgha, that family from which these three young men of family have gone forth from home into homelessness were to remember these three young men of family with a believing mind, then for a long time would there be welfare and happiness for that family. If, Dīgha, that group of families [**211**] . . . that village . . . that little town . . . that town . . . that district . . . all nobles . . . all brahmans . . . all merchants . . . all workers, were to remember these three young men of family with a believing mind, then for a long time would there be welfare and happiness for that village . . . that little town . . . that town . . . that district . . . all these nobles . . . all these brahmans . . . all these merchants . . . all these workers. And if, Dīgha, the world with its *devas*, with its Māras, with its Brahmās, if creation with recluses and brahmans, with *devas* and men, were to remember these three young men of family with a believing mind, then for a long time would there be welfare and happiness for the world with its *devas*, with its Māras, with its Brahmās, for creation with recluses and brahmans, with *devas* and men. See, Dīgha, how these three young men of family are faring along for the welfare of the manyfolk, for the happiness of the manyfolk, out of compassion for the world, for the good, the welfare, the happiness of *devas* and men."

Thus spoke the Lord. Delighted, Dīgha Parajana the *yakkha* rejoiced in what the Lord had said.

Lesser Discourse in Gosiṅga:
The First

32. GREATER DISCOURSE IN GOSIṄGA

(Mahāgosiṅgasutta)

[**212**] THUS have I heard: At one time the Lord was staying in a grove in the Gosiṅga sāl-wood together with many famous disciples who were elders: with the venerable Sāriputta and the venerable Moggallāna the Great and the venerable Kassapa the Great and

the venerable Anuruddha and the venerable Revata[1] and the venerable Ānanda and with other famous disciples who were elders. Then the venerable Moggallāna the Great, emerging from solitary meditation towards evening, approached the venerable Kassapa the Great; having approached, he spoke thus to the venerable Kassapa the Great: "Let us go, reverend Kassapa, we will approach the venerable Sāriputta so as to hear *dhamma*."

"Yes, your reverence," the venerable Kassapa the Great answered the venerable Moggallāna the Great in assent. Then the venerable Moggallāna the Great and the venerable Kassapa the Great and the venerable Anuruddha approached the venerable Sāriputta so as to hear *dhamma*. The venerable Ānanda saw the venerable Moggallāna the Great and the venerable Kassapa the Great and the venerable Anuruddha approaching the venerable Sāriputta so as to hear *dhamma*; having seen them, he approached the venerable Revata; having approached, he spoke thus to the venerable Revata: "Reverend Revata, some who are true men are approaching the venerable Sāriputta so as to hear *dhamma*; let us go, reverend Revata, we will approach the venerable Sāriputta so as to hear *dhamma*."

"Yes, your reverence," the venerable Revata answered the venerable Ānanda in assent. Then the venerable Revata and the venerable Ānanda approached the venerable Sāriputta so as to hear *dhamma*.

The venerable Sāriputta saw the venerable Revata and the venerable Ānanda coming in the distance; having seen them, he spoke thus to the venerable Ānanda: "Let the venerable Ānanda come; good is the coming of the venerable Ānanda who is the Lord's attendant, the Lord's companion. Delightful,[2] reverend Ānanda, is the Gosiṅga sāl-wood, it is a clear moonlight night, the sāl-trees are in full blossom, methinks *deva*-like scents are being wafted around. By what type of monk, reverend Ānanda, would the Gosiṅga sāl-wood be illumined?"

"In this case, reverend [**213**] Sāriputta, a monk comes to be one who has heard much, who masters what he has heard, who stores

---

[1] *Cf. A.* i. 24. *MA.* ii. 247 says Revata the Doubter is meant here, not Revata of the Acacia Wood (Khadiravaniya-Revata).

[2] *MA.* ii. 250 says delightfulness is twofold: that of woods and that of people. Here both kinds are meant, for the wood is full of flowers and scents, and here the highest person in the world, the All awakened one, is staying with 30,000 renowned monks.

what he has heard; those teachings which are lovely at the beginning, lovely in the middle, lovely at the end, which with the spirit and the letter declare the Brahma-faring which is completely fulfilled, utterly pure—such teachings come to be much heard by him, borne in mind, repeated out loud, pondered over in the mind, well comprehended by view; he teaches *dhamma* to the four assemblies with correct and fluent lines and sentences for the rooting out of (latent) propensities.[1] By a monk of such a type, reverend Sāriputta, would the Gosiṅga sāl-wood be illumined."

When this had been said, the venerable Sāriputta spoke thus to the venerable Revata: "It has been explained, reverend Revata, by the venerable Ānanda according to his own capacity. On this point we are now asking the venerable Revata, saying: "Delightful, reverend Revata, is the Gosiṅga sāl-wood. . . . By what type of monk, reverend Revata, would the Gosiṅga sāl-wood be illumined?"

"In this connection, reverend Sāriputta, a monk delights in solitary meditation, he is delighted by solitary meditation, he is intent on mental tranquillity within, his meditation is uninterrupted, he is endowed with vision, a cultivator of empty places.[2] By a monk of such a type, reverend Sāriputta, would the Gosiṅga sāl-wood be illumined."

When this had been said, the venerable Sāriputta spoke thus to the venerable Anuruddha: "It has been explained, reverend Anuruddha, by the venerable Revata according to his own capacity. On this point we are now asking the venerable Anuruddha: Delightful, reverend Anuruddha, is the Gosiṅga sāl-wood. . . . By what type of monk, reverend Anuruddha, would the Gosiṅga sāl-wood be illumined?"

"In this connection, reverend Sāriputta, a monk surveys the thousand worlds[3] with purified *deva*-vision surpassing that of men. Reverend Sāriputta, as a man with vision might survey a thousand concentric circles from the top of a long house, so, reverend Sāriputta, does a monk survey the thousand worlds with purified *deva*-vision, surpassing that of men. By a monk of such a type, reverend Sāriputta, would the Gosiṅga sāl-wood be illumined."

---

[1] *MA.* ii. 254 says there are seven. See *D.* iii. 254. Ānanda is called chief of those who have heard much at *A.* i. 23.

[2] As at *M.* i. 33. Revata is called chief of meditators at *A.* i. 24.

[3] *MA.* ii. 254, "thousand world-elements." Anuruddha is chief of those with *deva*-sight, *A.* i. 23.

When this had been said, the venerable Sāriputta spoke thus to the venerable Kassapa the Great: " It has been explained, reverend Kassapa, by the reverend Anuruddha according to his own capacity. On this point we are asking the venerable Kassapa the Great: Delightful, reverend Kassapa, is the Gosiṅga sāl-wood. . . . By what type of monk, reverend Kassapa, [**214**] would the Gosiṅga sāl-wood be illumined ?"

" In this connection, reverend Sāriputta, a monk is both a forest-dweller himself and one who praises forest-dwelling; he is an almsman himself and one who praises being an almsman; he is a rag-robe wearer himself and one who praises the wearing of rag-robes; he wears three robes himself and is one who praises the wearing of three robes; he is of few wishes himself and is one who praises being of few wishes; he is contented himself and is one who praises contentment; he is aloof himself and is one who praises aloofness; he is ungregarious himself and is one who praises ungregariousness; he is of stirred up energy himself and is one who praises stirring up energy; he is possessed of moral habit himself and is one who praises success in moral habit; he is possessed of concentration himself and is one who praises success in concentration; he is possessed of intuitive wisdom himself and is one who praises success in intuitive wisdom; he is possessed of freedom himself and is one who praises success in freedom; he is possessed of the knowledge and vision of freedom himself and is one who praises success in the knowledge and vision of freedom.[1] By a monk of such a type, reverend Sāriputta, would the Gosiṅga sāl-wood be illumined."

When this had been said, the venerable Sāriputta spoke thus to the venerable Moggallāna the Great: " It has been explained, reverend Moggallāna, by the venerable Kassapa the Great according to his own capacity. On this point we are now asking the venerable Moggallāna the Great: Delightful, reverend Moggallāna, is the Gosiṅga sāl-wood, it is a clear moonlight night, the sāl-trees are in full blossom, methinks *deva*-like scents are being wafted around. By what type of monk, reverend Moggallāna, would the Gosiṅga sāl-wood be illumined ?"

" In this connection, reverend Sāriputta, two monks are talking on Further *dhamma*;[2] they ask one another questions; in answering

[1] At *A*. i. 23 Kassapa the Great is chief of those who uphold the austere practices.

[2] *abhidhamma*.

one another's questions they respond and do not fail, and their talk on *dhamma* goes forward. By a monk of such a type, reverend Sāriputta, would the Gosiṅga sāl-wood be illumined."

Then the venerable Moggallāna the Great spoke thus to the venerable Sāriputta: "It has been answered by all of us, reverend Sāriputta, each one according to his own capacity. On this point we are now asking the venerable Sāriputta: Delightful, reverend Sāriputta, is the Gosiṅga sāl-wood, it is a clear moonlight night, the sāl-trees are in full blossom, methinks *deva*-like scents are being wafted around. By what type of monk, reverend Sāriputta, would the Gosiṅga sāl-wood be illumined?"

"In this connection, reverend Moggallāna, a monk has rule over mind, he is not under mind's rule; whatever attainment of abiding[1] he wishes [**215**] to abide in in the morning, in that attainment of abiding he abides in the morning; whatever attainment of abiding he wishes to abide in at midday, in that attainment of abiding he abides at midday; whatever attainment of abiding he wishes to abide in in the evening, in that attainment of abiding he abides in the evening. Reverend Moggallāna, as a king[2] or a king's chief minister might have a chest for clothes filled with differently dyed cloths, so that no matter which pair of cloths he wished to put on in the morning, he could put on that self-same pair of cloths in the morning; no matter which pair of cloths he wished to put on at midday, he could put on that self-same pair of cloths at midday; no matter which pair of cloths he wished to put on in the evening, he could put on that self-same pair of cloths in the evening—even so, reverend Moggallāna, a monk rules over mind, is not under mind's rule; whatever attainment of abiding he wishes to abide in in the morning, in that attainment of abiding he abides in the morning; whatever attainment of abiding he wishes to abide in at midday, in that attainment of abiding he abides at midday; whatever attainment of abiding he wishes to abide in in the evening, in that attainment of abiding he abides in the evening. By a monk of such a type, reverend Moggallāna, would the Gosiṅga sāl-wood be illumined."

Then the venerable Sāriputta spoke thus to these venerable ones: "It has been explained by all of us, your reverences, each one according to his own capacity. Let us go, your reverences, we

---

[1] *MA.* ii. 255 says worldly or other-worldly.

[2] Simile at *S.* v. 71; *A.* iv. 230.

will approach the Lord; having approached, we will tell this matter to the Lord; as the Lord explains it to us so will we remember it."

"Very well, your reverence," these venerable ones answered the venerable Sāriputta in assent. Then these venerable ones approached the Lord; having approached, having greeted the Lord, they sat down at a respectful distance. As he was sitting down at a respectful distance, the venerable Sāriputta spoke thus to the Lord:

"Now, Lord, the venerable Revata and the venerable Ānanda approached me in order to hear *dhamma*. And I, Lord, saw the venerable Revata and the venerable Ānanda coming in the distance, and on seeing [**216**] the venerable Ānanda, I spoke thus: 'Let the venerable Ānanda come; good is the coming of the venerable Ānanda who is the Lord's attendant, the Lord's companion. Delightful, reverend Ānanda, is the Gosiṅga sāl-wood, it is a clear moonlight night, the sāl-trees are in full blossom, methinks *deva*-like scents are being wafted around. By what type of monk, reverend Ānanda, would the Gosiṅga sāl-wood be illumined?' When I had spoken thus, Lord, the venerable Ānanda spoke thus to me: 'In this connection, reverend Sāriputta, a monk comes to be one who has heard much. . . . By a monk of such a type, reverend Sāriputta, would the Gosiṅga sāl-wood be illumined.'"

"It is good, Sāriputta, it is good. It is so that Ānanda, in answering you properly, should answer. For, Sāriputta, Ānanda is one who has heard much, who masters what he has heard, who stores what he has heard; those teachings which are lovely at the beginning, lovely in the middle and lovely at the end, which with the spirit and the letter declare the Brahma-faring which is completely fulfilled, utterly pure—such teachings come to be much heard by him, borne in mind, repeated out loud, pondered over in the mind, well comprehended by view; he teaches *dhamma* to the four assemblies with correct and fluent lines and sentences for the rooting out of (latent) propensities."

"When this had been said, Lord, I spoke thus to the venerable Revata: 'It has been answered, reverend Revata, by the venerable Ānanda according to his own capacity. On this point we are now asking the venerable Revata: Delightful, reverend Revata, is the Gosiṅga sāl-wood. . . . By what type of monk, reverend Revata, would the Gosiṅga sāl-wood be illumined?' When I had spoken thus, Lord, the venerable Revata spoke thus to me: 'In this connection, reverend Sāriputta, a monk delights in solitary meditation.

. . . By such a type of monk, reverend Sāriputta, would the Gosiṅga sāl-wood be illumined.' "

" It is good, Sāriputta, it is good. It is so that Revata, in answering you properly, should answer. For, Sāriputta, Revata is one who delights in solitary meditation, who is delighted by solitary meditation, he is intent on mental tranquillity within, his meditation is uninterrupted, he is endowed with vision, a cultivator of empty places."

[**217**] " When this had been said, Lord, I spoke thus to the venerable Anuruddha: ' It has been answered, reverend Anuruddha, by the venerable Revata according to his own capacity. On this point we are now asking the venerable Anuruddha: Delightful, reverend Anuruddha, is the Gosiṅga sāl-wood. . . . By what type of monk, reverend Anuruddha, would the Gosiṅga sāl-wood be illumined?' When I had spoken thus, Lord, the venerable Anuruddha spoke thus to me: ' In this connection, reverend Sāriputta, a monk surveys the thousand worlds with purified *deva*-vision. . . . By such a type of monk, reverend Sāriputta, would the Gosiṅga sāl-wood be illumined.' "

" It is good, Sāriputta, it is good. It is so that Anuruddha, in answering you properly, should answer. For, Sāriputta, Anuruddha surveys the thousand worlds with purified *deva*-vision, surpassing that of men."

" When this had been said, Lord, I spoke thus to the venerable Kassapa the Great: ' It has been answered, reverend Kassapa, by the venerable Anuruddha according to his own capacity. On this point we are now asking the venerable Kassapa the Great: Delightful, reverend Kassapa, is the Gosiṅga sāl-wood. . . . By what type of monk, reverend Kassapa, would the Gosiṅga sāl-wood be illumined?' When I had spoken thus, Lord, the venerable Kassapa the Great spoke thus to me: ' In this connection, reverend Sāriputta, a monk is both a forest-dweller himself and one who praises forest-dwelling. . . . By a monk of such a type, reverend Sāriputta, would the Gosiṅga sāl-wood [**218**] be illumined.' "

" It is good, Sāriputta, it is good. It is so that Kassapa, in answering you properly, should answer. For Sāriputta, Kassapa is a forest-dweller himself and is one who praises forest-dwelling . . . he is possessed of the knowledge and vision of freedom himself and is one who praises success in the knowledge and vision of freedom."

" When this had been said, Lord, I spoke thus to the venerable

Moggallāna the Great: 'It has been answered, reverend Moggallāna, by the venerable Kassapa the Great according to his own capacity. On this point we are now asking the venerable Moggallāna the Great: Delightful, reverend Moggallāna . . . by what type of monk, reverend Moggallāna, would the Gosiṅga sāl-wood be illumined?' When I had spoken thus, Lord, the venerable Moggallāna the Great spoke thus to me: 'In this connection, reverend Sāriputta, two monks are talking on Further *dhamma*; they ask one another questions; in answering one another's questions they respond and do not fail, and their talk on *dhamma* is one that goes forward. By a monk of such a type, reverend Sāriputta, would the Gosiṅga sāl-wood be illumined.'"

"It is good, Sāriputta, it is good. It is so that Moggallāna, in answering you properly, should answer. For, Sāriputta, Moggallāna is a talker on *dhamma*."[1]

When this had been said, the venerable Moggallāna the Great spoke thus to the Lord: "Then I, Lord, spoke thus to the venerable Sāriputta: 'It has been answered by all of us, reverend Sāriputta, each one according to his own capacity. On this point we are now asking the venerable Sāriputta: Delightful, reverend Sāriputta, is the Gosiṅga sāl-wood, it is a clear moonlight night, the sāl-trees are in full blossom, methinks *deva*-like scents are being wafted around. By what type of monk, reverend Sāriputta, would Gosiṅga sāl-wood be illumined?' When this had been said, Lord, the venerable Sāriputta spoke thus to me: 'In this connection, reverend Moggallāna, a monk has rule over mind. . . . [**219**] . . . By a monk of such a type, reverend Moggallāna, would the Gosiṅga sāl-wood be illumined.'"

"It is good, Moggallāna, it is good. It is so that Sāriputta, in answering you properly, should answer. For, Moggallāna, Sāriputta has rule over mind, he is not under mind's rule; whatever attainment of abiding he wishes to abide in in the morning, in that attainment of abiding he abides in the morning; whatever attainment of abiding he wishes to abide in at midday, in that attainment of abiding he abides at midday; whatever attainment of abiding he

---

[1] Moggallāna is called chief of those of psychic power, *A*. i. 23. *MA*. ii. 256 explains that "*abhidhamma*-men, having come to knowledge of subtle points, having increased their vision, can achieve a supermundane state." Non-*abhidhamma*-men get muddled between "own doctrine" (*sakavāda*) and "other doctrine" (*paravāda*).

wishes to abide in in the evening, in that attainment of abiding he abides in the evening."[1]

When this had been said, the venerable Sāriputta spoke thus to the Lord: " Now, by whom was it well spoken, Lord ?"

" It was well spoken by you all in turn, Sāriputta. But now hear from me by what type of monk the Gosiṅga sāl-wood would be illumined. In this connection, Sāriputta, a monk, returning from alms-gathering after the meal, sits down cross-legged, the back erect, having raised up mindfulness in front of him, and thinking: ' I will not quit this cross-legged (position) until my mind is freed from the cankers without any residuum (for rebirth) remaining.' By such a type of monk, Sāriputta, would the Gosiṅga sāl-wood be illumined."

Thus spoke the Lord. Delighted, these venerable ones rejoiced in what the Lord had said.

Greater Discourse in Gosiṅga:
the Second

33. GREATER DISCOURSE ON THE COWHERD

(Mahāgopālakasutta)[2]

[**220**] THUS have I heard: At one time the Lord was staying near Sāvatthī in the Jeta Grove in Anāthapiṇḍika's monastery. While he was there the Lord addressed the monks, saying: " Monks." " Revered one," these monks answered the Lord in assent. The Lord spoke thus:

" Monks, possessed of eleven qualities a cowherd cannot be one to take care of a herd of cattle and to make it prosperous. Of what eleven ? Herein, monks, a cowherd is not one who is versed in material shapes,[3] he is not skilled in (distinguishing) marks, he does not remove flies' eggs, he does not dress sores, he makes no fumigation,[4] he does not know what is a ford, he does not know

---

[1] *A*. i. 23, he is chief in great wisdom. [2] As at *A*. v. 347.

[3] Cannot recognise the animals by counting them or by their colour, *MA*. ii. 258.

[4] Against gadflies, mosquitoes, etc., so during the rains the harassed cows cannot eat as much grass as they require, *MA*. ii. 259.

what is a watering-place, he does not know what is a road, he is not skilled in pastures, he is one who milks dry, he pays no special respect to those bulls who are the sires and leaders of the herd. Monks, if a cowherd is possessed of these eleven qualities, he cannot be one to take care of the herd and make it prosperous.

Even so, monks, if a monk is possessed of eleven qualities, he cannot become one to reach growth, increase and maturity in this *dhamma* and discipline. With what eleven? Herein, monks, a monk is one who is not versed in material shapes, he is not skilled in (distinguishing) marks, he does not remove flies' eggs, he does not dress sores, he makes no fumigation, he does not know what is a ford, he does not know what is a watering-place, he does not know what is a road, he is not skilled in pastures, he is one who milks dry, he pays no special respect to those monks who are elders and have gone forth many a day and are the sires and leaders of the Order.

And how, monks, is a monk not versed in material shapes? Herein, monks, a monk in regard to material shape does not comprehend as it really is that all material shape is of the four great elements and that material shape is derived from the four great elements.[1] Even so, monks, is a monk not versed in material shapes.

And how, monks, is a monk not skilled in (distinguishing) marks? Herein, monks, a monk does not comprehend as it really is: A fool is marked by his deed, a sage is marked by his deed.[2] Even so, monks, is a monk not skilled in (distinguishing) marks.

And how, monks, is a monk not one to remove flies' eggs? Herein,[3] monks, a monk gives in to thought about sense-pleasures that has arisen, does not get rid of it, does not avert it, does not make an end of it, does not send it to non-existence. He gives in to thought of malevolence that has arisen . . . to thought of harming that has arisen . . . he gives in to evil unskilled mental objects that have constantly arisen, [**221**] he does not get rid of them, does not avert them, does not make an end of them, does not send them to non-existence. Even so, monks, is a monk one who does not remove flies' eggs.

And how, monks, is a monk one who does not dress a sore? Herein, monks, a monk, having seen material shape with the eye, is entranced by its general appearance,[4] is entranced by its detail.

---

[1] *M.* i. 185. [2] *A.* i. 102. [3] *Cf. M.* i. 11.
[4] *Vbh.* 372; and *cf. D.* i. 70; *A.* ii. 16; *K.S.* iv. 63.

Although coveting and dejection[1]—evil unskilled states—might get power over one who fares along with his organ of sight uncontrolled, he does not proceed to control it, he does not guard the organ of sight, he does not come to control over the organ of sight. Having heard a sound with the ear . . . having smelt a smell with the nose . . . having savoured a taste with the tongue . . . having felt a touch with the body . . . having cognised a mental object with the mind, he is entranced with the general appearance, he is entranced with the detail. Although coveting and dejection—evil unskilled states—might get power over one who fares along with his organ of mind uncontrolled, he does not proceed to control it, he does not guard the organ of mind, he does not come to control over the organ of mind. Even so, monks, is a monk one who does not dress a sore.

And how, monks, is a monk one who does not make a fumigation ? Herein, monks, a monk does not teach *dhamma* to others in detail as he has heard it, as he has borne it in mind. Even so, monks, is a monk one who does not make a fumigation.

And how, monks, is a monk one who does not know a ford ? Herein, monks, a monk who from time to time has approached those monks who have heard much, to whom the tradition has been handed down, experts in *dhamma*, experts in discipline, experts in the summaries, yet he does not question them, does not interrogate them, saying: 'How is this, revered ones ? What is the meaning of this, revered ones ?' These venerable ones do not disclose to him what was not disclosed, they do not make clear what was not made clear, and on various doubtful points in *dhamma* they do not resolve his doubts. Even so, monks, is a monk one who does not know a ford.

And how, monks, is a monk one who does not know a watering-place ? Herein, monks, a monk, while *dhamma* and discipline proclaimed by the Tathāgata are being taught, does not acquire knowledge of the goal,[2] does not acquire knowledge of *dhamma*, does not acquire the delight that is connected with *dhamma*. Even so, monks, is a monk one who does not know a watering-place.

And how, monks, is a monk one who does not know a road ? Herein, monks, a monk does not comprehend the ariyan eightfold Way as it really is. Even so, monks, is a monk one who does not know the road.

---

[1] *Cf. M.* i. 180.

[2] As at *M.* i. 37, ii. 206.

And how, monks, is a monk not skilled in pastures? Herein, monks, a monk does not comprehend as they really are the four arousings of mindfulness. Even so, [222] monks, is a monk one not skilled in pastures.

And how, monks, is a monk one who milks dry? Herein, monks, when householders with faith invite a monk to take[1] the requisites of robe-material, almsfood, lodgings and medicines for the sick, he does not know moderation in accepting such. Even so, monks, is a monk one who milks dry.

And how, monks, is a monk one who pays no special respect to the monks who are elders, gone forth many a day, the sires and leaders of the Order? Herein, monks, a monk[2] does not make friendliness as to acts of body rise up either openly or in private for those monks who are elders, gone forth many a day, the sires and leaders of the Order; he does not make friendliness as to acts of speech rise up either openly or in private, he does not make friendliness as to acts of thought rise up either openly or in private. Even so, monks, is a monk one who pays no special respect to the monks who are elders, gone forth many a day, the sires and leaders of the Order. Monks, possessed of these eleven qualities a monk cannot become one to reach growth, increase, maturity in this *dhamma* and discipline.

Monks, possessed of eleven qualities, a cowherd can become one to take care of a herd of cattle and make it prosperous. With what eleven? Herein, monks, a cowherd is versed in material shapes, he is skilled in (distinguishing) marks, he removes flies' eggs, he dresses sores, he makes a fumigation, he knows what is a ford, he knows what is a watering-place, he knows what is a road, he is skilled in pastures, he is one who does not milk dry, he pays special respect to those bulls who are the sires and leaders of the herd. Monks, if a cowherd is possessed of these eleven qualities, he can become one to take care of the herd and make it prosperous. Even so, monks, if a monk is possessed of eleven qualities, he can become one to reach growth, increase and maturity in this *dhamma* and discipline. Of what eleven? Herein, monks, a monk is one who is versed in material shapes, he is skilled in (distinguishing) marks, he removes flies' eggs, he dresses sores, he makes a fumigation, he knows what is a ford, he knows what is a watering-place, he

---

[1] *abhihaṭṭhuṃ pavārenti. Cf. abhiharati* at *Vin.* iv. 82, and see *B.D.* ii. 329, *n.* 2.

[2] As at *M.* i. 206.

knows what is a road, he is skilled in pastures, he is one who does not milk dry, he pays special respect to those monks who are elders and have gone forth many a day and are the sires and leaders of the Order.

And how, monks, is a monk versed in material shapes ? Herein, monks, a monk in regard to material shape comprehends as it really is that all material shape is of the four [**223**] great elements and that material shape is derived from the four great elements. Even so, monks, is a monk versed in material shapes.

And how, monks, is a monk skilled in (distinguishing) marks ? Herein, monks, a monk comprehends as it really is: A fool is marked by his deed, a sage is marked by his deed. Even so, monks, is a monk skilled in (distinguishing) marks.

And how, monks, is a monk one who removes flies' eggs ? Herein, monks, a monk does not give in to thought about sense-pleasures that has arisen, he gets rid of it, averts it, makes an end of it, sends it to non-existence. He does not give in to thoughts of malevolence that have arisen . . . to thoughts of harming that have arisen . . . he does not give in to evil unskilled mental objects that have constantly arisen, he gets rid of them, averts them, makes an end of them, sends then to non-existence. Even so, monks, is a monk one who removes flies' eggs.

And how, monks, is a monk one who dresses a sore ? Herein, monks, a monk, having seen material shape with the eye, is not entranced by its general appearance, is not entranced by the detail. Because covetousness and dejection—evil unskilled states—might get power over one who fares along with his organ of sight uncontrolled, he proceeds to control it, he guards the organ of sight, he comes to control over the organ of sight. Having heard a sound with the ear . . . having cognised a mental object with the mind, he is not entranced with its general appearance, he is not entranced with the detail. Because coveting and dejection—evil unskilled states—might get power over one who fares along with his organ of mind uncontrolled, he proceeds to control it, he guards the organ of mind, he comes to control over the organ of mind. Even so, monks, is a monk one who dresses a sore.

And how, monks, is a monk one who makes a fumigation ? Herein, monks, a monk teaches *dhamma* to others in detail as he has heard it, as he has borne it in mind. Even so, monks, is a monk one who makes a fumigation.

And how, monks, is a monk one who knows what is a ford ? Herein, monks, a monk who from time to time has approached those monks who have heard much, to whom the tradition has been handed down, experts in *dhamma*, experts in discipline, experts in the summaries, and questions them, interrogates them, saying: 'How is this, revered ones ? What is the meaning of this, revered ones ?' These venerable ones disclose to him what was not disclosed, they make clear what was not made clear, and on various doubtful points of *dhamma* they resolve his doubts. Even so, monks, is a monk one who knows what is a ford.

And how, monks, [**224**] is a monk one who knows what is a watering-place ? Herein, monks, a monk, while *dhamma* and discipline proclaimed by the Tathāgata are being taught, acquires knowledge of the goal, acquires knowledge of *dhamma*, acquires the delight that is connected with *dhamma*. Even so, monks, is a monk one who knows what is a watering-place.

And how, monks, is a monk one who knows what is a road ? Herein, monks, a monk comprehends the ariyan eightfold Way as it really is. Even so, monks, is a monk one who knows what is a road.

And how, monks, is a monk one who is skilled in pastures ? Herein, monks, a monk comprehends as they really are the four arousings of mindfulness. Even so, monks, is a monk one who is skilled in pastures.

And how, monks, is a monk one who does not milk dry ? Herein, monks, when a householder with faith invites a monk to take the requisites of robe-material . . . medicines for the sick, he knows moderation in accepting such. Even so, monks, is a monk one who does not milk dry.

And how, monks, is a monk one who pays special respect to the monks who are elders, gone forth many a day, the sires and leaders of the Order ? Herein, monks, a monk makes friendliness as to acts of body rise up whether openly or in private for those monks who are elders, gone forth many a day, the sires and leaders of the Order; he makes friendliness as to acts of speech rise up whether openly or in private, he makes friendliness as to acts of thought rise up whether openly or in private. Even so, monks, is a monk one who pays special respect to the monks who are elders, gone forth many a day, the sires and leaders of the Order. Monks, possessed of these eleven qualities, a monk can become one to reach growth, increase and maturity in this *dhamma* and discipline.'

Thus spoke the Lord. Delighted, these monks rejoiced in what the Lord had said.

Greater Discourse on the Cowherd:
the Third

34. LESSER DISCOURSE ON THE COWHERD

(Cūḷagopālakasutta)

[**225**] Thus have I heard: At one time the Lord was staying among the Vajjis at Ukkācelā on the banks of the river Ganges. While he was there the Lord addressed the monks, saying: "Monks." "Revered one," these monks answered the Lord in assent. The Lord spoke thus:

"Formerly, monks, an incompetent cowherd of Magadha in the last month of the rains at harvest time, without considering the hither bank of the river Ganges, without considering the further bank, drove his cattle across to the further bank in Suvidehā at a place where there was no ford. Then, monks. the cattle huddled together in the middle of the stream of the river Ganges, got into difficulties and misfortune there. What was the cause? It was, monks, that that incompetent cowherd of Magadha in the last month of the rains at harvest time, without considering the hither bank of the river Ganges, without considering the further bank, drove the cattle across to the further bank in Suvidehā at a place where there was no ford. Even so, monks, any recluses or brahmans who are unskilled about this world, unskilled about the world beyond, unskilled about Māra's realm,[1] unskilled about what is not Māra's realm,[2] unskilled about Death's realm,[1] unskilled about what is not Death's realm[2]—whoever think they should listen to these (recluses and brahmans) and put their faith in them, that will be for a long time for their woe and anguish.

Once upon a time, monks, a competent cowherd of Magadha in the last month of the rains at harvest time, having considered the hither bank of the river Ganges, having considered the further

---

[1] The triple stage of existence: *kāma, rūpa, arūpa, MA*. ii. 266.

[2] The nine transcendental things, *MA*. ii. 266.

bank, drove his cattle across to the further bank in Suvidehā at a place where there was a ford. First of all he drove across those bulls who were the sires and leaders of the herd—these, having cut across the stream of the Ganges, went safely beyond. Then he drove across the sturdy bullocks and young steers—these, also, having cut across the stream of the Ganges, went safely beyond. Then he drove across the half-grown bull-calves and heifers—these too, having cut across the stream of the Ganges, went safely beyond. Then he drove across the weaker calves—these too, having cut across the stream of the Ganges, went safely beyond. At that time there was a young new-born calf which, by following the lowing of its mother, also cut across the stream of the Ganges and went safely beyond. What was the cause of this ? It was, monks, that that cowherd of Magadha [**226**] in the last month of the rains at harvest time, having considered the hither bank of the river Ganges, having considered the further bank, drove his cattle across to the further bank in Suvidehā at a place where there was a ford. Even so, monks, any recluses or brahmans who are skilled about this world, skilled about the world beyond, skilled about Māra's realm, skilled about what is not Māra's realm, skilled about Death's realm, skilled about what is not Death's realm—whoever think they should listen to these (recluses and brahmans) and put their faith in them, that will be for a long time for their welfare and happiness.

Monks, like unto those bulls who were the sires and leaders of the herd, and who, having cut across the stream of the Ganges, went safely beyond, are those monks who are perfected ones, the cankers destroyed, who have lived the life, done what was to be done, laid down the burden, attained their own goal, the fetters of becoming being utterly destroyed, and who are freed by perfect profound knowledge. For these, having cut across Māra's stream,[1] have gone safely beyond.[2]

Monks, like unto those sturdy bullocks and young steers who, having cut across the stream of the Ganges, went safely beyond, are those monks who, by destroying the five fetters binding to this lower world, are of spontaneous uprising, and being ones who attain nibbāna there, are not liable to return from that world. For these also, having cut across Māra's stream, will go safely beyond.

---

[1] The stream of *taṇhā*, craving, *MA*. ii. 267.

[2] Beyond *saṃsāra* to nibbāna, *MA*. ii. 267.

Monks, like unto those half-grown bull-calves and heifers who, having cut across the stream of the Ganges, went safely beyond, are those monks who, by destroying the three fetters, by reducing attachment, aversion and confusion, are once-returners who, having come back again to this world once only, will make an end of anguish. For these also, having cut across Māra's stream, will go safely beyond.

Monks, like unto those weaker calves who, having cut across the stream of the Ganges, went safely beyond, are those monks who, by destroying the three fetters, are stream-attainers, not liable for the abyss, assured, bound for awakening. For these also, having cut across Māra's stream, will go safely beyond.

Monks, like unto that young new-born calf which, by following the lowing of its mother, also cut across the stream of the Ganges and went safely beyond, are those monks who are striving for *dhamma*, striving for faith. For these also, having cut across Māra's stream, will go safely beyond.

Now I, monks, [**227**] am skilled about this world, skilled about the world beyond, skilled about Māra's realm, skilled about what is not Māra's realm, skilled about Death's realm, skilled about what is not Death's realm. To those who think they should listen to me and place faith in me, there will be welfare and happiness for a long time."

Thus spoke the Lord; the Well-farer having said this, the Teacher then spoke thus:

"This world, the world beyond, are well explained by the one who knows,
And what is accessible by Māra and what is not accessible by Death.

By the Self-awakened One, comprehending, thoroughly knowing every world,
Opened is the door of the Undying[1] for reaching security—nibbāna.

Cut across is the stream of the Evil One, shattered, destroyed;
Let there be abundant rapture, monks, let security be reached."

Lesser Discourse on the Cowherd:
the Fourth

---

[1] The ariyan Way, *MA*. ii. 267.

35. LESSER DISCOURSE TO SACCAKA

(Cūḷasaccakasutta)

THUS have I heard. At one time the Lord was staying near Vesālī in the Great Grove in the hall of the Gabled House. Now at that time, staying at Vesālī was Saccaka, the son of Jains,[1] a controversialist, giving himself out as learned, much honoured by the manyfolk.[2] As he was going about Vesālī, he used to utter this speech: "I do not see that recluse or brahman, the head of a company, the head of a group, the teacher of a group,[3] even if he is claiming to be a perfected one, a fully Self-awakened one, who, when taken in hand by me, speech by speech, would not tremble, would not shake, would not shake violently, and from whose armpits sweat would not pour. Even if I were to take in hand, speech by speech, an insensate post, even that, when taken in hand by me, speech by speech, would tremble, would shake, would shake violently—let alone a human being."

Then the venerable Assaji,[4] having dressed in the morning, taking his bowl and robe, entered Vesālī for almsfood. Saccaka, the son of Jains, who was always pacing up and down, [**228**] always roaming about on foot,[5] saw the venerable Assaji coming in the distance; having seen him, he approached the venerable Assaji; having approached, he exchanged greetings with the venerable Assaji, and having exchanged greetings of courtesy and friendliness, he stood at a respectful distance. As he was standing at a respectful distance, Saccaka, the son of Jains, spoke thus to the venerable Assaji:

"How, good Assaji, does the recluse Gotama train disciples? And what are the divisions by which a great part of the recluse Gotama's instruction for disciples proceeds?"

"Thus, Aggivessana,[6] does the Lord train disciples, and by such

---

[1] On both sides, according to *MA*. ii. 268; but *M*. throughout this Sutta has *v.l.* Nigaṇṭhiputto, son of a Jain woman.

[2] As at *M*. i. 237.

[3] See *M*. i. 198.

[4] Sāriputta's teacher, *MA*. ii. 270; see *Vin*. i. 39 *f*.; one of the first five disciples.

[5] Stock, see *M*. i. 108, 237.

[6] Others addressed by this name (probably the name of a brahman clan, *DPPN*.) are Dīghanakha at *M*. i. 497, and the novice Aciravata at *M*. iii. 128.

divisions does a great part of the Lord's instruction for disciples proceed: 'Material shape, monks, is impermanent, feeling is impermanent, perception is impermanent, the habitual tendencies are impermanent, consciousness is impermanent. Material shape, monks, is not self, feeling is not self, perception is not self, the habitual tendencies are not self, consciousness is not self; all conditioned things[1] are impermanent, all things[2] are not self.' Thus, Aggivessana, does the Lord train disciples, and by such divisions does the great part of the Lord's instruction for disciples proceed."

"Indeed, we heard with disappointment,[3] good Assaji, those of us who heard that the recluse Gotama spoke like this. Perhaps we could meet the good Gotama somewhere, sometime, perhaps there might be some conversation, perhaps we could dissuade him from that pernicious view."

Now at that time at least five hundred Licchavis were gathered together in the conference hall on some business or other. Then Saccaka, the son of Jains, approached those Licchavis; having approached, he spoke thus to those Licchavis: "Let the good Licchavis come forward, let the good Licchavis come forward. Today there will be conversation between me and the recluse Gotama. If the recluse Gotama takes up his stand against me, as one of his well known disciples, the monk Assaji, has taken up his stand against me, even as[4] a powerful man, having taken hold of the fleece of a long-fleeced ram, might tug it towards him, might tug it backwards, might tug it forwards and backwards, even so will I, speech by speech, tug the recluse Gotama forwards, tug him backwards, tug him forwards and backwards. And even as a powerful distiller of spirituous liquor, having sunk his crate for spirituous liquor in a deep pool of water, taking it by a corner would tug it forwards, would tug it backwards, would tug it forwards and backwards, even so will I, speech by speech, tug the recluse Gotama forwards, tug him backwards, tug him forwards and backwards. And even as a powerful drunkard of abandoned life, [**229**] having taken hold of a hair-sieve at the corner, would shake it upwards, would shake it downwards, would toss it about,[5] even

---

[1] *sankhārā*, *cf. Dh.* 277.

[2] *dhammā*. These include, beside the *sankhārā* (conditioned things), the unconditioned nibbāna as well. *Sankhārā* are *anicca* and *dukkha*, but not nibbāna, so it is not a *sankhāra*. They are all, however, *anattā*.

[3] *dussutaṃ*.

[4] As at *M*. i. 374.

[5] As at *M*. i. 374; *S*. iii. 155; *A*. iii. 365. *S*. iii. 155 and *MA*. ii. 272 read correctly *nicchodeti*, see *PED*. and *JPTS*., 1917, p. 53.

so will I, speech by speech, shake the recluse Gotama upwards, shake him downwards, toss him about. And even as a full-grown elephant, sixty years old, having plunged into a deep tank, plays at the game called the 'merry washing,'[1] even so, methinks, will I play the game of 'merry washing' with the recluse Gotama. Let the good Licchavis come forward, let the good Licchavis come forward; today there will be conversation between me and the recluse Gotama."

Then some Licchavis spoke thus: "How can the recluse Gotama refute Saccaka, the son of Jains, when it is Saccaka, the son of Jains, who will refute the recluse Gotama?" Some Licchavis spoke thus: "How can he, being only[2] Saccaka, the son of Jains, refute the Lord when it is the Lord who will refute Saccaka, the son of Jains?" Then Saccaka, the son of Jains, surrounded by at least five hundred Licchavis, approached the Great Wood, and the hall of the Gabled House.

Now at that time several monks were pacing up and down in the open air. Then Saccaka, the son of Jains, approached these monks; having approached, he spoke thus to these monks: "Good sirs, where is this revered Gotama staying now? We are anxious to see the revered Gotama."

"Aggivessana, this Lord, having plunged into the Great Wood, is sitting down for the day-sojourn at the root of a tree." Then Saccaka, the son of Jains, together with a great company of Licchavis, having plunged into the Great Wood, approached the Lord; having approached, he exchanged greetings with the Lord; having exchanged greetings of friendliness and courtesy, he sat down at a respectful distance. And these Licchavis too—some having greeted the Lord, sat down at a respectful distance; some

---

[1] *saṇadhovika*, *v.l.* *sāṇadhovika*, literally hempen (or canvas) washing. *MA*. ii. 272 says "men play this game, which is great sport, by tying up handfuls of *saṇavāka* and sinking it in the water. Then they go there and taking a handful of the *saṇa* and saying, 'Right, left, front,' they give blows to planks, *phalaka*, in these directions, and then they wash, enjoying, drinking and eating sour gruel and strong drink and so on, which they have taken with them. The elephant king saw this game, and plunging into deep water, took up water with his trunk and sprinkled it on his body, his back, on both sides and between his thighs." Chalmers' "merry washing" gets the meaning well. See *DA*. 84 where *sāṇadhovana* is referred to as a game of the *caṇḍālas*, low class people.

[2] *bhavamāno*. *MA*. ii. 272: the meaning is that it is not possible for an ordinary human being to refute the Lord.

exchanged greetings with the Lord, and having exchanged greetings of friendliness and courtesy, they sat down at a respectful distance; some, having saluted the Lord with outstretched palms, sat down at a respectful distance; some, having made known their names and clans in the Lord's presence, sat down at a respectful distance; some, having become silent, sat down at a respectful distance. As he was sitting down at a respectful distance, Saccaka, the son of Jains, spoke thus to the Lord:

"I would ask the revered Gotama about a point if the revered Gotama grants me permission[1] to ask a question."[2]

"Ask, Aggivessana, [**230**] whatever you like."

"How does the good Gotama train disciples? And what are the divisions by which a great part of the good Gotama's instructions for disciples proceeds?"

"Thus do I, Aggivessana, train disciples, and by such divisions does the great part of my instruction for disciples proceed: Material shape, monks, is impermanent, feeling is impermanent, perception is impermanent, the habitual tendencies are impermanent, consciousness is impermanent. Material shape, monks, is not self, feeling is not self, perception is not self, the habitual tendencies are not self, consciousness is not self; all conditioned things are impermanent, all things are not self. Thus, Aggivessana, do I train disciples, and by such divisions does the great part of my instruction for disciples proceed."

"A simile occurs to me, good Gotama."

"Speak it forth, Aggivessana," the Lord said.

"Good Gotama, as[3] all seed growths and vegetable growths come to growth, increase and maturity because all depend on the earth and are based on the earth, and it is thus that these seed growths and vegetable growths come to growth, increase and maturity; as, good Gotama, all those strenuous occupations that are carried on depend on the earth and are based on the earth, and it is thus that these strenuous occupations are carried on; so, good Gotama, that person[4] whose self is material shape,[5] because it is based on material shape, begets either merit or demerit, this person whose self is feeling, because it is based on feeling, begets either merit or demerit, this person whose self is perception, because it is based

---

[1] *okāsaṃ karoti, cf. Vin.* i. 114. [2] As at *M.* iii. 15; *D.* i. 51; *A.* v. 39.

[3] As at *Miln.* 33. [4] *purisapuggala.* See *B.D.* iii, Intr., p. xxv *ff.*

[5] This is of course the very opposite of Gotama's teaching. *MA.* ii. 275 says *rūpaṃ attā assâ ti rūpattā.*

on perception, begets either merit or demerit, this person whose self is the habitual tendencies, because it is based on the habitual tendencies, begets either merit or demerit, this person whose self is consciousness, because it is based on consciousness, begets either merit or demerit."

"Can it be, Aggivessana, that you speak thus: Material shape is my self, feeling is my self, perception is my self, the habitual tendencies are my self, consciousness is my self"?

"But I, good Gotama, do speak thus: Material shape is my self, feeling . . . perception . . . the habitual tendencies . . . consciousness is my self. And so does this great concourse."

"What has this great concourse to do with you, Aggivessana? Please do you, Aggivessana, unravel just your own words."

"But I, good Gotama, speak thus: Material shape is my self, feeling is my self, perception is my self, the habitual tendencies are my self, consciousness is my self."

"Well then, Aggivessana, I will question you in return about this matter. You may answer me as you please. What do you think about this, [**231**] Aggivessana? Would a noble anointed king, such as King Pasenadi of Kosala or such as King Ajātasattu of Magadha, the son of the lady of Videhā, have power in his own territory to put to death one deserving to be put to death, to plunder one deserving to be plundered, to banish one deserving to be banished?"

"Good Gotama, a noble anointed king, such as King Pasenadi of Kosala or such as King Ajātasattu of Magadha, the son of the lady of Videhā, would have power in his own territory to put to death one deserving to be put to death, to plunder one deserving to be plundered, to banish one deserving to be banished. Why, good Gotama, even among these companies and groups, namely of the Vajjis and Mallas, there exists the power in their own territories to put to death one deserving to be put to death, to plunder one deserving to be plundered, to banish one deserving to be banished. How much more then a noble anointed king, such as King Pasenadi of Kosala or King Ajātasattu of Magadha, the son of the lady of Videhā? He would have the power, good Gotama, and he deserves to have the power."

"What do you think about this, Aggivessana? When you speak thus: 'Material shape is my self,' have you power over this material shape of yours (and can say), Let my material shape be thus, Let my material shape be not thus?"[1]

[1] *Cf. Vin.* i. 13.

When this had been said, Saccaka, the son of Jains, became silent. And a second time the Lord spoke thus to Saccaka, the son of Jains: " What do you think about this, Aggivessana ? When you speak thus: ' Material shape is my self,' have you power over this material shape of yours (and can say), Let my material shape be thus, let my material shape be not thus ?" And a second time Saccaka, the son of Jains, became silent. Then the Lord spoke thus to Saccaka, the son of Jains:

" Answer now, Aggivessana, now is not the time for you to become silent. Whoever, Aggivessana, on being asked a legitimate question up to the third time by the Tathāgata does not answer, verily his skull splits into seven pieces."[1]

Now at that time the *yakkha* Thunderbolt-bearer,[2] taking his iron thunderbolt which was aglow, ablaze, on fire, came to stand above the ground over Saccaka, the son of Jains, and said: " If this Saccaka, the son of Jains, does not answer when he is asked a legitimate question up to the third time by the Lord, verily I will make his skull split into seven pieces." And only the Lord saw this *yakkha* Thunderbolt-bearer, and Saccaka, the son of Jains. Then Saccaka, the son of Jains, afraid, agitated, his hair standing on end, [**232**] seeking protection with the Lord, seeking shelter with the Lord, seeking refuge with the Lord, spoke thus to the Lord: " Let the revered Gotama ask me, I will answer."

" What do you think about this, Aggivessana ? When you speak thus: ' Material shape is my self,' have you power over this material shape of yours (and can say), ' Let my material shape be thus, let my material shape be not thus ' ?"

" This is not so, good Gotama."

" Pay attention, Aggivessana. When you have paid attention, Aggivessana, answer. For your last speech does not agree with your first, nor your first with your last. What do you think about this, Aggivessana ? When you speak thus: ' Feeling . . . perception . . . the habitual tendencies . . . consciousness is my self,' have you

---

[1] As at *D.* i. 95.

[2] *Sakka devarājā,* not just any *yakkha, MA.* ii. 277. Sakka was a name for Indra, one of whose epithets was Vajirapāṇi, Thunderbolt in hand (Thunderbolt-bearer). According to C. E. Godage, *The Place of Indra in Early Buddhism, Ceylon University Review,* April, 1945, Vol. III, No. 1, p. 52, the above context and *D.* i. 95 " are the only instances in the Suttas in which Sakka comes in the guise of a Yakkha bearing a bolt." " Here, we see Sakka as a patron of the new religion." *Cf. Jā.* iii. 146, v. 92, vi. 155.

power over this feeling . . . perception . . . the habitual tendencies . . . consciousness of yours (and can say): ‘ Let my consciousness be such, let my consciousness not be such ’ ?”

“ This is not so, good Gotama.”

“ Pay attention, Aggivessana. When you have paid attention, Aggivessana, answer. For your last speech does not agree with your first, nor your first with your last. What do you think about this, Aggivessana ? Is material shape permanent or impermanent ?”

“ Impermanent, good Gotama.”

“ But is what is impermanent anguish or is it happiness ?”

“ Anguish, good Gotama.”

“ But is it fitting to regard that which is impermanent, anguish, liable to change as ‘ This is mine, this am I, [**233**] this is my self ’ ?”

“ This is not so, good Gotama.”

“ What do you think about this, Aggivessana ? . . . Is feeling . . . is perception . . . are the habitual tendencies permanent or impermanent ? . . . What do you think about this, Aggivessana ? Is consciousness permanent or impermanent ?”

“ Impermanent, good Gotama.”

“ But is what is impermanent anguish or is it happiness ?”

“ Anguish, good Gotama.”

“ But is it fitting to regard that which is impermanent, anguish, liable to change as ‘ This is mine, this am I, this is my self ’ ?”

“ This is not so, good Gotama.”

“ What do you think about this, Aggivessana ? Does he who is cleaving to anguish, attached to anguish, clinging to anguish regard anguish as ‘ This is mine, this am I, this is my self ’—and further, could he comprehend his own anguish or could he dwell having brought anguish to destruction ?”

“ How could this be, good Gotama ? This is not so, good Gotama.”

“ Aggivessana, as a man walking about aiming at the pith, seeking for the pith, looking about for the pith,[1] taking a sharp knife, might enter a wood; he might see there the stem of a great plantain tree,[2] straight, young, grown without defect; he might cut it down at the root; having cut it down at the root, he might cut off the crown; having cut off the crown, he might unroll the spirals of the leaves; but unrolling the spirals of the leaves, he would not even

---

[1] As at *S.* iii. 141, iv, 167; *cf. M.* i. 193.

[2] The plantain tree was the emblem of insubstantiality, for it has no pith or heartwood, see *S.* iii. 142.

come upon softwood, how then on pith? Even so are you, Aggivessana, when being questioned, cross-questioned and pressed for reasons[1] by me in regard to your own words, empty,[2] void, and have fallen short.[3] But these words were spoken by you, Aggivessana, to the company at Vesālī: 'I do not see that recluse or brahman, the head of a company, the head of a group, the teacher of a group, even if he is claiming to be a perfected one, a fully Self-awakened one, who, when taken in hand by me, speech by speech, would not tremble, would not shake, would not shake violently, and from whose armpits sweat would not pour. Even if I were to take in hand, speech by speech, an insensate post, even that, when taken in hand by me, speech by speech, would tremble, would shake, would shake violently—let alone a human being.' But it is from *your* brow, Aggivessana, that drops of sweat are pouring, and having soaked through your upper and inner robes, are falling to the ground. But there is not at present, Aggivessana, any sweat on *my* body." And the Lord disclosed his golden coloured body to that concourse. [**234**] When this had been said, Saccaka, the son of Jains, having become silent, having become ashamed, his shoulders drooped, his head cast down, sat down brooding, at a loss for an answer.

Then Dummukha,[4] the son of a Licchavi, knowing that Saccaka, the son of Jains, had become silent, had become ashamed, his shoulders drooped, his head cast down, brooding, at a loss for an answer, spoke thus to the Lord: "A simile occurs to me, Lord."[5]

"Speak it forth, Dummukha," the Lord said.

"Lord, it is like a lotus-tank,[6] not far from a village or little town, where there might be a crab. Then, Lord, several boys or girls, having come out from that village or little town, might approach that lotus-tank, and having approached, having plunged into that lotus-tank, having lifted the crab out of the water, might place it on the dry land. And whenever that crab, Lord, might thrust out a claw, as often might those boys or girls hack and break and smash it with a piece of wood or a potsherd. Thus, Lord, that crab with all its claws hacked and broken and smashed, could not become one to descend again to the tank as it used to do before. Even so, Lord, whatever the distortions, the disagreements, the

---

[1] As at *M*. i. 130. [2] *MA*. ii. 279, devoid of pith.

[3] *aparaddha*=*parājita*, defeated, *MA*. ii. 279. As at *M*. i. 440.

[4] *MA*. ii. 280, in spite of his name he was handsome.

[5] *bhagavā* of text should read *bhante*. [6] As at *S*. i. 123.

wrigglings[1] of Saccaka, the son of Jains—all these[2] have been hacked, broken and smashed by the Lord. And now, Lord, Saccaka, the son of Jains, cannot become one to approach the Lord again, that is to say desiring speech."[3]

When this had been said, Saccaka, the son of Jains, spoke thus to Dummukha, the son of a Licchavi: " You, Dummukha, wait, you, Dummukha, wait. Not with you am I conferring, I am conferring here with the good Gotama.

Let be, good Gotama, these words of mine and of other individual recluses and brahmans. Methinks this idle talk is regretted.[4] Now, to what extent does a disciple of the good Gotama come to be one who is a doer of the instruction, one who accepts the exhortation,[5] one who has crossed over doubt and, perplexity gone, fares in the Teacher's instruction, won to conviction, not relying on others ?"

" Now, Aggivessana, a disciple of mine in regard to whatever is material shape, past, future, present, subjective or objective, gross or subtle, low or excellent, distant or near, sees all material shape as it really is by means of perfect intuitive wisdom as: This is not mine, this am I not, this is not my self. **[235]** In regard to whatever is feeling . . . perception . . . the habitual tendencies . . . consciousness, past, future, present, subjective or objective, gross or subtle, low or excellent, distant or near, he sees all consciousness as it really is by means of perfect intuitive wisdom as: This is not mine, this am I not, this is not my self. To this extent, Aggivessana, a disciple of mine comes to be a doer of the instruction, an accepter of the exhortation, one who has crossed over doubt and, perplexity gone, fares in the Teacher's instruction, won to conviction, not relying on others."

" To what extent, good Gotama, does a monk become a perfected one, the cankers destroyed, one who has lived the life, done what was to be done, laid down the burden, attained his own goal, the fetter of becoming utterly destroyed, and is freed with perfect profound knowledge ?"

" Now, Aggivessana, a monk in regard to whatever is material shape, past, future, present, subjective or objective, gross or subtle,

---

1 These same three words are used at *M.* i. 446 of a horse being broken in, and are therefore differently translated.

2 *tāni. S.* i. 123 reads *sabbāni*, all. *M.* should be corrected to *sabbāni tāni.*

3 *vādâdhippāya*, a controversialist, *Fur. Dial.* i. 167.

4 *vilāpaṃ vilapitaṃ*, or " idly talked."

5 *ovādapatikara*, as at *M.* i. 491.

low or excellent, distant or near, having seen all material shape as it really is by means of perfect intuitive wisdom as: This is not mine, this am I not, this is not my self, becomes freed with no (further) attachment.[1] In regard to whatever is feeling . . . perception . . . the habitual tendencies . . . consciousness, past, future, present, subjective or objective, gross or subtle, low or excellent, distant or near, having seen all consciousness as it really is by means of perfect intuitive wisdom as: This is not mine, this am I not, this is not my self, he becomes freed with no (further) attachment. To this extent, Aggivessana, does a monk become a perfected one, the cankers destroyed, who has lived the life, done what was to be done, laid down the burden, attained his own goal, the fetter of becoming utterly destroyed, and is freed with perfect profound knowledge. Aggivessana, a monk with his mind freed thus becomes possessed of the three things than which there is nothing further:[2] the vision than which there is nothing further, the course than which there is nothing further, the freedom than which there is nothing further.[3] Aggivessana, a monk freed thus reveres, esteems, reverences, honours only the Tathāgata, saying: 'The Lord is awakened, he teaches *dhamma* for awakening; the Lord is tamed, he teaches *dhamma* for taming; the Lord is calmed, he teaches *dhamma* for calming; the Lord is crossed over, he teaches *dhamma* for crossing over; the Lord has attained nibbāna, he teaches *dhamma* for attaining nibbāna."[4]

When this had been said, Saccaka, the son of Jains, spoke thus to the Lord: **[236]** " Good Gotama, I was arrogant, I was presumptuous, in that I deemed I could assail the revered Gotama, speech by speech. Good Gotama, there might be safety for a man assailing a rutting elephant, but there could be no safety for a man assailing the revered Gotama. Good Gotama, there might be safety for a

---

[1] Here spelt *anuppādā*.

[2] *anuttariyāni*. *Cf. D.* iii. 219. At *D.* iii. 250, 281, *A.* iii. 284, 325, 452 the " six " are different except for the first.

[3] *MA.* ii. 281 explains that these are the wisdom, the course and freedom that are worldly or other-worldly. Or, the first is called right view of the way of arahantship, the second the factors of the remaining ways, and the third the freedom that is the highest fruit. Or, again, the first is called the vision of nibbāna for one whose cankers are destroyed, the second the eight factors of the Way, and the third the highest fruit. *DA.* iii. 1003 " refers these to categories of the Path, Fruits and Nibbāna, with alternative assignments," *Dial.* iii. 213, *n.* 4.

[4] As at *D.* iii. 54. Quoted *MA.* ii. 134.

man assailing a blazing mass of fire, but there could be no safety for a man assailing the revered Gotama. Good Gotama, there might be safety for a man assailing a deadly poisonous snake, but there could be no safety for a man assailing the revered Gotama. Good Gotama, I was arrogant, I was presumptuous, in that I deemed I could assail the revered Gotama, speech by speech. May the good Gotama consent (to accept) a meal with me on the morrow together with the Order of monks." The Lord consented by becoming silent.

Then Saccaka, the son of Jains, having understood the Lord's consent, addressed those Licchavis, saying: " Let the good Licchavis listen to me: the recluse Gotama is invited for a meal on the morrow together with the Order of monks. Prepare anything of mine that you think will be suitable." Then these Licchavis, towards the end of that night, prepared five hundred offerings of rice cooked in milk as the gift of food.[1] Then Saccaka, the son of Jains, having had sumptuous food, solid and soft, made ready in his own park, had the time announced to the Lord, saying: " It is time, good Gotama, the meal is ready." Then the Lord, having dressed in the morning, taking his bowl and robe, approached the park of Saccaka, the son of Jains; having approached he sat down on the appointed seat, together with the Order of monks. Then Saccaka, the son of Jains, with his own hand served and satisfied the Order of monks with the Lord at its head with the sumptuous food, solid and soft. Then Saccaka, the son of Jains, when the Lord had eaten and had withdrawn his hand from his bowl, having taken a low seat,[2] sat down at a respectful distance. As he was sitting down at a respectful distance, Saccaka, the son of Jains, spoke thus to the Lord:

" Whatever there is of merit or the accompaniment of merit[3] in this gift, good Gotama, let that be for the happiness of the donors."[4]

" There will be for the donors, Aggivessana, whatever attaches to the recipient of a gift of faith such as you who are not without

---

[1] *I.e.* food that might be given and so made " allowable," *kappiya*. The Licchavis had to know what was allowable and what not, and so they brought forward rice, *bhatta*, that could be brought forward, *MA*. ii. 283. The word *bhattâbhihāra* occurs at *S*. i. 82.

[2] A mark of respect.

[3] *puññamahī*. *MA*. ii. 283 *vipākakkhandhānaṃ yeva parivāro*, what makes up the accumulations of fruitions (in the future).

[4] Here the Licchavis.

attachment, not without aversion, not without confusion. [**237**] There will be for you, Aggivessana, whatever attaches to the recipient of a gift of faith such as me who am without attachment, without aversion, without confusion."[1]

Lesser Discourse to Saccaka:
the Fifth

36. GREATER DISCOURSE TO SACCAKA

(Mahāsaccakasutta)

THUS have I heard: At one time the Lord was staying near Vesālī in the Great Grove in the hall of the Gabled House. Now at that time the Lord came to be fully clothed[2] in the morning and, taking his bowl and robe, wished to enter Vesālī for almsfood. Then Saccaka, the son of Jains, who was always pacing up and down, always roaming about on foot,[3] approached the Great Grove and the hall of the Gabled House. The venerable Ānanda saw Saccaka, the son of Jains, coming in the distance; having seen him, he spoke thus to the Lord: " Lord, this Saccaka, the son of Jains, is coming, a controversialist, giving himself out as learned, much honoured by the manyfolk.[4] He, Lord, desires dispraise of the Awakened One, dispraise of *dhamma*, dispraise of the Order. It were good, Lord, if the Lord were to sit down for a moment out of compassion."[5] The Lord sat down on an appointed seat. Then Saccaka, the son of Jains, approached the Lord; having approached, he exchanged greetings with the Lord; having exchanged greetings of friendliness and courtesy, he sat down at a respectful distance. As he was sitting down at a respectful distance, Saccaka, the son of Jains, spoke thus to the Lord:

---

[1] *MA*. ii. 283 points out that the Licchavis gave to Saccaka, not to the Lord, but that Saccaka gave to the Lord.

[2] *I.e.* he had clothed himself in a dyed double-cloth, *rattadupaṭṭa*, (*cf. Jā*. iv. 379, *VvA*. 4), had fastened on his girdle, and had put his rag-robe over one shoulder, *MA*. ii. 284. It remained to take his outer cloak to put on when he entered Vesālī.

[3] Stock, as at *M*. i. 108, 227-28. [4] As at *M*. i. 227.

[5] For Saccaka, for he would see the Lord and hear *dhamma*, *MA*. ii. 284.

"There are, good Gotama, some recluses and brahmans, who dwell intent on the development of body,[1] not on the development of mind.[2] They acquire, good Gotama, a feeling of physical pain. If once upon a time, good Gotama, there had been acquired a feeling of physical pain, there may be paralysis of the legs, and the heart may burst, and warm blood may issue from the mouth, or one may come to madness, to mind-tossing.[3] This comes to be for one, good Gotama, when the mind conforms to the body, when it is under the rule of body. What is the cause of this? **[238]** It is the non-development of the mind.

But there are, good Gotama, some recluses and brahmans who live intent on the development of mind, not on the development of body. They acquire, good Gotama, a feeling of mental pain. If once upon a time, good Gotama, there had been acquired a feeling of mental pain, there may be a paralysis of the legs, and the heart may burst, and warm blood may issue from the mouth, or one may come to madness, to mind-tossing. This comes to be for one, good Gotama, whose body conforms to mind, is under the rule of mind. What is the cause of this? It is the non-development of body."

"But what have you, Aggivessana, heard about the development of body?"

"For example, Nanda Vaccha, Kisa Saṅkicca, Makkhali of the Cowpen[4]—these, good Gotama, are unclothed,[5] flouting life's decencies, licking (their hands after meals), not those to come when asked to do so, not those to stand still when asked to do so. They do not consent (to accept food) offered to (them) or specially prepared for (them), nor to (accept) an invitation (to a meal). They do not accept food straight from the cooking pot or pan, nor within the threshold, nor among the faggots, nor among the rice-

---

[1] *bhāvanā*, "development," more precisely mental development. *MA*. ii. 285 says *kāyabhāvanā* is called *vipassanā*, insight. Achieving this there is no mental disturbance.

[2] *cittabhāvanā* is called *samatha*, calm. There is no paralysis for the person intent on concentration. What the Jain says is not true; see *MA*. ii. 285.

[3] *Cf*. *S*. i. 125-6, and last phrase at *A*. iii. 119, 219; and "mind-tossing," *cittakkhepa*, at *Dh*. 138.

[4] These three "shining lights," *niyyātāro*, are mentioned at *M*. i. 524; *A*. iii. 384. All were *ājīvikas*, and are said at *MA*. ii. 285 to have achieved leadership over the extreme ascetics.

[5] Following passage also at *M*. i. 77.

pounders, nor when two people are eating, nor from a pregnant woman, nor from a woman giving suck, nor from one co-habiting with a man, nor from gleanings, nor near where a dog is standing, nor where flies are swarming, nor fish, nor meat. They drink neither fermented liquor nor spirits nor rice-gruel. They are one-house-men, one-piece-men, or two-house-men, two-piece-men, or seven-house-men, seven-piece-men. They subsist on one little offering, and they subsist on two little offerings, and they subsist on seven little offerings. They take food once a day, and they take food once in two days and they take food once in seven days. Then they live intent on the practice of eating rice at regular fortnightly intervals."

"But do they, Aggivessana, keep going on so little?"

"No, good Gotama. Now and then they eat very good solid food, partake of very good soft food, savour very good savourings, drink very good drinks. They build up their bodily strength with these, make their bodies grow and become fat."

"These, Aggivessana, attend later to what they had eschewed earlier; thus there is increase and loss for that body.[1] But what have you, Aggivessana, heard about the development of mind?" **[239]** But, Saccaka, the son of Jains, on being questioned by the Lord on the development of mind, did not succeed (in replying). Then the Lord spoke thus to Saccaka, the son of Jains:

"That which was first spoken of by you, Aggivessana, as the development of the body, that, in the discipline for an ariyan, is not the proper development of the body. For you, Aggivessana, do not know what is development of the body, so how can you know what is development of the mind? Yet, Aggivessana, hear how there comes to be one who is not developed as to body and not developed as to mind, developed as to body and developed as to mind; pay careful attention and I will speak."

"Yes, sir," Saccaka, the son of Jains, answered the Lord in assent. The Lord spoke thus:

"And how, Aggivessana, does one come to be not developed as to body and not developed as to mind? As to this, Aggivessana, a pleasurable feeling arises in an uninstructed ordinary man; he, being assailed by the pleasurable feeling, becomes addicted to pleasure and falls into addiction for pleasure. If that pleasurable feeling of his is stopped, a painful feeling arises from the stopping

---

[1] *Cf. S.* ii. 94.

of the pleasurable feeling; he, being assailed by the painful feeling, grieves, mourns, laments, beats his breast and falls into disillusion. This pleasurable feeling, Aggivessana, that has arisen in him, impinging on the mind, persists, because of the non-development of body; and the painful feeling that has arisen, impinging on the mind, persists, because of the non-development of mind. In anyone in whom, Aggivessana, there are these two alternatives thus: a pleasurable feeling that has arisen, impinging on the mind, persists, because of the non-development of body; and a painful feeling that has arisen, impinging on the mind, persists, because of the non-development of mind—he thus comes to be, Aggivessana, not developed as to body and not developed as to mind.

And how does there come to be, Aggivessana, one who is both developed as to body and developed as to mind? As to this, Aggivessana, a pleasurable feeling arises in an instructed disciple of the ariyans; he, being assailed by the pleasurable feeling, does not become addicted to pleasure nor does he fall into addiction to pleasure. If that pleasurable feeling of his is stopped and a painful feeling arises from the stopping of that pleasurable feeling, he, being assailed by the painful feeling, does not grieve, mourn, lament, he does not beat his breast, he does not fall into disillusion. This pleasurable feeling, Aggivessana, that has arisen in him, impinging on his mind, does not persist, because of the development of the body; and the painful feeling that has arisen, impinging on the mind, does not persist, because of the development of mind. In anyone in whom, Aggivessana, there are these two alternatives thus: a pleasurable feeling that has arisen, **[240]** impinging on the mind, does not persist, because of the development of body; and a painful feeling that has arisen, impinging on the mind, does not persist, because of the development of mind—he thus comes to be, Aggivessana, both developed as to body and developed as to mind."

"A believer thus am I in the revered Gotama. For the revered Gotama is both developed as to body and developed as to mind."

"This speech spoken by you, Aggivessana, is offensive and presumptuous, but yet will I answer you. When I, Aggivessana, had had the hair of my head and beard shaved, and had clothed myself in saffron garments and had gone forth from home into homelessness—that a pleasurable feeling arisen in me, impinging on my mind, could persist, or that a painful feeling arisen, impinging on my mind, could persist, such a situation could not occur."

"Is it then that a pleasurable feeling has not arisen in the good Gotama of such a nature that, having arisen, impinging on the mind, it could not persist? Is it then that a painful feeling has not arisen in the good Gotama of such a nature that, having arisen, impinging on the mind, it could not persist?"

"How could this not be, Aggivessana? Now, Aggivessana, before my Self-awakening while I was still the *bodhisatta*, not fully awakened, it occurred to me: Narrow is the household life, a path of dust, going forth is in the open, nor is it easy while dwelling in a house to lead the Brahma-faring completely fulfilled, utterly purified, polished like a conch-shell. Suppose now that I, having cut off hair and beard, having clothed myself in saffron garments, should go forth from home into homelessness? So I, Aggivessana, after a time, being young, my hair coal-black, possessed of radiant youth, in the prime of my life . . . (*repeat from M*.i. **163**. *l*. **28** *to p*. **167** *l*. **8**; *above, p*. **207** *to p*. **211**; *for monks substitute* Aggivessana) . . . So I, Aggivessana, sat down just there thinking: Indeed this does well for striving.

Moreover,[1] Aggivessana, three similes occurred to me spontaneously, never heard before: It is as if[2] there were a wet sappy stick placed in water; then a man might come along bringing an upper piece of fire-stick,[3] and thinking: 'I will light a fire, I will get heat.' What do you think about this, Aggivessana? Could that man, bringing an upper piece of fire-stick, and rubbing that wet sappy stick that had been placed in water (with it), light a fire, could he get heat?"

"No, good Gotama. What is the cause of this? It is, good Gotama, that such a stick is wet and sappy and that [**241**] it was placed in water. That man would only get fatigue and distress."

"In like manner, Aggivessana, whatever recluses or brahmans dwell not aloof from pleasures of the senses that are bodily, then if that which is for them, among the sense-pleasures, desire for sense-pleasure, affection for sense-pleasure, infatuation with sense-pleasure, thirst for sense-pleasure, fever for sense-pleasure —if that is not properly got rid of subjectively nor properly allayed, whether these worthy recluses and brahmans experience

---

[1] From here to *M*. i. 249=*M*. ii. 212 *ff*. *Cf*. *Mhvu*. ii. 121*ff*.

[2] As at *M*. iii. 95.

[3] *uttarāraṇī*, opposite *adharāraṇī*, *MA*. ii. 91, *SA*. iii. 241. The former word occurs at *M*. ii. 93 (a repetition of the above passage), *M*. ii. 152, iii. 95; *Miln*. 53.

feelings which are acute, painful, sharp, severe, they could not become those for knowledge, for vision, for the incomparable Self-awakening[1]; and whether these worthy recluses and brahmans do not experience feelings which are acute, painful, sharp, severe, they could not become those for knowledge, for vision, for the incomparable Self-awakening. This, Aggivessana, was the first parable that occurred to me spontaneously, never heard before.

Then, Aggivessana, a second parable occurred to me spontaneously, never heard before. It is as if, Aggivessana, a wet, sappy stick were placed on dry ground, far from water. Then a man might come along bringing an upper piece of fire-stick, and thinking: 'I will light a fire, I will get heat.' What do you think about this, Aggivessana? Could that man, bringing an upper piece of fire-stick, and rubbing that wet sappy stick that had been placed on the dry ground, far from water, light a fire, could he get heat?"

"No, good Gotama. What is the cause of this? It is, good Gotama, that that stick is wet and sappy although it had been placed on dry ground, far from water. So that man would only get fatigue and distress."

"In like manner, Aggivessana, whatever recluses or brahmans dwell not aloof from pleasures of the senses that are bodily . . . they could not become those for knowledge, for vision, for the incomparable Self-awakening. This, Aggivessana, was the second parable that occurred to me spontaneously, never heard before.

Then, Aggivessana, a third parable occurred to me [**242**] spontaneously, never heard before. It is as if, Aggivessana, a dry sapless[2] stick were placed on the dry ground, far from water. Then a man might come along bringing an upper piece of fire-stick, and thinking: 'I will light a fire, I will get heat.' What do you think about this, Aggivessana? Could that man, bringing an upper piece of fire-stick, and rubbing that dry sapless stick that had been placed on dry ground, far from water, light a fire, could he get heat?"

"Yes, good Gotama. What is the cause of this? It is, good Gotama, that that stick was dry and sapless and had been placed on dry ground far from water."

"In like manner, Aggivessana, whatever recluses or brahmans dwell aloof from pleasures of the senses that are bodily, then if that which is for them, among the sense-pleasures, desire for sense-pleasure, affection for sense-pleasure, infatuation with sense-

---

[1] As at *A*. ii. 200.

[2] *Cf*. *M*. iii. 95; *S*. iv. 161.

pleasure, thirst for sense-pleasure, fever for sense-pleasure—if this is well got rid of subjectively, well allayed, then whether these worthy recluses and brahmans experience feelings that are acute, painful, sharp, severe, indeed they become those for knowledge, for vision, for the incomparable Self-awakening; and whether these worthy recluses and brahmans do not experience feelings that are acute, painful, sharp, severe, indeed they become those for knowledge, for vision, for the incomparable Self-awakening. This, Aggivessana, was the third parable that occurred to me spontaneously, never heard before. These, Aggivessana, were the three parables that occurred to me spontaneously, never heard before.

It occurred to me, Aggivessana: Suppose now that I, with my teeth clenched,[1] with my tongue pressed against the palate, by mind should subdue, restrain and dominate my mind? So I, Aggivessana, with my teeth clenched, with my tongue pressed against the palate, by mind subdued, restrained and dominated my mind. While I was subduing, restraining and dominating my mind, with the teeth clenched, the tongue pressed against the palate, sweat poured from my armpits. It is as if, Aggivessana, a strong man, having taken hold of a weaker man by his head or shoulders, would subdue, restrain and dominate him. Even so, while I, Aggivessana, was subduing, restraining and dominating my mind by mind, with my teeth clenched, with my tongue pressed against the palate, sweat poured from my armpits. Although, Aggivessana, unsluggish energy came to be stirred up in me, unmuddled mindfulness set up, yet my [**243**] body was turbulent, not calmed, because I was harassed[2] in striving by striving against that very pain. But yet, Aggivessana, that painful feeling, arising in me, persisted without impinging on my mind.

It occurred to me, Aggivessana: Suppose now that I should meditate the non-breathing meditation?[3] So I, Aggivessana, stopped breathing in and breathing out through the mouth and through the nose. When I, Aggivessana, had stopped breathing in and breathing out through the mouth and through the nose, there came to be an exceedingly loud noise of winds escaping by the auditory passages. As there comes to be an exceedingly loud noise from the roaring of a smith's bellows,[4] even so when I, Aggivessana, stopped breathing in and breathing out through the mouth

---

[1] *M.* i. 120; *Jā.* i. 67.
[2] *padhānâbhitunnassa.*
[3] *appānaka jhāna*; *cf. M.* ii. 212; *Jā.* i. 67.
[4] *S.* i. 106.

and through the nose, there came to be an exceedingly loud noise of wind escaping by the auditory passages. Although, Aggivessana, unsluggish energy came to be stirred up in me, unmuddled mindfulness set up, yet my body was turbulent, not calmed, because I was harassed in striving by striving against that very pain. It was even in this wise, Aggivessana, that a painful feeling that had arisen in me persisted without impinging on my mind.

It occurred to me, Aggivessana: Suppose now that I should still meditate the non-breathing meditation? So I, Aggivessana, stopped breathing in and breathing out through the mouth and through the nose and through the ears. When I, Aggivessana, had stopped breathing in and breathing out through the mouth and through the nose and through the ears, exceedingly loud winds rent my head. As, Aggivessana, a strong man[1] might cleave one's head with a sharp-edged sword, even so when I, Aggivessana, stopped breathing in and breathing out through the mouth and through the nose and through the ears, exceedingly loud winds rent my head. Although, Aggivessana, unsluggish energy came to be stirred up in me, unmuddled mindfulness set up, yet my body was turbulent, not calmed, because I was harassed in striving by striving against that very pain. But yet, Aggivessana, that painful feeling, arising in me, persisted without impinging on my mind.

It occurred to me, Aggivessana: Suppose that I should still meditate the non-breathing meditation? So I, Aggivessana, stopped breathing in and breathing out through the mouth and through the nose and through the ears. When I, Aggivessana, had stopped breathing in and breathing out through the mouth and through the nose and through the ears, I came to have very bad headaches.[2] As, Aggivessana, a strong man [**244**] might clamp a turban on one's head with a tight leather strap, even so when I, Aggivessana, stopped breathing in and breathing out through the mouth and through the nose and through the ears, did I come to have very bad headaches. Although, Aggivessana, unsluggish energy came to be stirred up in me, unmuddled mindfulness set up, yet my body was turbulent, not calmed, because I was harassed in striving by striving against that very pain. But yet, Aggivessana, that painful feeling, arising in me, persisted without impinging on my mind.

---

[1] This and the following similes at *M*. ii. 193, iii. 259; *A*. iii. 380; *S*. iv. 56.

[2] *sīse sīsavedanā honti*, there were head-feelings in the head.

It occurred to me, Aggivessana: Suppose now that I should still meditate the non-breathing meditation? So I, Aggivessana, stopped breathing in and breathing out through the mouth and through the nose and through the ears. When I, Aggivessana, had stopped breathing in and breathing out through the mouth and through the nose and through the ears, very strong winds cut through my stomach. As, Aggivessana, a skilled cattle-butcher or his apprentice might cut through the stomach with a sharp butcher's knife, even so, Aggivessana, did very strong winds cut through my stomach. Although, Aggivessana, unsluggish energy came to be stirred up in me, unmuddled mindfulness set up, yet my body was turbulent, not calmed, because I was harassed in striving by striving against that very pain. But yet, Aggivessana, that painful feeling, arising in me, persisted without impinging on my mind.

It occurred to me, Aggivessana: Suppose now that I should still meditate the non-breathing meditation? So I, Aggivessana, stopped breathing in and breathing out through the mouth and through the nose and through the ears. When I, Aggivessana, had stopped breathing in and breathing out through the mouth and through the nose and through the ears, there came to be a fierce heat in my body. As, Aggivessana, two strong men, having taken hold of a weaker man by his limbs, might set fire to him, might make him sizzle up over a charcoal pit, even so, Aggivessana, when I had stopped breathing in and breathing out through the mouth and through the nose and through the ears, did there come to be a fierce heat in my body. Although, Aggivessana, unsluggish energy came to be stirred up in me, unmuddled mindfulness set up, yet my body was turbulent, not calmed, because I was harassed in striving by striving against that very pain. But yet, Aggivessana, that painful feeling, arising in me, persisted without impinging on my mind. In addition to this, Aggivessana, [**245**] *devatās*, having seen me, spoke thus: 'The recluse Gotama has passed away.' Other *devatās* spoke thus: 'The recluse Gotama has not passed away, but he is passing away.' Other *devatās* spoke thus: 'The recluse Gotama has not passed away, nor is he passing away; the recluse Gotama is a perfected one,[1] the mode of living of a perfected one is just like this.'

---

[1] *arahaṃ.* Either the *devatās* were mistaken, for at this time Gotama was not an arahant in its meaning of one who had done all there was to be done, or the term is here being used in a pre-Buddhist sense. *Cf. Jā.* i. 67.

It occurred to me, Aggivessana: Suppose now that I should take the line of desisting from all food? Then, Aggivessana, *devatās*, having approached me, spoke thus: 'Do not, good sir, take the line of desisting from all food. If you, good sir, take the line of desisting from all food, then we will give you *deva*-like essences to take in through the pores of the skin; you will keep going by means of them.' Then, Aggivessana, it occurred to me: Suppose that I should take the line of not eating anything, and these *devatās* were to give me *deva*-like essences to take in through the pores of the skin, and that I should keep going by means of them, that would be an imposture in me. So I, Aggivessana, rejected those *devatās*;[1] I said, 'Enough.'

It occurred to me, Aggivessana: Suppose now that I were to take food little by little, drop by drop, such as bean-soup or vetch-soup or chick-pea-soup or pea-soup? So I, Aggivessana, took food little by little, drop by drop, such as bean-soup or vetch-soup or chick-pea-soup or pea-soup. While I, Aggivessana, was taking food little by little, drop by drop, such as bean-soup or vetch-soup or chick-pea-soup or pea-soup, my body became exceedingly emaciated. Because I ate so little,[2] all my limbs became like the joints of withered creepers; because I ate so little, my buttocks became like a bullock's hoof; because I ate so little, my protruding backbone became like a string of balls; because I ate so little, my gaunt ribs became like the crazy rafters of a tumble-down shed; because I ate so little, the pupils of my eyes appeared lying low and deep; **[246]** because I ate so little, my scalp became shrivelled and shrunk as a bitter white gourd cut before it is ripe becomes shrivelled and shrunk by a hot wind. If I, Aggivessana, thought: 'I will touch the skin of my belly,' it was my backbone that I took hold of. If I thought: 'I will touch my backbone,' it was the skin of my belly that I took hold of. For because I ate so little, the skin of my belly, Aggivessana, came to be cleaving to my backbone. If I, Aggivessana, thought: 'I will obey the calls of nature,' I fell down on my face then and there, because I ate so little. If I, Aggivessana, soothing my body, stroked my limbs with my hand, the hairs, rotted at the roots, fell away from my body as I stroked my limbs with my hand, because I ate so little. And further, Aggivessana, men, having seen me, spoke thus: 'The recluse Gotama is black.' Other men spoke thus: 'The recluse Gotama is not black,

---

[1] *Cf. Jā.* i. 67.

[2] As at *M.* i. 80.

the recluse Gotama is deep brown.' Some men spoke thus: 'The recluse Gotama is not black, he is not even deep brown, the recluse Gotama is of a sallow colour.[1]' To such an extent, Aggivessana, was my clear pure complexion spoilt because I ate so little.

This, Aggivessana, occurred to me: 'Some recluses and brahmans in the past have experienced feelings that were acute, painful, sharp, severe; but this is paramount, nor is there worse than this. And some recluses and brahmans in the future will experience feelings that are acute, painful, sharp, severe; but this is paramount, nor is there worse than this. And some recluses and brahmans are now experiencing feelings that are acute, painful, sharp, severe; but this is paramount, nor is there worse than this. But I, by this severe austerity, do not reach states of further-men, the excellent knowledge and vision befitting the ariyans. Could there be another way to awakening ?'

This, Aggivessana, occurred to me: 'I know that while my father, the Sakyan, was ploughing,[2] and I was sitting in the cool shade of a rose-apple tree, aloof from pleasures of the senses, aloof from unskilled states of mind, entering on the first meditation, which is accompanied by initial thought and discursive thought, is born of aloofness, and is rapturous and joyful, and while abiding therein, I thought: 'Now could this be a way to awakening ?' Then, following on my mindfulness,[3] Aggivessana, there was the consciousness: This is itself the Way to awakening. This occurred to me, Aggivessana: 'Now, [**247**] am I afraid of that happiness which is happiness apart from sense-pleasures, apart from unskilled states of mind ?' This occurred to me, Aggivessana: 'I am not afraid of that happiness which is happiness apart from sense-pleasures, apart from unskilled states of mind.'

This occurred to me, Aggivessana: 'Now it is not easy to reach that happiness by thus subjecting the body to extreme emaciation. Suppose I were to take material nourishment—boiled rice and sour milk ?' So I, Aggivessana, took material nourishment—boiled rice and sour milk. Now at that time, Aggivessana, five monks[4] were attending me and (they thought): 'When the recluse

---

[1] *maṅguracchavi*, as at *M.* i. 429, ii. 33; *D.* i. 193, 242.

[2] According to *MA.* ii. 290 this was a ritual sowing, *vappamaṅgala.* See my art., *Early Buddhism and the Taking of Life, B. C. Law Volume, Part I*; also *Jā.* i. 57.

[3] *I.e.* of in-breathing and out-breathing, *MA.* ii. 291.

[4] *Cf. Vin.* i. 8 *ff.*; *M.* i. 171 *ff.*

Gotama wins *dhamma* he will announce it to us.' But when I, Aggivessana, took material nourishment—boiled rice and sour milk—then these five monks turned on me in disgust, saying: 'The recluse Gotama lives in abundance, he is wavering in his striving, he has reverted to a life of abundance.'

But when I, Aggivessana, had taken some material nourishment, having picked up strength, aloof from pleasures of the senses, aloof from unskilled states of mind, I entered on and abided in the first meditation which is accompanied by initial thought and discursive thought, is born of aloofness, and is rapturous and joyful. But yet, Aggivessana, the pleasurable feeling, arising in me, persisted without impinging on my mind. By allaying initial thought and discursive thought, with the mind subjectively tranquillised and fixed on one point, I entered on and abided in the second meditation which is devoid of initial and discursive thought, is born of concentration, and is rapturous and joyful. But yet, Aggivessana, the pleasurable feeling, arising in me, persisted, without impinging on my mind. By the fading out of rapture I dwelt with equanimity, attentive and clearly conscious, and I experienced in my person that joy of which the ariyans say: 'Joyful lives he who has equanimity and is mindful,' and I entered on and abided in the third meditation. But yet, Aggivessana, the pleasurable feeling, arising in me, persisted without impinging on my mind. By getting rid of joy and by getting rid of anguish, by the going down of former pleasures and sorrows, I entered into and abided in the fourth meditation which has neither anguish nor joy and which is entirely purified by equanimity and mindfulness. But yet, Aggivessana, the pleasurable feeling, arising in me, persisted without impinging on my mind.

With the mind composed thus, quite purified, quite clarified, without blemish, without defilement, grown soft and workable, fixed, immovable, [**248**] I directed my mind to the knowledge and recollection of former habitations . . . (*as at* p. 28 *above*). . . . Thus do I remember divers former habitations in all their modes and details. This, Aggivessana, was the first knowledge attained by me in the first watch of the night; ignorance was dispelled, knowledge arose, darkness was dispelled, light arose, even as I abided diligent, ardent, self-resolute. But yet, Aggivessana, the pleasurable feeling, arising in me, persisted without impinging on my mind.

With the mind composed thus, quite purified, quite clarified, without blemish, without defilement, grown soft and workable, fixed, immovable, I directed my mind to the knowledge of the passing hence and arising of beings . . . (*as at* p. 28 *above*). . . . Thus with the purified *deva*-vision surpassing that of men, do I see beings as they pass hence, as they arise, I comprehend that beings are mean, excellent, fair, foul, in a good bourn, in a bad bourn according to the consequences of their deeds. This, Aggivessana, was the second knowledge attained by me in the middle watch of the night; ignorance was dispelled, knowledge arose, [**249**] darkness was dispelled, light arose, even as I abided diligent, ardent, self-resolute. But yet, Aggivessana, the pleasurable feeling, arising in me, persisted without impinging on my mind.

With the mind composed thus, quite purified, quite clarified, without blemish, without defilement, grown soft and workable, fixed, immovable, I directed my mind to the knowledge of the destruction of the cankers . . . (*as at* p. 29 *above*) . . . When I knew thus, saw thus, my mind was freed from the canker of sense-pleasures and my mind was freed from the canker of becoming and my mind was freed from the canker of ignorance. In freedom the knowledge came to be that I was freed, and I comprehended: Destroyed is birth, brought to a close is the Brahma-faring, done is what was to be done, there is no more of being such or such. This, Aggivessana, was the third knowledge attained by me in the third watch of the night; ignorance was dispelled, knowledge arose . . . even as I abided . . . self-resolute. But yet, Aggivessana, the pleasurable feeling, arising in me, persisted without impinging on my mind.

Now I, Aggivessana, am aware that when I am teaching *dhamma* to companies consisting of many hundreds, each person thinks thus about me: 'The recluse Gotama is teaching *dhamma* especially for me.' But this, Aggivessana, should not be understood thus. For when a Tathāgata is teaching *dhamma* to others it is for the sake of general instruction. And I, Aggivessana, at the close of such a talk, steady, calm, make one-pointed and concentrate my mind subjectively in that first characteristic of concentration[1] in which I ever constantly abide."

"This is to believed of the good Gotama, for he is a perfected one, a fully Self-awakened One. But does the good Gotama allow that he sleeps during the day?"

---

[1] *samādhinimitta*, explained at *MA*. ii 292 as concentration on the fruit of voidness, *suññataphalasamādhi*.

"I allow, Aggivessana, that during the last month of the hot weather, returning from alms-gathering after the meal, having laid down the outer cloak (folded) into four, mindful and clearly conscious, I fall asleep on my right side."

"But this, good Gotama, is what some recluses and brahmans call 'abiding in confusion.'"

[**250**] "So far, Aggivessana, there is neither bewilderment nor non-bewilderment. But, Aggivessana, how there is bewilderment and non-bewilderment—listen to it, pay careful attention, and I will speak."

"Yes, sir," Saccaka, the son of Jains, answered the Lord in assent. The Lord spoke thus:

"In whoever, Aggivessana, those cankers are not got rid of that have to do with the defilements, with again-becoming, that are fearful, whose result is anguish, making for birth, ageing and dying in the future[1]—him I call bewildered. In whoever, Aggivessana, those cankers are got rid of which are connected with the defilements, with again-becoming, that are fearful, whose result is anguish, making for birth, ageing and dying in the future—him I call unbewildered. Those cankers of the Tathāgata, Aggivessana, that are connected with the defilements, with again-becoming, that are fearful, whose result is anguish, making for birth, ageing and dying in the future, these are got rid of, cut off at the root, made like a palm-tree stump so that they can come to no further existence in the future. Even as, Aggivessana, a palm-tree whose crown is cut off cannot come to further growth, even so, Aggivessana, got rid of, cut off at the root, made like a palm-tree stump so that they can come to no further existence in the future are those cankers of the Tathāgata that have to do with the defilements, with again-becoming, that are fearful, whose result is anguish, making for birth, ageing and dying in the future."

When this had been said, Saccaka, the son of Jains, spoke thus to the Lord:

"It is wonderful, good Gotama, it is marvellous, good Gotama, that while this was being said so mockingly[2] to the good Gotama, while he was being assailed by accusing ways of speech, his colour was clear and his countenance happy like that of a perfected one, a fully Self-awakened One. I allow that I, good Gotama, took

---

[1] *Cf. M.* i. 464; *A.* ii. 172.

[2] *āsajja āsajja*, as at *D.* i. 107; *cf.* also *A.* i. 172 and *G.S.* i. 156, *n.* Used not in an offensive sense at *M.* iii. 152.

Pūraṇa Kassapa in hand speech by speech, but he, when taken in hand by me, speech by speech, shelved the question by (asking) another, answered off the point and evinced anger and ill-will and discontent.[1] But while the good Gotama was being spoken to thus so mockingly and was being assailed by accusing ways of speech, his colour was clear and his countenance happy like that of a perfected one, a fully Self-awakened One. I allow that I, good Gotama, took Makkhali of the Cow-pen . . . Ajita of the hair-blanket . . . Pakudha Kaccāyana . . . Sañjaya Belaṭṭha's son . . . Nātha's son, the Jain, in hand, speech by speech, but he, when taken in hand by me, speech by speech, [**251**] shelved the question by (asking) another, answered off the point and evinced anger and ill-will and discontent. But while the good Gotama was being spoken to thus so mockingly and was being assailed by accusing ways of speech, his colour was clear and his countenance happy like that of a perfected one, a fully Self-awakened one. And if you please, we, good Gotama, are going now, for there is much to do, much to be done by us."

"Do now whatever you think it is the right time for, Aggivessana."

Then Saccaka, the son of Jains, having rejoiced in what the Lord had said, having given thanks,[2] rising from his seat, departed.

Greater Discourse to Saccaka:
the Sixth

---

[1] As at *M*. i. 442.

[2] *MA*. ii. 293 points out that although the Lord spoke two discourses to Saccaka he neither gained understanding (of the truths) nor went forth nor was established in the Refuges. But the Lord taught him *dhamma* for the sake of his future dwelling (*vāsana*, or, mental impressions). He saw that two hundred years after his own parinibbāna his teaching would be established in Ceylon. The Jain, having been reborn there, having gone forth and learnt the three Piṭakas, having made vision (*vipassanā*) grow, and having won arahantship, would be one whose cankers were destroyed.

37. LESSER DISCOURSE ON THE DESTRUCTION OF CRAVING

(Cūḷataṇhāsaṅkhayasutta)

Thus have I heard: At one time the Lord was staying near Sāvatthī in the Eastern Monastery in the palace of Migāra's mother. Then Sakka, the lord of *devas*, approached the Lord; having approached, having greeted the Lord, he stood at a respectful distance. As he was standing at a respectful distance, Sakka, the lord of *devas*, spoke thus to the Lord:

"Briefly, Lord, to what extent does a monk come to be freed by the destruction of craving, completely fulfilled, completely secure from the bonds, a complete Brahma-farer, complete as to his culmination,[1] best of *devas* and men ?"[2]

"As to this, lord of *devas*, a monk comes to hear: 'It is not fitting that there should be inclination towards any (psycho-physical) conditions.'[3] If, lord of *devas*, a monk comes to hear this, that 'It is not fitting that there should be inclination towards any (psycho-physical) conditions,' he knows all the conditions thoroughly; by knowing all the conditions thoroughly he knows all the conditions accurately; by knowing all the conditions accurately, whatever feeling he feels, pleasant or painful or neither painful nor pleasant, he abides viewing impermanence, he abides viewing dispassion, he abides viewing stopping,[4] he abides viewing renunciation in regard to those feelings. When he is abiding viewing impermanence, when he is abiding viewing dispassion, when he is abiding viewing stopping, when he is abiding viewing renunciation in regard to these feelings, he grasps after nothing in the world; not grasping he is not troubled; being untroubled he himself is

---

[1] *Cf. D.* ii. 283, where Sakka puts the same question; also *S.* iii. 13; *A.* v. 326.

[2] A term usually reserved for the Buddha or *Tathāgata*, but used as above at *A.* v. 326.

[3] *MA.* ii. 298 calls these the five *khandhas* (psycho-physical components), the twelve spheres (the six sense-organs and their appropriate kinds of sense-data), and the eighteen elements (see *e.g. Vbh.* 87; *Dhs.* 1333).

[4] Dispassion and stopping are twofold: dispassion for or stopping of destruction; and complete dispassion, complete stopping, *MA.* ii. 299.

individually attained to nibbāna,[1] [252] and he comprehends: 'Destroyed is birth, brought to a close is the Brahma-faring, done is what was to be done, there is no more of being such or such'. Briefly, it is to this extent, lord of *devas*, that a monk comes to be freed by the destruction of craving, completly fulfilled, completely secure from the bonds, a complete Brahma-farer, complete as to his culmination, best of *devas* and men." Then Sakka, the lord of *devas*, having rejoiced in what the Lord had said, having given thanks, having greeted the Lord, vanished then and there keeping his right side towards him.

Now at that time the venerable Moggallāna the Great was sitting down near the Lord. Then it occurred to the venerable Moggallāna the Great: "Now, did that *yakkha*, when he thanked the Lord for his words, grasp them or not? Suppose that I should find out whether that *yakkha*, when he thanked the Lord for his words, grasped them or not?" Then the venerable Moggallāna the Great, as a strong man might stretch out his bent arm or might bend back his out-stretched arm, vanishing from the palace of Migāra's mother in the Eastern Monastery, appeared among the *devas* of the Thirty-Three.

Now at that time Sakka, the lord of *devas*, equipped and provided with five hundred *deva*-like musical instruments,[2] was amusing himself in the One Lotus pleasure grove.[3] Sakka, the lord of *devas*, saw the venerable Moggallāna the Great coming in the distance; seeing him, having had those five hundred *deva*-like musical instruments stopped, he approached the venerable Moggallāna the Great; having approached, he spoke thus to the venerable Moggallāna the Great:

"Come, my good Moggallāna, you are welcome, my good Moggallāna; at last, my good Moggallāna, you take this occasion for coming here; sit down, my good Moggallāna, this seat is appointed." The venerable Moggallāna the Great sat down on the appointed seat. Sakka, the lord of *devas*, having taken a low seat, sat down at a respectful distance. The venerable Moggallāna the Great spoke thus to Sakka, the lord of *devas*, as he was sitting down at a respectful distance:

---

[1] As at *M*. i. 67; *S*. iii. 54. *MA*. ii. 299 says he himself attains nibbāna by the nibbāna of the defilements.

[2] *MA*. ii. 300, consisting of five kinds.

[3] Ekapuṇḍarīka *uyyāna*. *MA*. ii. 300 does not comment on this. See Ekapuṇḍarīka paribbājakârāma, near Vesālī, *M*. i. 481.

"In regard to the talk that the Lord spoke in brief to you, Kosiya,[1] on freedom by the destruction of craving, it were good even for me to hear portions of this talk."

"I, my good Moggallāna, am very busy, there is much to be done by me; both on my own account there are things to be done, and there are also (still more)[2] things to be done for the *devas* of the Thirty-Three. Further, my good Moggallāna, it was properly heard, properly learnt, [**253**] properly attended to, properly reflected upon, so that it cannot vanish quickly. Once upon a time,[3] my good Moggallāna, a battle was in full swing between *devas* and demons. In that battle, my good Moggallāna, the *devas* conquered, the demons were defeated. So I, my good Moggallāna, having won that battle and being victorious in the battle, when I came back from there built a palace named Vejayanta[4] (Victory). Now, my good Moggallāna, there are a hundred towers to the Vejayanta Palace, in each tower there are seven gabled houses, in each gabled house there are seven nymphs, and for each nymph there are seven attendants. Would you, my good Moggallāna, like to see the delights of the Vejayanta Palace?" The venerable Moggallāna the Great consented by becoming silent.

Then Sakka, the lord of *devas*, and the great rajah Vessavaṇa,[5] having put the venerable Moggallāna the Great in front of them approached Vejayanta Palace. The female attendants of Sakka, the lord of *devas*, saw the venerable Moggallāna the Great coming in the distance; on seeing him, shrinking and shy, each entered her own inner room. As a daughter-in-law[6] shrinks and is shy on seeing her father-in-law, even so did the female attendants of Sakka, the lord of *devas*, on seeing the venerable Moggallāna the Great, shrinking and shy, each enter her own inner room. Then Sakka, the lord of *devas*, and Vessavaṇa, the great rajah, made the

---

[1] "Probably one of the several clan names which are also names of animals" (owl), *DPPN*. *Cf. D.* ii. 270, *Ud.* 30, *Jā.* ii. 252. C. E. Godage, "Place of Indra in Early Buddhism," *University of Ceylon Review*, Vol. III, No. 1, p. 53 thinks Indra (=Sakka) may have become the tutelary god of that particular clan (the Kusikas) to have gained this epithet.

[2] *App'eva sakena . . . api ca devānaṃ yeva=na bahu . . . pana bahu, MA.* ii. 301.

[3] As at *D.* ii. 285.

[4] *Cf. Thag.* 1194-96; *S.* i. 234; *DhA.* i. 273.

[5] One of the names of Kuvera, a ruler over the *yakkhas*, his kingdom being to the north. *MA.* ii. 303 says he was a favourite of Sakka's.

[6] *Cf. M.* i. 186.

venerable Moggallāna the Great follow them into the Vejayanta Palace and roam about in it, and (they said): "My dear Moggallāna, see this delight of the Vejayanta Palace, and, dear Moggallāna, see that delight of the Vejayanta Palace." "This shines forth as a deed of merit formerly done by the venerable Kosiya, and people seeing anything delightful speak thus: 'Indeed it shines forth from the *devas* of the Thirty-Three, that is to say it shines forth as a deed of merit formerly done by the venerable Kosiya.'"

Then it occurred to the venerable Moggallāna the Great: "This *yakkha* lives much too indolently. Suppose that I were to agitate this *yakkha*?" Then the venerable Moggallāna the Great worked such a working of psychic power that with his big toe he made Vejayanta Palace tremble, shake and quake. [**254**] Then the minds of Sakka, the lord of *devas*, and of the great rajah Vessavaṇa and of the *devas* of the Thirty-Three were full of wonder and marvel, and they said: "Indeed, the great psychic power, the great majesty of the recluse is wonderful, it is indeed marvellous, inasmuch as with his big toe he makes this *deva*-like abode tremble, shake and quake." Then the venerable Moggallāna the Great, knowing that Sakka, the lord of *devas*, was agitated and astounded,[1] spoke thus to Sakka, the lord of *devas*:

"In regard to the talk that the Lord spoke in brief to you, Kosiya, on freedom by the destruction of craving, it were good even for me to hear portions of that talk."

"As to that I, my good Moggallāna, approached the Lord; having approached, having greeted the Lord, I stood at a respectful distance. As I was standing at a respectful distance, my good Moggallāna, I spoke thus to the Lord: 'Briefly, Lord, to what extent does a monk come to be freed by the destruction of craving, completely fulfilled, completely secure from the bonds, a complete Brahma-farer, complete as to his culmination, best of *devas* and men?' When this had been said, my good Moggallāna, the Lord spoke thus to me: 'As to this, lord of *devas*, a monk comes to hear: It is not fitting that there should be inclination towards any (psycho-physical) conditions. . . . Briefly, it is to this extent, lord of *devas*, that a monk comes to be freed by the destruction of craving, completely fulfilled, completely secure from the bonds, a complete Brahma-farer, complete as to his culmination, best of *devas* and

[1] *MA*. ii. 304 says this was due to joy.

men.' Thus, my good Moggallāna, did the Lord speak to me briefly on freedom by the destruction of craving."

Then the venerable Moggallāna the Great, having rejoiced in what Sakka, the lord of *devas*, had said, [**255**] having given thanks, as a strong man might stretch out his bent arm or might bend back his outstretched arm, vanishing even so from among the *devas* of the Thirty-Three, did he become manifest in the palace of Migāra's mother in the Eastern Monastery. Then soon after the venerable Moggallāna the Great had departed, the female attendants of Sakka, the lord of *devas*, spake thus to Sakka, the lord of *devas*:

"Good sir, is not this lord your teacher?"

"Good ladies, this lord is not my teacher, he is a fellow Brahma-farer of mine, the venerable Moggallāna the Great."

"It is a gain for you, good sir, that this fellow Brahma-farer of yours is of such great psychic potency, of such great majesty; certainly this lord is your teacher."

Then the venerable Moggallāna the Great approached the Lord; having approached, having greeted the Lord, he sat down at a respectful distance. As he was sitting down at a respectful distance, the venerable Moggallāna the Great spoke thus to the Lord:

"Lord, does the Lord know that just now he spoke in brief on freedom by the destruction of craving to a very powerful *yakkha*?"

"I know, Moggallāna, that Sakka, the lord of *devas*, approached me here; having approached, having greeted me, he stood at a respectful distance. As he was standing at a respectful distance, Sakka, the lord of *devas*, spoke thus to me, Moggallāna: 'Briefly, Lord, to what extent does a monk come to be freed by the destruction of craving, completely fulfilled, completely secure from the bonds, a complete Brahma-farer, complete as to his culmination, best of *devas* and men?' When this had been said, I, Moggallāna, spoke thus to Sakka, the lord of *devas*: 'As to this, lord of *devas*, a monk comes to hear: It is not fitting that there should be inclination towards any (psycho-physical) conditions. If, lord of *devas*, a monk comes to hear this, that "It is not fitting that there should be inclination towards any (psycho-physical) conditions," he knows all the conditions thoroughly; by knowing all the conditions thoroughly, he knows all the conditions accurately; by knowing all the conditions accurately, whatever feeling he feels, pleasant or painful or neither painful nor pleasant, he abides viewing impermanence, he abides viewing dispassion, he abides viewing stopping, he abides viewing renunciation in regard to those feelings. When he is abiding viewing impermanence . . . dispassion . . . stopping, when he is abiding viewing renunciation in regard to those feelings, he grasps after nothing in the world; not grasping he is not troubled; not being troubled he himself has individually attained nibbāna, and he comprehends: "Destroyed is birth, brought to a close **[256]** is the Brahma-faring, done is what was to be done, there is no more of being such or such." Briefly, it is to this extent, lord of *devas*, that a monk comes to be freed by the destruction of craving, completely fulfilled, completely secure from the bonds, a complete Brahma-farer, complete as to his culmination, best of *devas* and men.' I, Moggallāna, know that I spoke in brief thus on freedom by the destruction of craving to Sakka, the lord of *devas*."

Thus spoke the Lord. Delighted, the venerable Moggallāna the Great rejoiced in what the Lord had said.

Lesser Discourse on the Destruction of Craving:
the Seventh

38. GREATER DISCOURSE ON THE DESTRUCTION OF CRAVING

(Mahātaṇhāsaṅkhayasutta)

THUS have I heard: At one time the Lord was staying near Sāvatthī in the Jeta Grove in Anāthapiṇḍika's monastery. Now at that time a pernicious view[1] like this had accrued to the monk called Sāti, a fisherman's son: "In so far as I understand *dhamma* taught by the Lord it is that this consciousness itself runs on, fares on, not another." Several monks heard: "It is said that a pernicious

[1] For other "pernicious views" see *M.* i. 130, 326; *Vin.* ii. 25-6; *A.* v. 194. Here the view is one of Eternalism. This thera, as *MA.* ii. 305 calls Sāti, was not learned. He was a Jātaka-repeater, so he thought that, although the other *khandhas* were stopped now here, now there, consciousness ran on from this world to that beyond and from there to this world. It is inferred that he therefore thought consciousness had no condition, *paccaya*, for arising. But the Buddha had said if there is a condition it arises, with no condition there is no origination of consciousness. He therefore spoke as the Buddha did not, gave a blow to the Conqueror's Wheel, and was a thief in his dispensation. *MA.* ii. 305.

view like this has accrued to the monk called Sāti, a fisherman's son: 'In so far as I understand *dhamma* taught by the Lord it is that this consciousness itself runs on, fares on, not another.'" Then these monks approached the monk Sāti, a fisherman's son; having approached, they spoke thus to the monk Sāti, a fisherman's son: "Is it true, as is said, that a pernicious view like this has accrued to you, reverend Sāti: 'In so far as I understand . . . not another'?" "Even so do I, your reverences, understand *dhamma* taught by the Lord, that it is this consciousness itself that runs on, fares on, not another." Then these monks, anxious to dissuade the monk Sāti, a fisherman's son, from that pernicious view, questioned him, cross-questioned him, and pressed him for his reasons, saying: "Do not, reverend Sāti, speak thus, do not misrepresent the Lord; neither is misrepresentation of the Lord seemly, nor would the Lord speak thus. For, reverend Sāti, in many a figure is conditioned genesis spoken of in connection with consciousness [**257**] by the Lord, saying: 'Apart from condition there is no origination of consciousness.'"

But the monk Sāti, a fisherman's son, even although questioned, cross-questioned and pressed for his reasons by these monks, obstinately holding to and adhering to that pernicious view, decided: "Thus it is that I, your reverences, understand *dhamma* taught by the Lord, that it is this consciousness itself that runs on, fares on, not another."

And since these monks were not able to dissuade the monk Sāti, a fisherman's son, from that pernicious view, they approached the Lord; having approached, having greeted the Lord, they sat down at a respectful distance. As they were sitting down at a respectful distance, these monks spoke thus to the Lord: "Lord, a pernicious view like this has accrued to the monk Sāti, a fisherman's son: 'In so far as I understand . . . not another.' We heard, Lord: 'They say that a pernicious view like this has accrued to the monk called Sāti, a fisherman's son: 'In so far as I understand . . . not another.' Then we, Lord, approached the monk Sāti, a fisherman's son; having approached, we spoke thus to the monk Sāti, a fisherman's son: 'Is it true, as is said, reverend Sāti, that a pernicious view like this has accrued to you: In so far as I understand . . . not another?' When this had been said, Lord, the monk Sāti, a fisherman's son, spoke thus to us: 'Even so do I, your reverences, understand *dhamma* taught by the Lord . . . not another.' Then we, Lord, anxious to dissuade the monk Sāti, a fisherman's son, from that pernicious view, questioned him, cross-questioned him, pressed him for his reasons, saying: 'Do not, reverend Sāti, speak thus, do not misrepresent the Lord; neither is misrepresentation of the Lord seemly, nor would the Lord speak thus. For, reverend Sāti, in many a figure is conditioned genesis spoken of in connection with consciousness by the Lord, saying: Apart from condition there is no origination of consciousness.' But, Lord, the monk Sāti, a fisherman's son, even although questioned, cross-questioned and pressed for his reasons by us thus, obstinately holding to and adhering to that pernicious view, decided: 'Thus it is that I, your reverences, understand *dhamma* . . . not another.' And since, Lord, we were not able to dissuade the monk Sāti, a fisherman's son, from that pernicious view, we are telling this matter to the Lord."

Then the Lord addressed a certain monk, saying: "Come, [**258**] do you, monk, address the monk Sāti, a fisherman's son, in my name, saying: 'Sāti, the teacher is summoning you.' "

"Yes, Lord," and this monk, having answered the Lord in assent, approached the monk Sāti, a fisherman's son; having approached, he spoke thus to the monk Sāti, a fisherman's son: "The teacher is summoning you, reverend Sāti."

"Yes, your reverence," and the monk Sāti, a fisherman's son, having answered this monk in assent, approached the Lord; having approached, having greeted the Lord, he sat down at a respectful distance. The Lord spoke thus to the monk Sāti, a fisherman's son, as he was sitting down at a respectful distance:

"Is it true, as is said, that a pernicious view like this has accrued to you, Sāti: 'In so far as I understand *dhamma* taught by the Lord it is that this consciousness itself runs on, fares on, not another' ?"

"Even so do I, Lord, understand *dhamma* taught by the Lord: it is this consciousness itself that runs on, fares on, not another."

"What is this consciousness, Sāti ?"

"It is this, Lord, that speaks,[1] that feels, that experiences now here, now there, the fruition of deeds that are lovely and that are depraved."[2]

"But to whom, foolish man, do you understand that *dhamma* was taught by me thus ? Foolish man, has not consciousness generated by conditions[3] been spoken of in many a figure by me,

---

[1] *vado=vade*? (*PED*), and see *v.l.* at *M.* i. 552. *MA.* ii. 305 gives *vadati.*

[2] *Cf. M.* i. 8.

[3] *Cf. M.* i. 191.

saying: Apart from condition there is no origination of consciousness? But now you, foolish man, not only misrepresent me because of your own wrong grasp, but you also injure[1] yourself and give rise to much demerit which, foolish man, will be for your woe and sorrow for a long time."

Then the Lord addressed the monks, saying: "What do you think about this, monks? Can this monk Sāti, a fisherman's son, have even a glimmering of this *dhamma* and discipline?"

"How could this be, Lord? It is not so, Lord." When this had been said, the monk Sāti, a fisherman's son, sat down silent, ashamed, his shoulders drooping, his head bent, brooding, speechless. Then the Lord, understanding why the monk Sāti, a fisherman's son, was silent, ashamed . . . speechless, spoke thus to the monk Sāti, a fisherman's son:

"You, foolish man, will be known through this pernicious view of your own, for I will question the monks on it." Then the Lord addressed the monks, saying:

"Do you, monks, understand that *dhamma* was taught by me thus so that this monk Sāti, a fisherman's son, [**259**] because of his own wrong grasp not only misrepresents me but is also injuring himself and giving rise to much demerit?"

"No, Lord. For in many a figure has consciousness generated by conditions been spoken of to us by the Lord, saying: 'Apart from condition there is no origination of consciousness.'"

"It is good, monks, it is good that you understand thus *dhamma* taught by me to you, monks. For in many a figure has consciousness generated by conditions been spoken of by me to you, monks, saying: 'Apart from condition there is no origination of consciousness.' But this monk Sāti, a fisherman's son, because of his own wrong grasp, not only misrepresents me, but is also injuring himself and giving rise to much demerit. This will be for this foolish man's woe and sorrow for a long time.

It is because, monks, an appropriate condition arises that consciousness is known by this or that name: if consciousness arises because of eye and material shapes, it is known as visual consciousness; if consciousness arises because of ear and sounds, it is known as auditory consciousness; if, consciousness arises because of nose and smells, it is known as olfactory consciousness; if consciousness arises because of tongue and tastes, it is known as gustatory consciousness;

---

[1] *khaṇati*, to dig; *cf. Dh.* 247, 337. *Cf.* "wrong grasp" at *M.* i. 134.

if consciousness arises because of body and touches, it is known as tactile consciousness; if consciousness arises because of mind and mental objects, it is known as mental consciousness. Monks, as a fire burns because of this or that appropriate condition, by that it is known: if a fire burns because of sticks, it is known as a stick-fire; and if a fire burns because of chips, it is known as a chip-fire; and if a fire burns because of grass, it is known as a grass-fire; and if a fire burns because of cow-dung, it is known as a cow-dung fire; and if a fire burns because of chaff, it is known as a chaff-fire; and if a fire burns because of rubbish, it is known as a rubbish-fire. Even so, monks, when because of a condition appropriate to it consciousness arises, it is known by this or that name: when consciousness arises because of eye and material shapes, it is known as visual consciousness . . . [**260**] . . . when consciousness arises because of mind and mental objects, it is known as mental consciousness. Do you see, monks, that this has come to be ?"

"Yes, Lord."

"Do you see, monks, the origination of this nutriment ?"

"Yes, Lord."

"Do you see, monks, that from the stopping of this nutriment, that which has come to be is liable to stopping ?"

"Yes, Lord."

"From doubt, monks, does the perplexity arise: This that has come to be, might it not be ?"

"Yes, Lord."

"From doubt, monks, the perplexity arises: Might there not be an origination of that nutriment ?"

"Yes, Lord."

"From doubt the perplexity arises: By the stopping of that nutriment, might that which has come to be not be liable to stopping ?"

"Yes, Lord."

"By seeing as it really is by means of perfect intuitive wisdom, monks, that, This has come to be—is that which is perplexity got rid of ?"

"Yes, Lord."

"By seeing as it really is by means of perfect intuitive wisdom, monks, that, This is the origination of nutriment—is that which is perplexity got rid of ?"

"Yes, Lord."

"By seeing as it really is by means of perfect intuitive wisdom, monks, that, From the stopping of that nutriment that which has come to be is liable to stopping—is that which is perplexity got rid of ?"

"Yes, Lord."

"Thinking, 'This has come to be'—is there for you, monks as to this, absence of perplexity ?"

"Yes, Lord."

"Thinking, 'This is the origination of nutriment'—is there for you, monks, as to this, absence of perplexity ?"

"Yes, Lord."

"Thinking, 'From the stopping of this nutriment, this that has come to be is liable to stopping'—is there for you, monks, as to this, absence of perplexity ?"

"Yes, Lord."

"Thinking, 'This has come to be'—is it properly seen by means of perfect intuitive wisdom as it really is ?"

"Yes, Lord."

"Thinking, 'This is the origination of nutriment'—is it properly seen by means of perfect intuitive wisdom as it really is ?"

"Yes, Lord."

"Thinking, 'From the stopping of this nutriment, this that has come to be is liable to stopping'—is it properly seen by means of perfect intuitive wisdom as it really is ?"

"Yes, Lord."

"If you, monks, cling to, treasure, cherish, foster this view, thus purified, thus cleansed, then, monks, would you understand that the Parable of the Raft[1] is *dhamma* taught for crossing over, not for retaining ?"

"No, Lord."

"But if you, monks, do not cling to, do not treasure, do not cherish, do not foster[2] this view, thus purified, thus cleansed, then, monks, would you **[261]** understand that the Parable of the Raft is *dhamma* taught for crossing over, not for retaining ?"

"Yes, Lord."

"Monks, these four (forms of) nutriment[3] are for the maintenance of creatures that have come to be or for the assistance of those seeking birth. What are the four ? Material nutriment, whether coarse or fine, sensory impingement is the second, mental striving is the third, consciousness is the fourth. And

---

[1] *M.* i. 134. [2] Quoted at *MA.* ii. 109. [3] *Cf. S.* ii. 11 *ff.*

of these four (forms of) nutriment, monks, what is the provenance, what the source, what the birth, what the origin?[1] These four (forms of) nutriment, monks, have craving as the provenance, craving as source, craving as birth, craving as origin. And, monks, what is the provenance of this craving, what the source, what the birth, what the origin? Feeling is the provenance of craving, feeling is the source of craving, feeling is the birth of craving, feeling is the origin of craving. And what, monks, is the provenance of feelings, what the source, what the birth, what the origin? Sensory impingement is the provenance . . . the source . . . the birth . . . sensory impingement is the origin of feeling. And what, monks, is the provenance of sensory impingement . . what the source . . . what the birth . . . what is the origin of sensory impingement? The six (sensory) spheres are the provenance . . . the source . . . the birth . . . the six (sensory) spheres are the origin of sensory impingement. And what, monks, is the provenance of the six (sensory) spheres . . . what the source . . . what the birth . . . what is the origin of the six (sensory) spheres? Psycho-physicality[2] is the provenance . . . the source . . . the birth . . . the origin of the six (sensory) spheres. And what, monks, is the provenance of psycho-physicality . . . what the source . . . what the birth . . . what is the origin of psycho-physicality? Consciousness is the provenance . . . the source . . . the birth, consciousness is the origin of psycho-physicality. And what, monks, is the provenance of consciousness . . . the source . . . the birth . . . what is the origin of consciousness? The karma-formations are the provenance . . . the source . . . the birth . . . the karma-formations are the origin of consciousness. And what, monks, is the provenance of the karma-formations . . . what the source . . . what the birth . . . what is the origin of the karma-formations? Ignorance is the provenance . . . the source . . . the birth . . . ignorance is the origin of the karma-formations. So it is, monks, that conditioned by ignorance are the karma-formations; conditioned by the karma-formations is consciousness; conditioned by consciousness is psycho-physicality; conditioned by psycho-physicality are the six (sensory) spheres; conditioned by the six (sensory) spheres is sensory impingement; conditioned by sensory impingement is feeling; conditioned by feeling is craving; conditioned by craving is grasping; conditioned by grasping is becoming; conditioned by becoming is

---

[1] *Cf. M.* i. 67.

[2] *nāma-rupa*, name-and-shape.

birth; conditioned by birth, ageing and dying, grief, sorrow, suffering, lamentation and despair come into being. Such is the arising of this entire mass of anguish.

It has been said: 'Conditioned by birth is ageing and dying.' Is there ageing and dying for you, monks, conditioned by birth, or how is it as to this ?"

"Conditioned by birth, Lord, is ageing and dying. Thus it is for us as to this: 'Conditioned by birth is ageing and dying.'"

"It has been said: 'Conditioned by becoming is birth.' Is there birth for you, monks, conditioned by becoming, or how is it as to this ?"

"Conditioned by becoming, **[262]** Lord, is birth. Thus it is for us as to this: 'Conditioned by becoming is birth.'"

"It has been said: 'Conditioned by grasping is becoming.' Is there becoming for you, monks, conditioned by grasping, or how is it as to this ?"

"Conditioned by grasping, Lord, is becoming. Thus it is for us as to this: 'Conditioned by grasping is becoming.'"

"It has been said: 'Conditioned by craving is grasping.' Is there grasping for you, monks, conditioned by craving, or how is it as to this ?"

"Conditioned by craving, Lord, is grasping. Thus it is for us as to this: 'Conditioned by craving is grasping.'"

"It has been said: 'Conditioned by feeling is craving.' Is there craving for you, monks, conditioned by feeling, or how is it as to this ?"

"Conditioned by feeling, Lord, is craving. Thus it is for us as to this: 'Conditioned by feeling is craving.'"

"It has been said: 'Conditioned by sensory impingement is feeling.' Is there feeling for you, monks, conditioned by sensory impingement, or how is it as to this ?"

"Conditioned by sensory impingement, Lord, is feeling. Thus it is for us as to this: 'Conditioned by sensory impingement is feeling.'"

"It has been said: 'Conditioned by the six (sensory) spheres is sensory impingement.' Is there sensory impingement for you, monks, conditioned by the six (sensory) spheres, or how is it as to this ?"

"Conditioned by the six (sensory) spheres, Lord, is sensory impingement. Thus it is for us as to this: 'Conditioned by the six (sensory) spheres is sensory impingement.'"

"It has been said: 'Conditioned by psycho-physicality are the six (sensory) spheres. Are there the six (sensory) spheres for you, monks, conditioned by psycho-physicality, or how is it as to this?"

"Conditioned by psycho-physicality, Lord, are the six (sensory) spheres. Thus it is for us as to this: 'Conditioned by psycho-physicality are the six (sensory) spheres.'"

"It has been said: 'Conditioned by consciousness is psycho-physicality.' Is there psycho-physicality for you, monks, conditioned by consciousness, or how is it as to this?"

"Conditioned by consciousness, Lord, is psycho-physicality. Thus it is for us as to this: 'Conditioned by consciousness is psycho-physicality.'"

"It has been said: 'Conditioned by the karma-formations is consciousness.' Is there consciousness for you, monks, conditioned by the karma-formations, or how is it as to this?"

"Conditioned by the karma-formations Lord, is consciousness. Thus it is for us as to this: 'Conditioned by the karma-formations is consciousness.'"

"It has been said: 'Conditioned by ignorance are the karma-formations.' Are there karma-formations for you, monks, conditioned by ignorance, or how is it as to this?"

"Conditioned by ignorance, Lord, are the karma-formations Thus it is for us as to this: 'Conditioned by ignorance are the karma-formations.'"

"It is good, monks. Both you say this, monks, and I too say this: If this is, that comes to be; [**263**] from the arising of this, that arises, that is to say: conditioned by ignorance are the karma-formations; conditioned by the karma-formations is consciousness; conditioned by consciousness is psycho-physicality; conditioned by psycho-physicality are the six (sensory) spheres; conditioned by the six (sensory) spheres is sensory impingement; conditioned by sensory impingement is feeling; conditioned by feeling is craving; conditioned by craving is grasping; conditioned by grasping is becoming; conditioned by becoming is birth; conditioned by birth, ageing and dying, grief, sorrow, suffering, lamentation and despair come into being. Such is the arising of this entire mass of anguish. But from the utter fading away and stopping of this very ignorance is the stopping of the karma-formations; from the stopping of the karma-formations the stopping of consciousness; from the stopping of consciousness the stopping of psycho-physicality; from the stopping of psycho-physicality the stopping of the six (sensory) spheres; from the stopping of the six (sensory) spheres the stopping of sensory impingement; from the stopping of sensory impingement the stopping of feeling; from the stopping of feeling the stopping of craving; from the stopping of craving the stopping of grasping; from the stopping of grasping the stopping of becoming; from the stopping of becoming the stopping of birth; from the stopping of birth, old age and dying, grief, sorrow, suffering, lamentation and despair are stopped. Such is the stopping of this entire mass of anguish.

It has been said: 'From the stopping of birth is the stopping of ageing and dying.' Is there for you, monks, from the stopping of birth the stopping of ageing and dying, or how is it as to this?"

"From the stopping of birth, Lord, is the stopping of ageing and dying. Thus it is for us as to this: 'From the stopping of birth is the stopping of ageing and dying.'"

"It has been said: 'From the stopping of becoming is the stopping of birth . . .' [**264**] . . . 'From the stopping of ignorance is the stopping of the karma-formations.' From the stopping of ignorance is there for you, monks, the stopping of the karma-formations, or how is it as to this?"

"From the stopping of ignorance, Lord, is the stopping of the karma-formations. Thus it is for us as to this: 'From the stopping of ignorance is the stopping of the karma-formations.'"

"It is good, monks. Both you say this, monks, and I too say this: If this is not, that does not come to be; from the stopping of this, that is stopped, that is to say: from the stopping of ignorance is the stopping of the karma-formations . . . from the stopping of birth, old age and dying, grief, sorrow, suffering, lamentation and despair are stopped. Such is the stopping of this entire mass of anguish.

Now, would you, monks, knowing thus, seeing thus, [**265**] either run back to times gone by,[1] thinking: 'Now, were we in a past period,[2] were we not in a past period, what were we in a past period, how were we in a past period, having been what, what did we become in a past period?'"

"No, Lord."

"Or would you, monks, knowing thus, seeing thus, run forward into times to come, thinking: 'Will we come to be[2] in a future period, will we not come to be in a future period, what will we come

---

[1] *Cf. S.* ii. 26-7. [2] *Cf. M.* i. 8.

to be in a future period, how will we come to be in a future period, having been what, what will we come to be in a future period ?"

"No, Lord."

"Or would you, monks, knowing thus, seeing thus, come to be subjectively doubtful now about the present period, thinking: 'Am I, am I not, what am I, how am I, whence has this being come, wheregoing will it come to be?"

"No, Lord."

"Or would you, monks, knowing thus, seeing thus, speak thus: 'The Lord is oppressive[1] to us, but we speak out of respect to our Teacher' ?"

"No, Lord."

"Or would you, monks . . . speak thus: 'A recluse speaks thus to us, and recluses, but we do not speak thus' ?"

"No, Lord."

"Or would you, monks, knowing thus, seeing thus, look out for another teacher ?"

"No, Lord."

"Or would you, monks, . . . fall back on those which are the customs and curious ceremonies[2] of ordinary recluses and brahmans (thinking) these to be the essence ?"

"No, Lord."

"Do not you, monks, speak only of that which of yourselves you have known, seen[3] and discerned ?"

"Yes, Lord."

"It is good, monks. You, monks, have been presented by me with this *dhamma* which is self-realised, timeless, a come-and-see-thing, leading onwards, to be understood individually by the wise. Monks, this *dhamma* is self-realised, timeless, a come-and-see-thing, leading onwards, to be understood individually by the wise. What has been said has been said on account of this.

Monks, it is on the conjunction of three things that there is conception.[4] If there is here[5] a coitus of the parents, but it is not the mother's season and the *gandhabba*[6] is not present—for so long

---

[1] *MA.* ii. 309 says that here *garu* means *bhārika*, grievous, burdensome, to be followed unwillingly.

[2] *vata-kotūhalo-maṅgalāni*; *cf. A.* iii. 206, 439, and see *G.S.* iii. 151, *n.* 4.

[3] With the eye of intuitive wisdom, *MA.* ii. 309.

[4] *Cf. M.* ii. 157; *Miln.* 123; *Divy.* 1, 440.

[5] In this world of beings, *MA.* ii. 310.

[6] *MA.* ii. 310 explains *gandhabba* as the being who is coming into the womb

[**266**] there is not conception. If there is here a coitus of the parents and it is the mother's season, but the *gandhabba* is not present—for so long there is not conception. But if, monks, there is here a coitus of the parents and it is the mother's season and the *gandhabba* is present, it is on the conjunction of these three things that there is conception. Then, monks, the mother for nine or ten months carries the fœtus in her womb with great anxiety for her heavy burden. Then, monks, at the end of nine or ten months the mother gives birth with great anxiety for her heavy burden. When it is born, she feeds it with her own life-blood. For this, monks, is ' life-blood ' in the discipline for an ariyan, that is to say mother's milk. And, monks, when that boy has grown and has developed his sense-organs,[1] he plays at those which are games[2] for little boys, that is to say with a toy plough, tip-cart, at turning somersaults, with a toy windmill, with a toy measure of leaves, with a toy cart, with a toy bow. Monks, when that boy has grown and has developed his sense-organs he enjoys himself, endowed with and possessed of the five strands of sense-pleasures: material shapes cognisable through the eye . . . sounds cognisable through the ear . . . scents cognisable through the nose . . . savours cognisable through the tongue . . . touches cognisable through the body, agreeable, pleasant, liked, enticing, connected with sense-pleasures, alluring.

When he has seen a material shape[3] through the eye, he feels attraction[4] for agreeable material shapes, he feels repugnance for disagreeable material shapes; and he dwells without mindfulness aroused as to the body, with a mind that is limited;[5] and he does not

---

. . . the being about to enter the womb (*tatrûpakasatta*) . . . about to come into that situation, being driven on by the mechanism of *kamma*. See O. H. de A. Wijesekera, *Vedic Gandharva and Pali Gandhabba*, *Ceylon University Review*, Vol. III. No. 1, April, 1945, who suggests that *gandhabba* means a " saṃsāric being in the intermediate stage (between death and birth)."

[1] Here of course not in the sense of over-development or decay, as in old age, see *D.* ii. 305; *M.* i. 49; *S.* ii. 2, 42 *ff.*; but in the sense of growing out of babyhood into boyhood, as at *A.* v. 203.

[2] See *D.* i. 6; *Vin.* iii. 180 for these (and other) games, and notes at *B.D.* i. 316-17.

[3] *Cf. S.* iv. 120, 184.

[4] *sārajjati. MA.* ii. 311 says *rāgaṃ uppādeti. S.* iv. 120, 184 read *adhimuccati.*

[5] *parittacetaso.* The opposite, as given at *M.* i. 270, *S.* iv. 120, 186, is *appamāṇacetaso*, a mind that is boundless or immeasurable. *Cf. A.* i. 249: *paritto appâtumo appadukkhavihārī . . . aparitto mahattā appamāṇavihārī. MA.* ii. 311 explains *paritta* by *akusala*, unskilled.

comprehend that freedom of mind[1] and that freedom through intuitive wisdom as they really are, whereby those evil unskilled states of his are stopped without remainder. Possessed thus of compliance and antipathy,[2] whatever feeling he feels—pleasant or painful or neither painful nor pleasant— he delights in that feeling, welcomes it and persists in cleaving to it. From delighting in that feeling of his, from welcoming it, from persisting in cleaving to it, delight arises; whatever is delight amid those feelings, that is grasping; conditioned by grasping is becoming; conditioned by becoming is birth; conditioned by birth, old age and dying, grief, sorrow, suffering, lamentation and despair come into being. Such is the arising of this entire mass of anguish.

When he has heard a sound through the ear . . . smelt a scent with the nose . . . savoured a taste with the tongue . . . felt a touch with the body . . . known a mental object with the mind, he feels attraction for agreeable mental objects, [**267**] he feels repugnance for disagreeable mental objects; and he dwells without mindfulness aroused as to the body, with a mind that is limited; and he does not comprehend that freedom of mind . . . Such is the arising of this entire mass of anguish.

Now, monks, a Tathāgata arises in the world, a perfected one, a fully Self-awakened one . . . (*as above p.* 223, *to p.* 227) . . . [**268**] . . . [**269**] . . .

[**270**] He, by getting rid of these five hindrances—defilements of a mind, and weakening to intuitive wisdom—aloof from pleasures of the senses, aloof from evil unskilled states of mind, enters on and abides in the first meditation, which is accompanied by initial thought and discursive thought, is born of aloofness and is rapturous and joyful. And again, monks, a monk, by allaying initial and discursive thought, his mind subjectively tranquillised and fixed on one point, enters on and abides in the second meditation, which is devoid of initial and discursive thought, is born of concentration and is rapturous and joyful . . . the third meditation . . . the fourth meditation, which has neither anguish nor joy, and which is entirely purified by equanimity and mindfulness.

When he has seen a material shape through the eye, he does not feel attraction for agreeable material shapes, he does not feel

---

[1] Often connected with the immeasurable or boundless (*appamāṇa*) *brahmavihāras*.

[2] Quoted at *Kvu.* 485; *cf. A.* iv. 158; *S.* i. 111. Explained as "attachment as well as hatred" at *MA.* ii. 311.

repugnance for disagreeable material shapes; and he dwells with mindfulness aroused as to the body, with a mind that is immeasurable;[1] and he comprehends that freedom of mind and that freedom through intuitive wisdom as they really are, whereby those evil unskilled states of his are stopped without remainder. He who has thus got rid of compliance and antipathy, whatever feeling he feels—pleasant or painful or neither painful nor pleasant—he does not delight in that feeling, does not welcome it or persist in cleaving to it. From not delighting in that feeling of his, from not welcoming it, from not persisting in cleaving to it, whatever was delight in those feelings is stopped. From the stopping of his delight is the stopping of grasping; from the stopping of grasping is the stopping of becoming; from the stopping of becoming is the stopping of birth; from the stopping of birth, old age and dying, grief, sorrow, suffering, lamentation and despair are stopped. Such is the stopping of this entire mass of anguish.

When he has heard a sound through the ear . . . smelt a scent with the nose . . . savoured a taste with the tongue . . . felt a touch with the body . . . known a mental object with the mind, he does not feel attraction for agreeable mental objects, he does not feel repugnance for disagreeable mental objects; and he dwells with mindfulness aroused as to the body, with a mind that is immeasurable; and he comprehends that freedom of mind . . . Such is the stopping of this entire mass of anguish.

Do you, monks, bear in mind this freedom by the destruction of craving (taught) in brief by me, but (remember) that Sāti [**271**] the monk, a fisherman's son, is caught in the great net of craving, the tangle of craving."[2]

Thus spoke the Lord. Delighted, these monks rejoiced in what the Lord had said.

Greater Discourse on the Destruction of Craving:
the Eighth

---

[1] *Cf. A.* i. 249, *aparitto mahattā appamāṇavihārī.*
[2] *Cf. M.* i. 383.

39. GREATER DISCOURSE AT ASSAPURA

(Mahāassapurasutta)

Thus have I heard: At one time the Lord was staying among the Aṅgas; a township of the Aṅgas was called Assapura. While he was there the Lord addressed the monks, saying: " Monks." " Revered one," these monks answered the Lord in assent. The Lord spoke thus:

" ' Recluses, recluses,' so the people know you, monks, and you, on being asked: ' Who are you ?' should acknowledge: ' We are recluses.' Such being your designations, monks, such being your vocations, thus you should train yourselves, monks: ' We will go forward undertaking those things that are to be done by recluses,[1] that are to be done by brahmans; thus will this designation of ours become true and the vocation real; and the gifts of those things we make use of—robe-material, almsfood, lodgings, medicine for the sick—will come to be of great fruit, of great advantage to us; and this our going forth will come to be not barren but fruitful and growing.'

And what, monks, are the things to be done by recluses and to be done by brahmans ? Thinking: ' We will become endowed with modesty and fear of blame[2]—thus you should train yourselves, monks. But it may occur to you, monks: ' We are endowed with modesty and fear of blame—to this extent there is enough, to this extent it is done; attained by us is the goal of recluseship, there is nothing further to be done by us '—up to this very point you may come to find contentment. I protest to you, monks, I declare to you, monks: While you are aiming at recluseship, fall not short of the goal of recluseship[3] if there is something further to be done.

And what, monks, is there further to be done ? Thinking: ' Our **[272]** bodily conduct must be perfectly pure, clear, open, and without defects, controlled. But not on account of this perfectly pure bodily conduct will we exalt ourselves or disparage others'—thus must you train yourselves, monks. But it may occur to you, monks: ' We are endowed with modesty and fear of blame; our bodily conduct is quite pure—to this extent there is enough, to this

---

[1] *Cf. A.* i. 229; but *MA.* ii. 313 says different duties are given here (below, in next paragraph).

[2] *MA.* ii. 313-14 quotes *A.* i. 51.

[3] See *S.* v. 25, quoted *MA.* ii. 314.

extent it is done; attained by us is the goal of recluseship, there is nothing further to be done by us '—up to this very point you may come to find contentment. I protest to you, monks, I declare to you, monks: While you are aiming at recluseship, fall not short of the goal of recluseship if there is something further to be done.

And what, monks, is there further to be done? Thinking: 'Our conduct in speech must be perfectly pure, clear, open, without defects, controlled. But not on account of this perfectly pure speech will we exalt ourselves or disparage others '—thus must you train yourselves, monks. But it may occur to you, monks: 'We are endowed with modesty and fear of blame; our bodily conduct is perfectly pure; our conduct in speech is perfectly pure—to this extent there is enough . . . ' up to this very point you may come to find contentment. I protest to you, monks . . . if there is something further to be done.

And what, monks, is there further to be done? Thinking: 'Our conduct in thought must be perfectly pure, clear, open, and without defects, controlled. But not on account of this perfectly pure thought will we exalt ourselves or disparage others '—thus must you train yourselves, monks. But it may occur to you, monks: 'We are endowed with modesty and fear of blame; our bodily conduct is perfectly pure; our conduct in speech is perfectly pure; our conduct in thought is perfectly pure—to this extent there is enough . . . ' up to this very point you may come to find contentment. I protest to you, monks . . . if there is something further to be done.

And what, monks, is there further to be done? Thinking: 'Our mode of living must be perfectly pure, clear, open, and without defects, controlled. But not on account of this perfectly pure mode of living will we exalt ourselves or disparage others '—thus you must train yourselves, monks. But it may occur to you, monks: 'We are endowed with modesty and fear of blame; our bodily conduct is perfectly pure; our conduct in speech is perfectly pure; our conduct in thought is perfectly pure; our mode of living is perfectly pure—[**273**] to this extent there is enough . . . ' up to this very point you may come to find contentment. I protest to you, monks . . . if there is something further to be done.

And what, monks, is there further to be done? Thinking: 'We must be guarded as to the doors of the sense-organs; having seen a material shape with the eye we are not entranced by the general appearance, we are not entranced by the detail; for if one had the organ of vision uncontrolled, coveting and dejection, evil unskilled states of mind, might predominate. We will fare along for its control, we will guard the organ of sight, we will come to control over the organ of sight. Having heard a sound with the ear . . . having smelt a smell with the nose . . . having savoured a taste with the tongue . . . having felt a touch with the body . . . having cognised a mental object with the mind we are not entranced by the general appearance, we are not entranced by the detail; for if one had the organ of mind uncontrolled, coveting and dejection, evil unskilled states of mind, might predominate. We will fare along for its control, we will guard the organ of mind, we will come to control over the organ of mind'—this is how you must train yourselves, monks. But it may occur to you, monks: 'We are endowed with modesty and fear of blame; our bodily conduct is perfectly pure; our conduct in speech is perfectly pure; our conduct in thought is perfectly pure; our mode of living is perfectly pure, guarded are the doors of our sense-organs—to this extent there is enough . . .' up to this very point you may come to find contentment. I protest to you, monks . . . if there is something further to be done.

And what, monks, is there further to be done? Thinking: 'We must be moderate in eating, carefully reflecting must we eat, not for fun or pleasure or adornment or beautifying, but just enough for maintaining this body and keeping it going, for keeping it from harm, for furthering the Brahma-faring; with the thought: 'I am destroying old feeling, and I must not allow new feeling to arise, so that there will be blamelessness for me and living in comfort' —thus, monks, must you train yourselves. But it may occur to you, monks: 'We are endowed with modesty and fear of blame; our bodily conduct is perfectly pure; our conduct in speech . . . in thought . . . our mode of living is perfectly pure; guarded are the doors of our sense-organs; we are moderate in eating—to this extent there is enough . . .' up to this very point you may come to find contentment. I protest to you, monks . . . if there is something further to be done.

And what, monks, is there further to be done? Thinking: 'We must be intent on vigilance; during the day, pacing up and down, sitting down, we must cleanse the mind from obstructive mental objects; during the first watch of the night, [**274**] pacing up and down, sitting down we must cleanse the mind from obstructive mental objects; during the middle watch of the night, we must lie down on our right side in the lion posture,[1] placing one foot on the other, mindful, clearly conscious, attending to the thought of getting up again; during the last watch of the night, rising, pacing up and down, sitting down, we must cleanse the mind from obstructive mental objects '—thus, monks, must you train yourselves. But it may occur to you, monks: ' We are endowed with modesty and fear of blame; our bodily conduct is perfectly pure; our conduct in speech . . . in thought . . . our mode of living is perfectly pure; guarded are the doors of our sense-organs; we are moderate in eating; we are intent on vigilance—to this extent there is enough . . . ' up to this point you may come to find contentment. I protest to you, monks . . . if there is something further to be done.

And what, monks, is there further to be done? Thinking: ' We must be possessed of mindfulness and clear consciousness, acting with clear consciousness,[2] whether setting out or returning . . . whether looking down or looking around . . . whether bending back or stretching out (the arm) . . . whether carrying the outer cloak, the bowl, the robe . . . whether munching, drinking, eating, savouring . . . whether obeying the calls of nature, acting with clear consciousness when walking, standing, sitting, asleep, awake, talking, silent '—thus, monks, must you train yourselves. But it may occur to you, monks: ' We are endowed with modesty and fear of blame; our bodily conduct is perfectly pure; our conduct in speech . . . our conduct in thought . . . our mode of living is perfectly pure; guarded are the doors of our sense-organs; we are moderate in eating; we are intent on vigilance; we are possessed of mindfulness and clear consciousness—to this extent it is enough, to this extent it is done; attained by us is the goal of recluseship, there is nothing further to be done '—up to this very point may you come to find contentment. I protest to you, monks, I declare to you, monks: While you are aiming at recluseship, fall not short of the goal of recluseship if there is something further to be done.

And what, monks, is there further to be done? In this case, monks, a monk chooses a remote lodging[3] in a forest, at the root of a tree, on a mountain slope, in a wilderness, in a hill-cave, in a

---

[1] *MA*. ii. 316 gives four postures, or sleeping-ways, *seyyā*: that of those indulging in sense-pleasures, that of the *petas*, that of the lion, and that of the Tathāgata. *Cf. A.* ii. 244-45. But the Tathāgata's posture is that (assumed) during the fourth meditation. At *e.g. S.* iv. 184 the Lord lay down in the lion-posture.

[2] *Cf. M.* i. 57, 181.

[3] *Cf. A.* iii. 92 with what follows.

cemetery, in a forest haunt, in the open or on a heap of straw. Returning from alms-gathering after the meal, he sits down cross-legged, holding the back erect, having made mindfulness rise up in front of him. He, by getting rid of coveting for the world, dwells with a mind devoid of coveting, he purifies the mind of coveting. By getting rid of the taint of ill-will he dwells benevolent in mind, [**275**] compassionate for the welfare of all creatures and beings, he purifies the mind of the taint of ill-will. By getting rid of sloth and torpor, he dwells devoid of sloth and torpor; perceiving the light, mindful, clearly conscious, he purifies the mind of sloth and torpor. By getting rid of restlessness and worry, he dwells calmly, the mind subjectively tranquillised, he purifies the mind of restlessness and worry. By getting rid of doubt, he dwells doubt-crossed, unperplexed as to the states that are skilled, he purifies the mind of doubt.

Monks, as a man[1] after contracting a loan might set some affairs going, and if these affairs of his should succeed, and if he should pay off those old original debts, and if he had a surplus over with which to maintain a wife, it might occur to him: 'I, formerly, after contracting a loan, set some affairs going, and these affairs of mine succeeded so that I paid off those old original debts, and have a surplus over with which to maintain a wife.' He, from this source would obtain joy, he would reach gladness.

And, monks, as a man might be a prey to disease, in pain, seriously ill, and could not digest his food, and there were not strength in his body, but if after a time he were to recover from that disease and could digest his food and there were some strength in his body, it might occur to him: 'Formerly I was a prey to disease, in pain, seriously ill, and could not digest my food, and there was no strength in my body, but now I am recovered from that disease, I digest my food, there is some strength in my body.' He, from this source, would obtain joy, he would reach gladness.

And, monks, as a man might be bound in a prison, but after a time might be freed from those bonds, safe and sound, and with no loss of his property, it might occur to him: 'Formerly I was bound in a prison, but now I am freed from those bonds, safe and sound, and with no loss of my property.' He, from this source would obtain joy, he would reach gladness.

Monks, it is as if a man had been a slave, not his own master,

---

[1] *Cf. D.* i. 71 *ff.*

subject to others, not able to go where he liked, but who after a time were freed from that slavery, his own master, not subject to others, able to go where he liked; it might occur to him: 'Formerly I was a slave, not my own master, subject to others, not able to go where I liked, but now I am freed from that slavery, my own master, [**276**] not subject to others, able to go where I like.' He, from this source, would obtain joy, he would reach gladness.

Monks, as a rich and prosperous man[1] might travel on a road through a wilderness and after a time might emerge safe and sound and with no loss of his property, it might occur to him: 'Formerly I, rich and prosperous, travelled on a road through a wilderness, but now I have emerged safe and sound and with no loss of my property.' He, from this source, would obtain joy, he would reach gladness.

Even so, monks, does a monk regard these five hindrances that are not got rid of from the self as a debt, as a disease, as a prison, as slavery, as travelling on a road through a wilderness. But, monks, when these five hindrances are got rid of from the self, a monk regards them as debtlessness, as health, as freedom from the bonds, as liberty, as secure ground.

By getting rid of these five hindrances which are defilements of the mind and weakening to intuitive wisdom[2] then, aloof from pleasures of the senses, aloof from unskilled states of mind, he enters on and abides in the first meditation which is accompanied by initial thought and discursive thought, is born of aloofness, and is rapturous and joyful. He drenches, saturates, permeates, suffuses this very body with the rapture and joy that are born of aloofness; there is no part of his whole body that is not suffused with the rapture and joy that are born of aloofness. Monks, as a skilled bath-attendant or his apprentice, having sprinkled bath-powder into a bronze vessel, might knead it together with drops of water until the ball of lather has taken up moisture, is drenched with moisture, suffused with moisture inside and out, but there is no oozing—even so, monks, does a monk drench, saturate, permeate, suffuse this very body with the rapture and joy that are born of aloofness; there is no part of his whole body that is not suffused with the rapture and joy that are born of aloofness.

And again, monks, a monk by allaying initial and discursive

---

[1] *Cf. D.* i. 73 (somewhat different).

[2] *Cf. M.* i. 181. This sentence differs at *D.* i. 73.

thought, with the mind subjectively tranquillised and fixed on one point, enters on and abides in the second meditation which is devoid of initial and discursive thought, is born of concentration and is rapturous and joyful. He drenches, saturates, permeates, suffuses this very body with the rapture and joy that are born of concentration; there is no part of his whole body that is not suffused with the rapture and joy that are born of concentration. Monks, as a pool of water [**277**] with water welling up within it, but which has no inlet for water from the eastern side, no inlet for water from the western side, no inlet for water from the northern side, no inlet for water from the southern side, and even if the god did not send down showers upon it from time to time, yet a current of cool water having welled up from that pool would drench, saturate, permeate, suffuse that pool with cool water; there would be no part of that pool that was not suffused with cool water. Even so, monks, does a monk drench, saturate, permeate, suffuse this very body with the rapture and joy that are born of concentration; there is no part of his whole body that is not suffused with the rapture and joy that are born of concentration.

And again, monks, a monk by the fading out of rapture, dwells with equanimity, attentive and clearly conscious and experiences in his person that joy of which the ariyans say: 'Joyful lives he who has equanimity and is mindful,' and he enters on and abides in the third meditation. He drenches, saturates, permeates, suffuses this very body with the joy that has no rapture; there is no part of his whole body that is not suffused with the joy that has no rapture. As in a pond of white lotuses or a pond of red lotuses or a pond of blue lotuses, some white lotuses or red lotuses or blue lotuses are born in the water, grow up in the water, never rising above the surface but flourishing beneath it—these from their roots to their tips are drenched, saturated, permeated, suffused by cool water. Even so, monks, a monk drenches, saturates, permeates, suffuses this very body with the joy that has no rapture; there is no part of his whole body that is not suffused with the joy that has no rapture.

And again, monks, a monk by getting rid of joy and by getting rid of anguish, by the going down of his former pleasures and sorrows, enters on and abides in the fourth meditation which has neither anguish nor joy, and which is entirely purified by equanimity and mindfulness. He, having suffused this very body with a mind that is utterly pure, utterly clean, comes to be sitting down; there is no part of his whole body that is not suffused with a mind that is utterly pure, utterly clean. Monks, as a monk might be sitting down who has clothed himself including his head with a white cloth, no part [**278**] of his whole body would not be suffused with the white cloth. Even so, monks, a monk, having suffused this very body with a mind that is utterly pure, utterly clean, comes to be sitting down; there is no part of his whole body that is not suffused by a mind that is utterly pure, utterly clean.

He, with his mind thus composed, quite purified, quite clarified, without blemish, without defilement, grown soft and workable, fixed, immovable, directs his mind to the knowledge and recollection of former habitations . . . (*as at p.* 28 *above*). . . . Thus he remembers divers former abodes in all their modes and detail. Monks, it is as if a man should go from his own village to another village, and should go from that village to another village, and as if he should go back again from that village to his own village.[1] This might occur to him: ' Now I went from my own village to a certain village, there I stood in such a way, sat in such a way, spoke in such a way, became silent in such a way. And from that village I went to a certain village, there I stood in such a way, sat in such a way, spoke in such a way, became silent in such a way. Then I went back again from that village to my own village.' Even so, monks, does a monk remember various former habitations, that is to say one birth and two births. . . . Thus he remembers divers former habitations in all their modes and detail.

He, with his mind thus composed, quite purified, quite clarified, without blemish, without defilement, grown soft and workable, fixed, immovable, directs his mind to the knowledge of the passing hence and arising of beings. With the purified *deva*-vision . . . (*as at p.* 28 *above*). . . . [**279**] . . . Thus with the purified *deva*-vision, surpassing that of men, he sees beings as they pass hence or come to be; he comprehends that beings are mean, excellent, comely, ugly, well-going, ill-going according to the consequences of their deeds. Monks, it is as if there were two houses with doors[2] and a man with vision standing there between them might see people entering a house and leaving it and going back and forth and walking across. Even so, monks, does a monk with the purified

---

[1] *MA.* ii. 323 says these villages represent the three becomings mentioned in the recollection of former abodes (as is clear from the text).

[2] Facing one another, *MA.* ii. 323. This simile also at *M.* ii. 21, iii. 178, both in connection with *deva*-vision.

deva-vision, surpassing that of men, see beings as they pass hence, as they come to be, and comprehend of the beings that they are mean, excellent, comely, ugly, well-going, ill-going . . . according to the consequences of their deeds.

He, with the mind thus composed, quite purified, quite clarified, without blemish, without defilement, grown soft and workable, fixed, immovable, directs his mind to the knowledge of the destruction of the cankers . . . (*as at p.* 29 *above*). . . . When he knows thus, sees thus, his mind is freed from the canker of sense-pleasures, his mind is freed from the canker of becoming, his mind is freed from the canker of ignorance. In freedom the knowledge comes to be that he is freed, and he comprehends: Destroyed is birth, brought to a close is the Brahma-faring, done is what was to be done, there is no more of being such or such. Monks, it is like[1] a pure, limpid, serene pool of water in which a man with vision standing on the bank might see oysters and shells, also gravel and pebbles, and shoals of fish moving about and keeping still.[2] It might occur to him: This pool of water is pure, limpid, serene, here these oysters and shells, [**280**] and gravel and pebbles, and shoals of fish are moving about and keeping still. Even so, monks, a monk comprehends as it really is: This is anguish . . . he comprehends as it really is: This is the course leading to the stopping of the cankers. When he knows thus, sees thus, his mind is freed from the canker of sense-pleasures and his mind is freed from the canker of becoming and his mind is freed from the canker of ignorance. In freedom the knowledge comes to be that he is freed, and he comprehends: Destroyed is birth, brought to a close is the Brahma-faring, done is what was to be done, there is no more of being such or such.

Monks, this is called a monk who is a recluse, and who is a brahman, and who is washen, and who is expert in lore, and who is learned,[3] and who is an ariyan, and who is a perfected one. And how, monks, is a monk a recluse ? Evil, unskilled states that are connected with the defilements, with again-becoming, fearful, whose results are anguish, leading to birth, ageing and dying in the future are allayed in him. It is thus, monks, that a monk is a recluse.

And how, monks, is a monk a brahman ? Evil, unskilled states

---

[1] =*M*. ii. 22=*D*. i. 84=*A*. i. 9.

[2] MA. ii. 324 says the gravel and pebbles lie still; the other two groups both keep still and move about.

[3] *sottiyo*; or, cleansed. *Cf*. *Thag*. 221.

that are connected with the defilements . . . leading to birth, ageing and dying in the future are excluded by him. It is thus, monks, that a monk is a brahman.

And how, monks, is a monk washen? Evil, unskilled states that are connected with the defilements . . . leading to birth, ageing and dying in the future, are washed away by him. It is thus, monks, that a monk is washen.

And how, monks, is a monk expert in lore? Evil unskilled states that are connected with the defilements . . . leading to birth, ageing and dying in the future are understood by him. It is thus, monks, that a monk is expert in lore.

And how, monks, does a monk become learned? Evil unskilled states that are connected with the defilements . . . leading to birth, ageing and dying in the future, come to be vanished[1] from him. It is thus, monks, that a monk comes to be learned.

And how, monks, is a monk an ariyan? Evil unskilled states that are connected with the defilements . . . leading to birth, ageing and dying in the future, are far from him. It is thus, monks, that a monk is an ariyan.

And how, monks, is a monk a perfected one? Evil unskilled states that are connected with the defilements, with again-becoming, fearful, whose results are anguish, leading to birth, ageing and dying in the future, are far from him. It is thus, monks, that a monk is a perfected one.'

Thus spoke the Lord. Delighted, these monks rejoiced in what the Lord had said.

Greater Discourse at Assapura:
The Ninth

40. LESSER DISCOURSE AT ASSAPURA

(Cūḷaassapurasutta)

[**281**] Thus have I heard. At one time the Lord was staying among the Aṅgas; a township of the Aṅgas was called Assapura. While he was there the Lord addressed the monks, saying: "Monks."

---

[1] *nissuta.*

"Revered one," these monks answered the Lord in assent. The Lord spoke thus:

"'Recluses, recluses,' so the people know you, monks, and you, on being asked: 'Who are you?' should acknowledge: 'We are recluses.' Such being your designations, monks, such being your vocations, thus you should train yourselves, monks: 'We will follow those practices which are fitting for recluses; thus will this designation of ours become true and the vocation real; and the gifts of those things we make use of—robe-material, almsfood, lodging, medicines for the sick—will come to be of great fruit, of great advantage to us; and this our going forth will come to be not barren but fruitful and growing.'

And how, monks, does a monk come to be one who is not following the practice that is fitting for recluses? Monks, in any monk who is covetous, covetousness not got rid of; who is malevolent in mind, malevolence not got rid of; who is wrathful, wrath not got rid of; who is grudging, grudging not got rid of; who is hypocritical, hypocrisy not got rid of; who is spiteful, spite not got rid of; who is jealous, jealousy not got rid of; who is stingy, stinginess not got rid of; who is treacherous, treachery not got rid of; who is crafty, craftiness not got rid of; who is of evil desires, evil desires not got rid of; who is of wrong view, wrong view not got rid of—I, monks, say that if he does not follow the practice fitting for recluses, there is no getting rid of these stains on recluses, defects in recluses, faults in recluses, occasions for the sorrowful states, of what is to be experienced in a bad bourn. Monks, as a deadly weapon[1] for fighting with, double-edged and whetted sharp, may be covered and enveloped by his outer cloak—unto this do I, monks, liken this monk's going forth.

I, monks, do not say that the recluseship of one who wears an outer cloak depends merely on his wearing an outer cloak. I, monks, do not say that the recluseship of one who is unclothed depends merely on his being unclothed. I, monks, do not say that the recluseship of one living in dust and dirt depends merely on his living in dust and dirt. I, monks, do not say that the recluseship of one who bathes ceremonially[2] depends merely on the ceremonial bathing. I, monks, do not say that the recluseship of one who

---

[1] *maṭaja*; *v.l. mataja.*

[2] At *S.* iv. 312= *A.* v. 263 spoken of as brahmans of the west. *MA.* ii. 325 says they enter the water three times a day (to cleanse themselves of their wrong-doings).

lives at the root of a tree [**282**] depends merely on his living at the root of a tree. I, monks, do not say that the recluseship of one who lives in the open depends merely on his living in the open. I, monks, do not say that the recluseship of one who stands erect depends merely on his standing erect. I, monks, do not say that the recluseship of one who lives on a regimen[1] depends merely on his living on a regimen. I, monks, do not say that the recluseship of one who meditates on chants[2] depends merely on his meditating on chants. I, monks, do not say that the recluseship of one who has matted hair depends merely on his matted hair.

If, monks, the covetousness of one who is covetous and who wears an outer cloak could be got rid of merely by wearing an outer cloak, if the malevolence of mind of one who is malevolent . . . wrath of one who is wrathful . . . the grudging of one who is grudging . . . the hypocrisy of one who is hypocritical . . . the spite of one who is spiteful . . . the jealousy of one who is jealous . . . the stinginess of one who is stingy . . . the treachery of one who is treacherous . . . the craftiness of one who is crafty . . . the evil desires of one who is of evil desires . . . the wrong view of one who is of wrong view could be got rid of, then his friends and acquaintances, kith and kin, would make him wear an outer cloak from the very day that he was born, would encourage him to wear an outer cloak, saying: 'Come, you auspicious-faced,[3] become a wearer of an outer cloak, for on your being a wearer of an outer cloak the covetousness of one who is covetous will be got rid of, the malevolence of mind of one who is malevolent will be got rid of, the wrath . . . the evil desires of one who is of evil desires will be got rid of, the wrong view of one who is of wrong view will be got rid of merely by the wearing of an outer cloak.' But because I, monks, see here some wearers of an outer cloak who are covetous, malevolent in mind, wrathful, grudging, hypocritical, spiteful, jealous, stingy, treacherous, crafty, of evil desires, of wrong view, therefore I do not say that the recluseship of one who wears an outer cloak depends merely on his wearing an outer cloak.

---

[1] *MA*. ii. 325 saying he eats once a month or a fortnight. Also that all these practices are external to "this teaching," where a monk who wears a robe is not called "a wearer of an outer cloak", *saṅghāṭiko*. The only practices that Gotama's followers have in common with the crowd outside are dwelling at the root of a tree and in the open.

[2] *manta*.

[3] *bhadramukha*. Also at *M*. ii. 53, *S*. i. 74. See *K.S*. i. 100, *n*. 3. *MA*. ii. does not comment.

If, monks, the covetousness of one who is covetous and who is unclothed . . . the wrong view of one who is of wrong view and who is unclothed could be got rid of merely by being unclothed . . . merely by living in dust and dirt . . . merely by ceremonial bathing . . . merely by living at the root of a tree . . . merely by living in the open . . . merely by standing erect . . . merely by living on a regimen . . . merely by meditation on chants . . . merely by wearing matted hair, then on the very day that he was born friends and acquaintances, kith and kin, would make him wear matted hair, would encourage him to wear matted hair, saying: 'Come, you auspicious-faced, become a wearer of matted hair, for on your being a wearer of matted hair the covetousness of one who is covetous will be got rid of merely by wearing matted hair . . . [**283**] the malevolence of one who is malevolent in mind will be got rid of . . . the wrong view of one who is of wrong view will be got rid of.' But because I, monks, see some wearers of matted hair here who are covetous, malevolent in mind, wrathful, grudging, hypocritical, spiteful, jealous, stingy, treacherous, crafty, of evil desires, of wrong view, therefore I do not say that the recluseship of one who wears matted hair depends merely on his wearing matted hair.

And how, monks, does a monk become one following practices fitting for recluses?

In whatever monk who was covetous covetousness is got rid of, who was malevolent malevolence of mind is got rid of, who was wrathful wrath is got rid of, who was grudging grudging is got rid of, who was hypocritical hypocrisy is got rid of, who was spiteful spite is got rid of, who was jealous, jealousy is got rid of, who was stingy, stinginess is got rid of, who was treacherous, treachery is got rid of, who was crafty, craftiness is got rid of, who was of evil desires, evil desire is got rid of, who was of wrong view, wrong view is got rid of, I, monks, say that if he follows the practice fitting for recluses, there is a getting rid of those stains on recluses, defects in recluses, faults in recluses, occasions for the sorrowful states, of what is to be experienced in a bad bourn. He beholds the self purified of all these evil unskilled states, he beholds the self freed. When he beholds the self purified of all these evil unskilled states, when he beholds the self freed, delight is born; rapture is born from delight; when he is in rapture the body is impassible; when the body is impassible he experiences joy; being joyful, the mind is concentrated. He dwells, having suffused the first quarter with a mind of friendliness, likewise the second, likewise the third, likewise the fourth; just so above, below, across; he dwells having suffused the whole world everywhere, in every way with a mind of friendliness that is far-reaching, wide-spread, immeasurable, without enmity, without malevolence. He abides, having suffused the first quarter with a mind of compassion. . . . He abides having suffused the first quarter with a mind of sympathetic joy. . . . He abides having suffused the first quarter with a mind of equanimity . . . without enmity, without malevolence.

Monks, it is as if[1] there were a lovely lotus-pond with clear water, sweet water, cool water, limpid, with beautiful banks; [**284**] and if a man were to come along from the east, overcome and overpowered by the hot-weather heat,[2] exhausted, parched and thirsty, he, on coming to that lotus-pond, might quench[3] his thirst with water, might quench the hot-weather fever. And if a man were to come along from the west . . . from the north . . . from the south . . . from wherever a man might come along, overcome and overpowered by the hot-weather heat, exhausted, parched and thirsty, he, on coming to that lotus-pond, might quench his thirst with water, might quench the hot-weather fever. Even so, monks, if from a noble's family one has gone forth from home into homelessness and has come into this *dhamma* and discipline taught by the Tathāgata, having thus developed friendliness, compassion, sympathetic joy and equanimity, he attains inward calm—I say it is by inward calm that he is following the practices fitting for recluses. If from a brahman's family . . . if from a merchant's family . . . if from a worker's family . . . and if from whatever family he has gone forth from home into homelessness and has come into this *dhamma* and discipline taught by the Tathāgata, having thus developed friendliness, compassion, sympathetic joy and equanimity, he attains inward calm—I say it is by inward calm that he is following the practices fitting for recluses. And if one has gone forth from home into homelessness from a noble's family, and by the destruction of the cankers, having here and now realised by his own super-knowledge freedom of mind, the freedom through intuitive wisdom that are cankerless, entering on them, abides therein—he is a recluse through the destruction of the cankers. If from a brahman's family . . . if from a merchant's family . . . if from a worker's family . . . if from whatever family he has gone forth from

---

[1] *M.* i. 76. [2] *M.* i. 74.

[3] *vineyya*, might avert, drive or lead away.

home into homelessness, and by the destruction of the cankers, having realised here and now by his own super-knowledge freedom of mind, the freedom through intuitive wisdom that are cankerless, entering on them, abides therein—he is a recluse through the destruction of the cankers."

Thus spoke the Lord. Delighted, those monks rejoiced in what the Lord had said.

Lesser Discourse at Assapura:
The Tenth

The Greater Division of the Pairs:
the Fourth

V. THE LESSER DIVISION OF THE PAIRS

(*Cūḷayamakavagga*)

41. DISCOURSE TO THE PEOPLE OF SĀLĀ

(Sāleyyakasutta)

[285] THUS have I heard: At one time[1] the Lord, walking on tour among the Kosalans together with a large Order of monks, arrived at the brahman village of the Kosalans named Sālā. The brahman householders of Sālā heard: "It is said that the recluse Gotama, the son of the Sakyans, gone forth from the Sakyan family, and walking on tour among the Kosalans together with a large Order of monks, has reached Sālā, and that a lovely reputation has gone forth about the Lord Gotama thus: 'The Lord is perfected, wholly Self-awakened, endowed with (right) knowledge and conduct, well-farer, knower of the worlds, incomparable charioteer of men to be tamed, teacher of *devas* and men, the Awakened One, the Lord . . .[2] He teaches *dhamma* that is lovely at the beginning, lovely in the middle and lovely at the ending, with the spirit and the meaning, he proclaims the Brahma-faring, wholly fulfilled, quite pure. It were good to see perfected ones like this.' "

Then the brahman householders of Sālā approached the Lord; some, having approached, having greeted the Lord, sat down at a respectful distance; some exchanged greetings with the Lord; having exchanged greetings of friendliness and courtesy, they sat down at a respectful distance; some, having saluted the Lord with joined palms, sat down at a respectful distance; some, having made known their names and clans in the Lord's presence, sat down at a respectful distance; some, becoming silent, sat down at a respectful distance. As they were sitting down at a respectful distance, the brahman householders of Sālā spoke thus to the Lord:

"Now, what is the cause, good Gotama, what is the reason why some beings here at the breaking up of the body after dying arise in a sorrowful state, a bad bourn, the abyss, Niraya Hell? What is the cause, what the reason, good Gotama, why some beings here at the breaking up of the body after dying arise in a good bourn, a heaven world?"

"Householders, some beings here at the breaking up of the body after dying arise thus in a sorrowful state, a bad bourn, the abyss,

---

[1] As at *M*. i. 400-1. [2] See above, p. 223.

Niraya Hell because of faring by not-*dhamma*, an uneven faring. Householders, some beings here at the breaking up of the body after dying arise thus in a good bourn, a heaven-world, [**286**] because of faring by *dhamma*, an even faring."

"We do not understand in full the matter that has been spoken of in brief by the good Gotama, and whose meaning was not explained in full. It were good if the good Gotama were so to teach us *dhamma* that we might understand in full the matter spoken of in brief by the good Gotama, and whose meaning was not explained in full."

"Well then, householders, listen, pay careful attention, and I will speak."

"Yes, sir," these brahman householders of Sālā answered the Lord in assent. The Lord spoke thus:

"Threefold, householders, is the faring by not-*dhamma*, an uneven faring as to body; fourfold is the faring by not-*dhamma*, an uneven faring as to speech; threefold is the faring by not-*dhamma*, an uneven faring as to thought. And what, householders, is the threefold faring by not *dhamma*, the uneven faring as to body? In this case,[1] householders, a certain one makes onslaught on creatures, he is cruel, bloody-handed, intent on injuring and killing, without mercy to living creatures.[2] He is a taker of what is not given; whatever property of another in village or jungle is not given to him he takes by theft. He is a wrong-goer in regard to pleasures of the senses; he has intercourse with (girls) protected by the mother,[3] protected by the father, protected by the parents, protected by a brother, protected by a sister, protected by relations, who have a husband, whose use involves punishments,[4] and even with those adorned with the garlands of betrothal. Even so, householders, is the threefold faring by not-*dhamma*, the uneven faring, in regard to body.

And how, householders, does there come to be the fourfold faring by not-*dhamma*, the uneven faring as to speech? In this case, householders, a certain one is of lying speech; when he is cited and asked as a witness before a council or company or amid

---

[1] As at *M*. iii. 46; *A*. v. 264 *ff*. *Cf*. *Asl*. 97 *ff*.

[2] *M*. ii. 97, iii. 203; *A*. v. 289.

[3] See the ten kinds of women at *Vin*. iii. 139, and notes at *B.D*. i. 237.

[4] *saparidaṇḍa*. *MA*. ii. 330 says: "Whoever goes to the woman so and so thinking 'such is the punishment for him,' if punishments are instituted with regard to a village or house or street, that is called *saparidaṇḍa*." *Cf*. *Vin*. iii. 139.

his relations or amid a guild or amid a royal family, and is told: 'Now, good man, say what you know,' although he does not know, he says, 'I know,' although he knows, he says, 'I do not know'; although he has not seen, he says, 'I saw,' although he has seen, he says, 'I did not see.' Thus his speech becomes intentional lying either for his own sake or for that of another or for the sake of some material gain or other. And he is a slanderer; having heard something at one place, he makes it known elsewhere for (causing) variance among those (people)[1]; or having heard something elsewhere he makes it known among these people for (causing) variance among these (people). In this way he sows discord among those who are in harmony, or is one who foments those who are at variance. Discord is his pleasure, discord his delight, discord his joy, discord is the motive of his speech. And he is one of harsh speech.[2] Whatever speech is rough,[3] hard, severe on others, abusive of others, bordering on wrath, not conducive to concentration, [**287**] such speech does he utter. And he is a frivolous chatterer, one who speaks at a wrong time, one who does not speak in accordance with fact, one who speaks about what is not the goal, one who speaks about not-*dhamma*, one who speaks about not-discipline. He utters speech that is not worth treasuring; owing to its being at the wrong time it is incongruous, has no purpose, is not connected with the goal. Even so, householders, is the fourfold faring by not-*dhamma*, the uneven faring in regard to speech.

And what, householders, is the threefold faring by not-*dhamma*, the uneven faring as to thought? In this case, householders, a certain one comes to be covetous; he covets that which is the property of another, thinking, 'O that what is the other's might be mine'; he is malevolent in mind, corrupt in thought and purpose, and thinks, 'Let these beings be killed or slaughtered or annihilated or destroyed, or may they not exist at all.' And he is of wrong view, of perverted outlook, thinking, 'There is no (result of) gift,[4] there is no (result of) offering, no (result of) sacrifice; there is no fruit or ripening of deeds well done or ill done; there is not this

---

[1] *Cf.* opposite at *D.* i. 4 (of Gotama).

[2] *Cf.* opposite at *D.* i. 4; *Dhs.* 1343.

[3] *aṇḍaka.* *Cf.* *Bud. Psych. Ethics*, p. 349, *n.* 4. *MA.* ii. agrees with *Asl.* (there quoted).

[4] This is a "heretical" view; *cf.* *M.* i. 401, 515; *D.* i. 55; *S.* iii. 206. *MA.* ii. 332=*DA.* 165 says *n'atthi dinnaṃ* means there is no existence of the fruit of giving.

world, there is not a world beyond[1]; there is not a mother, there is not a father,[2] there are no spontaneously uprising beings;[3] there are not in the world recluses and brahmans who are faring rightly, proceeding rightly, and who proclaim this world and the world beyond, having realised them by their own super-knowledge.'[4] Even so, householders, is the threefold faring by not-*dhamma*, the uneven faring in regard to thought. Thus it is, householders, that as a result of faring by not-*dhamma*, the uneven faring, some beings here, at the breaking up of the body after dying, arise in a sorrowful state, a bad bourn, the abyss, Niraya Hell.

And threefold, householders, is the faring by *dhamma*, the even faring in regard to body, fourfold is the faring by *dhamma*, the even faring in regard to speech, threefold is the faring by *dhamma*, the even faring in regard to thought. And what, householders, is the threefold faring by *dhamma*, the even faring in regard to body? In this case, householders, a certain one, abandoning onslaught on creatures,[5] is restrained from onslaught on creatures; the stick laid aside, the sword laid aside, he lives scrupulous, merciful, kindly and compassionate to all living creatures. Abandoning taking what is not given, he is restrained from taking what is not given. He does not take by theft any property of another in village or jungle that is not given to him. Abandoning wrong-doing in regard to pleasures of the senses, he is restrained from wrong-doing in regard to pleasures of the senses; he does not have intercourse with (girls) who are protected by the mother, protected by the father, protected by the parents, protected by a brother, protected by a sister, protected by relations, who have a husband, whose use involves punishment, nor even with those adorned with

---

[1] *MA*. ii. 332=*DA*. i. 165: " when one is established in the world beyond, this world is not (' there is not this world '); when one is established in the world here, a world beyond is not (' there is not a world beyond '). All beings are cut off precisely here or there." Apparently there was no relation between the two worlds; in this deterministic view deeds done would not bring one to a world beyond—although this view apparently conceded that there was such a world.

[2] *MA*. ii. 332=*DA*. i. 165: " there is no existence of fruit of good or bad behaviour "—towards parents.

[3] *MA*. ii. 332=*DA*. i. 165: " having deceased, there are no arising beings "—meaning apparently there is no more birth for them, no more life.

[4] Here the " heretic " is speaking of the non-existence of omniscient Buddhas, *MA*. ii. 332.

[5] *Cf*. *D*. i. 4; *A*. v. 266.

the garlands of betrothal. Even so, householders is the threefold faring by *dhamma*, [**288**] the even faring in regard to body.

And what, householders, is the fourfold faring by *dhamma*, the even faring in regard to speech ? In this case, householders, a certain one, abandoning lying speech is restrained from lying speech.[1] When he is cited and asked as a witness before a council or company or amid his relations or amid a guild or amid a royal family, and is told: 'Now, good man, say what you know,' if he does not know, he says, 'I do not know'; if he knows, he says, 'I know'; if he has not seen, he says, 'I did not see,' if he has seen, he says, 'I saw.' Thus his speech does not come to be intentional lying either for his own sake or for that of another or for the sake of some material gain or other. Abandoning slanderous speech, he is restrained from slanderous speech. Having heard something at one place, he is not one for repeating it elsewhere for (causing) variance among those people, or having heard something elsewhere he is not one to repeat it to these people for (causing) variance among these people. In this way he is a reconciler of those who are at variance and one who combines those who are friends. Concord is his pleasure, concord his delight, concord his joy, concord is the motive of his speech. Abandoning harsh speech, he is restrained from harsh speech. Whatever speech is gentle, pleasing to the ear, affectionate, going to the heart, urbane, pleasant to the multitude—such speech does he utter. Abandoning frivolous chatter, he is restrained from frivolous chatter. He is one who speaks at a right time, who speaks in accordance with fact, who speaks about the goal, who speaks about *dhamma*, who speaks about discipline. He utters speech that is worth treasuring, with similes at a right time, purposeful, connected with the goal. Even so, householders, is the fourfold faring by *dhamma*, the even faring in regard to speech.

And what, householders, is the threefold faring by *dhamma*, the even faring in regard to thought ? In this case, householders, a certain one comes to be not covetous,[2] he does not covet the property of another, thinking, 'O, might that be mine which is the other's.' And he is not malevolent in mind, not corrupt of thought and purpose, but thinks, 'Let these beings, friendly, peaceful, secure, happy, look after self.'[3] And he is of right view, not of perverted outlook, thinking, 'There is (result of) gift,

---

[1] *Cf. M.* i. 179; *A.* v. 267. [2] *Cf. A.* v. 267 *f.*

[3] *attānaṃ pariharantu*; *cf. A.* ii. 3, 228, 253.

there is (result of) offering, there is (result of) sacrifice; there is fruit and ripening of deeds well done and ill done; there is this world, there is a world beyond; there is mother, there is father, there are spontaneously uprising beings; there are in the world recluses and brahmans who are faring rightly, proceeding rightly and who proclaim this world and the world beyond having realised them by their own super-knowledge.' Even so, householders, is the threefold faring by *dhamma*, the even faring in regard to thought. Thus it is, householders, that as a result of faring by *dhamma*, the even faring, some beings here at the breaking up of the body after dying arise in a good bourn, a heaven world.

[**289**] If, householders, a *dhamma*-farer, an even-farer should wish: 'O that I at the breaking up of the body after dying might arise in companionship with rich nobles,' this situation occurs when he, at the breaking up of the body after dying might arise in companionship with rich nobles. What is the cause of this? It is that he is a *dhamma*-farer, an even-farer. If, householders, a *dhamma*-farer, an even-farer should wish: 'O that I at the breaking up of the body after dying should arise in companionship with rich brahmans . . . with rich householders,' this situation occurs when he, at the breaking up of the body after dying, might arise in companionship with rich householders. What is the cause of this? It is that he is a *dhamma*-farer, an even-farer. If, householders, a *dhamma*-farer, an even-farer, should wish: 'O that I, at the breaking up of the body after dying, might arise in companionship with the *devas* belonging to the four Great Regents . . . with the *devas* of the Thirty-Three . . . with Yama's *devas* . . . with the Tusita *devas* . . . with the *devas* of creation . . . with the *devas* who have power over the creations of others . . . with the *devas* in the retinue of Brahmā . . . with the *devas* of light . . . with the *devas* of limited light . . . with the *devas* of boundless light . . . with the *devas* of brilliance . . . with the *devas* of splendour . . . with the *devas* of limited splendour . . . with the *devas* of boundless splendour . . . with the Subhakiṇṇa *devas* . . . Vehapphala *devas* . . . Aviha *devas* . . . Atappa *devas* . . . Sudassa *devas* . . . Sudassī *devas* . . . Akaniṭṭha *devas* . . . with the *devas* experiencing the plane of infinite ether . . . with the *devas* experiencing the plane of infinite consciousness . . . with the *devas* experiencing the plane of no-thing . . . with the *devas* experiencing the plane of neither-perception-nor-non-perception, this situation occurs when he, at the breaking up of the body after dying, might arise in companionship with the *devas* who experience the plane of

neither-perception-nor-non-perception. What is the cause of this? It is that he is a *dhamma*-farer, an even-farer.

If, householders, a *dhamma*-farer, an even-farer should wish: 'O that I, by the destruction of the cankers, might enter on and abide in that freedom of mind, that freedom through intuitive wisdom that are cankerless, having realised them here and now through my own super-knowledge,' this situation occurs when he, by the destruction of the cankers, might enter on and abide in the freedom of mind, the freedom through intuitive wisdom that are cankerless, having realised them here and now through his own super-knowledge. What is the cause of this? It is that he is a *dhamma*-farer, an even-farer."

[**290**] When this had been said, the brahman householders of Sālā spoke thus to the Lord: "It is wonderful, good Gotama, it is wonderful, good Gotama. As if one might set upright what has been upset, or might disclose what was covered, or might show the way to one who had gone astray, or bring an oil lamp into the darkness so that those with vision might see material shapes—even so in many a figure has *dhamma* been proclaimed by the revered Gotama. We ourselves are going to the revered Gotama for refuge, to *dhamma* and to the Order of monks. Let the revered Gotama accept us as lay-followers going for refuge from today forth for as long as life lasts."

Discourse to the People of Sālā:
the First

42. DISCOURSE TO THE PEOPLE OF VERAÑJĀ

(Verañjakasutta)

THUS have I heard: At one time the Lord was staying near Sāvatthī in the Jeta Grove in Anāthapiṇḍika's monastery. Now at that time brahman householders of Verañjā entered Sāvatthī on some business or other. The brahman householders of Verañjā heard: "It is said that the recluse Gotama, the son of the Sakyans, gone forth from the Sakyan family, is staying at Sāvatthī in Anāthapiṇḍika's monastery, and that a lovely reputation has gone forth about the Lord Gotama thus: 'The Lord is perfected, wholly Self-awakened . . . [**291**] . . .' " (*etc., as in the foregoing Discourse, substituting* Verañjā *for* Sālā, *to the end*).

Discourse to the People of Verañjā:
the Second

43. GREATER DISCOURSE OF THE MISCELLANY

(Mahāvedallasutta)

[**292**] Thus have I heard. At one time the Lord was staying near Sāvatthī in the Jeta Grove in Anāthapiṇḍika's monastery. Then the venerable Koṭṭhita the Great,[1] emerging from solitary meditation towards evening, approached the venerable Sāriputta[2]: having approached, he exchanged greetings with the venerable Sāriputta; having exchanged greetings of friendliness and courtesy, he sat down at a respectful distance. As he was sitting down at a respectful distance, the venerable Koṭṭhita the Great spoke thus to the venerable Sāriputta:

"Your reverence, one is called: 'Poor in intuitive wisdom, poor in intuitive wisdom.' Now what are the respects in which one is called 'Poor in intuitive wisdom,' your reverence ?"

"Your reverence, if it is said 'He does not comprehend, he does not comprehend,' therefore he is called 'Poor in intuitive wisdom.' What does he not comprehend ? He does not comprehend 'This is anguish,' he does not comprehend 'This is the arising of anguish,' he does not comprehend 'This is the stopping of anguish,'[3] he does not comprehend 'This is the course leading to the stopping of anguish.' If it is said, 'He does not comprehend, he does not comprehend,' your reverence, therefore he is called 'poor in intuitive wisdom.' "

---

[1] At *A.* i. 24 he is called chief of those who have mastery in logical analysis; cited at *MA.* ii. 337.

[2] At *A.* i. 23 called chief of those of great intuitive wisdom; cited at *MA.* ii. 335.

[3] He does not comprehend that the third truth, of stopping, is nibbāna. *MA.* ii. 338 points out that the first two truths are concerned with the "round" of rebirths, and the last two with what is not the "round" *vivaṭṭa*.

"It is good, your reverence," and the venerable Koṭṭhita the Great, having rejoiced in what the venerable Sāriputta had said, having thanked him, asked the venerable Sāriputta a further question:

"Your reverence, one is called 'Intuitively wise, intuitively wise.' Now what are the respects in which one is called 'intuitively wise,' your reverence?"

"Your reverence, if it is said 'He comprehends, he comprehends,' he is therefore called 'Intuitively wise.' And what does he comprehend? He comprehends 'This is anguish,' he comprehends 'This is the arising of anguish,' he comprehends 'This is the stopping of anguish,' he comprehends 'This is the course leading to the stopping of anguish.' If it is said, 'He comprehends, he comprehends,' your reverence, therefore he is called 'intuitively wise.'"

"Your reverence, it is called 'Discriminative consciousness,[1] discriminative consciousness.' Now in what respects, your reverence, is it called 'discriminative consciousness'?"

"Your reverence, if it said 'It discriminates,[2] it discriminates,' it is therefore called discriminative consciousness. And what does it discriminate? It discriminates pleasure and it discriminates pain and it discriminates neither pain nor pleasure.[3] If it is said 'It discriminates, it discriminates,' your reverence, therefore it is called 'Discriminative consciousness.'"

"That which is intuitive wisdom, your reverence, and that which is discriminative consciousness, are these states associated or dissociated? And is it possible to lay down a difference between these states, having analysed them again and again?"

"That which is intuitive wisdom, your reverence, and that which is discriminative consciousness, these states are associated, not dissociated, and it is not possible to lay down a difference between these states, having analysed them again and again. Whatever one comprehends, your reverence, that one discriminates; whatever one discriminates that one comprehends; **[293]** therefore these states are associated, not dissociated, and it is not possible to lay down a difference between these states, having analysed them again and again."

"That which is intuitive wisdom, your reverence, and that which is discriminative consciousness, what is the difference between these states which are associated, not dissociated?"

---

[1] *viññāṇa*. [2] *vijānāti*. [3] *Cf. M.* i. 59.

"That which is intuitive wisdom, your reverence, and that which is discriminative consciousness among these states that are associated, not dissociated, intuitive wisdom is to be developed, discriminative consciousness is for apprehending.[1] This is the difference between them."

"Your reverence, it is said, 'Feeling, feeling.' Now what are the respects in which it is called 'feeling,' your reverence?"

"Your reverence, if it is said, 'He feels, he feels,' it is therefore called 'feeling.' And what does he feel? He feels pleasure, and he feels pain, and he feels neither pain nor pleasure. If it is said, 'He feels, he feels,' your reverence, therefore it is called 'feeling.'"[2]

"Your reverence, it is said, 'Perception, perception.' Now what are the respects in which it is called 'perception,' your reverence?"

"Your reverence, if it is said, 'He perceives, he perceives,' it is therefore called 'perception.' And what does he perceive? He perceives what is dark green and he perceives what is yellow and he perceives what is red and he perceives what is white. If it is said 'He perceives, he perceives,' your reverence, it is therefore called 'perception.'"

"That which is feeling, your reverence, and that which is perception and that which is discriminative consciousness—are these states associated or dissociated? And is it possible to lay down a difference between these states, having analysed them again and again?"

"That which is feeling, your reverence, and that which is perception and that which is discriminative consciousness—these states are associated, not dissociated, and it is not possible to lay down a difference between these states, having analysed them again and again. Your reverence, whatever one feels, that one perceives; whatever one perceives that one discriminates; therefore these states are associated, not dissociated, and it is not possible to lay down a difference between these states, having analysed them again and again."

"What is knowable, your reverence, by purified mental consciousness isolated from the five sense-organs?"[3]

---

[1] *pariññeyyaṃ*; *cf. pariññeyya dhamma* at *S.* iii. 36. *MA.* ii. 342 keeps the view that there is no difference. For it says that discriminative consciousness being joined to intuitive wisdom should be developed with it, and that intuitive wisdom being joined to discriminative consciousness should be apprehended with it.

[2] *Cf. S.* iii. 69.

[3] That is, in the fourth *jhāna*.

"Your reverence, thinking, 'Ether is unending,' the plane of infinite ether is knowable by pure mental consciousness isolated from the five sense-organs; thinking, 'Consciousness is unending,' the plane of infinite consciousness is knowable; thinking, 'There is not anything,' the plane of no-thing is knowable."

"By what means does one comprehend a knowable mental object, your reverence?"

"One comprehends a knowable mental object, your reverence, by means of the eye of intuitive wisdom."[1]

"But what is intuitive wisdom for, your reverence?"

"Your reverence, intuitive wisdom is for super-knowledge, for apprehending,[2] for getting rid of."

[294] "But how many conditions are there, your reverence, for bringing right understanding[3] into existence?"

"There are two conditions, your reverence, for bringing right understanding into existence: the utterance of another (person) and wise attention.[4] Your reverence, these are the two conditions for bringing right understanding into existence."

"If right understanding is forwarded, by how many factors, your reverence, does there come to be the fruit of freedom of mind and the advantage of the fruit[5] of freedom of mind, and the fruit of freedom through intuitive wisdom and the advantage of the fruit of freedom through intuitive wisdom?"

"Your reverence, if right understanding is forwarded by five factors there comes to be the fruit of freedom of mind and the advantage of the fruit of freedom of mind, and the fruit of freedom through intuitive wisdom and the advantage of the fruit of freedom through intuitive wisdom: in this case, your reverence, right understanding is forwarded by moral habit, and it is forwarded by hearing,[6] and it is forwarded by discussion, and it is forwarded by calm and it is forwarded by vision. Your reverence, if right understanding is forwarded by these five factors, there comes to

---

[1] Wisdom that has become vision. *MA.* ii. 345 gives two kinds of wisdom, that of concentration and that of vision.

[2] *abhiññatthaṃ* and *pariññatthaṃ* also at *It.* p. 29. But *cf.* p. 352, above, where consciousness is for apprehending, *pariññeyya*.

[3] *MA.* ii. 346, the right understanding through vision, the right understanding of the Way.

[4] *MA.* ii. 346 cites Sāriputta as having heard a verse (*Vin.* i. 40) spoken by Assaji, as an example of hearing from another; and *paccekabuddhas* as coming to omniscience through their own wise attention.

[5] *Sn.* 256.

[6] *I.e.* hearing from others, learning.

be the fruit of freedom of mind and the advantage of the fruit of freedom of mind, and there comes to be the fruit of freedom through intuitive wisdom and the advantage of the fruit of freedom through intuitive wisdom."[1]

"And how many becomings are there, your reverence?"

"These three are becomings, your reverence: becoming of sense-pleasures, becoming of fine-materiality, becoming of immateriality."[2]

"How, your reverence, is there the recurrence of again-becoming in the future?"

"For those creatures who are hindered by ignorance, fettered by craving, delighting in this and that, there thus comes to be recurrence of again-becoming in the future."[3]

"But how, your reverence, is there not recurrence of again-becoming in the future?"

"By the fading away of ignorance, by the uprising of knowledge,[4] by the stopping of craving, there is thus no recurrence of again-becoming in the future"

"And what, your reverence, is the first meditation?"

"As to this, your reverence, a monk, aloof from pleasures of the senses, aloof from unskilled states of mind, enters on and abides in the first meditation which is accompanied by initial thought and discursive thought, is born of aloofness, and is rapturous and joyful. This, your reverence, is called the first meditation."

"Of how many factors, your reverence, is the first meditation?"

"Your reverence, the first meditation is five-factored: if a monk has entered on the first meditation there is initial thought and discursive thought and rapture and joy and one-pointedness of mind. Thus, your reverence, is the first meditation five-factored."

"Your reverence, in regard to the first meditation, how many factors are abandoned, how many factors are possessed?"

"Your reverence, in regard to the first meditation, five factors are abandoned, five are possessed: if a monk has entered on the first meditation, desire for sense-pleasure is abandoned, malevolence is abandoned, sloth and torpor are abandoned, restlessness and worry are abandoned, [**295**] doubt is abandoned, but there is initial thought and discursive thought, rapture and joy and one-pointedness of mind. Thus, your reverence, in regard to the first

---

[1] For, the Way to arahantship coming into being as a result of practising these five factors, gives the fruit, *MA*. ii. 346.

[2] *Cf. A*. i. 223; *S*. ii. 3, 65, 101; *Vin*. iii. 3.

[3] *Cf. A*. i. 223.

[4] As at *M*. i. 67; *S*. ii. 82.

meditation, five factors are abandoned, five factors are possessed."

"Your reverence, these five sense-organs,[1] different in range, different in pasture, do not react to the pasture and range of one another; that is to say the organ of eye, the organ of ear, the organ of nose, the organ of tongue, the organ of body. What is the repository[2] of these five sense-organs, different in range, different in pasture, which do not react to the pasture and range of one another? And what is it that reacts to their pasture and range?"

"Your reverence, these five sense-organs, different in range, different in pasture, do not react to the pasture and range of one another; that is to say the organ of eye . . . ear . . . nose . . . tongue, the organ of body. Of these five sense-organs, your reverence, different in range, different in pasture, not reacting to the pasture and range of one another, mind is the repository, and mind reacts to their pasture and range."

"Your reverence, these are the five sense-organs, that is to say, organ of eye . . . of ear . . . of nose . . . of tongue, organ of body. On what do these five sense-organs depend, your reverence?"

"Your reverence, these are the five sense-organs, that is to say, organ of eye . . . ear . . . nose . . . tongue, organ of body. Your reverence, these five sense-organs depend on vitality."[3]

"And on what does vitality depend, your reverence?"

"Vitality depends on heat."

"And on what does heat depend, your reverence?"

"Heat depends on vitality."

"Your reverence, we now understand the words of the venerable Sāriputta thus: 'Vitality depends on heat'; we now understand the words of the venerable Sāriputta thus: 'Heat depends on vitality.' What is the precise meaning to be attached to these words, your reverence?"

"Well then, your reverence, I will make a simile[4] for you. For by a simile some intelligent persons here understand the meaning of what has been said: As when an oil lamp is burning the light is seen because of the flame and the flame is seen because of the light, so, your reverence, vitality depends on heat and heat on vitality."

---

[1] *Cf.* the following passage with *S.* v. 217 *f.*

[2] *paṭisaraṇa* also resort, arbiter, as at *M.* i. 310, iii. 9, or underlying principle.

[3] *āyu*; *MA.* ii. 349 says *jīvitindriya*. *Cf. Chānd. Up.* 6. 8. 4, 6.

[4] As at *M.* i. 148.

"Now, your reverence, are these properties of vitality[1] states that are to be felt, or are the properties of vitality one thing, states that are to be felt another ?"

[296] "Your reverence, these properties of vitality are not themselves states to be felt. If, your reverence, these properties of vitality were themselves states to be felt, no emergence[2] could be shown for a monk who had won to the stopping of perception and feeling. But because, your reverence, the properties of vitality are one thing and states to be felt another, therefore the emergence of a monk who has won to the stopping of perception and feeling can be shown."

"In regard to this body, your reverence, when how many things are got rid of, does this body lie cast away, flung aside like unto a senseless log of wood ?"[3]

"In regard to this body, your reverence, when three things are got rid of: vitality, heat and consciousness, then does this body lie cast away, flung aside like unto a senseless log of wood."

"What is the difference, your reverence, between that dead thing, passed away, and that monk who has attained to the stopping of perception and feeling ?"

"Your reverence, the bodily activities[4] of that dead thing, passed away, have been stopped, have subsided, the vocal activities[5] have been stopped, have subsided, the mental activities[6] have been stopped, have subsided, the vitality is entirely destroyed, the heat allayed, the sense-organs are entirely broken asunder. But that monk who has attained to the stopping of perception and feeling, although his bodily activities have been stopped, have subsided, although his vocal activities have been stopped, have subsided, although his mental activities have been stopped, have subsided, his vitality is not entirely destroyed, his heat is not allayed, his sense-organs are purified. This, your reverence, is the difference

---

[1] *āyusaṅkhāra*. *MA*. ii. 350 *āyum eva*. *Cf*. *D*. ii. 106; *Ud*. 64; *A*. iv. 311; *S*. ii. 266

[2] *I.e.* from this (ninth) attainment, that of the stopping of perception and feeling.

[3] *Cf*. *S*. iii. 143, quoted *MA*. ii. 351; *cf*. *Dh*. 41; *Thag*. 468; *M*. Sta. 66.

[4] Defined in next Discourse, *M*. i. 301, and similarly at *MA*. ii. 351: in-breathing and out-breathing. *Cf*. *S*. iv. 294-97.

[5] Thought-conception and discursive thought. The "ariyan silence" ensues when these are stopped.

[6] Feeling and perception.

between a dead thing, passed away, and that monk who has attained to the stopping of perception and feeling."

"And how many conditions are there, your reverence, for the attainment of the freedom of mind which has neither anguish nor joy?"

"There are four conditions, your reverence, for the attainment of the freedom of mind which has neither anguish nor joy. In this case, your reverence, a monk by getting rid of joy, by getting rid of anguish, by the going down of his former pleasures and sorrows, enters on and abides in the fourth meditation which has neither anguish nor joy, and which is entirely purified by equanimity and mindfulness. These, your reverence, are the four conditions for attaining the freedom of mind which has neither anguish nor joy."

"How many conditions are there, your reverence, for the attainment of the freedom of mind that is signless?"

"There are two conditions, your reverence, for the attainment of the freedom of mind that is signless: paying no attention to any signs, and paying attention to the signless realm.[1] These, your reverence, are the two conditions for the attainment of the freedom of mind that is signless."

"How many conditions are there, your reverence, for the persistence of the freedom of mind that is signless?"

"There are three conditions, your reverence, for the persistence of the freedom of mind that is signless: [**297**] paying no attention to any signs, and paying attention to the signless realm, and a preceding preparation. These, your reverence, are the three conditions for the persistence of the freedom of mind that is signless."

"How many conditions are there, your reverence, for emergence from the freedom of mind that is signless?"

"There are the two conditions, your reverence, for emerging from the freedom of mind that is signless: paying attention to all signs, and not paying attention to the signless realm. These, your reverence, are the two conditions for emergence from the freedom of mind that is signless."

"Your reverence, whatever is immeasurable freedom of mind[2] and whatever is freedom of mind that is naught[3] and whatever is freedom of mind that is void and whatever is freedom of mind that

---

[1] This is nibbāna, *MA.* ii. 352. *Nimitta* (signs) and *animitta* refer to experiential phenomena (*i.e.* to conditioned existence), and their absence.

[2] This appears to refer to the *brahmavihāra*, see below.

[3] *Cf.* *Sn.* 1113-1115. "Naught because of the non-existence of any (*kiñcana*) basis for meditation," *MA.* ii. 353.

is signless—are these states different in connotation and different in denotation, or are they identical in connotation while being different only in denotation ?"[1]

"Your reverence, whatever is immeasurable freedom of mind and whatever is the freedom of mind that is naught and whatever is freedom of mind that is void and whatever is freedom of mind that is signless—there is a method according to which these states are different in connotation as well as being different in denotation; and, your reverence, there is a method according to which these states are identical in connotation while being different in denotation. And what, your reverence, is the method according to which these states are different in connotation as well as being different in denotation ? As to this, your reverence, a monk abides having suffused the first quarter with a mind of friendliness, likewise the second, likewise the third, likewise the fourth; just so above, below, across; he dwells having suffused the whole world everywhere, in every way with a mind of friendliness, that is far-reaching, wide-spread, immeasurable, without enmity, without malevolence. He dwells having suffused the first quarter with a mind of compassion . . . with a mind of sympathetic joy . . . with a mind of equanimity, likewise the second, likewise the third, likewise the fourth; just so above, below, across; he dwells having suffused the whole world, everywhere, in every way with a mind of equanimity that is far-reaching, wide-spread, immeasurable, without enmity, without malevolence. This, your reverence, is called immeasurable freedom of mind.[2]

And what, your reverence, is the freedom of mind that is naught ? As to this, your reverence, a monk passing quite beyond the plane of infinite consciousness, thinking, 'There is not anything,' enters on and abides in the plane of no-thing. This, your reverence, is called the freedom of mind that is naught.

And what, your reverence, is the freedom of mind that is void ? As to this, your reverence, a monk forest-gone or gone to the root of a tree or gone to an empty place, reflects thus: 'This is void of self[3] or of what pertains to self.'[4] [**298**] This, your reverence, is called the freedom of mind that is void.

---

[1] *Cf. M.* iii. 145 *f.* in connection with immeasurable and widespread freedom of mind.

[2] *Cf. M.* iii. 146.

[3] *MA.* ii. 353, the self that composes an individual or man.

[4] *I.e.* the requisites of robe-material and so on, *MA.* ii. 353. *Cf. S.* iv. 54, 296; *Kvu.* 67, 579.

And what, your reverence, is the freedom of mind that is signless? As to this, your reverence, a monk, by paying no attention to any signs, entering on the concentration of mind that is signless, abides therein. This, your reverence, is called the freedom of mind that is signless. This, your reverence, is the method according to which these states are different in connotation as well as differing in denotation.

And what, your reverence, is the method according to which these states are identical in connotation while being different in denotation? Attachment, your reverence, is productive of the measurable, hatred is productive of the measurable, confusion is productive of the measurable. For a monk whose cankers are destroyed, these are got rid of, cut off at the roots, made like a palm-tree stump so that they can come to no further existence in the future. To the extent, your reverence, that freedoms of mind are immeasurable,[1] unshakable freedom of mind is shown to be their chief, for that unshakable freedom of mind is void of attachment, void of hatred, void of confusion. Attachment, your reverence, is something (obstructive),[2] hatred is something (obstructive), confusion is something (obstructive).[3] For a monk whose cankers are destroyed, these are got rid of, cut off at the roots, made like a palm-tree stump so that they can come to no further existence in the future. To the extent, your reverence, that freedoms of mind are naught, unshakable freedom of mind is shown to be their chief, for that unshakable freedom of mind is void of attachment, void of hatred, void of confusion. Attachment, your reverence, is productive of signs, hatred is productive of signs, confusion is productive of signs. For a monk whose cankers are destroyed these are got rid of, cut off at the roots, made like a palm-tree stump so that they can come to no further existence in the future. To the extent, your reverence, that freedoms of mind are signless,[4] unshakable freedom of mind is shown to be their chief, for that unshakable freedom of mind is void of attachment,

---

[1] *MA.* ii. 354 gives twelve: four *brahmavihāras,* the ways and fruits—and also nibbāna.

[2] *kiñcana.* *MA.* ii. 354 says that when passion has uprisen it does something (*kiñcati*) to a man, it crushes him, or obstructs him.

[3] *Cf. D.* iii. 217, *tayo kiñcanā.*

[4] "These number thirteen: vision, the four (concentrations) which are formless, the four ways, the four fruits. Vision is signless because it removes the signs of permanence, joy and self. The next four are signless because of the non-existence (in them) of the sign of form. The ways and fruits are

void of hatred, void of confusion.[1] This, your reverence, is the method according to which these states are identical in connotation while being different in denotation."

Thus spoke the venerable Sāriputta. Delighted, the venerable Koṭṭhita the Great rejoiced in what the venerable Sāriputta had said.

Greater Discourse of the Miscellany:
the Third

44. LESSER DISCOURSE OF THE MISCELLANY

(Cūḷavedallasutta)

[**299**] THUS have I heard: At one time the Lord was staying near Rājagaha in the Bamboo Grove at the squirrels' feeding place. Then the layfollower Visākha approached the nun Dhammadinnā;[2] having approached, having greeted the nun Dhammadinnā, he sat down at a respectful distance. As he was sitting down at a respectful distance, the lay follower Visākha spoke thus to the nun Dhammadinnā:

"Lady, it is said, 'Own body,[3] own body.' Now, lady, what is called 'own body' by the Lord?"

"Friend Visākha, these five groups of grasping are called 'own body' by the Lord, that is to say, the group of grasping after material shape, the group of grasping after feeling, the group of grasping after perception, the group of grasping after the habitual tendencies, the group of grasping after consciousness. These five groups of grasping, friend Visākha, are called 'own body' by the Lord."

---

signless through the non-existence of the defilements which produce signs. Nibbāna too is simply signless," *MA*. ii. 355.

[1] *MA*. iii. 355 notes that void freedom of mind is not treated separately, for "void of attachment" and so on has come in everywhere.

[2] In his time as a householder Visākha had been Dhammadinnā's husband, *MA*. ii. 355; *PvA*. 21; *KhpA*. 204; *DhA*. iv. 229. She is called the chief teacher of *dhamma* among the women disciples, *A*. i. 25. A verse is ascribed to her at *Thīg*. 12 (*cf*. *Dh*. 218).

[3] *sakkāya*. *MA*. ii. 358 makes Dhammadinnā say, "I have not long gone forth. How should I know about 'own body' or 'other's body'?"

"It is good, lady," and the lay follower Visākha, having rejoiced in what the nun Dhammadinnā had said, having thanked her, asked the nun Dhammadinnā a further question:

"Lady, it is said, 'The uprising of own body, the uprising of own body.' Now, lady, what is called 'the uprising of own body' by the Lord?"

"Whatever, friend Visākha, is the craving[1] connected with again-becoming, accompanied by delight and attachment, finding delight in this and that, namely the craving for sense-pleasures, the craving for becoming, the craving for annihilation, this, friend Visākha, is called 'the uprising of own body' by the Lord."

"Lady, it is said, 'The stopping of own body, the stopping of own body.' Now, lady, what is called 'stopping of own body' by the Lord?"

"Whatever, friend Visākha, is the stopping, with no attachment remaining, of that self-same craving, the giving up of it, the renunciation of it, the release from it, the doing away with it, this, friend Visākha, is called 'The stopping of own body' by the Lord."

"Lady, it is said, 'The course leading to the stopping of own body, the course leading to the stopping of own body.' Now, lady, what is called 'the course leading to the stopping of own body' by the Lord?"

"This ariyan eightfold Way itself, friend Visākha, is called 'the course leading to the stopping of own body' by the Lord, that is to say perfect view, perfect thought, perfect speech, perfect action, perfect way of living, perfect endeavour, perfect mindfulness, perfect concentration."

"Do those five groups of grasping, lady, (comprise) the whole of grasping? Or is there a grasping apart from the five groups of grasping?"

"No, friend Visākha, these five groups of grasping (comprise) the whole of grasping, [**300**] and there is no grasping apart from the five groups of grasping. Whatever, friend Visākha, is the attachment and desire for the five groups of grasping, that is grasping after them."

"But how, lady, does there come to be (wrong) view as to own body?"

"In this case, friend Visākha, an uninstructed average person, taking no count of the pure ones, not skilled in the *dhamma* of the

---

[1] *Cf. M.* i. 48-9.

pure ones, untrained in the *dhamma* of the pure ones, taking no count of the true men, not skilled in the *dhamma* of the true men, untrained in the *dhamma* of the true men, regards material shape as self[1] or self as having material shape[2] or material shape as in self[3] or self as in material shape[4]; he regards feeling as self . . . he regards perception as self . . . he regards the habitual tendencies as self . . . he regards consciousness as self or self as having consciousness or consciousness as in self or self as in consciousness. Thus, friend Visākha, does there come to be (wrong) view as to own body."

"But how, lady, does there not come to be (wrong) view as to own body?"

"In this case, friend Visākha, an instructed disciple of the pure ones, taking count of the pure ones, skilled in the *dhamma* of the pure ones, well trained in the *dhamma* of the pure ones, taking count of the true men, skilled in the *dhamma* of the true men, well trained in the *dhamma* of the true men, does not regard material shape as self nor self as having material shape nor material shape as in self nor self as in material shape; he does not regard feeling as self . . . he does not regard perception as self . . . he does not regard the habitual tendencies as self . . . he does not regard consciousness as self nor self as having consciousness nor consciousness as in self nor self as in consciousness. Thus, friend Visākha, does there not come to be (wrong) view as to own body."

"But what, lady, is the ariyan eightfold Way?"

"This, friend Visākha, is the ariyan eightfold Way, that is to say, perfect view, perfect thought, perfect speech, perfect action, perfect way of living, perfect endeavour, perfect mindfulness, perfect concentration."

"But, lady, is the ariyan eightfold Way composite[5] or incomposite?"

"The ariyan eightfold Way, friend Visākha, is [**301**] composite."

"Now, lady, are the three classes arranged in accordance with

---

[1] *MA*. ii. 360 quotes a passage from *Pṭs*. i. 143 where such a person regards material shape and self as identical (not two, *advaya*) like the flame and hue of a lighted lamp.

[2] As a tree has a shadow, *cf*. *Pṭs*. i. 144.

[3] As a scent is in a flower, *cf*. *Pṭs*. i. 145.

[4] As a jewel is in a casket, *cf*. *Pṭs*. i. 145.

[5] *saṅkhata*. *MA*. ii. 361 explains by *cetito kappito pakappito āyūhito nibbattito samāpajjantena samāpajjitabbo*, thought out, arranged, fixed, cultivated, produced, to be entered on by entering it.

the ariyan eightfold Way or is the ariyan eightfold Way arranged in accordance with the three classes ?"

"Friend Visākha, the three classes are not arranged in accordance with the ariyan eightfold Way, but the ariyan eightfold Way is arranged in accordance with the three classes. Whatever, friend Visākha, is perfect speech and whatever is perfect action and whatever is perfect way of living—these things are arranged in the class of Moral Habit. And whatever is perfect endeavour and whatever is perfect mindfulness and whatever is perfect concentration—these things are arranged in the class of Concentration. And whatever is perfect view and whatever is perfect thought—these things are arranged in the class of Intuitive Wisdom."[1]

"And what, lady, is concentration, what are the distinguishing marks of concentration, what are the requisites for concentration, what is the development of concentration ?"

"Whatever, friend Visākha, is one-pointedness of mind, this is concentration; the four arousings of mindfulness are the distinguishing marks of concentration; the four right efforts are the requisites for concentration; whatever is the practice, the development, the increase of these very things, this is herein the development of concentration."

"And how many activities[2] are there,[3] lady ?"

"There are these three activities, friend Visākha: activities of body, activities of speech, activities of mind."

"And what, lady, is activity of body, what activity of speech, what activity of mind ?"

"In-breathing and out-breathing, friend Visākha, is activity of body; initial thought and discursive thought is activity of speech; perception and feeling is activity of mind."

"But why, lady, is in-breathing and out-breathing activity of body, why is initial thought and discursive thought activity of speech, why is perception and why is feeling activity of mind ?"

"In-breathing and out-breathing, friend Visākha—these are bodily things dependent on the body, therefore in-breathing and out-breathing is activity of body. Having first had initial thought

---

[1] Quoted *Asl.* 305.

[2] *saṅkhāra*; here with a different sense from *sankhārā* as one of the *khandhas*, and meaning function or formation. "Being dependent on body it is put together (*saṅkharīyati*) by the body, produced by it," *MA.* ii. 364; and similarly for speech and thought.

[3] *Cf.* the following with *S.* iv. 294.

and discursive thought, one subsequently utters a speech, therefore initial and discursive thought is activity of speech. Perception and feeling—these are mental things, dependent on mind, therefore perception and feeling is (each) activity of mind."

"And how, lady, does there come to be the attainment of the stopping of perception and feeling?"

"Friend Visākha, it does not occur to a monk who is attaining the stopping of perception and feeling: '*I* will attain the stopping of perception and feeling,' or '*I* am attaining the stopping of perception and feeling,' or '*I* have attained the stopping of perception and feeling.' For, his mind has been previously so developed in that way[1] that it leads him on to the state of being such."[2]

[**302**] "But, lady, when a monk is attaining the stopping of perception and feeling, what things are stopped first: activity of body or activity of speech or activity of mind?"

"Friend Visākha, when a monk is attaining the stopping of perception and feeling, activity of speech is stopped first,[3] then activity of body,[4] then activity of mind."[5]

"And how, lady, does there come to be emergence from the attainment of the stopping of perception and feeling?"

"Friend Visākha, it does not occur to a monk who is emerging from the attainment of perception and feeling: '*I* will emerge from the attainment of the stopping of perception and feeling,' or '*I* am emerging . . . ' or '*I* have emerged from the attainment of the stopping of perception and feeling.' For his mind has been previously so developed in that way that it leads him on to the state of being such."

"But, lady, when a monk is emerging from the attainment of the stopping of perception and feeling, what things arise first: activity of body or activity of speech or activity of mind?'

"Friend Visākha, when a monk is emerging from the attainment of the stopping of perception and feeling, activity of mind arises first, then activity of body, then activity of speech."

"Lady, how many impingements[6] assail a monk who has emerged

---

[1] He thinks "At that time I will become (or, I must be) without mind, (*acittaka*, unconscious)," *MA*. ii. 365.

[2] So a mind developed in this way leads the man on to a state of suchness, *tathattāya*, a state of unconsciousness, *MA*. ii. 365.

[3] In the second *jhāna*.

[4] In the fourth *jhāna*.

[5] In the inner stopping, *antonirodhe*, *cf*. *MA*. ii. 349.

[6] *phassa* is the awareness, cognition or reaction dependent on the impinge-

from the attainment of the stopping of perception and feeling ?"

" Friend Visākha, when a monk has emerged from the attainment of the stopping of perception and feeling three impingements assail him: impingement that is void,[1] impingement that is signless,[2] impingement that is undirected."[3]

" When, lady, the mind of a monk has emerged from the attainment of the stopping of perception and feeling, towards what does his mind tend, slide and gravitate ?"

" Friend Visākha, the mind of a monk who has emerged from the attainment of the stopping of perception and feeling tends, slides and gravitates towards aloofness."[4]

" How many feelings are there, lady ?"

" There are these three feelings, friend Visākha: Feeling that is pleasant, feeling that is painful, feeling that is neither painful nor pleasant."[5]

" And what, lady, is feeling that is pleasant, what feeling that is painful, what feeling that is neither painful nor pleasant ?"

" That, friend Visākha, which is experienced, whether by body or mind, and is pleasant and agreeable, this is a pleasant feeling. That, friend Visākha, which is experienced, whether by body or mind, and is painful and disagreeable, this is a painful feeling. That, friend Visākha, which is experienced, whether by body or mind, and is neither agreeable nor disagreeable, this [**303**] is a feeling that is neither painful nor pleasant."

" But, lady, how is pleasant feeling pleasant, how painful ? How is painful feeling painful, how pleasant ? How is neutral feeling pleasant, how painful ?"

" Friend Visākha, pleasant feeling is that where pleasantness is lasting, pain variable; painful feeling is that where pain is lasting,

---

ment or impact of sense-data on their appropriate sense-organ; see *M*. i. 111.

[1] It is seen to be not-self, *MA*. ii. 367. *Cf*. *MA*. ii. 113 where *anattā* is *suññata*, empty.

[2] Impermanent, *MA*. ii. 367.

[3] Not directed to ill, for he understands ill to be *rāga*, *dosa* and *moha*. In fact, in meditation, he realises that nibbāna is void of attachment, hatred and confusion, unmarked or not " signed " by them, not directed towards them, *MA*. ii. 367. On the three terms of the text, see *Vin*. iii. 93, and *B.D.* i. 161, *n*. 3 for further references.

[4] *I.e.* nibbāna, *MA*. ii. 367.

[5] *Cf*. *S*. iv. 205.

pleasantness variable; neutral feeling is pleasant as to knowing, painful as to not knowing."

"But, lady, what tendency lies latent in pleasant feeling, what tendency lies latent in painful feeling, what tendency lies latent in neutral feeling?"

"Friend Visākha, a tendency to attachment lies latent in pleasant feeling; a tendency to repugnance lies latent in painful feeling; a tendency to ignorance lies latent in a neutral feeling."[1]

"But, lady, does a tendency to attachment lie latent in all pleasant feeling? Does a tendency to repugnance lie latent in all painful feeling? Does a tendency to ignorance lie latent in all neutral feeling?"

"Friend Visākha, a tendency to attachment does not lie latent in all pleasant feeling, a tendency to repugnance does not lie latent in all painful feeling, a tendency to ignorance does not lie latent in all neutral feeling."

"But, lady, what is to be got rid of in pleasant feeling? What is to be got rid of in painful feeling? What is to be got rid of in neutral feeling?"

"A tendency to attachment, friend Visākha, is to be got rid of in pleasant feeling; a tendency to repugnance is to be got rid of in painful feeling; a tendency to ignorance is to be got rid of in neutral feeling."

"But, lady, is a tendency to attachment to be got rid of from every pleasant feeling? Is a tendency to repugnance to be got rid of from every painful feeling? Is a tendency to ignorance to be got rid of from every neutral feeling?"

"No, friend Visākha, a tendency to attachment is not to be got rid of from every pleasant feeling, a tendency to repugnance is not to be got rid of from every painful feeling, a tendency to ignorance is not to be got rid of from every neutral feeling. In this case, friend Visākha, a monk, aloof from pleasures of the senses, aloof from unskilled states of mind, enters on and abides in the first meditation which is accompanied by initial thought and discursive thought, is born of aloofness, and is rapturous and joyful. It is by this means that he gets rid of attachment, no tendency to attachment lies latent there. In this case, friend Visākha, a monk reflects thus: 'Surely I, entering on it, will abide in that plane which the ariyans, entering on, are now abiding in.' From setting up a

[1] *Cf. S.* iv. 208.

yearning for the incomparable Deliverances [**304**] there arises, as a result of the yearning, distress; it is by this means that he gets rid of repugnance, no tendency to repugnance lies latent there. In this case, friend Visākha, a monk, by getting rid of joy, and by getting rid of anguish, by the going down of his former pleasures and sorrows, enters on and abides in the fourth meditation which has neither anguish nor joy and which is entirely purified by equanimity and mindfulness. It is by this means that he gets rid of ignorance, no tendency to ignorance lies latent there."

"But, lady, what is the counterpart[1] of pleasant feeling?"

"Friend Visākha, the counterpart of pleasant feeling is painful feeling."

"And what, lady, is the counterpart of painful feeling?"

"Friend, Visākha, the counterpart of painful feeling is pleasant feeling."

"And what, lady, is the counterpart of neutral feeling?"

"Ignorance, friend Visākha, is the counterpart of neutral feeling."

"And what, lady, is the counterpart of ignorance?"

"Knowledge, friend Visākha, is the counterpart of ignorance."

"And what, lady, is the counterpart of knowledge?"

"Freedom, friend Visākha, is the counterpart of knowledge."

"And what, lady, is the counterpart of freedom?"

"Nibbāna, friend Visākha, is the counterpart of freedom."

"And what, lady, is the counterpart of nibbāna?"[2]

"This question goes too far, friend Visākha, it is beyond the compass of an answer. Friend Visākha, the Brahma-faring is for immergence in nibbāna, for going beyond to nibbāna, for culminating in nibbāna.[3] Friend Visākha, if you so desire, having drawn near the Lord, ask him about this matter. As the Lord explains, so will you remember."

Then the layfollower Visākha, having rejoiced in what the nun Dhammadinnā had said, having thanked her, rising from his seat, having greeted her, keeping his right side towards her, drew near the Lord; having drawn near, having greeted the Lord, he sat down at a respectful distance. As he was sitting down at a respectful distance, the layfollower Visākha told the Lord the whole of the conversation he had had with the nun Dhammadinnā. When he

---

[1] *paṭibhāga*, analogy, equal, comparable to.

[2] *Cf. Miln.* 316; *appaṭibhāga nibbāna*; and *MA*. ii. 370, *nibbānaṃ nām'etaṃ appaṭibhāgaṃ*.

[3] *Cf. S.* v. 218.

had been told, the Lord spoke thus to the layfollower Visākha: " Clever, Visākha, is the nun Dhammadinnā, of great wisdom, Visākha, is the nun Dhammadinnā. If you had asked me, Visākha, about this matter, I too would have answered [**305**] exactly as the nun Dhammadinnā answered;[1] and this is indeed the meaning of that; thus do you remember it."[2]

Thus spoke the Lord. Delighted, the layfollower Visākha rejoiced in what the Lord had said.

Lesser Discourse of the Miscellany:
the Fourth

45. LESSER DISCOURSE ON THE (WAYS OF) UNDERTAKING DHAMMA

(Cūḷadhammasamādānasutta)

THUS have I heard: At one time the Lord was staying near Sāvatthī in the Jeta Grove in Anāthapiṇḍika's monastery. While he was there the Lord addressed the monks, saying: " Monks." " Revered One," these monks answered the Lord in assent. The Lord spoke thus:

" These four, monks, are (ways of) undertaking *dhamma*.[3] What four ? There is, monks, the undertaking of *dhamma* that is happiness in the present but results in suffering in the future. There is, monks, the undertaking of *dhamma* that is both suffering in the present as well as resulting in suffering in the future. There is, monks, the undertaking of *dhamma* that is suffering in the present but results in happiness in the future. There is, monks, the undertaking of *dhamma* that is both happiness in the present as well as resulting in happiness in the future.

And what, monks, is the undertaking of *dhamma* that is happiness in the present but results in suffering in the future ? There are, monks, some recluses and brahmans who speak like this and are

---

[1] This Sutta therefore ranks as the Conqueror's speech, not as the disciple's speech, *MA*. ii. 371.

[2] *Cf*. *S*. iv. 374 where the Lord explains certain matters exactly as the nun Khemā had done.

[3] *Cf*. below, p. 373; *D*. iii. 229.

of these views: 'There is no fault in pleasures of the senses.'[1] These come to indulgence[2] in pleasures of the senses; these gratify themselves with girl-wanderers who tie their hair into top-knots; these speak thus: 'How can these worthy recluses and brahmans, seeing future peril among sense-pleasures, speak of getting rid of sense-pleasures, lay down a full knowledge of sense-pleasures?' Saying: 'Happiness is in the young, soft and downy arms of this girl-wanderer,' these come to indulgence in pleasures of the senses.

These, having come to indulgence in sense-pleasures, at the breaking up of the body after dying arise in a sorrowful state, a bad bourn, the abyss, Niraya Hell. Here they experience feelings that are painful, sharp, acute. They speak thus: 'These worthy recluses and brahmans, seeing future peril in sense-pleasures, speak of getting rid of sense-pleasures and lay down a full knowledge of sense-pleasures. But we, because of sense-pleasures, [**306**] are experiencing these feelings that are painful, sharp, acute, their provenance being sense-pleasures.' It is as if, monks, in the last month of the hot weather, a creeper's seed-pod should burst and a seed of the creeper, monks, should fall at the root of a sāl-tree. Then, monks, the *devatā* residing in that sāl-tree, afraid, agitated, might fall a-trembling.[3] Then, monks, the friends and acquaintances, the kith and kin of that *devatā* who resides in that sāl-tree—*devatās* of parks, *devatās* of groves, *devatās* of trees, *devatās* residing in medicinal herbs, grasses and woods—gathering together and assembling might give comfort thus: 'Do not be afraid, revered one, do not be afraid, revered one. For a peacock might swallow this creeper's seed or a deer might consume it or a forest-fire might burn it or workers in the wood might remove it or white ants might eat it, or it might not germinate.' But, monks, if neither a peacock should swallow this creeper's seed nor a deer consume it . . . nor white ants eat it, it might germinate. Rained on heavily by the monsoon clouds, it might grow apace, and a young, soft and downy creeper, clinging to it might fasten on to that sāl-tree. Then,

---

[1] *Cf. A.* i. 266.

[2] *pātabyataṃ*, derived at *MA.* ii. 371 from *piv*, to drink. *Cf. G.S.* i. 244, *n.* 2. *MA.* says the pleasures of the senses are to be enjoyed according to one's likes.

[3] At the thought that the creeper, sprung from the seed, would cover the tree with its leaves, and because of the great weight the tree would fall to the ground in a gale or heavy rain, be broken, and the *devatā* destroyed, *MA.* ii. 372.

monks, it might occur to the *devatā* residing in that sāl-tree: 'Why then, did these worthy friends and acquaintances, kith and kin: *devatās* of parks . . . herbs, grasses and woods, seeing future peril in this creeper's seed, gathering together and assembling, give comfort thus: "Do not be afraid, revered one, do not be afraid, revered one. For a peacock might swallow this creeper's seed . . . or it might not germinate"? Pleasant is the touch of this young, soft, downy and clinging creeper.' It might cover that sāl-tree; when it had covered that sāl-tree, it might form a canopy above it, it might produce dense undergrowth;[1] when it had produced a dense undergrowth it might strangle every great branch of that sāl-tree. Then, monks, it might occur to the *devatā* residing in that sāl-tree: 'It was because of seeing this future peril in the creeper's seed that those worthy friends and acquaintances, kith and kin—*devatās* of parks . . . grasses and woods—gathering together and assembling, gave comfort thus: "Do not be afraid . . . for a peacock might swallow this creeper's seed **[307]** or a deer . . . or it might not germinate." For I, because of this creeper's seed, am experiencing painful, sharp, acute feelings.' Even so, monks, there are some worthy recluses and brahmans who speak thus and are of these views: 'There is no fault in pleasures of the senses.' These, come to indulgence . . . '. . . their provenance being sense-pleasures.' This, monks, is called the undertaking of *dhamma* that is happiness in the present but results in suffering in the future.

And what, monks, is the undertaking of *dhamma* that is both suffering in the present as well as resulting in suffering in the future? Here, monks, there is some unclothed (ascetic), flouting life's decencies . . . (*as at p.* 103 *to p.* 105 *above*) . . . **[308]** . . . and he is intent on the practice of going down to the water to bathe up to three times in an evening. He, at the breaking up of the body after dying, arises in a sorrowful state, a bad bourn, the abyss, Niraya Hell. This, monks, is called the undertaking of *dhamma* that is both suffering in the present as well as resulting in suffering in the future.

And what, monks, is the undertaking of *dhamma* that is suffering in the present but results in happiness in the future? Here, monks, there is someone who is full of attachment by nature and who constantly experiences suffering and grief born of attachment; he

---

[1] *oghanaṃ janeyya*, explained as *heṭṭhā ghanaṃ janeyya* at *MA*. ii. 372, "it might produce denseness below. Climbing aloft and encircling the whole tree, then falling downwards again, it might touch the earth."

is full of hatred by nature . . . full of confusion by nature, and constantly experiences suffering and grief born of confusion. With suffering and with grief, his face covered with tears and crying, he fares the Brahma-faring[1] that is utterly fulfilled, utterly pure. He, at the breaking up of the body after dying arises in a good bourn, a heaven world. This, monks, is called the undertaking of *dhamma* that is suffering in the present but results in happiness in the future.

And what, monks, is the undertaking of *dhamma* that is both happiness in the present as well as resulting in happiness in the future? Here, monks, someone is not full of attachment . . . full of hatred . . . full of confusion by nature. He does not constantly experience suffering and grief born of attachment . . . hatred . . . **[309]** confusion. He, aloof from pleasures of the senses, aloof from unskilled states of mind, enters into and abides in the first meditation which is accompanied by initial thought and discursive thought, is born of aloofness, and is rapturous and joyful . . . the second meditation . . . the third meditation . . . enters on and abides in the fourth meditation which has neither anguish nor joy, and is entirely purified by equanimity and mindfulness. At the breaking up of the body after dying he arises in a good bourn, a heaven world. This, monks, is called the undertaking of *dhamma* that is both happiness in the present as well as resulting in happiness in the future. These, monks, are the four (ways of) undertaking *dhamma*."

Thus spoke the Lord. Delighted, these monks rejoiced in what the Lord had said.

Lesser Discourse on the (Ways of) Undertaking *Dhamma*:
The Fifth

---

[1] *MA*. ii. 373 says his teachers and preceptors give commands for punishments which cause pain and grief, and further says it is due to *kamma* that one person is full of attachment and so on and another not.

46. GREATER DISCOURSE ON THE (WAYS OF) UNDERTAKING DHAMMA

(Mahādhammasamādānasutta)

THUS have I heard: At one time the Lord was staying near Sāvatthī in the Jeta Grove in Anāthapiṇḍika's monastery. While he was there the Lord addressed the monks, saying: "Monks." "Revered one," these monks answered the Lord in assent. The Lord spoke thus:

"For the most part, monks, beings wish like this, desire like this, intend like this: 'O may unpleasant, unenjoyable, disagreeable things dwindle away, O may pleasant, enjoyable, agreeable things grow much,' Monks, unpleasant, unenjoyable, disagreeable things grow much in those beings of such wishes, such desires, such intentions; pleasant, enjoyable, agreeable things dwindle away. As to this, what do you, monks, take to be the cause?"

[**310**] "Things for us,[1] Lord, are rooted in the Lord, have the Lord for conduit, the Lord for arbiter.[2] It were good indeed, Lord, if the meaning of this speech of the Lord's were explained; having heard the Lord, monks would remember."

"Well then, monks, listen, attend carefully, I will speak."

"Yes, Lord," these monks answered the Lord in assent. The Lord spoke thus:

"In this case, monks, the uninstructed average person, taking no count of the pure ones, unskilled in the *dhamma* of the pure ones, untrained in the *dhamma* of the pure ones, taking no count of the true men, unskilled in the *dhamma* of the true men, untrained in the *dhamma* of the true men, does not know what things should be followed, does not know what things should not be followed, does not know what things should be associated with, does not know what things should not be associated with. Not knowing what things should be followed . . . should not be followed . . . should be associated with, not knowing what things should not be associated with, he follows things that should not be followed, he does not follow things that should be followed, he associates with things that should not be associated with, he does not associate with

---

[1] As at *M*. i. 317, 465, iii. 115; *A*. i. 199, iv. 158, 351, v. 355.

[2] *Bhagavanpaṭisaraṇā*; *cf*. *M*. iii. 9 *dhammapaṭisaraṇā*, and *M*. i. 295 *mano paṭisaraṇa*.

things that should be associated with. While he is following things that should not be followed, not following things that should be followed, associating with things that should not be associated with, not associating with things that should be associated with, unpleasant, unenjoyable, disagreeable things grow much, pleasant, enjoyable, agreeable things dwindle away. What is the reason for this ? This is so, monks, for one who is unintelligent[1] about this.

But, monks, the instructed disciple of the pure ones, taking count of the *dhamma* of the pure ones, skilled in the *dhamma* of the pure ones, well trained in the *dhamma* of the pure ones, taking count of the true men, skilled in the *dhamma* of the true men, well trained in the *dhamma* of the true men, knows what things should be followed . . . should not be followed . . . should be associated with, knows what things should not be associated with. Knowing what things should be followed . . . should not be followed . . . should be associated with . . . should not be associated with, he follows things that should be followed, does not follow things that should not be followed, does not associate with things that should not be associated with, associates with things that should be associated with. While he is not following things that should not be followed, following things that should be followed, not associating with things that should not be associated with, associating with things that should be associated with, unpleasant, unenjoyable, disagreeable things dwindle away, pleasant, enjoyable, agreeable things grow much. What is the cause of this ? This is so, monks, for one who is intelligent about this.

Monks, there are four (ways of) undertaking *dhamma*[2]. What are the four ? There is, monks, the undertaking of *dhamma* that is both suffering in the present as well as resulting in suffering in the future. There is, monks, [**311**] the undertaking of *dhamma* that is happiness in the present but results in suffering in the future. There is, monks, the undertaking of *dhamma* that is suffering in the present but results in happiness in the future. There is, monks, the undertaking of *dhamma* that is both happiness in the present as well as resulting in happiness in the future.

As to this, monks, that undertaking of *dhamma*[3] that is both suffering in the present as well as resulting in suffering in the

---

[1] A foolish, blind worldling, *MA*. ii. 375.

[2] *Cf*. above, p. 368.

[3] Not obeying the five precepts; *MA*. ii. 375, based on text p. 313 below.

future: if anyone is unintelligent about this, ignorant, he does not comprehend as it really is: This undertaking of *dhamma* is both suffering in the present as well as resulting in suffering in the future. Unintelligent about this, ignorant, not comprehending it as it really is, he follows it, he does not avoid it. While he is following it, not avoiding it, unpleasant, unenjoyable, disagreeable things grow much, pleasant, enjoyable, agreeable things dwindle away. What is the cause of this ? It is so, monks, for one who is unintelligent about this.

As to this, monks, that undertaking of *dhamma* that is happiness in the present but results in suffering in the future: if anyone is unintelligent about this, ignorant, he does not comprehend as it really is: This undertaking of *dhamma* is happiness in the present but results in suffering in the future. Unintelligent about this . . . pleasant, enjoyable, agreeable things dwindle away. What is the cause of this ? It is so, monks, for one who is unintelligent about this.

As to this, monks, that undertaking of *dhamma* that is suffering in the present but results in happiness in the future; if anyone is unintelligent about this, ignorant, he does not comprehend as it really is: This undertaking of *dhamma* is suffering in the present but results in happiness in the future. Unintelligent about this, ignorant, not comprehending it as it really is, he does not follow it, he avoids it. While he is not following it, avoiding it, unpleasant, unenjoyable, disagreeable things grow much, pleasant, enjoyable, agreeable things dwindle away. What is the cause of this ? It is so, monks, for one who is unintelligent about this.

As to this, monks, that undertaking of *dhamma* that is both happiness in the present as well as resulting in happiness in the future; if anyone is unintelligent about this, ignorant, he does not comprehend as it really is: This undertaking of *dhamma* is both happiness in the present as well as resulting in happiness in the future. Unintelligent about this . . . he does not follow it, he avoids it. While he is not following it, avoiding it, [**312**] unpleasant, unenjoyable, disagreeable things grow much, pleasant, enjoyable, agreeable things dwindle away. What is the cause of this ? It is so, monks, for one who is unintelligent about this.

As to this, monks, that undertaking of *dhamma* that is both suffering in the present as well as resulting in suffering in the future; if anyone is intelligent about this, wise, he comprehends as it really is: This undertaking of *dhamma* is both suffering in the present as well as resulting in suffering in the future. Intelligent about this, wise, comprehending it as it really is, he does not follow it, he avoids it. While he is not following it, avoiding it, unpleasant, unenjoyable, disagreeable things dwindle away, pleasant, enjoyable, agreeable things grow much. What is the cause of this? It is so, monks, for one who is intelligent about this.

As to this, monks, that undertaking of *dhamma* which is happiness in the present but results in suffering in the future; if anyone is intelligent about this, wise, he comprehends as it really is: This undertaking of *dhamma* is happiness in the present but results in suffering in the future. Intelligent about this . . . pleasant, enjoyable, agreeable things grow much. What is the cause of this? It is so, monks, for one who is intelligent about this.

As to this, monks, that undertaking of *dhamma* that is suffering in the present but results in happiness in the future; if anyone is intelligent about this, wise, he comprehends as it really is: This undertaking of *dhamma* is suffering in the present but results in happiness in the future. Intelligent about this, wise, comprehending it as it really is, he follows it, he does not avoid it. While he is following it, not avoiding it, unpleasant, unenjoyable, disagreeable things dwindle away, pleasant, enjoyable, agreeable things grow much. What is the cause of this? It is so, monks, for one who is intelligent about this.

As to this, monks, that undertaking of *dhamma* that is both happiness in the present as well as resulting in happiness in the future; if anyone is intelligent about this, wise, he comprehends as it really is: This undertaking of *dhamma* is both happiness in the present as well as resulting in happiness in the future. Intelligent about this . . . pleasant, enjoyable, agreeable things grow much. What is the cause of this? It is so, monks, for one who is intelligent about this.

[313] And what, monks, is the undertaking of *dhamma* that is suffering in the present and results in suffering in the future? In this case, monks, someone, even with suffering, even with grief, becomes one to make onslaught on creatures; and because of the onslaught on creatures he experiences suffering and grief. Even with suffering, even with grief, he becomes one who takes what was not given and because of taking what was not given he experiences suffering and grief. Even with suffering, even with grief, he becomes one to behave wrongly in regard to sense-pleasures . . . he becomes a liar . . . a slanderer . . . a harsh speaker . . . a frivolous talker . . . he becomes covetous . . . malevolent in thought

. . . of wrong view; and because of his wrong view he experiences suffering and grief. He, at the breaking up of the body after dying uprises in a sorrowful state, a bad bourn, the abyss, Niraya Hell. This, monks, is called the undertaking of *dhamma* that is both suffering in the present as well as resulting in suffering in the future.

And what, monks, is the undertaking of *dhamma* that is happiness in the present but results in suffering in the future? In this case, monks, someone, even with happiness, even with pleasure becomes one to make onslaught on creatures; and because of his onslaught on creatures he experiences happiness and pleasure. Even with happiness, even with pleasure, he becomes one who takes what is not given . . . who behaves wrongly in regard to sense-pleasures . . . who is a liar . . . a slanderer . . . [**314**] . . . a harsh speaker . . . a frivolous talker . . . covetous . . . malevolent in thought . . . of wrong view; and because of his wrong view he experiences happiness and pleasure. He, at the breaking up of the body after dying, uprises in a sorrowful state, a bad bourn, the abyss, Niraya Hell. This, monks, is called the undertaking of *dhamma* that is happiness in the present but results in suffering in the future.

And what, monks, is the undertaking of *dhamma* that is suffering in the present but results in happiness in the future? In this case, monks, someone, even with suffering, even with grief, abstains from onslaught on creatures; and because of his abstaining from onslaught on creatures he experiences suffering and grief. Even with suffering, even with grief, he is one who abstains from taking what was not given . . . who abstains from wrong behaviour in regard to sense-pleasures . . . who abstains from lying . . . slander . . . from harsh speech . . . from frivolous talk . . . he is one who is not covetous . . . not malevolent in thought . . . [**315**] . . . who is of right view; and because of his right view he experiences suffering and grief. He, at the breaking up of the body after dying, arises in a good bourn, a heaven world. This, monks, is called the undertaking of *dhamma* that is suffering in the present but results in happiness in the future.

And what, monks, is the undertaking of *dhamma* that is both happiness in the present as well as resulting in happiness in the future? In this case, monks, someone, even with happiness, even with pleasure, is one to abstain from onslaught on creatures; and because of his abstaining from onslaught on creatures he experiences happiness and pleasure. Even with happiness, even with pleasure, he abstains from taking what was not given . . . from wrong behaviour in regard to sense-pleasures . . . from lying . . . from slander . . . from harsh speech . . . from frivolous talk . . . he is not covetous . . . not malevolent in thought. . . . Even with happiness, even with pleasure he is of right view; and because of his right view he experiences happiness and pleasure. He, at the breaking up of the body after dying, arises in a good bourn, a heaven world. This, monks, is called the undertaking of *dhamma* that is both happiness in the present as well as resulting in happiness in the future. These, monks, are the four undertakings of *dhamma*.

Monks, it is as if there were a bitter gourd infused with poison. Then a man might come along, anxious to live, anxious not to die, anxious for happiness, averse from suffering, and someone might speak thus to him: 'This bitter gourd is infused with poison; if you like, drink; [**316**] but while you are drinking, it will please you neither with its colour, scent, nor taste, and when you have drunk you will come to death or to suffering like unto death.' He might drink without heeding him, he might not give it up. While he was drinking, he might not be pleased either with the colour, scent or taste, and when he had drunk he might come to death or to suffering like unto death. I, monks, say that this undertaking of *dhamma* is similar, that is to say the undertaking of *dhamma* that is both suffering in the present as well as resulting in suffering in the future.

Monks, it is as if there were in a drinking-bowl[1] a beverage that has colour, scent and taste, but into which poison has been infused. Then a man might come along, anxious to live, anxious not to die, anxious for happiness, averse from suffering,[2] and someone might speak thus to him: 'My good man, in this drinking-bowl is a beverage that has colour, scent and taste, but poison has been infused into it. If you like, drink, and while you are drinking you will be pleased with the colour, scent and taste, but when you have drunk you will come to death or to suffering like unto death.' He might drink without heeding him, he might not give it up. While he was drinking he might be pleased with the colour, scent and taste, but when he had drunk he would come to death or to suffering like unto death. I, monks, say that this undertaking of *dhamma* is similar, that is to say the undertaking of *dhamma* that is happiness in the present but results in suffering in the future.

---

[1] *Cf. S.* ii. 110.

[2] As at *M.* ii. 261; *S.* v. 170.

Monks, it is as if ammonia were infused into various medicines.[1] Then a man might come along suffering from jaundice, and someone might say to him: 'My good man, this is ammonia infused into various medicines. If you like, drink, but while you are drinking it you will be pleased neither with the colour, scent nor taste, but when you have drunk you will become eased.' He might drink, heeding him, he might not give it up. While he was drinking he might not be pleased either with the colour or scent or taste, but when he had drunk he might become eased. I, monks, say that this undertaking of *dhamma* is similar, that is to say the undertaking of *dhamma* that is suffering in the present, but results in happiness in the future.

Monks, it is as if milk and honey and oil and sugar were mixed together. Then a man might come along suffering from dysentery, and someone might say to him: 'My good man, [**317**] this is milk and honey and oil and sugar mixed together. If you like, drink; while you are drinking you will be pleased with the colour, scent and taste; and when you have drunk you will become eased.' He might drink, heeding him, he might not give it up. While he was drinking, he might be pleased with the colour, scent and taste, and when he had drunk he would become eased. I, monks, say that this undertaking of *dhamma* is similar, that is to say the undertaking of *dhamma* that is both happiness in the present as well as resulting in happiness in the future.

Monks, as in[2] the last month of the rains, at harvest time when the sky is clear, without a cloud, and the sun, ascending in the firmament and driving away the darkness from all the sky, shines forth, and is bright and brilliant—even so, monks, is this undertaking of *dhamma* that is both happiness in the present as well as resulting in happiness in the future, because, having driven away the opposing tenets of the ordinary recluses and brahmans, it shines forth and is bright and brilliant."

Thus spoke the Lord. Delighted, these monks rejoiced in what the Lord had said.

Greater Discourse on the (Ways of) Undertaking *Dhamma*:
the Sixth

---

[1] *Vin.* i. 58, 96; *It.* p. 103.

[2] *S.* iii. 156, v. 44; *It.* p. 20.

47. DISCOURSE ON INQUIRING

(Vīmaṁsakasutta)

THUS have I heard: At one time the Lord was staying near Sāvatthī in the Jeta Grove in Anāthapiṇḍika's monastery. While he was there the Lord addressed the monks, saying: " Monks." " Revered one," these monks answered the Lord in assent. The Lord spoke thus:

" Monks, an inquiring[1] monk, learning the range[2] of another's mind, should make a study[3] of the Tathāgata so as to distinguish whether he is a fully Self-awakened One or not."

" For us,[4] Lord, things are rooted in the Lord, have the Lord for their conduit, the Lord for their arbiter. Well for us, Lord, if the Lord would reveal the meaning of this saying; having heard the Lord, the monks will remember."

" Very well, monks; listen, attend carefully [**318**] and I will speak."

" Yes, Lord," these monks answered the Lord in assent. The Lord spoke thus:

" Monks, an inquiring monk, learning the range of another's mind, should study the Tathāgata in regard to two things: things cognisable through the eye and through the ear,[5] thinking: 'Do those that are impure states cognisable through the eye and the ear exist in a Tathāgata or not?' While he is studying this he knows thus: 'Those impure states which are cognisable through the eye and the ear do not exist in a Tathāgata.' After he has studied this and knows thus: 'Those impure states which are cognisable through the eye and the ear do not exist in a Tathāgata,' he then studies further, thinking: 'Do those that are mixed states[6] cognisable through the eye and the ear exist in a Tathāgata or not?' While he is studying this he knows thus: 'Those mixed states cognisable through the eye and the ear do not exist in a Tathāgata.'

---

[1] *MA*. ii. 378 distinguishes three kinds of inquiring; here inquiring about the Teacher is meant.

[2] Here *pariyāya* is explained by *vāra*, track, and *pariccheda*, range or limit, *MA*. ii. 378.

[3] *samannesanā*, search, quest.

[4] As at *M*. i. 309, *etc*.

[5] *MA*. ii. 380, the Teacher's bodily conduct is cognisable through the eye, his speech through the ear.

[6] *MA*. ii. 381, those which are sometimes " dark " and sometimes " bright."

After he has studied this and knows thus: 'Those mixed states cognisable through the eye and the ear do not exist in a Tathāgata,' he then studies further, thinking: 'Do those that are absolutely pure states cognisable through the eye and the ear exist in a Tathāgata or not?' While he is studying this he knows thus: 'Those which are absolutely pure states cognisable through the eye and the ear exist in a Tathāgata.' After he has studied this and knows thus: 'These absolutely pure states which are cognisable through the eye and the ear exist in the Tathāgata,' he then studies further, thinking: 'Has this venerable one been possessed of this skilled state for a long time or only for a short time?' While he is studying this he knows thus: 'This venerable one has been possessed of this skilled state for a long time, this venerable one has not been possessed of it for only a short time.' After he has studied this and knows thus: 'This venerable one has been possessed of this skilled state for a long time, this venerable one has not been possessed of it for only a short time,' he then studies further: 'Do there exist any perils for that venerable monk who has attained to fame and won renown?'

Monks, there are some perils that do not exist here for a monk until he has attained to fame and won renown. It is, monks, after a monk has attained to fame and won renown that some perils exist for him here. While he is studying this he knows thus: 'Although the venerable monk has attained to fame and won renown, some perils do not exist for him here.' After he has studied this and knows thus: 'Although this venerable monk has attained to fame **[319]** and won renown, some perils do not exist for him here,' he then studies further: 'Does this venerable one refrain out of fearlessness, does not he refrain out of fear?[1] Is it because, through the destruction of attachment, that, being without attachment, he does not follow pleasures of the senses?' As he is studying this he knows thus: 'This venerable one refrains out of fearlessness, this venerable one refrains not out of fear; he does not follow pleasures of the senses because, through the destruction of attachment, he is without attachment.'

If, monks, others should question this monk thus: 'What are the venerable one's facts, what his evidence by reason of which the venerable one speaks thus: "This venerable one refrains out of

---

[1] The worldling has four fears, the "learner" (*sekha*) three, so he is restrained out of fear. But there is not even one fear for him whose cankers are destroyed, *MA*. ii. 385.

fearlessness, this venerable one refrains not out of fear; he does not follow pleasures of the senses because, through the destruction of attachment, he is without attachment"?' Monks, a monk answering properly would answer thus: 'This venerable one, whether staying in an Order or staying alone,[1] whether those near him are progressing well, whether they are progressing badly, whether they lead a group, whether they are engaged with any material things here or whether they are unstained by any material things here—this venerable one does not despise them because of this.[2] This have I heard face to face with the Lord, this have I learnt face to face with him: "I am restrained out of fearlessness, I am not restrained out of fear; without attachment because of the destruction of attachment, I do not follow pleasures of the senses."'

Monks, the Tathāgata should himself be further questioned hereon: 'Do those impure states cognisable through the eye and through the ear exist in the Tathāgata or not?' Monks, in answering,[3] a Tathāgata would answer thus, 'Those impure states cognisable through the eye and through the ear do not exist in a Tathāgata.' 'Do those mixed states cognisable through the eye and through the ear exist in a Tathāgata or not?' Monks, in answering, a Tathāgata would answer thus: 'Those mixed states cognisable through the eye and through the ear do not exist in a Tathāgata.' 'Do those absolutely pure states cognisable through the eye and through the ear exist in a Tathāgata or not?' Monks, in answering, a Tathāgata would answer thus: 'Those absolutely pure states cognisable through the eye and through the ear exist in a Tathāgata. This is my path, this my pasture[4] and no one is like (me) in this.'[5] Monks, a disciple should draw near a teacher who speaks like this so as to hear *dhamma*. From further to further, from excellence to excellence, the Teacher teaches him *dhamma*, what is dark and what is bright, with their counterparts.[6] As, monks, the Teacher gradually teaches

---

[1] Temporarily (half a month or three months), for solitary meditation, as is implied by the references given (to *S*. v. 320, 325) at *MA*. ii. 386.

[2] All are alike to the *muni* (sage). The verse stating this is found at *MA*. ii. 387; *DhA*. i. 146, and *cf*. *Miln*. 410.

[3] There is no "aright" (*sammā*) as at *Fur. Dial*. i. 229, for a Truth-finder could not do otherwise than speak aright, as noticed at *MA*. ii. 387.

[4] *etapatho 'ham asmi etagocaro*. *MA*. ii. 387 gives *etapātha* as another reading, and explains by "utter purity of living and morality."

[5] In purity of moral habit without craving, *MA*. ii. 387.

[6] *sappaṭibhāga* appears to mean *savipāka*, with their results, fruits.

dhamma to the monk, from further to further, from excellence to excellence, what is dark and what is bright with their counterparts, so does he gradually by his superknowledge of point after point of *dhamma* come to fulfilment in *dhamma*. He has [**320**] confidence in the Teacher, that: 'The Lord is a fully Self-awakened One, well taught is *dhamma* by the Lord, the Order fares along well.' Monks, if others should ask that monk: 'But what are the venerable one's facts, what the evidence by reason of which he speaks thus: "The Lord is a fully Self-awakened one, well taught is *dhamma* by the Lord, the Order fares along well?"' that monk, monks, answering rightly would answer thus: 'I, your reverences, drew near the Lord so as to hear *dhamma*. The Lord taught me *dhamma* from further to further, from excellence to excellence, what is dark and what is bright with their counterparts. As the Lord gradually taught me *dhamma* from further to further, from excellence to excellence, what is dark and what is bright with their counterparts, so did I gradually by my superknowledge of point after point in *dhamma* come to fulfilment in *dhamma*. I have confidence in the Teacher, that: "The Lord is a fully Self-awakened One, well taught is *dhamma* by the Lord, the Order fares along well."'

"Monks, in anyone in whom faith in the Teacher is established, rooted, supported by these methods,[1] by these sentences, by these words,[2] that faith is called reasoned, based on vision,[3] strong; it is indestructible by a recluse or brahman or *deva* or Māra or a Brahmā or by anyone in the world. Thus, monks, does there come to be study of the Tathāgata's *dhamma*, and thus does the Tathāgata come to be well studied in the proper manner."

Thus spoke the Lord. Delighted, these monks rejoiced in what the Lord had said.

Discourse on Inquiring:
The Seventh

---

[1] *MA*. ii. 388, by his inquiries as to the Teacher.

[2] As at *M*. i. 114; *cf*. *S*. v. 219.

[3] *MA*. ii. 388 here says: based on the way of stream-attainment; it is the basis of faith; the faith of a stream-attainer cannot be destroyed by Māra.

48. DISCOURSE AT KOSAMBĪ

(Kosambiyasutta)[1]

THUS have I heard: At one time the Lord was staying near Kosambī in Ghosita's monastery. Now at that time, the monks of Kosambī, disputatious, quarrelsome, contentious,[2] lived wounding another with the weapons of the tongue.[3] They neither convinced one another nor came to be convinced themselves, nor did they win one another over or come to be won over themselves.[4] Then [**321**] a certain monk approached the Lord; having approached, having greeted the Lord, he sat down at a respectful distance. As he was sitting down at a respectful distance, that monk spoke thus to the Lord:

"Now, Lord, the monks of Kosambī, disputatious, quarrelsome, contentious, are living wounding one another with the weapons of the tongue. They neither convince one another, nor are they convinced themselves; they do not win one another over, nor are they won over themselves."

Then the Lord addressed a certain monk, saying: "Come you, monk, summon these monks in my name, saying: 'The Teacher is summoning you.'"

"Yes, Lord," and this monk, having answered the Lord in assent, approached those monks; having approached, he spoke thus to those monks: "The Teacher is summoning the venerable ones."

"Yes, your reverence," and those monks having answered that monk in assent, approached the Lord; having approached, having greeted the Lord, they sat down at a respectful distance. The Lord spoke thus to those monks as they were sitting down at a respectful distance:

"Is it true, as is said, that you, monks, are disputatious, quarrelsome, contentious, and live wounding one another with the weapons of the tongue? That you neither convince one another nor are convinced yourselves, that you neither win one another over nor are won over yourselves?"

---

[1] Called at *MA*. ii. 389 and *DA*. i. 123 Kosambakasutta, "Discourse to the monks of Kosambī." At *MA*. i. 176 and *DA*. i. 123 it is cited as a discourse which arose out of a quarrel.

[2] *Cf. Vin*. i. 341, 352 *ff*., *M*. iii. 152 *f*.

[3] *Cf. Ud*. 6[7].

[4] *Cf. Vin*. i. 337 *f*.

"Yes, Lord."

"What do you think about this, monks? At the time when you, disputatious, quarrelsome, contentious, live wounding one another with the weapon of the tongue, is a friendly act of body[1] offered[2] your fellow Brahma-farers, both in public and in private? Is a friendly act of speech . . . Is a friendly act of thought offered your fellow Brahma-farers, both in public and in private?"

"No, Lord."

"Then it is to be said, monks, that at that time when you, disputatious, quarrelsome, contentious, live wounding one another with the weapons of the tongue—at that time no friendly act of body . . . of speech . . . no friendly act of thought is offered your fellow Brahma-farers, either in public or in private. Therefore, knowing what, seeing what, is it that you, foolish men, disputatious, quarrelsome, contentious, **[322]** live wounding one another with the weapons of the tongue? You neither convince one another nor are convinced yourselves, neither do you win one another over nor are won over yourselves. So this, foolish men, will be for a long time for your woe and sorrow."

Then the Lord addressed the monks, saying: "Monks, these six things are to be remembered;[3] making for affection, making for respect, they conduce to concord, to lack of contention, to harmony and unity. What six? Herein, monks, a monk should offer his fellow Brahma-farers a friendly act of body both in public and in private. This is a thing to be remembered, making for affection, making for respect, which conduces to concord, to lack of contention, harmony and unity. And again, monks, a monk should offer a friendly act of speech . . . an act of thought . . . both in public and in private. This is a thing to be remembered. . . . And again, monks, whatever those lawful acquisitions, lawfully acquired, if they be even but what is put into the begging bowl—a monk should be one to enjoy sharing such acquisitions, to enjoy them in common with his virtuous fellow Brahma-farers. This too is a thing to be remembered . . . unity. And again, monks, whatever those moral habits that are faultless, without flaw, spotless, without blemish, freeing, praised by wise men, untarnished, conducive to concentration—a monk should dwell united in virtues such as

---

1 *mettaṃ kāyakammaṃ.*

2 *paccupaṭṭhita,* offered, presented.

3 *dhammā sārāṇīyā*; *MA*. ii. 394 *saritabbayuttā,* that should be remembered. Also at *M*. ii. 250 *f*.; *A*. iii. 288; *D*. ii. 80, iii. 245.

these with his fellow Brahma-farers, both in public and in private. This too is a thing to be remembered . . . unity. And again, monks, whatever view is ariyan,[1] leading onwards, leading him who acts according to it to the complete destruction of anguish—a monk should dwell united in a view such as this with his fellow Brahma-farers, both in public and in private. This too is a thing to be remembered; making for affection, making for respect, it conduces to concord, to lack of contention, to harmony and unity. Monks, these are the six things to be remembered, making for affection, making for respect, which conduce to concord, to lack of contention, to harmony and unity.

And, monks, of these six things to be remembered, this is the topmost, this the roof-plate, this the dome,[2] that is to say whatever view is ariyan, leading onwards, leading him who acts according to it to the complete destruction of anguish. As, monks, in a house with a peaked roof, this is the topmost, the roof-plate, the dome, that is to say the peak, even so, [**323**] monks, of these six things to be remembered, this is the topmost . . . to the complete destruction of anguish.

And what, monks, is that view which is ariyan,[3] leading onwards, and which leads him who acts according to it to the complete destruction of anguish? Herein, monks, a monk who is forest-gone or gone to the root of a tree or gone to an empty place, reflects like this: 'Now, have I a subjective obsession, not got rid of, owing to which I, if my mind were obsessed by it, could not know, could not see (things) as they really are?' If, monks, a monk is obsessed by addiction to sense-pleasures, to this extent is his mind obsessed. If, monks, a monk is obsessed by malevolence . . . sloth and torpor . . . restlessness and worry . . . doubt, to this extent is his mind obsessed. If, monks, a monk centres his thought on this world, to this extent is his mind obsessed. If, monks, a monk centres his thought on the world beyond, to this extent is his mind obsessed. If, monks, a monk, disputatious, quarrelsome, contentious, lives wounding with the weapons of his tongue, to this extent is his mind obsessed. He comprehends thus: 'I have no subjective obsession, not got rid of, owing to which I, if my mind were obsessed by it,

[1] Connected with the Way, *MA*. ii. 401.

[2] As at *A*. iii. 10.

[3] Here the view of the Way (or stage) of stream-attainment, *MA*. ii. 401. So, it is said at the end of this Discourse, the seven kinds of knowledge enumerated in it pertain to a stream-attainer.

could not know, could not see (things) as they really are; my thought is well directed towards awakening as to the truths.' This is the first knowledge won by him, ariyan, transcendental, not in common with average men.

And again, monks, the ariyan disciple reflects thus: 'While I am following, developing, maturing this view, I gain calm for myself, I gain quenchedness[1] for myself.' He comprehends thus: 'While I am following, developing, maturing this view, I gain calm for myself, I gain quenchedness for myself.' This is the second knowledge won by him, ariyan, transcendental, not in common with average men.

And again, monks, an ariyan disciple reflects thus: 'Is there another recluse or brahman—outside here—who is possessed of a view such as I am possessed of?'[2] He comprehends thus: 'There is no other recluse or brahman—outside here—**[324]** who is possessed of a view such as I am possessed of.' This is the third knowledge won by him, ariyan, transcendental, not in common with average men.

And again, monks, the ariyan disciple reflects thus: 'Am I too possessed of the kind of propriety a man is possessed of who is endowed with right view?' And what kind of propriety, monks, is a man possessed of who is endowed with (right) view? This is propriety, monks, for a man endowed with (right) view: Whatever kind of offence he falls into he makes known the removal[3] of such an offence, for he confesses it, discloses it, declares it quickly to the Teacher or to intelligent fellow Brahma-farers; having confessed, disclosed and declared it, he comes to restraint in the future.[4] Just as an innocent little baby lying on its back quickly draws back its hand or foot if it has touched a live ember—even so, monks, this is propriety for a man endowed with (right) view . . . restraint in the future. He comprehends thus: 'I too am possessed of the kind of propriety which a man is possessed of who is endowed with (right) view.' This is the fourth knowledge won by him, ariyan, transcendental, not in common with average men.

---

[1] *nibbuti*, explained at *MA*. ii. 401 as *kilesavūpasama*, allayment of the defilements.

[2] *I.e.* a view of one who has attained the stage of stream-entrant.

[3] By confession or by a formal act of the Order (*saṅghakamma*); *MA*. ii. 402. He does not keep his offence concealed.

[4] The view that future restraint or control results from confession is often met with in the *Vinaya-* and *Sutta-piṭakas*.

And again, monks, the ariyan disciple reflects thus: 'Am I too possessed of the kind of propriety a man is possessed of who is endowed with (right) view?' And what kind of propriety, monks, is a man possessed of who is endowed with (right) view? This is propriety, monks, for a man endowed with (right) view: If he is zealous concerning those manifold things[1] which are to be done for fellow Brahma-farers, he then becomes of strong aspiration for training in the higher moral habit, for training in the higher thought, for training in the higher intuitive wisdom. Just as a cow with a young calf, while she is pulling the grass keeps an eye on the calf—even so, monks, this is propriety for a man endowed with (right) view . . . for training in the higher intuitive wisdom. He comprehends thus: 'I too am possessed of the kind of propriety a man is possessed of who is endowed with (right) view.' This is the fifth knowledge won by him, ariyan, transcendental, not in common with average men.

[**325**] And again, monks, the ariyan disciple reflects thus: 'Am I too possessed of the kind of strength a man is possessed of who is endowed with (right) view?' And what kind of strength, monks, is a man possessed of who is endowed with (right) view? This is strength, monks, for a man endowed with (right) view: While *dhamma* and discipline proclaimed by the Tathāgata are being taught, having applied himself, paying attention, concentrating with all the mind, he listens to *dhamma* with ready ear.[2] He comprehends thus: 'I too am possessed of the kind of strength a man is possessed of who is endowed with (right) view.' This is the sixth knowledge won by him, ariyan, transcendental, not in common with average men.

And again, monks, the ariyan disciple reflects thus: 'Am I too possessed of the kind of strength a man is possessed of who is endowed with (right) view? And what kind of strength, monks, is a man possessed of who is endowed with (right) view? This is strength, monks, for a man endowed with (right) view: While *dhamma* and discipline proclaimed by the Tathāgata are being taught, he acquires knowledge of the goal, he acquires knowledge of *dhamma*, he acquires the rapture that is connected with

---

[1] Greater and lesser duties, the former comprising the making and dyeing of robe-material, keeping the shrine clean, and duties in the Observance-hall and so on. The lesser duties comprise putting out water for washing the feet, oil and so forth. Alternative lists are then given, *MA*. ii. 402.

[2] *Cf. M*. i. 445, iii. 201; *S*. i. 112; *Ud*. 80; also *Vin*. i. 103, etc.

dhamma.[1] He comprehends thus: 'I too am possessed of the kind of strength a man is possessed of who is endowed with (right) view.' This monks, is the seventh knowledge won by him, ariyan, transcendental, not in common with average men.

Thus, monks, propriety has come to be well sought by an ariyan disciple who is possessed of seven factors for realising the fruit of stream-attainment. Possessed of seven factors thus, monks, an ariyan disciple is possessed of the fruit of stream-attainment."

Thus spoke the Lord. Delighted, these monks rejoiced in what the Lord had said.

Discourse at Kosambī:
the Eighth

49. DISCOURSE ON A CHALLENGE TO A BRAHMĀ

(Brahmanimantaṇikasutta)

[326] THUS have I heard: At one time the Lord was staying near Sāvatthī in the Jeta Grove in Anāthapiṇḍika's monastery. While he was there the Lord addressed the monks, saying: "Monks." "Revered one," these monks answered the Lord in assent. The Lord spoke thus:

"At one time I, monks, was staying at Ukkaṭṭhā in the Subhaga Grove near the great sāl-tree.[2] At that time, monks, an evil wrong view[3] came to have accrued to Baka the Brahmā[4] like this: 'This[5] is permanent, this is stable, this is eternal, this is entire, this is not liable to passing away, this is not born, does not age, does not die, does not pass away, does not uprise, and there is not another further escape from this.'[6] Then did I, monks, knowing with my mind the reasoning in the mind of Baka the Brahmā, as a

---

[1] *M.* i. 37, 221.

[2] As at *M.* i. 1; quoted *Kvu.* 559.

[3] An eternalist view, *MA.* ii. 405.

[4] At *S.* i. 142, *Jā.* iii. 358 this Baka episode appears to occur in Sāvatthī.

[5] According to *MA.* ii. 405, "this" is a *Brahmaṭṭhāna*.

[6] "Further" there are, however, three stages in meditation, four ways, four fruits, and nibbāna, *MA.* ii. 405.

strong man might bend back his outstretched arm or might stretch out his bent arm, so, vanishing from near the great sāl-tree in the Subhaga Grove at Ukkaṭṭhā, did I appear in that Brahma-world. Monks, Baka the Brahmā saw me coming in the distance; seeing me, he spoke thus: 'Come, good sir, you are welcome, good sir. At last, good sir, you make this occasion for coming here.[1] But this, good sir, is permanent, this is stable, this is eternal, this is entire, this is not liable to passing away, this is not born, nor does it age or die or pass away or uprise, and there is not another further escape from this.' When this had been said, I, monks, spoke thus to Baka the Brahmā:

'Indeed, Baka the Brahmā is steeped in ignorance, indeed, Baka the Brahmā is steeped in ignorance, inasmuch as he says "permanent" although it is indeed impermanent, "stable" although it is indeed instable, "eternal" although it is indeed not eternal, "entire" although it is indeed not entire, "not liable to passing away" although it is indeed liable to passing away, and because in regard to what is born, and ages and dies and passes away and uprises, he says: "This is not born, nor does it age or die or pass away or uprise," and although there is another further escape, he says: "There is not another further escape."'

Then, monks, Māra the Evil One, having entered a certain company of Brahmās,[2] spoke thus to me: 'Monk, monk, do not meddle with this, do not meddle with this. For, monk, this Brahmā is a Great [**327**] Brahmā,[3] Victor, Unvanquished, All-seeing, Controller, Lord, Maker, Creator, Chief, Disposer, Master, Father of all that have become and will be. Monk, there were recluses and brahmans in the world before you who scorned extension, loathed extension, who scorned cohesion, loathed cohesion, who scorned heat, loathed heat, who scorned motion, loathed motion, who scorned creatures, loathed creatures, who scorned *devas*, loathed *devas*, who scorned Pajāpati, loathed Pajāpati, who scorned Brahmā, loathed Brahmā[4]—these at the breaking up of the body, at the cutting off of life, were established in a low group.[5] But, monk, there were recluses and brahmans in the world before you,

---

[1] As at *M*. i. 252, 481.

[2] *MA*. ii. 405 says he was not able to enter among Great Brahmās or among priests of the Brahmās.

[3] Following sequence of terms at *D*. i. 18; first six also at *It*. p. 15.

[4] For the sequence: extension to Brahmā, see *M*. i. 1 *ff*.

[5] *kāya*. *MA*. ii. 406 says they were reborn in the four woeful ways.

who lauded extension, delighted in extension, who lauded cohesion . . . heat . . . motion . . . creatures . . . *devas* . . . who lauded Pajāpati, delighted in Pajāpati, lauded Brahmā, delighted in Brahmā—these at the breaking up of the body, at the cutting off of life, were established in an excellent group.[1] On account of this do I, monk, speak thus: "Please do you, good sir, do exactly what Brahmā says to you, do not go beyond Brahmā's word. If you, monk, should go beyond Brahmā's word, it will be with you, monk, as with a man who might beat back approaching glory[2] with a stick, or, monk, as with a man who might miss[3] the earth with his hands and feet as he was falling down hell's precipices. Please do you, good sir, do exactly what Brahmā says to you, do not go beyond Brahmā's word. Do not you, monk, see the seated company of Brahmā ?"' And so, monks, Māra the Evil One conducted me to the company of Brahmā. When he had spoken thus, I, monks, spoke thus to Māra the Evil One:

'I, Evil One, know you; do not think that I do not know you. Māra, you are the Evil One. And whoever, Evil One, is a Brahmā, and whatever are Brahmā-companies, and whatever are Brahmā-conclaves, all are in your grasp, all are in your power. It occurs to you thus, Evil One: Let this one too be in my grasp, let this one too be in my power. But I, Evil One, am not in your grasp, I am not in your power.'

When I had said this, monks, Baka the Brahmā spoke thus to me: 'But I, good sir, say "permanent" because it is permanent, [**328**] I say "stable" because it is stable, I say "eternal" because it is eternal, I say "entire" because it is entire, I say "not liable to passing away" because it is not liable to passing away, and of what is not born, does not age, die, pass away and uprise, this is just what I say: This is not born, it does not age, it does not die, it does not pass away, it does not uprise; and because there is not another further escape, I say, There is not another further escape. There were, monk, recluses and brahmans in the world before you who practised austerities for a term as long as your whole life. These would know thus: either, if there is another further escape: There is another further escape; or, if there is not another further escape: There is not another further escape. So I, monk, say this to you: You will never see another further escape however

[1] *MA*. ii. 406, in the Brahma-world.

[2] *siri*, luck, glory, prosperity. *MA*. ii. 406 says nothing.

[3] *virāgeyya*. *MA*. ii. 406-7 reads *virādheyya*.

much you may go in for toil and trouble. But if you, monk, would ascertain[1] extension, you will become near to me,[2] reposing on my substance,[3] to be done to as I will, dwarfed.[4] If you would ascertain cohesion . . . heat . . . motion . . . creatures . . . *devas* . . . Pajāpati . . . Brahmā, you will become near to me, reposing on my substance, to be done to as I will, dwarfed.'

'But I too, Brahmā, know this: If I were to ascertain extension . . . cohesion . . . heat . . . motion . . . creatures . . . *devas* . . . Pajāpati . . . Brahmā, I will become near to you, reposing on your substance, to be done to as you will, dwarfed. Moreover I both comprehend your bourn, Brahmā, and I comprehend your splendour:[5] Baka the Brahmā is of great psychic power thus, Baka the Brahmā is of great majesty thus, Baka the Brahmā is of great fame thus.'

As far as moon and sun revolve in their course
And light up all the quarters with their radiance,
So far extends the thousand-world system:
Here your sway is exercised.
But do you know the distinctions ?[6]
The passionate and dispassionate likewise ?
The becoming thus, the becoming otherwise,
The coming and the going of beings ?[7]

'It is thus that I, Brahmā, both comprehend your bourn and comprehend your splendour: Baka the Brahmā is of great psychic power thus, Baka the Brahmā is of great majesty thus, [**329**] Baka the Brahmā is of great fame thus. But there are, Brahmā, three other classes which you do not know, do not see, but which I know and see. There is, Brahmā, the class called Radiant ones from which you have passed away, uprising here; but because of your very long abiding[8] (here), the recollection of it is confused, and

---

[1] *I.e.* in meditation, *ajjhosati*.

[2] *opasāyika*. *MA*. ii. 407 gives *samīpasaya*. [3] *vatthusāyika*.

[4] *bāhiteyyo*. This is obscure. To be sent out, degraded; or, as *paṭibāheti*, to be kept off, shut off, warded off. *MA*. ii. 407 *jajjharikāgumbato pi nīcataro lakuṇṭakataro kātabbo bhavissasi*, weakened, degraded, dwarfed.

[5] *juti*. This spelling seems to be faulty for *cuti* (given as v.l. at *M*. i. 557 and also as v.l. for *muṭi* at *MA*. ii. 36 in quoting the above passage); see *P.E.D.* But *MA*. ii. 408 gives *ānubhāva*.

[6] *paroparaṃ*. *MA*. ii. 408 says the high and low, the poor and excellent.

[7] *Cf*. *Jā*. i. 132, ii. 313; *A*. i. 227; *DA*. ii. 659.

[8] *nivāsa*, abode, residence; *cf*. *pubbenivāsa*, former abodes or habitations, or former births.

because of that *you* neither know nor see it; *I* know and see it. Thus I, Brahmā, am not merely on an exact equality with you as regards super-knowledge; how could I be lower, since I am indeed greater than you? There is, Brahmā, the class called Lustrous ones . . . the class called Vehapphala, which *you* neither know nor see, but which I know and see. Thus again I, Brahmā, am not merely on an exact equality with you as regards super-knowledge; how could I be lower, since I am indeed greater than you?

'I, Brahmā, knowing extension to be extension, to that extent knowing that which is not reached[1] by means of the extensity of extension, do not think: It is extension,[2] (of self) in (regard to) extension, (of self) as extension, extension is mine'—I do not salute extension. Thus again I, Brahmā, am not merely on an exact equality with you as regards super-knowledge; how could I be lower, since I am indeed greater that you?

I, Brahmā, knowing cohesion . . . heat . . . motion . . . creatures . . . *devas* . . . Pajāpati . . . Brahmā . . . the Radiant ones . . . the Lustrous ones . . . the Vehapphalas . . . the Overlord[3] . . . I, Brahmā, knowing the all to be the all, to that extent knowing that which is not reached by the allness of the all, do not think: "It is all, (of self) in (regard to) all, (of self) as all, all is mine"—I do not salute the all. Thus again I, Brahmā, am not merely on an exact equality with you as regards super-knowledge; how could I be lower, since I am indeed greater than you?'

'If, through the allness of the all[4] that is not reached by you, good sir, take care lest it be vain for you, lest it be empty. Discriminative consciousness which cannot be characterised,[5] which is unending, lucid in every respect,[6] cannot be reached through the extensity of extension, the cohesiveness of cohesion, heat's hotness, motion's movement, creatures' creaturehood, *devas*' *deva*-hood, Pajāpati's Pajāpatihood, the Brahmās' Brahmahood, the Radiant ones' radiance, the Lustrous ones' lustre, the Vehapphalas' Vehapphalahood, [**330**] it cannot be reached through the Overlord's overlordship, it cannot be reached by the allness of the all. And now I am vanishing from you, good sir.'

---

[1] *ananubhūtam*; *MA*. ii. 412 calls it nibbāna.

[2] *Cf. M*. i. 1.

[3] *abhibhu*.

[4] *MA*. ii. 412 says the Brahmā meant the Imperishable, *akkhara*, whereas the Teacher meant his own body.

[5] *MA*. ii. 413, "invisible."

[6] This sequence also at *D*. i. 223, where last phrase reads *sabbato pahaṃ*, while *M*. reads *sabbatopabhaṃ*. See *Dial*. i. 283, *n*. 2.

'Now, Brahmā, you vanish from me if you are able.'

Then, monks, Baka the Brahmā saying, 'I will vanish from the recluse Gotama, I will vanish from the recluse Gotama,' was nevertheless unable to vanish from me. When this had been said, I, monks, spoke thus to Baka the Brahmā: 'Now I am vanishing from you, Brahmā.'

'Come, good sir, you vanish from me if you are able.' Then I,[1] monks, having resolved a psychic resolve like this:[2] 'May Brahmā and Brahmā's company and Brahmā's conclave hear the sound of me without seeing me,' disappeared and spoke this verse:

> Having seen danger in becoming itself,
> And becoming seeking dis-becoming,[3]
> I saluted not becoming
> Nor grasped after any delight.

Then, monks, Brahmā and Brahmā's company and Brahmā's conclave were filled with wonder and amazement, and said: 'Wonderful, good sirs, marvellous, good sirs, is the great psychic power, the great majesty of the recluse Gotama; indeed before now there has not been seen or heard another recluse or brahman of such great psychic power, of such great majesty as this recluse Gotama, a son of the Sakyans, gone forth from a Sakyan family. For a people delighting in becoming, delighted with becoming, revelling in becoming, he has indeed pulled up becoming with its root.'

Then, monks, Māra the Evil One, having entered a certain Brahma-conclave, spoke thus to me: 'If you, good sir, know thus, if you have understood[4] thus, do not communicate it to disciples[5] or to those who have gone forth; do not teach *dhamma* to disciples or to those who have gone forth; do not crave for disciples or for those who have gone forth. Monk, there were recluses and brahmans in the world before you, claiming to be perfected ones, fully self-awakened ones; these communicated to disciples and to those who had gone forth; they taught *dhamma* to disciples and to those who had gone forth; they craved for disciples and for those

---

[1] To end of the verse, quoted at *Vism.* 394.

[2] As at *Vin.* i. 16; *D.* i. 106; *S.* iii. 92, etc.

[3] Or "annihilation," *vibhava*.

[4] *anubuddha*, or awakened. *MA.* ii. 415 says, "if you have understood (*anubuddho*) the four truths thus by yourself."

[5] *MA.* ii. 415 calls these householders.

who had gone forth. These, having communicated to disciples and to those who had gone forth, having taught *dhamma* to disciples and to those who had gone forth, having craved for disciples and for those who had gone forth, at the breaking up of the body, at the cutting off of life, were established in a low group.[1] Monk, there were recluses and brahmans in the world before you, claiming to be perfected ones, fully self-awakened ones; [**331**] these did not communicate to disciples or to those who had gone forth; they did not teach *dhamma* to disciples or to those who had gone forth; they did not crave for disciples or for those who had gone forth. These, not having communicated to disciples or to those who had gone forth, not having taught *dhamma* to disciples or to those who had gone forth, not having craved for disciples or for those who had gone forth, at the breaking up of the body, at the cutting off of life, were established in an excellent group.[2] So I speak thus to you, monk: Please do you, good sir, dwell untroubled and intent on abiding in ease here and now.[3] What is skill is not pointing out,[4] good sir, so do not instruct others.'

When this had been said, I, monks, spoke thus to Māra the Evil One: 'I know you, Evil One, do not think: He does not know me. Evil One, you are Māra. You do not speak to me thus, Evil One, because you are friendly and compassionate; you speak to me thus, Evil One, because you are not friendly, not compassionate. And you think thus, Evil One: Those to whom the recluse Gotama teaches *dhamma* will get beyond my reach. Although those recluses and brahmans, Evil One, who claimed: "We are fully self-awakened ones," were not fully self-awakened ones, nevertheless I, Evil One, who claim, "I am a fully self-awakened one," am indeed a fully self-awakened one. For, Evil One, whether a Tathāgata is teaching *dhamma* to disciples, he is such a one; whether, Evil One, a Tathāgata is not teaching *dhamma* to disciples, he is such a one; whether, Evil One, a Tathāgata is communicating it to disciples, he is such a one; whether, Evil One, a Tathāgata is not communicating it to disciples, he is such a one. What is the reason for this? Evil One, in a Tathāgata those cankers which are connected with the defilements, with again-becoming, fearful, whose results are anguish, which make for birth, ageing and dying

---

[1] *MA*. ii. 415, in the four woeful ways.

[2] *MA*. ii. 415 instancing a Brahma-world. [3] *Cf. Vin*. ii. 188.

[4] *MA*. ii. 415, reading *akkhānaṃ* instead of text's *akkhātaṃ*, says it is skill not to point out, exhort or teach *dhamma* to others; this is best.

in the future, these are got rid of, cut off at the root, made like a palm-tree stump so that they can come to no further existence in the future.[1] Evil One, as a palm-tree whose crown has been cut off cannot put forth growth again, even so, Evil One, in a Tathāgata those cankers which are connected with the defilements, with again-becoming, fearful, whose results are anguish, which make for birth, ageing and dying in the future, these are got rid of, cut off at the root, made like a palm-tree stump that can come to no further existence in the future.'

Because of Marā's failure to persuade (me) and because of the invitation to a Brahmā, a synonym for this homily is therefore A challenge to a Brahmā."

Discourse on a Challenge to a Brahmā:
the Ninth

50. DISCOURSE ON A REBUKE TO MĀRA

(Māratajjaniyasutta)

[**332**] Thus have I heard: At one time the venerable Moggallāna the Great was staying among the Bhaggas in Sumsumāragira in Bhesakaḷā Grove in the deer-park. Now at that time the venerable Moggallāna the Great was pacing up and down in the open. Now at that time Māra the Evil One, entering the venerable Moggallāna the Great's belly, got into his stomach. Then it occurred to the venerable Moggallāna the Great: " Now why is my belly heavy as if it were heaped full?"[2] Then the venerable Moggallāna the Great, having come down from the place for pacing up and down in, having entered the dwelling-place, sat down on a seat made ready. As he was sitting down, the venerable Moggallāna the Great reflected carefully about himself. Then the venerable Moggallāna the Great saw that Māra the Evil One, having entered his belly, had got into his stomach; seeing him, he spoke thus to Māra the Evil One:

"Get out, Evil One; Evil One, get out; do not annoy a Tathāgata

---

[1] As at *M*. i. 250, 280.

[2] *māsācitam*. See *VbhA*. 510 (on *Vbh*. 386), and *PED*.

or a Tathāgata's disciple, lest for a long time there be woe and sorrow for you."

Then it occurred to Māra the Evil One: "This recluse speaks thus not even knowing, not even seeing me: 'Get out, Evil One, Evil One, get out. Do not annoy a Tathāgata or a Tathāgata's disciple, lest for a long time there be woe and sorrow for you.' Even his teacher could not know me so quickly, so how can this disciple know me ?"

Then the venerable Moggallāna the Great spoke thus to Māra the Evil One: "But I do know you, Evil One. Do not you think: He does not know me. You, Evil One, are Māra. It occurred to you, Evil One: This recluse speaks thus not even knowing, not even seeing me: 'Get out, Evil One; Evil One, get out. Do not annoy a Tathāgata or a Tathāgata's disciple, lest for a long time there be woe and sorrow for you.' Even his teacher could not know me so quickly, so how can this disciple know me ?"

Then it occurred to Māra the Evil One: "It is because this recluse knows and sees me that he speaks thus: 'Get out, Evil One; Evil One, get out. Do not annoy a Tathāgata or a Tathāgata's disciple, lest for a long time there be woe and sorrow for you.'"

Then Māra the Evil One, [**333**] having gone out through the venerable Moggallāna the Great's mouth, stood against the door.[1] Then the venerable Moggallāna the Great saw Māra the Evil One standing against the door; seeing him, he spoke thus to Māra the Evil One: "Indeed I do see you now, Evil One. Do not think: He does not see me; it is you, Evil One, standing against the door. Once upon a time, I, Evil One, was the Māra called Dūsin;[2] as such Kāḷī was the name of my sister, you were her son, thus you were my nephew. Now at that time, Evil One, Kakusandha, the Lord, the perfected one, fully self-awakened one, had uprisen in the world. Now, Evil One, Vidhura and Sañjīva were the pair of disciples which was the chief, the lucky pair of Kakusandha,[3] the Lord, the perfected one, the fully self-awakened one. Of all the disciples, Evil One, of Kakusandha, the Lord, perfected one, fully self-awakened one, there was none there equal to the venerable Vidhura in regard to teaching *dhamma*. It was because of this,

---

[1] *paccaggaḷe aṭṭhāsi. PED.* "stuck in his throat." *MA.* ii. 416 says *paṭi-aggaḷe aṭṭhāsi. Aggaḷaṃ vuccati kavāṭaṃ.*

[2] At *Vism.* 229 is said to have died untimely as his life-current was cut off by *kamma.*

[3] *D.* ii. 4; *S.* ii. 191; *Budv.* XXIII. 20; *Jā.* i. 42.

Evil One, that the venerable Vidhura's name came to be Vidhura, the Peerless. But the venerable Sañjīva, Evil One, forest-gone, gone to the roots of trees and gone to empty places, with no trouble attained the stopping of perceiving and feeling. Once upon a time, Evil One, the venerable Sañjīva was sitting at the root of a certain tree attaining the stopping of perceiving and feeling. Then, Evil One, cowherds, goatherds, yeoman farmers, travellers,[1] saw the venerable Sañjīva sitting at the root of that tree attaining the stopping of perceiving and feeling; having seen him, it occurred to them: 'Indeed it is wonderful, indeed it is marvellous, that this recluse is just sitting dead. Come, we will cremate him.' Then, Evil One, these cowherds, goatherds, yeomen farmers, travellers, having collected grass and sticks and cow-dung and having heaped them over the venerable Sañjīva's body, lit the fire and departed. Then, Evil One, the venerable Sañjīva, having emerged towards the end of that night from that attainment, having shaken his robes, having dressed in the morning, taking his bowl and robe, entered a village for almsfood. Evil One, those cowherds, goatherds, yeomen farmers and travellers saw the venerable Sañjīva walking for almsfood; having seen him, it occurred to them: 'Indeed it is wonderful, indeed it is marvellous that this recluse who was just sitting dead—that he has come back to life.'[2] **[334]** It was because of this, Evil One, that the venerable Sañjīva's name came to be Sañjīva, the Quick.

Then, Evil One, it occurred to the Māra Dūsin: 'I simply do not know either the coming or the going of these monks who are of moral habit, lovely in character. Suppose I were to visit brahmans and householders (and say): "Come, do you revile, abuse, vex, annoy the monks who are of good moral habit, lovely in character, for it is likely that when they are being reviled, abused, vexed and annoyed by you there will be a change of heart so that Dūsin the Māra might get a chance over them."' Then, Evil One, the Māra Dūsin visited brahmans and householders (and said): 'Come, do you revile . . . chance over them.' Then, Evil One, those brahmans and householders who had been visited by the Māra Dūsin reviled, abused, vexed and annoyed the monks who were of good moral habit, lovely in character, saying: 'But these little shaveling recluses are menials, black, the offscourings of our kins-

---

[1] As at *Vin.* iv. 108.

[2] *paṭisañjīvito.* This feat is called *samādhivipphārā iddhi;* see *Budv. A.* 26, *Vism.* 380-81, *Pts.* ii. 212.

man's feet.[1] They say, We are meditatives, we are meditatives, and with their shoulders drooping, with their faces cast down, as if drugged,[2] they meditate, they meditate absorbed, they meditate more absorbed, they meditate quite absorbed.[3] As an owl on the branch of a tree when tracking a mouse meditates, meditates absorbed, meditates more absorbed, meditates quite absorbed, so do these little shaveling recluses, menials, black . . . meditate quite absorbed. And as a jackal on the bank of a river when tracking fish meditates, meditates absorbed, meditates more absorbed, meditates quite absorbed, so do these little shaveling recluses . . . meditate quite absorbed. And as a cat on the edge of a refuse heap when tracking a mouse[4] meditates, meditates absorbed, meditates more absorbed, meditates quite absorbed, so do these little shaveling recluses . . . meditate quite absorbed. And as an ass at the edge of a refuse-heap, its burden removed, meditates, meditates absorbed, meditates more absorbed, meditates quite absorbed, so do these little shaveling recluses, menials, black, the offscourings of our kinsman's feet, saying: We are meditatives, we are meditatives, with their shoulders drooping, with their faces cast down, as if drugged, meditate, meditate absorbed, meditate more absorbed, meditate quite absorbed. Evil One, nearly all the people who passed away at that time, at the breaking up of the body after dying arose in a sorrowful state, a bad bourn, the abyss, Niraya Hell.

[**335**] Then, Evil One, Kakusandha, the Lord, perfected one, fully self-awakened one, addressed the monks, saying: 'Monks, brahmans and householders have been visited by the Māra Dūsin (who said): "Come, do you revile, abuse, vex, annoy the monks who are of good moral habit, lovely in character, for it is likely that when they are being reviled, abused, vexed and annoyed by

---

[1] *M.* ii. 177; *D.* i. 90; *S.* iv. 117. *MA.* ii. 418=*DA.* 254 refers to the brahman theory of the origin of the four castes, and says recluses sprang from the soles of Brahmā's feet.

[2] *madhurakajāta.* Not here, as more frequently, combined with *kāyagata*; *cf. D.* ii. 99; *S.* iii. 106; *A.* iii. 69. See *K.S.* iii. 90, *n.* 2. *MA.* ii. 418 gives *ālasiyajāta*, slothful, lazy.

[3] *jhāyanti pajjhāyanti nijjhāyanti apajjhāyanti.* As at *M.* iii. 14. *MA.* ii. 418 says these prefixes have an increasing emphasis. Therefore the final one would not be "de-trance" (Chalmers), for the *a*- would not be privative; the prefix would be *apa*-, and would denote a rather more advanced state than those denoted by the other prefixes.

[4] *S.* ii. 270.

you there will be a change of heart so that Dūsin the Māra might get a chance over them." Come, do you, monks, abide, having suffused the first quarter with a mind of friendliness, likewise the second, likewise the third, likewise the fourth; just so above, below, across; abide having suffused the whole world, everywhere, in every way with a mind of friendliness, that is far-reaching, wide-spread, immeasurable, without enmity, without malevolence. Abide, having suffused with a mind of compassion . . . with a mind of sympathetic joy . . . with a mind of equanimity the first quarter, likewise the second, likewise the third, likewise the fourth; just so above, below, across; abide having suffused the whole world, everywhere, in every way with a mind of equanimity that is far-reaching, wide-spread, immeasurable, without enmity, without malevolence.'

Then, Evil One, these monks, forest-gone and gone to the roots of trees and gone to empty places, thus exhorted, thus instructed by Kakusandha, the Lord, perfected one, fully self-awakened one, abided, having suffused with a mind of friendliness the first quarter, likewise the second . . . the third . . . the fourth; just so above, below, across; they abided having suffused the whole world, everywhere, in every way, with a mind of friendliness that was far-reaching, widespread, immeasurable, without enmity, without malevolence. They abided, having suffused with a mind of compassion . . . with a mind of sympathetic joy . . . with a mind of equanimity the first quarter, likewise the second, likewise the third, likewise the fourth; just so above, below, across; so that they abided having suffused the whole world, everywhere, in every way with a mind of equanimity that was far-reaching, widespread, immeasurable, without enmity, without malevolence.

Then, Evil One, it occurred to the Māra Dūsin: 'Even although I am working thus, I do not know the coming or the going of these monks who are of good moral habit, lovely in character. Suppose I were to visit brahmans and householders (and say): "Come, do you reverence, revere, respect, honour the monks who are of good moral habit, lovely in character, [**336**] for it is likely that when they are being reverenced, revered, respected and honoured by you, there will be a change of heart, so that Dūsin the Māra can get a chance over them." ' Then, Evil One, the Māra Dūsin visited these brahmans and householders (and said): 'Come, do you reverence, revere, respect and honour these monks who are of good moral habit, lovely in character, for it is likely that when they are being reverenced, revered, respected and honoured by you, there will be a change of heart so that Dūsin the Māra can get a chance over them.' Then, Evil One, these brahmans and householders who had been visited by Dūsin the Māra, reverenced, revered, respected and honoured those monks who were of good moral habit, lovely in character. Evil One, nearly all the people who passed away at that time, at the breaking up of the body after dying arose in a good bourn, a heaven world.

Then, Evil One, Kakusandha, the Lord, perfected one, fully self-awakened one, addressed the monks, saying: 'Monks, brahmans and householders have been visited by the Māra Dūsin (who said): "Come, do you reverence, revere, respect, honour those monks who are of good moral habit, lovely in character, for it is likely that when they are being reverenced, revered, respected and honoured by you there will be a change of heart so that Dūsin the Māra can get a chance over them." Come, do you, monks, dwell beholding what is unlovely in the body,[1] conscious of the cloying of food,[2] conscious of there being no delight in the whole world,[3] beholding[4] the impermanence of all constructions.'[5] Then, Evil One, these monks, forest-gone, gone to the roots of trees and gone to empty places, being exhorted thus, being instructed thus by Kakusandha, the Lord, perfected one, fully self-awakened one, dwelt beholding what is unlovely in the body, conscious of the cloying of food, conscious of there being no delight in the whole world, beholding the impermanence of all constructions.

Then, Evil One, Kakusandha, the Lord, perfected one, fully self-awakened one, having dressed in the morning, taking his bowl and robe, entered a village for almsfood with the venerable Vidhura as his attendant. Then, Evil One, Dūsin the Māra, having visited a certain young man, having taken up a stone, gave a blow to the venerable Vidhura's head; his head split. Then, Evil One, the venerable Vidhura with his head broken and dripping with blood, even so [**337**] followed close after Kakusandha, the Lord, the perfected one, fully self-awakened one. Then, Evil One, Kakusandha, the Lord, perfected one, fully self-awakened one, looked around with the "elephant-look."[6] and thought: "Indeed, this Dūsin the Māra does not know moderation." While he was looking

---

[1] *MA*. ii. 420 cites *A*. iv. 46-7.
[2] *MA*. ii. 420 cites *A*. iv. 49.
[3] *MA*. ii. 420 cites *A*. iv. 50.
[4] *MA*. ii. 420 cites *A*. iv. 51.
[5] *Cf*. *A*. iii. 79, 83, 143.
[6] That is, not merely twisting the neck from this side to that, but turning the whole body.

around, Evil One, Dūsin the Māra deceased from that place and arose in the Great Niraya Hell. Evil One, there are three appellations of that Great Niraya Hell: it is called "Belonging to the sphere of the Six Sensory Impingements"[1] and it is called "The Meeting of the Spikes"[2] and it is called "The Separate Feelings." Then, Evil One, the guardian of Niraya Hell, having approached me, spoke thus: 'When, good sir, spike shall meet spike within your heart, then you should understand this: There will be a thousand years of boiling in Niraya Hell for me.' Then I, Evil One, for many years, for many a hundred, for many a thousand years, boiled in that Great Niraya Hell. After ten thousand years of that Great Niraya Hell itself, feeling a feeling called *vuṭṭhānima* (pain), I was boiled in Ussada (Hell). Because of this, Evil One, my body came to be such, like a man's; my head came to be such, like a fish's."

[3]What was that Niraya Hell like where Dūsin was boiled
For striking the disciple Vidhura and the brahman[4] Kakusandha ?
It was that of the hundred iron spikes, all suffered separately—
This[5] was the Niraya Hell where Dūsin was boiled
For striking the disciple Vidhura and the brahman Kakusandha.
Whatever monk, the Awakened One's disciple, understands this—
Dark One, for striking such a monk you go to suffering.[6]
Mansions[7] stand for an eon in the middle of the sea,
The hue of beryl-stones,[8] brilliant, glowing, radiant;
There dance full many nymphs in divers hues.
Whatever monk, the Awakened One's disciple, understands this—
Dark One, for striking such a monk you go to suffering.
Whoever, urged on by the Awakened One, watched by the Order of monks,
With his great toe shakes the palace of Migāra's mother[9]—

---

[1] See *S.* iv. 125. [2] See *Jā.* vi. 453.

[3] At *Thag.* 1187-1208 these verses are ascribed to Māra.

[4] Brahman here of course in the sense of arahant.

[5] *MA.* ii. 422 says this is described in the *Devadūta Sutta*, *M.* iii. 178; *cf. A.* i. 138 *ff.*

[6] = *Thag.* 25.

[7] *MA.* ii. 422 says they are to be understood as in *Vv.* and *Pv.*

[8] Or, lapis lazuli, *veḷuriya*.

[9] *MA.* ii. 422 refers us to *Pāsādakampanasutta* (*S.* v. 269).

Whatever monk, the Awakened One's disciple, understands this—
Dark One, for striking such a monk you go to suffering.
Whoever with his great toe shakes Vejayanta Palace,[1]
Rigid through psychic power and strongly moves the *devatās*—
[**338**] Whatever monk, the Awakened One's disciple, understands this—
Dark One, for striking such a monk you go to suffering.
Whoever inquires of Sakka in the Vejayanta Palace,
'Have you, friend, found the freedoms by the destruction of craving?'[2]
To whom Sakka truthfully answers the question put to him—
Whatever monk, the Awakened One's disciple, understands this—
Dark One, for striking such a monk you go to suffering.
Whoever inquires of Brahmā in conclave in Sudhammmā's hall,[3]
'Do you,[4] friend, even today hold those views which formerly were views of yours?
Do you see the passing radiance in the Brahma-world?'[5]
To whom, Brahmā truthfully answers (those questions) in succession:[6]
'Good sir, those views are not mine which formerly were views of mine;
I see the passing radiance in the Brahma-world;
How could I say today: I am permanent, eternal?'—
Whatever monk, the Awakened One's disciple, understands this—
Dark One, for striking such a monk you go to suffering.

---

[1] *MA*. ii. 422 refers us to *Cūḷataṇhāsankhayavimuttisutta* (*M*. i. 251; *Cf*. *S*. i. 234 *f*.).

[2] *M*. i. 255.

[3] See *M*. *Sta*. 49 (referred to by the Comy. as *Bakabrahmasutta*) and *S*. i. 142. *MA*. ii. 422 also says that Sudhammā's hall is here meant to be in the Brahma-world, not in the Tāvatimsa abode, but there is no *deva*-world without its Sudhammasabhā. The whole Brahma-world was one glory, *MA*. ii. 423.

[4] As at *S*. i. 145.

[5] *I.e.* the radiance of Sāriputta, Moggallāna, Kassapa the Great and so on as they were sitting in the Lord's effulgence in the Brahma-world, having attained the condition of heat. *MA*. ii. 423 and see *S*. i. 145.

[6] *anupubbaṃ yathātathaṃ*, as at *Sn*. 600. *Thag*. 1199 reads (as in previous stanza) *pañhaṃ puṭṭho*.

Who, by deliverance,[1] has gained great Neru's[2] peak,
The forest[3] of the Eastern Videhas,[4] and whatever men sleep on the ground[5]—
Whatever monk, the Awakened One's disciple, understands this—
Dark One, for striking such a monk you go to suffering.
Verily, a fire does not think, 'I am burning a fool,'
For the fool is burnt by assailing the blazing fire;
Even so, you, Māra, by assailing the Tathāgata,
Will yourself burn yourself like a fool touching a fire.
Māra[6] acquires demerit for assailing a Tathāgata.
But do you not think, Evil One: Evil does not mature for me?
The evil done (by you) must be heaped up[7] for a long time, End-maker.
Māra, turn away from the Wake,[8] have no hopes among the monks.

Thus did a monk tilt at[9] Māra in the Bhesakaḷā Grove,
Wherefore that dejected fiend[10] vanished then and there."[11]

Discourse on a Rebuke to Māra:
the Tenth

Lesser Division of the Pairs:
the Fifth

TOLD ARE THE FIRST FIFTY

---

[1] *MA*. ii. 423, deliverance through *jhāna*.

[2] A mountain in Himavā, at *Jā*. iii. 247. Neru, Sineru, Meru are different mountains.

[3] Jambudīpa (India), *MA*. ii. 423.

[4] One of the four great continents (or islands).

[5] The men of Aparagoyāna and Uttarakuru; the former is one of the four great continents, the latter a mythical region. Bu. here refers to *Nandopanandadamana*. See *Jā*. v. 126.

[6] Also at *S*. i. 114.

[7] *karoto cīyati pāpaṃ; v. ll. karoto te nijiyati, karoto casati*. *Thag*. 1207 reads *karato te miyyate pāpaṃ*. *Cf. pahūtaṃ cīyate puññaṃ*, *Sn*. 428.

[8] *buddhamhā*. No need to translate this as "the awakened mind," or to annotate: "applied to a disciple." On the contrary it is in opposition to the disciples, the "monks" of the next phrase. Māra, in point of fact, followed Gotama from the day of his enlightenment to that of his parinibbāna.

[9] *aghaṭṭesi, v.ll. asaddhesi, asajjesi; Thag*. 1208 *atajjesi* (which is perhaps best).

[10] *yakkha*.

[11] Last line also at *Sn*. 449; *cf. Vin*. i. 21, 22.

INDEXES

I.—TOPICS

Abiding, living (*vihāra*), 260 *f.*, 267, 270; in comfort, 161, 259 *ff.*, 327; in confusion, 304; in ease, 30, 42, 52 *f.*, 394; in equanimity, 107; peaceful, 53
Acquisitions, 384
Activities (*saṅkhārā*), 68, 72, 176, 211, 356, 363
Agriculture, 113
All, the (*sabba*), 392
Almsfood, 13, 17, 37, 41, 48, 137 *ff.*, 163, 216 *f.*, 226, 257 *ff.*, 274, 325, 335, 400; to be thrown away, 17
Aloof, 103, 187, 266, 295 *f.*; -ness, 18 *ff.*, 22, 105, 187, 266, 365 (*see also* Meditation)
Anger, discontent, 34 *ff.*, 305
Angry, displeased, 132, 134, 159 *f.*, 162 *f.*
Anguish, xxii; and ignorance, 68; beset by, 238 *ff.*, 247 *ff.*; cleaving to, 286; destruction of, 91 *f.*, 96, 108, 286, 385; end of, 16, 43, 58 *ff.*, 156, 182, 279; ender of, 70; freed from, 87 *f.*; stopping of, 19 *n.*, 237 *f.*, 320, 324; truths of, 12 *f.*, 81, 230 *f.*, 350 *f.* (*see also* Meditation)
Animal birth, 98 *ff.*
Annihilation (*vibhava*), 60, 64 *n.*, 87, 180 *n.*, 361, 393 *n.*; -ists, 11 *n.*, 60 *n.*, 87 *n.*
Ant-hill, 183 *ff.*
Anxiety, 175 *f.*
Ardour, *etc.*, 132 *ff.*
Ariyan, 3 *f.*, 29, 44, 52 *f.*, 57 *ff.*, 91, 95, 103, 108, 120, 174, 226 *ff.*, 259 *f.*, 322, 334 (*see also* Quest, Silence, View, Way)
Arrow, 114
Ascetic (*tapassin*), 103; -ism, xii
Assail, to, 143, 147
Attachment, 133, 143, 380 *f.*; and aversion (hatred), confusion, 32 *ff.*, 42, 86 *f.*, 93, 182, 279, 291, 359, 360 *f.*; and repugnance, shunning, 58, 61 *ff.*, 143, 147, 366
Awakened One(s), 223, 232, 401 *ff.*; confidence in, 46, 232 *ff.*; dispraise of, 291; eye of, 213 (*see also* Confidence, Self-awakened)
Awakening, 20 *f.*, 22, 42, 120, 135, 148, 182, 207, 209 *f.*, 289, 301, 386; seven links in, 15, 80

Bank, further and hither, 173, 277
Barrier lifted, 178
Backsliding, 19 *f.*, 39
Bathe, to, 204; ceremonially, 49, 335, 370
Battle, 114
Becoming (*bhava*), xviii *f.*, 6 *f.*, 60, 62 *f.*, 64 *n.*, 87, 317 *f.*, 354, 361, 393; again-, 60, 179, 211, 217, 304, 334, 354, 361; attachment to, 143, 147; canker of, 10, 12, 29, 48, 303, 333; fetters of, 6, 181, 278, 288 *f.*; thus and otherwise, 391; and non-becoming, 142 *f.* (*see also* Annihilation)
Beds, high, large, 225
Being(s) (*bhūta*), 5, 8; (*satta*), 28, 44, 71, 82, 94 *f.*, 110, 152, 179 *n.*, 343 *f.*, 391
Bewilderment, 304
Beyond, the, 173, 278 *f.*
Bile, phlegm, *etc.*, 74, 233
Birth, 62, 178 *f.*, 318; ageing and dying, 7 *f.*, 12, 60 *f.*, 87, 205 *ff.*, 211, 217, 238 *ff.*, 247 *ff.*, 304, 333 *f.*, 394; destroyed is birth, *etc.*, 29, 48, 51, 90, 178, 229, 303, 307, 311, 333; former (*see* Habitations)
Blemish, 31 *ff.*, 131
Blow with hand, *etc.*, 114, 160, 232
Boat, 173
Bodhisatta, xviii, 22, 28 *n.*, 103 *n.*, 120, 148, 207, 295

Body, 27, 42, 150, 185, 232, 300, 330 *ff.*, 337, 356; activity of (*saṅkhāra*), 68, 72, 356, 363; attachment to, 133 *f.*; contemplation of, 83 *ff.*; development of, 292 *ff.*; own, 13, 360 *f.*; what is unlovely in, 400; divers bodies, 258
Body, speech, *etc.*, 22 *f.*, 28 *f.*, 44, 55, 68, 95, 115, 122, 185, 325 *f.*, 344 *ff.*, 356, 363, 384
Bolts withdrawn, 178 *f.*
Bourn, good, bad, 29, 44 *f.*, 46, 94, 98 *f.*, 101, 103, 343, 346, 348, 370 *f.*, 376 *f.*, 398, 400; Baka's, 391; five, 98
Brahma, xx *ff.*; -attainment, xx *f.*; -become, xxii, 144; -vihāra, xx, *see under* Friendliness, mind of, *etc.*; -wheel, 93 *ff.*; -world, xxi, 43, 92, 212, 263, 389, 402
Brahma, -farer(s), xxii, 14, 37 *f.*, 40, 41, 53, 125, 127, 132, 134, 143 *f.*, 187 *f.*, 193 *f.*, 208, 210, 258, 306 *f.*, 310, 384 *ff.*; -faring, xxii, 13, 103, 133, 135, 189 *f.*, 193, 207, 209, 216, 222, 224, 252, 265, 295, 327, 367, 371; branches, pith, *etc.* of, 239 *ff.*; brought to a close, 29, 48, 51, 90, 178, 229, 303, 307, 311, 333; goal, pith, culmination of, 245, 253;
Brahman(s), 97, 114, 141 *f.*, 183 *ff.*, 220 *ff.*, 245 *ff.*, 325, 333, 397 *ff.*; householders, 343, 349
Breaking through, 135
Breathing in, out, 71 *f.*, 91 *n.*, 297 *ff.*, 363
Bridge, 173
Buddha(s), xviii *ff.*, 3 *n.*, 204 *n.*, 205 *n.*; -seat, 205 *n.*
Burden: dropped, 178 *f.*; laid down, 6, 181, 278; set aside, 96 *ff.*, 103

Calm, 174 *n.*, 338, 353, 386; -ed, 299 (*see* Tranquillity)
Cankers (*āsava*), xxiii; and ignorance, 69 *f.*; destroyed, xx, 5 *n.*, 6, 96, 141 *n.*, 181, 186, 203, 219, 252, 261, 278, 359; destruction of, 9, 29, 45, 95, 99, 102 *f.*, 136 *ff.*, 229, 303, 333, 338 *f.*, 349; got rid of, 304, 394 *f.*; mind freed from, 29, 48, 229, 271, 303; seven ways for getting rid of, 9 *ff.*; three, 10, 12, 29, 48, 303, 333; uprising, stopping of, *etc.*, 29, 69 *f.*, 229
Carpenter, 153
Causal: occasion, relation, 93 *f.*, 174 *ff.*; uprising, 211
Cause, 232
Cemetery, 74 *f.*, 106, 116 *f.*, 227
Characteristics (*nimitta*), five, 153, 155
Chariot, 161, 192, 220, 222; -eer, 223
Clear consciousness, 328
Clod of earth, 160, 232
Cloth to sit on (*nisīdana*), 189
Cobra (*nāga*), 184, 186
Comfort, *see* Abiding in
Companion (*dutiya*), 259
Compassion, 27, 30, 56, 110, 152, 204, 213, 263, 291; mind of, 48, 338, 358, 399; -ate, 160, 164, 166, 224
Comport oneself, 227, 232
Comprehend, to, 350 *f.*
Concentration, 15, 22, 25, 80, 94, 96, 150, 187, 208 *f.*, 266, 303, 363, 384; success in, 241 *ff.*, 249 *ff.* (*see also* Meditation)
Conception (*gabbhassâvakkanti*), 321 *f.*
Concord, 225, 347, 384
Condition (*paṭicca*), xxiv, 237, 313 *f.*; (*paccaya*), 312
Conditioned Genesis, xx, 60 *ff.*, 89 *f.*, 236 *f.*, 312 *f.*, 317 *ff.*
Confidence: in *Buddha*, *Dhamma*, *Saṁgha*, 46 *f.*, 221, 228 *ff.*, 382; (without *saṁgha*), 85, 89; (*dhamma* only), 57
Confidently (*vissattha*), 218 *f.*
Consciousness, 59, 67, 90, 179, 311 *ff.*, 316, 351 *f.*; infinite, 5, 53, 202, 219, 252, 348, 358; mental, 352 *f.*; sections of, 236 *f.*, 314 *f.*; as a *khandha*, 232, *and see under* Material shape; in Conditioned Genesis, 312 *ff.*, 317 *ff.*
Constructions (*saṅkhārā*), 400
Contending (with), 141 *ff.*
Control: (*saṁvara*) of (sense-) organs, 227, 327; (*vinaya*) of desire, 237
Cough, to, 204
Counterpart (*paṭibhāga*), 367
Coveting, 329; and dejection, 273, 275, 327
Covetous, 23, 335 *ff.*, 345, 347, 375 *f.*; -ness, 23, 71, 226 *f.*, 273, 335 *ff.*
Cowherd, 105 *f.*, 151, 271, 274, 277, 397
Cows, 106, 151

Craving, 16, 52 *n.*, 59 *f.*, 64, 86 *f.*, 89 *f.*, 133 *f.*, 142 *f.*, 156, 179, 317, 354, 361; body derived from, 232; destruction of, 176, 211, 306 *ff.*, 324, 402
Crops, 194 *ff.*
Cross-ed over, 289; doubt, 227, 288, 329; entanglement, 203, 219; -ing over, 173, 190 *f.*, 203, 289, 316
Cross-legged, 271, 329

Dancing, *etc.*, 225
Deathless, -ness, 71 *n.*, 144, 212 *f.*, 215 *f.*
Decoy, 151 *f.*
Deeds, 11, 28, 44, 49, 94 *f.*, 122, 229, 272, 313
Deer, 151 *f.*, 194 *ff.*, 198 *ff.*, 217 *f.*
Defilements, 46, 304, 333 *f.*, 394
Delight, 60, 186, 337; (*nandi*), 7
Deliverances (*vimokkhā*), 42, 94, 367, 403
Demerit, 170 *f.*, 314
Demons (*asura*), 308; (*parajana*), 196 *f.*
Departed (*peta*), 42, 98, 100
Desire, 160, 174 *n.*; and attachment, 237 *f.*; and aversion, confusion, 153 *ff.*
Desires, evil, 125, 127, 335 *ff.*
Desiring little, 187
Detesting, 105
Deva(s), 5, 96, 98, 110, 112, 133, 135, 179, 183 *f.*, 223, 262, 306, 308 *f.*, 348 (*listed*), 389 *ff.*; -hearing, 43, 93; -vision, 28, 44, 95, 99 *f.*, 214, 229, 265, 303, 332; -world, 98
Devatā(s), 213 *f.*, 262, 299 *f.*, 369, 402
Dhamma, xix *f.*, 3 *f.*, 26 *n.*, 48, 91 *ff.*, 119, 163, 167 *ff.*, 173 *f.*, 176, 181 *f.*, 207 *ff.*, 224, 311 *ff.*, 316, 361 *f.*, 372 *f.*, 387; -become, 144; confidence in, 47, 57 *ff.*, 85, 89, 221 *f.*, 232 *ff.*, 382; delight connected with, 47, 273, 387; dispraise of, 291; disquisition on, 40, 110; doubts about, 132, 134, 273; experts in, 273; faring by, 344, 346 *ff.*; fulfilment in, 382; heirs of, 16 *f.*; knowledge of, 47, 273, 387; -lord, 144; -men, 85 *f.*, 89; speaker on, 141 *n.*, 225, 347; strivers, 182, 279; talk on, 188 *f.*, 203 *ff.*, 221 *f.*, 259; -teaching, 109, 111, 396; true, 57 *ff.*; -wheel, 215; as 'Conditioned Genesis,' 237; as deep, *etc.*, 211; as 'lovely at the beginning,' *etc.*, 224, 265; as refuge, 30, 50, 230, 233, 349; as 'well-taught,' *etc.*, 47, 221 *f.*, 228 *ff.*, 321, 382; to drink, 40; to hear, 264; to master, 171 *f.*; to teach, 35 *f.*, 95 *f.*, 103, 246, 265, 273, 289, 303, 381 *f.*, 383 *f.*; nine divisions of, 171; ways of undertaking, 368 *ff.*, 373 *ff.*; and discipline, 89, 91, 132, 134 *f.*, 161, 207, 209, 338, 387; not-, 344 *ff.*; Further- (*abhidhamma*), 266
Difficult to speak to, 125 *f.*
Diligent, ardent, self-resolute, 28 *f.*, 50, 148 *ff.*, 222, 259, 302 *f.*
Disciple(s), 16 *ff.*, 109 *f.*, 120, 152, 176, 184, 193, 221, 228 *ff.*, 280 *f.*, 283, 386 *ff.*, 393 *f.*, 396, 401 *ff.*; instruction for, 280 *f.*
Discipline, 52 *ff.*, 293, 322; speaker on, 225. *See under* Dhamma and discipline
Discriminate, to (*vijānāti*), 351
Dispassion, -ate, 8, 176, 178, 209 *f.*, 212, 306, 310 *f.*
Disputations, quarrelsome, 383 *ff.*
Disquisition, on *dhamma*, 40, 110, 148; on expunging (and 3 others), 56; on the Forest Grove, 136; of the Honey-ball, 148; Hair-raising, 110
Doubt, 13, 132, 134, 190 *f.*, 193, 288, 315. *See also* Hindrances
Dwelling (*agāra*), 236

Earth, 164
Ease, *see* Abiding in
Ease of bed, *etc.*, 133, 135
Easy to speak to, 127 *f.*, 163
Efforts, four, 363
Egg, 97, 136
'Eights', 106
Elders, doctrine of the, 208 *f.*
Elements, four great (*dhātu*), 4 *ff.*, 67, 74, 185, 231, 272, 275
Elephant, 14, 205 *f.*, 221, 223, 282, 289; foot, 230; footprint, tracker, forest, 220, 223; -look, 400
Empty places, 41 *ff.*, 56-7, 71, 152, 265, 358, 385, 397
Energy, 15, 25, 27, 32 *f.*, 40, 55, 80, 103 *n.*, 185, 187, 208 *f.*, 266;

feeble, 40; unsluggish, 151, 232, 297 *ff.*
Epithets of the Buddha, 212 *f.*
Equanimity, 107, 232 *ff.*; mind of 48, 338, 358, 399. *See also* Awakening, seven links *and* Meditation
Escape, 48, 77 *n.*, 87, 112, 115, 117, 217 *f.*, 388 *ff.*
Essence (*sāra*), 321. *See also* Pith
Eternal (the), 11, 174 *ff.*, 388 *ff.*
Eternalists, 11 *n.*, 87 *n.*, 311 *n.*, 388 *n.*
Ether, infinite, 5, 53, 202, 219, 252, 261, 348
Even-farer, -faring, xx, xxii, 344, 346 *ff.*
Evil One, 152, 198 *ff.*, 217 *ff.*, 393 *ff.*, 395 *ff.* *See also* Māra
Exalt (extol) oneself and disparage others, to, 24, 125, 127 *ff.*, 238 *ff.*, 248 *ff.*, 325 *f.*
Exertion (*āyoga*), 161; (*ussoḷhi*), 135
Exist, that (which) does not, 175 *f.*
Existent entity, 180
Expunging, 18, 52 *f.*, 56
Extension (*paṭhavī*), 4, 6 *f.*, 74, 231 *f.*, 389 *ff.*
Eye(s), of affection, 258 *f.*; of an Awakened One, 213; *with* ear, *etc.*, 13, 66, 79, 112, 121, 186, 226, 236 *f.*, 355; to close 154; little dust in, 212 *f.*

Faith, 22, 39, 54, 94 *n.*, 160, 182, 205, 208 *f.*, 224, 238 *ff.*, 247 *ff.*, 277, 279, 382; gift of, 290
Fan, 236
Faring-on (*saṁsāra*), 108, 179
Fear, 97, 150, 195, 199, 380 *f.*; and dread, 22 *ff.*, 42; -lessness, 96, 380 *f.*
Feeling(s), 99 *ff.*, 111, 121 *f.*, 293 *f.*, 296 *ff.*, 301 *ff.*, 306, 310, 317, 323 *f.*, 327, 352, 365 *ff.*, 369; satisfaction, peril in, *etc.*, 118 *f.*; as application of mindfulness, 71, 75 *f.*; in definition of 'mind', 66; in 'Conditioned Genesis', 64 *f.*, 90, 317 *ff.*; *with four other khandha*, 232, *and see* Material Shape
Fetter(s), 12 *f.*, 16, 79, 156, 178 *f.*; five, 43, 179, 181, 278; three, 42, 182, 279
Fire, 109, 295 *f.*, 403; -stick, 295 *f.*
Flag laid low, 178 *f.*
Food, 107, 300; cloying, 400; gift of, 290
Ford, 204 *n.*, 210 *f.*, 271, 273 *f.*, 276, 277 *f.*
Forest, 22 *ff.*, 195, 199, 227, 328, 358, 385, 397; -dweller, 266; grove, 136 *ff.*, 151; lodgings, 22 *ff.*
Forgetfulness, 154 *ff.*
Forked: path, 183, 185; stick, 172
Formations (*saṅkhārā*), 67 *f.*, 90, 317
Freed, 6 *f.*, 29, 48, 87, 178 *f.*, 229, 288 *f.*, 303, 306 *f.*, 337
Freedom, 6 *n.*, 29, 48, 178, 187 *f.*, 229, 266, 289, 303, 308 *f.*, 324, 333, 367, 402; of mind, xx, 45, 95, 99, 102 *f.*, 199, 244-5, 253, 323 *f.*, 338 *f.*, 349, 353, 357 *ff.* (*various kinds*); through wisdom, xx, 45, 95, 99, 102 *f.*, 323 *f.*, 338 *f.*, 349, 353; unshakable, 211, 217; as to things of time, 243 *f.*
Friendliness: as to acts of body, speech, thought, 258, 274, 276, 384; mind of, 23, 48, 91 *n.*, 160, 163 *f.*, 166, 337, 358, 399
Fulfilment (*niṭṭhā*), 228 *ff.*
Further: escape, 48, 388 *ff.*; from . . . to . . ., 381; nothing, 289; to be done, 325 *ff.*
Further-men, states of, 91 *f.*, 95, 103, 108, 216, 259 *ff.*, 301

Gains, honours, fame, 24, 238 *ff.*, 248 *ff.*, 252
Games for children, 322
gandhabba, 321 *f.*
Garlands, *etc.*, 225
Glimmering (*usmīkata*), 170, 314
Gifts, 325, 335
Goal (*attha*), 144, 163 *ff.*, 171, 181, 193 *n.*, 222, 225, 245; knowledge of, 47, 273, 387
Going forth, the (*pabbajjā*), 50, 222, 224, 325, 335; one gone forth, 22, 137 *ff.*, 224, 238, 338, 393 *f.*
Gold and silver, 205 *f.*, 225
Good (*attha*), 151 *f.*
Grasp: right, 172; wrong, 170, 172, 314
Grasping, 86 *f.*, 176 *f.*, 317 *ff.*, 323; five groups, 78 *f.*, 186, 231, 236 *f.*, 360 *f.*; four kinds, 63 *f.*, 88 *ff.*; not, 72 *ff.*, 90, 306, 311

Grass-torch, 165
Greed, 20, 46, 119 *f.*
Grieve, mourn, lament, *etc.*, 175 *f.*

Habitations, former, 28, 44, 94, 229, 302, 332
Habitual tendencies (*saṅkhārā*): as a *khandha*, 232, *and see under* Material Shape
Hair of head, body, etc., 73 *f.*, 231
Happiness (*sukha*), 123 *f.*, 301
Head, 163, 400
Heat, 4, 6 *f.*, 74, 231, 234 *f.*, 389 *ff.*, 402 *n.*
Heaven, 29, 45, 182, 343, 348, 371, 376 *f.*, 400
Hermitage, 203 *f.*
Higher, more excellent things, 250 *ff.*
Hindrances (five), (23 *f.*), 77 *f.*, 185, 227, 323, (329), 330, (354), (385)
Honey-ball, 148
Horses, 161
Hot weather, 99 *ff.*, 151, 195, 199, 235, 338, 369
Household life, dusty, 224
Householder(s), 86, 97, 114, 221, 224, 343 *ff.*, 349, 397 *ff.*
Hunger and exhaustion, 17 *f.*, 148
Hurt, -ful, 118; self-, of others, 149

'I', 232
'I am', 58 *f.*, 179, 232
'I will be annihilated,' *etc.*, 176
'If this is . . .', 319 *f.*
Ignorance, 9 *n.*, 58 *f.*, 68 *ff.*, 90, 143, 147, 152, 178, 185, 317, 354, 366 *f.*, 389; canker of, 10, 12, 29, 48, 303, 333
Ill (*dukkha*), 122 *f.*
Immeasurable, 48, 338, 357 *ff.*, 399
Impermanence, 232, 234 *ff.*, 306, 310 *f.*, 400
Impermanent, *etc.*, 118, 177 *f.*
Incomprehensible (*anupalabbhamāna*), 177
Injure oneself, to, 170 *f.*
Insight, 151 *n.*, 174 *n.* *See* Knowledge and insight
Instruction (*sāsana*), 193, 288

Joy, 120 *f.* *See also* Meditation

King, 113 *ff.*, 284
khandha, 5 *n.*, 29 *n.*, 31 *n.*, 51 *n.*, 62 *n.*, 72 *n.*, 78 *n.*, 94 *n.*, 311 *n.*
Knowledge (*vijjā*), 9 *n.*, 58 *f.*, 90, 354, 367; the three, xxi, 28 *f.*, 44 *f.*, 94 *f.*, (151), 228 *f.*, 302 *f.*; (*ñāṇa*), 296; doctrine of, 208 *f.*; seven, 386 *ff.*
Knowledge, profound (*aññā*), 6 *f.*, 81 *f.*, 96, 181, 278, 288 *f.*
Knowledge and insight (*or*, vision), 91 *f.*, 95, 103, 108, 122, 190, 211, 213 *f.*, 216 *f.*, 242 *ff.*, 250 *ff.*; ariyan, 91 *f.*, 95, 103, 108, 216, 258 *ff.*, 301

Lady, ageing and dead, 116 *f.*
Lair (*āsaya*), 196 *ff.*, 200 *f.*
Layfollower(s), 36 *f.*; acceptance as, 30, 230, 253, 349
Learner, 185
Legal question, 159 *f.*
Life: coming back to, 397; cutting off of, 389 *f.*, 394; four modes of, 97; of abundance, 215 *f.*; -principle and body, 200
Lion: -posture, 328; -roar, 85, 93 *ff.*
Liquid element (*āpo*), 4, 6 *f.*, 74, 231, 233 *f.*, 389 *ff.* (cohesion)
Living creatures (water, without), 17, 259
Loathliness, 105
Lodgings, 13, 37, 41, 137 *ff.*, 163, 274, 325, 335; remote, 22 *ff.*, 37, 42 *n.*, 227, 328
Lord (*bhagavā*): epithets, 144; things rooted in the, 372, 379
Lying speech, *etc.*, 54, 58, 143, 147, 224, 344 *f.*, 347

Man with vision, 99 *ff.*, 154, 239 *ff.*, 246 *f.*, 332 *f.*
Mastery, 195 *ff.*
Material shape(s), 67, 111, 133 *f.*, 154, 164, 271 *f.*; craving for, 64; passing beyond perception of, 202, 218-19, 252, 261; satisfaction, peril in, *etc.*, 116 *f.*; *with* 'eye, ear,' *etc.*, 79, 112, 121, 186, 217, 226, 236, 272 *f.*, 322 *ff.*, 326 *f.*; *with four other khandha*, 78 *f.*, 174 *f.*, 177 *f.*, 181, 186, 231, 236, 281, 283 *ff.*, 288, 360, 362
Material things (*āmisa*), 16 *f.*, 76, 198 *ff.*

Meal, 290; at one session, 161, 225; remains of a, 259
Meditate, meditate absorbed, *etc.*, 398
Meditation (*jhāna*), xx *f.*, 27 *f.*, 42, 52 *f.*, 72 *n.*, 94, 118, 151, 201 *f.*, 218, 227 *f.*, 243 *n.*, 251 *f.*, 259 *f.*, 301 *f.*, 323, 330 *f.*, 371; the first, 354, 366; the fourth, 357, 367; non-breathing, 297 *ff.*; uninterrupted, 41
Men: born as, world of, 98, 123
Mental: barrennesses, 132 *ff.*; objects, states (*dhammā*), 71, 77 *ff.*, 151, 237; striving, 316
Merit, 290, 309
Middle Course, 20 *f.*
Mind, 71, 132 *ff.*, 150, 179, 228 *f.*; activity of, 68, 356, 363; composed, *etc.*, 28, 229, 332; contemplating the, 76 *f.*; defilements of, 46, 119; development of, 15, 292 *ff.*; freed, 289, 333; immeasurable, 324; limited (*paritta*), 322 *f.*; obsessed, 385; one, 258; one-pointed, 151, 153 *ff.*, 232, 303, 363; perverted, 160, 164, 166; rule over, 267; subdued, *etc.*, 297; suffusing body, 331 *f.*; -tossing, 292; as repository, 355; to be subdued, *etc.*, 155; to cleanse, 327 *f.*; to comprehend with, 99 *ff.*, 262; with attachment, *etc.*, 43 *f.*, 76 *f.*, 93. *See also* Freedom of mind
Mind-and-matter, 66 *f.*, 90
Mindfulness, 25, 27, 55, 109, 136 *ff.*, 151, 161, 208 *f.*, 227, 271, 301, 322 *ff.*, 328 *f.*; applications of, xv, xix, 71 *ff.*, 109, 274, 363; unmuddled, 25, 151, 232, 297 *ff.*; as link in awakening, 15, 80. *See also* Meditation
Minds of other beings, 43, 93
Mine, 4, 175, 232, 345, 347. *See also* 'This is (not) mine'
Misrepresent, to, 168 *ff.*, 180, 312 *f.*
Moat filled, 178 *f.*
Moderate in eating, 327
Modesty, 325 *ff.*
Moisture-born, 97 *f.*
Monks, 36 *f. passim*; elders, of middle standing, *etc.*, 19; group of five, 214 *ff.*, 301 *f.*
Moral habit, 41 *ff.*, 48 (53 *f.*), (58), 85, 89, 96, 132 *n.*, 133, 135, 187, (224 *ff.*), 226 *f.*, 266, 353, 363, 384, 397, 399; higher, *with* thought, wisdom, 387; purity of, 189 *f.*; success in, 240 *ff.*, 248 *ff.*
Mother, 322
Motion (*vāyo*), 4, 6 *f.*, 74, 231, 235 *f.*, 389 *ff.*
Musical instruments, 307

Naked ascetic, 39, 214 *f.*
Name-and-form. *See* Mind-and-matter
Neither-perception-nor-non-perception, 5, 53, 174 *n.*, 202, 209 *f.*, 219, 252, 261, 348
Nibbāna, xviii, 5 *ff.*, 9 *n.*, 15 *n.*, 20 *f.*, 43, 48 *n.*, 71, 90, 91 *n.*, 99, 102 *n.*, 132 *n.*, 149 *f.*, 176, 182, 192, 206 *f.*, 209 *ff.*, 217, 278 *f.*, 289, 307, 311, 365 *n.*, 367; without attachment (*anupādā*), 190 *f.*, 193
Nihilist (*venayika*), 180
Nobles, brahmans, etc., 221, 338, 348
No-thing, plane of, 5, 53, 202, 208 *f.*, 219, 252, 261, 348, 358
Non-return -er, -ing, 48 *n.*, 81 *f.*, 181 *n.*
Not yours, 181
Nuns, 36 *f.*, 159 *f.*
Nutriment (*āhāra*), 315 *f.* *See also* Sustenance
Nymphs, 308

Oblation, 108 *f.*
Obligations, 41
Obsess, to, 141 *f.*
Obsessions, 143, 145 *ff.*
Ocean, 234
Offence (*āpatti*), 34, 386
Old age and dying, 8, 12, 61, 87, 205 *ff.* *See also* Birth, ageing and dying
Once-returner, 42, 182, 279
Onslaught on creatures, *etc.*, 53, 58, 224 *ff.*, 344, 346, 375 *f.*
Open (air), 106, 151, 224, 227
Openly and in private, 258, 384
Order (of monks), 30; confidence in, 47, 221 *f.*, 228 *ff.*, 382; doubts about, 132, 134; dispraise of, 291
Ordination, 50
Outer cloak, 335 *f.*

Paccekabuddha(s), 3 *n.*
Parable, 151, 192, 198 *ff.*; of Raft, 173, 316; of Saw, 166 *f.*, 232
Passion of delight, 152, 186

Past, the, 122; *with* future, present, xxi, 10 *f.*, 320 *f.*
Peace (*santi*), 207, 209 *f.*
Peaceful Abidings, xxi, 53
Peacock, 369
Perception(s), 48, 53, 66, 141 *ff.*, 219, 352; of material shapes, *etc.*, 202, 218-9, 252; of sense-pleasures, 171; *as a khandha*, 232, *and see also* Material shape
Perfected one(s) (*arahant*), 6 *f.*, 51, 152, 181, 185, 212, 215 *f.*, 222 *f.*, 262, 278, 280, 288 *f.*, 299, 334, 343, 393 *f.*
Perfection, 9 *n.*, 30
Peril, 153 *f.*, 156, 206 *f.*, 211, 217, 369 *f.*, 390. *See under* Satisfaction
Permanent, 11, 174 *ff.*, 388 *ff.*
Perplexity, 143, 185, 315 *f.* *See also* Doubt
Pillar pulled up, 178 *f.*
Pith, 144, 238, 246, 286
Plantain tree, 286
Ploughing, 301
Possession (*pariggaha*), 176
Postures, four, 26 *f.*, 30 *n.*, (72 *f.*), 154 *f.*, 223
Pride, 3 *n.*, 8 *n.*, 16, 52 *n.*, 87 *n.*, 143, 147, 156
Propriety (*dhammatā*), 386 *ff.*
Psychic power, xxi, 309, 391, 393, 402; bases of, 135; forms of, 43, 92
Punishments, various, 115
Pure: in body, speech, *etc.*, 22 *f.*
Pure ones (*ariya*), 3 *f.*, 10, 12, 174, 178
Purity: of moral habit, mind, *etc.*, 189 *ff.*; through food, *etc.*, 107 *ff.*
Purpose (not) fulfilled, 238 *ff.*

Quarrelling, 143, 147
Quest: ariyan, unariyan, 205 *ff.*; -er, 207, 209 *f.*

Raft, 173; Parable of the, 173 *f.*, 316
Rains, 187
Rapture (*pīti*), 120 *f.*, 151 *f.*
Recluse, 85, 97, 141 *f.*, 180, 221 *f.*, 325, 335, 338 *f.*, 396; stains on, 335, 337; -ship, 39 *f.*, 325, 333, 335 *ff.*
Recluses and brahmans, 23 *ff.*, 107 *ff.*, 117 *ff.*, 141 *f.*, 180, 184, 198 *ff.*, 217, 224, 277 *f.*, 292, 295 *ff.*, 301, 304, 321, 368, 378, 389 *f.*, 393 *f.*
Refectory, 35 *f.*, 259
Refuge (threefold), 30, 50, 230, 253, 305 *n.*, 349
Refute, to, 221 *f.*
Release as to time, timeless things, 243 *f.*
Remembered, six things to be, 384 *f.*
Remorse, 142 *f.*; -ful, 57, 152
Renunciation, 76 *n.*, 148, 150, 306, 310 *f.*
Reprove, to (for an offence), 34 *f.*; -d, 126 *f.*, 129 *f.*
Resort (for alms), 14, 41
Revile, abuse, to, 180, 232, 397 *f.*
Rites and customs, 63
Road (*magga*), 151
Robe (-material), 13, 37, 41, 137 *ff.*, 163, 204, 226, 274, 325, 335; householder's, 38; rag-, 37, 266; three, 266
Roots of trees, 56, 71, 151 *f.*, 189, 223, 227, 328, 336 *f.*, 358, 385, 397

Sāl-tree, 3, 369 *f.*, 388 *f.*
Saṁsāra, 9 *n.*, 91 *n.*
Saṅkhārā, xxiv *ff.* *See under*: Activities, Constructions, Formations, Material shape (as a *khandha*: 'habitual tendencies')
Satisfaction, peril, escape, 87, 112 *ff.*, 217 *f.*
Saw, Parable of the, 166 *f.*, 232
Scrutinise, to (*upaparikkhati*), 153 *f.*, 156
Seat, not an (allowable), 14
Sects, founders of, 245
Security (from bondage), 6, 96, 135 *f.*, 136 *ff.*, 151 *f.*, 206 *f.*, 211, 217, 279, 306 *f.*
Seen, heard, sensed, *etc.*, 174
Self (*attā*), xxi, (4), 9 *n.*, 11, 30, 72 *n.*, 128 *f.*, 205 *ff.*, 211, 217, 224, 257, 337, 347, 358, 362, 403; not-, 9 *n.*, 11, 181, 281, 283; theory of, 51, 63, 88 *f.*, 176 *f.* *For* my self, not my self *see also* 'This is (not) mine'
Self: -awakened (ones), 7, 22, 89, 96, 152, 185, 215 *f.*, 221 *ff.*, 228 *ff.*, 262 *f.*, 280, 379, 382, 393 *f.*; -awakening, 8, 30, 295 *ff.*
Sense: bases, 62 *n.*, 65 *f.*, 79 *f.*, 90; faculties, 39 *f.*; impingement (*phassa*), 59, 65 *f.*, 90, 316 *f.*; *phassa* with four *khandha*, 232; -organs, 13, 226 *f.*, 326, 355 *f.*

Sense-pleasures, 27, 60, 63, 64 *n.*, 77 *f.*, 88 *f.*, 111, 120, 133 *f.*, 142 *f.*, 151, 168 *ff.*, 295 *ff.*, 344, 346, 361, 369, 380, 385; canker of, 10, 12, 29, 48, 303, 333; five strands of, 5 *n.*, 112, 121, 186, 198, 217, 322; satisfaction, peril in, *etc.*, 111 *ff.*, 120 *f.*; thought of, *with* malevolence, harming, 15, 148 *ff.*, 272, 275. *See also* Hindrances, Meditation.
Sensory reactions, 202, 218-9, 252
Shaveling, 397 *f.*
Shrines, 26
Signless, 357 *ff.*, 365
Silence, ariyan, 205, 356 *n.*
Similes, *see* Index II
Skill, -ed; unskill, -ed, 23 *ff.*, 40, 55 *ff.*, 58, 120, 129 *ff.*, 143, 147, 153 *ff.*, 161, 230, 233 *f.*, 236; their roots, 58
Skull splits, 285
Slave-woman, 162 *f.*
Sleep, of Gotama, 303 *f.*
Sloth, 238 *ff.*; and torpor, *see* Hindrances
Snake, 290
Something to be done, 151, 192
Sower, 194 *ff.*, 198
Space, 164 *f.*
Speaker at right time, *etc.*, 163, 225, 347
Speaking, five ways of, 163 *ff.*
Speech: activity of, 68, 356, 363; evil, 160, 164, 166; slanderous, harsh, *etc.*, 225, 245, 247, 375; ways of, 163 *ff.*, 304 *f.*; to break into, 259. *See also* Body, speech, *etc.*
Spontaneous uprising, 43, 97 *f.*, 181-2, 278
Stopping (*nirodha*), 8, 176, 209 *f.*, 212, 306, 310 *f.*, 315 *f.*, 319 *f.*, 324; of perception and feeling, xxi, 203, 219, 252, 356 *f.*, 364 *f.*, 397
Stream: against the, 212; -attainer, 42, 182, 279, 382 *n.*, 385 *n.*, 386 *n.*; -attainment, 388; Māra's, 278 *f.*; of the Ganges, 278 *f.*
Strength, 387 *f.*
Striving, 132 *ff.*, 211, 214 *ff.*, 295, 297 *ff.*
Stumbling-block, 48, 96, 167 *ff.*
Such: a one (*tādisa*), 394; state of being, 364
Super-knowledge (*abhiññā*), 20 *f.*, 50, 99, 102 *f.*, 207-8 *ff.*, 216, 222, 392
Sustenance (*āhāra*), 59. *See also* Nutriment
Suttas, alternative titles of, xvi
Sweat, 287, 297
Sympathetic joy, mind of, 48, 338, 358, 399
Synonym, 151 *f.*, 185, 198

Tamed, 289
Tathāgata, xiii, xvii, 4 *n.*, 7 *f.*, 89, 92 *ff.*, 109, 112, 125 *n.*, 144, 152, 176, 179 *f.*, 184 *f.*, 212, 215, 223 *f.*, 227 *ff.*, 262, 273, 285, 289, 303 *f.*, 323, 338, 387, 394 *f.*, 395 *f.*, 403; after dying, 200; untraceable, xvii, xxi, 179; footprint of, xxi, 227 *ff.*; four convictions of, 96; ten powers of, 93 *ff.*, to be studied, 379 *ff.*; as path and pasture, 381
Teacher, 18 *f.*, 35, 85, 89, 132, 134, 144, 152, 188, 193 *f.*, 214 *f.*, 257, 387
Teaching, 166, 232
Teeth clenched, 155 *f.*, 297
Temporal, to seize the, 55 *f.*, 126, 128 *ff.*
Test a meaning, to, 171 *f.*
Theft, by, 344, 346
'There is (no) (result of) gift,' *etc.*, 345, 347 *f.*
Thief, thieves, 113 *f.*, 156, 232
Things (*dhammā*), 281; to be followed, *etc.*, 372 *f.*; to be remembered (six), 384 *f.*; conditioned (*saṅkhārā*), 281; rooted in the Lord, 372, 379
'This is (not) mine,' *etc.*, 52, 174 *f.*, 177 *f.*, 231, 233, 235, 286, 288 *f.*
'This the world this the self,' *etc.*, 174 *ff.*
Thought (*citta*), 136 *ff.*; arising of, 55 *f.*; *see also* Body, speech, *etc.* higher (*adhicitta*), 153; (*vitakka*), 148 *ff.*, 153 *ff.*, 160; of sense-pleasures, 171
Time, release as to things of, 243; (timeless), 244
Time, right, wrong, 163, 165 *f.*, 225, 347
Tongue against palate, 155 *f.*, 297
Track not discernible, 181
Train oneself, to, 160, 163 *ff.*
Training, 39 *f.*, 132, 134, 224, 387; rules of, 41, 45
Tranquillity, 41, 209 *f.*, 265

Truth, Truths, 4 *n.*, 20 *n.*, 70 *n.*, 81, 224, 230, 350 *f.*, 386

Unborn, the, 206 *f.*, 211, 217
Understanding (or View), right, 353. *See also* Way, eightfold
Undying, the, 206 *f.*, 211, 217, 279

Victor (*jina*), 215
View(s), 51 *f.*, 57, 63, 87 *ff.*, 96, 141, 143, 174, 176 *f.*, 386 *ff.*; ariyan, 385; perfect, 9 *n.*, 55, 57 *ff.*; as to purity, 107 *ff.*; purity of, 189 *ff.*; right, 347; 'there is (no) gift,' *etc.*, 345, 347; two, 87; 'this the world this the self,' *etc.*, 174; 'world is (not) eternal,' *etc.*, 200; wrong, pernicious, 11 *ff.*, 29, 51 *n.*, 167 *ff.*, 281, 311, 335 *ff.*, 345, 361 *f.*, 388
Vigilance, 327
Village, 161, 210 *f.*, 221 *f.*, 233, 235, 259; confines of, 151
Vision, 41, 265, 289, 296 *f.*, 353. *See also* Knowledge and insight
Vitality and heat, 355 *f.*
Void, 357 *ff.*, 365
Volition, 59, 66
Vulture-trainer, 167 *ff.*

Wanderers, 85 *f.*, 111 *f.*, 220, 222; girl, 369
Washen, 334
Washing: inner, 48; 'merry,' 282; water for, 259
Water-snake, 172
Way, 9 *n.*, 15 *n.*, 42 *n.*, 178 *n.*, 190 *f.*, 193, 301; eightfold, 20 *f.*, 59 *ff.*, 152, 273, 360 *ff.*; fourfold, 243 *n.*; not the, 190 *f.*, 193; wrong, 152
Wealth, 224
Weapon, 143, 147, 160, 232
Well-farer, 18, 46, 92, 143, 212
Wisdom (intuitive), xix, 25 *f.*, 48, 52, 55, 96, 108 *f.*, 121, 148, 149 *f.*, 171, 178, 185, 187, 203, 209, 217, 219, 231, 233, 235, 252, 266, 288 *f.*, 315 *f.*, 350 *ff.*, 363; lucidity of, 109, 220. *See also* Freedom through wisdom
Wise attention, 10 *ff.*, 353
Wish, the, 34 *ff.*; to, 41 *ff.*
Womb, 97, 322
Women, different kinds, 344
World, 71, 141, 164 *ff.*, 174 *ff.*, 182, 184, 198 *ff.*, 212 *f.*, 223, 277 *ff.*, 338, 348, 385, 399 *f.*; entanglement in, 203, 219; is (not) eternal, *etc.*, 200; of men, 98; theory of, 51; thousand-, 391
Worldly (*gehasita*), 160
Wrath, 125 *ff.*, 185

yakkha, 262, 285, 307, 209 *f.*

II.—SIMILES

ANT-HILL, *etc.*, 183
archer, 109

bath attendant, 330
beating back glory, 390
bird on the wing, 43, 92, 226
body thrown aside, 74 *f.*
bronze bowl, 35 *f.*, 37 *f.*
burning lamp, 355
burnt baby, 386

carcase round neck, 154
catskin bag, 165
cattle butcher, 74, 299
cesspool, 100
chest for clothes, 267
cloth, 46, 48
concentric circles, 265
cow and calf, 387
cowherd, 151, 271 *ff.*
crab, 287
creeper and tree, 369
crossing Ganges, 278 *f.*

daughter-in-law, 233, 308
deer, 106; -decoy, 151 *f.*; in forest, 217 *f.*; herd of, 199 *ff.*
delineating shapes, 164
distiller, drunkard, 281
dream, 168

elephant playing, 282
elephant's foot, 230; footprint, 220 *ff.*
enclosed space, 236

even, uneven fords, roads, 55

felloe, 39
fire (different kinds of), 315

gold, 48
grasping water-snake, 172
grass torch, 168

hen and eggs, 136
honey-ball, 148

impaling stake, 168

Jeta grass, twigs, *etc.*, 181

log of wood, 356
long house, 101
lotus-pond, 102, 213, 331
lump of meat, 168

making earth not earth, 164
man coming to lotus-pond, 338
man contracting a loan, with disease, in prison, *etc.*, 329 *f.*
man fully clothed, 332
man going from village to village, 332
man sunk into mud, 56
man with vision, 99 *ff.*, 154, 239 *ff.*, 246 *f.*, 332 *f.*
medicine, 378
milk, honey, *etc.*, 378
milk and water, 258 *f.*
missing the earth, 390

not wanting to see, 154

owl, jackal, cat, ass meditating, 398

peg, knocking out, 153
pit of embers, 168
pith, 144, 238 *ff.*, 246 *ff.*, 286
poisoned gourd and drinking bowl, 377
pool of water, 331, 333
provision bag, 74

raft, 173
reflection in a mirror, 131
relays of chariots, 192

sāl-wood, 161
saw, 166
seed and vegetable growths, 283
setting upright, *etc.*, 30, 50, 230, 253, 349
skeleton, 168
skilled groom, 161
slaughter house, 168
smith's bellows, 297
snake's head, 168
something borrowed, 168
stick, wet and dry, 295 *f.*
strong man, 155, 212, 281, 297, 298, 299, 307, 310, 389
sun, 378

torch setting fire to Ganges, 165
tree, 100 *f.*
turner, 72
two houses, 332

weapon, 335

young woman or man, 40, 154

III.—NAMES

Abhidhamma, 171 *n.*
Aciravatī, river, 204
Aggivessana, 280 *ff.*, 292 *ff.*
Ajātasattu, 284
Ajita Kesakambalin, 245, 305
Āḷāra the Kālāma, xxii, 207 *ff.*, 213 *f.*
Ambapālī's Grove, 91 *n.*
Ānanda, xvi, 147 *f.*, 203 *f.*, 264 *f.*, 291
Anaṅgaṇavatthusutta, 31 *n.*
Anāthapiṇḍika's monastery. *See under* Sāvatthī
Aṅgas, 325, 334
Anguttara, x *f.*
Anuruddha, 257 *ff.*, 264 *f.*
Ariṭṭha, 167 *ff.*
Assaji, 280
Assapura, 325, 334

Bāhukā, river, 49
Baka the Brahmā, 388 *ff.*
Bakabrahmasutta, 402 *n.*
Bamboo Grove, 3 *n.*, 187, 360

Basham, A. L., 39 *n.*, 245 *n.*
Benares, 214 *f.*
Bhagavadgītā, xix
Bhaggas, the, 124, 395
Bhikkhupātimokkha, 124 *n.*
Bimbisāra, 123 *f.*, 220 *n.*
Blind Men's Grove, 3 *n.*, 183, 189
Brahmā(s), xx, 5, 48 *n.*, 96 *f.*, 112, 141 *f.*, 179, 184, 223, 262, 382, 389 *ff.*, 398 *n.*, 402; Great, *etc.*, 389
Brahmā Sahampati, 212 *f.*
Buddhadatta, A. P., 214 *n.*
Buddhaghosa, xvi, xxvi

Chalmers, Lord, ix, xi *f.*, xiv, xxiii, 103 *n.*, 184 *n.*, 220 *n.*, 282 *n.*, 398 *n.*
Coomaraswamy, A. K., xxiii
Cunda the Great, 51 *ff.*

Dasgupta, S., xxiv *f.*
Devadatta, 141 *n.*, 238
Dhammadinnā, 360 *ff.*
Dhammapada, xi, 171 *n.*
Dīgha-Nikāya, xiv *f.*
Dīgha Parajana, 262 *f.*
Dummukha, 287 *f.*
Dūsin Māra, 396 *ff.*

Eastern: Monastery, Park, 203 *f.*, 306, 310; Porch, 204
Ekapuṇḍarīka uyyāna, 307

Ganges, 165, 277 *ff.*
Gayā, 214
Geiger, W., xix
Ghosita's monastery, 383
Giribbaja, 39 *n.*
Godage, C. E., 285 *n.*, 308 *n.*
Godhika, 179 *n.*
Gosiṅga sāl-wood, 257, 263 *ff.*
Gotama, xvi, xviii *f.*, xxvi, 22, 30, 91 *f.*, 95, 103, 111, 123 *f.*, 180, 215 *f.*, 220 *ff.*, 230, 245, 253, 280 *ff.*, 299 *ff.*, 343, 349, 393, 403 *n.*
Gotamakasutta, 8 *n.*
Great Grove, Wood, 3 *n.*, 141 *f.*, 280, 282, 291
Great Regents, 97, 98 *n.*

Hair-raising Disquisition, 110

Inda, 179
Isigili, 121
Isipatana, 214 *f.*

Jains, 121 *ff.*, 280
Jāṇussoṇi, 21, 220, 222 *f.*, 230
Jeta Grove, 3 *n.*, 181, 189 *n.*, *and see under* Sāvatthī
Jīvaka's Mango Grove, 91 *n.*

Kaccāna the Great, xiv *n.*, 143 *ff.*
Kakusandha, Buddha, xxv, 396, 398 *ff.*
Kāḷī, slave-woman, 162 *f.*
Kāḷī, 396
Kammāssadhamma, 70
Kapilavatthu, 119, 141 *f.*, 187 *n.*
Kassapa, Buddha, 183 *n.*, 204 *n.*
Kassapa the Boy (Kumārakassapa), 183 *f.*
Kassapa the Great, 263 *f.*, 266, 402 *n.*
Khemā, 368 *n.*
Kimbila, 257 *ff.*
Kisa Saṅkicca, 292
Kosalans, 343
Kosambī, 383
Kosiya, 308 *f.*
Koṭṭhita the Great, 350 *f.*
Kurus, 70

Licchavi(s), 91, 281 *f.*, 290
Lomahaṁsa, *-jātaka*, *-napariyāya*, 110 *n.*
Lustrous (*subhakiṇṇā devā*), 392

Magadha, 210, 212, 277
Mahā- and *Cūḷa-* in titles, xi *ff.*
Mahāmāyā, 28 *n.*
Mahānāma, 119 *ff.*
Mahā-puṇṇamā-sutta, xii, 171 *n.*
Mahinda, 220 *n.*
Makkhali Gosāla, 245, 292, 305
Majjhima-nikāya, ix *ff.*, 174 *n.*
Mallas, 284
Māra(s), 5 *n.*, 96 *f.*, 112, 152, 179 *n.*, 184, 198 *ff.*, 218 *f.*, 223, 277 *ff.*, 382, 389 *f.*, 393 *ff.*, 395 *ff.*; 's stream, 278 *f.*; unseen by, 202 *f.*, 218 *f.* *See also* Evil One
Migāra's mother, palace of, 203 *f.*, 306, 310, 401
Moggallāna, 32, 38, 124, 131, 263 *f.*, 266 *f.*, 307 *ff.*, 395 *f.*, 402 *n.*
Moliyaphagguna, 159 *f.*
Mount Vulture Peak, 121, 238
Mūlapariyāyajātaka, 3 *n.*, 8 *n.*

Nādikā, 257
Nāgasamāla, xvi, 110
Nanda Vaccha, 292
Nandiya, 257 *ff.*
Nāthaputta, 122, 246, 305
Nerañjarā, 210 *n.*
Neru, 403
Neumann, E. K., ix, xi, 184 *n.*
Niraya Hell, 29, 44, 95 *ff.*, 103, 115, 343, 346, 369 *f.*, 375 *f.*, 398, 401; appellations of, 401
Nyanatiloka, xxiv *n.*

Pajāpati, 5, 179, 389 *ff.*
Pakudha Kaccāyana, 245, 305
Paṇḍu's son, 39
Papañcasūdanī, x, xvi
Pāsarāsi-sutta, 203 *n.*
Pasenadi, 192, 220 *n.*, 284
Pilotika, 220
Piṅgalakoccha, 245 *f.*, 253
Puṇṇa, Mantāṇī's son, 188 *f.*, 193
Pūraṇa Kassapa, 86 *n.*, 245, 305
Pure Abodes, *devas* of the, 109

Radiant (*ābhassarā devā*), 391 *f.*
Rājagaha, 39, 121, 187 *f.*, 238, 360
Rammaka, brahman, 203 *ff.*
Revata, 264 *f.*
Rhys Davids, T. W., ix, xii, xiv, xxiii
Rhys Davids, Mrs., xxv

Saccaka, 280 *ff.*, 291 *ff.*
Sāketa, 192
Sakka, 220 *n.*, 285 *n.*, 306 *ff.*, 402
Sakka-pañha-sutta, 171 *n.*
Sakyans, 119, 141
Sālā, 343
Samīti, 39
Sañjaya Belaṭṭhaputta, 245, 305
Sañjīva, 396 *f.*
Sankhārabhājanīya-sutta, 171 *n.*
Sammādiṭṭhi-sutta, 171 *n.*
Saṁyutta, x *f.*
Sāriputta, xxvi, 18, 21, 31 *f.*, 39 *f.*, 57 *ff.*, 91 *ff.*, 188 *f.*, 193 *f.*, 220 *n.*, 230, 263 *ff.*, 350 *f.*, 402 *n.*
Sāti, 311 *ff.*, 324
Satipaṭṭhāna Suttas, xiv *f.*
Sāvatthī, 16, 21, 31, 41, 45, 51, 57, 85, 111 *f.*, 132, 136, 148, 152, 159, 161, 167, 183, 188, 192, 194, 203, 220, 230, 245, 271, 306, 311, 349, 350, 368, 372, 279, 388
Sīhanāda Suttas, xii *ff.*
Soma, Bhikkhu, 57 *n.*, 70 *n.*
Stick-in-Hand, 141 *f.*
Subhadda, 245 *n.*
Subhaga Grove, 3, 388 *f.*
Sudhammasabhā, 402
Suṃsumāragira, 124, 395
Sundarika-Bhāradvāja, 49 *f.*
Sunakkhatta, 91 *f.*
Suttanipāta, xxvi, 171 *n.*
Suvidehā, 277 *f.*

Tagore, Rabindranath, xxiii *n.*
Thera-therī-gāthā, 171 *n.*
Thirty-Three, *devas* of the, 97, 307, 309 *f.*
Thomas, E. J., xxiv
Thunderbolt-bearer (Vajirapāṇi), 285

Uddaka, Rāma's son, xxii, 209 *f.*, 214
Ukkācelā, 277
Ukkaṭṭhā, 3, 388
Upaka, 214 *f.*
Upatissa, 193
Uppalavaṇṇā, 220 *n.*, 226 *n.*
Uruvelā, 210, 214
Ussada, 401

Vacchāyana (Pilotika), 220, 222
Vajji(s), 262, 277, 284
Vatthasutta, 45 *n.*,
Vedalla-suttas, 171 *n.*
Vedehikā, 162 *f.*
Vehapphalā (*devā*), 392
Vejayanta palace, 308 *f.*, 402
Verañjā, 349
Vesālī, 91 *f.*, 141 *n.*, 280, 291
Vessavaṇa, 308 *f.*
Vidhura, 396 *f.*, 400 *f.*
Vinaya, 171 *n.*
Visākha, 360 *ff.*
Visākhā, 220 *n.*

Wijesekera, O. H. de A., 322 *n.*
Winternitz, M., xxv *n.*

IV.—SOME PALI WORDS IN THE NOTES

abhikkanta, 183
ativela, 159
āpo, 4
eḷamugā, 25
ossavane, 236
kālakiriya, 61
caṅgavāra, 184
deva, 5
paṭhavī, 4
pariyāyā, 3, 8
bhava, 87, 142
bhūtā, 5
magga, 20
vado vedeyyo, 11
vana, 3
veda, 47
saṇadhovika, 282
samayavimokkha, 243
so loko so attā, 174